EXECUTIVE DECISION MAKING

THE IRWIN SERIES IN MANAGEMENT

Consulting Editor   JOHN F. MEE, *Indiana University*

EXECUTIVE DECISION MAKING

by MANLEY HOWE JONES, M.B.A., D.C.S.

Professor of Business Management

Illinois Institute of Technology

1962 · REVISED EDITION

RICHARD D. IRWIN, INC.

HOMEWOOD, ILLINOIS

REVISED EDITION

First Printing, June, 1962

Library of Congress Catalogue Card No. 62–16525

PRINTED IN THE UNITED STATES OF AMERICA

This book is for

T. S. J.

PREFACE TO FIRST EDITION

THIS BOOK is intended for men and women who wish to improve their effectiveness as executives. It has been written primarily for use in an advanced undergraduate college course or a graduate course, and for use by companies in their executive development programs. At the same time I have tried to keep in mind the needs of men who wish to read the book by themselves at their leisure.

Those readers who are looking for neatly packaged answers, or for statistical data on how executives behave, or for a description of business as an institution will be disappointed in this book; it is not for them. My intent has been to provide an approach to orderly thinking —to bring together and develop some concepts that will be of use as tools to an executive in solving some of his specific everyday and long-run problems. Because many of these tools are elusive—the book deals largely with intangibles—I have not hesitated to spend whatever time was necessary to clarify the concepts. But most readers, even those with no experience in business, will soon discover they have been using a majority of the ideas intuitively and unconsciously as tools. All I have done is attempt to describe these ideas in words, make them more precise, and organize them into an orderly pattern. The book simply offers new ways of looking at familiar things— "systematized common sense." The purpose has been to integrate in one framework a body of knowledge that men usually learn by ear. It is hoped that this may shorten the process of gaining the insight and confidence a man needs if he is to become an effective leader.

There is a tendency among executives to feel that their own companies and industries are unique. This is true to a certain extent, but the executives of most companies also have a wide range of common problems. This book is confined to these problems. As my ideas for the book took shape, I eventually found that most of their common problems fell rather readily under three headings—decision making, gaining acceptance of their decisions, and planning and putting their plans into effect. Nevertheless, not all of these would stay neatly classified in the pockets; they are actually interrelated and most of them overlap. But that's the way the business world is and I could not do much about it.

I believe the concepts developed here for solving these problems

vii

are almost equally applicable in all types of organizations. The chief reason is that people are very much alike, no matter where they work. I have written the book, however, from the point of view of executives in medium-sized manufacturing companies. More specifically, in my comments and examples I have had in mind firms with somewhere between 100 and 3,000 to 5,000 employees, and annual sales running between $250,000 and perhaps $25,000,000 or $30,000,000. Readers who work for larger or smaller firms, or for a wholesaler, a retailer, a bank, a church, a school, a labor union, a governmental agency, or a voluntary or nonprofit organization may find this distracting at times, but they should have little trouble in recalling examples drawn from their own experience and transposing and using the concepts in their own organization.

My objective has been to write a practical book in problem solving. The ideas are drawn primarily from my twenty years experience as a businessman in three quite diverse industries, and more lately from my work as a business consultant and from teaching college students and young executives through the use of a wide range of business cases, including some prepared at the Harvard Business School. But I have also adapted for my purposes several ideas, approaches, and conclusions developed by specialists in the fields of sociology, cultural anthropology, social psychology, economics, history, philosophy, politics, logic, religion, the arts, and engineering and science, even though at first sight these subjects may seem foreign to a book on management. I am not an expert in any of these fields (nor need the reader be), so I beg the indulgence of the real experts for my frequent oversimplification of their tools. Most of the concepts that I have pre-empted, and those I offer here for the first time, were gradually revised as a result of my own observation of the application of these ideas in the business world and of incisive suggestions made by businessmen, young executives, and students who have taken the course covering the material in this book.

I am greatly indebted to many people. Throughout the book I have drawn heavily upon ideas developed and employed by the faculty of the Harvard Business School; this is particularly true of Part III. In writing Parts I and II, I was also strongly influenced by Chester I. Barnard: *The Functions of the Executive* (Cambridge: Harvard University Press, 1938) and Herbert Simon: *Administrative Behavior* (New York: The Macmillan Co., 1947), though I have taken the liberty of revising many of their concepts, adding details of my own, and restating their ideas in less abstract terms.

Rough drafts of parts or all of the manuscript have been read and criticized to its great benefit by several men. In particular I wish to thank Dr. Paul C. Greene, psychologist and Director of Student Counseling Service, University of Illinois, Chicago Branch, who went through the next to final draft in its entirety and to Donald Ghent, personnel administrator for Flexonics Corporation, Maywood, Ill., who read most of those chapters. To Elmer Burack, production control manager, Federal Tool Corporation, Chicago, and to Norman Francis, engineer for the Link-Belt Corporation, Chicago, Illinois, both of whom have taught the course using the manuscript as a basis, I am equally indebted. In addition, I owe much to the following people who read and criticized one or more chapters at various stages in the evolution of the manuscript: J. E. Ratner, Vice-President of Campbell-Mathun, Inc., Minneapolis; Dr. Paul R. Trumpler; Dr. Samuel K. Workman, Dr. Gerald J. Matchett, Mr. Cecil R. Glaves, and Dr. Donald W. Smithburg, all of the faculty of the Illinois Institute of Technology; Dr. Lura Teeter; Messers Robert E. Elsas, Controller of American Breeders Service, Chicago, E. M. Meneough, President of Meneough Advertising Agency, Des Moines, Edwin L. Fox, Vice-President and General Manager of Foxbilt Feeds, Des Moines, and Charles S. Varner, Superintendent of Schools, Johnston, Iowa. I have not always taken the advice of these many readers, a fact which probably accounts for some of the book's shortcomings. To all my warmest thanks for their encouragement and help.

But probably my family deserves the most appreciation; without their forbearance and help I would not have been able to write this book. To my wife, Thelma, I am especially indebted; her judgment and her eye for the right word have greatly benefited the book. Our college-age children, Gregory, Karin, and Delight have likewise made many pertinent suggestions.

MANLEY HOWE JONES

CHICAGO
February, 1957

PREFACE TO REVISED EDITION

IN THIS revised edition, I have placed more emphasis than before on the book's conceptual framework. Those of us who are in management cannot lay claim to a tidy body of theory, one that is as widely accepted as, for instance, the economist's theory of the firm. Nevertheless this new edition does set out a consistent system of reasoning about behavior in the firm based on a body of rather widely accepted concepts which have here been integrated into subsystems—subsystems which, in turn, form an interrelated whole. It weaves into a pattern an internally consistent set of analytical tools, each of which, according to most students of management, will help an executive solve certain of his problems.

The revisions were more extensive than I had expected. Since the publication of the first edition there has been an ever-increasing stream of research studies and writings in the field. I have included references to many of these and have incorporated new findings. The most noticeable change is the new chapter (4); there I have set down some of the uses and limitations of operations research models for executive decision making. The book's concepts and underlying philosophy have not been materially changed, however. Other revisions were made with a view to explaining some of the concepts more clearly. And in the chapter on formal organization structure, I have gone back to the somewhat more conventional ideas of structure and line and staff.

I am not only indebted to the researchers and writers in the field but to the scores of students at IIT and to faculty members in many schools who have generously taken the time to restudy the book and suggest changes. There are too many men to name; hence I can only acknowledge them here as my valued collaborators and offer my warmest thanks.

M.H.J.

CHICAGO
March, 1962

xi

TABLE OF CONTENTS

PART I

DECISION MAKING

DECISION MAKING is probably the most characteristic task of the executive. All executives, high and low, work on decisions constantly; ordinarily, an executive must contend with several at the same time. Hundreds of decisions, perhaps thousands, are made in a company every day.

The majority of the people in most organizations feel that they are under constant pressure to make decisions; frequently, they feel obliged to make them immediately. Practically every man in a company is called upon to make certain decisions that provide the basis for (or at least a part of the basis for) the actions of others. Other men await those decisions so that they can get on with their own work. Even small decisions play an essential part in the pattern of company activity. Each man knows that if he neglects to make the decisions expected of him or consistently makes "poor" ones, his associates will think he has failed them; they will start criticizing and may eventually begin to ignore him. This pressure is felt by all men who make decisions affecting others, regardless of whether or not they are executives.

Decision making is by no means confined to executives. A janitor decides where in the room to sprinkle the sweeping compound, where to start his sweeping, and when. He has several alternatives to choose from in making each of these decisions. The mechanic on a lathe decides whether to increase or decrease the flow of the coolant he uses, and by how much. In making such decisions, these men use an approximation of the framework we shall explore in Part I—though (need we add?) quite unconsciously, and only in a very sketchy fashion. Everyone in an organization makes decisions, regardless of how high or low in the hierarchy he may be.

Decisions range all the way from the simple ones affecting only the decider to extremely complex ones which will affect many people. We make some of our simpler decisions so frequently that they become habitual. In taking out a cigarette and lighting it, a smoker seldom notices that he has chosen between alternative means (smoking or not smoking) of attaining some goal he has in mind. Whether or not to sharpen a pencil is ordinarily a more consciously made decision, though still a relatively simple one. Decisions that affect other people—such as a family expedition to the movies or a change of location of the desks in an office—are more complex. Comparatively speaking, a supervisor's decisions typically affect relatively few individuals. The decisions of a middle-level executive usually concern more people and are more complicated. The chief executive's decisions, for the most part, will be the most intricate of all and will frequently affect the lives of a large number of men and women.

Irrespective of a man's level in the hierarchy, he consciously or unconsciously takes certain distinguishable steps in making a decision. For instance, he sets goals; periodically looks over the means he has already chosen (decided upon) for achieving those goals; and notes which of these earlier decisions will have to be changed, and the ones he has not yet made. In making a new decision, he first conceives some promising alternatives and then tries out each one in his imagination in an attempt to foresee the wanted and unwanted consequences of adopting it; he often checks these predictions of consequences to see whether they are reasonably reliable, weights them to make sure that he sees them in perspective and is not attaching too much importance to trivial ones, and anticipates the reaction of others to each of the alternatives. Finally, he tries to choose the one that will provide the greatest amount of wanted consequences and a minimum of unwanted consequences. This, in brief, is the decision-making process which we shall explore in Part I of the book.

For the most part, executives have little idea of how they make their decisions. Nor is such knowledge of any importance to men who have already "arrived"; for them, learning about the decision-making process would be a waste of time and effort, though it might be of some academic interest. They are already able to cope with the uncertainties and imponderables they must take into consideration; thus, they feel confident of their decisions. But the majority of men, especially those on the way up the ladder, feel less self-assured. The job of anticipating the unknown—predicting wanted and unwanted consequences where no solid predictions are possible, a vital feature of decision making—poses the greatest hurdle. Part I of this book offers no crystal ball, no formula, for making decisions. Instead, the objectives are to uncover and explore the steps men ordinarily take unconsciously in making a decision; to learn a little about performing those steps more thoroughly than is our wont, especially those where the unknown plays a large role; and to view these steps as parts of an orderly framework.

Chapter 1   GOALS AND MEANS-END STAIRCASES

THE TERMS *executive* and *decision* seem to call up a variety of pictures in people's minds. Each man has known a somewhat different group of executives and has encountered a different set of decisions. So before exploring the details of executive decision making, perhaps an effort should be made to describe the way in which the two terms will be used in this book.

We shall think of an executive as a man whose duty is to guide the behavior of others; he is able to plan the goals of the group he heads and organize its activities into effective means of attaining those goals; he has the ability to reach decisions about goals and means which will stand up when reviewed, to gain acceptance of those decisions, and to put them into effect.[1] He may be serving as a section head supervising only two or three people, or a department head, or a chief executive, though he need not necessarily hold the formal title of head of the group of men he supervises. Characteristically, he is the man to whom the others turn for solutions of their problems.

We shall think of a decision as a course of action chosen by the decider as the most effective means at his disposal for achieving the goals or goal he is currently emphasizing—for solving the problem that is bothering him. Note that a decision is something quite apart from the actual performance of the act that has been decided upon; it is a conclusion that a man has reached as to what he (or others) should do later—sometimes only a moment later. It is a solution selected after examining several alternatives—chosen because the de-

---

[1] This definition closely corresponds with the three main topics of this book—"Decision Making," "Gaining Acceptance of Decisions," and "Planning and Putting Plans into Effect."

The quite specific and often quite unfamiliar definitions employed in this book are designed to help us see and explain phenomena or behavior encountered in diverse situations which at first sight seem totally different but actually are basically the same. The definitions are repeated in brief form in the glossary for easy reference.

cider foresees that the course of action he elects will do more than the others to further his goals and will be accompanied by the fewest possible objectionable consequences. We would all like to make decisions we can feel proud of. One test of a good decision is whether it still looks like a wise one when we re-examine it later. The key problem is to make a realistic appraisal of the many probable results of taking a certain action *before these results have occurred*. At the moment this description probably sounds rather abstract; but as we progress, it will become more meaningful.

Most of us occasionally have trouble making up our minds; we may go through periods when we wonder if our indecisiveness may have become chronic. Sometimes we vacillate because we cannot be sure about the consequences of our decisions; we have not yet lived through the experience of seeing the results, so that we feel insecure. On other occasions, after dwelling on the problem for a time, we may become overwhelmed by the many imponderables we discover. For instance, not all the consequences of a decision to marry a certain woman or to accept a certain job are readily apparent at the time the decision must be made; and the intangibles we have to take into consideration loom large. Consequently, we are afraid that the choices we make will turn out to be disappointing.

Sometimes, we look with envy on men we know who seem to make decisions without apparent effort and who somehow manage to make good ones. They probably could not explain how they do this, for they have never bothered to analyze the process; they make their decisions quite unconsciously, yet they undoubtedly go through certain steps. In this chapter, an attempt will be made to begin uncovering these steps.

Although none of us can expect to be right 100 per cent of the time, I am quite convinced that nearly everyone can learn to make decisions comfortably, and can greatly improve those he makes by mastering certain steps in the decision-making process and consciously putting to work what he learns. This process[2] is relatively easy to understand

---

[2] There are many variants of this decision-making process, so that the one described in Part I should really be called *a* decision-making process. Operations research and game theory are two that may interest the reader. The former will be put to work in Chapter 4. Students wishing to go further into these and other approaches will find descriptions of some of the more abstruse concepts in Albert H. Rubenstein and Chadwick J. Haberstroh (eds.), *Some Theories of Organization* (Homewood, Ill.: The Dorsey Press, Inc., and Richard D. Irwin, Inc., 1960). See Section Six, entitled "Decision Making," especially the introduction and articles 33, 34, and 35.

once it is broken down into separate concepts and the characteristics of each are understood. Most of us use these concepts constantly, though in a somewhat haphazard fashion; in fact, in Part I, we shall be examining the details of six concepts, giving them names, exploring their uses, and fitting them together in an orderly framework so that eventually we can employ them deliberately. Quite often, a man becomes impatient when trying to make a decision—even an important one. I am advocating that we slow down much of our decision making, at least until we have mastered the steps—the concepts— and have gained some practical experience in using them consciously. When these steps become our own instead of something learned from a book, when we begin to use them automatically, it is quite easy once again to make decisions with dispatch.

We shall use the term *concept* to mean a description of the details of an idea, together with a mental picture of the ways its unique details fit together and act upon one another to form an integrated whole. As we advance through Part I, we shall see that each of the six concepts is made up of a number of smaller, more detailed concepts. For this reason, we shall often use the term *conceptual subsystem* or simply *subsystem* when we refer to such a group of small related concepts. And it eventually becomes clear that these six subsystems of concepts in turn form an over-all conceptual framework, a framework for decision making. Together, these are intended to provide a young executive with a realistic frame of reference which will enhance his effectiveness in his organization.[3]

The paramount purpose of the present chapter is to probe far enough into the first two of these conceptual subsystems—the idea of goals and the idea of means-end staircases—to permit us to utilize them tellingly as decision-making instruments. Every man has in mind some goals he would like to achieve; and he probably also has in mind some means he plans to employ in achieving his goals. But few of us bother to *clarify* our own (or our company's) goals to a point where we can see them distinctly and thus see exactly where we

---

[3] Actually, when we get into Parts II and III, we discover that the over-all decision-making framework which we shall explore in Part I is only one segment of a much more comprehensive conceptual framework of executive action. Each of those Parts will have its own subsystems, and all three Parts are of a piece. For a general statement of this idea of subsystems which make up a larger conceptual framework see Talcott Parsons, *Essays in Sociological Theory* (Glencoe, Ill.: Free Press, 1954), pp. 212–19. If Professor Parsons' statements and style seem somewhat elusive, turn for a touchstone to C. Wright Mills, *The Sociological Imagination* (New York: Oxford University Press, 1959), pp. 25–33.

want to go. We are often equally vague about the means we intend to employ. Consequently, few of us secure as much benefit as we might from these two tools.

Although we are concerned in this book with company goals and decisions, we can learn a great deal about them by examining men's *personal* goals and decisions. Fortunately, personal decisions and company decisions are made in the same way—the concepts of goals and means-end staircases, for example, are utilized in both. Moreover, most of the executive's decisions have to do with people. In fact, the decisions made in behalf of the company as an organization and the personal decisions of the men and women in the company are so closely bound together that it would be unrealistic to try to separate them. An organization is made up entirely of *people*.

THREE TYPES OF GOALS

Once we see our goals clearly and describe them, some appropriate means of furthering them will usually come to mind. When we know what we want, we can choose our means more accurately, and waste little effort on unproductive means; we shoot at a selected target. Moreover, a decision that advances some of our specific *permanent* goals will usually seem wise later; when we look back over what we have done, the chances are that we shall have few regrets because these goals have not changed in the interim and a decision that furthered them some time ago still makes good sense. We may realize later that we might have made a somewhat better choice of means; but, at any rate, the one we selected has advanced us a step nearer our objectives. We usually regret a decision made to advance a fleeting whim. At best, we have wasted our efforts in carrying it out; at worst, we have imperiled our more permanent goals.

Pushing our thinking a step further and distinguishing three types of goals helps to sharpen our ideas of our goals and thus our ability to make wise decisions. We shall consider *ultimate* goals, *intermediate* goals, and *those goals that rest on the steps of the staircases leading up to the intermediate goals;* goals of the third type are the ones that make up what we shall call the *means-end staircases.* The first two types of goals are the relatively permanent, far off ones mentioned above. The third type consists of the lesser, more immediate goals we set. These are so arranged on the stair steps that each goal, once achieved, will serve as a means of furthering the goal resting on the step just above it on the staircase. The goal on the highest of these steps serves as a means of achieving one or more of the intermediate goals. In the next few pages, we shall explore these three types of goals rather thoroughly, for these are actually decisions we have made—decisions as to the goals we shall attempt to attain.

Some brief examples of decisions will indicate what is meant by these three types of goals and will serve as a preview for a somewhat more thorough investigation. In each example, we shall begin with the third type of goal—those lying rather far down on a staircase. Bear in mind that these names are simply ones we are giving to the goals we ordinarily use unconsciously in making our decisions.

Let us, for a moment, watch a man who is planning a vacation, a man who is now at a sporting goods store selecting some fishing tackle. The immediate goal he apparently has in mind is to catch some fish (some big ones, of course); and he is in the process of choosing the best means of achieving that goal—choosing from the many alternatives before him the lines and lures that will most likely produce the results he wants. He is imagining himself fishing from a boat on the lake where he will spend his vacation and is mentally trying out the more promising lures to see which will most likely entice the fish to strike. But if he sharpens his goal—sets as his goal the catching of some bass or wall-eyed pike—he is in a position to make much more telling decisions.

For another example of the use, in decision making, of this third type of goal, let us observe a salesman as he gets ready to leave his hotel room for the day's work. His immediate goal (we hope) is to mail some large orders to the company this evening. He looks over his records of the accounts in the city, recalls his last visits with them, and then decides which of these customers will probably give him the best orders. He is selecting a group of means. On the other hand, he may conclude that his most important goal for the day is to get some rest and that the best means of achieving this goal is to sleep all morning and go to a movie in the afternoon. Afterward, of course he may regret these decisions as to his day's goal and means because, in retrospect, he realizes that they did little to further his own or his company's rather permanent goals. Nevertheless, once he has set his goals clearly, the decision as to the means comes quite naturally.

An executive follows much the same procedure. Were we to live inside the mind of a chief executive this morning, we might discover him recalling that he has lately noticed that one of his subordinates, a department head, has frequently made company decisions which have not stood up. He is now checking back to see if his earlier impression is correct. He finally concludes that this subordinate (an important means now being employed) will not be equal to the job of carrying out the tasks lying ahead of that department. So he sets as his short-term goal the selection of a more telling means, a stronger department head. With this in mind, he begins casting about for a new man, a new means, and eventually makes his choice from the most promising candidates available. Perhaps we see his mind crystallizing a second goal—finding a place for the old department head—and searching for a means of realizing this goal, too.

The fisherman's and the salesman's decisions were relatively easy ones, since their goals were quite specific and obvious from the beginning. The executive, however, had not yet formulated his objective when we first met him; his decision, therefore, turns out to be more complex. (He also had to take more facts and imponderables into consideration.) Yet, once he had crystallized and stated his goal, he was well along the way to deciding what means to employ—what action to take. All three men made their decisions in the same way, however.

Although the goals of the fisherman, the salesman, and the executive served as the immediate touchstone for the decisions we saw them making, the men also undoubtedly looked upon the achievement of those goals as means of attaining still "higher" goals—of moving to the next higher step on the staircase. For example, as a result of catching some big fish, the fisherman will be able to brag to his friends about his skill as an angler, a "higher" goal. If the salesman sends in a sheaf of orders, he will impress his sales manager with his sales ability. Finding a top-flight department head (a goal, as we saw) will serve as a means of strengthening the company's organization; and strengthening the organization will help the company compete more effectively. Boasting to friends, impressing the boss, strengthening the organization are illustrations of intermediate goals. The men undoubtedly took these intermediate goals into consideration, along with their "lower," more immediate goals, in making their decisions. They each knew that once they had achieved the goal they had set that morning, it would in turn serve as a means of reaching their intermediate goals. Even though these higher objectives were probably so buried in the subconscious levels of their minds that the men were only dimly aware of them, these are certainly very specific things they knew they would like to achieve.

These intermediate goals, however, in turn serve as means of achieving still higher goals—ultimate goals. Perhaps the fisherman and the salesman have in mind the ultimate goal of gaining a reputation among their associates for being very intelligent and capable; the executive may have in mind the gaining of prestige for his company—prestige among potential customers and competitors.

Chronologically speaking, the three men probably chose their highest goals (their ultimate goals) some years earlier—to achieve reputation or prestige, we have said. Then they moved down the staircase—sought a means of attaining their ultimate goals and hit upon the intermediate goals mentioned above as means of reaching the ultimate goals they had set. With their intermediate goals in mind, they then chose the goals stated in the original examples as the best means available that day for achieving the intermediate goals they had set earlier. In our more detailed examination of the three types of goals, we shall start at the top with ultimate goals and work down the staircases.

Ultimate Goals

Though ultimate goals are the last to be achieved, they are the ones that really initiate many of our decisions; they spur us to make decisions and thereafter carry them out. If we were able to keep our ultimate goals clearly in mind at all times (or at any rate, if we were to take them out and dust them off once in a while), and if we then consciously made decisions that would advance these goals, there is little question that our decision making would improve, for the choices we made would then fall into an interrelated pattern; they would serve as complementary means of reaching a single, rather permanently desired destination.

Probably all of us have adopted or chosen some ultimate goals, some far-off goals, even though they are usually quite nebulous and we seldom think much about them. Many of us would say that our goal is happiness—that we should welcome a climate of general auspiciousness in our lives. Others less fortunate than we may take a grimmer view—that of survival, for example. But whatever our own ultimate goals may be, they represent our idea of something almost perfect, something we should like to enjoy forever. We think of these as our aspirations, our dreams. They are conditions or situations that, in our eyes, are much better than our present ones. These goals are what we have in mind when we say, "Wouldn't it be wonderful if things were like that?" and then go on to describe what "that" is. We could then *be* what we had always wanted to be and feel confident that we could flourish.[4]

Our ultimate goals are by no means confined to those we want for ourselves as individuals. We also visualize and strive for more perfect situations for the groups to which we are warmly attached— our family, for example, or our company, or our nation.

Each individual's picture of what he thinks would be wonderful for him or his group will differ in certain respects from that of every other man. And the same is probably true for every company; for, as can be readily imagined, companies differ, as do individuals. Yet despite this marked variety in ultimate goals, there are some that are rather widely held. Moreover, a further examination reveals some notable similarities in the goals of an individual and a company. Indeed, the same phrases can frequently be used to describe the ultimate goals of both. As an illustration, both might set as an ultimate goal one or more of the following:

To better fulfill one's own (or the company's) potentials by utilizing skills and capacities to the full.

To prosper.

To grow in importance in the eyes of others—that is, to gain prestige, reputation, respect, admiration.

To get along with the least possible trouble or effort.

To live in peace with others.

To help people to flourish.

To have the freedom to pursue what it (he) considers the best means of achieving this wonderful, perfect thing that it (he) wants—freedom of choice.

To be able to cope with unforeseen contingencies.

To gain stability and security for the future.

To maintain and perpetuate itself—or himself and his family.

To enjoy a perfect life.[5]

---

[4] These goals may be ideal or perfect situations which we realize we can never attain, but this does not deter us from setting them and struggling to reach them. We are sure that we shall be better off if we only partially achieve them than if we had made no attempt.

[5] At first sight, this list of ultimate goals may seem somewhat unreal. One reason is that characteristically these high goals are elusive and intangible ideas and are therefore difficult to put into words. Another reason is that the above statements have been framed rather broadly, so that they could be used to depict the goals of both individuals and companies. As a matter of fact, these statements also describe some of the ultimate goals of a family, a political party, a government, a trade union, or a church. "Making profit" or "making a lot of money," which some readers may think should be listed as ultimate goals, will be included among intermediate goals; we shall think of those activities as means of achieving some of the ultimate goals. In Chapter 5 we shall probe further into personal goals, and in Part III we shall go quite thoroughly into the complex task of working out goals and means for companies.

In this book, we shall often use the term *future welfare* to summarize a company's or an individual's *ultimate goals*—use it almost synonymously. The words *future welfare* are broad enough and flexible enough to encompass the lists of the ultimate goals of all individuals and all companies; we can pour into this term the *details* of the picture of the perfect situation which men and companies are seeking. The *future* can be thought of as a time several years hence or as a period immediately ahead. Most of the examples of ultimate goals listed above would be considered far-off goals, which will take time to achieve. But the ultimate goal could be a near-by one. A man *could* look upon loafing, or having a good time, as his ultimate goal—a very realistic picture of the perfect situation and one that is immediately achievable. In this book, however, we shall ordinarily think of the future as a period several years ahead.

If this idea of ultimate goals and future welfare is to become meaningful to a man for the purpose of making everyday decisions in particular cases, however, it is essential that he do two things. First, he must determine and see clearly the *specific* ultimate goals which he and his organization are seeking, and among these, the ones that seem to him (it) most important. The goals listed just above are intended only for illustration. To make good decisions, men (and companies) must select goals that have real meaning *to them;* and they must convert the vague images in their minds into more explicit mental pictures, which they can frame in words. The idea is useful only when these goals are visualized as *specific* things wanted by a *particular* person (or a *particular* company). Secondly, he (or it) must also move down a step to what we are calling the intermediate goals—to the means of achieving the ultimate goals. This brings us a step nearer the point where we can take some action.

Intermediate Goals

In trying to attain ultimate goals, men and organizations set somewhat lesser goals for themselves—intermediate goals. These are the means of achieving their ultimate goals. These intermediate goals lie next to the ultimate goals; the deciders feel confident that if they can achieve these, their ultimate goals will almost inevitably and automatically be attained. Developing new products, finding a new group of customers, or making a profit may serve as a *company's intermediate* goals, which in turn are means that the company can use to further one or more of its ultimate goals and thus secure its future welfare. A government may be seeking its future welfare by working for peace or engaging in a war. A man may be seeking the future welfare of his family by seeing that his children go to college.

Here are a few examples of intermediate goals sometimes pursued by an individual:

To have a happy and contented home life.
To rise in his profession or get a better job in the company.
To be a good husband and father.
To increase his effectiveness in his work.
To become a leader in his community or in his groups.
To live according to Christian ideals.
To do work that will give him a great deal of satisfaction—constructive work, such as solving problems.
To have job security, make a lot of money, and build financial reserves.
To gain freedom from physical toil and boring tasks.[6]

Similarly, the executives of a company set intermediate goals, ones they predict, if achieved, will ensure the company's future welfare. *In addition* to the three intermediate company goals already mentioned—developing new products, finding new customers, and making a profit—the company may be attempting to do one or more of the following:

To become a leader in its industry, a leader, for example, in creating and launching new products.
To grow larger—expand.
To improve its position in its own industry—that is, to secure a larger percentage of the business done by its industry.
To increase productivity and lower the company's costs.
To gain a reputation for quality products—or for low-priced products.
To accumulate a financial reserve which will enable the company to weather a depression.
To increase sales.
To ensure the welfare of its employees.
To find and fill a given niche in the business world, one in which it can flourish.[7]

These intermediate goals are actually *decisions*—courses of action chosen, often unconsciously, from among several alternatives in the belief that they will serve as relatively permanent and effective

---

[6] Incidentally, no man can judge whether the intermediate goals (or, for that matter, the ultimate goals) which another man has chosen will give that man the greatest satisfaction. A man's goals may seem stupid to the onlooker, but they never look foolish to the one who has done the choosing.

In Western Europe where many companies are owned and operated by long-established families, a company's ultimate goal is frequently to further the reputation, renown, and wealth of the families.

[7] In Part III, we shall devote particular attention to this last-named goal.

means of achieving some of the ultimate goals. The executives are quite sure that if their company can realize most of its intermediate goals, its welfare will be more fully assured. The same can be said of a man's decisions as to his personal intermediate goals.

Intermediate goals are much easier to use than ultimate goals. Not only are they by nature more explicit, as already explained, but they can also be framed in definite terms to fit the particular company or individual, and can be described so that men can form a clear mental image of them. Instead of setting down a *general* intermediate goal such as "to become a leader in the industry," the executives can set as their goal "to become a leader like Acme Corporation"; or instead of saying, "We want to improve our position in the industry," they can decide that "Our aim is to get 5 per cent of the industry's volume." How to attain these intermediate company goals or achieve a personal intermediate goal such as "securing a job as a department head in the company," while difficult enough, is nevertheless much easier to decide than how to attain such ultimate goals as gaining prestige or prospering.

Intermediate goals ordinarily complement one another; each one helps to further several of the ultimate goals the decider has chosen. Moreover, the intermediate goals chosen by the company should promote the ultimate goals of the individual members of the organization as well as those of the company itself. Building up the financial backlog of the company, for example, not only forwards the company's goals but also serves as a means of providing security for its employees during a recession or depression and as a means of achieving some of the stockholders' ultimate goals.

It should be pointed out here that the terms *intermediate goals* and *ultimate goals* (or for that matter, the term *goals that lie on the staircase*) will not serve as a watertight classification system. So far as I know, there are no universals—no goals that everyone agrees are ultimate, or any that all people would classify as intermediate. Each man will have his own list. In your eyes, probably some of the intermediate goals listed earlier—living according to Christian ideals, for instance—should be included among the ultimate goals; and some of the ultimate goals should perhaps be listed as intermediate. You may also feel that some of the goals mentioned are of no importance whatsoever. Nor can we expect everyone to agree on the order of their relative importance. One man would list "being a good husband and father" as a topmost intermediate goal and place "becoming a leader in the community" far down, whereas another man would reverse the positions. Moreover, we change our minds about our goals and means. At one time in life, we may think of making a million dollars as our ultimate goal; whereas, later, we may think of helping future generations as our ultimate goal and of making a fortune as an intermediate goal. (Most of us soon discard as unrealistic the idea of becoming a millionaire.) Similarly, the executive in a company may at one time consider filling a given niche in the economy, filling it better than competitors, as the intermediate goal; whereas, at another time, this is replaced by the goal of surviving—weathering a financial crisis, for instance.

Fortunately, in making decisions, there is no need for a general classification system for goals, or for a list of universally accepted goals. All we need is the concept of clear-cut goals. As pointed out earlier, at this juncture in our examination of the decision-making process, the key job of the man is to visualize *his own* or *his company's* ultimate goals clearly and then discern the specific intermediate goals he has decided to employ. These are relatively permanent goals. Nevertheless, even these goals are not so concrete as we should like for our purposes; the lesser goals farther down on the means-end staircases are even more explicit, as we saw earlier in our observation of the fisherman, the salesman, and the executive.

Goals That Lie on the Means-End Staircases

We shall think of a means-end staircase as a set of steps on which rest statements of a man's or a company's lesser goals, statements arranged so that each serves as a means of attaining the goal resting on the step above it and as a goal when we are trying to decide on a means to place on the step just below it. We shall visualize the topmost step resting "against" one or more of the intermediate goals. The goal on this top step is a decision we have made as to a means we expect will be effective in achieving one or more of the intermediate goals we have chosen. When making each of these decisions, we view it as a means; but thereafter we look upon it as a goal and in turn try to find (decide upon) a means of realizing it. Then as soon as we can decide on this last-named means, we place it on the next step below that goal. This, in turn, becomes a goal, and so on down the staircase. Diagram 1 should make this clearer. Notice in the diagram that the intermediate and ultimate goals are shown as a part of the staircase. These were originally discussed separately, chiefly for the purpose of emphasis.

Success in furthering a long-term goal depends upon finding effective means (courses of action) which we can employ relatively soon. In a clearly framed means-end staircase, *each* step is an action which meets these tests:

1. It is the best means available for achieving the goal on the step above it.
2. It is a cause which is powerful enough to produce the step (goal) on the step above it.
3. It serves as a goal for selecting an effective means to be placed on the step below it.
4. It is a decision that has not yet been carried out.

It will be seen that a staircase is much more complex than a series of goals arranged according to the chronological sequence in which we expect to achieve them. Developing a new product will precede the launching of its advertising campaign, but it is not a means of achieving that goal; obtaining a bachelor's degree will ordinarily precede getting married, but these two statements are parts of two quite different staircases; they may meet the fourth test but not the other three.

A means-end staircase is really a way of viewing the decisions we have already made but have not yet carried out—a way of connecting them up in an orderly pattern to make sure that all the steps necessary for reaching our objectives are included. We make most of our decisions on the run, in what appears to be a helter-skelter fashion. But even so, a careful examination of our decision will usually disclose that the majority can be fitted together into means-end staircases. In diagramming a stairway, we are merely arranging these old decisions as a series of stair steps, so that each one serves as a means of reaching the step just above it and as a goal for the step below it. None of us really makes very many of these decisions in an orderly sequence, starting first with the ultimate goals, then working downward a step at a time to successively lower means. Nor is this essential. The means-end concept is not intended as a description of the *order* in which an intelligent, logical man should make his decisions, though when we deliberately set out to make a decision, we sometimes do use such an orderly procedure, as will be seen shortly. We are not so concerned at this point in the discussion with the sequence in which these decisions are made. Rather, the means-end staircase concept is to be looked upon as a tool for reappraising our decisions before actually putting them into effect.

Several means-end staircases are customarily employed simultaneously by men and companies. An examination of prior decisions and an attempt to frame these into staircases will reveal that a distinguishably different staircase is being employed as a means of achieving each of the intermediate goals. Moreover, the goal on the topmost step of a staircase is usually serving as a means of achieving more than one of the immediate goals. And certain of the steps contained in one staircase may serve as a means of furthering certain other steps in *other* staircases. Some of these details are shown in Diagram 1. In the second paragraph below, we shall investigate an example of a single staircase; but bear in mind there that the company is undoubtedly employing several others at the same time. If this were not true, the company would fail in its objective of staying in business.

As already indicated, we do not always make our decisions in a piecemeal fashion. Once in a while, we *deliberately* form means-end staircases, albeit without a full consciousness of what we have been doing. All of us probably begin to construct one whenever we come across an intermediate goal we want very much to reach. In such a case, we generally work from the top down in a rather orderly fashion. We first visualize the intermediate goal and then seek out a likely means of achieving it. But we soon discover that we cannot employ that means today; it is not available immediately; we shall first have to produce it. So we set that as a goal and go about finding a means that will give us that result. Then we realize that even this new "lower" means must be preceded by, and produced by, still another action. If we are really serious about attaining the intermediate goal, we continue this process of constructing lower and lower steps until we find a means that we can initiate today. Our minds usually go through such a procedure at lightning speed. This is especially true on those occasions when we are constructing rather simple staircases but quite extensive flights of steps also frequently come to mind very quickly.

The executive we met earlier, who was choosing a new department head, was apparently using this rather orderly method of working down from the top of the stairway. His frame of thinking, shorn of details, was probably somewhat as follows. We said that his ultimate goal was to ensure his company's future welfare, and let us suppose that the intermediate goals he had in mind were to increase the company's sales and to increase the company's prestige in the industry. Both of these intermediate goals are decisions that he and his associates had reached earlier. He then apparently asked himself, "How can I achieve these intermediate goals?" (he doubtlessly would not use our vocabulary) and thereupon began looking around

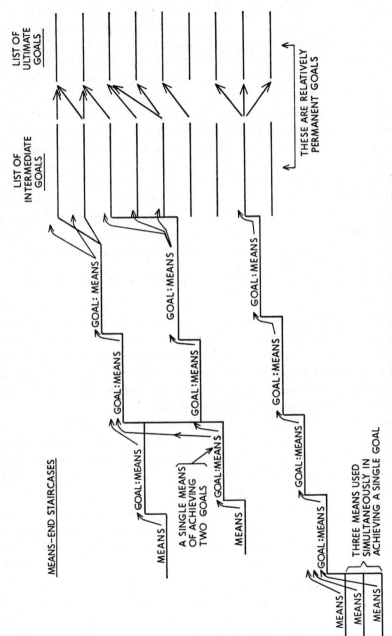

MEANS-END STAIRCASES

LIST OF INTERMEDIATE GOALS

LIST OF ULTIMATE GOALS

GOAL: MEANS

A SINGLE MEANS OF ACHIEVING TWO GOALS

MEANS

THREE MEANS USED SIMULTANEOUSLY IN ACHIEVING A SINGLE GOAL

THESE ARE RELATIVELY PERMANENT GOALS

DIAGRAM 1. Means-End Staircases and Permanent Goals

for a means. He seems to have decided (though this was not mentioned in the earlier example) that one means would be to improve the company's product. He then thought of this means (improving the product) as his highest goal in the staircase he is forming, and began searching for a means (cause) which would produce that goal (a wanted result); then he decided that strengthening the personnel in the product development department would be the best means. He now begins thinking of the latter as a goal instead of a means and seeks a means (a cause) that will produce a stronger department. In the example we used, he had decided to hire a new department head as a means of reinvigorating the department and was using this as his day's goal, one lying quite far down on his staircase. In the example, he was at the stage of choosing (deciding) among the various alternatives (several possible men) in an effort to find the best means of achieving the goal of improving the department's personnel, which in turn would serve as a means of securing improved products.

USES OF THE CONCEPTS OF GOALS AND STAIRCASES

Knowing ourselves as we do, we can be fairly sure that we shall seldom go to the trouble of actually writing down our own or our company's goals and drawing diagrams on paper of the staircases except, possibly, when we are working on a decision that is of overwhelming importance to us. Nevertheless, these two concepts, if kept in the mind, can be put to good use, for they help us to proceed with the decision-making process more deliberately.

Two uses have already been mentioned. First, each lower step is more concrete than the one above it; by pushing our thinking down the stairway, we eventually find goals that are relatively definite. With these in mind, we can usually discover some concrete means of achieving them. Second, the decisions made within this framework of thinking are more likely to stand up well when examined in retrospect, for they are all made with a view to advancing the comparatively permanent intermediate and ultimate goals. We need to be particularly careful that our decisions lying far down in the means-end staircases are judicious ones because we usually act on these immediately; and once they have been put into effect, there is little chance of undoing them. These actions may prevent us from achieving some of the goals we really want. Deciding to marry and start a family immediately upon graduation from high school may, for instance, virtually preclude a college education.

Third, this concept enables us to reappraise our earlier decisions

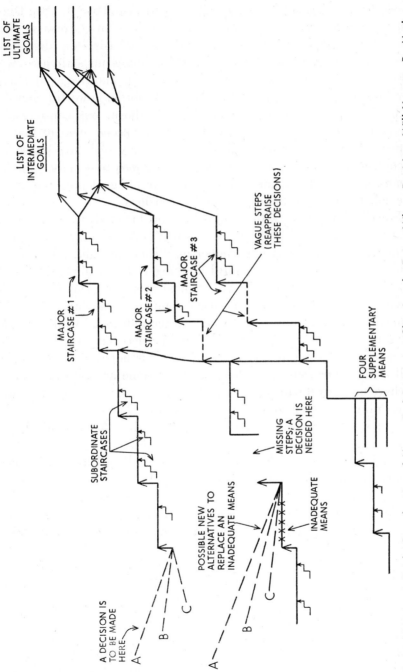

DIAGRAM 2. A Fairly Complex Set of Means-End Staircases, Showing the Points Where Decisions Will Have to Be Made

and thus to make sure that each will, in fact, be the most effective means at our disposal for achieving the goal just above it. (See Diagram 2.) When we arrange our prior decisions on staircases—the ones we have made in the past on a patchwork basis—we often discover *weak* or *inadequate* steps. Upon examining our staircases, we may conclude that, in the light of our present knowledge and experience, some of our earlier decisions will not be powerful enough to produce the results resting on the step above; our cause-result predictions now seem unreliable. Or it may become evident that a better alternative is now available. Or we may find that we shall need to employ several means simultaneously instead of only a single means, as we first thought, in order to attain the goal just above. So one job is to revise these unrealistic decisions.

Equally important, with such a diagram in mind, we can detect *missing* or *vague* steps—decisions to which we have so far given little or no thought. A surprising number may come to light. Most of us tend to do a great deal of wishful thinking—"Everything will come out all right," or "That'll be no problem at all; we can forget it." We often say, "I'll be president of the company some day," or "Our company will some day be the leader in the industry," without troubling to think out realistically *each* of the necessary specific steps we must take. Some of us seem to expect (or hope) that our goals will achieve themselves, or that chance or some agency over which we have no control will supply the missing means. Chance *does* sometimes play a part (in our day dreams chance plays a major role); but when we are honest with ourselves, we realize that we shall have to rely on ourselves to initiate most of the means. If there is a weak or a missing step, the chances are that we shall fail to achieve our higher goals.

In addition to uncovering the inadequate and missing steps, the idea of a staircase points out the decisions at the lower end of the staircase which have not yet been made—the ones that we can make and act on today or tomorrow.

Finally, the concept of goals and means provides a tool for determining what the problem facing us really *is*—for discerning *near*-term goals and means. Experienced executives often point out that the most difficult task in making company decisions is to define the problem—that once the problem is clearly stated, it is half solved; when this is accomplished, the solutions usually turn out to be relatively easy. *In almost every instance the executives will find that the problem they now face originated because the company is failing to attain some goal they had set at an earlier date.* More specifically, they are now trying to learn why they have failed to achieve their aim. When they originally set the goal, they decided to employ certain means which they expected would produce the result they wanted. But they now discover that they miscalculated; some of the means they adopted at that time have evidently failed. Once these inadequate means are located, they can be discarded and new ones chosen—ones which, along with other means the company is now employing, will more surely achieve the wanted goal. These inadequate means frequently lie rather far down on one of the staircases.

Let us observe how this works by attending a conference of company executives called to deal with a sales volume problem. Probably the first statement of the problem would be, "Our sales are too low; we should be running at least $100,000 a month." Here, the men are pointing out that they have not been achieving one of the intermediate goals they had set. This is not much help, however, for all they can conclude from this is, "We've got to get out and sell more"; everyone knows that already. So they take another look, perhaps naming the specific actions they have been taking to maintain sales volume. Here, they are moving down a step on their staircase—from their intermediate goal (high sales volume) to the highest of the goals in the several stairways they have been employing. The next question is, "Where are we falling down; which of these means—these highest goals—have proved unequal to the job?" Perhaps the men will conclude that the products are not standing up—that certain competitors have introduced improved products—and as a consequence the company is losing customers. This suggests a revamping of the product research department, a specific problem with which the executives can cope. In fact, a moment ago, we were watching an executive struggle with the decisions connected with this very problem— namely, finding a new department head for product research.

Or one of the executives may point out that sales in two of the territories have declined noticeably, which suggests that the supervisors or salesmen in these territories may need more help from the home office; or if the men in those territories seem hopelessly unequal to the task of raising their sales volume, perhaps new men should be hired. Incidentally, this may explain why our salesman friend set "sending in some big orders" as his goal for the day. His problem was better defined at the outset than those of the executives under consideration here, but it originated because he was not achieving the goals that he and his sales manager had set some weeks earlier.

The idea of goals (three distinguishably different types) and the employment of the staircase concept carries us a goodly distance toward our objective of making wise decisions. However, only by practicing the use of these two conceptual subsystems as instruments in our everyday decision making will they become meaningful and valuable. If we merely read about these in a book, we shall be wasting our time. They remain intellectual playthings for us until the moment when, as a result of constant use, each of the specific concepts drops down into the unconscious levels of the mind, so that we can begin to use them automatically instead of deliberately. The same is true of the other four major concepts of decision making which we shall be investigating in the remaining chapters of Part I. We are now well on our way toward gaining a mastery of our first set of subsystems.

PROBLEM

Goals and Means-End Staircases

Prepare a diagram that sets out:

1. A list of your own ultimate goals—a list of your aspirations. Place this at the upper right-hand edge of the sheet. Your goals should be much more real than those listed on pp. 12 and 14.
2. A list of your intermediate goals—means that are peculiarly yours because of your capacities, means you presently think of as the most effective ones you could employ in achieving your ultimate goals. These are ones that you believe, if achieved, will almost inevitably result in furthering one or more of your ultimate goals. Connect some of these up with some of your ultimate goals by drawing lines.
3. Attach two means-end staircases to two or more of these intermediate goals, placing on each step of these staircases a statement that will meet all of the following tests:
   a) It is the best means available for achieving the goal on the step above it.
   b) It is a cause which is powerful enough to produce the goal on the step above it.
   c) It serves as a goal for selecting an effective means to be placed on the step below it.
   d) It is a decision that has not yet been carried out.
   Note: Include a minimum of four steps in each of the two staircases called for in Part 3, above. On the bottom step of *one* of these staircases, write in: "To get the most out of the course of study in which this book is being used." In that staircase, your job is to write in appropriate goals on the other steps. In the other staircase, you are given a free hand to write in

whatever goals you want. Each step in both staircases must conform to Parts 3 *a*, *b*, *c*, and *d*.

From the above, it is evident that although the time sequence of the achievement of the goals you have placed on each step is important, that is by no means the only thing you must take into consideration.

Chapter **2**   # THE CREATIVE PROCESS

SEEING the goals clearly, arranging our prior decisions on staircases, and looking for inadequate or missing steps so that we can pinpoint the decisions we must now make, brings us to the stage where we can put to work the creative process, the third subsystem of concepts related to decision making. The objective here is to learn to create ideas for promising alternatives, which we shall consider later when we embark on the task of choosing the best alternatives to replace the inadequate or missing steps shown in Diagram 2 (p. 21). For it will be your responsibility as an executive to recognize company problems early and conceive solutions promptly.

A decision can be only as good as the best of the alternatives taken into consideration. For this reason, it behooves us to spend time conceiving alternatives that hold great promise. Even though we conscientiously select the best one before us, if we consider only those alternatives that first pop into the mind, the chances are that the decision will look unwise in retrospect.

In this chapter, our hope will be to brush away some of the mystery commonly associated with the process and put it to work for us—to get some insight into what it is and to transform what is ordinarily an unconscious process into a conscious, deliberately directed one. As we shall use the term, the creative process consists of framing ideas for new or heretofore unthought-of alternatives—for new means of achieving goals which will solve a problem better than those already at hand. We saw an example of this in Chapter 1 where we watched the chief executive grappling with a problem in his product development department and trying to conceive a solution to it.

If we can fathom what steps a person's mind takes in conceiving heretofore unthought-of ideas, we should be able to direct our minds to take those steps. My experience with executives and students leads me to believe that the creative process can be taught. In fact, I am convinced that it is an essential step in making decisions that will look good in retrospect; and as I have already said, I believe decision making can be taught. I do not subscribe to the generally held belief that inventiveness is an entirely God-given ability which people either have or do not have, that it consists of a blinding light of inspiration, the genesis of which is unfathomable. Teachers of the plastic arts and of singing have repeatedly shown that they can markedly impove a child's ability to create. This is not to say that all men can become equally creative; but by securing an understanding of the creative process and deliberately putting it to work, a man can augment whatever creative ability he may have. It should be pointed out at the start, however, that the mental processes of innovation are not known. Even though we may be able to describe approximately what our minds do unconsciously in the creative process, and thus what steps we want our minds to take, this does not guarantee that we shall all be able to guide our minds as we should wish.

THE EXECUTIVE'S TASK OF CREATING

Although we shall be chiefly concerned here with the task of creating rather complex ideas, the term *creative process*, as we are using it, also includes the creation of quite unsophisticated ideas for means of achieving those goals that lie far down on the staircase—those lying at the left in Diagram 2 (p. 21). For instance, the fisherman we watched in the sporting goods store (p. 9) was doing that—creating an idea of what lures would be best. The janitor we met in the Introduction to Part I was creating a step that rested low on the company's staircase when he figured out a new method of sprinkling the sweeping compound or a new point from which to begin sweeping the room. A machinist is creating when he thinks of a way of setting a new shape of casting in his grinder. An office clerk is creating when she discovers for herself how to handle an unfamiliar piece of information. It will be seen that practically everyone creates—at least in the sense in which we are using the term here—even though most of us would never think of dignifying some of these everyday activities with such a pretentious word. The creative process in these lower levels can usually be completed in a few moments. As we move upward toward the ultimate goals, the creative process becomes more complex and requires more time. We shall devote our attention to these somewhat complex creative activities.

Laymen frequently suppose that an executive's task is simply to decide between the alternatives presented to him by subordinates. But typically, the routine alternatives they suggest do not offer a fully satisfactory solution of the problem at hand. Conceiving better alternatives than those a subordinate originates is a major responsibility of an executive. And he is *forced* to be creative when asked: "What shall I do? Here are the three alternatives I ordinarily consider in handling a job of this kind; but as I see it, none of them will work very well here."

A good *chief* executive is also constantly called upon to create new alternatives. For one thing, it is his responsibility to take the initiative in creating pictures of new intermediate goals and developing ideas for new or improved ways of achieving them; his subordinates and the stockholders are particularly dependent on him for this. Ordinarily, the chief executive can create better alternatives than his subordinates because he can see the whole picture of the organization and is thus able to foresee the effect on each part of it when an extensive new program is inaugurated. Similarly, when he is confronted with the conflicting needs of two apparently opposite groups in his organization—the production department and the sales department, for example—we want him to evolve a new and better plan which will meet the needs of both groups. Moreover, he is in a position to create a new plan which cuts through red tape; he will know which of the rules or policies already established for governing the organization can be changed or broken.

Regardless of his position in the hierarchy, an executive's task is to create values, to create intangible satisfactions which are of enormous import to society. His contributions to society flow primarily from this creative ability. Curiously enough, in this respect, his task is not much different from that of a writer, or a composer, or a painter. He and they are trying to create new means—new satisfactions, new values—which they hope will interest others.[1] He is trying (or should be trying) to produce intangible values or satisfactions for his subordinates—for instance, a work environment and treatment which will give them satisfactions—and he and all his associates are trying to create products that will prove valuable to customers. He is often told, however, that what he creates is *un*desirable (material things are undesirable) or at least somewhat

---

[1] In his book, *Realms of Value* (Cambridge, Mass.: Harvard University Press, 1954), p. 3, Ralph Barton Perry explains that "a thing—anything—has value, or is valuable in the original or generic sense, when it is the object of interest—any interest. Or whatever is an object of interest is *ispo facto* valuable."

"lower," less desirable than the creations that "feed the spirit"—the ones produced by men in the fields of art, philosophy, or religion, for example. This point of view, it seems to me, is an unjustifiably narrow one.[2]

The executive's task of creating solutions to problems is a perennial one. The problem of creating better means of furthering people's goals will always be present, for as we saw in Chapter 1, they are always seeking better ones. Moreover, the accelerating rate of change in our society will place a higher premium than ever on the creativity and originality of businessmen.

The creative process of the chief executive is a particularly lonely one. A characteristic plaint is that he finds himself an isolated man, even though he is surrounded by people who talk and argue almost incessantly, and even though he often makes his final decisions in conjunction with a group of associates. In order to create plans and programs that will fit the needs of all the groups who look to him for leadership, however, he must periodically close his ears to the special claims of each, lift himself out of the center of the situation, and view the picture as would a detached outsider. The advice of men outside his organization—such as his banker, his attorney, or a professional business consultant, men with whom he can talk freely and with whom he can think—can be of inestimable help. Yet, in the last analysis, he must resolve these problems alone; for he, and only he, can know and sense all the ramifications of the decision he is trying to create. As Coleridge so aptly phrases it, he is "forever Voyaging through strange Seas of thought alone."

LEVELS OF CREATIVE OUTPUT

We are all aware that some people are more creative than others. Among artists, writers, mathematicians, scientists, and statesmen, the creative ability ranges all the way from those conceivers of vast

---

[2] No one is in a position to be dogmatic about which group of creators or which type of created thing contributes more or better satisfactions to society. A man has every right to have strong opinions about what he values most; but the amount of satisfaction one man gets from working in a congenial atmosphere, or from using a paper box to protect a newly purchased radio, or from consuming a bottle of liquor, or from sleeping in a comfortable bed, or from eating, can—for all anybody knows—be as great as some other man's satisfaction from hearing Mozart's String Quartet in A Major (K. 464) flawlessly played, from reading a passage from Spenser's *Faerie Queene*, or from gaining some new insights from a philosophical writer or scientist. There is no way of divining or of generalizing about what gives another man the greater satisfaction, or, for that matter, what is the better or more desirable satisfaction for that other individual or for society. In any case, all of us need and want some of *each* of these values. At a given hour, one need may be paramount; and at another time, some other need may predominate.

new ideas explaining and resolving a major enigma which has been baffling the best thinkers of the world, or of ideas for satisfying much more effectively than ever a deeply felt need of the world's people, on down to the pedestrian practitioner. The pedestrian man sees only isolated pieces of information and usually leaves most of them scattered about gathering dust in the attic of his mind. He has not learned to use these facts fully. He seldom asks himself what causes produced the facts he has accumulated, nor has he tried to guess what consequences might be expected to flow from a given fact. As a minimum, a creator must be able to frame pieces of information into statements of cause-result relationships. A creator should be able to go a step further and classify his facts and his ideas about the relationships between these facts into homogenous, related groups, so that they can be kept in order in the mind.

We shall probably never know exactly why there are wide differences between people in their ability to create. Perhaps the kind of guidance and encouragement they received accounts for some of the disparity. Almost all children start out with an overwhelming curiosity. They are forever seeking light on cause-effect relationships to explain what they see about them. The habit of asking questions is probably the foundation on which the creative process is built. Children ask what makes the sun shine, how babies are born, what makes the rain. Some parents and teachers have the patience to explain the cause-result relationships clearly, and they may go a step further and help the child to connect this newly recognized cause-result relationship with other facts he already understands. Possibly this helps to foster the habit of creating. On the other hand, some children seem to need very little guidance. They discover cause-result relationships for themselves by watching what happens around them, by experimenting, and by reading. In any case, once the habit of noticing cause-result relationships is established, it will probably persist; once the child has experienced the exhilaration accompanying creative activity, he will want to experience it again and again.

Conversely, the parent or teacher who answers the child's questions by saying, "That's just the way it is," or "Because it says so in a book I once read," or "Don't bother me with unimportant questions," could set up an almost opposite pattern of behavior. The child associates a painful rebuff with an attempt to create. Here, he is also being told, in effect, that it is a waste of time to try to discover cause-result relationships; everything happens because of chance or because an authority says so, and consequently it must be true. But this does not mean that an adult who in his childhood may have built up the latter type of thinking pattern cannot alter it and thereby improve his creative ability.

To foster creativity, a company's executives can deliberately establish an encouraging atmosphere and can try to guide men's minds into creative channels that will further the company's goals. New ideas are likely to abound where executives set an example by showing that the creation of new ideas is proper behavior, by adopting some of the more promising ideas even though they are not sure bets, and by rewarding the innovators. But it is also their duty to orient these people and direct them into fruitful projects by showing them specific goals the company would like to achieve and the boundaries they must work within. The more clear cut the goals, the greater the chances that a suitable means will be found. To be productive, the creative men must also know the practical limitations; for instance they must know something about the ability of the company's personnel to carry out a new project they are considering, the cost of carrying it out, and sense whether it is likely to pay for itself in the long run. Creating just *any* idea is not very difficult, but creating a *workable* idea that the organization can adopt requires mental discipline of a high order.[3]

First, then, the amount of encouragement and guidance an individual receives may influence his creativity. Secondly, the character and amount of his creative output probably depends a great deal on the level of his inherent mental ability. The amount of information he can recall and keep in his mind at one time about a particular subject is one measure of this. He must also have the ability to manipulate or rearrange the information into meaningful relationships. He must be able to shift it around and then ask himself what would happen if two or more of the facts not usually found together were placed in juxtaposition. If he is to create, he must think of pieces of information as dynamic, movable, visual images; they are not inert, static elements which have already been assigned their permanent place in the scheme of things. The possibilities of making new combinations are infinite.

Probably a third essential is drive. We all know men who without doubt are adept at the task of creating and who obviously have the ability to do so, yet nothing happens; they create practically nothing. So far, there seems to be no completely satisfactory explanation for

---

[3] How this is done will be explored in Chapter 14, where the work of the product development department will be scrutinized.

the differences in drive among people. The amount of a man's creative ability probably depends heavily on the height of the goals he has set, and even more on how badly he wants to achieve them. Perhaps the drive may have arisen from some preadulthood experiences. A man may have set a high goal, a goal of becoming famous, for example, because he read about and admired a famous person. He may want to achieve such a goal very badly because someone once belittled him and he thereupon determined to prove his worth. Or in some cases the drive may be the result of the heady experience attending the creative process, an exhilaration he may have experienced in his formative years. I believe that in most cases the man with great drive expects to enjoy a rise in status if he creates a large amount of high-level product—expects that his future welfare will be assured if he achieves the big goal he has set. The creator is usually confident he is creating values that will be highly esteemed by his fellow men, the unborn as well as the living.

This drive seems to induce constructive discontent, a willingness to disagree with the current solutions of problems—which is itself a mark of a creative person. Drive undoubtedly helps sustain the emotional and intellectual self-discipline a creator needs while he is bringing a new idea to fruition. And it gives him the fortitude and dedication he needs to work at the frontiers, knowing that his innovations will be challenged by those who dislike change or who fear that the new idea will jeopardize their welfare.

Creative activity appears to be one of the most intoxicating of all activities. Executives with a high degree of drive to create frequently experience the same sense of excitement as writers, musicians, or painters. The drive is so great that such men *have* to create; they feel frustrated if anything stands in their way or stalls this creative process.[4] Butterflies in the stomach, ulcers, and nervous breakdowns appear when they are thwarted.

As can be inferred from what has been said so far, a good executive must be a thinker as well as a doer. Although we usually look upon him as a doer, it is apparent that a highly effective executive must also be a philosopher, a thinker, a creator; he needs many of

---

[4] Wives of executives will testify to this. Their husbands are often in the throes of creating; and when they are going through the process, they are usually so abstracted or touchy that their wives are tempted to tell them to stay at the office instead of coming home. Worry, incidentally, is a manifestation of an attempt to create a solution to a problem.

the characteristics commonly associated with a retiring, ivory-tower sort of person, the so-called "dreamer."

STAGES IN THE CREATIVE PROCESS

What we shall explore is really *a* description of the creative process. This happens to be the only one I have come across in my reading, in my talks with other men, and in my personal experiences. No executive that I know of has written an account of his own creative processes;[5] but from what I have seen, I am quite certain that the creative processes of many executives are essentially the same as those used by men in the fields of the arts and sciences and those described by psychologists; we shall therefore draw heavily upon their reports. The chief difference is that businessmen create many of their new ideas for alternatives at conferences, whereas the others more often create in solitude.

Let us glance briefly at an example to get a quick preview of this creative process. The one we shall examine is the creation of the idea of the potter's wheel. Since its origins are lost in history, we shall have to imagine what took place. Before the invention of the potter's wheel the craftsman, in fashioning a clay vessel, had to build up the sides with successive handfuls of clay and laboriously smooth them with his fingers—a slow process which produced ill-shaped pots. At first, the tedious work and lopsided appearance of the pots were problems that only vaguely troubled him; he merely felt a sense of frustration that he could not define. But eventually, he began to recognize these as definite problems; and once he could visualize what was wrong, he was in a position to formulate concrete goals and conceive some solutions. Thereafter, he probably began to observe closely how his hands and fingers moved—that after placing each handful of clay, he slid his right hand around the sides of the finished vessel to smooth it and, at the same time, turned the pot in the opposite direction with his left hand. He had now put two pieces of information together. Then one day, perhaps, he noticed that the flat stone on which he customarily did his work suddenly began to rotate somewhat freely; upon examination, he discovered beneath it a small pebble—a cause that seemed to account for the result he had ob-

---

[5] But see A. T. Collier and James Hillier, "Creativity: What Lessons Can We Learn From Scientists?" an article by a scientist and a businessman in Dan H. Fenn, Jr., *Management's Mission in a New Society* (New York: McGraw-Hill Book Co., Inc., 1959).

served. He had now put together two further pieces of information which might be germane to the problems he had recognized. A few nights later, while half asleep, he found himself reviewing these— visualizing his hand movements when the flat stone was lying solidly on the ground and the way the stone turned when it rested on the pebble. Suddenly he caught a new vision, conceived a new idea. Why not deliberately place a pebble beneath the stone? The next day he tried this out—tested his idea. But he found that it did not work so well as he had expected (the table tipped awkwardly), and he concluded that he must improve on his solution. Possibly he discovered that he could use a larger and more spherical pebble, chip a circular recess in the center of the underside of the stone, and thus secure freer rotation and less tipping. Eventually, he explained his new idea to others—undoubtedly bragging a bit about his resourcefulness. These seem to be the approximate steps most men go through in creating a new alternative.

At the risk of making the creative process appear to consist of a simple sequence of steps such as those just described, with each of the separate activities fitting tidily into its own pigeonhole—when actually there is no formula, and the parts merge into one another —we shall explore the process in six stages. As a matter of fact, as we explore each of these stages in the pages that follow, we shall probably have trouble keeping each one firmly in its own place:

1. The stage of confusion.
2. The stage of gathering information.
3. The stage of incubation—of thinking about and organizing the information.
4. The stage of illumination—the actual act of creating the new idea.
5. Rechecking—reappraisal and revision.
6. Communication of the idea.

New ideas usually are not created by moving in an orderly sequence from the first stage to the sixth, but this approach should give us some useful insights. On occasion, in this investigation to follow, we shall examine some of the experiences of creators in the field of the arts and sciences, and tie these in with the executive's tasks.[6] In these pages, I have incorporated, as an extra tool, a description of a

---

[6] The framework I use here for the creation of ideas connected with the arts and sciences has been greatly influenced by the writings of John Livingston Lowes, especially *The Road to Xanadu* (Boston: Houghton Mifflin Co., 1927), his study of Coleridge's creative processes. The methodological approach I use in connection with the executive is strongly influenced by the one developed and used at the Harvard Business School. Both follow essentially the same underlying pattern.

methodological and somewhat mechanical approach. I have taught this to many students and young executives over the years; it is designed to help an executive to create a solution to a particular problem his company faces.[7]

The Stage of Confusion

The first stage is likely to be an uncomfortable one for us, a period of confusion and uneasiness during which we gradually recognize that we face a problem that must be solved, and then eventually crystallize it. There are doubtless many types of confusion, but most of us are quite familiar with at least two. One type occurs when we have become engulfed by a mass of details that seem to make no sense, and we feel impelled to solve the problem of how they go together.

The other is the confusion we experience when we do not know how to proceed—when we discover we are not achieving one of our important goals and must find a new means, or when we are casting about for a means of achieving a newly discovered and very exciting new goal. The executives who met to deal with the problem of low sales (p. 23) in the beginning were doubtless in this first stage, the stage of confusion, and were caught up in this second type of confusion.

---

[7] The six stages just enumerated correspond reasonably well with those that certain psychologists have sorted out. One well-known psychologist, in a book attempting to synthesize the findings of all psychologists, summarizes the stages in the creative process thus:

1. Sensitiveness to a need. The mind begins with the recognition of a small need (a goal) and endeavors to satisfy the need by pushing further and further until the individual begins to create.
2. He begins a long period during which he accumulates experiences that become richer and richer, especially in relation to the above need.
3. Usually, in a moment of excited self-direction toward the goal an integration of the accumulated material takes place—an integration in which both conscious and unconscious experiences have been drawn upon. Often, the illumination produces a picture of the whole which is the answer to the long quest.
4. As the answer is reconsidered, it becomes evident that certain needs are not fulfilled; and certain weaknesses appear. Then follows a period of polishing and reworking until a reasonable result is hammered out.

The foregoing is from Gardner Murphy, *Personality: A Biosocial Approach to Origins and Structure* (New York: Harper & Bros., 1947), pp. 464–66. See also F. S. C. Northrup, *The Logic of the Sciences and Humanities* (New York: Macmillan Co., 1947), especially chaps. i and ii.

The process we are discussing here is essentially the same as James Harvey Robinson's description of what he calls "creative thought," which he explores in *The Mind in the Making* (New York: Harper & Bros., 1921), (Sec. 5, chap. ii. "This kind of meditation," he says, "begets knowledge, and knowledge is really creative inasmuch as it makes things look different from what they seemed before . . . it is that peculiar species of thought which leads us to *change* our minds."

Usually, the beginning of this stage of confusion is marked by an inner unrest, a vague awareness that something is not quite clear or that something is amiss. We are not yet conscious of exactly what the trouble is, but we have a feeling that we should do something. Sometimes, we never get beyond this stage; we either sit there in our puddle of confusion or shrug and forget it. If the problem forebodes some serious harm to our welfare, or if the glimpse of the new opportunity is alluring enough, we may become dimly aware of physical discomfort. At first, we may refuse to admit to ourselves, much less to anyone else, that a problem is agitating us.

In time, however, the mental and physical discomfort may force us to admit that there is a problem and begin to recognize its general nature. In the first-named type of confusion, we realize that several of the facts we have in mind seem to be contradictory—if one is true, then another cannot be true; or even though the facts all relate to a given subject, they simply do not fit together in any logical, interrelated pattern. We seem to like orderliness; and when we can find none, we are troubled. But once we have admitted to ourselves that we are confused, and then have gone a step further and confided this to someone else, we are on our way out of the first stage and ready to enter the stage of fact gathering.[8]

In the second type of confusion, the one in which we grow increasingly aware that we may fail to achieve a major goal we had counted on or may miss a very promising opportunity, but can see no solution, the discomfort may become almost unbearable. The following are examples of situations that alert us to oncoming trouble—produce confusion because we do not clearly see how to cope with a problem. We may gradually realize that we are not going to get the job promotion that we had been counting on. We may feel uneasy about the way our boss has been acting toward us; maybe he does not speak to us except when it is absolutely necessary. Or if we are higher in the management hierarchy, we may be worried because sales are declining, the morale of our subordinates has been deteriorating, or an unsolved problem is holding up an important project. Many of us worry about the welfare of a group to which we are loyal—our family or church, for example; about the chances that our political party will lose the next election or that a war will come.

---

[8] One of the most brilliant men I have ever known, an attorney with whom I worked for some years as a consulting economist, moved through the stage of confusion very quickly. When he was confused or vague, he recognized and admitted it at once, and then set about the job of becoming *un*confused.

Sometimes, some of us remain so confused that we abandon all hope and try to escape; the problem seems so complicated, so difficult to deal with, that we cannot force ourselves to cope with it realistically. We retire into a dream world we have created, a world where the problem does not exist, in the belief that we have created a solution.

But the creator in whom we are interested faces the problem and conceives solutions that will actually deal with it. He sees that one of his goals is not being achieved, tries to determine which of the means have proved inadequate, and creates ideas for more effective means.

For an executive, the stage of confusion normally serves as a trigger to unleash his drives. When he sees that his company's accomplishments are not going to be up to the standards or goals that had been set, he knows a problem is developing. It is his responsibility to react to these novel and unexpected situations—to recognize approaching problems, clarify, crystallize, and present the salient problems (leaving aside the fringe problems) and appraise their probable effect on the company. He may, for example, gradually become aware that the number of skilled mechanics in the community is dwindling. His task is to determine if this is a problem, and, if it is going to be a big problem, begin well in advance to conceive means of securing more mechanics by going through the remaining stages of the creative process.

The Stage of Gathering Specific Information

Once we realize the existence of our problem and have stated it clearly, we are on our way out of the stage of confusion. If we intend to create an idea for a solution, however, we shall need a goodly fund of specific, pertinent information. The more concrete this is, the more useful it will be. All of us gather a mass of heterogeneous information quite accidentally in our day-to-day living; our task is to select the relevant pieces of information and seek out additional specifics which seem germane.

This is what a scientist is doing when he tries to create a new idea. From the mass of specific information he has accumulated in his day-to-day work, he selects facts that are relevant to the problem he faces, determines what pieces seem to be missing, and goes on a hunting expedition for those. He then crystallizes his problem more clearly and determines which pieces of old information are relevant (concentrating perhaps on information that seems to him contradictory or exhibits no unifying pattern) by asking himself questions about the "how's" and "why's" of each piece. This points to the additional information which he must seek out—to the causes and results that he does not yet know. Some of the information he uses will be factual, some of it will be simply an approximation of fact, and some of it will be opinion; but in each case, it must be concrete.

Similarly, most business executives also unthinkingly gather odd bits of specific information which later prove valuable in creating new ideas. They pick up facts, approximate facts, and opinions about competitors, conditions in the industry, customers, people's ideologies, and political and economic conditions over the country; they observe and hear what is happening in the company. The executive accumulates company facts such as these: "Our inventories are down 7 per cent compared with a year ago." "Four mechanics quit last month." "Our annual gross margin has increased from $427,000 to $503,000." Approximations or near-facts may be accurate enough for some purposes: "That incident happened about a year ago." "I'd say there are about four or five thousand on hand." "It looks as though our competitors are raising their prices." Opinions are useful, too, though the executive must be aware that they cannot be relied upon fully: "The men down in the shipping room are working hard for Joe Sapolski." "Dave McGrath seems to be losing his punch." "I think our sales will increase about 10 per cent next year." "Business conditions should steadily improve from now on."

When faced with a problem that is becoming uncomfortable, executives select and gather specifics in much the same way as the scientist does. In our session in Chapter 1 (p. 23), when we met with the executives who were worried about the low sales volume, we found that the men's progress became rapid once they recognized what the problem was. They started out by examining the pieces of information that made no sense to them—asked themselves why they were losing certain orders and why sales in a particular territory were low. This led them to select other pertinent pieces of information from their own recollection and to seek out new information which might account for those results. Theirs was a deliberate, self-directed activity.

Some of the great creative writers have also made a practice of initiating their creative processes by starting out with images of specifics. Coleridge, Goethe, Shakespeare, and Chaucer deliberately gathered concrete information to supplement what they had already accumulated and gradually found a pattern into which it would fit.

Coleridge read avidly all the first-hand accounts of early sea voyages he could find. From these, he stored away in his mind those specific words and phrases which described actual phenomena. After these lay in the well of his mind for a time, they were organized and coalesced into *The Rime of the Ancient Mariner*. Practically every word and phrase, every minute picture in the *Rime*, can be traced to its origin—to the page where Coleridge found it.[9]

Goethe also relied heavily on specifics; and he, too, wove these into an integrated, logical pattern, as indicated by his famous answer to those who kept asking what idea he sought to embody in Faust.

It wasn't, on the whole, my way, as a poet to strive after the embodiment of something abstract. I received within myself impressions—impressions of a hundred sorts, sensuous, lively, lovely, many-hued as an alert, imaginative energy presented them. And I had as a poet nothing else to do but mold and fashion within me such observations and impressions, and through a vivid representation to bring it about that others should receive the same impression, when what I had written was read or heard.[10]

"There," says Lowes, "we have it again in a nutshell: the phantasmagoria of the concrete world; the poet's mind like a sensitized film, alive to impressions; the impulse to give these impressions form, and to communicate." Shakespeare and Chaucer relied upon specifics gathered from stories written by earlier authors. These provided a sequence of causes and results (plot) which served as a magnet for the information they had gathered from their own observations of people's behavior, specifics that would give life to the original stick-like characters they found in those stories.

Once the problem is crystallized, the confusion that formerly existed as a blur, a dark void, begins to take on a recognizable shape. The novelist or philosopher begins looking for additional specifics which he perceives will be necessary to give more content and unity to the book he has sketched out in his mind. The composer begins to look for additional combinations of notes to go with those he has already accumulated and selected; without them the composition that seemed so pregnant in his mind will be fragmentary—will have no emotional impact. The scientist begins looking for additional facts germane to the problem he wants to solve, so that he can create a hypothesis.

---

[9] The origins of these words and phrases are traced by Lowes in *The Road to Xanadu, op. cit.* The book is highly recommended to those who would pursue the creative process further. Lowes's concluding chapter, "Imagination Creatix," is especially stimulating.

[10] Quoted from Lowes, *Convention and Revolt in Poetry* (Boston: Houghton Mifflin Co., 1919), p. 4.

Once the executive's problem is determined, he too begins searching for applicable information. He will discover many relevant details in his own mind, though some may have sunk below the conscious level; he must dredge these up before he can use them, exhume them from the unconscious. Usually, these details are insufficient; and he must go on hunting excursions for additional information. Here, he is actually searching for cause-result relationships—answers to such questions as why this happened, or what result we should expect from such and such a situation. Equally valuable, this quest may uncover ideas for a solution to our problem that may eventually spark the stage of illumination.

Note taking is of considerable help during this period when the facts and other specifics are being drawn from the executive's own experience and, through questioning or reading, from the experiences or findings of others.[11] The creative process is often given a generating push when the creator makes notes to himself. Without such notes, he frequently either forgets the specifics entirely or else uses them unconsciously in reaching his conclusion. Our common practice is to throw away the details that underlie our conclusions because we have no further use for them. As a consequence, in explaining our ideas to others, we make generalized statements which to us are self-evident; but to others, these statements seem to be merely leaps in the dark because they have not visualized the specifics we used.[12]

Incubation—Thinking about and Organizing the Information

In working at this third stage, that of incubation, we are trying to bring some order out of the many pieces of information we have accumulated. Here, we want to guide our minds in taking four steps: (1) putting the detailed pieces of information together into statements of cause-result relationships—putting two and two together; (2) checking the reliability of each statement; (3) gaining some perspective as to which cause-result relationships will have the greatest bearing on the problem; and (4) organizing these cause-result statements into three or four homogenous groups. We are actually doing a great deal of creating at this stage—creating small, subsidiary ideas—so we shall touch briefly on the creative act here.

[11] Many authors, composers, and painters keep notebooks to help them recall in detail the specifics they come across; their practice is to catch the picture at the moment it becomes sparkling and clear in their minds, so that they can reproduce it later.

[12] The reader will undoubtedly notice several instances of such lapses in this book. These notes also come in handy during the incubation stage and (as we shall find later, in Chapter 5) in employing proof to gain acceptance of our newly created alternative.

When we get to the fourth stage, where we are actually formulating a new alternative, we shall explore it more fully.

Although concrete information is essential if a man is to create, the information often adds to our confusion; we sometimes lose our way in the details.

Facts may swamp the imagination and remain unassimilated and untransformed. This sometimes happens with the masters. . . . Even Dante and Milton and Goethe sometimes clogged their powerful streams with the accumulations of the scholar who shared bed and board with the poet. . . . But when the stuff that Professors and Doctors are made on has been distilled into quintessential poetry, then the passing miracle of creation has been performed. . . . The imagination sees . . . the endless flux of the unfathomed sea of facts and images—but it also sees the controlling form. . . . The imagination in the field of science, for example, is slowly drawing the immense phenomena within the unfolding conception of an ordered universe. Its operations in the field of science are essentially the same as in the field of literature.[13]

When the executive is trying to think about and organize *his* information, he is coping with the same sorts of problems.

We do not know how the mind organizes and synthesizes the information. Yet we know that after a period of protracted, conscious study, we can lay away in our minds the pertinent pieces of information; and that after a period of incubation the relationships between them become obvious for the first time. Possibly Wordsworth's explanation that he was writing of things remembered in tranquility opens up a central idea of what happens. Much of this process seems to take place when we are performing other activities, usually routine ones. For many people the synthesis occurs extemporarily while traveling to work, mowing the lawn, taking a walk, or performing a routine job at the office. It often occurs at night when lying half awake. Usually, these are only fragmentary, fleeting insights; but later, they can gradually be added up into a whole. There is no way to turn on the spigot. It is almost impossible for the creator of a complex idea to sit down at his desk and say, "Now I am going to solve this problem," or "now I am going to create," the way one sets out to solve a practical engineering or arithmetical problem by the use of a formula.

Time seems to be essential if the process is to bear fruit—a period of time which permits the mind to recall and to put together, experimentally, in a number of alternative relationships, those parts which

<hr>

[13] Quoted from Lowes, *The Road to Xanadu, op. cit.* pp. 427–32.

seem germane to the problem at hand. During the incubation period, we endeavor to work out new and better arrangements of the parts until one is eventually found that seems to encompass all the parts naturally so that they fit together into an integrated whole. The creator of complex ideas is working with many unknowns, the organization of which is in each case unique; he is working at the frontiers. Whether he be a scientist, an engineer, an artist, a writer, or an executive, he must work out many new relationships; and this requires time.[14] Ideally, the executive's incubation period should be a very long one, though the pressure to make a decision promptly seldom permits this. His task of visualizing these relationships is particularly time-consuming because most of the details he must employ consist of his predictions of how people will behave in the future, and these are difficult to uncover.

Though we can train our minds to take the four distinguishable steps of the incubation stage, virtually no one takes these in a neat, orderly sequence. We do not *first* frame *all* the pieces of information into cause-result statements, connecting all the pieces together in pairs; nor do we then test the reliability of each; nor when (and only when) these statements are all framed and tested, do we weight them (or rank them) in the order of their pertinence; nor do we wait until this is completed to sort them into homogeneous groups. Our minds do all this on a catch-as-catch-can basis and in no particular order. And few of us perform these steps thoroughly unless we are forced to do so. These steps are what we should *like* to direct our minds to do at this stage, but they need not be done in any particular sequence. Indeed, we have already found that our minds are no respecters of the neat, orderly six-stage system we have devised in this chapter to describe what the mind does when it is creating—we have already had to look at the fourth stage, the stage of illumination, for example, even though at this point we are only part way through the third stage.

Framing Cause-Result Statements.   Only after a fact, or an approximation, or an opinion has been framed into a cause-result statement containing a second piece of information does it become useful for creative purposes.[15] These statements may be made up of

---

[14] We shall see later that the coalescence frequently takes place in a blinding flash, but this usually has been preceded by a long incubation period.

[15] In the next chapter, we define these cause-result statements more fully and give them the name "premise." As a matter of fact, we shall there explore all four of the steps in the incubation stage more fully.

any combination of two facts, approximations, or opinions. For example, a statement may contain two facts, or an opinion and an approximation, or an approximation and a fact, and so on. It may contain one piece of information the creator has already accumulated and another he has figured out himself. Upon observing a piece of information, he may suddenly realize he knows the *cause* that produced the result described by that piece of information; conversely, he may suddenly realize that he knows of a *result* that will probably flow from the situation described in a piece of information he already has; in this case, he thinks of the piece of information as a cause. Incidentally, a given piece of information may appear as a cause in one of these statements and as a result in another.

Essentially, what the mind is doing here is making images of causes and their results. To get a clearer view of this, let us put together some of the pieces of information used as examples in the second stage. "Because inventories are up seven per cent (cause), we should be in a position to handle the expected increase in sales volume (result)." "Four machinists quit last month (result), indicating that the morale of the department must be low (cause)." These are examples of statements using only the information we accumulated a few pages ago. Here is an example of a new cause-result statement made up of one fact already gathered and a newly found result. "Four machinists quit last month (cause); as a consequence, we will run into difficulty handling the increased business (result)." Notice also that "four machinists quit" is used as a result in one statement and as a cause in another. These cause-result relationships are just as easily forgotten as the separate pieces of information; it is useful to write down phrases that will help us to recall how the two related pieces fit together.

Once we see that cause-result relationships will help explain and illuminate our problem, it is easier to establish the habit of watching for them. Past experience and the recollection of it is of inestimable value in framing these statements, though what really matters is what one has *learned* from that experience. "Genius," says William James, "is the capacity of seeing relationships where lesser men see none." But at the moment, we must remind ourselves that we are only part way through the incubation stage. Only after we have related these cause-result statements to one another and to the central issue do they become useful.

Checking the Reliability of Each Statement. Once we have formed these statements, we usually suppose that they are undoubtedly true

—that the separate pieces of information are true representations of the actual circumstances and that the cause we have stated will produce the results we visualized. However, an executive can seldom find *any* statements that are demonstrably true; he must often be content with rather loose and unprovable statements, recognizing that they are approximations. Were we dealing only with inanimate mechanical objects—a printing press, for example—we could devise quite accurate cause-result statements: "When this lever moves, it will turn that wheel." But an executive must characteristically predict what a particular person or group of people will do if he hopes to reach a solid conclusion—no easy matter. And he must be reasonably sure that these statements are reliable. But even though he is quite certain that the results he envisages will really come true, will really flow from the cause, he should recheck them.

The invalid cause-result relationships disclose themselves more readily than one might expect. For instance, in the light of his past experience, a man notices that he feels uneasy or unsure of some of the relationships he is taking into consideration; these are the ones he should recheck. Asking other people their opinions of what cause-result relationships, if any, they think exist between two pieces of information that he questions helps a man to verify cause-result statements. Often he encounters two sets of what appear at first to be inconsistent cause-result relationships; upon further questioning, however, it turns out that they form a pattern entirely consistent with others known to be reasonably reliable. In such a case, both are probably reliable. Other statements do not correspond with what is known to be true and must therefore be labeled "probably unreliable." All the statements an executive keeps should fall into a consistent pattern. After he has checked the reliability of the piece of information used as a cause, the one used as a result, and the statement of the relationship between the two, and has then checked the consistency of the several statements with one another, he should be able to tell how solid his footing is. He subconsciously discards the unreliable statements.

Weighting. Selecting the most pertinent cause-result statements and weighting these, the third of the four steps in this incubation stage, helps an executive to eliminate the unimportant ones and gain some perspective about the ones retained. After most of the cause-result relationships seem to have been brought to light, it will almost always become apparent that some of those caught during the hunting expeditions are trivial. Upon reexamining them with the problem before him, he realizes that some either have no pertinence to the central question or else, when laid alongside the others, appear to play such a minor role that they can be eliminated without much loss. This reduces the number of ideas the executive must cope with when the time comes to create his solution to the main problem. The creator can then range the ones he keeps in the order of their importance. Those that will probably have the greatest impact on the goals sought —the problem to be resolved—would be listed at the top, and the others ranked in descending order. It is very easy to lose perspective and give great weight to cause-result statements which eventually turn out to be of little real significance.

Grouping the Statements. The fourth task during this incubation period is to sort the cause-result statements into three or four homogeneous groups—into a manageable form, so that the creator can cope with them. His objective here is to find a few topics under which all the cause-result statements may be listed without distorting them. This usually requires disciplined thinking. In looking over his notes of images he has seen, he will eventually find that most of them fall rather naturally into a few groups under a few headings. Even those that appear to argue *against* some tentative ideas he may now have for a promising new alternative will fall into these groups. The task is to switch the cause-result statements around—combine them in various ways—until three or four headings are discovered that will encompass all of them.

The groupings for each of the many problems an executive must resolve will differ. For one problem, he may find that his notes can be classified quite well under the names of each of the several groups of people (a specific group of customers, a group of employees, and the company's jobbers, for example) whose reactions have to be considered in resolving the particular problem at hand. In another problem, these notes may fall naturally under such headings as expected sales volume, manufacturing capacity, variable and fixed expenses, and executive's reactions. The information he gathers determines the categories; the categories do not determine the information we should try to find. It is almost fatal to try to force these mental images into preconceived classifications or into groups which "the book," a professor, or some other authority says they ought to fall into. This results in distortion—in a twisting of the information gathered; as a result, the proposed solution to the problem turns out to be so academic and unreal that it is virtually useless as a possible decision.

With these homogeneous groups, we are endeavoring to bring some order out of chaos. We are trying to devise what might be likened to an instrument case, one suitable for a complex instrument with all kinds of curious bulges, a case for an instrument that is unique. The case is not, however, a part of the instrument itself.[16] Once we have found an orderly arrangement, we can tick the groups off on the fingers of one hand and thus remember the three or four big parts which make up the whole; and a further look at these headings will help to remind us of the several details we listed under each.[17] At this point, we often discover heretofore unsuspected interrelationships among the cause-result statements included within each classification. By this time, we are also beginning to get a sense of the whole; we see an allover composition made up of many interrelated parts.

The Stage of Illumination

In the three stages thus far explored, our minds have been accumulating and organizing the stuff needed to reach the culminating fourth stage, the stage of illumination. Our objective now is to conceive a new, better solution, a newly seen alternative. Sometimes, as we near the end of the incubation stage, our minds slide effortlessly to a solution. More often, we must at least nudge our minds.

Inducing the Mind to Think. Once in a while, to solve a complicated problem, we must deliberately force our minds to do hard thinking. When this is required it is helpful to begin by revisualizing the framework of cause-results which the mind has gradually conceived and observe the workings of the whole and the parts; we look both at the problem and at the relationships of the now-well-organized mass of information pertinent to it. As we walk around the problem and visualize it in its setting, we gain a more penetrating perspective, see its inner structure and operation more clearly. And while observing from a fresh perspective this model of reality which our mind has constructed, we *may* decide to reorganize our newly found picture once again; we discover that by regrouping some of the cause-result statements we can better see their meaning and role.

If this observation of the whole structure and its operation fails to produce a solution, we may employ a more mechanical approach to start a new ferment in the mind, namely, endeavor to draw useful

---

[16] Lecomte du Noüy uses this simile in *The Road to Reason* (New York: Longmans, Green & Co., 1948), p. 169.

[17] The reason for trying to include all cause-result statements within no more than three or four groups is that most of us can readily recall only that many; we encounter difficulty remembering five or more.

conclusions from each of the three or four homogeneous groups. Here we first *force* our minds to pick out two or three possible solutions, even though we know that none will be very satisfactory. Then we try each one out by observing what would occur were it adopted; the cause-result statements included under each topic will suggest many of the results of adopting each solution. Recall that we have already thought some about the reliability of these results—whether they will really flow from the causes—and their relative impact on our goals. Our task now is to frame a conclusion relative to *each topic* which summarizes the results we foresee would occur if one, then another, of the solutions were put into effect. If, for example, one of our topics were headed "customers," we might try to summarize their probable reactions to solution A—for instance, "Our customers will like solution A quite well"—then to solution B—"customers in the South will like solution B, but most others will dislike it." If one of the topics were costs, we would try to write similar statements— "Solution A will increase our manufacturing costs by about 5 per cent," and so on. These procedures clearly call for mental discipline.

For convenience, such conclusions will, in this book, always be called "subconclusions." As an aid in reviewing his thinking processes, the creator should make notes of the two or three not quite suitable preliminary solutions he was trying out and the subconclusions he drew for these. When these are laid together, he may suddenly see a more satisfactory solution.

We should now be in a position to create a new idea—a visual image for a realistic course of action. By this time the originative process should be working at full blast, and the mind should be teeming with ideas for solutions.

At this point we are dealing chiefly with the time when all the separate steps fall into an integrated pattern and the mind sees a solution to its problem. Our mind will not be content with just any solution; it automatically discards solutions which have obvious drawbacks and keeps searching until it finds a "good idea." It is trying to conceive a solution that is feasible in the light of the situation in which the individual or organization finds itself. Actually, at each of the earlier stages the mind has also been creating; clearly, we have been trying to separate into compartments a process that is inseparable. During the information-gathering and the incubation stages the creator was giving the facts and his problem his undivided, absorbed attention, though probably intermittently. He was saying, "Given these facts, what hypotheses, what pattern, best unifies them and best illuminates the world I will be living in?"[18] As we noted earlier, "the imagination sees all things in one. It sees . . . the unfathomed sea of facts and images—but it also sees the controlling form."[19] The creator has been voyaging through chaos and reducing it to clarity and order. The six-stage approach used here is simply a tool for inducing creative activity.

Sometimes, the difficult task, surprisingly enough, is not that of creating an idea for the final solution (the ideas often come pell-mell); but, instead, the task of *not* creating one; in other words, the difficult task may be to hold off "seeing all things in one" until after the first three stages have been completed—until all the information is in and has been appropriately weighted and organized. Jumping to a conclusion about the pattern found and the solution to the problem results in decisions that almost always look unwise in retrospect. This, incidentally, is a hazard of testing out those not quite satisfactory solutions intended to induce ferment in our minds. Jumping to a conclusion is nevertheless understandable. In our anxiety to create, we often accept the first over-all unifying pattern we see, believing it to be the only one. Moreover, once we have found a solution, we feel that we can leave off the painful task of thinking. We shall return to this problem of jumping to conclusions when we get into the fifth stage, the task of reappraising and revising.

The Creative Mind at Work. Overstreet[20] defines imagination as "a synthesis of new ideas from elements experienced separately. It is not, as is so often thought, a process of making something out of nothing. Imagination is rather a process of making new wholes out of familiar parts." Buermeyer, in a book dealing with the arts, calls it "the reorganization of those impressions or facts so as to extract . . . their meaning and value."[21]

Lecomte du Noüy, the biologist and philosopher of science, points out that the salient feature of creativeness in the scientific field is the creation of hypotheses[22] or, as we should say, of tentative new alternatives.

---

[18] Adapted from a statement by James Bisset Pratt, quoted by David Elton Trueblood, *The Logic of Belief* (New York: Harper & Bros., 1942), p. 8

[19] Lowes, *The Road to Xanadu, op. cit.*, p. 432.

[20] H. A. Overstreet, *The Mature Mind* (New York: W. W. Norton & Co., Inc., 1949), p. 64.

[21] Laurence Buermeyer, *The Aesthetic Experience* (Merion, Pa.: Barnes Foundation, 1924), p. 89.

[22] Noüy, *op. cit.*, p. 77. In the quoted passage, the words in brackets are ones I have added.

In his words:

. . . the man of science who cannot formulate a hypothesis is only an accountant of phenomena. Hypothesis is the stamp imprinted by the human mind on the simple succession of facts. Through the intermediary of our senses, extended by our instruments, nature furnishes rough phenomena which follow each other in time. [Cause-result relationships?] Our intelligence grasps this enumeration and tries to create a plausible fairy story in which each event plays a plausible part in the birth of subsequent events and is a consequence of past events. [Means-end staircase?] This fairy story is the hypothesis, the fundamental tool of scientific work. It rests entirely upon one of the most extraordinary qualities of the human mind, imagination— science could not exist without it. It is not a method for it cannot be transmitted. [Note that I think it can, to some extent, be taught.] It is the result of an individual gift, which cannot be specifically differentiated from literary or philosophical genius. The more facts it covers, the greater its value. . . .

Later he points out (p. 79):

Imagination bolstered by facts is the mother of hypothesis, and hypothesis is the soul of science. It would, therefore be useful to develop imagination.[23]

In creating an idea, a hypothesis, our mind seems to fling itself beyond the known into the not-yet-known, using as a jumping-off place the information, cause-results, and ideas it already knows. The hypothesis we conceive is a possible solution to the problem that originally confused us. In conceiving a hypothesis, both we and the scientists seem to be aided by immersing ourselves for a time in the problem and the information pertinent to it. The hypotheses that we are trying to conceive in this chapter, however, differ in one major respect from those conceived by men in the physical sciences. They gather and organize information as a basis for reaching a *general* conclusion (or a law) that will be *universally* true; they seek a successful working hypothesis that, when properly employed, will yield right answers or solutions in every instance. In contrast, because we deal with people instead of atoms, we can with confidence use our solution for only one problem—one particular group of people in one company at one time in their lives. (Be reminded that

---

[23] Several artists, writers, and scientists have written descriptions of their creative experiences; and some of these have been reprinted in anthologies. One such, edited by Brewster Ghiselin, is called *The Creative Process* (Berkeley: University of California Press, 1952); and another is Rosamund E. M. Harding, *An Anatomy of Inspiration* (Cambridge Eng.: W. Heffer & Sons, Ltd., 1940). Morris I. Stein and Shirley J. Heinge, in their *Creativity and the Individual* (Glencoe, Ill.: The Free Press, 1960), summarize some 300 books and articles from the fields of psychology and psychiatry. Also see "Creativity" in *Carnegie Corporation of New York Quarterly*, Vol. IX, No. 3 (July, 1961), for a résumé of some recent studies of creative individuals.

we are trying to create quite complex ideas for use near the tops of staircases; we can quite easily conceive fairly useful hypotheses for steps near the foot of a staircase.) People are not so homogeneous as atoms, consequently their behavior is not so predictable—except perhaps in their muscular behavior, and in performing routine tasks.

The actual creative experience often seems to take place all in one moment, without any apparent preliminary effort. Perhaps this and our tendency to do much of our thinking at the unconscious level has led to the common belief that inspiration strikes. "Our thought," as James Harvey Robinson says in another connection, "moves with such incredible rapidity that it is impossible to arrest any specimen of it long enough to have a look at it." Gardner Murphy also speaks of a blinding flash of inspiration; the concept of the whole is born in a moment. John Dewey[24] describes this process as a readjustment of observations made in the past which often come in a flash following a period of prolonged painful thinking on the parts and which produce a new orientation, a new insight. It is a process of welding together the elements, no matter how diverse, into a new and completely unified experience.

Lowes[25] explains the all-in-a-moment creative experience somewhat further in a description of one of his own experiences:

> Once called, they [the facts] came pell mell as if the fountains of the deep were broken up. Moreover, to my certain knowledge, most of them had never come into conjunction in the field of my consciousness before . . . the panorama was set in motion and unrolled without my will. For a moment I simply allowed the images to stream, then I deliberately assumed control. For, when an hour later, I came back to write, I saw that here like manna from heaven was grist for my mill. The sentences about the world of images at the center of which we lived stood already on the page, and the skeleton of a plan was in my head. . . . I have now consciously selected and rejected among the crowding elements of the phantasmagoria, and the elements accepted have been fitted into my design. The streamy nature of association has been curbed and ruddered.

But despite our attempt to perceive the nature of the process of creation by separating it into stages and retracing the footsteps of men in the creative arts, it is evident that we have not found out how the mind of man can and does create. We can only get glimpses into this creative process and, by deliberately gathering information and inducing incubation, try to smooth the path so that the creative proc-

---

[24] John Dewey, *Art as Experience* (New York: Minton, Balch & Co., 1934). See pp. 266–69 particularly.

[25] Lowes, *The Road to Xanadu, op. cit.*, pp. 430–31.

ess will flow unimpeded. We do not know how it is triggered. As Lowes says, "It is true beyond possible gainsaying that the operations we call creative leave us in the end confronting a mystery. But that is the fated terminus of all our quests."[26] The mind produces answers that grow out of the totality of all the impressions that have lain in the creator's mind; some of these are his own experiences, but many are garnered from his reading and conversations. Relatively few lie at the conscious level of his mind; most have long since become submerged. And each one is weighted by the creator in accordance with his own prediction of the impact that each of these cause-result relationships will likely have on the problem he is solving—on his own or his group's welfare.[27] The mind can, without apparent effort, organize, test, and weight a mass of specific information, much of which lies beneath the conscious level and little of which is subject to mathematical measurement.

Perhaps this process has something in common with what some people call "intuition." Women are supposed to possess this, and men say that executives often make their decisions intuitively. Perhaps their perception can be attributed to their extreme sensitivity to the impressions—the pieces of information—they have gathered, their ability to recall and put together these impressions and thus use them as premises. These cause-result relationships are ordinarily so subtle that the creator of the idea has difficulty in framing them for his personal use and almost overwhelming difficulty in explaining them fully to others, even when he can see them clearly in his mind's eye. Yet the cause-result relationships which the creator sees are so real to him and he is so sure of them that he can act upon them with confidence.[28]

Cultivating Creativity. There are several practices which a man can follow in an effort to enhance the fruits of his creative ability. In my work with young executives and students, I sometimes sug-

---

[26] *Ibid.*, p. 428.

[27] The cause-result relationships which are never brought up out of the unconscious probably have just as much effect upon the new ideas we create as do those lying at the conscious level. Freud and Jung's pioneer work in this field seems to have stood up fairly well.

[28] In this chapter, we have been talking almost exclusively about mental images— of cause-result relationships which have occurred or may occur. These ocular spectra, to use Coleridge's term, are for the most part images of intangible, nonphysical things. My psychologist friends tell me, however, that some people use images of *symbols*—words or signs, for example—instead of mental images of abstract or real things. Some creators make up nonsense words or symbols of their own to stand for a set of cause-result relationships. Lord Kelvin used these. One of their problems, then, is to translate these into English when the time comes to communicate them.

gest three. One is to practice the rather matter-of-fact aproach we
have been exploring—seeing the problem, gathering facts, framing
them into cause-result statements, testing and weighting them, and
organizing these into homogeneous groups. This usually results in a
gradually dawning idea for a reasonably solid solution. Another is to
retrace some of our own creative experiences, preferably rather simple ones. The trick here is to recognize the experience immediately.
The path must be recalled at the very moment the new idea appears
because within two or three minutes, all trace of it is obliterated. A
new alternative conceived to solve a simple everyday problem which
lies far down on a staircase is best for this purpose because the thinking sequence there can be retraced rather easily.

A third method is to practice what we might call "deliberate-
thinking." Although we cannot sit down and say, "Now I'm going to
create," we *can* deliberately observe; and we can then ask ourselves
what someone else might consider were foolish questions about what
we observe, and put these pieces of information into juxtaposition.
This is a characteristic procedure of the scientist; he asks why a chair
should be designed the way it is. The chain of thinking starts when
two ideas, heretofore seen separately, are thrown together for the
first time and we observe a new cause-result relationship. This seeing
of two pieces of information in a new light often occurs while reading; we can tell there has been such a conjunction when we discover
that we cannot recall what we have just read. (I hope you will encounter several such experiences while reading this book.) What has
happened is that something the author has said suddenly connects up
with something we already know; we see both these ideas in a new
light. To get the full benefit from this spark, we should immediately
stop reading, take another look at the newly noted cause-result relationship, and then force ourselves to think of a *new* result that would
or could flow from what we have just seen. We say to ourselves, "If
this were to happen, what result would flow from it?" Then we take
another step and another, forming a means-end chain (instead of a
means-end staircase) that is headed toward no particular goal. Often, we shall hit upon some collateral chains before we are through.
It is time to call a halt when our minds wander into means-end chains
which end in trivia—which have to do with the beauty of a movie
star, for instance. After completing this exploration, it is fruitful to
retrace as many of the steps as possible, starting with the spark that
set us off. In this way, we can observe what we did and do it again.
Frequently, the new ideas uncovered in these unintentional and in-

tentional excursions unexpectedly stand us in good stead later. The new paths through the gray matter of the brain can be retraced rather quickly whenever those ideas are needed in resolving a pressing problem.

Rechecking: The Reappraisal and the Revision into Polished Form

The fifth stage is the one in which the executive reappraises his newly created idea and revises and polishes it to make sure that it will stand up when it is put into practice. We have already seen that a man should hold off his final decision about adopting the newly created alternative, even though at first sight it seems perfect to him. Regardless of whether the solution to the problem has come in a blinding flash or has been more deliberately evolved by methodically building it piece by piece and organizing the pieces, it often turns out to be unrealistic in certain respects when viewed later. All of us have gone through the disillusioning experience of realizing that a solution which looked wonderful the night before is really quite impracticable upon re-examination the next morning. In reappraising it, we discover that we had overlooked some unsolved subsidiary problem lying far down on the staircase we had hastily conceived to carry out the new solution; or some unwanted consequences show up which would make the new alternative much less desirable than it seemed at first. We discover we shall have trouble securing the necessary funds, for instance, or that someone on whom we must count to carry out part of the project will oppose this proposal because it will lower his prestige. Sometimes, we can find nothing seriously wrong; our mind has done an almost perfect job of creating.[29]

If, at the time of reappraisal, we are watching for some of the characteristic pranks our minds play on us, we can usually locate weaknesses and then make realistic revisions. Maybe we have overlooked the obvious, the *big* thing—for example, the long-term goals we are trying to achieve. Merely stating the obvious often lends perspective. Our minds sometimes mislead us into giving great weight to a cause-result statement that is unimportant and little or no weight to a very important one. We frequently become enamored of certain information which really concerns side issues. Conversely, we may dis-

---

[29] We expect that some unforeseen "bugs" will show up, of course, when we put the "perfect" idea into effect; but we rely on our ingenuity to solve these minor problems when we actually meet them. Scientists, artists, and businessmen seem to do this regularly. If we waited to clear up *all* the subsidiary problems beforehand, we should probably never get around to putting the idea into effect.

cover that some of the cause-result relationships we originally discarded as insignificant or nongermane now loom up as salient ones. Or we may have used certain cause-result relationships unthinkingly or perhaps even unconsciously. These can be detected because they are vague; the procedure is to break the statement down into its specific causes and results and thus make them more concrete. Reviewing our notes also aids us in uncovering our mental slips. We shall not stop here for examples of these lapses. The reader will be able to furnish illustrations from his personal experiences.

An executive can nearly always employ almost all of his original idea for his solution if he goes about revising it carefully; indeed, he can often improve it. Such revisions in the details enable the executive to get the fullest value from his idea. Frequently, after speculating upon the solution, he uncovers many new, illuminating relationships totally unnoticed while he was intent on the exciting experience of shaping the idea. He also often discovers unexpectedly that the plan will concurrently serve as a means of achieving other goals—of solving some other elusive problems which have been disturbing him and his associates, other than the problems he set out to solve—or it can be made to do so if slight revisions are made.

An effective way to revise the new idea is to put it to work in the mind—put it into operation. The executive can try out his alternative —imagine that it has now been put into effect—and if it does not work to his complete satisfaction, if weaknesses gradually become apparent, he can revise it. If this revision does not work, he can make further revisions until he finds one that satisfies him; if he concludes that he cannot immediately solve some part of the problem, he should lay such a feature aside for further incubation.

Communicating the new idea and the concrete details lying beneath it, the subject to which we next turn, offers still another way of reappraising, revising, and polishing the idea.

Communicating the Idea

In Part II, there will be a chapter devoted to communication, so that we need not spend much time on the sixth and final stage. But this does not mean that communication is unimportant. A newly created idea is useless unless it is imparted to others.

Complex ideas such as those we have been talking about are very difficult to communicate. Perhaps this explains the high correlation revealed in many psychological tests between an extensive vocabulary and success as an executive. An executive is working with intangibles, and these are so elusive that most men have trouble describing them in concrete terms. A good executive must be articulate. His task is to delineate these ideas so clearly that his hearers will be able to form similar pictures in their own minds. Upon hearing or reading what he says, they must be able to nod their heads and say to themselves, "Yes, I recognize that; it is real; it makes sense to me."

Perhaps the key to communication lies in a man's ability to form and hold in his mind images of the *details* of his whole idea—hold them out at arm's length, as it were—and then to describe in an orderly way exactly what he sees there. In these pages, we have spent a good deal of thought on sharpening the images to a point where even the intangibles can be described in concrete terms. If he has the vocabulary to portray these concrete intangibles, his description of the ideas flows easily from his tongue or his pen. As Lowes expressed it, ". . . here like manna from heaven was grist for my mill." And to requote Goethe, "I had . . . nothing else to do but mold and fashion within me such . . . impressions, and . . . bring it about that others should receive the same impression, when what I had written was read or heard."

The executive's job of communicating is similar to that of an artist —a writer, for example. Each must create the image in all its complexity—create in his own mind the picture of people feeling things and doing things—and then describe all of them in detail with words that precisely and fully convey this ocular spectrum to others. Men like Tolstoy, Thomas Wolfe, or Thomas Mann stand above many of their fellow writers in this ability to paint detailed mental pictures of people and their motives and actions, in their capacity to hold these details clearly in the mind's eye, and in their skill in searching out the words necessary to convey these images with exactitude to others.

Regardless of his level in the hierarchy, relatively few of the ideas for new alternatives which an executive is called upon to create are as complex as those with which we have been working in this chapter, so that if the reader has been able to say, "Yes, I comprehend what has been said, and it makes sense to me," he should be able to cope with lesser problems more easily than before. He has gained some grasp of the concept of creating ideas for new alternatives.

These six stages of the creative process constitute our third conceptual subsystem.

Chapter 3 THE USE OF
PREMISES IN
MAKING DECISIONS

IN THIS chapter the task of actually making the decisions will be explored. Here we put to work the fourth subsystem of concepts, the concept of premises, the use of factual premises and value premises as instruments for choosing between alternatives. In Chapter 1, we first worked with the subsystem we called the concept of goals (ultimate, intermediate, and those lying on the means-end stair), underlining the necessity for choosing meaningful ones and making them as explicit as possible. Then we dealt with the idea of arranging these goals on a staircase, so that we could uncover any vague, or inadequate, or missing steps that would likely be crucial in achieving our higher goals. That second subsystem enabled us to pinpoint those decisions in need of revision or those that had not yet been made. In Chapter 2, we set as our objective the creation of ideas for new alternatives, which we could lay alongside the more obvious ones we had already thought of. We used the creative process, the third subsystem, to bring to light the most promising alternatives, so that we could be reasonably sure that the one we finally decided to insert in the staircase would be the best available.

From this point on, we are jumping off into the unknown. It is at this juncture that the fourth subsystem, which we shall call the premise concept, begins to play its role. The decision maker knows about past events, but he cannot know about the future. Yet he is chiefly concerned with what will occur in the period ahead—with what would occur if he were to adopt one of the alternatives. His responsibility here is to probe the unknown, to make the invisible visible.[1] The premise concept is an instrument for imagining in detail what the results of choosing an alternative would be.

[1] See "How Businessmen Make Decisions," *Fortune* (August, 1955), for an illuminating description of the process used by some executives.

56

The objective in making a decision, whether a personal decision or a company decision, is to choose from among the most promising alternatives the one (or ones) that will produce the greatest aggregate amount of wanted consequences and the smallest amount of unwanted consequences. In order to determine which is best, most of us ordinarily test out each alternative in turn by imagining that each (but not the others) has already been put into effect; and then we try to foresee in detail what the probable desirable and undesirable results or consequences of adopting that alternative would be. When these two steps have been completed, we are in a position to compare the alternatives. This is the practice we shall examine here; we shall break it apart and probe the elements of this process in an effort to turn what is typically an unconscious procedure into a conscious one.

The statements of wanted consequences and unwanted consequences are what we shall call "premises." All of us employ premises in making decisions, even though we never think much about them. They simply flit through our minds as mental images. If we are alone when we are trying to reach a decision, we make no attempt to describe the premises. When several men work together on a decision, each one tries to express in words the consequences he foresees. But whether these thoughts are spoken or unspoken, a decision maker is saying, in effect, "If I were to put into effect the first (or the second, or the third) alternative, I would expect such-and-such results to follow, all of which I consider desirable; and I anticipate these other results, which seem to me undesirable."

The alternative we choose should not only serve as the best means of furthering the goal just above it on our means-end staircase. It should also help to advance *other* goals we have in mind—our own, our associates', and our organization's intermediate and ultimate goals as well as other goals lying on lower steps of some of the several means-end staircases. We frequently refer to these consequences that further other goals as desirable side effects. In making a decision, our aim should be to select a means that will further several goals simultaneously. In this way the benefits from the chosen course of action are greatly multiplied.

We are also seeking the alternative that will produce the least amount of injurious effects on those higher goals. Sometimes, we close our eyes to undesirable side effects—and live to regret the oversight.

Virtually every alternative we consider will produce both wanted and unwanted consequences. We should (but seldom do) look with skepticism upon an alternative that seems to us either all black or all white. It behooves us to take a second look at any such proposal, for the chances are that we have made up our minds too early—have decided to accept or reject it before examining the consequences realistically. We sometimes become so enamored of a new alternative we have uncovered that we unconsciously magnify the desirable ends it will serve and block out of our minds all the results we do not want to see.

Before making the final decision, it will also be advisable to check the reliability of our predictions of those consequences we envisage. Otherwise, we may find later that some of the results we had depended upon fail to materialize. Breaking down a premise into its elements, then examining the premise for its factual and value characteristics, provides a tool for checking the reliability of the premises we have gathered—for testing our detailed predictions of what will occur. In addition, it will be necessary to assign relative weights to the premises we uncover—to determine which premises will probably have a marked impact on the goals we cherish and which ones will have only a slight effect. Weighting provides us with some perspective as to the relative importance of the anticipated wanted and unwanted consequences.

The first steps, however, are (1) to uncover the premises germane to each alternative—imagine in detail the specific results—and then (2) to list them according to whether they are wanted or unwanted. Diagram 3 shows a useful way to visualize the location of premises in relation to the several possible alternatives we have under consideration, one of which we intend to insert permanently on our staircase.[2]

In this chapter, we shall be thinking mainly about the decision making of middle-level executives. What is said applies equally well,

---

[2] Many of the ideas contained in the first chapter and in this one have been touched upon by John Dewey in one or more of his many books. In his *Quest for Certainty* (New York: Minton, Balch & Co., 1929), for example, he refers to several of the concepts in general terms: means and ends, goals (purpose), predictability, cause and effect, values, solutions to problems. Chapter VIII is particularly interesting in this connection. It is almost impossible to quote from any of his books however, for his ideas are so embedded in the whole of his writing, and the concepts are framed in such a fragmentary manner, that individual sentences are almost useless when lifted out of context. Herbert Simon, in his *Administrative Behavior* (New York: Macmillan Co., 1947), leans heavily upon Dewey, as does almost every other writer who is attempting a marriage between man's ethical decisions and his practical everyday decisions. Ralph Barton Perry, in his *Realms of Value* (Cambridge, Mass.: Harvard University Press, 1954), employs a philosophical and logical approach which parallels in certain respects the one used in these chapters (see chap. i, pp. 79, 124, 395 ff.). The framework used here is an adaptation of what is often called "scientific logic," broadened to include predictions of occurrences for which no measurements are available, predictions of the unknown.

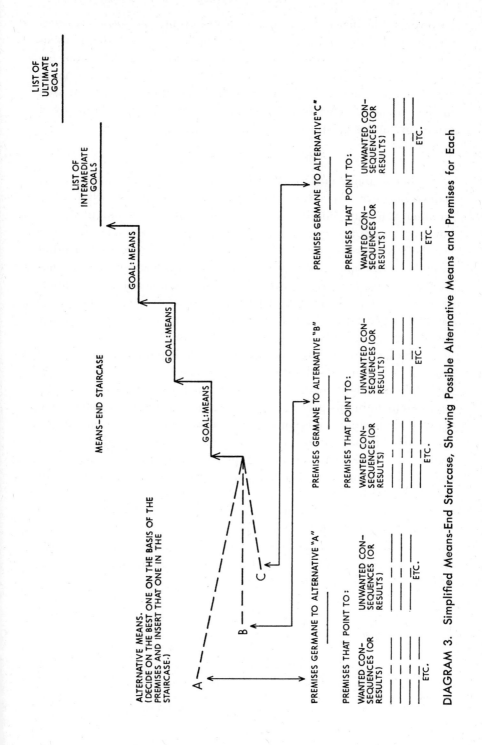

DIAGRAM 3. Simplified Means-End Staircase, Showing Possible Alternative Means and Premises for Each

however, to the decisions of all executives, from supervisors of small sections containing only three or four people up to the top executives and the chief executive. This is pointed out to avoid confusion, because the term "the executive" will continue to be used. It should also be emphasized that even though this term will frequently be used in the singular, actually most company decisions are made by a group or, at least, approved by a group.

THE PREMISE CONCEPT

We noted above that premises are statements of our ideas of the wanted or unwanted consequences which we believe would flow from an attempt to put into effect a certain alternative. For our purposes, however, it will be necessary to sharpen that definition. As we shall use the term here, a premise is a statement containing a description of both a cause and a result which we deem pertinent to the alternative we are examining. But even that description is not quite explicit or accurate enough for our purposes. A premise is really composed of three elements: a *cause,* a *result, and* the *causal connection* which we believe exists between the cause and the result.[3]

In a majority of the premises we formulate, a phrase describing the alternative under consideration serves as the *cause* element. Such a *cause* phrase might read, "If we carry out this proposal . . ." The *result* element in this premise would be a phrase describing one of the wanted or unwanted consequences we visualized when testing out the alternative in our mind. So the complete premise would read as a sentence: "If we carry out this proposal (the cause), the morale of the men in the product development department (for example) will rise (the result)."

One of the main premises pertinent to each alternative would be some variant of the following general statement: "If we adopt this alternative, we shall achieve the goal resting on the step just above," for that is the problem we first set out to resolve. (An actual premise, of course, would state the specific cause and result.) However, as we saw earlier, most of the *other* premises we uncover in our tryout of the alternative will refer to effects on *other* goals we have in mind, mostly those lying higher up on the means-end staircases, and those

---

[3] The only dictionary definition of a premise at all similar to the concept developed in these pages will be found in Funk and Wagnall's (unabridged) *Standard Dictionary:* "A proposition which serves as a ground for a conclusion; a judgment leading to another conclusion." No textbook on logic that I know uses the definition employed here. It differs markedly from the terms *major premise* and *minor premise* used in Aristotelian logic.

of other individuals or organizations which would be affected. The adoption of almost any alternative will produce several results. Moreover, as we shall have occasion to see in the examples used later, *causes* other than the alternative itself frequently come to light during such a tryout. And the result element appearing in one premise may serve as the cause element in another premise.

The idea of a third element, the causal connection between the cause and the result, is somewhat more elusive. The causal connection is the *inference* contained in the premise as to the relationship that exists between the cause and the result. This third element is seldom stated in so many words in the premise, words we can actually point to; it is usually only implied in the premise statement. It is simply an idea that we convey when we link two pieces of information or ideas together, one serving as a cause, the other as a result. It is an invisible thing which lies between the cause and the result. We can see the connection in our mind even though no actual words have been used to express it, because it rests upon some experiences we have had, or upon what we have read or heard. In the premise, "If we carry out this proposal, the morale of the men in the product development department will rise," the causal connection would lie in the blank space shown. In our mind's eye, we can visualize the result flowing from the cause. The foregoing brief description of the middle element, the one we are calling a causal connection, undoubtedly leaves the idea somewhat vague; but we shall return to it later. The idea will become more explicit when we explore the task of testing the reliability of premises and weighting them. Equally important, the usefulness of the three elements as tools should then become more apparent.

Actually, we were using the premise concept in the chapter on "The Creative Process."[4] Recall that during the second stage, where we were gathering specific information germane to the problem troubling us, we were going on a hunting expedition for relevant facts, approximations, and opinions. In the first step of the third stage, the incubation stage, we began framing these into premises; we were organizing our separate pieces of information into cause-result statements pertinent to the problem. But whereas there we used them as a foundation for creating an idea for a new alternative, here we are using them to test out the three or four best alternatives which have already come to mind, *including* any newly created ones. We are

---

[4] Some of the other ideas examined in that chapter, such as weighting and organizing the premises, will also be examined more fully here.

beginning here with the alternative and working back to the premises, whereas there we were beginning with the premises and working up to the alternative. Note, in passing, that the decision maker who has created an idea for a new alternative has already accumulated the premises relating to it; accordingly, in making his decision, he has only to recapture these and use them again in comparing that alternative with the others.

Although the reliability of the premises a man takes into consideration has a great deal to do with the outcome of his decision—how well it will stand up—the *actual* soundness (or truth) of his prediction of outcome has nothing to do with whether the man uses it as a premise. If a man takes into consideration a three-part statement such as that described, it is still a premise in his eyes, whether or not it finally proves to be reliable. Of course, no one uses a premise he thinks is unreliable; he automatically throws it away. He keeps and uses only those premises he believes will turn out to be true, only those describing results he expects will actually occur.

Many pertinent premises come to light once we visualize the people, organizations, or things which would be affected were the alternative adopted. Our procedure is to conduct an experiment in our minds. We begin by recalling the characteristic behavior of these people and objects, and the conditions in which they now exist. Then, in our imagination, we put into effect the possible new course of action and "watch" their reactions to the change. This provides explicit (though not necessarily accurate) pictures of their probable response—of some significant consequences.

Clearly, an executive must make his decisions with a recognition of the effect of the decision on the goals of a wide range of people and organizations. For instance, a decision to build a second plant on the West Coast would doubtless affect our dealers, our customers, our competitors, our salesmen, work force, and executives, our cash assets, our profits, our bankers, and our stockholders. A young man's decision to go to graduate school would affect his family, the company, if any, for which he works, perhaps the men in his car pool, the companies he will work for in the future, his bank account, the academic standards of the university, and so on. In Chapters 4 and 5, we shall probe further into the task of gathering premises by anticipating the effects on people and things of adopting an alternative.

Ordinarily, the more premises we take into consideration, the better our decision will be, *provided* that we have before us the most promising alternatives, *and* provided that the premises used for each are reasonably reliable, that the most significant ones have been considered, and that the premises are assigned their appropriate weights. In going through these steps, we say we are "thinking things over." Going through a detailed analysis such as the one to be described in this chapter would, of course, prove a waste of time in those cases where the decisions will have little impact on our future—for instance, a decision about whether to use a small or large sheet of paper for a message. However, when we foresee that the rightness or wrongness of a decision will have a marked effect on our own welfare or on that of an organization to which we are loyal, this extra effort in making the decision is well spent. Most of us tend to make our big decisions without sufficient forethought and as a result are often disappointed when we carry them out and observe the actual consequences.

Illustration of the Task of Gathering Premises

By sitting in on a conference of company executives called for the purpose of deciding whether or not to raise the price of one of the company's products, we can observe men gathering premises. Each man contributes the premises that come to his mind when he tries out the alternative. The alternative the men have met to discuss is "to raise the price." They are evidently already familiar with the premises germane to other alternatives, such as "to keep the present price" and "to lower the price."

The discussion begins with one man stating, "If we raise the price, I'm pretty sure we'll sell just about as many as in the past." Another man adds, "If general business conditions keep on improving, our competitors will probably raise their prices, too." Then others join in. "If those raw material costs keep going up, as I think they will, our margin between selling price and out-of-pocket costs per unit is going to be cut to a point where we won't have anything left to cover overhead and profits." "If our sales continue to drop, we'll have a lot of idle equipment and layoffs in Department M." "If we raise the price, our salesmen will have to spend most of their time arguing over prices instead of talking about the product." "If we raise the price, that customer in Cincinnati will kick; the account will still buy from us, but they'll give most of their business to somebody else." (This last one is really three premises in one sentence—a single cause and three results.)

These "if . . . then" statements used above are very cumbersome; most people usually frame their premises in shorter and more direct form. The discussion continues. "Our salesmen will probably meet with opposition at first (cause) and as a result may become discouraged." "Raising the price (cause) will encourage the union president to ask for pay raises when contract negotiations start next month (the result)." "That (the request for pay increases, a cause) would give Fred and his assistants in the industrial relations department a good deal of extra trouble, and they are already overworked." "I wonder how the increased price will affect our income taxes." (This speaker and the next one are hunting for information with which to frame some pertinent premises; these are not yet premises.) "Will the antitrust division raise questions about the price increase, as they did with the competitor in Buffalo three years ago?" "If we raise the price, the total amount of this item contributes toward overhead and profits will increase rapidly, provided that sales stay up." "Remember the last time we raised the price, we lost that account in Birmingham." (That is a premise referring solely to the past.) "Raising the price will mean we must issue a revised price list; and all the salesmen have been booking orders for future delivery of this product, so we will have to figure out a date for the change and how to handle those future orders." (Note here that the speaker is unconsciously telling the others that he has tentatively agreed to go along with a price increase.) "By setting August 1 as the date, we can get the announcement out to the men in plenty of time."

Sometimes, we express only a cause *or* a result (not both), because we suppose the other person is so familiar with our thinking that he will supply the other elements we have in mind. "The salesmen won't like it." (The cause, unexpressed, is "if we raise the price.") "The cost-estimating department will have to revise some of its formulas for markups." "We can't get the revised list to the printer in time." "I'm worried about the effect of this on the sales of our other lines." "That competitor in Cleveland is likely to make a big point of the fact that we have raised the price." On the surface, it would appear these men are thinking only with isolated, separate pieces of information. But the speakers, at least, have all *three* parts of a premise in their minds, even though they express only one element; they expect the hearers to furnish the results that would flow from the statements, or the causes that produced them. Misunderstandings often arise when the speaker expresses only a part of the premise because the hearer often supplies an unintended cause or result.

CLASSIFYING PREMISES ACCORDING TO WHETHER THEY POINT TO WANTED OR UNWANTED CONSEQUENCES

Once the premises relevant to an alternative are brought to light, they can be classified into two groups. One list would contain only those premises which point to that alternative's probable wanted or enjoyable results or consequences; and the other, those pointing to its unwanted or painful consequences. To illustrate this, a few of the premises uncovered earlier at the pricing conference are set out below.

PREMISES PERTINENT TO "RAISE THE PRICE" WHICH POINT TO:

WANTED CONSEQUENCES	UNWANTED CONSEQUENCES
If we raise the price, we will sell just as many as before.	If we raise the price, the salesmen will have to spend most of their time arguing over prices instead of talking about the product.
If general business conditions keep on improving, our competitors will probably raise their prices, too.	Raising the price will encourage the union president to ask for pay raises.
The amount of money available to cover overhead and profits should increase.	The men in the cost-estimating department will have to revise their mark-up formulas.
And so on.	If our sales continue to decline, we'll have a lot of idle equipment in Department M.
	And so on.

The foregoing illustrates the first two steps in the procedure men follow in examining one of the alternatives they are considering— namely, uncovering the premises and classifying them according to whether they refer to wanted or to unwanted consequences, whether they further our goals or retard them.

To make a comparison of the several alternatives under consideration, most of the premises germane to *each* alternative would, of course, have to be uncovered and then classified as illustrated above. The objective, as indicated earlier, is to discover the alternative with the greatest aggregate amount of wanted results and the least amount of unwanted results.

When the alternatives being investigated are diametrically opposed—raise the price *versus* lower the price—many (though by no means all) of the wanted consequences pertinent to one will prove to be almost identical with the unwanted consequences of the other. Examples of alternatives used by the logicians are usually opposites because this simplifies the exposition. But in real life, there are frequently several alternatives available, each with its own set of premises. For instance, the premises relating to the three alternatives stated at the beginning of the example used above (raise the price, lower the price, or keep it unchanged) would each have a somewhat different set of premises, as would price rises (or reductions) of, say, 5 per cent, 25 per cent or 90 per cent. And bear in mind that, in many situations, two or more alternatives can be simultaneously employed as means. If one means is not powerful enough to achieve the goal above it, others can frequently be employed to supplement it.

TESTING THE RELIABILITY OF PREMISES: THE CONCEPT OF FACTUAL AND VALUE PREMISES

One of the chief reasons why our decisions occasionally look unwise when viewed in retrospect is that some of the premises we used were unreliable; our predictions of the consequences proved to be wrong. We find later that we jumped to the conclusion that certain results would flow from a given cause. In making a major decision, it is essential to recheck the reliability of at least the more important premises—the ones that will have the greatest impact on the welfare of the company and its members. The pre-eminent one in the pricing discussion was, "If we raise the price, I'm pretty sure we'll sell just as many as in the past." If this turns out to be *in*valid—if the company should sell considerably fewer units as a result of the higher price—its intermediate goal of financial well-being would be seriously harmed. On the other hand, it is not so necessary to check the reliability of premises that will have relatively little effect on the welfare of the company and its members. For instance, if the premise, "The cost estimators will have to revise some of their pricing formulas," should prove wrong, the company and its members will suffer very little harm.

The idea that a premise is made up of three elements—a cause, a causal connection, and a result—and that these elements can each be either predominantly factual or predominantly value (please do not attempt yet to attach any definitions to these two terms)[5] supplies a useful tool for testing the reliability of the important premises we have uncovered in our imaginary tryout of an alternative. In trying to appraise the reliability of a premise, it is helpful at the outset to *think of each of the three elements as a separate piece of information and in this initial stage to examine each one by itself without any*

---

[5] We shall use special definitions for the words *factual* and *value* throughout this book, but do not worry about those yet; they will be explained later in the chapter. As a temporary touchstone the following may be helpful: A factual element is one that is measured objectively, and a value element is one that is measured subjectively.

reference whatsoever to the other two elements. Our central task at this point will be to determine *how* each separate element is *measured* —objectively or subjectively. Once we see clearly how these separate elements are measured, our feet are on more solid ground; we are in a much better position to put the three elements back together and reach a conclusion about the extent to which we can depend upon the premise. In this way, we can anticipate whether most of the results we foresaw will really come true, or whether we are unconsciously deceiving ourselves into *thinking* they will (or will not) occur.

As we shall see shortly, an appraisal of the nature of each of the three elements in a premise—whether they are each predominantly factual or predominantly value—enables us to determine whether the premise *as a whole* is mostly of a factual or a value nature. This, in turn, helps to pinpoint and describe the uncertainties connected with the decision. The idea of the two types of premises (factual and value) will also be used extensively in the later chapters of this book, where we attempt to cope with some of the imponderables an executive commonly encounters.

If all three of the elements in all the pertinent premises we uncover were indubitably factual in nature, we could feel fairly secure in our decisions. Everything we anticipated—all the wanted and unwanted consequences—would actually transpire; and no unexpected, unpleasant surprises would come to light. However, as we shall see when we begin examining value elements and value premises, there are relatively few completely factual premises available to us in everyday life. In fact, the majority of the premises we must take into consideration are predominantly value in character. A premise may have only two elements that are measured *objectively*, or one, or none. Yet these premises in which one (or even all three) of the elements is measured *subjectively* may be just as reliable as the purely factual premises; and they typically describe causes and results that are even more important to us and our organization than factual ones. Nevertheless, factual elements and factual premises play a significant role in most decision making; our chief regret is that so few can be found.

Factual Elements and Factual Premises

To understand the meaning of the word *factual* as we are using the term, we have to *dismiss* from our minds the commonly held definition of a fact—namely, something that has occurred, or could occur, or will occur. Rather, the question we are asking ourselves here is:

How has the element in the premise statement been described? Or more exactly, *what kinds of measures* are being used by the speaker and his hearers?

As we shall use the term, a factual element in a premise is either a cause, a causal connection, or a result which is described or measured by the speaker and his hearers with an objective measuring rod, one that, figuratively speaking, they could hang on the wall. The men who are visualizing the idea contained in the element are employing essentially the same standard, the same units of measurement. "If we should raise the price to $10 . . ." would be an example of a factual *cause* element; and ". . . we should sell about 5,000 of those units next year" would be a factual *result* element. When these words are spoken, the speaker and his hearers all see the same image of the units—a pile of ten dollars and a pile of, for instance, 5,000 pairs of shoes.

A factual element need not necessarily be stated in numerical terms, though it frequently is. When describing a physical object, words can convey a reasonably precise image. "That customer in Cincinnati" and "issue a revised price list" would be examples of factual elements described in words. They are explicit; each man sees virtually the same picture. Typically, it is rather easy to convey the precise characteristics of physical objects or of physical actions. We can touch and see these; and in many instances, we have adopted measures for delineating them. Some intangibles can also be described by commonly used measures—*time,* for instance. But the point here is that the element is completely factual when (and only when) the speaker and his hearers are all using the same "external" or objective measures and consequently all are picturing essentially the same image. The speaker has demonstrated the element.

The idea of a *factual cause* element or a *factual result* element can be perceived without too much trouble. The description of the element is explicit. The idea underlying a factual *causal connection* is somewhat more complex than the one underlying a factual cause or result, though it is basically the same.

We can distinguish between a factual and a value *causal connection* by asking ourselves what types of measures the speaker and his hearers are using to *test and determine* whether the asserted relationship exists—test whether the result will actually flow from the cause, as the premise implies. If the men are using numbers or the movement of physical objects to demonstrate or test the connection, the causal connection would be classified as factual. For instance, if the men were mentally reviewing some pertinent empirical data, such as statistical information culled from past studies of the connection between this particular cause and effect, or if they were using other publicly available information to demonstrate or to determine whether a connection exists, we would say the causal connection is factual. Similarly, the connection would be called factual if the men at the meeting were demonstrating or testing by visualizing the operation of physical objects. Everyone who hears the premise *sees* whether the result will flow from the cause, even though no actual words are to be found in the premise statement to describe the causal connection; the connection is observable, but it exists only in the mind.[6]

Metallurgy offers an example of a premise that is almost purely factual—one in which all three elements are measured objectively. We know that if a certain alloy is heated to a given temperature (the cause in the premise), it will expand a given amount. This cause is usually measured in degrees of temperature and the result in millimeters. The speaker and his hearers would all visualize the cause and result in the same way. The readings of size at various temperatures can also be tabulated and then be presented graphically in the form of a clean-cut line, as in Diagram 4. This line running through the various points represents the causal connection between the sev-

---

[6] For a modern day physicist's explanation of this elusive idea of causal connection, see Norwood Russel Hanson, *Patterns of Discovery* (Cambridge, Eng.: The University Press, 1958), pp. 60–64 or his chapter on Causality. Hans A. Riechenback points out in *The Rise of Scientific Philosophy* (Berkeley: University of California Press, 1951), p. 157, that "the idea of causality has stood in the foreground of every theory of knowledge of modern times." At the same time, no physicist today supposes we live in a mechanical universe where a neat, precise result always flows from a given cause; the results of experiments, when graphically presented, look more like the dots shown in Diagram 5 (p. 70). My physicist friends tell me that the physicists' three major conceptual frameworks live compatibly side by side. For some purposes, Newtonian physics, whose central tenet is strict causality, provides laws of inestimable value in predicting occurrences. For other (larger) worlds, they may use as frameworks in their thinking the Einstein general theory of relativity. For other problems, they may employ the quantum theory, with its basic philosophy of indeterminancy of the results that will be induced by a cause; probability theory is a facet of the quantum theory.

In this book we are leaning most on Newton's cause-effect, stimulus-response concept, though we shall make no attempt to formulate laws of cause and effect that are supposed to work in the same way in all comparable situations. Our framework also partakes slightly of the central tenet of the quantum theory, indeterminancy. However, because we are trying to predict only one result instead of millions, we cannot use the laws of chance with their statistical descriptions of the results that a given cause produces, as in the quantum theory; we are very much aware, as are physicists, that we cannot predict the *next* consequence—the next flip of the coin—with accuracy.

Readers interested in pursuing these ideas of indeterminacy further will find the Riechenback book stimulating—especially pages 157–65. An earlier but very insightful book, is J. W. N. Sullivan, *The Limitations of Science* (New York: Mentor Books, 1933).

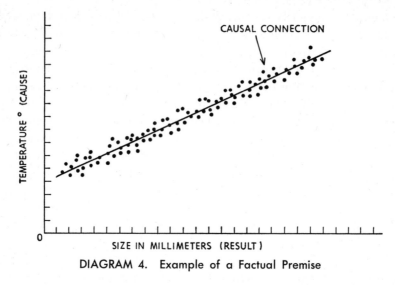

DIAGRAM 4.   Example of a Factual Premise

eral causes and results; it is an illustration of a factual causal connection.[7]

Such an analysis of the *elements* also enables us to identify a factual *premise*. As would be expected, a factual premise is made up of elements that are predominantly factual. We can fix this idea in our minds more firmly by reviewing the metallurgy example. Both the cause and the result are clearly factual; they are measured or described (and thus demonstrated) by the reader and the author (by you and me) with yardsticks that are objective—with uniform, standardized, objective yardsticks employed by many people. Similarly, the causal connection is factual; a vast amount of experimentation and statistical data lies beneath the statement of the relationship between the cause and the result, and both you and I either consciously or unconsciously use these data in rough form to test or demonstrate the existence of the averred connection contained in "If we heat the alloy, it will expand."

Thousands of such factual premises have been developed by physical scientists and engineers as aids in predicting the results that would accompany the adoption of certain alternatives they have under consideration. These normally are expressed as mathematical

---

[7] By the way, this *is* a premise, though we seldom recognize it as such. When choosing between different alloys for a piece of equipment that he is designing, an engineer would consider the effect of the expansion of the metal on the piece of equipment and, in addition, the consequences of its weight, rigidity, strength, rust resistance, aesthetic appearance, and so on.

equations; the independent variables correspond with our causes and the dependent variables correspond with our result.

Businessmen can also frequently uncover factual premises, especially when they are dealing with material, tangible things. In making a decision about shipping an order, some of the predominantly factual premises which a sales manager and a production manager might use are as follows: "If we ship a thousand of these to that Chicago customer, we won't have enough for the Cincinnati account; we have only 1,100 on hand. We wouldn't be able to deliver the Cincinnati order by May 1, as promised, because we won't be able to produce and assemble the parts by then. We have ten machines, and they each can produce about a hundred E 19 parts a day. Four of the mechanics who work regularly on those machines quit last month. (The two preceding premises are incompletely stated.) We could shift Ben and Louie over to the other machines; but they are slow, and we'd have a great many rejects. If we place the order now, we might be able to get delivery on three tons of the stainless steel tubing in two weeks."

In the foregoing example the two executives (and other men also) will probably agree on the amount, the size, or other specific characteristics of the causes and of the results mentioned; they use approximately the same objective, widely adopted measuring sticks. And they and the other men will also mentally test and demonstrate the existence of the causal relationships by making some rough arithmetical calculations and observing the working of the men and equipment to determine whether the relationships implied in the statements correspond with their own past experience. Nevertheless, the *only* purely factual premise is the first one; in that, all three of the elements are measured objectively. The causal connections in the others contain some value characteristics. (Remember that we have not yet attempted to describe the special meaning we shall attach to this word *value*.) Moreover, the executives recognize that these predictions are only rough approximations; and they also know that new and unforeseen factors will enter the picture. Yet the premises are accurate enough for their present purposes, and decisions based on these predictions will probably prove wise.

Were all the premises that a businessman must take into consideration as clear and as obviously reliable as the ones used so far as examples, executives would seldom suffer from ulcers. Scholars have been developing the field of operations research to cope with complex factual premises, relying heavily on mathematical equations to express the three elements of these premises. But the trouble is that businessmen and scholars are obliged to look askance at a great many factual premises; even those that contain both a factual cause and a factual result frequently turn out to be wrong. Most people who see a statement asserting that a factual result will be produced by a factual cause jump to the conclusion that the causal connection has been measured and tested or demonstrated objectively and found to be true by the man who made the statement. They assume that it is a solid prediction, only to discover later, when they have observed the *actual* results, that it should have been rechecked. In the premise, "If we raise the price $10, profits will increase by $15,000," it may be possible to demonstrate the causal connection by arithmetic; but only the uninitiated would accept it as a solid prediction. Profits are the result flowing from many causes; price is only one of the causes.

Elements and Premises Containing Both Factual and Value Characteristics

Although we have so far dealt mostly with examples of premise elements which would be called *purely* factual—almost 100 per cent factual—we measure and test the majority of those we use and hear in everyday life and in business with a combination of objective and subjective measuring sticks. Indeed, many of the pieces of information we use as elements *cannot* be measured objectively; the only measures that we have available for them are subjective in nature, as we will see when we take up value premises. But simply because the elements in a premise are expressed with less than perfect precision does not mean that the premise is invalid or that we should discard it.

The premise, "By setting August 1 as the date (for the price change), we can get the announcement out to the men in plenty of time," offers examples of three elements, each of which contains differing percentages of factual measuring rods, although they are nevertheless all predominantly factual in nature. The cause element, "By setting August 1 as the date," would be almost entirely factual; everyone attending the meeting would use the same objective standard and see the same visual image.

But the result element, "we can get the announcement out to the men in plenty of time," would probably be judged only 70 or 80 per cent factual. In other words, of the several measures the men use, about three fourths would be called "factual" (see Diagram 5). Incidentally, these percentages in Diagram 5 are being used here only as a temporary convenience in grasping the idea that we use a va-

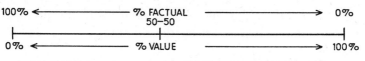

DIAGRAM 5. The Factual and Value Premise Continuum

riety of measuring rods for most elements, and that a portion of them are objective and a portion are subjective. The executives attending the meeting would use *days* and *hours* to measure "time." However, they doubtless use only *approximately* the same yardsticks for the word *plenty*. Evidently this element is by no means purely factual; though each man at the conferences will use some objective measures—hours, for instance—he will also use some of his own personal and unique experiences as yardsticks when visualizing or measuring the word "plenty" in this element. The result element in this premise is evidently much less factual than the cause element, although it is still predominantly factual.

In measuring the *causal connection* between the cause and the result expressed in the above premise the men also probably are using a larger portion of factual standards than value standards. Perhaps about three fifths of their measures would be termed objective. They probably mentally tested the causal connection by making some quick estimates of the amount of work involved in getting out the announcement and how much other work the men had ahead of them; most of the men at the conference undoubtedly used time as a measure of these, and *approximately* the same set of measures. But notice that the causal connection implied in the statement would be rather difficult for the men to test or demonstrate conclusively because the men are each drawing heavily upon their own ideas of the amount of work involved in this job and of the backlog of other work to be done.

When this premise we have used as an example is viewed as a whole, when all three of the elements are brought back together and seen as a triumvirate, we should probably judge the *premise as a whole* to be predominantly factual—certainly more than half factual, though probably less than two thirds factual. Incidentally, this percentage is *not* determined simply by adding up the percentages of the three elements and dividing by three; we need to *give most weight to the causal connection*, for, as we have seen, that one plays a dominant role in every premise. In any case, all we can really do is to place a finger on the scale shown in Diagram 5 (p. 73), and say, "I think *this* element of the premise would fall about *here, that* one about *here*, the *third* one at *that* point; and the premise as a whole would fall about *there* on the diagram."

Value Elements and Value Premises

It is evident from the several references made already to value elements and value premises that the term *value*, as we are using it, has nothing to do with the valuableness or worth of the element or of the premise. A value *element* is a piece of information which the speaker and his hearers measure with their own privately designed measuring rods instead of with objective or factual standards. A value *premise* is one in which these personal standards are used much more than objective standards in attempting to measure the three elements.

These value measures are the personal measuring systems that each man has developed on his own and carries around inside himself. They are his own inventions. Ordinarily, he employs them in trying to describe intangibles—nonmaterial things such as ideas, or people's feelings and behavior.[8]

We are frequently obliged to employ some of our own personal yardsticks when we ourselves express, or when we hear others express, the three elements of a premise. The reason is that in many cases there are no generally accepted objective measures for all the elements in the multifarious premises which we find germane to an alternative. For instance, we often have to use such words as *high morale, a good reputation, success, satisfaction,* or *disappointment*

---

[8] To avoid confusion, in this book, we shall *not* use the rather widely used term *value judgment*. Nevertheless, our term *value premise* has a good deal in common with it—in particular, the idea of personal standards. But although, as far as I can find, there is no fully agreed-upon definition of a value judgment, apparently it is a much broader term than ours. It encompasses several of the ideas that we have been examining separately in these chapters. For example, it is used to describe a person's measure of unmeasurable things—a *beautiful* girl, an *honest* man; or of things they haven't troubled to measure— "The pavement is very slippery." In these cases, it is used as one *element* of what *we* call a premise—a cause or result that is measured with value standards, the other half of which is unexpressed. It is also often used to describe the decision a man reaches after comparing some of those alternatives for the goals that rest high on the staircase— "Following Christ's pattern of living is better than making money"; here, value judgment is being used to assign relative ranks or weights to ultimate or intermediate goals. Sometimes, it is used to describe a person's belief that certain causes will produce certain results—a causal connection: "If I make a million dollars, my future will be secure." "If I follow my church's instructions, I will go to heaven." "If the country goes Republican, we shall be better off." Nevertheless, the common denominators which bind all these types of value judgments together are that all the statements are based on the experiences accumulated by the individual involved and that each person carries around a different picture in his mind. As a matter of fact, we have been using value judgments freely throughout these first three chapters.

in our premises. In testing out an alternative, we recognize that consequences involving ideas such as the foregoing will occur if the alternative is adopted and that they will have to be considered if we are to make a realistic choice or decision. Words like these also serve as causes in some of our premises. And in order to employ them, a man has to have a mental image of them; otherwise, he can attach no meaning to the words. But the point here is that since there are no generally accepted objective or factual yardsticks for these, each man must develop his own; he has to measure these subjectively.

The words just used—high morale, and so on—are measured almost exclusively by value standards. Here is an example of a premise in which all three of the elements are predominantly of a value nature: "If I work hard, I will be a success." There are no universal standards for "working hard"; the image called up by these words will differ for each man. The same is true of the word *success*.

Moreover, every man who hears this premise stated will have to use his own experiences instead of neatly tabulated statistics to *demonstrate* and *test* whether there is a *causal connection;* in fact, the causal connection is very hard to describe and demonstrate. When appraising it, each man looks back to his own experiences; they provide him with information (data) which he first revises to take account of any differing circumstances, and then employs in an effort to test or demonstrate whether working hard will bring success to the particular man who made the assertion. Each hearer makes such revisions because he recognizes that in this type of situation, the past, taken literally, is not entirely reliable as a demonstration or test of what will occur in the future.

All of us have gradually accumulated a battery of subjective measures for many of the causes, causal connections, and results of the premises we voice and hear. Each man has built these personal measures *out of the sum of his total experience.*[9] We suppose that we know them intuitively; but they come from sources obscured by time, which have long since dropped into the subconscious levels of our minds.

Nearly all of us tend to think of our own value measures as factual or objective. We also presuppose that our hearers have in mind the same visual images as the ones we have developed out of our

---

[9] David Hume, in his "Enquiry Concerning Human Understanding," Sec. IV, Part I, points out that these causal connections can only be based on experience. Actually the causal connections we have called factual are also based on experience, the experience of specialists; but those men have rigorously described most of them by numbers after measuring them.

own experience. The fact is, however, that each man's personal measures differ, sometimes radically, from those of every other man. We should be hard put to describe and demonstrate our own personal measures to others so that they would see them exactly as we do.

The immediate objective of the preceding discussion of value *elements* is to provide a basis for recognizing a value *premise* when we see one; in a later section, we shall get to our key task of checking the reliability of a value premise. A value premise is one in which the three elements, when viewed as a whole, seem to be measured predominantly by the speaker's and hearers' own private standards. And here again, just as was the case in examining mixed premises, the percentage of value characteristics in the premise cannot be determined by taking an average of the percentages of the three elements; the causal connection must be given the greatest weight. In fact, a premise the cause and result elements of which are almost purely factual may be of a predominantly value nature because of the way in which the causal connection must be measured or demonstrated.

Let us now analyze more carefully an example of a premise that is of a predominantly value nature: "The salesmen are likely to meet with opposition from customers (cause); as a result, they will become discouraged." The men we watched at the pricing conference we attended, the men who were considering the possibility of raising the price, would all have in mind the same physical characteristics of the customers and salesmen, but they would doubtless measure the term "opposition" in the cause element with yardsticks they each carry around within themselves. There is no external measure for describing "opposition"; in fact, no yardsticks have ever been devised for the idea of opposition. Each man at the conference will have a somewhat different, though perhaps quite explicit, idea of what constitutes opposition. Moreover, each one's image of the *amount* of opposition the men will encounter will differ. The same is true of the result element—especially the words "become discouraged." In this premise, both the cause and the result are very largely composed of value characteristics—perhaps 70 per cent. But they also have used some factual measures; these, we are estimating, would constitute roughly 30 per cent of those they were using.

The middle element in this premise, the causal connection, is also of a predominantly value nature. That the result will flow from the cause on this particular occasion would be almost impossible to test or demonstrate conclusively, and there are no reliable statistics available because no two men and situations are alike and this particular situation has never before occurred. Yet each man can *see* that there is a causal connection; he carries his yardsticks around in his mind, using his similar experiences as measures. And naturally, each man has adopted a somewhat different set of yardsticks to determine whether this result will be produced by the cause. We should probably agree that most of the measures used by these men to visualize the causal connection are value measures—perhaps 90 per cent of them; the remaining 10 per cent might be based on objective measures used in common.

Based on our appraisal of the three elements, we should judge this premise to be very dominantly of a value nature, perhaps 85 or 90 per cent or thereabouts. When the three elements are put back together, the character of the premise becomes readily apparent. All the elements, as well as the premise as a whole, would fall far to the right of the 50-50 mark on the continuum in Diagram 5 (p. 73).

But the fact that this particular premise is of a preponderantly value nature does not mean that it should be discarded. This one is of great importance to the welfare of the company, its salesmen, and its customers. And it is probably almost as reliable as the factual premises discussed earlier. The men at the conference, at least those with sales experience, could put themselves in the shoes of the salesmen—imagine the salesmen talking with the customers and facing criticism—and feel the discouragement that would result. They know it would occur. (Be aware that we have yet to explore the subject of reliability, however.)

Value premises must nevertheless be used with great caution because they are frequently unreliable. Whenever we see one, especially one that refers to wanted or unwanted consequences which will have a marked bearing on future welfare, we should recheck it for reliability. For example, we concluded a few pages back that the premise, "If we raise the price, the sales will remain about the same," was a very important one; yet it is of a predominantly value nature. The point here, however, is that the men making the decision dare not take it for granted that the cause in an important premise like this one will produce the result stated in the premise. Before naively accepting this premise as reliable, they should check back over their own experiences to see whether, under the particular conditions they will encounter in the months ahead, they can really visualize sales volume remaining constant when the price is raised.

One of the main responsibilities of an executive (or for that matter, of anyone who makes decisions) is to recognize a value premise when he encounters one, probe its weaknesses and limitations, and take these into consideration. If he does this, the chances are that he will not be misled by them. The results he anticipated when examining the alternative he chose will turn out about as he had expected.

The term *value premise* will be used hereafter as a short term for *any* premise that seems to be *predominantly* of a value nature when viewed *as a whole*—any premise that would fall to the right of the 50-50 mark in Diagram 5 (p. 73)—without indicating the amount of value or factual components contained in the value premise. We shall use the term *factual premise* in the same way—for those premises falling to the left of the midpoint on the continuum. But bear in mind that such a classification of premises into these either-or categories tends to obscure the important fact that in everyday life we employ both factual and value measurements in practically every element and in every premise.

Value Premises and the Executive

In most of our decisions, we have to rely heavily on value premises because factual premises are not available for all the consequences we must take into consideration. Despite the extraordinary amount of numerical data now made available by electronic computers and governmental agencies, executives are constantly faced with this problem. Finding dependable premises for consequences that affect the company's topmost goals is particularly difficult. As executives express it, they are compelled to make most of those decisions on the basis of inadequate facts. They may know what results were produced by what causes in the past, but when making a decision to be implemented in the period ahead they are *forced* to use value premises, forced to predict the unknown and the intangible, to predict where prediction would seem impossible. Moreover, if they confine themselves to factual premises and omit value premises, their decisions turn out to be unrealistic, for they have only a partial picture of the consequences. Choosing an alternative solely on the basis of factual premises would be naive. After such a decision is put into effect, many unforeseen wanted and unwanted consequences would emerge—consequences that should have been anticipated at the time the decision was made.

Simply because all the elements in a premise cannot be (or have not been) described and measured accurately does not mean that the premise is irrelevant or should be discarded. From what has been said, it can be seen why value premises frequently have a much greater impact than factual premises on the future welfare of the company and its members. The result elements of these value premises usually refer to goals lying near the top of the staircase, and virtually all those goals are of a value nature.[10]

Generally speaking, the higher a man's position in the company hierarchy, the more value premises he must consider. For men at the bottom of the hierarchy—workmen in the machine shop or book-keepers, for instance—the majority of the premises needed in making their decisions are factual in nature. They employ premises relating to how machines will operate and how they must move their hands—not only seeable but measurable elements. Many of the causes and results are concrete, tangible objects. Frequently, the decisions made by their immediate superiors are also based primarily on predictions of what machines will do and the consequences of the physical hand movements; but they must also employ some value premises. For instance, in deciding which of his men to choose for a particularly difficult task, such as resetting a sensitive piece of packaging equipment that is not working right, the foreman needs to visualize how the two or three most promising men would handle the job—what each man would do, and how well each would like the job. If the foreman knows his men quite well, he can readily uncover the necessary value premises. To him, they are fairly obvious. Decisions at this lower level are relatively easy. The men require only a few premises; most of the ones they employ are factual; and their value premises are comparatively simple. The majority of their premises impinge upon goals lying on steps near the bottom of the means-end staircase, and these are frequently concrete.

As a man rises in the hierarchy, the premises he needs for decision making steadily grow more numerous and more complex; and the proportion of value premises increases strikingly. As he advances to higher positions in the company, he deals with decisions that rest higher and higher on the staircases. The result elements in a large proportion of his premises refer to relatively high goals which can

---

[10] A decision or a conclusion based almost entirely on value premises can be, and often is, just as solid as one based mostly on factual premises. If all, or practically all, of the most heavily weighted value premises form a consistent pattern—point toward choosing a given alternative—we can be fairly certain that our decision is a good one.

be measured only with value standards, and the causal connections are likewise dominantly of a value nature. Here, he requires a great many complicated value premises; few, if any, factual premises can be uncovered, for the results he is interested in are not only intangible but have not yet occurred. Also these decisions take longer to carry out—cover a longer time span; hence, because he is predicting consequences that lie farther into the future, he has more trouble framing reliable premises. Yet he must feel sure of the results he uses in his premises, even though he is dealing with imponderables.

But no matter whether the executive is located low in the organization, or high, he can profit from becoming aware of value premises. Once a man low in the hierarchy forms the habit of noticing value premises he is more likely to double-check, use them with caution, and thus make more perceptive day-to-day decisions. This gives a man confidence in the employment of such premises and practice in using them, thus preparing him for a more responsible position. A good executive is one who has the courage to base his decisions upon value premises as well as factual premises.

Most of our value premises lie at the subconscious levels of our minds, but this does not mean that we do not use them regularly. Once in a while, they flash through to the conscious levels of our minds, although usually their passage is so swift that we scarcely notice them. When an executive speaks about "getting the feel" of a situation, he is actually gathering value premises. An effective executive can dredge them out of the subconscious and frame the elusive ideas into words, so that he and his associates can visualize them and test them, and thus use them deliberately and consciously in making decisions.

Most men have had more experience with value premises than they realize. All of us employ them constantly in making personal decisions—decisions relating to the family's welfare, for example. However, a man's willingness to search out value premises in his work and his ability to use them with assurance largely determine his success as an executive. (Chapter 5 is devoted to this difficult task.) An executive simply uses more such premises, and more intricate ones, than most other people. He has to train his mind to retain and describe these, keep asking questions that will add to his store, and provide himself with an orderly framework into which he can insert the new premises he gathers. In this way, he has them available when he is called upon to consider an alternative. That this is not an overwhelming task is because the mind works with lightning speed. When the mind is making a rather simple decision requiring only a few moments, it actually gathers, visualizes, organizes, and weights a considerable array of premises. In making more complex decisions, the only difference is that a longer incubation period is required. The greater an executive's responsibility, the more thoroughly he must train his mind to employ value premises with rapidity and sureness.

Some men never learn how to cope with value premises. A man who feels insecure in using them, and therefore relies largely upon factual premises for fear his recommendations will prove wrong, nearly always makes bad decisions—ones that are *really* wrong. Actually, his decisions are seldom accepted because they seem unrealistic to his more perceptive associates. To such a man, value premises seem to exhibit no general pattern which he can hold in his mind; to him, they appear to be an unfathomed sea of chaos. Consequently, he is always searching for formulas, for the "word," for principles that will bring some order out of chaos: "Seven ways to assure your success as an executive," or "Ten tried and true principles for getting along with people." But when he attempts to apply these principles to a particular problem, they ordinarily fail him; he senses that his decisions, based on the premises contained in the principles, are unrealistic and must be discarded. To add to his difficulties, the principles are so fragmentary in nature that he can seldom find one to fit the problem he faces. Men who employ the concept of operations research and include only selected factual premises in reaching their tentative decisions, frequently encounter trouble in making "good" decisions, as we shall see in the next chapter.

Sometimes a man who has carefully schooled himself to deal *only* with factual premises feels ill at ease when using value premises.[11] Engineers, physicists, biologists, chemists, mathematicians, accountants, and statisticians, for instance, trained as they often are to employ only factual elements and premises in their research and rigorously to exclude all others when reaching their decisions, usually are selected as executives only after they have demonstrated that they

---

[11] Lecomte du Noüy in *The Road to Reason* (New York: Longmans, Green & Co., 1948), points out that there is an unscientific belief among some physical scientists, engineers, psychologists, and social scientists that the only premises they should use are those for which the three elements can be measured—the facts and principles or theories found by looking through a microscope or by measuring with a micrometer, or by weighing on a delicate scale, or by counting in other ways—and that they have, perhaps unwittingly (and unfortunately), foisted this idea upon the lay public.

can gather and use value premises with confidence. An inexperienced man with scientific training often fails as an executive because he tends to throw away as useless all premises except those that are almost purely factual. To him, value premises are no good; they are emotional and thus unscientific; they cannot be incorporated into an equation as independent or dependent variables, nor are they really trustworthy; therefore he feels obliged to leave them out. If value premises are forced upon his attention, he tends to give them little weight—brushes them aside as of little importance. What is more, he fails to realize that certain value premises may be needed in making a given decision and thus seldom even attempts to seek them out; in fact, he would not know where to look for them even if he were aware of their importance.[12]

TESTING THE RELIABILITY OF PREMISES

In testing the reliability of any premise, regardless of whether it is predominantly factual or value, the paramount problem is to be as sure as possible that the relationship claimed to exist between the cause and the result elements actually will exist when the alternative is adopted. The question is, will the result actually occur. Perceiving *how* the cause produces the result minimizes the chances of jumping to a wrong conclusion about the reliability of a premise; such perception minimizes the chances of accepting as true an assertion about the connection existing between two pieces of factual or value information which in reality have little or no cause-result relationships. Our problem is to immerse ourselves in the environment that we think will exist and try to observe *how* the result is brought about by the cause, see how the result is produced.

I have been told that, over the past years, there has been a close correlation between the stork population in Denmark each year and the number of babies born there each year; but I still do not believe that storks deliver babies. There may be a notable mathematical correlation between the changes in the length of women's skirts from one year to the next and the changes in the annual rainfall in California; but the amount of rainfall is not "seeable" as a cause for changes in the length of skirts, and much less is it "seeable" as a result of changes in skirt lengths. I cannot see how a black cat walk-

---

[12] The reader who wishes to pursue further the problems encountered in handling factual and value elements may turn to Olaf Helmer and Nicholas Rescher, "On the Epistemology of the Inexact Sciences," *Management Science*, Vol. 6 (October, 1959), pp. 25–52.

ing across my path will produce bad luck. Such statements do not correspond with my own experience.

Deliberately testing the reliability of the causal connection also minimizes the practice of wishful thinking—our tendency to suppose that the alternative chosen will actually produce all of the results that are wanted, and that most of the unwanted results that have been uncovered can be brushed aside with impunity.

The task of testing the reliability of the important factual and value premises can be described rather quickly now that we have a foundation. In fact, all we need do now is to summarize what has already been said. The central problem is to determine *ahead of time* whether the results we anticipate will *actually* flow from the causes mentioned,—whether the predicted result will *actually* come true in this particular case.

To sharpen our thinking about reliability, it will be helpful here to point up the distinction between two of the ideas we have been using—the idea of a factual or value causal connection, and the idea of the reliability of a premise. When determining whether a causal connection is factual or value, we ask ourselves how the speaker and his hearers have *tested or demonstrated the connection*—whether they are using objective measuring rods or their own personal standards. When determining whether a premise is reliable or un-reliable—whether the result will actually occur—we are examining the *answers we got when we conducted that mental test;* in this latter act, we are trying to determine how true the prediction will be, not how the relationship was measured.

Fortunately we are not concerned with whether the result will *always* occur in *all* instances: We are not trying to frame general principles or laws. Ours is a more modest objective, namely, to foresee whether the particular cause will actually bring about the particular result stated in the premise under the set of conditions we believe will exist when or if the alternative is put into effect.

It is easiest to begin the test with an examination of the cause and the result elements. A *number* that is used as a cause or result can be readily verified by referring back to the source from which it came. Frequently, a *word description* of a physical object poses somewhat more difficulty—"a heavy load," "a company that cuts prices." In cases like these, where the standards used by the speaker in measuring the object are left vague, the elements can be verified by asking what the speaker means; quite often, this leads to a more explicit description, one that the speaker and hearer can agree upon.

Where the cause or the result is an idea, an intangible, one for which no agreed-upon objective measurements have yet been devised— "prestige" or "kindness," for example—an agreement about what is meant can sometimes be reached by comparing it with a familiar example: "as much prestige as a Supreme Court Justice enjoys" or "as kind as Lincoln." These, of course, can never be fully verified; but at least the men start out with the same mental image of what they are talking about and can then apply their own personal measurements more precisely. The objective of the procedure described in this paragraph is to make the causes and the results as explicit as possible—to eliminate ambiguity and thus avoid misunderstanding —as an aid in checking the premise.

A clear understanding of the meaning of the cause and the result in a premise lightens the task of testing the causal connection. The more precise they are, the easier it is to visualize whether the result will actually flow from the cause. Once we have framed careful visual pictures of the causal connection, we are in a much better position to determine whether the claimed result will occur. Equally pertinent, we also now have some basis for an opinion as to the *amount* we can expect of that result: Whether we shall get only a small amount or a large amount.

We can expect inanimate objects to behave in the future as they have in the past, so that the causal connections of these can usually be verified. Nevertheless, factual premises made up largely of numerical data, with the causal connection demonstrated and proved by elaborate mathematical calculations or statistics, are frequently deceptive. "Giving the men a raise of 10 per cent should increase their production of parts 416A and 5ZE by about 8 per cent" may be based on careful calculations of the results of past pay raises in the factory, but this does not prove that this particular premise is reliable. The man who makes such calculations is almost forced to assume that the particular set of conditions and worker attitudes which existed when pay raises were introduced in the past will exist in the future. But we are quite sure these will change. If they do, his estimate of the result will almost certainly be wrong; actually, the men's level of production is a result which is influenced by, or produced by, a combination of several causes, including pay rates, all of which must be taken into consideration.

Most of the important premises describe the goals and the expected actions or responses of people; it is here that we most often encounter difficulty. Because the success of an executive rests heavily on his ability to predict what other people would do were he to adopt a given alternative, we shall devote an entire chapter to this task— Chapter 5. He cannot afford to employ faulty premises when predicting the responses of customers, dealers, workers, fellow executives, and so on. The fact that certain people have responded in a certain way in the past, and that there are statistics available to support the statements, does not mean they will necessarily so behave in the future. So in testing the reliability of these premises, we have to rely on our own experiences and those of our associates. We have to fall back on value premises which we have found valid in the past. No one can be completely sure of a causal connection which is of a dominantly value nature, though men may hold convictions bordering on certainty that the cause *will* produce the anticipated results. Recognizing that men and women are subjected to an ever-changing barrage of influences and visualizing the *particular* circumstances which will influence the men in question will aid us in checking the reliability of these causal connections.

Clearly, then, one way to improve our tests of the reliability of factual and value premises is to give more thought to the people who will be affected. Another is to uncover our unnoticed assumptions. These are easily overlooked—and very treacherous. The task is to bring these to light and verbalize them, then frame premises that will keep these in the foreground. We may unthinkingly assume that we can readily find effective means of achieving a goal. For example, the president of the company who decided to replace the head of the product research department (pp. 9, 18, 23) was assuming he could readily hire a better man than the present head. Upon noting and then questioning this assumption, he might frame a premise such as "Finding a good replacement will entail a lot of work." This is an unwanted consequence to which he would attach considerable weight. We also sometimes assume that we have really found what the problem is. The men at the conference (p. 23) were assuming that they knew the reasons why sales were too low—poor product development, and low sales in one territory. Upon recognizing and verbalizing this, they might decide to include a premise such as "Improving our products (or hiring new salesmen) may make no difference whatsoever in our sales." And we all frequently assume that most of our colleagues will enthusiastically welcome our newly conceived alternative. But perhaps most prevalent and treacherous is the assumption that conditions will not change. We saw in Chapter 1 that our executives assumed that competitors would make no changes in their activities, but later concluded they had made a mistake which produced serious consequences.

Despite our every effort, we shall certainly err at times in predicting consequences. Knowing this, we can take our mistakes philosophically. Certainly some of our carefully wrought premises turn out to be wrong because of unseen forces at work; and conditions outside our control may notably influence a few of the results. We also have to recognize that in case we should *unconsciously* choose an alternative, we tend to notice its wanted consequences and overlook its unwanted consequences.

Nevertheless, we can expect that the majority of our predicted results will occur if we have honestly examined the elements in each premise. And we should be capable of appraising a premise's weaknesses and limitations, and thus know how much we can rely upon it.

WEIGHTING THE PREMISES

The fourth subsystem's pattern of interconnected concepts is now beginning to take form—the concepts clustered around the premise concept, a key tool in the decision-making process. At the outset we pictured our special definition of a premise, and worked on the task of gathering premises that we thought would be pertinent to each alternative. After that we listed each alternative's premises according to whether they referred to desirable or undesirable consequences. Next we probed the ideas of factual and value and eventually were able to cope reasonably well with the task of appraising the reliability of premises. Now we turn to weighting, the next-to-the-last task in the decision-making process. We here try to determine which premises will have a great impact on our goals, which a fairly heavy effect, which a light impact, and which a trivial influence on our own welfare or on that of our company and our associates. Once we are able to weight an alternative's premises, we can gain a fairly realistic idea of the *aggregate* weight of the alternative's several wanted and unwanted consequences. When this has been done for each of the alternatives, we are in a position to compare them and make our decision.

The weight we assign to a premise—or perhaps we should say, the *rank* we assign to it, for we have no way of computing its actual weight—is largely determined by: (1) whether the goal it affects is high or low on the staircase, (2) the amount of the impact it will have on that goal, and (3) the reliability we think the premise has.

In other words, we unconsciously assign the highest rank to a premise whose consequences, in our opinion, will either advance or imperil the goals which we prize most highly, will have a very strong beneficial or harmful impact on them, and is quite reliable—will, almost certainly produce the wanted or unwanted result stated in the premise. Whether the premise refers to wanted or unwanted consequences has no bearing on the rank or weight we assign to it. At the opposite extreme, we give little or no weight to a premise that will affect a goal lying on a low step of some staircase that holds little interest for us, will have little impact on that goal, either harmful or helpful, and will probably not come true anyway.

One method of assessing the weight or rank of a premise is to ask ourselves what would happen to us, our company, and its members if its consequence failed to come about. Earlier, when we were dealing with the question of validating premises, it was pointed out that the premise, "If we raise the price, I'm pretty sure we'll sell just as many as we have in the past," was undoubtedly a salient one— that, of the consequences mentioned by the men, this one would have more effect on the company's welfare than any of the others. This consequence bears heavily on one of the company's main intermediate goals—namely, making a profit—and the men seemed to think it would be fairly reliable; it would therefore be ranked high. On the other hand, consequences such as, "We can't get the copy for the price list to the printer's on time," and "The cost-estimating department will have to revise its formulas," would have relatively little effect on the long-term goals; even though they are more reliable than the former premises, these would be ranked low in the list.

The men may have given only modest weight to the premise "Raising the price will encourage the union president to demand pay raises," reasoning that there was only a small likelihood of this and that if he did use the price increase as an argument it would not be very potent as a means of achieving a pay raise. They might give considerably more weight to the premise, "Our salesmen will probably meet with opposition at first and as a result may become discouraged." They are reasonably sure this unwanted consequence will occur and it will temporarily reduce the drive of the salesmen and thus adversely affect the company's sales, a goal lying quite high on the staircase; but the effect of this on that goal will be temporary and probably not very great, hence it would be ranked among the medium-weighted premises.

Of course, men frequently differ in the relative weights they accord the premises brought to light in a discussion. Each man has his own ranking system for the goals. At the pricing conference, several of the men undoubtedly ranked the company's profit goals highest and therefore gave greatest weight to premises relating to those goals. But the man responsible for printing the price list may have attached greatest importance to the goal, "Get the price list out on time" (perhaps he was once severely criticized for failure and is uneasy about his job); and he therefore attaches greatest weight to premises relating to that goal. These variances in the ranking of goals in part account for differences in opinion—for differences in the decisions each man reaches—even in those cases where all the men have the same premises in mind. Also, most men consciously or unconsciously take into consideration and give great weight to premises that they never mention openly, and this, too, accounts for differences in decisions.

Despite these differences, however, in the majority of cases, men find a reasonably wide area of agreement as to which of the premises germane to a particular alternative are the most significant, once this topic has been brought into the discussion. At least, the men thus become aware of which premises are most important with respect to their own, their associates', and the company's long-term goals. Once this has been threshed out, they can each assign their own ranks to the premises related to each alternative.

Numbering all those premises pertinent to an alternative according to their relative importance—assigning No. 1 to the most significant premise, No. 2 to the second, and so on down the list—helps in visualizing and remembering their relative weights. But notice that we have made no attempt to measure or quantify the weights. There is no way of objectively measuring or weighting them, for we are here dealing with matters that can be compared only by using our own experience.

These premises are assigned a *single* series of ordinal numbers, *irrespective* of whether they refer to wanted or to unwanted results. Thus, one of the premises pointing to a wanted consequence might be ranked first; two others pointing to unwanted effects might be ranked second and third; and so on. This enables a man to gain perspective. When he has done this for the premises relating to each alternative, he is in a position to make his decision.

MAKING THE DECISION

Actually, our decision making is likely to start while we are still gathering premises. As soon as we discover that one or more of the consequences of adopting an alternative would seriously harm us, our associates, or our organization, we drop that alternative immediately. For example, we quickly rule out alternatives which we foresee would be impractical or might lead to bankruptcy. And we almost automatically abandon any alternative that would be censured by our associates, our community, or by society; or would violate laws, or our own ethical or moral precepts. Most of us would immediately discard the alternative of stealing as a means of getting a new car.

In most instances, however, the choice of the best alternative is not always so readily apparent and so neat. Whether we are acting as individuals or executives, our decisions will normally have to be compromises. The best ones we can find will harm some of our own goals and will usually be distasteful to some of the people or organizations who are affected. Our responsibility is to find an alternative that will help as much as possible to further as many diverse goals as possible. The one we choose may not advance a particular goal as much as some other alternative might, but we select it because we think that by and large it will help most goals some, and will not seriously jeopardize any important goals. A decision to end a strike by agreeing to a small pay raise would be an example.

Equally troublesome, most decisions, especially those for the higher steps on the staircases, call for a cluster of ancillary decisions. Among these subordinate decisions would be a determination of what means will be needed to implement the main decision. These, once made, are placed on the steps of the subordinate staircases shown in Diagram 2 (p. 21), and on lower steps of the main staircase. In addition we have to decide *who* will carry out these subordinate decisions and when these various steps are to be completed.[13]

We now are ready for the culminating step, namely, choosing between the surviving alternatives, including any alternatives we may have newly created and the alternative (the means) if any, that we are already using. We have been going through a reasoning process. "The object of reasoning," to quote Charles S. Pierce, the philosopher, "is to find out, from a consideration of what we already know, something else we do not know." We are nearing our objective of

---

[13] An interesting firsthand account of the steps a company took in making a quite complex decision—a decision as to whether to buy electronic data-processing equipment, which brand to buy, and how to put it to work—will be found in an article by Richard M. Cyert, Herbert A. Simon, and Donald B. Trow, "Observation of a Business Decision," *Journal of Business*, 29, 1956. This is reprinted in Arthur H. Rubenstein and Chadwick J. Haberstroh, *Some Theories of Organization* (Homewood, Ill.: The Dorsey Press, Inc., and Richard D. Irwin, Inc., 1960).

discovering what we did not know before—the best solution to our problem, the best means of achieving the goal on the step above. Incidentally, despite the American penchant for change, we frequently decide that our present course is still the best, despite its manifest unwanted consequences. We decide to stay on in school, for example, despite all the disadvantages.

As indicated earlier, our objective is to find the solution that will yield the greatest aggregate weight of wanted consequences and the smallest amount of unwanted consequences. The *number* of premises listed as wanted and unwanted consequences under each alternative is *not* significant in choosing the alternative. Two or three wanted consequences may far outweigh a long list of trivial unwanted consequences. A re-examination of the premises brought to light at the pricing conference we attended will disclose that relatively few wanted results were mentioned; most were unwanted. Yet my own guess is that the men finally decided to raise the price because, in their eyes, the three or four wanted consequences far outweighed the many unwanted results they considered.

The decision is easy to make in those instances where one alternative will clearly provide a greater amount of wanted consequences and less unwanted results than any other alternative. Under such circumstances, a decider can feel reasonably confident that his decision will stand up—provided, of course, that he has employed steps such as those we have so far examined in these first three chapters.

At one time or another, most of us encounter five kinds of difficulties in making decisions. Although these are vexing, they are not insurmountable; in fact, we have already developed tools for resolving several such difficulties.

One kind arises when two or more alternatives seem equally satisfactory. To resolve this impasse, the best thing to do is to toss a coin, so that we can get on with the job of putting one of the alternatives into effect. If both (or all) will serve equally well, the choice is a matter of indifference. A second difficulty arises when it becomes clear that no *single* alternative we have examined is going to be a sufficiently strong cause or means. In such cases, it may be advisable to employ the two or three best alternatives simultaneously. In working with alternatives, we often suppose that if we use one, we cannot use the other—that it is an either-or decision. We noted earlier that books on logic nearly always set up examples in which the choice of one automatically excludes the other, for these are easy to work with; in real life, however, we seldom face such tidily packaged alternatives.

A third difficulty frequently encountered is that the unwanted causes and consequences often loom so overwhelmingly large and disagreeable that they immobilize us.[14] Ranking the premises helps to resolve this difficulty; as we have seen, one or two premises pointing to a decision to accept an alternative may be of such paramount consequence that they will offset a large number of unwanted effects. And stating the obvious, as we saw in exploring the creative process, frequently brings to the forefront of our minds those ideas we know are important; these are sometimes overlooked in our search for premises; we become so enmeshed in details that we lose sight of the big goals. Some of us seem to feel that it is somehow beneath the dignity of a man of our stature, a man of subtle intellect, to state obvious facts or goals and to frame them into premises that are already manifest; answers to the question, "What are we trying to do?" for example, often clear the mind and turn up salient premises.

Organizing the premises into three or four homogeneous groups helps in coping with a fourth difficulty—confusion as a result of an overabundance of premises. We used this idea in the third stage of the creative process. At the pricing conference, we uncovered only a few premises; but if more premises had been brought to light, we could probably have classified some under "what our customers would do," others under "what our salesmen would do," still others under "what our competitors would do," and the rest under "the effect on our company." On the basis of the several premises relating to each of these topics, we could have reached subconclusions about the effects upon, and the reactions of, the members of each group were we to adopt alternative A, or B or C. After weighting the impact of each of these three or four *sub*conclusions, we should be able to reach a clear-cut decision as to whether the price should be raised. Incidentally, this procedure of organizing related premises into separate groups often helps us to uncover premises we would otherwise have overlooked—especially the unwanted consequences.[15]

Sometimes, it becomes evident that *none* of the alternatives we have in mind will prove satisfactory. This is a fifth type of difficulty. After examining the alternatives, we begin to realize that they will all be accompanied by too many undesirable effects. Or it becomes clear that none of the alternatives will be strong enough to produce

---

[14] Incidentally, if we overlook these unwanted consequences—or, having come across them, close our eyes to them—the decision is readily made; the alternative then looks so attractive that there is no question that it will work. In such a case the difficulties arise *after* the decision is put into effect.

[15] See Appendix A—"Check List for Writing Business Reports"—for suggestions on organizing premises.

the results we seek—achieve the goals we have in mind. In these cases, we face a problem, one that troubles us greatly; and we must either go through the process of creating a new alternative or revise the most promising alternative of those under consideration so that it will be equal to the job lying ahead.

SUMMARY

This concept of premises provides the executive with tools for dealing with the unknown—for coping with the imponderables and the uncertainties he encounters in making a decision. At first sight the job of sorting out and examining these intangibles seems baffling; but the tools contained in the concept of premises turn out to be quite simple, once the details and their interrelationships are understood. A premise, as we define it, is a statement consisting of three elements —a cause, a causal connection, and a result. The first step is to try out in the mind each of the alternatives we have conceived and thus uncover the premises germane to each. The next step is to separate the premises pertaining to each alternative according to whether they point to desirable or undesirable effects on the goals we prize. The third step is to probe the unknowns—that is, to check the reliability of our detailed predictions of what would occur in case an alternative were adopted. A moment ago, when we began testing each of the three elements of premises for factual and value characteristics, it became evident that relatively few of the premises an executive must consider are purely factual and indubitably valid as predictions. The majority are partially or almost entirely measured with personal yardsticks. These predictions, which deal with the unknown, the invisible, may be as true as a purely factual premise; but to avoid being misled, we need to check them carefully and use them with a full recognition of their possible weaknesses. So the fourth step is to test the reliability of the salient premises. The fifth step is to weight (rank) the premises pertaining to each alternative with a view to ascertaining which ones will have the greatest impact on the goals we cherish most and which will have the least effect, thus gaining perspective as to which are the most important. The concluding step is to determine which alternative will provide the greatest total amount of wanted results and the least amount of unwanted results.

The four subsystems of concepts that we have been working with in Chapters 1, 2, and 3—goals, staircases, the creative process, and premises—when integrated into a single encompassing conceptual framework, should enable us to understand and improve our decision making. However, as already indicated, we shall double back in our next two chapters. In Chapter 4, we shall look into the field of mathematical decision making, a relatively new field whose practitioners are attempting to introduce more rigor in the use of factual premises. In Chapter 5, we shall work on the task of gathering value premises, particularly those intended to predict the responses of people; thus far we have skirted this most difficult and elusive task.

Once we have the over-all decision-making framework in hand, we shall be in a position to begin, thereafter, to cope with some of the typical kinds of decisions an executive must handle, decisions designed to solve a specific problem the company currently faces. For instance, in Parts II and III, we shall be learning to decide what type of authority to use in a particular instance, what changes should be made in the company's formal organization structure to help solve a problem, what the company's long-term goals should be, and how to implement those goals.

PROBLEM

CHOOSING BETWEEN ALTERNATIVES: DECISION MAKING

The Frisch Electronics Company* of South Bend, Indiana, was organized in 1942 to design and manufacture electronic instruments and equipment. During and after World War II, it had confined its attention to government contracts. The company concentrated on specially designed television, radio, and radar receivers; radio relay equipment; frequency control devices for communication sets; and other highly complex electronic devices, most of which were classified as "top secret" by the government.

In the spring of 1960, the president, Mr. Stanley Frisch, a graduate of Massachusetts Institute of Technology, expressed the belief that his company had lately been drifting. Shortly before the end of the war, he and his executives had attempted to uncover suitable peacetime products; but because of the availability of subcontracts for government orders, the project was all but forgotten. Early in 1960, however, it seemed probable that government purchases of electronic equipment would soon be reduced—at least the type which the company could supply. As a consequence, Mr. Frisch felt that the problem of conversion to civilian products could no longer be postponed. This had become evident to him in April, he explained, during a period of enforced rest following a mild heart attack. He commented that although the inaction had irked him, at least the doctors could not make him stop thinking.

The company had grown rapidly since its inception. A corps of imaginative and extremely competent electronics engineers had been brought to-

---

* In this case, all names, a few of the facts, and the location of the company have been altered to avoid disclosure of the company's identity.

gether and welded into a productive team. These were led by a German scientist, Dr. Hans Bloch, who had left his fatherland in 1935.

Mr. Jack Monroe headed the manufacturing department. The government orders were all special orders; no two were alike; they called for no more than 100 pieces of equipment. Virtually all the parts needed for the equipment were purchased; in fact, the majority of the items could be bought from wholesalers. Whenever specially designed parts were required, the engineers drew up blueprints and specifications and placed the orders with manufacturers. Nevertheless, the company found it necessary to employ several highly skilled machine tool operators who could handle fabrication jobs which required close tolerances on small parts. The assembly work was done largely by women, approximately 100 in all, who were trained by the company. As a result of months of practice, some of the women had become remarkably dextrous and proficient. The executives believed that their morale was high.

The financial problems were handled by the president with the help of his chief accountant, Mr. Calvin Jerome, a man who had taken over the accounting department in 1946 and straightened out the accounting system.

There was no sales organization; Mr. Frisch was responsible for negotiating most of the government contracts. One of the engineers, Mr. Alex Johns, had frequently expressed the opinion that a sales force was needed.

Over the past fifteen years the company had shown a reasonably consistent profit, but most of the earnings had been plowed back into laboratory equipment and buildings.

Upon his return to work early in May, the president prepared a memorandum setting out some of the details of the program he had thought through while in the hospital and distributed copies to each of the three departmental managers. A few days later, at a meeting of these men, he explained that during his enforced vacation, he had worked out several possible plans, but that he had chosen the one described because it seemed the most realistic of any he could devise. The purpose of the meeting was to go through the plan and make any needed modifications. The memorandum is reproduced below.

SUGGESTED PROGRAM

FRISCH ELECTRONICS COMPANY

S. J. Frisch
5–23–60

OUR LONG-RUN OBJECTIVES

We want to do more than simply stay in business. We want to flourish and expand in the years ahead. Our objective is to make the Frisch Electronics Company the leading firm in the industry. In my opinion, the best way to achieve leadership is to build a solid reputation for quality products; I see no point in trying to be the largest company in the industry.

POLICIES THAT WILL IMPLEMENT THESE OBJECTIVES

1. Keep our engineering staff vital and productive.
2. Find new peacetime markets for nonmilitary products that we can design and manufacture.
3. Begin to build a sales organization to market those products.
4. Make sure that the men and women we employ think Frisch Electronics Company is a good place to work.

SUGGESTIONS FOR CARRYING OUT THE ABOVE POLICIES

1. The engineers:

a) As far as possible, assign our engineers to projects that will challenge them.
b) Ask each engineer to turn in every two weeks some idea for a commercially feasible product—one for householders or one for use in industry.
c) Keep watching for young engineers and scientists who are well trained and imaginative, and bring these to the attention of Dr. Bloch.

2. Prospective customers and the products they can use:

a) All of us should make a concerted effort to think of definite *kinds* of customers who can use products we are able to design and manufacture.
b) Our job also is:
   (1) To examine the products those buyers now use.
   (2) To determine wherein the products they now use fall short of solving the problems they face.
   (3) To suggest types of electronic devices which might solve these problems for them.
c) The ideas for new products we already have under consideration should be reappraised.
d) Possibly we should assign a man to head up and co-ordinate this work of finding promising markets and conceiving products the buyers will want.

3. Sales organization:

a) Appoint a sales manager. I am not yet sure what his qualifications should be. We have two alternatives here: to ask Mr. Alex Johns to be sales manager, or to go outside for a man.
b) We will have to start looking around for salesmen, but I think we should make no decisions here until we have selected our markets and chosen our new products.

4. The welfare of our semiskilled and skilled plant and office employees:

a) Reappraise our pay rates every six months, and keep these in line with rates in the South Bend area.
b) Maintain regular employment. On second thought, maybe we should reconsider this one. Perhaps we should follow a policy of irregular employment. There is a great deal to be said on both sides.
c) Try to avoid being paternalistic, but nevertheless watch to see that employees' grievances are heard and that appropriate corrective action is taken.
d) Recognize any outstanding work that is done, and compliment the employees.

Study the case carefully, mastering it to a point where you feel as though you had worked with the company for some years and knew most of the employees quite well. You are to appraise the following two alternatives mentioned in Part 4 (*b*) by Mr. Frisch—"maintain regular employment," or "maintain irregular employment." Follow the directions listed below. At the end of your report, you are to choose one of these as the second of the four bottom steps on the means-end staircase No. 4, as set out in Mr. Frisch's memorandum.

1. Your first job is to think out and write down eight or ten premises you believe are pertinent to each of the two alternatives, ones the executives who are attending the meeting will probably consider in making this decision. Fix one alternative in mind and try it out, then turn to the other. Use the following directions. Each of your premise statements should be framed as a sentence reading, "If . . . , then . . . ," which:

a) Includes a phrase following the "if" which serves as a cause. (This first element in some, but not all, of your premises for the first alternative might read, "If we maintain regular employment . . .")
b) And includes a phrase following the "then" which reads as a result that you think might flow from the cause (the *third* element of your premise).
c) And also includes a "causal connection" between the cause and the re-

sult; this *second* element in the premise is not stated in words but is to be inferred from reading the sentence. (Later, we shall drop the rather cumbersome "if" and "then" phraseology.)

NOTE: When writing your report answer questions 1 and 2 together to save busy-work recopying.

2. Arrange the premises pertinent to each of the *two* alternatives in two lists, one containing those premises which refer to the desirable consequences (or results) of adopting the alternative, and the other listing those premises which refer to undesirable consequences. You will have four lists in all—two for each alternative. Some of them will undoubtedly refer to goals other than "making sure of the welfare of the employees"—the No. 4 in Mr. Frisch's outline—for instance, goals appearing in the company's list of "long-term objectives" (its intermediate goals) and goals appearing in some of the other means-end stairs which Mr. Frisch described. But your premises should *not* be confined to these.

3. Pick out of your lists one premise which is predominantly factual, and explain why you think so by analyzing *each* of its three elements. (You may have trouble finding a predominantly factual premise; but try to pick one in which at least one of the three elements is dominantly factual, and explain why that element seems factual to you. To avoid becoming confused, choose a premise with a single cause and a single result. Indicate your idea of where each element would fall on the scale in Diagram 5 (p. 73). Then do the same for the premise as a whole. Finally, indicate how reliable you think the premise is and explain why you think so.

4. Select from your lists a premise which is of a predominantly value nature, and explain why you think so by analyzing *each* of its three elements, following the detailed instructions in Question 3.

NOTE: In Questions 3 and 4, carefully appraise the reliability of these two premises you have analyzed. Will the result stated in the premise *really* flow from the cause you mention? In other words, how reliable are these premises? Recall that a value premise can be just as valid and reliable as a factual premise.

5. Weight the premises you listed under each of the two alternatives. That is, rank the premises pertaining to each alternative according to their probable relative impact on the future welfare of the company and its employees and customers, giving the one that will have the greatest impact the top position and the most trivial one (make up a trivial one if you have to) the bottom position. You need not rewrite the lists called for in Question 2. Simply rank these premises, using only two series of numbers— one series for all the premises germane to the first alternative, and the second series for the premises pertinent to the second alternative. Explain why you ranked your two No. 1 premises at the top and your two last premises at the bottom.

6. On the basis of the premises you have set down and the weight you have assigned them, which of the two alternatives provides the greatest *total* amount (or total weight) of wanted consequences and the least total amount of unwanted consequences? In other words, which would you decide the company should adopt? Explain why.

Chapter 4

MATHEMATICS
AND NUMERICAL
PREMISES

OPERATIONS RESEARCH, a relatively
new concept, attempts to introduce the methods of mathematics and
natural science into executive decision making. It is a body of analytical tools designed for calculating certain of the consequences
of adopting an alternative—usually the profits or the costs—and
thus determining which alternative would prove most desirable from
the profit or cost standpoint. More generally speaking, it deals with
the problem of maximizing certain wanted consequences (profits, for
instance) or minimizing certain unwanted consequences (costs, for
instance).

It is ordinarily used as an aid in making major decisions where the
three elements of the most heavily weighted premises can be cast into
factual form. As its name implies, it is intended primarily for top
management decisions having to do with the operating level of the
organization and with physical objects and their behavior. Thus,
operations research fits into Part I, the Decision-making Process,
at two points. It can be used in making decisions to be inserted on
the lower steps of the company's means-end staircases; normally
these are management decisions about how to carry out measurable
physical activities. And its use is confined to purely factual premises. Although its proponents will argue that it can be used for value
premises, we shall have reason to doubt its efficacy there.

We shall first inquire into the nature of operations research. Then,
in the second part of the chapter, we shall explore its uses in business decision making.

THE NATURE OF OPERATIONS RESEARCH

Operations research is actually a way of thinking, not a single
method. It uses any tools from any academic discipline. Building

and using models, usually mathematical models, however, holds a central position; our examination, therefore, will be confined to these. We shall nevertheless use our own terminology and not that of the mathematician.

The Idea of a Model

A model is an attempt at representing some segment of real life and explaining, in a simplified manner, the way that segment operates. It omits those determinants (causes) that the model builder thinks have only a minor influence on the segment's operation and concentrates on what he believes are the chief influences. In operations research, problems are usually analyzed by means of a mathematical model. In many models—wherever appropriate—the chief determinants are woven together into a formula which shows the relationships that appear to exist between them. For example, the formula might describe some of the costs of producing and storing a product and be designed to determine the size of run (lot size) that will cost the least.

A highly simplified version of a formula designed to determine the least costly lot size—a formula that is much simpler than is usually employed—might read as follows:

$$\frac{D\,CS}{Z} + \frac{Z\,CP\,CI}{2} = \text{total cost}$$

For our illustration, we shall assume:

Where
Z = number of parts that could be produced in one run   250 units
CS = total setup cost per run   \$50
CI = carrying cost per dollar of inventory investment for one year   6%
CP = cost of part per unit   \$2
D = yearly sales   500 units

Using this formula, we find that if we produce in lot sizes of 250, for instance, the cost of setup per year would be \$100 (500 × \$50 ÷ 250) and the interest cost of carrying the inventory would be \$15 (250 × \$2 × .06 ÷ 2—dividing by 2 gives us the *average* cost for a year). The total annual carrying cost in this example would be \$115. The costs of other lot sizes can be calculated in exactly the same way by changing the 250 lot-size figure (changing the Z); we can then compare the costs and determine which would be cheapest. We have assumed that two annual costs will vary with the size of the run: setting up the machine (the total setup cost per year) and the inventory holding costs (the total annual cost of interest). A third cost, the cost of raw materials, parts, and labor that we have invested in each *unit,* is also included in the formula, but this is used merely to determine the value of the inventory; we assume that variable costs per unit will not vary with the lot size.

These equations usually show on one side the more significant causes and their relative weight and on the other side the result that flows from the causes. In economic terminology, the input factors are placed on one side and the resulting output on the other. In mathematical terminology, the independent variables are the causes or means and the dependent variable is the result or objective we are seeking.

In order to frame a mathematical model, all the pertinent causes and their weights, the causal connections, and the result must be measurable and be expressed in quantitative form. As intimated earlier, the three elements of the premise must be virtually 100 per cent factual. Equally important, these premises must be entirely reliable. We would prefer that the causal connection be statistically demonstrable; but at least we must be certain that in our company, during the period under consideration, the consequences set out in the formula will actually occur. Any causes, causal connections, and results that must, in part, be measured with value standards will have to be left out of the equation; if these are included, the equation loses its mathematical precision.

A model stands in place of and is a simplified representation of a quite complex set of relations. Economic theory employs models— admittedly very simple ones; for instance, it uses formulas, usually presented graphically, showing the amounts and relationships of supply, demand, and price, or marginal cost and marginal revenue. The diagrams are models showing what economists deem to be the main determinants (but by no means *all* the determinants) of prices and how the determinants relate to each other. Many of the operations researchers' models are adaptations of the economists' models. In Chapter 1, the staircase diagram we were using was also a simplified model representing one feature of the behavior of executives in deciding on the steps for a plan of action. A model is a succinct statement of what goes on in a segment of the complex real world; thus, the user is better able to grasp the main features of the structure and the way they operate.

Once the model is conceived, the operations researcher (who, as will soon be seen, must be an imaginative and highly trained mathematician as well as a man who knows how the company actually operates) begins to experiment with it. For instance, he may watch the results when the size of the manufacturing lot (the Z in our simplified formula) is increased or decreased. He manipulates, on paper, the causes (the independent variables), using them as stimuli, and observes (calculates) the results, the effect on the dependent variable. The objective is to see which alternative, which combination of the various causes or means, will yield the greatest amount of the result he seeks—usually, in operations research, either the lowest cost or greatest profit.

Conceiving a Suitable Model

The task of creating a mathematical model which, though simplified, will represent approximately the way things work in the actual segment of the company under study, calls for both a mastery of what really goes on in the company and the imaginative use of advanced mathematics to describe those activities. The problem is to discover the causes and results that are significant *and* the mechanism or system underlying the observed relationships between the causes and results. Deciding which data to employ (which costs are significant, for instance), quantifying these cause and result elements, gathering and tabulating data, and making tests to find out exactly how the cause elements actually affect the result (through the use of correlation studies, for instance) likewise demand imagination. We shall return in a moment to this task of creating a new model.

A few standard formulas for some of the most prevalent types of problems have been developed by operation researchers. We have already been introduced to a highly simplified version of one used to determine economical lot sizes. This happens to be the type of problem where some costs decline and others simultaneously rise, and the objective is to find the point where the sum of the costs is least. As we saw, to get the most economical lot size for any product in the company's line, the actual cost data for each of our products is substituted for the symbols in the formula and the answer is calculated. Frequently the calculations are extremely long and complex, in which case an electronic computer will be used. To handle these calculations, the computer's mechanism is specially set up (programmed) to go through the sequence of calculations called for in the formula.

In addition to models for determining the most economical lot sizes, the operations researchers have developed a conceptual frame-

work called engineering economics which is designed to aid in making choices from among long-term capital investment alternatives. For instance, it can be used in deciding which of two machines—the best new one or the one now owned—will cost the least in the period ahead. The experts have worked out formulas which enable them to compare all the expected costs of the best new machine (this would include its installation costs, interest on the investment, and expenses of operation, such as labor and maintenance, minus its resale value at the end of its useful life)—compare these with similar costs of the piece of equipment now owned. The mathematical computations include a technique by which the two sets of data can be made comparable in all respects.

So much for standard formulas. Frequently it is necessary to design a model that will fit the company's peculiar needs. Conceiving a reliable formula from scratch, a formula in which the results always describe approximately what will occur, is a major task. Briefly, the problem is to analyze the behavior of the segment under scrutiny—see in detail the forces that move the system—measure and describe those forces, and represent them in a model, preferably a mathematical formula. Such a formula is, of course, based on past performance, and assumes that the dominant forces (causes) that moved the system in the past will continue to move it in the future and that the relative impact of each will remain unchanged. In some systems this would be true; our formula for determining the minimal cost of carrying the inventory would be an example. We assumed there would be only two influences—the interest and setup costs—and we knew the impact they would each have on the cost would be the same in the future as in the past. In other systems this would not be true. Spending $100,000 for six quarter page advertisements in each of three magazines A, C, and T may produce a large sales volume on one occasion, but these causes may produce virtually no sales on a later occasion. From our recent examination of the idea of premises, we learned that people's behavior cannot be reliably predicted with a formula.

We can now see that the development of a mathematical model consists of several steps. As previously noted, the researcher begins by defining the problem that the executives want to solve—the problem of minimizing costs of manufacturing and storing each product in our product line, for instance, or of determining where to locate a warehouse in order to minimize transportation costs, or deciding whether to buy a new machine. These results, the dependent variables, must be cast in number form. The researcher then looks for, and lists, the causes that most strongly influence the results; these will eventually become the independent variables. His next task is to describe these numerically, perhaps by observing and tabulating what he sees. In addition, he determines the relative impact of each of the inputs. On the basis of this study of the chief causes, he seeks to create in his mind's eye a moving visual image of the behavior of the *causal side* of the equation which gives due weight to the relative importance of each of the causes. A further examination of this empirical data will also help suggest to a mathematician the prevailing causal connections between the causes and the result, thus giving him ideas about the character of the *result side* of the equation. He may, for instance, try to plot the data on a graph or otherwise search for correlations or relationships.

By this time, he has gone through the first three stages of the creative process and he should be ready for the fourth stage: From all this, he begins to create in his mind an equation that will express with fair reliability the relationships he sees among the independent variables and between them and the dependent variable. The task now is to generalize—to convert this pattern of activity into a formula by couching it in mathematical symbols which are suggested by the arrays of actual data. For example, he may eventually find that in practice his company uses n units of means D, uses the square of means F, and always reduces means L by an amount K; this, he finds, gives the cost, C.

But before finally adopting the model, he will try to test its reliability (this is stage five of the creative process) by substituting recent data for the causal elements in the formula and observing any discrepancies between the model's answers and the known recent results—what has actually happened lately when these causes have occurred—and revising the formula where necessary. When he is satisfied, he puts his formula to use by running his "experiments." His procedure is to substitute a wide range of numbers for the symbols in the formula—lot sizes from 1 to 1,000, for instance.[1]

OPERATIONS RESEARCH AND THE EXECUTIVE

The foregoing will give us an idea of what an operations research model is like and how a researcher creates and uses a model. But our

---

[1] The mathematically oriented student who wishes to probe further should turn to C. West Churchman, Russell L. Ackoff, and E. Leonard Arnoff, *Introduction to Operations Research* (New York: John Wiley & Sons, Inc., 1957); and to Harold Bierman, Lawrence E. Fouraker, Robert K. Jaedicke, *Quantitative Analysis for Business Decisions* (Homewood, Ill.: Richard D. Irwin, Inc., 1961).

objective is not to become a specialist in this field; instead we want to find out how an executive can use it as a tool in decision making. To this end, we shall first see how the mathematical formulations dovetail with the conceptual framework we have been building. Thereafter, we shall look into the uses of operations research, become aware of the problems we must cope with when we employ it, find out what it can do efficiently and what it cannot do well, and try to appraise its future possibilities.

Similarities in the Reasoning Processes

As we have seen, operations research ties in very tightly at certain points with the decision-making framework we are using. The two differ in their emphasis and to some extent in the causes and consequences they take into consideration. But the basic ideas lying beneath these decision-making procedures are the same. In operations research, a staff specialist constructs a simplified mathematical description in symbol form of what goes on in the segment of the company that is under observation, tries out a number of alternatives in this model (tries out several lot sizes, for instance), notes the consequences (the costs of each alternative), compares these answers and chooses the one that comes nearest to achieving the goal— lowest cost, in our example.

Our approach parallels this but is more complex. Our procedure has been to construct and hold in our minds a rather complete picture of the *actual* details of the segment's structure, and create detailed images of how the structure operates, including the behavior of both the people and the things that serve as means. While holding this quite complete picture of the real world in our minds, we conceive and try out three or four alternatives by imagining we have put each one to work in our visual image of the actual environment. As we run off these mental experiments, we make notes of the several consequences of adopting each alternative. After weighting and comparing the wanted and unwanted consequences produced by each alternative, we choose the best one.

We can see that the basic decision-making procedures are identical. The differences arise chiefly from the precise mathematical reasoning the researchers have chosen to impose upon themselves and the limitations this places on the causes and consequences they are able to take into consideration. In this book we have, of course, been observing and trying to foresee the causes and responses of factually describable things, and we have given appropriate weight to factual premises. But we have chosen each of our premises on the basis of the amount of impact or weight it will have (this includes its reliability), regardless of whether it was factual or value. In fact, because we thought men's ideas, goals, and behavior produced consequences that were of notable import in deciding on a course of action, we sought out premises the elements of which were partially or wholly value; and we could readily include premises in which one element was factual and the others predominantly value.

In contrast, the men using operations research are constrained, though not obliged, to disregard any premise which is partially or wholly value, regardless of its weight. To achieve their objective they must choose their premises on the basis of how factual each premise is and the amount and reliability of the available data describing its elements. Nevertheless, they are well aware that decisions cannot be made solely on the basis of formulas found in handbooks and that life in a company has only a slight resemblance to a machine's operation. They also know that there are relatively few reliable constants in a business firm and that it is possible to find the values of only a small portion of the constants; it is therefore not possible to turn the crank and read off the final answers. But we must be on guard against the understandable tendency of operations research men to weight their own premises very heavily and either overlook or give little weight to other premises an executive may consider important. This does not mean that these men are unaware of the importance of value elements and premises.[2] They merely assume that management will supply these—will add "judgments" which make allowances for these as well as for the oversimplification of the model—when making the final decision. For instance, a formula may tell us which combination of causes (which alternative) will be the least costly, but we may also want to take into consideration the number of men we must hire or other factual results. These premises relating to costs are of cardinal importance in many situations, but just because an alternative will cost least in the pe-

---

[2] Several men are now attempting to find publicly accepted measuring rods or universal standards for measuring what is unmeasurable. See, for example, C. West Churchman's *Prediction and Optimal Decision* (Englewood Cliffs, N.J.: Prentice-Hall, Inc., 1961); David W. Miller and Martin K. Starr, *Executive Decisions and Operations Research* (Englewood Cliffs, N.J.: Prentice-Hall, Inc., 1960), particularly chap. 5; and Chris Argyris, *Understanding Organizational Behavior* (Homewood, Ill.: The Dorsey Press, Inc., 1960), chap. iv. Frank M. Bass, et al., *Mathematical Models and Methods in Marketing* (Homewood, Ill.: Richard D. Irwin, Inc., 1961), also includes several examples of such attempts. Perhaps the most fertile of all is a slender volume by Herbert A. Simon, *The New Science of Management Decision* (New York: Harper & Brothers, 1960).

riod ahead does not necessarily mean we choose that one. To make a good decision we usually need to take many consequences into consideration, and a majority may be of a value character. For instance, increasing the lot size may force us to increase our already overlarge borrowings for inventories, may clutter up the shipping room aisles and slow down deliveries, may produce irritation among the stock clerks, and may cause a dozen other wanted and unwanted consequences.

Uses of Operations Research

While mathematics imposes quite severe limitations, the chief value of operations research lies in its mathematical orientation. First of all, it can be very useful in forcing us to frame factual premises. We are sometimes unwilling to take the trouble to sort out and, where possible, quantify the factual elements and thereafter reason our way through to a point where we can frame reliable factual premises. It also helps the executive to study the factual means and goals which are germane to a problem, *provided* these were uncovered and included in the formula. And the specific causes or means that are included in the formula tells him what additional data, if any, he needs for the formula in order to make his decision. In addition, the formulation of the mathematical equations may oblige him to uncover and reappraise some of the assumptions that he has normally made when forming a decision. All this presupposes, however, either that the executive is mathematically inclined and has the time and patience to understand what is included in the formula and how close it comes to representing the actual operation, or else that the operations research staff man is capable of observing, verbalizing, and quantifying most of the significant premises and means and goals that are actually employed in the segment of the company under study and is aware of how close his equation comes to reality.

But doubtless most important, operations research enables us to take into consideration the influence of several numerically described causes *simultaneously*—calculations which the human mind, unaided, could not handle. Without a linear programming formula, for instance, we should never be able to determine precisely which lot size will yield the lowest combination of costs, or the location of a plant which would minimize the combined inbound and outbound transportation costs. Without engineering economy formulas we would find it difficult to take into consideration the precise effects of the wide variety of costs and assumptions that we should consider when deciding on a new piece of equipment. Operations research provides a method of solving certain business problems of great complexity, problems which executives have heretofore had to solve almost intuitively.

As we look back, it becomes evident that we can expect some success in the use of operations research where the following conditions are present: when the causal connection between the independent and dependent variables are clear cut—usually for decisions resting on the low steps of the staircases or for technological or physical processes where the causes and results are likely to be relatively tangible and measurable; when these relationships can be described with some accuracy by mathematical formulations; and, as we shall see shortly, when rather complete and reliable statistical data are available for the chief variables or can be obtained at a reasonable cost.

Operations research techniques have been used with some success in handling types of problems such as the following: deciding on inventory levels (we have used this problem as one of our examples); determining the best location for a plant or warehouse from the point of view of freight costs; calculating the most economical combination of inputs (raw materials) to achieve a certain result—in feed manufacturing, for instance, the cheapest combination of protein feed ingredients such as soybean meal, cottonseed meal, and linseed meal to secure a feed of a given level of protein (least-cost input model); and in deciding when to replace equipment (engineering economics). However, it can also aid in deciding how to schedule production orders to minimize the amount of wasted machine time (waiting line problems), and it was used in executive training to construct and operate models designed to help predict the actions of competitors (game theory).

Problems Frequently Encountered

If we are to secure usable answers from operations research we must be willing to deal honestly with the troublesome problems it poses. Gathering reliable data about the past and preparing estimated data of the future are two; estimating the costs of making an operations research study and determining whether to spend the money on such a study is another; verbalizing our assumptions and making allowances for them in the calculated answers is a fourth— here we are concerned with the reliability of the answers. And, finally, if operations research is to have a future for businessmen, its practitioners must be realistic about claims of its usefulness, for this is tied into the problem of building management's confidence in it.

Gathering useful and accurate data about past performance is no easy matter. Yet this is essential, for the answers we get will be no better than the reliability of our numerical data—their completeness and accuracy in measuring and representing what has actually been occurring in the segment of the company under scrutiny. To the man who has never dug into a company's original cost records or its accounting data, the determination of the cost of setup or the cost of raw materials, labor, and machine time per unit would appear easy. But many companies do not prepare cost data, and those that do are obliged to make arbitrary allocations of overhead expenses. In any case, the data are seldom available in exactly the form needed. Consequently, in practice we must be content, often, with approximate data or even with estimates, simply because no better figures are available and the time and cost of compilation prohibit a special study to gather real data.

But thus far we have been talking about determining *past* costs and sales, whereas we are really interested only in *future* costs and *future* production and sales. We must answer questions such as these: Should we use estimates of next year's costs of raw materials, and if so, what premises should we employ in making the estimate? Should we allow for the fact that the machine is getting older? That it is to be replaced by a modern machine? In our sales data we encounter similar problems. Our sales of an item next year will largely depend on future business conditions, the product improvements introduced by our competitors, the prices we set, and the efforts of our sales force; we can be sure that customers will form such information into premises when deciding whether to buy our unit. In estimating our sales we have to foresee the changes in these determinants and sense the weight our customers will attach to each of these causes and results.

The point is, if the cost figures or sales figures which we use in our equation prove wrong—regardless of whether they describe past circumstances or are estimates of the future—our decision as to which alternative (lot size) would be cheapest will also turn out to be wrong; we place an order for an uneconomical lot size.

Because next year's figures will almost certainly differ from last year's—figures for such items as sales volume, prices, production, costs of raw materials, and so on—we are frequently obliged to use estimated figures when trying out our alternatives. Actually, this is common practice in industry; executives regularly use estimated figures that take into account the influences of future events. When we employ the relatively flexible premises that we studied in Chapter 3, our minds seem to make the adjustments almost spontaneously, but when these are employed in a formula, we often feel uneasy and wish we had some "hard" figures.

In using operations research we also have to reconcile ourselves to the thought that most of the key data are not "facts." Instead they are conclusions based largely on value premises; as we just saw, next year's sales estimates and cost estimates must be based on people's future behavior. This holds for engineering economy formulas as well as for other operations research formulas. A key figure in equipment replacement is the probable obsolescence rate of the equipment —what its useful life will be. This obsolescence rate involves at least two estimates based on value premises: how soon technological improvements will render the machine obsolete and how soon the equipment will become useless because of a decline in the sale of the products it is designed to produce. These two estimates, based upon value premises, provide premises for predicting how many units will be produced on the equipment before it must be discarded. Similarly, in our lot-size formula, the key figures of expected costs and annual sales must rest heavily on value premises; these must be estimated for next year. Once these key figures are determined, we can proceed with the mathematical computations. As executives, we must *not* allow ourselves to be misled into supposing the answers which the formulas supply are solidly based on fact and scientific reasoning.

It is evident from what we have just seen that we can usually cope with the task of gathering data and preparing estimated data, though it is clearly a major problem. Estimating the costs of using an operations research study to make a decision and determining which decisions warrant such expenditures is a third major problem. Estimating the size of the problem of securing data—we have just been through that—will be fairly easy for a man who knows the company's records and understands what will be needed. On the basis of this he can estimate the man-hours required for gathering the data. The question the executives must then answer is this: Will the premises developed by the operations research studies produce decisions which will save the company more than the cost of the study? Clearly, many of the decisions an executive must make are so simple that good ones can be made in a few moments without forming a mathematical model, and many fairly complicated decisions can be made by using the rather straightforward decision-making procedure developed in this book. Generally speaking, the costs of gathering data and conceiving and testing a model make operations research of practical use only when the executives are making very complex one-shot decisions involving large expenditures or when the company expects to use the formula to make many repetitive decisions which, in the aggregate, involve large expenditures, decisions requiring masses of data that can be programmed and fed into a computer.

A fourth problem, verbalizing our assumptions and *determining the reliability of the equation* as a predictor of the consequences poses a more sophisticated problem. Earlier—in Chapter 3—we were dealing with this same task; we saw that where we had a factual cause and result, and where we had a body of statistical data which demonstrated the presence of a tight causal connection (data which proved that the result always followed the introduction of the cause), we could feel quite confident that the result would come true. In Diagram 4 (p. 70), for example, we saw the connection between the amount of heat and the expansion of metal. But we also found that merely asserting that a result would flow from a cause, even though cause and result were both factual, did not make it true. Choosing the plant location that would have reduced the cost of freight by 15 per cent in the past would not necessarily yield the same savings in the years ahead.

The reliability of an equation which is made up entirely of purely factual elements can be partially determined by examining the assumptions that are made. Allowing for the assumptions that are knowingly incorporated would appear to be easy, though it is not. We need to make a note of our assumptions that certain conditions will exist—that business conditions will remain the same, for instance, that there will be no strikes or slowdowns in the plant, or that our salesmen's morale will remain high. We need to question any assumption that the *system's* behavior in the future—the behavior of the men and machines, for example—will always be the same as in the past. We *know* that most conditions will differ from those existing in the past and we must allow for these changes. Equally important, we shall want to reappraise periodically our assumption that we can still ignore the less important forces (causes) which we had deliberately omitted from the equation to keep it simple enough for our mathematical tools. If we fail to revise our unrealistic assumptions, we can be certain that the calculated consequences will not come true.

The assumptions that we *unknowingly* use pose even greater problems than the assumptions we recognize. For instance, a recent college graduate steeped in economic theory may automatically tend to assume that the chief models used in microeconomics, the models of perfect competition, monopolistic competition, monopoly, and so on are fairly accurate representation of the way companies actually operate, just because he knows no other framework. And he, or a mathematician unfamiliar with the actual operating practices in the segment under study, may automatically assume that the only significant causes are the observable physical ones, whereas some of these may be trivial or even misleading. Even the more experienced men in the office may unthinkingly assume that the workers in the plant will operate their equipment at the rated capacity even though we know that the members of informal groups regularly set their own production quotas and vary these in the light of the backlog of unfilled orders. Similarly, they may make the unrealistic assumption that there will always be just enough orders on hand to keep all the men and equipment busy all the time when, in fact, the orders seldom exactly match the productive capacity. It is also easy to assume that the company can automatically sell all it makes—that all we have to do is find the lowest manufacturing cost and set our prices competitively. Also, men who have not had long experience tend to assume that there will be no side effects on other goals as a result of introducing changes. And they are likely to assume that the change which benefits the company (a change, for example, that increases its profits), will be enthusiastically welcomed and promptly adopted by the workers.

Most deeply buried, in many cases, is the assumption that the equation, once it is conceived, represents the actual behavior accurately—or a realistic abstraction of it. We realize that the symbols are simply representations of the real things, but we assume that the real things—the men and machines, for instance—can be just as easily and precisely manipulated by arithmetic as are the symbols. Moreover, we assume that the real things which we include in the formula behave in a mechanical manner, following the neat cause-effect laws of Newtonian physics. On top of that, with the formula's symbols arrayed in an equation and the internal consistency of its mathematical logic clearly demonstrable, it *looks* scientific and, therefore, we assume it is quite accurate. Not many men would raise question about such an equation.

Both the operations researcher and the executive can easily forget to appraise the reliability of the equations they use. As executives, our task is to bring to light the many noticed and unnoticed assumptions and mentally revise the computed answers to allow for them.

The Future of Operations Research

Once we understand the limitations of these mathematical models, we can use them with considerable confidence. In solving problems in which only purely factual premises are required and where reliable data are available, they are above reproach. However, they fall down when people must be considered. Though we know that there are some discoverable uniformities in men's behavior, we also know that we have no way of measuring human thoughts and motives; we know that men are notably unpredictable, and that their individual webs of influence and action are so complex that the behavior of people in general is not reducible to a formula. For these reasons, we are obliged to recognize that operations research is of little help in framing reliable value premises. We have no way of either measuring the elements objectively or manipulating them mathematically.

We are well aware that if we are to make decisions that will stand up when reappraised six months or six years hence, we shall have to include the pertinent value premises along with the purely factual premises which are brought to light when we prepare an operations research study. Our procedure should be to examine the three or four most desirable alternatives turned up by experimenting with the mathematical model and try to foresee the effects on *other* goals of adopting each alternative—its effect on the company's reputation, its labor relations, its sales volume, its ability to attract and retain effective executives, and so on. In our final decision we may find ourselves giving little weight to the results calculated by the operations researcher either because we think they will not come true or because they will have only a minor impact on our long-term goals.

We can see that operations research may play a useful role in decision making, but that *alone* it is not flexible enough or broad enough to handle most decisions. We have also found that it does not provide a science of management as some of its proponents would have us believe. Indeed, its future as an accepted executive tool may depend on a willingness of its supporters to shield operations research from the overly enthusiastic claims of the highly specialized staff people who advocate its use. It is evident that the concept provides a very useful tool, but we do not have here a major breakthrough, a comprehensive decision theory. As we have noted, the applications are rather limited. Where the approach is applicable, we cannot expect the precision in measurement and certitude of cause and effect attained in the natural sciences, even though we use symbols and manipulate them in sophisticated equations. Although its proponents always caution the reader that operations research will give only a preliminary and not necessarily accurate answer, they, especially the mathematicians, sometimes tend to place much more confidence in the tool than do executives. Some seem to become enamored of the elegance of their mathematical formulation and forget that it is simply one of several means to an end.

Not only will the future of operations research depend on a willingness to make modest claims about its efficacy so that executives will not be disappointed in the results they get, but also its future will heavily depend on the acceptance by executives of the idea of mathematical models and a recognition by researchers of the limitations of models. Unfortunately, in order to reduce a problem to a size where it can be formulated in mathematical terms, the mathematician frequently must prune and simplify the model to a point where, in the eyes of a practical executive, it yields unrealistic answers, or at best, answers whose reliability he questions. While a simplified model may be useful even though it gives the wrong answers (because it provides unexpected insights), few executives have the patience, the perception, or the highly developed mathematical skills necessary to follow the complex mathematical reasoning or to make the necessary mental revision in the answers. Moreover, a man who has had as much as two or three years of college mathematics but no longer uses it every day, eventually becomes rusty.

In view of these mathematical hurdles and the problems men must cope with when they employ it, the acceptance by executives may be slow. In any case, it is an analytical tool to be used with care. Operations research could easily turn into a sterile intellectual game played only by unsophisticated men. But it *should* prove of considerable value to executives. We must, in any case, keep our minds open in appraising newly created tools such as this one.

Operations research provides a fifth conceptual subsystem. We now turn to a sixth, the concluding subsystem of our decision-making framework, namely, anticipating the decisions of others.

Chapter *5*   ANTICIPATING THE DECISIONS OF OTHERS

THAT AN executive must depend heavily upon value premises, and that probing for them calls for considerable insight, became evident in Chapter 3. Among the more elusive and important value premises are those that *other* individuals will employ when they are deciding how they will respond to the alternative the executive proposes. If, on the basis of the premises they would use, he anticipates perfunctory responses or outright opposition from certain men or groups upon whom he will have to depend to carry out the proposal, he must take this into consideration in making his decision. He will want to incorporate this information with his other premises at the time he finally chooses his alternative.

The most obvious way to gather ideas about men's probable reactions is, of course, to ask them ahead of time what they would think of the proposal. The procedure frequently discloses some of the value premises the men would use, and ones to which the executive must attach some weight. Typically, however, a man is unwilling to lay bare *all* of his inmost thoughts. Exposing his secret hopes and fears would leave him vulnerable; and anyway, it's "just not done." He discloses only the premises he thinks others would deem "proper." Those that mean the most to him, the ones to which he attaches greatest weight, are seldom expressed; consequently, the executive usually uncovers only a part of the picture by asking questions. Moreover, this procedure takes time; and for this reason, it is impractical in those cases where the proposal will impinge upon a large number of individuals and several groups.

The first half of this chapter will be devoted to the task of uncovering these unstated premises used by *individuals* whom we know personally. What we shall be talking about can be summarized in the word *empathy*—feeling *with* the other man. The objec-

113

tive here will be to investigate some techniques for living inside another man's skin—for thinking as he will think and feeling as he will feel when he is making up his mind—and in this way gathering value premises pertinent to the alternative we have under consideration. The men we observed at the pricing conference were attempting to do this. They were putting themselves in the shoes of several of the people who would be affected in the event that the prices were raised—some of the individual customers, the salesmen, the union president, and individual personnel and cost accounting men, for instance. The purpose was to uncover the value premises those people would use and thus anticipate their reactions.

The second half of the chapter will be devoted to uncovering the premises of *groups* of people who will be affected by the proposal under consideration, groups with whom we have little face-to-face contact.

No man should expect to become letter perfect in anticipating the decisions of others. But I believe that a man can teach himself to be more perceptive and thus reduce the number of wrong guesses he makes by the deliberate use of some of the ideas developed here.

DISCOVERING THE GOALS AND PREMISES OF INDIVIDUALS IN THE ORGANIZATION

Whether we like it or not, people's personal goals play a dominant role in company decision making. When a man is making company decisions or deciding to accept and carry out company decisions proposed to him, he examines them in part with a view to whether they will further his own goals. Yet he may also derive great personal satisfaction from helping his organization and its members to attain their goals. To most of us, the experience of making a decision (or acting on another's decision) that contributes in a major way to the company's welfare is frequently a memorable one. Equally important, carrying out such a decision helps a man to ensure his own welfare. He can feel more confident than before that his subordinates, associates, superiors, and the men in other groups in the company will want him to stay on; perhaps they will even propose that he be given heavier responsibilities or a better job and more pay. This is a rather typical pattern of thinking, used by everyone from the office boy up to the president.

Management sometimes says that an employee should be interested solely in the welfare of the company. But in my opinion, it is neither improper nor unethical for a man to work in behalf of his personal goals, so long as he furthers the company goals and does not injure his fellow men. People join an organization because this is one of their best means of ensuring their welfare. If the personal goals of the members are not served, the men depart for greener pastures; and the company languishes.

An understanding of the personal goals of our associates, subordinates, and superiors, and those of the men in other groups in the organization whose cooperation must be secured, enables us to make better company decisions. A decision that advances the long-term goals both of the men in the company and of the company itself will stand up when it is reviewed later. Men's ultimate and intermediate goals are very real to them and very important—even those half-forgotten ones which have sunk down into the unconscious level in their minds. When men are faced with the task of making or carrying out a company decision, these goals often pop into their minds; and they check to see whether the proposed alternative will further these goals. The goals are so real that they serve as a partial guide in making many of their company decisions. All of us do this, even those of us who are completely dedicated to the goals of our organization.

How Men Set Their Goals

Though sweeping generalizations about men's needs and aspirations are not of much use in determining the goals of an individual, the following may provide a rough framework for the bewildering variety of goals and means adopted by mankind. There is some indication that a man (or a society) first seeks goals designed to fill his most elementary needs; then, as these are realized, he adopts successively more sophisticated goals and means, though, if he is to flourish, he must continue to pursue his earlier ones. Thus, were we able to learn where he stands in mankind's hierarchy of attainment, we should be able to approximate his set of goals.[1] This generalization suggests that men's first needs are physiological and biological. If a man manages to find a means of adequately fulfilling these needs, he may next try to work out a second staircase, a staircase designed to preserve his life, property, and position. Once these goals near achievement, he may seek means to satisfy his social needs—

---

[1] The following is an elaboration of an idea developed by Abraham S. Maslow, "Psychological Data and Value Theory," in A. S. Maslow (ed.), *New Knowledge in Human Values* (New York: Harper and Brothers, 1959), pp. 123–24, and his *Motivation and Personality* (New York: Harper and Brothers, 1954).

association, friendship, and love. Next he tries to satisfy his ego needs—achieve independence, reputation, and honor. Finally, if he succeeds in establishing means-end staircases for each of the foregoing goals, he may, as the culmination of all this, attempt to work out a pattern of means for achieving self-fulfillment—a set of staircases designed to help him realize his potentials for creativity. His goals and means are cumulative, because he does not dare abandon any of those he adopted earlier; if he does, his carefully erected world begins to crumble. Of course, a man (or a social group) may stop at any one of these levels; his opportunities, capacities, and will for achievement determine how far he goes.

The problem is to determine the current goals of a particular individual. He may have adopted some or all of those just mentioned, though probably they do not neatly fall into the pattern. A realization that each person has a somewhat different set of ultimate goals and that these can be lumped together under "the achievement of their future welfare" is also of some help in trying to perceive the goals of fellow workers. But as we saw in Chapter 1, what drives one man will leave another man unmoved. Only when an executive is able to visualize the real personal goals of a fellow worker do these become useful to him in making company decisions.

A man's intermediate and ultimate goals may *not* be any of those very vague high ones mentioned in Chapter 1. His ultimate goals are really those that rest at that point on his staircases *beyond which he has not imagined he could go*—a point beyond which he has not yet bothered to create an idea for a higher goal. As a child, he may have said he wanted to be a fireman or a pilot. At that stage of his life, he had envisaged no higher goal. Then as he grew older, he saw new horizons, new goals, such as graduating from high school, then perhaps graduating from college. And in high school and college, he possibly caught glimpses of what he thought of as still higher steps on the staircase. So he began (spasmodically!) shaping his nearby goals into means of achieving some of those newly seen ultimate goals.

A grown man who is realistic about his abilities nevertheless will tend to keep his mind on nearby goals which he knows are within his compass. Most men constantly watch for opportunities that will serve as means of achieving some higher goals, however. A well-adjusted individual will probably choose goals that will challenge him but, at the same time, ones for which he can build realistic means-end staircases, each step of which he is fairly sure he can attain. Then as these are achieved, he can keep setting higher goals on these staircases, each new goal designed to further his future welfare more fully than the ones already attained. While he is concentrating on these nearby goals, he can (and should) also have tucked away in the back of his mind one or two big aspirations, so that he can be setting some of his nearby goals (choosing opportunities) in line with these aspirations in the event that he should finally decide to pursue them seriously. The big goals should not dominate his life, however; indeed, as he grows in maturity, he may decide that some other new goal he has more recently discovered may serve his future welfare better than the original one. In a word, a man's goals are constantly changing.[2]

A man's ideas for his personal, long-term aspirations do not arise out of thin air. The goals he adopts are actually decisions, probably arrived at during his youth, based on premises he can no longer recall. They were created by him out of a vast mass of specific premises accumulated over a period of years, conceived in his mind's eye by unconsciously going through the several stages of the creative process we explored (though by no means so methodically). A man selects from, and coalesces, the ideologies he has encountered in reading about, hearing about, and observing the ultimate and intermediate goals which others have adopted—the pattern of social behavior he has seen around him—and noting how well these have worked as means of achieving welfare. Taken together, a man's ultimate and intermediate goals usually form *some* kind of pattern, though not necessarily an entirely consistent one; they constitute his philosophy of life. Most of these goals have long since dropped into the unconscious levels of his mind; and in any case, he lacks the vocabulary that would be required to explain their subtleties.

The point here is that an executive needs to be constantly aware of the fact that his associates have acquired goals that are very real to them. He can be reasonably sure that when he proposes a course of action, which will affect some of the goals and means they cherish, they will test it out in their minds in an effort to foresee what it will do to those goals.

The Art of Listening

One of the most effective methods for uncovering the goals of a man, and thus his probable reaction to a new alternative, is the

---

[2] Carl Rogers, *Client Centered Therapy* (Boston: Houghton Mifflin Co., 1951), and Robert W. White, *Lives in Progress* (New York: Henry Holt and Co., Inc., 1952), are two among many excellent books which bring to bear on the study of the individual and his goals the insights developed by psychologists, psychiatrists, and sociologists.

simple art of listening instead of talking—listening with the eyes as well as the ears. We often become so engrossed in ourselves and our own ideas that we do all the talking and forget that, as an executive, one of our tasks is to learn what other men think. Listening with empathy goes beyond merely asking a man for his reactions to a particular proposal; it is primarily a matter of trying to *be* the other person, of seeing the proposal from his point of view by living inside his mind for a time and recording in the mind what his goals probably are and what means he thinks will further them. We also get glimpses of his goals and means by listening to the sentiments he expresses and drawing inferences from these and from his reactions to the behavior of others. In these ways, we can gradually accumulate a good deal of information about the value premises a man customarily uses.

Presuming Each Man Thinks He Acts Rationally

A second approach is to recognize that each decision a man makes always looks completely rational and logical to him at the moment he makes it. At that time, he had some goals; and he had a problem. In deciding what action to take, he considered the alternatives and the premises that came to his mind (some he considered consciously and the rest unconsciously); and he chose what he predicted would be the best means of achieving those goals.[3]

By thinking back over the decisions a man has made in the past and trying to understand why he chose those alternatives, we can frequently uncover many of his goals and value premises. If, to us, the decisions another man has made do not appear completely understandable, completely rational when viewed through his eyes—if we often say to ourselves, "I don't see why he did it *that* way"—the probabilities are that either we are not fully aware of his goals and premises or else we are mistaken in our idea of the relative weight he assigns to each. Once we have recognized that a man always acts in what seems to *him* a rational manner—that his action will carry

---

[3] Later, he may think of other alternatives and other premises which he *should* have considered, and perhaps he may recall some he knew but forgot about at the moment he was making his decision; thus, he may *eventually* conclude that his decision was irrational. Nevertheless, the course of action he decided upon at the time looked right to him on the basis of the alternatives and premises he was then using. Even when a man is acting emotionally, in a fashion that we ordinarily label irrational—for example, when one man pokes another man on the nose or "gets mad" at another—he is choosing what to him is a logical course of action; choosing to use force appears to him the best means he has of furthering his goal of inducing the other to acquiesce. Notice that in these cases the man's decision is usually accompanied by a second decision—to act immediately.

him a step upward, not downward—we gain insights into his goals; and we are in a position to anticipate his probable reactions to a specific decision we want him to accept.

Looking into the Reservoirs from Which Men Draw Their Premises and Goals

Mentally surveying a man's background offers a third and much more sophisticated method of uncovering his personal goals and premises. It is a truism that each man is a product of the influences that have shaped his life. However, if this approach is to be meaningful, these influences must be sorted out. For unless we become aware of some of the specific ideas a man has picked out and adopted from the society of which he is a part, we can make but little progress in attempting to anticipate his responses. Uncovering and separating those ideas is no easy task. At best, they are more elusive than we would wish; and in any case, they are all closely entwined in a man's mind. Moreover, men who have been subjected to approximately the same influences will not behave exactly alike. So even though this approach serves the executive as a useful tool, it needs to be used with caution.[4]

The chief reason for trying to perceive the reservoirs from which a man draws his goals and premises is that when we ask him to embark on a new project, we know he will imagine for the moment that he has already accepted and will attempt to foresee the wanted and unwanted consequences—the effect on his goals. We all do this. He will ask himself, "What will my wife say? Will my family like it, or will they tell me, 'They gave you a bum deal, Dad. They don't think much of you around the company, so you'd better begin looking for another job.'" Will he expect that his status will be lowered or raised in the

---

[4] One characteristic pitfall in using this approach is that in our anxiety to catalogue a man and be done with it, we label him on the basis of fragmentary comments we have heard; generally, a man's pattern of goals is far too varied to be accurately described by a few catch phrases. A second pitfall is that we tend to assume that if one man with a certain background responds to a particular situation in a certain way, all others with that background will behave similarly. We often generalize from a single sample—jump to the conclusion that because Joe Petrone, a workman who is a member of the Italian community in town, says, "I think you've got a good idea," all the other Italian workmen will respond in the same way. Statements such as, "My wife told me *she* wouldn't like it, and she used to be a secretary," seldom provide valid bases for concluding that most secretaries will react in the same way. Yet premises such as these are frequently accorded great weight in making a decision—and later found to be completely erroneous. Similarly, a statement that 57.6 per cent of the workmen interviewed at 14 representative plants said they like to hear music at work may well prove misleading when applied to a particular plant, even though the psychologist who made the study used the best possible methods of choosing his sample and interviewing.

eyes of his fellow workers, his friends and neighbors, and the members of his outside organizations? Is there a chance that what he has been asked to do will clash with the moral and ethical codes he has inherited from his parents and his church? And what will the effect be on his and his family's everyday needs, which are largely dependent on his income? A man is willing to reveal premises relating to his economic welfare, but he seldom mentions these others because he feels slightly ashamed to find himself considering them and giving them rather heavy weight.

Although, as indicated earlier, men are individuals, nevertheless those who have shared the same experience are likely to adopt similar goals, means, and premises and thus to respond somewhat alike. Most of us, as we go about our daily lives, think that our behavior differs radically from that of everyone else—even from those in our own circle—for we are looking for differences. But an onlooker who views people through the eyes of an anthropologist—a man from Mars as it were—notes marked similarities in the behavior of men with the same type of background. For instance, there will be some uniformities in the behavior traits of skilled craftsmen, of scientists, and of professional men, and in those of men who have inherited the same religious or social philosophies.

As one well-known anthropologist points out:[5]

. . . the principal claim which can be made for the culture concept as an aid to useful action is that it helps us enormously toward predicting human behavior. One of the factors limiting the success of such predictions thus far has been the naïve assumption of a minutely homogeneous "human nature." In the framework of this assumption all human thinking proceeds from the same premises; all human beings [the world over] are motivated by the same needs and goals. [On the other hand] in the cultural framework we see that, while the ultimate logic of all people may be the same . . . the thought process departs from radically different premises—especially unconscious or unstated premises. Those [analysts] who have the cultural outlook are more likely to look beneath the surface and bring the culturally determined premises to the light of day. . . .

Knowledge of a culture makes it possible to predict a good many actions of any person who shares that culture. . . . If one knows how a given culture defines a certain situation, one can say that the betting odds are excellent that in a future comparable situation, people will behave along certain lines and not along others. If we know a culture, we know what the classes of individ-

---

[5] Clyde W. Kluckhohn, *Mirror for Man* (New York: McGraw-Hill Book Co., Inc., 1949), p. 39. In the quoted passages, I have added the words in brackets for purposes of clarification.

uals within it expect from each other—and from outsiders of various categories. We know what types of activity are held to be inherently gratifying.

Among the origins or reservoirs from which a man draws ideas for his personal goals, means, and value premises are: his biological, social, and psychological needs; the goals of the organizations to which he is loyal; and his cultural heritage. The last named, the one referred to in the above quoted passage, is by far the most complex and subtle.

His Biological, Social, and Psychological Needs. Fortunately, for our purposes, in these three areas men behave very much alike; biologists and experts in the fields of social and physiological psychology and sociology have sharpened our pictures of the goals, means, and premises men draw from this reservoir.[6] Clearly, such basic goals as adequate food, health, shelter, and clothing (the things we need for physical survival) provide premises for many of our own and our associates' decisions—company decisions as well as personal ones. We ask ourselves, Which of the alternatives under consideration will further these goals most and injure them least? Note, in passing, that economic security provides a means of supplying these needs.

There is a close interconnection between a man's biological needs and his psychological and social needs; so, in these next paragraphs, we shall weave them together. In order to fill his biological needs it is essential, in these days, that a man depend upon, and that he be accepted as a part of, a social group. His physical welfare is largely determined by the role the members permit him to play in his groups. Some of his psychological needs, such as feeling important and being wanted, are likewise supplied by the groups of which he is a member. Equally significant, if he really works in behalf of his groups, he can anticipate, and he can lead his friends to expect, that his future role in the group will eventually become even more important than at present, and that his biological, psychological, and social needs will consequently be served even better in the future than in the past. The executive can expect that all his fellow workers will constantly seek such means as a method of improving their lot in the future.

---

[6] Readers interested in probing these needs as well as the reservoir of men's cultural heritage will enjoy the following three books: Gardner Murphy, *Personality, A Biosocial Approach to Origins and Structures* (New York: Harper & Bros., 1947); Robert W. White, *op. cit.*, and Carl Rogers, *op. cit.*, particularly chap. 11. I know of no studies of men's organizations as sources of their goals.

A man's recognition that he must secure some measure of approval from a group on which he depends largely accounts for one of the central drives found in nearly all men—namely, ego-satisfaction. This is a personal psychological need related to self-esteem, self-confidence, and a need for recognition and a "good" reputation, though it cannot be neatly separated from the biological and social needs already emphasized. The ego-satisfactions we secure flow from the approbation of our fellow men. Probably all of us test out our own decisions and those we are asked to carry out by visualizing whether they will increase or decrease our ego-satisfactions. We are asking, If I do this, will I look bigger or smaller, enjoy greater prestige or less, in the eyes of others and in my own eyes?

In our framework, earning a good income, a pervasive goal, indeed, is actually a means. First of all, it serves as a means of taking care of our biological needs. However, if the income is reasonably large, a man may also use it to increase his ego-satisfactions and gain social approbation.

The Organizations to Which He Is Loyal.   The goals he adopts to take care of his personal needs are dominantly self-centered; those drawn from this second reservoir are strongly oriented toward the needs of others—his family, friends, and organizations. He wants to make sure that what he does will further the *goals* of the people and organizations to which he is loyal. Probably the chief organization is his family. If he suspects that the decision under consideration may affect the welfare of his wife and children, he will test out its impact on them with considerable care. Similarly, a man who is loyal to his union's goals, or to the goals and standards of the profession in which he has been trained, or to the goals of his particular church, or to those of his community or country, will sometimes pause to visualize the impact of the proposal on the chief goals of those organizations.

In addition to his family, his professional or work organizations, and his social, civic, self-improvement, and recreational organizations, many men are very loyal to the department and the company for which they work. In deciding how he will respond to a proposal we make, he will try to imagine whether it will help or harm the goals of those organizations.

If our proposal harms one of his organizations to which he is *not* particularly loyal, he will probably acquiesce. But if he believes the proposal will notably harm a major goal of an organization to which he is very loyal, we can be sure that sidetracking our proposal will become a goal of his. To him, the wanted consequence of circumventing us will greatly exceed the unwanted consequences.

The task of gathering the premises that men derive from membership in these organizations is less difficult than might be expected. In most cases, we already know the organization's distinguishing goals. Each organization, whether it be a family, a union, a professional society, a fraternal organization, a community organization, a university or a club, has developed a philosophy and a way of doing those things the members are most concerned with, a way its members believe is the right way. One method for uncovering the premises a member derives from these sources is to imagine that we are accompanying him to meetings of his various organizations for the purpose of "seeing" what his fellow members will say to him when they hear about the decision we have proposed he help carry out. Will it further the organization's goals, or will it harm them? Walking around with him arm in arm, as it were, while he talks with his fellow members actually takes only a few moments when done in the imagination; yet the visits will usually reveal several goals and premises which would otherwise remain hidden.

Cultural Heritage as a Reservoir of Goals and Premises. The reservoir we shall call cultural heritage lies deep within each man. It is fed by springs whose sources are obscure; and we draw upon this reservoir unwittingly. Into this goes all the experiences passed down to us from preceding generations, all the training in living which we unconsciously accumulate as a member of a human society.

Despite our best intentions, our decisions and responses are probably influenced more by the particular sociocultural matrix in which we grew up and by the emotional conditioning and the drives we then accumulated than by our highly trained intellects. While young, we unconsciously learned about goals and the unwanted and wanted consequences of certain courses of behavior from the precepts and talk that grew out of our living and working with others. For instance, most of us have adopted, without questioning, the ideas our *parents* inherited; because these were used unconsciously as guides or standards of behavior during our childhood and youth, they have stayed with the majority of us most of our lives.

Actually, a man's cultural heritage can be said to be the sum of three inextricably entwined influences—(1) his ethnic or nationality heritage, (2) his religious and moral heritage, and (3) the political, social, and economic philosophies he has adopted.

A man's national or ethnic heritage supplies him with many of his premises. A man from a family with a foreign or an American background unconsciously carries through his life (and seldom questions) some of the patterns of living that his ancestors found effective as means of ensuring their welfare. In the United States, for instance, "success" has become a dominant note in our pattern of living. While not all Americans, or all Scotsmen, Welsh, Mexicans, Norwegians, or Germans from the old country, will behave alike (generalizations about them are seldom entirely valid), nevertheless people in certain ethnic groups do seem to have taken on some national characteristics —their own particular goals, means, and premises, which they have tested over a long period and found good, ones that the families frequently weight heavily in making decisions. For example, the majority of people from a certain country may have found that working with their hands from dawn to dark and saving carefully provides the most effective way of ensuring welfare; while those from another ethnic group may have found that doing the least work possible will give them the greatest satisfaction.

A second place to look in a man's cultural heritage for hints about his value premises is his religious and moral philosophy, the philosophy he uses as a guide in his relationships with the individuals he meets every day. (Incidentally, this, together with his social philosophy, which will be discussed shortly, supplies him with what he vaguely calls his "principles"; if he acts contrary to these precepts, he notices that his conscience troubles him.) When a deeply religious man is asked to accept (or to make) a company decision, the chances are that he will try it out in his mind to see if it will further the goals enunciated by the Prophets of the Old Testament and by Christ in the New Testament. Many of his premises are drawn from the Ten Commandments and from the Sermon on the Mount. Even a man who considers himself unreligious frequently includes some of these religious precepts in what would be called his "moral code"—his ideas of duty, and of justice and honesty in dealing with others. Benjamin Franklin's Poor Richard framed many less lofty precepts which have become embedded in our moral philosophy. In addition to these, we have inherited many other moral beliefs:[7] "Individualism, that is, the survival of the fittest, is the law of nature." "Restrictions on individual freedom are bad and kill initiative." "Honesty is the best policy." "Education is a fine thing." "No man deserves to

---

[7] The ones quoted here are largely taken from Robert S. Lynd, *Knowledge for What?* (Princeton, N.J.: Princeton University Press, 1939), chap. iii, "The Pattern of American Culture."

have what he hasn't worked for." "People shouldn't be allowed to starve, even though they don't have a job or money." "A man owes it to himself and his family to make as much money as he can." "All men have been created free and equal." "Everyone should try to be successful."

Not all men, of course, adopt exactly the same religious philosophies or the same moral codes. Nor do all people rule themselves with equal rigor by the codes they follow. But even though all of us are forced to compromise our religious and moral codes once in a while—in real life, we find that we cannot always act solely on the basis of our principles—nevertheless, we do have to live with ourselves. We have to maintain our self-respect, our integrity. If a man does things—carries out decisions—that violate his religious and moral codes, his conscience begins to nag at him; he cannot feel at ease with himself, or his job, or his world. Sometimes, a man discovers that there exists a basic conflict between his own moral or religious codes and the codes underlying the policies of his company. Such an individual faces heartbreaking alternatives: He must either find a new job with an organization whose ethical standards accord with his own (how does a man go about finding such a company?) or remain and compromise his principles. In the latter case, if he is to live in some comfort, he must bend and shift his own codes and try to deceive himself (and his family and friends) into thinking that the company's moral codes are right and that he still maintains his integrity; this is no easy task.

A third feature of a man's cultural heritage is the political, economic, and social philosophy he has accepted as a guide to his behavior. This is quite often, though by no means always, simply an extension to very large groups of people—to mankind in general or to certain segments of society—of those religious and moral precepts he has developed as a guide for his person-to-person relationships. Most men have adopted rather definite social and political philosophies. For instance, they have quite definite ideas of the role the government should play in the advancement of the general welfare and the specific projects it should undertake. Some believe strongly that the lot of all men in the world should be bettered, and that almost all of our institutions, including the government, should be dedicated to that end; whereas others believe in rugged individualism—that each individual should fend for himself. In testing out a proposed company decision, the men holding the view that men should help one another will frequently check unconsciously to foresee whether it will advance the welfare of society in general. The men holding the second philosophy will automatically check the proposal to see if it fosters "creeping socialism"; if it does, they will oppose it.

In most cases a man's nationality traits, his religious and moral codes, and his political, social, and economic philosophy are rather fixed by the time he reaches maturity, the result of the ideas that he has unconsciously absorbed. But the point here is that every man has accumulated some body of ideas which he uses as a guide. Though these may be sketchy and inconsistent, he usually believes firmly in the ideas he has inherited; and he draws upon these for elements in many of the value premises which he thinks of in reaching some of his company decisions. By listening and watching, an executive can gradually build a picture of the premises a fellow worker uses regularly. Even though the cause-result statements the man frames from his maxims can never be proved, he is completely convinced that they are not only important to his welfare but valid; thus, they are weighted heavily when he makes decisions. To him, these are just as binding as the laws of the realm, even though there is no agency to enforce them. Any attempt on the part of the executive to change these ideas would probably prove abortive—for, to the man, they are self-evident, nonarguable. An executive who becomes involved in the question of whether these are proper ideas to hold, or whether they are right or wrong, moral or immoral, misses the main issue at hand—namely, to which premises from these sources this man will give greatest weight when he is deciding whether to accept this proposal.[8]

Men's drives to achieve those goals which they derive from their loyalty to their outside organizations, the ideals and behavior patterns which they have accumulated from their cultural heritage and from their own needs as biological, psychological, and social beings, are frequently very powerful ones. But their drives to hold on to what they already have may be even more powerful. A man will often fight a proposed decision with every weapon he can muster if he feels that, by accepting the proposed change, he is going to lose some of the things he cherishes. For instance, a man whose family or ancestors

---

[8] The executive must be wary about naïvely accepting what a man *says* are his principles. A man may give lip service to precepts that he knows are popular, and he may offer them as reasons for his stand on an issue on those occasions when he knows that his real reasons are so unacceptable that he dare not reveal them.

have gone through some cataclysmic experience which has almost wrecked their lives—a depression or a war, for example—or a man whose family has been ostracized by the community for one reason or another, will automatically oppose any move that might conceivably lead to a repetition of that experience. Many of the codes that he uses as guides of behavior are framed in terms of taboos—statements of unethical or immoral behavior which he must eschew. Here are some examples: "No man should attempt to push others around." "We should not covet what is another's." "We should never misrepresent, never make statements to employees or customers or to the government which are untrue." "Nobody should get a 'bum' deal." A man is not always willing to voice these ideas, fearing that others will think them trivial as compared with the welfare of the company. These nevertheless serve as red flags, as deeply grounded warnings, which tell him, "If I accede—if I do this thing—the results will be harmful to the ideals and to the people I am loyal to; see, here are some of the premises (the past experiences and the moral precepts) that prove it." Usually, he is but dimly aware of his taboos; they have dropped down to the unconscious level of his mind. Nevertheless, if an executive flagrantly disregards these unwanted consequences which the men weight heavily, the repercussions are likely to be even more serious than if his decisions merely fail to advance the men's goals.

We may as well face the fact that the task of anticipating those value premises which a man or group in the company will weight most heavily calls for a high degree of empathy and considerable time. Moreover, we cannot expect to make accurate predictions on each occasion, even though we faithfully use the tools of analysis so far explored in this chapter. Nevertheless, (1) listening to what the other man says, (2) presupposing that every man believes that he acts rationally, and (3) probing the contents of the three chief reservoirs from which each man draws some of his fundamental goals and premises—his own biological, psychological and social needs, the goals of the organizations to which he is most loyal, and the three facets of his cultural heritage—does help an executive to uncover important premises which he would otherwise overlook.

The use of another tool, closely related to the foregoing—the concept of informal groups—which will be investigated in Chapter 9, enables the executive to reduce this task to manageable size; men who have adopted similar goals and premises often coalesce into informal groups and hence can be studied as a group instead of as individuals. But that will have to wait. In the second half of this chapter, we turn to the task of anticipating how large groups in the organization will respond to a proposal.

THE INDUCEMENT-CONTRIBUTION CONCEPT

The inducement-contribution concept provides the executive with still another tool, one that is useful in bringing together and organizing those premises other members of the company will use in considering a proposed alternative. It is particularly helpful in gathering the premises of *the groups in the company* whose members he does *not* know personally. In addition, it aids in organizing and simplifying the all but overwhelming mass of other men's premises which he must frequently consider—their practical, everyday premises as well as their idealistic ones, their factual premises as well as their value premises. Here, instead of living inside the skins of the men by viewing them as individuals or as members of *informal* groups, we are classifying them into groups according to the types of contributions they make to the organization—salesmen, plant workers, customers, stockholders, and so on—and imagining what the responses of these groups will be.

The inducement-contribution concept is really a variant of the already familiar idea of the wanted and unwanted consequences of adopting a proposal. It is a tool for (1) examining a tentatively chosen alternative by first looking at it through the eyes of each of the several groups of people whose contributions are essential to the welfare of the company and (2) then examining it from the standpoint of the company. The objective is to make sure ahead of time that each of those groups whose goals will be affected by the proposal will *actually* make the contributions to the company which the decider has in mind. The men at the pricing conference we attended some time back were looking at certain contributing groups (as well as at individuals), though in a somewhat hit-or-miss fashion, by trying to imagine the salesmen's, the cost department's, and the union's responses to the price increase they were considering.

The undiscerning executive frequently either overlooks the premises that the various contributing groups will weight heavily; or else he tends to assume that if a proposal will advance the company's goals, the groups will each automatically accept and act upon it with enthusiasm. After putting his decision into effect, however, he discovers that one or more of the groups is unwilling to make the expected contributions; and as a result the company suffers. Old customers begin to slip away, or labor turnover increases in the plant, or maybe the bank refuses to cooperate. When this happens, the inducements that the company receives in the form of contributions from the now-dissatisfied member groups are reduced instead of increased because the members of those groups feel that their goals are no longer served as fully as in the past.

Classifying Members of the Organization into Groups Based upon Similarity in Their Contributions

Practically every company decision which an executive makes— whether he be low in the hierarchy, or a member of top management —will have *some* effect upon the welfare of at least one or two of the groups listed below and, in some cases, on almost all of the groups. For instance, a given decision may harm or help one or more of these groups: the various types of customers served by the company; the company's distributors and dealers; its salesmen; its advertising staff; the designers who handle product development; the groups of workmen in the several fabricating and assembly departments; maintenance men; groups who handle production planning, scheduling, or quality control; the union; the men in personnel work; those in the shipping and receiving departments; the accountants; the company's bank; its raw material and equipment suppliers; its transportation companies; or its stockholders. *In this book we shall think of all these groups as members of the organization.* According to this definition, employees are by no means the only members. The criterion of membership according to this special definition is whether a group is called upon to make contributions to the company either in the form of services or money—a much broader concept than the commonly used definition of company membership. With such a check list before him, an executive is in a position to make mental notes of all the groups whose company relationships will be changed when the proposal is put into effect.

All the member groups must feel that they are getting what they would call a "good deal." To anticipate how they would respond to a certain new proposal, the executive has to imagine himself a member of each group and then compare his newly *proposed* alternative with the *program now in effect*, from their point of view. (The members, of course, are unaware of other alternatives the executive has already tentatively discarded.) If, in their opinion, the new proposal offers them a greater amount of wanted consequences (inducements) than the current program, and/or if it seems to be accompanied by a smaller amount of unwanted consequences (contributions), they will tend to give it their wholehearted support. They will gladly make the contributions to the company which are called for under the new proposal; on the basis of the premises they have gathered and their weighting system, they conclude that the new proposal will further their own goals as well as those of the company; and the executive can expect that group to accept and act upon it wholeheartedly.

The Concept of Inducements and Contributions

In this concept of inducements and contributions, the idea of inducements is an almost exact counterpart of the idea of wanted consequences. The cause element of most of the premises used by contributing groups would read, "If we carry out the proposed change," though this element would probably not be stated. And, depending on the group, the result elements might, for example, read "the work will be easier," "the product will serve our needs better," "our prestige will go up," "our families will be better off," "our friends in the union and our neighbors will approve of us," "we'll get more pay," "we'll make more profit," and so on. Such are some of the inducements certain member groups might directly or indirectly receive from the company as a result of accepting a proposed change.

On the other hand, the idea of contributions is somewhat more sophisticated than that of unwanted consequences. True, the majority of the contributions a group would be called upon to make to the company would be viewed by them as unwanted consequences of acceding to the proposal. For instance, coping with more troublesome problems, working harder, or—in the case of customers—paying higher prices, would certainly constitute unwanted consequences in the eyes of certain groups. In many cases, however, the men like to make certain contributions to the company. For example, an opportunity to make more decisions might be looked upon as an inducement by the accountants or salesmen; yet, clearly, this would contribute to the welfare of the company. However, certain other groups may be reluctant to make this sort of contribution—would consider making more decisions an unwanted consequence.

One of the main objectives in using the inducement-contribution concept when making a decision is to be as sure as possible (1) that the members of each group feel that the sum of the inducements they will receive will definitely outweigh the sum of the contributions they will be asked to make, and (2) that they anticipate that the *difference* or *spread* between the total inducements they will receive and the total contributions they must make under the new proposal will be *greater* than (or at least equal to) the spread they now enjoy under the current program. Such an analysis usually discloses that the members' *non*monetary inducements and contributions—those that are measured with their value standards—are of as much importance to them as their monetary and material ones. If, in the eyes of the group, their total inducements under the new plan will exceed what, to them, will be their total contributions by a *greater* amount than under the old plan, the executive can be reasonably sure that the members of the group will cooperate (see Diagram 6A).

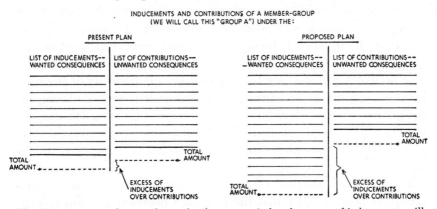

INDUCEMENTS AND CONTRIBUTIONS OF A MEMBER-GROUP
(WE WILL CALL THIS "GROUP A") UNDER THE:

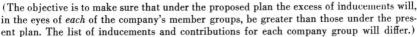

(The objective is to make sure that under the proposed plan the excess of inducements will, in the eyes of *each* of the company's member groups, be greater than those under the present plan. The list of inducements and contributions for each company group will differ.)

DIAGRAM 6A. Schematic Framework for Listing and Comparing the Inducements and Contributions of Each of the Company's Member Groups

If the men in a group anticipate that the spread will be smaller under the new plan, the executive can predict that the members of the group will reduce their contributions to the company in order to keep the spread enjoyed under the new program equal to the spread enjoyed under the old. In other words, if to them the difference between their inducements and contributions is reduced, the executive is likely to be disappointed in the group's contributions to the company; they will contribute less than he had expected when he first conceived the new alternative.

In the case of an employee group, he can expect that many of the men will do their work perfunctorily; labor turnover in the group may also increase because some men will decide to join a competing organization which offers a wider spread between inducements and contributions. Likewise, under such circumstances, a group made up of customers or dealers will reduce their total contributions to the company; in fact, the executive can expect some of these members to sever their connections with the company and join a competing company which offers a wider spread.

To avoid becoming lost in details in making decisions that affect several contributing groups, the executive may find it convenient to employ a classification device—to list for each group the more important consequences he believes its members consider pertinent to each of the two alternatives (the present program and the new proposal), as in Diagram 6A. Listing the members' ideas of their inducements in the left-hand column and their contributions in the right-hand column, somewhat like entries in a ledger, and then weighting these without formally assigning numerical weights (just as we did in Chapter 3), will help the executive predict with reasonable accuracy which of the two alternatives the majority of the members of each group will prefer—which one will provide them with the greatest excess of inducements over contributions. He can also predict which groups, if any, will probably oppose the proposal and, as a consequence, make less of a contribution to the company than he had originally expected.[9]

But the main purpose of the foregoing analysis of the member groups is to make sure that the proposed decision will advance the *company's* welfare better than the means presently employed. The new proposal may as well be discarded immediately unless there is a likelihood that the company as an entity, as well as its members, will be better off—that it, too, will enjoy a greater spread between the inducements it actually receives from its members (their contributions) and the contributions it must make to them (their induce-

---

[9] When a company conducts an *actual* trial run instead of an imaginary one in an effort to get a better idea of how a certain group will react, it is carrying this procedure a step further. For instance, companies frequently try out a new product or a new advertising theme in a representative city before deciding to adopt it in all territories; or they test out a new method of assembly in a small representative section in the manufacturing department. The presumption is that the entire group of members will respond in about the same way as the sample on which the experiment was conducted.

Lying half way between the two extremes of an imaginary tryout and an actual physical test are two methods of research—interviews in which people are asked their opinions, and motivation research. Marketing research men use both to appraise customer's responses, but similar studies can also be made of the probable responses of employee groups. Marketing research interviews are conducted in the same way as the opinion polls familiar to newspaper readers; and the answers are cast in statistical form. In motivation research, the objective is to uncover the goals and premises people use *unconsciously* when they buy one product and discard another. Using depth interviews and traditional projective devices such as sentence completion and interpretation of ambiguous pictures, they try to probe those three dim reservoirs we have been examining.

ments). A study of the *member* groups' inducements and contributions, such as that just described, provides premises for making reasonably realistic predictions about the contributions the member groups will *actually* make to the *company,* and of the inducements the company will need to offer them in order to make sure of these contributions.

Such an analysis helps to ward off wishful thinking—forces us to be realistic about that brilliant new idea we conceived just as we were going to sleep last night. It forces us to recognize that the inducements the company receives (the ones that serve as means of furthering its welfare) are what the members view as their contributions— the nonmonetary, monetary, or material contributions made by its members: the decision making and the manual work contributed by its employees and dealers, for example; or the raw materials furnished by its suppliers; or money furnished by stockholders, banks, and customers. The new proposal should increase the flow to the company of such inducements. Or, at any rate, it should widen what the company thinks of as the *spread* between the sum of the material and *in*tangible inducements it receives from all its member groups and what it must give up to them in the form of contributions, particularly those costly contributions measured primarily in terms of

INDUCEMENTS AND CONTRIBUTIONS OF THE COMPANY UNDER THE:

PRESENT PLAN   PROPOSED PLAN

LIST OF ITS INDUCEMENTS	LIST OF ITS CONTRIBUTIONS	LIST OF ITS INDUCEMENTS	LIST OF ITS CONTRIBUTIONS
(THESE ARE THE CONTRIBUTIONS NOW BEING MADE BY ALL THE MEMBER-GROUPS, AS SET OUT IN DIAGRAM 6A.)	(THESE ARE THE INDUCEMENTS NOW BEING OFFERED TO ALL THE MEMBER-GROUPS, AS SET OUT IN DIAGRAM 6A.)	(THESE ARE THE CONTRIBUTIONS ANTICIPATED FROM ALL THE MEMBER-GROUPS, AS SET OUT IN DIAGRAM 6A.)	(THESE ARE INDUCE-MENTS THE COMPANY PLANS TO OFFER ALL THE MEMBER-GROUPS, AS SET OUT IN DIAGRAM 6A.)

TOTAL AMOUNT

EXCESS OF THE SUM OF ALL ITS INDUCEMENTS OVER THE SUM OF ALL ITS CONTRIBUTIONS

TOTAL AMOUNT

TOTAL AMOUNT

EXCESS OF THE SUM OF ALL ITS INDUCEMENTS OVER ITS CONTRIBUTIONS

TOTAL AMOUNT

DIAGRAM 6B. Schematic Framework for Listing and Comparing the Company's Inducements and Contributions money (in the case of employees and suppliers) and in terms of goods (in the case of customers) (see Diagram 6B).[10]

An Example of the Use of the Inducement-Contribution Concept as a Tool for Predicting

What has been said about the inducement-contribution concept so far has doubtless made it sound abstract and impractical. To get down to earth again, let us examine one of the decisions made at the meeting we attended earlier—where the executives decided to improve one of the company's products—and try to predict how that plan will work. We shall quickly check the probable effects of this proposal on four of the groups of members whose welfare will be affected by the decision, and then the effect on the company itself. What follows will serve as an illustration of the application of the concept, even though it is somewhat pat and oversimplified.

Probably the company's present and potential consumers will welcome the new proposal for an improved product once they see or hear about it. Presumably, it will fit their needs more fully than the old one, so that their inducements to join the organization (become consumer members) will be greater than before. Moreover, it is unlikely that they will be asked to make greater contributions than in the past; the price asked, for example, probably will be increased very little, or possibly not at all. It seems reasonable to expect that new customers will join the organization when the product is marketed and that the total contributions from customers will increase.

The company's salesmen probably will also give the proposal their wholehearted support. It will increase the inducements they receive; they can now secure orders from customers who have not been buying, so that their sales records will look better. This, in turn, will raise their prestige or status in the eyes of friends and other salesmen; and if they are paid commissions, their money income will increase. At the same time, the amount of effort they will be called upon to contribute will probably be less. Their task of finding and transmitting premises that prospective customers will weight heavily in deciding

---

[10] This inducement-contribution concept is an adaptation of what is more generally known as the "equilibrium concept." Gradually, over the last half century, almost all of the physical and social sciences have developed adaptations of the equilibrium concept and have employed these extensively as tools of analysis. I have chosen to call my adaptation an "inducement-contribution analysis" because I want to emphasize that we do *not* want equal inducements and contributions but, instead, *greater* inducements than contributions.

whether to buy should be less onerous than before. The salesman will say, "It'll be a cinch to sell this new item; it'll almost sell itself."

The men in the product development department will probably be pleased with the proposal, too. It will raise their inducements. Their new job gives them a chance to do some creative work in solving a troublesome problem—the problem being, "The company can't sell the old product." It gives them prestige—status among their professional friends both within the company and outside—if they can say, "I helped to design that new product; it's a beauty; it does everything but talk." Even though they get no raise in pay, their inducements will be greater. However, the contributions they will be called upon to make to the company under the new program will also be greater (not the same, as was the case with customers; or less, as was the case with salesmen). Nevertheless (and this warrants emphasis), it is possible that, in *their* eyes, the contributions they are now asked to make will be *less*—less of a burden to them, more fun to make—than those they had been making. This would be true if their former jobs were dull, routine ones requiring little creative ability: routine testing of parts or end products before shipment, for instance. Under such circumstances, the contributions they are now asked to make would, in their eyes, be less disagreeable than under the old program. So we can conclude that here, too, the inducements that these men will receive will be greater; and the contributions that they are asked to make will be less than at present. To their way of thinking, the spread between inducements and contributions will be greater than at present.

The men in the plant, on the other hand, will probably dislike the new plan; the present program would be preferable. Their inducements will not increase. There will not be any higher pay; and they will not gain much, if any, prestige. At the same time, they will be called on to make greater contributions than before. They will have to make many unfamiliar decisions, some of which will try their patience, in putting the new product into production. In addition, they will have to change many of their old routines, which they have learned so well that they can now almost do them in their sleep. In their eyes, their spread has been narrowed; the inducements will remain about level, but the men will be called upon to make greater contributions. Consequently, we can expect opposition from the men in the plant. At the time the plan is proposed, they will probably try to find reasons why it will not work; and after the changeover in the plant is made, we can anticipate that they will consciously or unconsciously see to it that several troublesome incidents occur, things that we should not expect to happen. They will reduce their contributions to the company to a point where the spread between their inducements and contributions is about equal to that under the old program. We are obviously going to have to take further steps to gain this group's wholehearted acceptance—and shall have to postpone the task of solving this problem until we get into Part II of this book, where we deal with the task of gaining acceptance of decisions.

Finally, let us examine the effect of the proposal on the company.[11] If all goes as planned—that is, if we have included all the required steps in our means-end staircases, and if we manage to accomplish all the steps—the company should benefit from the proposed change. On the one hand, the inducements it receives from the member groups in the form of contributions should be greater than before. Sales should increase (greater total dollar contribution from consumers), and the contribution that the new product makes to annual fixed overhead and profit (unit sales volume for the year multiplied by the gross margin per unit) should be greater than for the old product. The inducements that the company will receive from the actual contributions made by the salesmen and the research men are also going to be greater; the number of sales made per salesman's call should increase, and the value to the company of the work done by engineers under the new plan should be greater than under the old. But the men in the plant will probably contribute less, at least for a time. Production will be unexpectedly low; and rejects will increase, for the reasons already noted. Nevertheless, the sum of the inducements that the company receives will probably increase.

On the other hand, in the eyes of the company, the contributions it must now make to these groups will be practically the same as before. Or, more exactly, it will not have to spend much more money; and the other contributions it makes to member groups will cost the company nothing. Salaries will not have to be increased (though possibly additional engineers will have to be hired); and the out-of-pocket costs of parts, fabrication, and assembly should not increase materially. Thus the company would be better off financially; the spread between its income and expenses should widen. Equally important for its future welfare, the company is making some extra contributions to three of the member groups which cost very little,

---

[11] Here, we are employing the ideas set forth in Diagram 6B. In the preceding paragraphs, those depicted in Diagram 6A were used.

but which, to the members, are major inducements. For example, the consumers get a product that satisfies their needs better; and the salesmen and the research men gain some status. However, the main point here is that this rise in the members' inducements almost always leads them, often quite unconsciously, to increase their nonmonetary and monetary contributions to the company. Thus, we can feel quite sure that the company will be better off than before; its spread will be wider because the inducements it will receive will be greater than before (provided that we can get the problem in the plant straightened out), and the contributions it will make in terms of money will remain about the same.

Some Uses of the Inducement-Contribution Concept

Contrary to what one might expect, it does not follow that when the company gives its members more inducements, it has less for itself. The wise executive tries to conceive an alternative that will provide the members with more monetary and material (as well as psychic) income and, at the same time, give the company more profits. The example set out in the preceding paragraphs provides an illustration of how the various member groups *and* the company can all benefit from a well-conceived new means.

This anomaly arises from two circumstances. One is that the organization's products are fashioned by groups of members who are specializing—specializing in a coordinated way. As a consequence, their production *per worker* is greater than the product of a Robinson Crusoe who works alone. In the United States, we have made striking progress in employing specialization and mass production to increase the excess of inducements a man receives compared with his contributions in the form of time and effort. For example, he now has to work approximately half as many minutes as in 1900 to buy a pound of meat, a pair of shoes, and so on. So far as we can see, we have not yet approached the upper limits in the possibilities for increasing the spread through the use of specialization and mass production.

The other circumstance is that an organization, as a result of its very existence as a social group, can furnish its members with a wide range of valuable means of achieving their personal goals, none of which cost the company much in the way of money. It is interesting to note that in spite of the reputation this nation has for managerial efficiency, we have not yet seriously attempted to employ these nonmaterial means which a company has at its disposal for increasing the inducements that men feel they should receive. Working together in harmony affords most men a great deal of satisfaction. Quite often, the members also derive fun from the banter and conversation that goes on. In addition, membership in most organizations gives a man status in the eyes of his friends and acquaintances. But there is an even greater opportunity in many companies to *reduce the contributions* that the members feel they are making. Reducing the friction that exists in the company is an example. The frustration that men endure when things go wrong and the unpleasant task of trying to untangle the resulting mess constitute contributions that most men weight heavily; they resent making these painful and unnecessary contributions day after day.[12] We should expect tough-minded executives to pay much greater attention than they do to these nonmonetary inducements and contributions which the members consider important, because the money cost to the company is negligible. More careful planning and decision making are the only things required. But most executives seem to be only dimly aware of this opportunity.

Making sure that the members, as well as the company, will benefit is one use of the inducement-contribution concept. The concept also enables us to frame two quite solid and interesting generalizations which the executive can employ. Both have already been mentioned. One is that when he reduces the men's inducements, they will *reduce* their contributions to the company in an effort to restore the balance. Often, this is done quite unconsciously, though frequently the men act consciously. If, for example, the men in a group are denied a means they once possessed for advancing their welfare (a privilege, for instance), some men may deliberately try to make blunders in their work or slow down production. When this occurs, their supervisors find that it is nearly impossible to induce the men to raise their contributions back to the former level. The men will protect one another by swearing that the mistakes were accidental and that they were working at top speed, or according to the standards in "the book."

The second generalization is that the executive can predict that the members will almost automatically *raise* their contributions to the company to keep them in line with any increases in the inducements they feel they are receiving. When the executive increases the group's inducements—and these inducements are by no means solely monetary or material inducements, as we have seen—he can expect

---

[12] See Chris Argyris, *Understanding Organizational Behavior* (Homewood, Ill.: The Dorsey Press, Inc., 1960), especially pp. 14–22, and Melville Dalton, *Men Who Manage* (New York: John Wiley & Sons, Inc., 1959), pp. 195–98.

both the quality and the amount of their decision making and other work to mount rapidly. For example, when the men feel that their inducements are large, they will usually think more about the effects of their acts upon the company and its several member groups, and will choose a way that will work out well for everyone, instead of taking an indifferent attitude. What is more, they will handle the work willingly and often with less effort. Thus they *feel* that their contributions are actually *less* than before, and the spread is widened still further. An executive can use these two rather general statements of consequences with considerable confidence in laying plans and testing them out.

The inducement-contribution analysis can also be used to uncover premises useful to executives in solving some of the troublesome problems which their company is encountering. In a company plagued by a high labor turnover and low morale in certain departments, the probabilities are that, in the eyes of the men, the inducements they are receiving are little greater than the contributions required of them, and that competing companies offer a larger spread to men doing work like theirs. The same will probably be found to be true of a company that is losing position in its industry; an analysis can be made to see if its competitors are offering more inducements to consumers and channels of distribution and/or demanding fewer contributions of them. The premises so brought to light will serve as a basis for deciding what the *specific* problem is, what new or improved means the company must introduce to induce new members to join its organization, and what it must do to influence its present members to increase their contribution.

Such an analysis sometimes helps in determining what concessions, if any, management should make to unions. Here, the job of the executive is to compare the inducements offered and the contributions demanded of its workmen in each group with those demanded of men handling similar jobs in other companies, for the purpose of deciding what extra inducements should be offered (money may not be the key inducement) to secure a high level of contributions. Sometimes, especially during the negotiation of a contract, his job is to predict whether the men might reduce their contributions (and by how much) if they are *not* given a pay raise or certain fringe benefits.

On the other hand, an inducement-contribution analysis may disclose that the inducements now allocated to a group could be reduced (instead of raised) with little adverse effect upon the group's contributions, or that the amount of contributions demanded of them could be increased. The company may be offering customers a product that is too high in quality; if they do not need or want the extra quality, this inducement can be lowered with but little adverse effect on sales volume. In examining the company's wholesalers and retailers, it may become evident that all the contributions that the company requires from them, such as carrying stock and offering it to prospective retailers or consumers, would be obtained even if their discounts were cut. Discounts (the inducements offered jobbers and retailers) can usually be reduced when, as a result of long-term advertising and customer experience, the company's product has become so firmly established in the consumer members' minds that the channels of distribution no longer have to do much selling. The analysis may reveal that the prices charged certain types of customers are too low, or that the distributors would be willing to do a more active job of selling with no increase in discounts.

It is of some importance for executives to note, in passing, that many workers think that some of the company's staff men and some of their bosses, especially those near the top, contribute practically nothing to the organization.[13] Executives and staff men produce nothing tangible that the workmen can handle and see; and frequently, those intangibles they do see the "higher-ups" produce seem to them either useless or downright harmful to their own or the company's goals—decisions such as "Don't smoke in this corridor," or "Hereafter use Form 19B instead of 19A in your reports." A characteristic comment runs like this: "Those guys sit in their plush offices smoking dollar cigars and doing nothing but gab and look out of the window." To offset this, executives should watch for opportunities to spell out what they contribute—for instance, those company goals or departmental goals which they have conceived and the means that they have introduced for achieving those goals. In many instances, executives erroneously assume that these contributions are so self-evident that they need not be mentioned.

But, in the eyes of the workers, the staff men and executives are not the only ones who sometimes have "soft" jobs. In virtually every company, there are certain jobs located far down in the hierarchy which are known as "easy berths." When an executive notices one of these jobs, it is his responsibility to demand increased contributions from the men or to decrease the monetary inducements given them. The

---

[13] Maybe some staff men and executives do not contribute much! Each man would do well to ponder what contributions he makes and compare these with the contributions others make and with the inducements he receives.

men will probably continue doing their jobs as well as before; but if they do not, good replacements can usually be found. Such a step also produces some very desirable side-effects: The contributions of the more conscientious workers will ordinarily rise.

SUMMARY

Sensitivity to the needs and thoughts of others—empathy—can be learned. Once a man recognizes the value of living inside other people as a method of foreseeing how they will think and feel about a proposal, and once he perceives some instruments for going about it and then gets some practice in using them, he usually makes rapid progress. At least, that has been my experience in teaching the ideas developed in this chapter. The tools we have investigated are really rather obvious ones: listening carefully; recognizing that men will always act rationally in the light of their goals and premises; delving into their personal reservoirs from which they draw premises—their biological, psychological, and social needs, the organizations to which they are loyal, and their cultural heritage; and examining the effects of a proposal on the inducement-contribution balances of the various member groups whose contributions are essential to the welfare of the company. A young man just entering a company can use the value premises thus uncovered almost as much as does a top executive.

But, even though we can improve our ability to predict the response of an individual or a group, we must recognize that we cannot be sure. The man himself is the only one who knows the premises and goals of his private world, though in his daily life, he is probably conscious of only that part of the iceberg lying above the surface. Moreover, the number of influences that bear on his decision (or on a group's decision) to accept or reject a proposal is so large that we must leave out the majority of the lesser ones; when we thus simplify, we are likely to impede our understanding and reach somewhat shaky conclusions or explanations. Yet as long as we keep a sense of humility, base our conclusions on the best premises we can readily muster, and recognize that our conclusions are tentative, we should not go too far astray.

POSTLUDE FOR PART I: PRACTICAL RATIONALITY IN DECISION MAKING

In this postlude, we shall draw together the six conceptual subsystems into an over-all conceptual framework for decision making.

We shall also explore and illustrate another concept—the concept of rationality in decision making; this should offer us some new insights. It turns out that the concept of rationality is simply an integration of the six conceptual subsystems we explored in Part I. In all five of these chapters, we have really been trying to learn to make rational decisions.

We shall be using a quite specific definition of rationality. Briefly, we define it thus: taking into consideration most of the pertinent and important goals and alternatives, and the heavily weighted premises, but limiting ourselves to those we are able to consider in the time we have available for making the decision. As we shall see in a moment, this is a definition of what we shall call *practical* rationality. It differs from other definitions in that instead of the dichotomy of rational versus irrational, it has to do solely with the *degree* or *amount* of rationality in a decision—with whether the decision maker is using a short list of hurriedly selected goals, alternatives, and premises and omitting many that are important (very little rationality) or using a great many of the most significant goals, alternatives, and premises (a great deal of rationality). It ties in with our thought earlier in the chapter that when making a decision a man always tries to be rational—always seeks to attain a goal, and considers some alternatives and at least a few of the premises pertinent to each; but an impulsive choice of some alternative such as punching his opponent on the jaw will probably seem to us (and to him, in retrospect) to have only a small amount of rationality. Our idea of rationality is much broader than the economist's definition now in popular use—the maximization of utility, maximization of goods or services secured, or of profit or income. That one deals only with those things offered in the market place.

A decision or an act can be judged as to its rationality only when it is viewed in terms of the goals it is intended to further. As we are using the term, rational behavior cannot be judged in a vacuum; it is not something we can evaluate a priori. The question must be asked, "Rational for what?" Taking a fishing trip would not be very rational as a means of securing food for the family; it would be cheaper to go out and buy the fish. Yet, viewed as a means of refreshing the spirit, it is entirely rational.

Complete or Perfect Rationality

To make a *completely* rational decision, instead of one that is only *practically* rational, would be a colossal undertaking; in fact, it would be so huge that we would be acting unrationally if we were to embark on such a task. Let us allow our imagination to roam a bit to see what would be involved. We should first of all have to create visual images of all the possible ultimate goals which all the people in the world might be able to conceive and of all the possible intermediate goals which might serve as means of achieving those ultimate goals. Then, for each of the thousands of intermediate goals, we should need to conceive staircases and examine all the possible alternatives for each step. To choose the best alternatives for each step, it would be necessary for us to visualize and predict accurately all the wanted and unwanted consequences for every presently living person and all unborn generations for all time to come. Then we should have to weight the premises accurately and choose the alternative(s) that would produce the greatest good for the greatest number —the greatest amount of wanted and the fewest unwanted consequences for everyone who will be living on earth. Obviously, no one could expect to be completely rational by this definition. Several lifetimes would have to be spent at the task, and probably it could never be completed.

Practical Rationality

In this book, we are trying to be more *practical* about rationality —and perhaps more rational. Compared with the standard just described, ours is a rather limited attempt; yet, for our purposes, this less ambitious level serves our needs reasonably well. Spending a great deal of time and effort in trying to find and carry out a course of action that would maximize one or two goals, but would leave little time for making other major decisions would be less rational than spreading our efforts more thinly over several decisions.[14]

We were actually introduced to the ideas that we are here incorporating in our framework of rational decision making when we first examined ultimate goals of companies in general and of people in general; recall that we soon became more practical—narrowed this down to the particular goals of a specific company and of specific individuals, primarily the members of the organization. Then we turned to intermediate goals—the means that a specific company and the specific people in the company plan to employ in achieving their

---

[14] Simon's idea of "bounded rationality" is akin to our idea of practical rationality. It is succinctly put in James G. March and Herbert A. Simon, *Organizations* (New York: John Wiley & Sons, Inc., 1958), pp. 140–41. Also see C. West Churchman, *Prediction and Optimal Decision* (Englewood Cliffs, N.J.: Prentice-Hall, Inc., 1961), chap. 8.

ultimate goals. The concept of semipermanent ultimate and inter-mediate goals helped us to make rational decisions which would stand up when examined later. And by arranging our past decisions as steps on staircases, it was possible to discover which, if any, of our earlier decisions (decisions about goals we had not achieved) were not so very rational—unequal to the job of achieving the goal on the step above—and which necessary means were missing. No attempt was made to recheck an earlier decision unless a casual inspection showed it to be inadequate. In this way, we reduced the number of new decisions and thus the number of new alternatives which we had to conceive.

In the chapter on "The Creative Process," we were attempting a rational approach to the problem of creating ideas for new alternatives which we could add to the more obvious and familiar ones when the time came to choose the best means of achieving the goal just above. The six stages of the creative process we investigated—the stages of confusion, information gathering, organization and incubation of the information, crystallization of a new alternative which would include and unify all the information gathered, reappraisal and revision, and communication—served as a means of creating an idea for a new and practical solution of a problem that was troubling us, a workable means of achieving the goal we had in mind.

For each of the missing or inadequate steps, we then examined and compared only the three or four most promising alternatives, including those already familiar to us and any new ones we may have conceived. But we tried to make sure that we *did* consider the most promising ones. In the third chapter, we embarked on the task of trying out each alternative in our minds in an effort to uncover the wanted or unwanted consequences of each, paying particular attention to those premises which would have the greatest impact on the goals of the company and its members. Here, we employed the premise concept, using the idea of its three elements—the cause, the causal connection, and the result—to uncover any unreliable premises. The concept of factual elements and factual premises, and of value elements and value premises, pointed up the need to be wary about our predictions of what would occur—wary that our predictions were not simply statements of our hopes or fears. We began to realize that there are few really factual premises. Indeed, we discovered that, to be rational, we had to take into consideration what other people might call irrational premises—the value premises which introduce men's emotions into our decisions and are measured by the individual's own standards instead of by objective ones. After weighting the premises germane to each alternative, we were in a position to make a moderately rational choice—a decision that would most likely achieve the goal just above, would implement several of the other goals on the staircases, and would produce a minimum of unwanted repercussions.

Then, having grasped the four conceptual subsystems that made up our idea of the decision-making process—goals, staircases, creating ideas for alternatives, and the use of premises—we examined factual premises and value premises separately. In Chapter 4, we explored the uses of mathematical formulations of factual premises in an attempt to give more rigor to the predictions contained in those premises. We were encouraging mathematically trained men to gather statistical descriptions of factual causes, causal connections, and results connected with an activity of one segment of the company's activity and then to use these empirical data as a basis of working out equations. These equations would describe the quantifiable aspects of the past behavior—the causes and accompanying effects observed in that particular activity in the past—and would thus describe the consequences that would occur in the future if some variant of those particular causes were introduced into the system.

Further examination revealed that we would usually be acting with a low degree of rationality were we to confine our premises to those we could express as formulas. For a few decisions—those in which most of the significant causes and results could be expressed in cardinal numbers—the procedure would be quite rational. In the majority of our important decisions, however, we found that value premises were of great importance; omitting these would be highly unscientific and unrational in most cases; we felt obliged to include the goals, alternatives, and premises that can be measured only with our personal measuring rods. Excluding these, as would be necessary were we to confine ourselves to mathematical descriptions, would clearly result in unrational decisions.

In Chapter 5, we began to realize that in order to make a rational decision, we must expand our list of premises to include those considered by the individuals and groups who would be affected by our proposal. We noted that each man believes his decisions are rational at the moment he makes them and that each man probably acts rationally in the light of the premises he draws from the organizational, cultural, and other influences which have shaped his life, including those that have dropped down into the unconscious levels of his mind. In an effort to reappraise the decision to see if it was as rational as it originally appeared, we then tested it out on the several member groups whose cooperation would be required, in an effort to anticipate whether each contributing group would feel that its inducement-contribution balance would be bettered. It became apparent that if the several groups felt that accepting and carrying out the proposal enthusiastically would be a logical way of furthering their own welfare or, at worst, that their welfare would not be jeopardized, the decision would probably turn out to be a wise one from the point of view of the company; the company's inducement-contribution balance would be bettered. The inducement-contribution analysis also enabled us to bring together in one place and organize most of the premises and concepts we were dealing with in the earlier chapters, so that we could view them as a whole and thus reach more intelligent decisions.

Rationality and the Executive

Most young men and many older men make mediocre executives because they employ only a small amount of rationality. They fail to take fully into consideration the company's and the members' goals and long-term means; they keep reusing the old alternatives, adopting them through habit instead of periodically appraising them anew; and when they do think up a new alternative, they fail to foresee all the interdepartmental effects of their proposal, and thus have trouble getting their proposals adopted. More than that, many men fail to sense the changes going on in the world outside the company, and ignore the need to make proposals that are attuned to those trends.

On the other hand, none of us should subject ourselves to the strain of making *all* our decisions as rationally as proposed here; we should soon buckle under the pressure. Moreover, the grim strait-jacket we must impose upon ourselves when we consider only long-term goals soon beeomes boring, and our friends begin to look upon us as a thinking machine whom they respect but cannot seem to love because we are too perfect. However, taking almost everything into consideration has its rewards, as we have seen. And the suspense of watching to see whether a decision we are proud of will turn out as we had hoped is as thrilling as reading an adventure story. We gain a great deal of satisfaction when we find that all ends well in spite of the vicissitudes of the journey. But acting on impulse, taking into consideration the goal of having fun—for instance, deciding to do something for the sheer fun it will afford us and other members of the organization—has therapeutic value for everyone. This, too, in a very real sense is rational.

Nevertheless, as a man rises toward the top in his organization, he can no longer permit himself the luxury of making many snap decisions or ones based on "hunch," for blunders at the higher levels on the means-end staircase leave permanently harmful marks on the company. One of the objectives of these five chapters on decision making has been to slow down the decision-making process and raise its separate components from the unconscious to the conscious levels of the mind. We have been trying to convert what is typically a rather disorderly, hurried, hit-or-miss thinking process into an orderly and rather thorough one. It is important to reiterate, however, that all this will prove abortive if these steps are thought of merely as something to be learned and remembered. The ideas will soon be forgotten unless we immediately begin watching for opportunities to use them in our daily lives. Most of us have to employ them consciously at first. But they really become fruitful only after we reach the point where the process becomes habitual and quite unconscious. Once it has become a visceral activity instead of an intellectual game, we can also regain speed in making our decisions; and—equally important—the chances are that we can feel proud of most of the decisions we make.

It is commonly said that if 51 per cent of a top executive's decisions turn out all right, he has done a good job. In my opinion, this is an unnecessarily low goal, even for a man who has no intention of becoming a thinking machine. I should say that all the decisions made by the chief executive and his associates as to the company's ultimate and intermediate goals must be farsighted ones, and that something like 80 per cent of their decisions for those steps they decide to insert near the top of the company's means-end staircases should stand up well when examined in retrospect. (This does not mean, however, that each of these decisions must be *perfect;* a good decision could be only 75 or 90 per cent perfect or achieve only a part of the goal that had been set and still look wise when reappraised later.) If the top executives and middle-level and lower-level executives make some mistakes in those decisions lying nearer the bottom of the means-end staircases, or in subsidiary staircases, the consequences will not be so serious. Indeed, executives seem to follow an unwritten rule that they will overlook one another's mistakes at this level; these must often be made hurriedly. However, inasmuch as the decisions lying near the bottom of the staircase are rather easily made because they are relatively concrete compared with those above them, the percentage of good decisions at these levels should also be much higher than 50 per cent.

PROBLEM

ANTICIPATING THE DECISIONS OF OTHERS

The Midwest Feed Manufacturing Company* of Aurora, Illinois, a family partnership founded in 1914, produced a highly concentrated livestock feed which it distributed to livestock growers through some 600 feed dealers located in the nine states of the corn belt. Approximately 15 executives and office employees worked in the offices of the company; the adjacent plant employed about 15 men who did unskilled work; and the sales staff consisted of about 75 men who traveled the nine-state territory.

By 1961, sales had risen about tenfold as compared with 1939. Despite two-shift operation, the original feed-mixing plant no longer had the capacity to take care of the heavy demand efficiently. Because of recent mergers among competitors, the management expected some reduction in sales; but the inadequate facilities of the plant, in view of the anticipated level of sales, led to a decision to abandon the old plant and build a new plant. The old plant was useless.

The decision to build opened an opportunity to reappraise the question of the city in which the offices and the plant would be located. Because of changes made from time to time in the types of raw materials used in the feed formulas, freight costs had become an important consideration; freight costs, it was known, would vary from location to location. In the early days of the company the freight costs were not of great significance, principally because of the small tonnage then moving through the plant, the local nature of the business, the character of the raw materials used at the time in the feed formulas, and the high retail price per ton of feed the company could charge in relation to the cost of ingredients. Over the years the formulas for the company's concentrated feeds had been markedly altered to include a high percentage by weight of protein-bearing ingredients such as soybean meal, produced mainly in Iowa and Illinois; cottonseed meal produced in the south; linseed meal, produced in Minnesota; and salt, calcium phosphate and other products shipped from various origins. Also, during that period, retail prices were sharply reduced in relation to costs of the raw materials so that raw materials now made up a much larger percentage of the final selling price than before. As a consequence, freight costs on these incoming raw materials and on the outgoing feeds had become a major factor, running about 10 per cent of sales.

The assistant general manager for Midwest, with the advice of a Chicago consulting firm which had made operations research studies for three other companies, compiled from the company's 1960 records the average inbound

---

* The company's actual name and location differ from those stated in the case.

freight cost per ton of ingredients (length of haul times rate per mile) the average outbound freight cost of a ton of feed, and the company's average freight savings per ton resulting from its milling-in-transit privileges in Aurora. In those cases where the suppliers prepaid the freight and quoted a delivered price, he used published rail tariff schedules to calculate the freight. To bring his figures up to date, he modified the freight costs of ingredients to reflect recent changes in the company's sources of supply and tried to allow for the increasing use of trucks for the delivery of feed. He also contemplated the possibility of allowing for possible changes in the feed formulas over the next few years—recent research in animal nutrition was bringing to light many improvements in formulas—but he finally abandoned this idea.

He then secured, from railroads serving the midwest, similar data on freight costs for seven other medium-sized cities in Illinois and Iowa—mostly those served by two or more railroads. The consulting firm then worked out a general formula designed to determine, for any plant location, what the total freight cost per ton would be from the various sources of ingredients to the final destination of the feed. Next, the formula was programmed for a computer, and the data for each city, including Aurora, was introduced into it to determine which city would have the lowest total freight cost per ton. The results showed that a plant located in Peoria, Illinois would provide a somewhat greater freight saving than the other cities.

The Midwest executives predicted that as a result of the new competition the company would suffer a reduction in tonnage of 25 per cent in the period ahead and about the same reduction in the current profit margin per ton. The assistant general manager, using this estimate and the freight cost study as a basis, calculated that the savings in freight for a plant located in Peoria would increase the profits by about 15 per cent over what they would be if the new plant were built in Aurora. If competition made further price reductions necessary, the freight savings would play an even greater part in the net profit picture.

The men who had some say in the final decision on the location of the plant were as follows:

The founder and principal partner, a man aged 68, no longer very active in the company. He was a member of the Chamber of Commerce and the Rotary Club, active in the trade association of feed manufacturers whose headquarters was located in Aurora, and active in church affairs. He and his wife enjoyed a wide circle of friends. In 1938, as a result of his growing anxiety about the plight of the farmer, he had left the Republican Party and ran for Congress on the Democratic ticket. He lost the election by a few hundred votes.

The general manager, young son of the founder, a partner, and the titular as well as actual chief executive of the company. He had grown up in Aurora and had attended an Illinois liberal arts college, where he majored in chemistry. He had a young family not yet of school age.

The assistant general manager, who had more recently moved to Aurora. He had been trained in business administration at the Harvard Business School and for some years had served as an executive in another company. He was the father of three children in grade school.

The sales manager, who in earlier years had moved from city to city. He had—since moving to Aurora—become active in the local advertising club and in church affairs. He was primarily responsible for a rapid growth in the sales and dealer organizations, and he felt a strong loyalty to the men in these groups. His family had grown up. He frequently expressed concern about the growing influence of the federal government and the "creeping socialism" he saw in the United States.

The plant superintendent, who had left high school to work and had grown up with the company. His children were in high school. The relationship between the superintendent and the plant employees was a particularly close one. He was proud of his working-class background, but he was very loyal to the company.

In reaching a decision, the above five men discussed the study of freight costs at length. The general manager and the assistant general manager understood the reasoning that lay beneath the operations research formula fairly well, though not its mathematics. They and the three other men eventually indicated that they thought the estimate of freight savings was reasonably accurate.

The assistant general manager, the sales manager, and the plant superintendent were paid attractive salaries, plus a bonus at the end of each fiscal year based on a percentage of the earnings of the company. The bonuses had sometimes amounted to as much as half of the salaries. The partners received the balance of the profits. It was expected that profits would decline in the postwar period.

Before answering the questions below, perhaps you had better check the reliability of the assistant general manager's crucial premise, "If we move to Peoria I estimate that profits will be 15 per cent more than if we build in Aurora." Analyze its three elements to determine how factual each one is, especially the causal connection; then, on the basis of your analysis, make up your own mind about whether the cause will actually produce the result. Finally, before starting to write, examine the premise through the eyes of each of the five men named above and determine what they each think of its reliability; do they think that moving to Peoria will really produce 15 per cent more profits.

1. Select two of the four men described above (exclude the general manager).
    a) Go around with each of them on a visit to each of the groups or organizations they belong to, examine the goals of these groups or organizations and list the premises (arrange them according to wanted and unwanted consequences) that these men are likely to gather from each of these organizational reservoirs in trying to decide whether to recommend moving to Peoria or staying in Aurora. Then mention two or three premises each might draw from the two other types of reservoirs discussed in pages 121 to 126, naming the reservoir.
    b) How do you think they would weight each of their premises? Why?
    c) Which location would you expect each of the men to recommend to the general manager?
2. In what way does this case, and your answers to Parts 1 *a*, *b*, and *c*, illustrate practical rationality (or lack of it) in the decision-making process?

PART II

GAINING
ACCEPTANCE
OF DECISIONS

THE EXECUTIVE'S task of gaining acceptance of the decisions he has made is just as essential to the company's welfare as making the decisions in the first place. Unless he can induce others to accept and act on his company decisions, all his efforts to make wise ones are wasted.

Gaining acceptance of his company decisions plays an equally important role in furthering a man's personal welfare. Typically, each time he makes a successful attempt, he finds it easier to gain acceptance of his next proposal. If he consistently fails, the conviction begins to grow among his colleagues that most of his decisions are unsound; his friends eventually get into the habit of brushing aside his proposals. As a consequence, he soon loses his effectiveness as a leader. Thus, an executive cannot afford to fail in the task of guiding the behavior of others.

Of the three main tasks of the executive explored in this book, that of getting his

proposals accepted is probably the most frustrating of all. It is undoubtedly the most difficult and least understood of his tasks, and
it is here that the executive most often fails. By comparison, decision
making is a relatively straightforward job, once the several steps are
mastered. True, we can describe and master some concepts designed
to aid in gaining acceptance; hence it is easy enough to learn what
should be done. However, in a face-to-face situation, especially where
much depends on our ability to convince the other man, these concepts are likely to fly out of the window; we lose our heads.

Knowing we have failed when such a conference ends is vexing
enough, but it is even more disturbing to suppose that we have convinced an associate and then to discover later that we have not. We
are perplexed by the failure. Characteristically, in a situation of this
kind, the man argues for a few moments, then eventually nods and
says, "Yes, that's a fine idea," or else says nothing definite but allows
us to suppose that he is convinced. In any case, he does nothing about
it. Such a pocket veto is a difficult problem with which to cope.

Once an executive, together with his associates, has chosen a course
of action as the best one for advancing the company's goals, he cannot
afford to be indecisive. Once the decision has been made, it is his responsibility to see that the plans are fully understood and carried
out by his subordinates, even though there is some opposition. In the
preceding chapter, we saw that by anticipating the responses of others
at the time the decision itself is being framed, the task of gaining
acceptance can be greatly eased. Nonetheless, there are limits to the
amount of inducements a company can offer its members; and in any
case, there are always some men who conclude, on the basis of their
premises, that the company would be injured if the proposed course
of action were adopted. The executive's task is to take the steps
necessary to ensure that virtually all members feel they *want* to make
the contributions called for by the proposal.

No man can expect to be uniformly successful, but learning how
to go about gaining acceptance can reduce his failures. Our objective
in Part II will be to probe some of the typical problems an executive
encounters and to investigate some concepts that will serve as tools
for coping with them. The five conceptual subsystems we shall explore—authority, leadership, communication, the use of the company's informal groups, and the use of its formal organization structure—are closely entwined. Our procedure will be to pull these apart,
master the details of each, then put them back together in an in-
telligible framework. By the time this has been completed, we shall

have made considerable progress in consciously using these tools, so that we can eventually employ them as unconscious, habitual modes of behavior. But basically, we shall again be making decisions —deciding about how to induce others to adopt our proposals. The successful use of each concept rests upon an understanding of the concepts developed in Part I.

Chapter **6**   AUTHORITY

IN THIS first chapter of Part II, we shall probe the task of deciding which type of authority we should employ to induce a given person to carry out a given proposal—which type will yield the most wanted consequences and the least unwanted. The details of the authority concept tie back into the conceptual subsystems of the decision-making process. And we shall eventually find that the various parts of this chapter form a subsystem of their own. But our main problem is to learn to use these subsystems effectively.

All of us attempt to exercise authority. We frequently try to induce others to adopt and follow our proposals. We endeavor to influence the behavior of the members of our family, for example, and of our subordinates, our associates, and even our bosses. In trying to induce these people to change their behavior, we are attempting to exercise authority over them. Occasionally, we succeed; but most of us fail more often than we should like. In this chapter, we shall investigate three very specific tools or concepts which should help us to increase the number of our successes. Needless to say, these concepts are by no means foolproof; they are to be thought of as aids in gaining wholehearted acceptance of our proposals.

The names we shall give the three concepts or tools are:
1. The estimated width of the zone of acceptance.
2. Authority: There are three types of authority discussed in this chapter; these we shall call:
   a) Simple authority.
   b) Proof.
   c) Sanctions.
3. The amount of wholeheartedness and contributions to be expected as a result of an attempt to exert authority.

We shall depend most upon item No. 2, the concept of authority. In this book, we shall discard the commonly used layman's definitions of authority. As a preliminary description of our definition, the following statement will prove helpful: Authority is an attempt—a successful attempt—to guide the behavior of another individual. In

155

trying to exercise authority, we sometimes use simple authority (merely ask the other person to act as we suggest); at other times we use proof (supply premises that point to the wanted consequences of acting as proposed); and at other times we use sanctions (make threats of punishment or offers of rewards).

The idea of authority used here is really what some people might call *informal* authority, as opposed to delegated or *formal* authority, the kind of authority a man is given when he is formally appointed to a job. It is evident that we are not talking here about the traditional view of authority—the authority that inheres in an official position or the "authority" of a noted specialist whose views are widely accepted. According to our definition, the amount of authority that we have is not determined by the amount of authority our superiors may have conferred on us or by how much we know, but instead by our ability to induce our associates, subordinates, and superiors to carry out our proposals.[1]

The other two concepts serve as supplementary tools for deciding ahead of time which of the three types of authority to employ. Before mentioning our proposal, and before attempting to exercise authority, we first (if we practice foresight) try to anticipate how the other person will take our recommendations—whether that individual's zone of acceptance for our proposal will be narrow, medium, or very wide. This gives us an idea of which type of authority should be employed to induce the other person to change his behavior. But before attempting to exercise authority, we *also* use concept No. 3—try to anticipate the amount of wholeheartedness we can expect from him, and the extent of his contribution to the company once we have employed what we consider the most appropriate type of authority and he has actually started to carry out the proposal. It will be noted that all three concepts are utilized *before* anything is said to the man. They are also interdependent; to gain the full benefit of each, the three concepts should be employed simultaneously.

Although we shall, in this book, approve of executives who exercise authority over their subordinates, we should be mindful of the harmful effects as well as desirable results. The wanted consequences loom large. The superior is responsible for achieving certain company goals. This means that he cannot allow his men to do entirely as they choose; his task is to induce them to carry out their regular

---

[1] See Merton J. Mandeville, "The Nature of Authority," in *Journal of the Academy of Management*, Vol. 3, No. 2 (August, 1960), for an explication of the several ideas of authority now in use.

assignments conscientiously. And, what is more difficult, he is responsible for inducing them to change their comfortable work habits whenever better means of achieving the company's goals are found. Evidently a certain amount of control and direction is essential. Much of the time, in a department where morale is reasonably high, this company goal-oriented authority is exercised in a quite easy and normal atmosphere. But when the men's goals and the company's goals are incompatible, we can expect conflict even in well run departments. In such instances, the company's goals (somewhat modified, perhaps, to meet the subordinates' needs), will usually have to take precedence if the company is to flourish.[2]

Upon occasion, such conflicts and strains produce wanted consequences; they may induce the stage of confusion which, in turn, may eventually force someone to create a better solution. In such an atmosphere a man is more likely to achieve his full growth, instead of merely to vegetate—*providing,* of course, the frustrations do not overwhelm him.

But we dare not overlook the unwanted consequences of the exercise of authority by a superior. These touch close to one of the most baffling problems of a democratic society; if a man's goals and the company's (or society's) goals are in conflict, to what extent should the individual's take precedence? We are talking here about individual freedom, the freedom to dissent, to be a nonconformist, versus the pressure for conformity: the desire to be one's own boss and make one's own decisions, versus doing what one is told to do. Working with others to achieve a common goal calls for compliance, for submission to the will of the group. We need this conformity much of the time to get the world's work done; yet we also want to encourage the nonconformist, for it is he who often asks embarrassing questions about the status quo and thus foments improvement and change.

ZONES OF ACCEPTANCE AND A PREVIEW OF THE OTHER TWO MAJOR CONCEPTS

In trying to influence the behavior of another person we often unconsciously first imagine what his reaction to our proposal would be. Before blurting out our newly conceived alternative, we estimate

---

[2] See, for instance, Melville Dalton, *Men Who Manage* (New York: John Wiley & Sons, Inc.), pp. 263–64, and Malcolm P. McNair, "Thinking Ahead: What Price Human Relations?" *Harvard Business Review,* Vol. 35, No. 2 (April–May, 1957), reprinted in Harold Koontz and Cyril O'Donnell (eds.), *Readings in Management* (New York: McGraw-Hill Book Co., Inc., 1959).

the width of his zone of acceptance and govern our statements accordingly. Before trying to induce our boss to give us a pay raise, we first imagine his response to the idea and then decide what we shall say to him. We know that to do otherwise might result in failure.

In attempting to anticipate a man's first reaction to our proposal, we are employing the concept that we are naming *the width of the zone of acceptance*. For convenience, we shall use the word *receiver* for the man whose behavior is being influenced; he is on the receiving end. The man who makes the proposal—who attempts to exert authority—will be called the *giver*.

Our prediction of the width of our receiver's zone of acceptance for our new proposal is based upon our idea of the goals and premises he already possesses, premises we uncover by using the group of concepts —the idea of reservoirs, for instance—we developed in Chapter 5 when learning to anticipate the decisions of others. By using the premises we thus gather, we can frequently anticipate his offhand response with considerable accuracy. We can predict whether his zone will be quite wide (we anticipate that the wanted consequences he thinks of will greatly outweigh the unwanted consequences—he is wide-open to the proposal), or medium in width (to him the wanted and unwanted consequences are of about equal weight), or narrow (the unwanted results far outweigh the wanted ones—he will scarcely listen to us).

We shall visualize the measuring rod for the width of the receiver's zone of acceptance as a horizontal line calibrated from zero to 100 per cent, with 100 per cent lying to the right. The wider the zone, the further it extends toward the 100 per cent mark; the widest zone would extend from zero all the way to 100 per cent. These percentages are introduced here merely as a shorthand method of depicting something that cannot be measured. Bear in mind that no one could possibly say that a man's zone would be 60 per cent in width because we (and he) must use our personal measures. The zone, by the way, can be negative in width—a minus percentage. This measure is shown as the topmost line of Diagram 7.

That the width of the receiver's zone will differ for each of our proposals should be emphasized. His mind may be wide open to one of our proposals; his zone extends to nearly 100 per cent. For another decision we want him to accept, his zone may be narrow—extending only a short distance to the right of zero per cent—less than 25 per cent in width; he is reluctant but not adamant about accepting. And frequently, the man's zone of acceptance will be medium wide, ex-

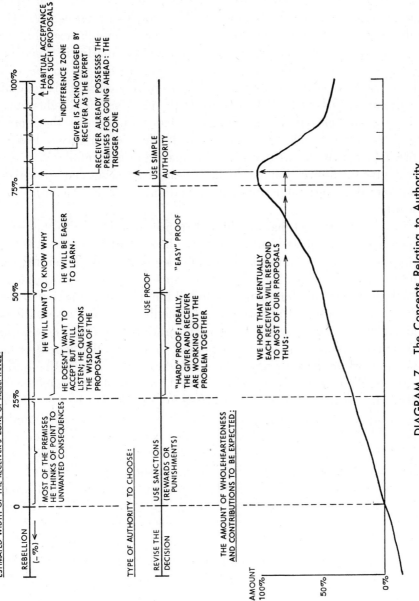

DIAGRAM 7. The Concepts Relating to Authority

tending to a point lying somewhere between 25 and 75 per cent on the scale—say, about 65 per cent in width. We anticipate that he will probably accept, but first he will ask questions and want some answers. He will want to know *why;* some of his premises say, "Go ahead and do it," but others point to unwanted consequences. Before accepting, he wants to resolve these questions. Finally, in some instances, we can predict that no matter what we say or do, he will never really accept our proposal; it falls entirely outside his zone of acceptance, falls to the left of zero. If the premises he weights most heavily point clearly to *not* doing as bidden—if in his eyes the contributions he must make in carrying out the decision greatly outweigh the inducements he will receive—he may refuse point-blank, or he may give the impression that he has assented yet never actually carry out our decision; both would be rebellion as we are defining the word.

We would predict that an old and respected mechanic in the company's machine shop would have a wide zone of acceptance for a proposal made by the president that he be given a gold watch for his long and meritorious service. But his zone of acceptance would be medium wide if his foreman were to tell him to help the maintenance crew for a month or so; he would undoubtedly have some reservations about this decision and would most certainly want to know why. Were the foreman, or even the president, to tell him that hereafter he was to work in the warehouse, his zone of acceptance would be quite narrow; the unwanted consequences would outweigh the wanted ones. If his foreman (or the president) were to tell him that henceforth he is to operate his lathe in such and such a manner, his zone would probably be negative in width. "Nobody can tell me how to do my job." The unwanted consequences of allowing others to guide his behavior in handling the work in which he is supposed to be an expert would greatly outweigh the wanted ones. He would be admitting to his family and fellow workers that he is not the skilled craftsman they had once believed. He might not openly refuse, but he would "forget" these instructions.

Errors in estimating the receiver's zone of acceptance account for most of our failures in attempts to exercise authority. Once we have estimated the width with some degree of accuracy, we are in a position to select the appropriate type of authority. If we anticipate a wide zone, we can expect *simple* authority to work. All we need to do is to ask the receiver to do our bidding or tell him what we want done; we can expect him to go ahead without hesitation. If we anticipate a medium-width zone of acceptance, *proof,* a second type of authority will be most effective; here, we are giving him a picture of the goals we have in mind, the means that we want him to contribute (that is, the proposal we are making to him), and the premises we took into consideration at the time we decided to make this proposal. When we transmit these goals and premises, we are using proof; we customarily call them *our reasons.* We expect him to agree to contribute the means we have in mind after hearing what we have to say.

In those cases where we anticipate a narrow zone, the chances are that we shall have to employ *sanctions,* a third type of authority; we offer him personal rewards if he does as he is told and threaten punishment if he does not. We are inserting into his inducement and contribution columns some sanctions (rewards or punishments) which we have in our pocket in the expectation that these will widen the spread between his inducements and contributions to a point where he will follow our directions. If we expect a negative-width zone, we had better change our proposal before voicing it; there is little we can say or do to change his mind. How the concepts of zone of acceptance and of authority fit together is shown in Diagram 7 (p. 159).[3] In a few moments, we shall go considerably further into the concept of authority.

To this preview of the different types of authority and their relationship to the concept of the zone of acceptance, we shall add a preview of the third main concept—the estimate of the amount of wholeheartedness and contributions we may expect. This estimate is also made ahead of time. We imagine that we have used the appropriate type of authority—have spoken to the receiver—and that he has added to his own fund of premises the premises he picks up from hearing what we have said; on the basis of this, we make a prediction of what his wholeheartedness and contributions to the company will be. When executives are trying to exercise authority, their objective is to elicit a high level of contributions; they are hoping to induce the receiver to do his best—to use 100 per cent of his ability in carrying out their proposal. The "amount" of wholeheartedness and contributions we can normally expect after employing any one of the three types of authority is shown in the bottom graph of Diagram 7. (In this graph the percentage is shown on a vertical scale instead of a horizontal one.) Great wholeheartedness and large contributions

---

[3] The statements contained in this paragraph and the ideas that underlie Diagram 7 are based only on my own observations. They are to be thought of only as useful generalizations.

are represented by 100 per cent, the highest level of this line. Thus the graph, when read from *right* to left, shows that, generally speaking, we can expect the receiver to do a fairly good job—carry out the proposal at about 60 per cent of his ability—not 100 per cent, as might be thought at first—when we use simple authority, provided, of course, that his zone of acceptance is wide. If his zone is of medium width and we employ proof, we can expect his contributions to be much closer to 100 per cent of his ability—a large amount of wholeheartedness and contributions. If we have to employ sanctions, we may expect rather low contributions; the man "will drag his feet," will go through the motions but will make small contributions, which will just about match the low level of inducements he feels he is receiving. And, of course, if there is passive or outright rebellion, there will be no contributions or, more likely, harmful or negative contributions.

THE IDEA OF AUTHORITY

It is already evident that we are using a special definition for the word *authority*. According to our definition, authority is a successful attempt by one person to guide the behavior of another in a chosen direction. An authority relationship exists when the receiver modifies or alters his behavior in the direction desired by the giver. If the receiver's behavior is not so altered or modified, no authority relationship exists; this would constitute an unsuccessful attempt to employ authority; the receiver has rebelled.

As a tool for grappling with the task of gaining acceptance, this special definition is much more realistic and flexible than those commonly used. Many people think of bosses as the only ones who influence the behavior of others, the only ones who exercise authority; they picture authority as originating only at or near the top of the hierarchy and gradually percolating down to the bottom. But according to our definition, the question of who has the title of boss and which man is supposed to report to whom is immaterial.[4] The authority we are talking about pervades every organization. This kind of authority actually is exercised to some extent by everyone in a company. It is exerted upward as well as downward and is also exercised diagonally through the organization. Subordinates often at-

---

[4] The appointment of a boss—the bestowing of *formal* authority (that is, assigning to a man the responsibility for a specific task over a period of time)—will be taken up in Part III, where we deal with putting plans into effect. The authority discussed in this chapter has to be *won*. It depends on the consent of the governed.

tempt to induce their bosses to carry out their decisions and frequently succeed in doing so; they "boss" their appointed bosses. Men are also successful at times in their efforts to influence the behavior of their fellow workers in their own departments and elsewhere in the organization. Undoubtedly, bosses exercise authority downward more often than subordinates exert authority upward or diagonally; but all of them try to influence the behavior of others. Such an authority relationship may exist between *any* two people in an organization.

This authority relationship we are investigating here exists only during the moment when one of the two men is exercising authority over the other. It is short-lived and quite fluid. Seldom does one man constantly act as a giver and the other only as a receiver. In one situation a man down low in the hierarchy may be acting as the giver, and the receiver may be the man above him in the hierarchy. In another situation, their positions may be reversed; the one "above" may be exercising authority—the so-called "normal" relationship. The same thing occurs in the authority relationships between two fellow workers. When Carl and Louie are discussing baseball, Carl may play the role of the giver and Louie the receiver; whereas a moment later, when machine tools are the topic, their roles may be reversed.

To gain some insight into how people exercise authority, let us explore three examples, one a rather elementary one, the other two more complex. The boss's secretary is endeavoring to exert authority over her boss when she asks him to sign a requisition for pencils. An authority relationship exists at the time he signs; his secretary has influenced his behavior. She apparently knew his zone of acceptance would be very wide, so she used simple authority. Probably the reason he accepts is that he is aware that she, not he, has the premises necessary to make this decision. She is the expert on this occasion. He is willing to accept her decision, her order; he uses her decision as a basis for his action—namely, signing. This is an example of upward-moving authority as well as simple authority.[5]

For a more complex example, one that illustrates the employment of authority diagonally upward and the use of proof, we shall go to the machine shop. A man from the cost department has just handed the foreman a record of the costs of yesterday's completed jobs,

---

[5] The boss is actually using the secretary's instructions as one element of a premise; he immediately frames it into a three-part premise and then uses it as the basis for deciding what action to take—for example, "If I sign this requisition, we'll have enough pencils on hand." Of course, he may also have considered others ("If I sign, we'll overspend our budget") ; but he evidently gave these less weight.

pointing out that the cost of one was far higher than the original estimate. He goes further and compares that cost with the cost of other similar jobs recently completed. Although he does not say, "You are to investigate the cause for the discrepancy and correct the situation," the foreman is quite aware of this intention. In this example the cost man presents some facts with the obvious intention of influencing the foreman's behavior; he expects the foreman to frame factual premises from these and then reach the conclusion, "I'll make sure this doesn't happen again." For purposes of illustration, let us say that the foreman does take this action—that the cost man succeeds in exercising authority. Evidently, on this occasion the cost man accurately predicted that the foreman's zone of acceptance would be medium in width. On the basis of this, he realized that considerable proof would be needed; and consequently, he brought together the premises he had originally taken into consideration in reaching his own conclusion and communicated these to the foreman.

For our third example—an illustration of an unsuccessful attempt to exercise authority diagonally upward—let us imagine a young and inexperienced cost man trying to exert authority over the same foreman. He too has discovered that the cost of one of yesterday's jobs was abnormally high. Probably his first thought is, "I wish I could force that foreman to keep these costs in line." He is vaguely aware that the foreman's zone of acceptance will be narrow and that sanctions will be required; threatening punishment, however, would be unrealistic, for both he and the foreman know that the threat could not be carried out. Simply to *ask* the foreman to watch expenses would likewise produce no results. Proof, then, is his only alternative. Inasmuch as the figure on the cost sheet is his only proof, he presents that. The foreman growls that the figure must be wrong: "Go back and check it." Since the young man has no further proof, he returns to his desk, defeated. Even though the cost man eventually demonstrates that the figure is valid, the attempt may still end in failure. The foreman may refuse to act, perhaps using a pocket veto, because he is taking into consideration a number of other premises, several of which point to unwanted results which he weights heavily; so he concludes that he should take no action. Had the cost man on this occasion attempted to use more extensive proof—had he mentioned other premises which he had in mind, ones the foreman obviously was not taking into consideration—his venture might have met with success.

When we observe an authority relationship in which the boss is the *giver* and the subordinate the receiver (the "normal" relationship), we see these same things occurring. A boss frequently estimates his subordinate's zone of acceptance and, on the basis of this estimate, chooses the appropriate type of authority—simple authority, proof, or sanctions. And once in a while, his subordinates—in effect—say, "No," when he asks or orders them to do certain things, either because his proposals lie entirely outside their zone of acceptance or because he has attempted to employ the wrong type of authority.

To avoid becoming confused in analyzing a given situation, for the purpose of determining whether an authority relationship exists between two people, it is essential to keep our eyes on those two persons only. The secretary's attempt was successful, even though her boss may fail later in trying to induce the storeroom clerk to deliver the pencils. *His* failure to establish an authority relationship with *his* receiver has no bearing on whether the secretary's attempt was successful. The test is whether the receiver *attempted* to carry out the indicated action and not whether he succeeded in carrying it out.[6] Furthermore, on those occasions when we are attempting to employ authority, we must scrutinize the *specific* receiver whom we are trying to influence, and the *specific* proposal we are making, if we are to lay realistic plans for gaining the receiver's acceptance. Generalizations about how most people will act or about how a certain receiver responds to *all* the decisions we ask him to carry out are seldom valid.

SIMPLE AUTHORITY

As has been already indicated, the term *simple authority* will be used here to describe an authority relationship in which the receiver employs the giver's request or instructions as his *sole* or *salient* piece of information in framing his premises for deciding what to do; he uses practically no premises of his own or, at least, gives very little weight to his own. In employing simple authority, we often say, "Would you mind doing . . . ," "Would you please . . . ?" "This is the way to do it," or "Why don't you do it this way?" Most of us would prefer to use simple authority because, *if* it works, it saves both time and trouble. We need not go to the bother of using proof, arguments, spankings, or lollipops. The difficulty is that sim-

---

[6] However, when a receiver is deciding whether to accept a proposal, he often takes into consideration the premises he uncovers when he envisages the width of the "third" man's zone of acceptance for his giver's proposed decision. A subordinate asks himself, "Will my men be able to live with my boss's proposal, or will it muddle up their work so badly they'll get fighting mad?" Executives often jump to the conclusion that if their subordinates readily accept, the job will be done—that all their subordinates have to do is use simple authority or sanctions on the men down in the hierarchy in order to gain wholehearted acceptance. Obviously, the task is not always so simple.

ple authority does not always work. The receiver may ignore our directions; or if he does follow them, his contributions may be relatively low, far below his ability. He does the job perfunctorily, though he may do it promptly enough and without resentment.

By breaking up the widest zone of acceptance into four zones, we can make reasonably accurate predictions about whether a man will respond to simple authority in a given situation. Instead of visualizing a single broad zone extending from zero to a point anywhere between 75 and 100 per cent, we shall think of *one* of these zones as extending from zero to a point lying anywhere between about 95 and 100 per cent; a second reaching to any point between approximately 88 and 95 per cent; a third, 80 to 88 per cent; and a fourth, 75 to about 80 per cent. These four divisions of the 75 to 100 per cent zone, together with some names and descriptions of them, are shown at the right of the top line in Diagram 7 (p. 159).

The widest of the four zones, the one extending from zero to about 95 or 100 per cent, we shall call the *habitual acceptance zone.* In every organization we can expect to find some receivers who are anxious to please or who will accept and carry out *some* proposals almost without thinking, a kind of conditioned reflex which is the result of a pattern of behavior ingrained during childhood; certain proposals made to these men will fall into their habitual acceptance zones. The model child of past generations was the one who always did as he was told, promptly and willingly; the parents never had to explain why (proof) or employ sanctions to gain acceptance. Over the centuries, businessmen, army officers, and church leaders have likewise praised those who accepted without questioning; dominance of the parent or the official and submission of the subordinate was then a pervading pattern. For the receivers who would not accept, they employed sanctions. Rigid parental discipline has lately been giving way to proof—the practice of providing the children with premises, so that they may act appropriately on their own initiative. Despite this shift, however, acceptance without critical examination of the instructions of the boss at home or at work is still a dominant characteristic in interpersonal relationships. "Isn't everyone *supposed* to have a boss and obey him?"[7] A man who has been so con-

---

[7] Company rules and regulations are conspicuous examples of directions that are often habitually accepted. They, too, are instructions or orders—even though they are permanent ones which are used repeatedly as guides to behavior. Some may be standard practice instructions, often referred to as "the bible," or they may be unwritten rules handed down by the older to the newer employees. Ordinarily, these are accepted by receivers as unchangeable decisions.

ditioned is likely to have a very wide zone of acceptance for the majority of the instructions he is given.

We shall call the next widest zone the *indifference zone*. This is the zone of a receiver when the particular action he is asked to carry out makes little difference to him. This and all the other work he might do are equally dull to him; hence the one he is told to do is a matter of indifference. He uses more premises in this zone than in the widest one, but the premises he considers indicate that the proposed action will have little or no adverse effects on his goals. He has no particular interest in the company's goals, but he assumes that the proposal will advance them; otherwise, so he reasons, he would not be asked to perform the task.

Into the third widest zone, that extending from zero to around 80 or 88 per cent, fall those proposals where the receiver acknowledges to himself that the giver is much more of an expert than he. If the receiver recognizes that the giver has accumulated many premises, whereas he is a novice with few or none, he is likely to take the expert's word—accept and act on the expert's decision without much questioning. Also, when the receiver realizes that the premises are difficult to master and he lacks the interest, or time, or the ability to master them, the chances are that he will defer to the expert; it is much easier. A workman in the plant will frequently take the metallurgist's word or his foreman's word that he should do such and such. The premises he has gathered in the past point to the conclusion that those men are more expert than he in making certain types of company decisions. When the nonexpert recognizes that the expert's decision will be better than his own, he accepts it as a guide for his own behavior and responds to simple authority.[8]

The narrowest of these four zones, the one extending to between 75 and 80 per cent on the continuum, is the most interesting and fruitful of all. Into this one fall those proposals for which the receiver has already accumulated a great many premises, most of which point toward accepting. We shall call this the *trigger zone*. The giver's instructions merely act as a trigger to unleash the contributions the receiver is asked to make to the company. To an onlooker, it appears that simple authority has been employed; but actually, this is more akin to proof. Into this zone would fall a proposal to take some action in behalf of the company which the receiver immediately

---

[8] As we shall see in the next chapter, this *expert* zone of acceptance (as well as the *habitual acceptance* and *indifference* zones) has a good deal to do with leadership. Incidentally, leadership is a relatively permanent authority relationship.

sees would also further his personal goals. A salesman would already possess a great many premises which point to accepting a proposal to write up a large order a customer has laid in his lap; he has already accumulated the necessary premises. The proposed act serves as a common means of achieving his own and his company's goals. Into this zone would also fall those proposals which the two men have talked over at an earlier date. Here, the giver has already furnished the receiver with the premises for accepting the proposal; and the receiver has already concluded, on the basis of these and his own premises, that he will carry out the proposal when the giver tells him that the time is ripe. In both these cases the only new premise is the instruction to go ahead—the trigger. The giver is quite aware that the receiver already possesses the necessary basic premises, so he does not bother to verbalize them.

We can expect simple authority to be effective in any one of the four situations just described; we can feel rather confident that the receiver will take the action we propose. Unfortunately, however, simple authority does not always produce a high level of contributions and wholeheartedness. (See the bottom graph in Diagram 7, p. 159). In fact, if the proposal falls into *either* of the *two widest* zones—habitual acceptance or indifference—and we use simple authority, the man will likely set his goal thus, "Do the job with the least possible effort and as quickly as possible, without regard to how well it is done." To him, doing the job well enough to "get by"— well enough to prove that he has done the job, but not at the top of his ability—is a better means of furthering his welfare than doing it carefully. He contributes at about 40 per cent of his ability. He sees no reason to "kill himself." Many employers complain that their employees always either respond in this way or have *very narrow* zones and contribute even less.

If the proposal falls into the *third*, or *expert*, zone—the one where the giver is the expert and the receiver the novice—he will also do the job and will probably try to do it as well as he can (better than in the first two situations). But he has to go about it blindly; he does not fully understand what he is doing and why, so his contributions are only moderately greater than in the first two cases, and certainly at a lower level than his real ability would indicate—perhaps at 60 or 75 per cent of his ability. But when the *fourth* situation exists, where the receiver has already accumulated and thought through a great many premises and has reached a decision identical with the giver's, we can expect him to do the job wholeheartedly and carry it out to the best of his ability. His inducements are very high; and in his mind the contributions he is asked to make seem relatively small; doing the job is fun.

It will be seen by referring to Diagram 7 (p. 159) that, as this widest zone of acceptance becomes narrower (that is, this zone of acceptance where simple authority can be employed), the receiver's wholeheartedness and his contributions to the company become higher. At the 75 per cent point on the zone of acceptance line, he is contributing very close to 100 per cent of his ability, or a "100 per cent amount."

SANCTIONS

Thus far in our discussion, we have been moving from the far right toward the left on the three graphs in Diagram 7. We shall continue doing so but shall omit *proof* for the moment and go on to *sanctions* and then to *rebellion*.

If it appears that the receiver will be quite reluctant to accept our proposal and act on it—in other words, if we expect a zone that is less than 25 per cent in width—we shall probably have to employ sanctions to gain acceptance. We can anticipate unwilling acceptance, accompanied by resentment. This is a case where most of the premises the receiver thinks of by himself point to unwanted consequences; he sees relatively few premises which tell him to carry out the proposal other than the rewards the giver will hand him if he accepts, or the penalties the giver will impose if he does not.

Sanctions are rewards or punishments meted out to the receiver by the giver at his discretion. They may not be stated in words; implied sanctions are almost as effective as outright statements. Almost every man in an organization carries some of these around in his pocket, and he can lay these on one side or the other of his receiver's inducement-contribution balance whenever he chooses. They are *not* the *normal* results inherent in, and flowing naturally from, the task in the company's means-end staircase which the receiver is asked to carry out. They are *extraneous,* often quite personal, rewards or penalties. The giver uses these at his discretion to gain conformance, knowing that they will have a strong impact on the receiver's personal goals.

That a superior has certain sanctions which he can place on his subordinate's scales is a familiar idea. At the time of his appointment, he was assigned the responsibility for handling a certain job. Coupled with that, usually, is the privilege of using sanctions to get the job done. He knows that if he uses these with discretion and within certain limits, his superiors will back him up. When it is warranted, he can praise or criticize a subordinate. In some cases, he can say or imply, "If you don't do what you're told, I'll get somebody who will," or "I'll see that you don't get a raise." He can also say, "If you do carry out my proposal, I'll help you to get that job you want." Incidentally, the sanctions used by the boss, together with *formally bestowed* authority, are what most people think of when they hear the word *authority*.

It is not so widely recognized that subordinates also carry sanctions around in their pockets and that they often employ them with telling effect on their superiors—a case of the exercise of authority upward in the hierarchy. Unions possess these sanctions; within limits, they can bestow or withhold rewards or inflict punishments; strikes, threats of strikes, and slowdowns can greatly influence the behavior of a company's executives. It is also true that *individuals* located far down in the hierarchy possess some very effective sanctions. They can reduce their contributions—the amount and quality of work they do for their boss, for instance—or they can criticize or even ostracize him; and they can do the same with any other man whom they are attempting to influence. Intermittent slowdowns, carelessness in handling equipment, and deliberate mistakes are examples of sanctions that are commonly used.

Unspoken or implied sanctions are just as real and compelling as spoken ones. When a man gives orders or commands, he usually indicates by his tone of voice that sanctions will be used if the receiver does not jump when told. Actually, the thought of possible sanctions also plays a role—though at times a minor one—when the zone of acceptance is wide and *simple* authority is being employed. But there, these sanctions are given little weight; whereas in a case where sanctions play the dominant role, they are given great weight by both the giver and the receiver.

Fear of possible punishment constitutes one of the chief reasons why some men are reluctant to make company decisions—why they often prefer to be guided by their boss's decisions. They are afraid that they will "catch hell" if they make a mistake; or they are afraid that their own decisions will be reversed by the boss. A man who is frequently forced to renege on his commitments or promises to others soon loses the respect of those men. What is more, he loses confidence in himself. Men also often take refuge in the company rules and regulations—accept and transmit the decisions set down in what they call "the book"—in order to make sure that their decisions will stand up.

A domineering, desk-pounding executive, given to stating his decisions with an air of finality in a brusque, loud voice, also implies that sanctions will be employed if the receivers do not accept without question. The receiver is cowed into keeping to himself the premises he believes are pertinent, premises he thinks point to a quite different decision. He knows that they will be brushed aside; the boss will not, even for a moment, play the role of receiver. The subordinate is afraid that if he does speak up, the boss will "get mad" and retaliate by withholding raises or promotions.[9] To my mind, the only satisfactory course of action open to a man with a boss of this kind is to begin a determined search for a new job, either in another department or in another company.

Nevertheless, the imposition of sanctions, or even an implied threat of sanctions, will often induce a receiver to take the action desired—provided, of course, that the threat is not an empty one. But unfortunately, the use of sanctions does not ensure that the job will be well done. Characteristically, the employment of sanctions induces a minimum of wholeheartedness and contributions to the company. (We are now looking at the *left-hand* end of the *bottom* graph in Diagram 7, p. 159). By using sanctions, a superior can command (and get) the physical presence of a man—can coerce him into spending his time at his desk or at his machine and going through certain motions. Sanctions are almost useless, however, as a means of motivating a man's *mind* and *spirit* to work in behalf of the company. A man usually cuts down on the work he does—on the quantity as well as the quality of his company decisions—when sanctions are employed. We have all seen instances of the very effective techniques used by an unwilling or resentful receiver in coping with a boss who tries to exact acceptance through sanctions. When a worker's inducements are reduced by his boss, he reduces his contributions accordingly.

Although an executive should think twice about possible unwanted consequences before deciding to employ sanctions, he should nevertheless use them unhesitatingly when he foresees that the receiver would otherwise rebel—when he knows that the receiver will *not* respond to simple authority or proof and he has not been able to create

---

[9] Quite a number of young executives, especially those in production departments, tell me their bosses act this way. Although further questioning sometimes reveals that some men simply imagine that their bosses would flare into anger if crossed, their conclusions seem frequently to be based upon solid premises.

an acceptable revision of his proposal. If the executive is to win and to maintain his leadership, he must make sure that the majority of his decisions are carried out.

There are some indications that sanctions will become less and less effective in the years to come. Labor legislation, the growth of labor unions, and grievance procedures are only three of several instruments fashioned by employees to limit the bosses' indiscriminate use of punishments. These, together with the wealth of job opportunities during periods of economic prosperity, are steadily reducing the effectiveness of sanctions. The recurrent criticism made by businessmen that "the help today is so independent that we can't get a lick of work out of them," whereas "in the old days, we could always get good help," is but one manifestation of these changing employee attitudes.

REBELLION—NO AUTHORITY

Rebellion, as we saw, lies outside the zone of acceptance, to the left of zero on our zone-of-acceptance continuum; this is the area where we measure the width of the zone in terms of "minus" percentages. Rebellion need not be elaborated on here, for we have already seen how it works and why people rebel. The receiver concludes that he should not carry out our proposal because, according to his premises and the weights he assigns them, his own future welfare (or the welfare of the group or the company to which he is loyal) would then be seriously imperiled. Not accepting is a more desirable alternative than accepting as a means of achieving the goals he has chosen. When we foresee rebellion as the reaction to our proposal, there is probably little we can do to gain acceptance.

To avoid failure in this case, the only alternative is to revise our proposal before mentioning it to the receiver. With a little extra forethought, it is often possible to revise an otherwise acceptable proposal, so that it will serve as an almost equally effective means of achieving the company's goals and at the same time further some of the receiver's goals.

In many instances the "arguments" (unwanted consequences) brought up by our receiver clearly indicate that he will not accept our proposal. But frequently, those who rebel keep quiet about their intentions; they conveniently forget to carry out the giver's proposal. Insubordination with the outward appearance of conformance is a widely practiced and subtle art. Coping with these pocket vetoes calls for considerable finesse. If we suspect that our superior is using a pocket veto, we are obliged to determine, without asking direct questions, whether he has decided to do nothing or has not yet gotten around to considering our proposal. If the receiver is our subordinate, we must think twice about trying to force compliance, because if he is actually rebelling, our attempt will doubtless prove abortive. Probably, in most cases, when we suspect the pocket veto is being used, we should quietly drop our proposal (surmising now that it was a mistake), and hope, by saying nothing, to let others know that we are willing to drop it. To retrieve our prestige and rewin the authority we have lost, we shall have to go back through the creative process to evolve a more suitable solution.

PROOF AS A TYPE OF AUTHORITY

So far, we have been dealing with those occasions when we anticipate that the receiver's zone of acceptance will be either very wide, quite narrow, or negative in width. But on most occasions, we predict that our receiver's zone will be of medium width—will extend to some point falling between 25 and 75 per cent on the zone-of-acceptance continuum. We believe that he will eventually accede, but he will want to know why before deciding about carrying out our wishes. According to Diagram 7 (p. 159), when this occurs, we shall find proof the appropriate type of authority. Proof is undoubtedly the most complex of the three types of authority and the most difficult to employ; hence, we are examining it last.

In using proof, we are attempting to change our receiver's mind. Our objective is to have him think *with us* and thus eventually conclude, on his own, that our proposal is both logical and desirable. We are explaining how it will work—describing the goal sought, and the wanted and unwanted consequences of adopting the proposal. We are inviting him to try out our decision in his own mind under our guidance. In presenting a new idea we have created, or one that is new to the receiver, proof is the most effective tool available for gaining acceptance. And it is almost the only tool we have for really convincing a man that he is wrong; simple authority and sanctions may produce the *appearance* of wholehearted conversion, but not the real thing.

One reason for the effectiveness of proof is that it crystallizes ideas in the receiver's mind. Ideas are undoubtedly the most powerful drives known to mankind; once an idea for a goal is clearly seen and it becomes evident that the goal will serve as a means of achieving some higher goal, a man's drives seem to be unleashed. Proof can be used to disclose goals the receiver had not glimpsed and to demonstrate that these goals can and should be achieved. Proof also enables the receiver to do his proposed job intelligently. A receiver who goes through the explanation with his giver becomes familiar with the details of the proposal and visualizes precisely what part he is to play in the new program—what means he is to provide. In addition, he can see how his new actions will be related to the new duties of his associates. The presence or absence of these niceties of integration in carrying out a program makes a great deal of difference in its eventual success. But the chief reason for using proof is that when it is successful, it produces wholehearted acceptance and a relatively high level of contributions. Proof discloses the many inducements that the new proposal affords. If the receiver really wishes to enjoy these inducements, he will automatically raise his contributions to the company.

The chief disadvantages are that proof requires much more time, forethought, and patience than either simple authority or sanctions. On the other hand, once proof has been established, the giver can thereafter save time—can employ simple authority (pull the trigger) when he next makes the same sort of proposal to the receiver. For as a result of this earlier use of proof, the receiver's zone of acceptance for that proposal is widened to a point just beyond 75 per cent; he already possesses the premises he needs for going ahead.

Breaking down this middle zone of acceptance into two zones, and dividing proof into two types—*easy proof* and *hard proof*—aids in employing proof effectively. Actually, however, this division is in one respect rather artificial, for we should really visualize all this as a continuum instead of as two distinct classifications: When the receiver's zone measures about 75 per cent in width, he will demand relatively little proof; but as this zone gradually narrows to 25 per cent in width, more and more proof will be required. Nevertheless, broadly speaking, if we anticipate that the receiver will ask for an explanation because he is eager to learn (a zone falling between 50 to 75 per cent), we can safely use *easy proof*. If, on the other hand, we predict that he will want to know why, because he questions the wisdom of the proposal (a zone 25 to 50 per cent in width—a case where he foresees several heavily weighted unwanted consequences), we must be prepared to use what we are calling *hard proof*.

Proof for the Receiver Who Is Eager to Learn—Easy Proof

If a receiver *wants* to learn what the giver (the expert) can teach him because he sees this as a means of achieving some of his goals, his zone will be quite wide—approaching 75 per cent. To him, learning why the company has decided to put out a new product, or why it should retrain its salesmen, or how to go about revising the layout of the desks in the office, serves as means of attaining his goals.

Generally, if we have correctly anticipated our receiver's response —perhaps by looking into the reservoirs from whence he draws his goals and premises—and have succeeded in revising our decision beforehand, so that it will further some of his own goals as well as the company's, the receiver's zone of acceptance will be quite wide (65 to 75 per cent); and our task is comparatively easy. All we need do is to unfold the new vista we have created in our own mind—take him up the staircase we have conceived.

Our first step is to describe the goals at the top of the staircase and explain the means and goals that will be needed for the lower steps. This would consist of describing the goals so clearly that the receiver can almost touch and smell them, and describing the staircase so concretely that the receiver can walk with us up to the goal. We are here carrying out the sixth stage of the creative process—communicating the new idea. He can now see exactly what actions must be taken and which duties he will have to perform when the proposal is put into effect. We may also mention two or three of the more obvious wanted consequences of adopting some of the means as well as the main decision. But we must be *sure* to show him the briars, rocks, and other barriers on the staircase—the *unwanted* consequences. Eventually, he will discover these for himself, anyway. If he is not prepared for them, he will lose a great deal of his enthusiasm as soon as they become apparent; and he will automatically reduce his contributions. But a receiver who has glimpsed the goals, tried out the steps on the staircase in his mind, and found them good in spite of the difficulties he has seen, will probably carry out the proposal wholeheartedly.[10]

We frequently assume that such a simple explanation of the goals and means will convert others to our way of thinking. In most cases, however, our associates, subordinates, and superiors are much less impressed with our new brain child than we; we discover that their zones are somewhat narrower than we had anticipated. If our initial description of the proposed goal and means has not convinced him, we shall be obliged to go further into proof—turn to a second approach, the problem-solving approach. Here, after completing the

---

[10] An understanding of the reservoirs a man draws upon not only helps us revise our proposal but it helps us to cut down the amount of time we must devote to gaining the man's acceptance through proof. For with his background in mind, we can see which aspects of the goals and means to emphasize and which ones to discard because they hold no interest for him.

first step, we go back a bit to the problem we set out to solve. Our task now is to secure agreement that this problem is an important one (that our failure to achieve the goal we are worried about will hurt us), that the means we have thus far been using to achieve that goal have proved ineffective (this caused the problem) and that, in view of the conditions we think the company will be facing in the period ahead, we believe the new means we are proposing should be adopted. Here, resolving the problem becomes the goal we both seek. In this second step, we point to other wanted consequences of adopting the proposed means, sketch in some of the lower goals on the staircase, and mention some of their wanted and unwanted consequences. Possibly by using the problem-solving approach, the receiver will begin to see the wisdom of the new proposal.

Actually, it is so difficult to make accurate estimates of the exact width of these two middle zones that it would be foolhardy to embark on easy proof before we are prepared to penetrate to a third level, in case this becomes necessary. Here, we offer the receiver several of the more important premises we considered when we first reached our decision, instead of naming only a few. When we penetrate to this third level, however, we are likely to leave him confused and impatient with the many details we are asking him to digest, so that it behooves us to keep these within bounds. One way is to present the premises in an orderly manner by grouping them according to the topics to which they relate, and stating the subconclusions we ourselves reached at the time we created the plan. We are already familiar with this procedure.[11] Or we might mention the factual premises first and present our value premises afterward. We might also try to reduce the number of premises by selecting and emphasizing those premises with which the man is most familiar, ones he derives from his heritage and work experience, and ones he is most likely to accept as reliable. What we are doing here is briefly presenting our subconclusions one by one, along with the main premises for these.

As long as the new goals and premises pictured by the giver are consonant with those the receiver has already seen and knows intimately, he will ordinarily accept them. But the moment he is offered goals or premises that seem incompatible with those he has already tested out and found good, a red flag goes up in his mind. When the new and old premises are inconsistent—when they do not square with

---

[11] We are here simply giving an oral report instead of a written one. For ideas about the form of such an oral report, see Appendix A (pp. 542–44).

one another, when they are in conflict—the executive runs into trouble. Here we have to employ *hard proof*.

Using Proof When the Receiver Questions the Wisdom of the Proposal—Hard Proof

Whereas in the preceding paragraphs we were trying to educate our receiver, here we are trying to re-educate him. We are aware that his zone will be comparatively narrow—25 to 50 per cent in width. We realize that he has already partially made up his mind about what he should do and that he will question our proposal; in fact, he may believe that he is somewhat more of an expert on the proposal than we. Our task is to change his mind by inducing him to accept the goals and means we think are important. When we are in the position of a subordinate and are trying to change our boss's mind, or when we are attempting to exercise authority over receivers on the same level as we, or those located diagonally upward, we must frequently resort to re-education. In an illustration used earlier, our cost accountant was endeavoring to re-educate the foreman of the machine shop. Re-education is also the chief task of salesmen and advertising men; they are always striving to change the behavior of some potential customer who has already partly made up his mind and who considers himself more of an expert than they in deciding what he *really* needs.

Inducing such a man to accept wholeheartedly a view that differs from his own obviously requires considerable sensitivity and perception. Once our receiver fixes in his mind some goals and premises he is sure are pertinent to the decision at hand, they are not easily dislodged. This is particularly true if he has already publicly committed himself to a proposal that differs from our own. In such cases, in trying to substitute our goals and premises for his, we have to be watchful to maintain his prestige and avoid making him look foolish. If he senses that his status is endangered, he will brush aside our premises, keep reiterating his old ones, and try to think up new premises pointing only to the wanted consequences of his original conclusion and the undesirable results of ours. His goals and premises may be trivial or invalid, but that is immaterial to him; more than that, he usually manages to think up new premises faster than we can break down his old ones. All chance of gaining his acceptance is lost when this occurs; the discussion turns into an argument. So the critical step in hard proof is to induce the receiver to reason his *own* way to the conclusion that certain of his goals and premises should be changed. It is essential that we establish an atmosphere of cooperative search for a solution; only then can we expect to gain his wholehearted acceptance. Obviously, the task of re-educating people should be essayed only after we have prepared carefully.

In offering *hard proof*, it is ordinarily necessary first to go through the three steps already described in connection with *easy proof*— (1) show the man our vision of the goal and the staircase; (2) get agreement that the problem is important and that the proposed means will not only solve it but will yield several other wanted consequences; and (3) set out in an orderly way the more obvious premises we used.

If we have not convinced him in the course of this presentation, we should by this time at least know the places where he became confused and the specific points with which he disagreed. He may say frankly that he does not understand, or he may vigorously question a statement; his facial expressions and tone of voice may be even more revealing. The giver must listen with both his ears and his eyes, and then make mental notes of the questions that trouble his receiver.

There are four approaches worth mentioning here as aids in clearing up misunderstanding and disagreements and thereby securing acceptance.[12] The first two approaches are amplifications of two that we have just used. One is to bring out the two or three alternatives and the very specific premises we considered in reaching our decision, then suggest he make a choice. As was noted in the chapter on the creative process, as decision makers we tend to throw away our premises once we have used them. They are no longer of any worth to us because we have already reached our conclusion. But our receiver is lost if he does not have these.[13] Unless we state the premises we used, our conclusions seem to him only glittering generalities pulled out of thin air.

---

[12] The two sections of this chapter dealing with proof (we are now in the second of the two) are closely tied up with problems of communication, which is the subject of Chapter 8. About midway through that chapter (pp. 222–23), we shall investigate several barriers to communication. Perhaps the reader will want to glance at those now. They supplement the ones mentioned here.

[13] Curiously enough, we usually write down and preserve the mathematical computations, that is, the arithmetic or factual premises we use in reaching an answer to a problem, especially if we intend to prove to another that our conclusion is correct; yet we seldom bother to make notes of the value premises we use at the time we make a complex decision, even though they are much harder to reconstruct afterwards and much more difficult for others to comprehend. Recall in this connection our earlier emphasis on note taking.

Secondly, here, even more than when we are employing *easy proof,* it is necessary to organize our premises into three or four homogeneous groups with subconclusions for each. If we present our premises in an orderly way, the receiver can afterward remember our three or four subconclusions—tick them off on his fingers—and these, in turn, help him to recall several of our premises. As a consequence, he is able to recheck the decision later, and he can (if he accepts the decision) explain to others why he agrees.

A third way to avoid confusion and disagreement is to maintain control and direction of the discussion. We must be careful to keep on the topic under discussion. This is often difficult because receivers frequently interrupt with questions; and these, in turn, lead into irrelevant bypaths. In this connection, it helps to mention that we plan to investigate one segment of the problem at a time—item A first (and hold to that one until it has been explored) and then go on to the next, item B, and finally to item C. If we fail to keep to the subject, there is little chance of getting anything accomplished. Moreover, if we fail to direct and control the discussion, it frequently turns into an argument. Our purpose is not to conduct a debate. As mentioned earlier, when a discussion degenerates into an attempt by each man to think up arguments—premises—that support only his own point of view, all chance of success is lost. We should so set the stage that the receiver recognizes that the two of us are exploring the problem together—thinking together—each one contributing premises that are pertinent, regardless of whether they are "for" or "against" our own preconceived point of view.

Finally, after presenting our proposal and mentally noting the points of disagreement, it is helpful to restate and emphasize the points of agreement. The ultimate and intermediate goals which we both have in mind need *not* necessarily be identical, but we do need to agree that the proposed means will advance whatever goals we each have in mind. The questions at issue, then, are (1) whether the proposed means will advance our respective goals and (2) whether, when the wanted and unwanted side-effects on the other goals are brought into the picture, this proposal is the most desirable alternative.

So eventually, the problem of using hard proof resolves itself into the task of getting agreement on the goals and reappraising the premises we have both been using. Our job is to correct any invalid premises the receiver may have been using and to recheck the reliability of our own with his help. The factual premises can be checked rather quickly. The main problems are to reach agreement on the reliability of the value premises and the weights we each assign the factual and value premises. In the chapter on the use of premises in decision making, we spent a good deal of time on this task, so that it is now a familiar one. We, as the giver, cannot assume that we have a corner on the premises, nor that our value premises are the only reliable and important ones. The testing of premises calls for a certain amount of humility on our part. This brief discussion completes our investigation of the use of hard proof.

In these pages, we have been exploring the use of proof in gaining the acceptance of an *individual* receiver. Frequently, however, we are confronted with the task of inducing a committee or some other *group* to accept a proposal. If we anticipate that the men's zone of acceptance will be medium in width, it is advisable to present our proof informally to some of the individuals *prior* to the meeting instead of waiting to present it "cold" at a formal group meeting. The first man to approach would be the one most likely to suspend disbelief while we are explaining our salient premises and conclusions. After correcting the weaknesses in our proposal which are brought to light in this discussion, we can then introduce the idea to two or three other open-minded men in the hope that after hearing our story, they too will make suggestions and eventually agree with us. (This is a refinement of the "rechecking" and "communication" stages of the creative process.) By this time, most of the "bugs" in the proposal will have been discovered and removed; we are now in a position to present it at the formal session with considerable confidence of its acceptance.

That proof is difficult to achieve and requires time and patience is not to be doubted. Yet, without the use of proof, probably no company would last very long. The contributions made to a company whose executives depend solely on simple authority and sanctions to influence people's behavior would be very small indeed. The benefits of proof are so great that it is ordinarily worth the extra trouble to employ this approach. No one can expect to be immediately successful in every attempt, but it may be consoling to realize that we are not the only ones who fail once in a while. Stories of the problems encountered by the creators of some of the world's most magnificent ideas—those of Christ or Socrates, for example—testify to the difficulty of re-educating people. Many great scientists—Galileo, for instance—also encountered resistance. That their newly created hypotheses were ultimately accepted after proof had accumulated testifies to the slow but sure success of this method of gaining acceptance. Most executives can recall instances of company proposals that were shelved when first presented, yet were eventually accepted, the result of the gradual impact of proof.

In this chapter, our attention has been centered on the task of influencing the behavior of others. It should be re-emphasized that the three tools we have investigated are supposed to be used *before* we make our proposal. We are *imagining* that we have made the proposal and are now estimating the width of the receiver's zone of acceptance, choosing the type of authority which will induce him to carry it out, and anticipating the amount of his wholeheartedness and contributions after he has added to his original premises the new ones he picks up when he hears what we say to him and how we say it. The salient features of the chapter are summarized in Diagram 7 (p. 159), so that these need not be repeated here.

But nowhere have we called attention to the idea that after we have exercised the appropriate type of authority, a receiver's zone of acceptance for a proposal may widen. If, through the use of either easy or hard proof we succeed in convincing a receiver with a narrow zone that he should accept a proposal, he automatically moves toward the trigger zone. He now has most of the pertinent premises and since the preponderance of these point to accepting, we can expect him to work at perhaps 80 or 90 per cent of his capacity when he carries out the proposal. Revising the proposal when we foresee rebellion may also induce him to widen his zone for a course of action that will help the company. But it is rather doubtful if the use of rewards or punishments will effectuate such a change. To reduce stresses and conflicts in the department, we should like most of our proposals to fall into either the trigger zone or the zone where the receiver is eager to learn. Yet as we saw, this course produces some unwanted consequences; without conflict, a group usually becomes self-satisfied.

Additionally, we should underline the idea that regardless of which type of authority is employed, the receiver must feel convinced *after* the authority has been inserted in the picture that behaving as proposed is a *logical* (rational) move for him. After visualizing the sanctions that may be thrown into his inducement or contribution columns, it must seem logical to him to allow the giver to guide his behavior. He must feel the same way after proof has been offered or after simple authority has been employed. If the proposed course of action seems illogical to the receiver after considering his own original premises and those he formed from what the giver says, he simply rebels—conveniently forgets or openly refuses. When this occurs, the giver is further away from his immediate objective of guiding the receiver's behavior than if he had made no attempt.

We can also anticipate failure if we try to use the wrong type of authority. If we employ simple authority where proof or sanctions are called for, we can expect rebellion; the same thing will occur when sanctions are necessary and we attempt to use proof. Furthermore, if we make a practice of using sanctions (punishments in particular) when the size of our receiver's zone calls for simple authority or proof, we shall also *eventually* find ourselves confronted with rebellion. Our receiver grows more and more irritated with these unnecessary commands and their undertone of threats. Each time we attempt to exercise authority and fail, we lose ground in our endeavors to win leadership.

This chapter provides a foundation for the next one, the chapter on leadership. It is also closely connected with the succeeding chapter on communication. Much of our success in gaining leadership depends upon our ability to employ authority; and if we are to exercise authority, we must be able to communicate our goals and premises to others. Clearly, this authority subsystem is closely tied up with subsystems yet to be explored, as well as those we opened up in Part I.

PROBLEM
EXERCISING AUTHORITY

The president of Gould Metal Company, Mr. James Gould, had recently found that his work load was growing too heavy.* To get some relief, he was considering several courses of action, among them the creation of a new office, vice-president of sales, and the selection for this position of a man capable of assuming full responsibility for planning and carrying out an aggressive sales program. He had in mind two men, both already executives in the sales department—Mr. Nicholas Willard, sales manager of the aircraft sales department, and Mr. Eugene Hemple, sales manager of the department which sold flexible metal tubing and expansion-compensating devices. Mr. Gould had worked closely with these men over a period of several years; hence he knew their strengths and shortcomings quite thoroughly. Nevertheless, he was not yet sure whether either man would be capable of handling the heavy responsibilities of the new office.

Since its founding at the turn of the century, Gould Metal Company had established a reputation as a leading manufacturer of flexible metal devices and ducts. These units were accordian-like pieces of thin-walled tubing employed as joints, elbows, or connecting links in pipes used for carrying liquids

* All the names and certain of the facts in this case have been disguised.

such as oil, water, and chemicals, and gases such as air, steam, and exhaust fumes. If required, these could be designed to withstand high pressures, high temperatures, and corrosive action. The units were used to connect up two misaligned pipes, to compensate for contraction and expansion in pipe lines, to permit necessary vibrations at the connection between two pipes, and to carry liquids or gases from a stationary pipe to a moving part of a machine. The company offered its line in bronze, steel, stainless steel, and other alloys, and in a variety of sizes, weights, shapes, and strengths.

Gould sold these devices to a wide range of manufacturers. Among these were producers of machine tools, oil burners, dry cleaning, pressing, and laundry equipment, diesel and other stationary engines, air or gas compressors; and manufacturers of heavy equipment for the oil, chemical, and paper industries. These industries were served by Mr. Hemple's organization; together they accounted for about half the sales. The company also sold to manufacturers of aircraft and missiles which were served by Mr. Willard's organization; they accounted for about 40 per cent of the sales. Most of the orders were for custom-made items designed and fabricated to each customer's specifications. The orders usually called for between 5 and 500 units. The company also manufactured a few standard metal hoses and bellows and carried them in stock; these brought in about 10 per cent of the sales.

During World War II and the Korean War, the company had expanded rapidly, largely the result of subcontracts for flexible tubing, joints, and ducts used in military equipment. One year the sales had amounted to $9,000,000. By 1954, however, sales dropped substantially and losses began to mount alarmingly. Business improved somewhat in 1955 and 1956 but again turned down in 1957. Finally, in 1958, to insure the survival of the company, Mr. Gould decided to retrench sharply. Some men—especially the middle-level executives, supervisory personnel, and engineers—seeing the company's plight, left of their own accord; others, including workers in the manufacturing department, were dismissed. Mr. Gould felt that the men and women who remained were reasonably good employees but he thought that morale, which had dropped precipitously as a result of this shake-up, was not yet back to par.

After 1958, sales again improved and with the reduction in overhead expenses, the company managed to show either a small profit or a small deficit. Nevertheless, Mr. Gould was uneasy; the low profits worried him of course; but what troubled him most was that the company was no longer getting its previous share of the available business.

The chief problem seemed to lie in the sales department, the department with which Mr. Gould normally identified himself. A nephew of the founder, he had started his career as a salesman for the company, then after a few years of seasoning was appointed sales manager. After 1937 when Mr. Gould was elected to the presidency, this post had remained vacant; however, he continued to carry the responsibility for the sales department work and to make most of the decisions.

Mr. Willard and Mr. Hemple reported directly to him. Both had started out as office salesmen, were then sent on the road as field sales engineers and after gaining experience as field sales supervisors in charge of branch offices, had been brought into the central office to handle the administrative sales work.

The field sales engineers of Mr. Willard's department worked as closely as possible with the design engineers of the aircraft and missile companies to make sure that Gould Metal Company had an opportunity to bid on the very complex and highly specialized duct work used in the engines and fuselage. The specifications and designs were closely guarded secrets, and included rigid specifications requiring careful machining and hand work.

Mr. Hemple's field sales engineers tried to induce OEM's (original equipment manufacturers) to install the company's hoses and bellows in the equipment they produced and sold. For instance, one man was currently trying to get the design engineers of a kitchen gas range manufacturer to adopt Gould bellows; apparently he was making only moderate progress. The men also worked with mill supply houses and other distributors, showing their salesmen how to sell standard hose—and sometimes the simpler bellows and expansion joints—to small users, mostly maintainance departments of manufacturing companies which needed repair parts quickly and bought infrequently.

Besides supervising the field sales engineers, the two sales managers supervised their office salesmen, a group of younger, less experienced men. Each office salesman was paired with a field sales engineer and acted as that outside man's alter ego in the central office.

The two sales managers frequently sought advice from Mr. Gould. They did this in part because Mr. Gould usually had some quite practical suggestions. But a more important reason for adopting this practice was their fear that they would make a wrong decision and that it would be reversed. They saw one another several times a day and often talked over their more difficult problems; at these sessions their usual procedure was to conceive three or four possible solutions then try to determine which one would be best, all things considered.

Usually, Mr. Gould took the lead in proposing new plans. Sometimes, however, if Mr. Gould were ignoring an acute problem, the two men would take the initiative; together they would work out and recommend a course of action and explain to Mr. Gould why they advocated it. For instance, one day the two went to Mr. Gould with a proposal for raising the salaries of the office salesmen. They knew this was not included in the current budget, but they explained that the turnover among these men was so high, the problems of training the men to handle the work were so great, and the losses in company reputation from an inexperienced man's mistakes were so serious that it would pay to raise the salary scale. In addition, they showed a tabulation of the men's present salaries, salaries for comparable jobs mentioned in newspaper help-wanted ads, a list of the proposed salaries, the extra cost per year, and a suggestion for a specific salary schedule. At the end of their presentation, Mr. Gould asked them whether this proposal would fit in with the company-wide job classifications and salary schedules, and if not, what would occur in the other departments if it were adopted. When they admitted they had not thought about this side-effect, he suggested they talk with the personnel man.

As already indicated, Mr. Gould made the decisions that his two sales managers brought to him, and in addition he worked out new sales plans. To get action on these he would call formal meetings of the Sales Executive Council, made up of himself, as chairman, the two product sales managers, and Mr. Mack, the advertising manager. His written notice of the meeting was always accompanied by an agenda listing 20 or 30 items. Everyone was free to suggest an item but virtually all the topics were Mr. Gould's. The meetings lasted for two hours and because of the pressure of time, they moved very fast. Mr. Gould would ask for comments on an agenda item then put it to a vote.

At one such meeting, a quite typical one, Mr. Gould proposed that new distributors for the standard metal hoses should be lined up in the Pacific Northwest. Mr. Hemple, seeing that a response was expected, said, with some hesitation, that he thought this a very good idea and Mr. Willard and Mr. Mack nodded concurrence. Mr. Gould then remarked, "Well, that's decided. Now Hemple, go after Merle (the salesman in that territory) and get him started. Report back to this committee a month from today. I'll make a note to put your report on our agenda for that date."

Later, after this particular meeting, Mr. Hemple told Mr. Willard that he doubted if he should speak to Merle about the boss' proposal. "Merle could do the job all right, but I have already piled a lot of tough and urgent jobs on him—enough to keep him running for the next three months. Anyway, the Chief and I have badgered him so much lately that I'm afraid he'll get discouraged and quit."

The next item on the meeting's agenda read "Booklet for the Marine Market." Mr. Gould immediately assigned Mr. Mack the task of writing the copy and designing a layout for presentation to the committee by the middle of next month. The other items were covered and disposed of in a similar fashion.

At these meetings each member of the committee reported on his own department's progress and new sales plans. And the president also told the men about new developments elsewhere in the company, particularly changes in the practices of other departments. For instance, at this particular meeting, he reported that the manufacturing department had tightened its inspection procedures, and the accounting department had changed certain of its standard practice instructions (known as SPI's). He also said that the engineering department would have its newly designed metal corrugating equipment ready in about a month and that the company's purchasing agent had been instructed to reduce raw material inventories by about 20 per cent in the next 60 days in order to rebuild the company's bank balance and reduce accounts payable.

In addition, he pointed out that the factory was getting far behind on deliveries. He further reported that in an effort to improve deliveries he had told the production manager to use whatever pressure was needed to get the orders out. This, he told the committee, was followed by a slowdown in the plant. Thereupon, he had called the business agent of the union and asked the agent to "get after the boys"—that the men were violating the no-strike, no-slowdown clause in the labor contract. The agent said he would look into the matter, but Mr. Gould observed that production seemed to be slower than ever.

At the end of the meeting, he examined his date book and asked if a meeting on Thursday the nineteenth would be agreeable.

To secure new business, Mr. Mack prepared advertisements which were regularly run in trade magazines. He selected those which were normally read by design engineers and maintenance men in the industries which could profitably use flexible hose and bellows. Typically, these advertisements illustrated how manufacturers could use hoses or expansion joints, described the advantages of Gould's units, and urged the reader to write for engineering advice on his problems. When an inquiry came in, the office salesman for that territory dictated a letter of acknowledgment, sent a marked catalogue, and forwarded a copy of his letter to his field sales engineer in the territory.

If the lead looked promising, a sales engineer would call when next in the vicinity. But the sales engineers secured most of their leads from conversations with other salesmen in the territory, men whom they met in waiting rooms who sold supplies or equipment to manufacturers which were likely prospects for Gould products. At times they would also make "cold" calls on what they thought might prove a promising account. And once in a while Mr. Willard or Mr. Hemple sent them detailed information about a company which looked like a good new prospect. These leads forwarded by their sales managers had proved uniformly good.

Finding new prospects, the task just described, was probably the sales engineers' crucial task. However, it was only the beginning; lining up an order demanded careful work on the part of several men. Over the years, Mr. Gould and the sales managers had evolved the following procedure for securing and handling orders:

1. Upon finding a company which could use a Gould product, the sales engineer first located the men in the company who actually decided which supplier's hose or bellows to buy.

2. He would then try to determine the problems that troubled the prospective customer—particularly the shortcomings of the customer's present methods of coping with the problems—learn what standards or requirements the unit would have to meet, and on the basis of this, decide whether Gould could solve the problem, and (if the answer was "yes"), determine which type of unit to recommend.

3. He next tried to induce the prospect to give him a formal request for specifications, blueprints, and a price quotation for this unit that he had recommended. To do this, he normally had to explain in detail the advantages of the proposed Gould unit and convince the prospect that he could depend on the company to fulfill its promises. (This step, and No. 2, usually required considerable finesse, especially if the prospect had never heard of Gould or had once placed an order and was dissatisfied with the way Gould had handled it.)

4. Thereafter, he forwarded the prospect's formal request for a quotation, together with the necessary specifications, the requested delivery date, and any other pertinent information to the office salesman, or, if it was a good-sized bid, to his sales manager; they, in turn, passed

it to the engineering division where a design engineer worked out a detailed design, prepared drawings and specifications, and listed the parts and materials required.

5. This information was then sent to the production department for estimates of labor time and machine time and a suggested delivery date in case the buyer accepted the bid.

6. These accumulated data were all sent to the cost estimating department where the out-of-pocket costs were computed and flat percentage markups for overhead and profit were added, using standard percentages determined by Mr. Gould and the two sales managers.

7. Finally, the office salesman received all these data. On the basis of prices recently secured for similar orders, the information supplied by salesmen about competitors' prices, and the importance to Gould of securing this particular order, the office salesman (or more likely, his sales manager) would determine a price to quote. This usually differed from the price computed in No. 6. The sales manager was required to review only quotations of over $500, but the office salesmen were often uncertain about the price to quote and accordingly the sales manager ended up setting most of the prices.

8. If the order was small, the office salesman mailed the quotation to the prospect; but if large, he sent it to the sales engineer who presented it in person. In the latter case, the sales engineer was taught to feel out the customer before presenting the bid; if he suspected that the price was too high, he would call his sales manager and talk over the possibility of a lower offer. This task of price negotiation required a high level of sophistication.

9. If the customer accepted the bid, the production planning department inserted the new order in its production schedule for delivery on the date agreed upon.

10. The office salesman, and possibly the customer, the sales engineer, and the sales manager followed up to insure delivery as promised.

Of the sixteen field sales engineers, two had worked for the company since 1946; most of the others had been hired within the past three or four years. All but three or four could now handle their part of this ten-point sales program quite effectively, as a result of the constant stream of help and advice that they had received from their respective sales managers over the years. Nevertheless, they still frequently forgot to send their design engineers some of the essential specifications that the new unit would have to meet.

These sales engineers looked upon their sales managers as highly skilled salesmen and gladly took their bosses' suggestions. These salesmen also recognized that Mr. Hemple and Mr. Willard consistently fought the salesmen's battles in the home office. For instance, when prompt delivery was necessary to secure an attractive order, or when an overdue order was needed immediately by an irate customer, the sales managers would work with the factory men to secure special concessions on delivery dates.

The sales managers were plagued by many problems. The most pervasive was broken delivery promises. Very few orders were shipped on time even though the factory allowed itself 10 or 15 weeks for delivery. Both men spent an hour or two each day either talking in person or on the phone with the production manager, trying to persuade him to work out new schedules and dates that would keep the customers partially satisfied. The production manager and the sales managers were frequently at loggerheads; the production manager complained that as a result of the sales managers' frequent changes in priorities, his production schedules had to be completely recast every few days, his costs were unbelievably high, and his department was getting further behind than ever in its deliveries. The office salesmen spent even more time than the sales managers on the tasks of expediting orders and coordinating the necessary revisions in shipping instruction occasioned by the delays. When they could not get satisfaction from the factory scheduling department, they would ask their sales manager to handle the problem. They usually received several phone calls each day from customers and salesmen, inquiring about delivery dates.

Equally troublesome were the two problems of training the office salesmen to make wise decisions and building their self-confidence. Most of these men had recently attended college and were hired with the promise of jobs as field sales engineers. The newer men learned the office salesmen's duties from the more experienced men in the group. The latter not only helped the less experienced but acted as informal assistants to the sales managers, and handled the more important accounts. The office salesmen also used as a guide an office salesman's manual that had been prepared for the company by a marketing consultant; this explained methods of dealing with many of the more common problems they encountered. They were given no formal training because the work load—especially the stream of pressing telephone calls and letters—was so heavy that no one felt free to take time out for meetings. The sales managers knew that the men at times made ill-conceived decisions, some of which were costly. However, the chances of really serious mistakes were reduced because the men avoided the difficult decisions by giving their bosses the correspondence and memos which related to those decisions which they knew they were not capable of making; they also handed over many of the complicated problems that demanded more than usual care and analysis before a decision could be made. But as a consequence of this practice, there was always a thick pile of unfinished work on the desks of both sales managers; and Mr. Hemple's in particular, grew thicker as the week progressed, even though he took home a sheaf of the most urgent problems each night. Over the weekend, he would try to catch up.

Both sales managers were vaguely aware that they were being appraised. And they also knew, from comments made by Mr. Gould, that he hoped to delegate authority to someone. Mr. Hemple sensed that the president was sometimes irked with him; this, he thought, stemmed from the fact that he was reluctant to make major decisions, that he had made a few rather bad mistakes, and he was usually behind in his work. He once confessed to Mr. Willard, after a few too many cocktails, that he was fearful of being fired. Mr. Willard felt somewhat the same way, but was more self-confident; he thought his decisions stood up fairly well when looked at in retrospect but he was not always able to take the initiative in decision making. Nor was he as successful as he would have liked in conceiving plans for getting more business and gaining the support of the president for these plans.

Mr Gould believed that his need to be relieved of pressure—particularly of the task of conceiving improved sales plans and carrying them out—was so urgent that he should decide about a vice-president of sales within the next two or three weeks.

1. Give three examples from this case of the use (or attempted use) of authority—first, where simple authority was employed; second, when the implied or outright threat of sanctions was dominant; and third, where proof was employed. (In the case, there are 20 or more examples of the use—or attempted use—of authority.) Try to choose one instance, at least, which was an attempt to exercise authority "upward," and one that was unsuccessful. If you wish, combine Part 1 and Parts 2a and 2b in your report.

2. *a*) For each of these three examples, name the proposal the giver is making to the receiver; name the giver and the receiver; and indicate the type of authority each giver was trying to use.

   b) In each instance, explain why you concluded that the example is an illustration of simple authority, or proof, or sanctions, by comparing it with our definitions of these terms.

3. Take one of the three examples you have chosen; imagine that, as yet, nothing has been said to the receiver about the proposal; and try to anticipate what the receiver's first response would be to the proposal, thus:

   a) List a few of the premises (according to wanted and unwanted consequences) that would occur to the receiver when he first learns of this proposal and the weights he would probably assign them.

   b) In view of the premises you listed in Part 3a, and the way you believe the receiver would weight each of them, what is your estimate of the width of the receiver's zone of acceptance for that proposal? Explain briefly the reasoning that lies beneath your estimate.

4. In the light of your answer to Part 3b, and the type of authority *actually* employed by the giver, predict the amount of the receiver's wholeheartedness in carrying out the proposal. Explain how you reached your conclusion.

5. What type of authority would *you* have used had *you* been the giver in the example you have examined? Why?

Chapter 7   LEADERSHIP

THIS CHAPTER on leadership grows out of, and is to be read as an integral part of, the other chapters in this book. What we shall explore here should not be looked upon as a separate and exhaustive treatment of leadership. For, in reality, this entire book is devoted to various phases of achieving leadership; a successful executive must of necessity be a leader. This discussion simply brings together and utilizes a few of the concepts we are investigating and throws a somewhat different emphasis on some of them.

As already indicated, leadership is closely tied up with the authority concept we have been using. There is no clear line separating the two. Nevertheless, we can distinguish between them. When we use the term *authority,* we are thinking about spasmodic reciprocal attempts of individuals to guide each other's behavior. In contrast, *leadership* consists of a continuing series of successful attempts by one person to influence the behavior of a group.

A man gradually wins leadership by successfully exercising authority on many occasions. Individuals accept a man *wholeheartedly* as their leader only after he has repeatedly and successfully used proof, and in this way has established the idea in the men's minds that he is more capable of making decisions than they. After this has occurred many times, the men gradually widen their zones of acceptance to a point where most of the leader's proposals fall into what we called the *trigger zone.* In fact, some of his receivers (we shall frequently call the receivers *followers* in this chapter) may eventually adopt even wider zones for virtually all his proposals. Using his past successes as a basis, they may conclude that they should automatically and habitually allow him to guide their behavior. Others may become his followers because the proposals are a matter of indifference to them, or because they were taught to obey, or because blindly accepting the leader's proposals is much easier than thinking through the problem and conceiving a solution by themselves. Securing leadership solely through the use of sanctions is a risky business, for this—especially the use of punishments—often ultimately leads to rebellion. Captain Bligh, in Nordoff and Hall's novel, *Mutiny on the Bounty*, provides an interesting example of such rebellion.

But once a follower has chosen his leader, he is anxious to be proud of him. A follower enjoys bragging about his leader to his family, relatives, and friends. In fact, a man who is very loyal to his leader will defend him vehemently against any criticism. His own status grows each time he proves to others that his leader foresaw everything, and that his leader's decisions were brilliant ones. His own judgment in accepting the leader is vindicated; and, in addition, his own future is assured.

Ordinarily, we observe and study leaders after they have achieved great prestige; we attempt in this way to find out how they manage to wield their power over their followers. But no man steps into the leader's chair at one stride. Even political dictators, such as those who periodically rise to dominate nations, begin their careers by gradually winning leadership over a small group. In this case the members eventually become fanatical followers; these loyal men accept the leader's proposals without question and carry them out with blind zeal. To gain the pinnacle of dictatorial domination of a people, such a leader customarily uses this loyal group as an instrument for threatening punishment or offering rewards to other groups as means of gaining nation-wide acceptance of his proposals, for the purpose of eventually gaining the unquestioning(?) obedience of an entire people. A dictator is an example of one type of leader. Our discussion will be confined to leadership in a company and to leadership based on the wholehearted consent of the governed.

Leadership is admittedly a difficult thing to pin down. Many writers have attempted to probe the reasons why one man becomes a leader and another does not; and many men have attempted to explain how to go about becoming a leader, but relatively little is known about this subject.[1] Nevertheless, in the preceding chapters,

---

[1] Sometimes, writers on the subject offer platitudes or write in such vague, general terms that the reader is left unsatisfied. Indeed, this chapter may strike the reader in the same way, especially if the general statements and terminology used here fail to evoke visual images of the specific concepts we probed in the earlier chapters. Sociologists have made substantial contributions to the understanding of this subject. *Studies in Leadership: Leadership and Democratic Action*, Alvin W. Gouldner (ed.) (New York: Harper & Bros., 1950), is a collection of studies prepared by some thirty-four sociologists; most of the studies are based on the various writers' own observations of leaders at work in particular organizations. George C. Homans, *The Human Group* (New York: Harcourt, Brace & Co., 1950), chap. 16, provides a summary of another sociologist's conclusions about the task of a leader, conclusions based on studies of leaders in five quite diverse types of organizations. Also see Chester I. Barnard, *Organization and Management* (Cam-
(*Footnote continued on next page.*)

we have been accumulating ideas that may help us open up the question.

We can make a few useful generalizations about the type of person a leader is, but we should recognize that leaders rise in response to particular situations and they lead a particular group of people. This is as true of executive leaders as of others. To meet the needs of these groups and the needs of the company, executive leaders are obliged to behave in a variety of ways. Members of the following groups would each require a different type of leader: a group of day laborers; the editors in a book publishing house; a group of research and development people; a group of skilled machinists; a group of business executives.

Not only do the groups call for different types of leaders, but a particular leader will vary the type of authority he uses to fit the particular situation. On occasion, he may employ sanctions—act in an authoritarian manner, use a substantial amount of direction and control—in an effort to further the goals of his group. But for projects where he believes his followers are capable of making reasonably good decisions, he may use the permissive or laissez-faire type of leadership—exercise very little direction and control. In another situation—for instance, where the group is beset by a problem that requires premises from all the members—he may employ democratic leadership, encourage the group to make decisions with him as a partner. Moreover, there are degrees of leadership; as we shall see when we study informal groups, a group may have its chief leader, but it also has lesser leaders. And in one type of situation one man in the group may assume leadership and in other situations other men may become the group's leader. Evidently, we must be chary of generalizations about the characteristics or traits of leaders or which type of leadership is best.

Yet as long as we keep in mind the heterogeneity of leaders and their tasks we can safely frame some generalizations. In this chapter,

bridge: Harvard University Press, 1949), chap. iv, and Chris Argyris, *Personality and Organization* (New York: Harper & Brothers, 1957), chap. viii, both of which throw light on leadership. Conclusions based on long-term studies of leadership are set out in Carroll Shartle, *Executive Performance and Leadership* (Englewood Cliffs, N.J.: Prentice-Hall, Inc., 1956), and in Robert Tannenbaum, Irving R. Meschler, and Fred Massarik, *Leadership and Organization* (New York: McGraw-Hill Book Co., Inc., 1961). Philip Selznick, *Leadership in Administration* (Evanston: Row, Peterson and Co., 1957), is an easily read book which provides substantial insight. For an excellent brief summary of the chief leadership concepts, see Warren G. Bennis, "The Revisionist Theory of Leadership," *Harvard Business Review*, Vol. 39, No. 1 (January–February, 1961). The idea of three types of leadership—authoritarian, laissez faire, and democratic—briefly mentioned later in this chapter is used as a framework by many students of leadership.

we shall first examine three aptitudes that a leader seems to need. Then, after noting that a man may try to use status symbols, formal authority, social position, and wealth as methods of acquiring leadership, we shall look into six methods of winning leadership. Finally, we shall touch on reasons why some men fail to win leadership. These concepts make up our second subsystem of Part II. Bear in mind that we are here primarily interested in executive leadership.

SOME APTITUDES OF LEADERS

Some people seem to have unconsciously developed certain aptitudes which appear to be associated with leadership. We shall look into three. But be aware that we do not know whether these are the most important ones, though common observation would indicate they stand high. Moreover, we have no way of proving that these aptitudes will bring about leadership nor that the greater our aptitude in these four fields, the greater will be our success as a leader; these three may help cause the result (leadership), but the causal connections are all predominantly value.

Aptitude for Creating Ideas for Goals and Means

First, a leader usually has a flair for creating ideas for realistic goals and means that his followers will accept with enthusiasm, goals that will stir their blood. He is out in front of his followers looking toward the horizon and disclosing new vistas. He should also have a gift for crystallizing their aspirations in words and conceiving plans for realizing them. These are essentials whether he is acting as a leader of a street-corner gang or of a nation, the leader of a small section or a department in a company, or its president. By foreseeing the nature of his group's future environment, finding therein a niche in which his group can flourish, then going a step further and proposing a set of staircases for filling that niche well, and supplying the members of his group with the premises he used in choosing the proposed goal and means, he provides them with a basis for believing that the goal on the horizon can really be theirs.[2] From the foregoing, it is evident that a leader must spend a great deal of his time living in the future.

Yet he also needs skill in setting goals that will *conserve* the group even while changing it. Frequently, this includes ideas for warding off threats from outsiders. And to preserve the group, he may, at

---

[2] The tasks described in this sentence will be discussed in Part III, "Planning and Putting Plans into Effect."

times, have to be a realist and reconcile the group's goals and the company's goals, or more accurately, create ideas for means which will further the goals of both. For the men in the group know that if they make but little contribution to the company, they will soon be out of a job. A leader will be accepted to the extent that he helps his followers further their welfare.

An Aptitude for Believing His Group Can Flourish

A leader must *care*. He should feel confident that his group's, or his section's, his department's, or his company's niche is important —that filling it well will serve as a means of furthering some very desirable ultimate goals—and that by changing his men's activities in certain ways, his group can fill that niche. He must see his group's goal clearly, feel convinced that it is attainable, and want intensely to achieve that goal; he is forever thinking and talking about it, and creating ideas for new and more effective means of realizing it. But more than that, he shows his followers that he expects them to work to their full capacity in behalf of the group's goals. If he is indifferent, they will be indifferent. If he is unsure, they will be unsure.

And perhaps the drive we thought accounted in part for a man's creativity also induces a man to seek leadership. In this instance, he is winning the approval of others by showing a dedication to the group. A leader with strong drives will carry on despite disappointments; he is willing to live with the frustrations of only partial success, or even defeat. A leader with a strong sense of mission will, when defeated, learn from his mistakes and start anew to fulfill his mission.

An Aptitude for Making Things Happen

He has a flair for carrying through. "Taking charge," taking the initiative in carrying out the group's activities, seems a quite normal procedure to him in view of his aptitude for conceiving goals for the group and his sense of mission in carrying them out.

An aptitude for gaining acceptance of his proposals—educating and re-educating his followers, or more generally speaking, a flair for choosing the type of authority appropriate to the particular receiver(s) and the particular situation(s)—serves as a very effective means of making things happen. Equally important, if he is to carry out his group's goals, he needs to be adept at exercising authority over those people *outside* his group who worry for fear they might be hurt by his proposed changes.

He must be willing to carry out the plan in the face of indifference or even active opposition. Seldom will all the members of his group agree that all the plans he proposes are always the best ones available. Nor will all his receivers always deem these to be the most effective means of achieving their own personal goals. Moreover, gaining wholehearted acceptance is frequently a slow process—the receivers often need months to think through the new premises and accept them—so that the leader must often plunge ahead with his plan before everyone has accepted it, expecting them to catch up later as best they can. If necessary, he is willing to take the calculated risk of resorting to threats of punishment and losing some of his followers in order to get the plan under way. His task is not to supervise the slow disintegration and perhaps ultimate eclipse of his group; it is his responsibility to see that the group flourishes.

An executive who must be constantly urged to take action gradually loses his leadership to the man who is prodding him. A leader does not dare wait for problems to be brought to him; he does not sit back and let things happen or wait for someone else to make something happen. Instead, he goes out and hunts for what needs doing—for problems to be solved. He is a *reformer* at heart.

Our discussion of three aptitudes found in leaders throws the spotlight on some basic differences between a man who is solely a creator and a man who is a creative executive leader. The former derives his satisfaction from the creation of the idea (and a great satisfaction it can be); while the latter, once having created the idea, or once having glimpsed an exciting idea created by another, cannot rest until he has gained acceptance of it and has put it to work.

The man who is chosen to hold a new, higher position in an organization, whether it be section head, or department head, or chief executive, finds it necessary to change his perspective—to take a broader view than before. In his old job, he was responsible for seeing that his own subordinates made their contributions wholeheartedly; his job also called for complete loyalty to that group. Now, however, he must widen his horizon. He must henceforth further the welfare of the several groups for which he is responsible and at the same time avoid favoritism toward any group. This change in viewpoint is often hard to acquire, but it is essential if a man is to win leadership in his new job.

UNCRITICAL ACCEPTANCE OF A MAN AS A LEADER

We may as well face the fact that people many times accept a man as a leader without much judicious evaluation of his ability. A title of director, a pretentious office, grey hairs at the temples, a battery of telephones on the desk, or a rug on the floor does impress people. These are symbols of leadership which play a large role, though they by no means prove that the man is a leader. As will be strongly underlined later, *real* leadership cannot be conferred by a man's superiors; it has to be won.

Men frequently accept an appointed superior as their leader because everybody is supposed to have one—habitual acceptance. The man who has been formally appointed or has already been accepted by others as the boss enjoys a marked advantage in attempting to establish leadership. In the absence of premises pointing to the contrary, a subordinate naturally assumes, at least initially, that the man has been chosen to sit in the leader's chair because men higher up in the organization believe that he will be equal to the job.

Age also seems to have something to do with leadership. Young men in a company are likely to assume that the older men have been able to garner a much wider range of premises than they, and that the older men can organize and use these premises to reach conclusions. That an older man does not always possess such ability is something that almost all of us can testify to, although we are usually willing to give him the benefit of the doubt in our first associations with him.

The control of large sums of money will at times enable a man to secure at least some degree of leadership, partially because most of us—in America, at least—assume that the acquisition of money is proof of success in the past. The possession of money also provides a man with some telling sanctions—the ability to give or withhold monetary rewards. Where the man in charge is the owner as well as the chief executive, the subordinates sometimes accept his leadership on the basis of indifference: "It's his money," they say, with a shrug, "and if he wants to spend it that way, it's his business."

In each of these instances the subordinate accepts his superior's leadership, accepts it uncritically, through habit or indifference. Here, the subordinate's zone of acceptance characteristically extends far to the right on our scale; and at the outset, at least, even a new boss can frequently use simple authority. The zone of acceptance can quickly narrow to the point of rebellion, however, if the men discover that the boss has little foundation beneath his leadership.

But leadership cannot be conferred any more than can authority. A man who has been appointed to a position of leadership and fails to win it is soon reduced to a rather pathetic figurehead. A section head, or department head, or even a president may have been appointed initially because no one else was immediately available or because his superiors believed that he would eventually learn to handle the job adequately, only to find later that they were mistaken. When he fails to win the respect of his superiors, they brush aside most of his proposals. A man's subordinates are usually even more perceptive than his superiors about his qualities as a leader. Gradually, as they discover that their superior is unable or unwilling to make what they think are good decisions, they turn to someone else. Once an informal leader takes over, and once the titular head *also* loses the respect of his *superiors,* he loses touch with what is going on in the company. To regain his lost leadership, he may resort to the use of sanctions or to distortion of the truth; he may even stoop to stealing his subordinates' ideas and passing them on as his own. All of us have encountered executives who have failed to win leadership in their jobs; we sometimes call them "stuffed shirts." Frequently, such a man is left in office despite his ineffectiveness because his superiors are reluctant to demote him or discharge him. Being human, they feel a responsibility for the welfare of a man who has served the company faithfully in the past.

WINNING LEADERSHIP

We shall center our attention on the executive's task of winning actual leadership after having been appointed head of a section or department—after his superiors have vested him with formal authority. Inducing his subordinates to select him as their real leader is his foremost problem; but he must also win the approbation of his superiors. His is thus the unenviable task of conceiving programs that will further his subordinate's goals, and in addition, those of his superiors and his company. We want him to be both an informal and a formal leader.

Readers of this book are well aware that leadership cannot be won by simply following a list of suggestions. The six suggestions we shall scrutinize in the next few pages are only intended to provide some insights into certain features of this challenging task. To win leadership, we need to make ideas such as these a part of our natural behavior and eventually entwine them with aptitudes such as those we discussed earlier.

Keeping Attuned to What Is Going on

Our first responsibility is to keep in touch with what is going on in our department. We can make considerable progress as soon as we become perceptive enough to recognize and interpret the meaning of the messages that our subordinates consciously or unconsciously send to us. These help us understand why the men are thinking, behaving, and speaking as they are, and what changes are going on in their emotional climate.[3] When we add to those messages the insights from our guesses about the goals and value premises each man draws from the three main reservoirs we explored in Chapter 5 —his biological, social, and psychological needs, his cultural heritages, and the goals of the organization to which he is loyal—we have at hand some fundamental premises for many of our difficult administrative decisions.

And all the foregoing, together with a sense of which pieces of information are currently important to the men, will help tell us what we must do and what we cannot do if we are to establish our leadership. After we have lived for a time with the men, we begin to know their sentiments and thinking patterns, and we then almost unconsciously include premises derived from *their* premises and goals when we are trying to create and select goals and means that they and our superiors will welcome.

Gathering this information about what is going on in the department takes time—and also patience and sensitivity. A leader has to be available; if his followers see little of him, he quickly loses touch. Some researchers have concluded that the leader of a group is the person who has the most "interactions" (encounters) with others both inside and outside the company.[4]

Building a Long Series of "Good" Decisions

As already indicated, a man establishes leadership (or fails to do so) through the decisions he has made. He begins building his reputation as a decision maker when he first joins the organization. His fellow workers and his boss cannot avoid forming an opinion of his ability, for they live with him; his decisions, even the small ones,

---

[3] The messages flow through the informal channels of communication that we shall encounter in Chapter 9.

[4] See, for instance, William Foote Whyte, *Men At Work* (Homewood, Ill.: The Dorsey Press, Inc. and Richard D. Irwin, Inc., 1961), pp. 161–62, and A. Zaleznik, C. R. Christensen, and F. J. Roethlisberger, *The Motivation, Productivity, and Satisfaction of Workers* (Boston: Harvard University, Division of Research, Graduate School of Business Administration, 1958), pp. 215–17. Incidentally, the tabulations made by those researchers of the number of interactions they observed are attempts to quantify behavior (here, leadership) which is ordinarily measured by value standards. When we studied operations research in Chapter 4, we became concerned about the problem of including these data in our mathematical equations.

have an effect upon them. They will tolerate some mistakes, too; his reputation for making good decisions is not seriously injured if he learns from these, learns which alternatives and premises he overlooked, and takes them into consideration next time. A man who has gradually built a long series of decisions that have stood up when examined in retrospect gains leadership among his associates.

A man can rather easily gauge the success of his own attempts (or of another man's attempts) to achieve leadership. When he observes that more and more often his subordinates, associates, and superiors consult with him and are willing to suspend judgment while he is offering his premises, he can feel confident that he is making progress. When those men no longer question his decisions in a given field, when they no longer insist on knowing why, he has become the expert, has achieved leadership in that field. When he is acknowledged as an expert in *several* of the fields that interest his group, he is on his way to becoming his *group's* leader instead of a leader (expert) in only one field.

Willingness on the part of others to suspend judgment without the necessity of going through proof appears to be a key factor in establishing leadership. This is granted to a man by his superiors, associates, and subordinates only after he has repeatedly demonstrated that he has been right in the past. (Perhaps this explains why we sometimes become enraged when other men try to prove that we were wrong!) A decision to suspend judgment about a man's proposals is usually arrived at unconsciously, but it is nevertheless based on very real premises. A man's associates pick these up by observing how he has coped with smaller problems or problems of a similar nature in the past. If he has repeatedly solved those intelligently, they reason that he should be capable of resolving the new problems they now see before them. They are confident that they can henceforth accept his decisions without bothering to analyze the premises and reason through to their own conclusions each time, as would be necessary if they were less confident of his judgment.

The foregoing paragraphs in part explain why meticulous attention has been given to intelligent decision making in this book. Moreover, we are now beginning to see some of the reasons (premises) for the rather unsupported statement made earlier that an executive cannot afford to fail very often in attempting to gain acceptance, cannot afford rebellion. And here we also see unfolding the grounds for what may have seemed to be an overconcern with the task of predicting the width of a man's zone of acceptance each time, and the revision of the decision to a point where one or another of the three types of authority—simple authority, proof, or sanctions (preferably the first two)—could be used successfully.

Even though a leader who has established himself is in a position to employ simple authority most of the time because his followers will readily accept the majority of his proposals, he should nevertheless use it sparingly. Were he to depend solely on simple authority, his men would gradually become automatons who blindly go through the motions and, in consequence, contribute at a level that is below their abilities. A leader has to "recharge their batteries" once in a while by employing proof, even though simple authority would induce prompt action. And manifestly, each time he makes a new proposal to a follower, he should offer proof. The chief advantage enjoyed by the established leader, as compared with a man who is still trying to win leadership, is that he is obliged to spend less time on proof. He has already proved that his decisions are usually good ones.

Employing More Alternatives and Premises than Other People Use

Consistently considering more alternatives (and where necessary, creating ideas for new ones) and employing more premises than others is a second way of winning leadership. We are attempting to behave more rationally—per Chapter 5—than others. We have opportunities to demonstrate this ability when our associates, subordinates, or superiors are faced with problems they are trying to solve and come to us for advice. It need not be labored here that taking into consideration more alternatives and premises should enable a man to help his fellow workers reach decisions that will stand up. Once men discover someone who is able and willing to help them solve their intractable problems, they turn to him again and again. In this uncertain world, there are so few things which men can count on that they instinctively cling to any solid rock.

The main problem here is to accumulate a stockpile of premises and alternatives against the time when they may be needed. One way of deliberately doing this was touched upon obliquely in the chapter on the creative process. Basically, this calls for an inquiring mind—watching for new pieces of information and framing them into newly seen premises. Some of the premises, as well as ideas for new alternatives, come from reading and thinking about the probable acts of those people outside the company whose behavior will affect the company—for instance, the actions of competitors, or of Congress (legislation), or what housewives and businessmen are doing about buying (general economic conditions). Others are discovered while reading books and articles in our specialized field. New ones are frequently perceived while "talking shop" with men in competing companies or with the company's attorney, its banker, and its outside accountants. If a man is perceptive, the accumulation of these heterogeneous pieces of information induces the stage of confusion, which, in turn (we hope), will lead to the creation of new alternatives that may come in handy at a later date.

By observing what goes on in the company and asking questions, a man can gather many premises that may prove useful later. Living inside the skins of the men in his department as a technique for discovering the goals and value premises they commonly use has already been discussed at length. And informal and formal talks with men in other departments provide insights into the premises those men ordinarily take into consideration. With these in mind a man can, with reasonable accuracy, anticipate the consequences that would flow from adopting a given alternative.

Many of these accumulated premises and alternatives can be recalled and considered when a subordinate asks for help on a baffling problem. They aid in testing out those alternatives the subordinate submits for consideration and in creating ideas for new ones to solve the problem.

An appointed superior also wins leadership by helping his men to secure the missing premises they require. He knows to whom he can go outside the department or outside the company for this information and what channels (what specific people) he can go *through* to get it. To obtain the necessary information, he may have to resort to deception; or he may be forced to go through devious and unconventional channels, or break the company rules; but he *does* get the data they need. For example, if another department holds some information needed by a subordinate in making a decision and the head of that department, jealous of his prerogatives, will not share it, the leader will resort to subterfuges in order to "shake it loose" for his man.

The main point of the foregoing is that a leader never fails to help his followers to solve their problems. In this way, he not only reinforces their confidence in his leadership but keeps his section or department running smoothly and (we will hope) sees that his men make wise decisions.

This procedure of deliberately setting out to employ more premises and alternatives than others also helps a man to win leadership among his superiors and associates. Scheduled conferences, where the problems to be considered are announced ahead of time, offer an exceptional opportunity. To establish leadership here, he must prepare carefully; he must do his thinking ahead of time. Few men are capable of exploring a problem thoroughly on the spur of the moment at a formal meeting—capable of gathering all the pertinent premises, weighting them, and thus reaching a conclusion—and even fewer are able to organize and express their ideas clearly without having thought through the problem ahead of time. All of us have had occasion to chide ourselves with: "I wish I'd thought of that (a newly seen premise or alternative) during the meeting." It is said that careful preparation prior to meetings largely accounted for the strong impact which John D. Rockefeller, a man of unimpressive appearance and physique, made on the owners of competing companies to whom he proposed merger during the early years when his company was yet small. He gathered more facts and near-facts than others, gathered many pertinent ones which no one else had thought of, and then demonstrated their relevance and relationships. He formed these into premises as a basis for conceiving a new alternative and reached his decision prior to the meeting. At the meeting, he was then able to state his proposed decisions and his premises clearly.

A young man attempting to achieve leadership can use this approach with telling effect—though he must make sure that he actually *does* employ all the pertinent premises. One of the amazing things about most meetings is that few of the men who attend have thought much about the problem ahead of time. The man who has made some preparation, even though he be young, stands out conspicuously. The writing of telling reports, a task to which we have already alluded, provides still another opportunity for establishing leadership among superiors and associates.

Winning Leadership through Group Decision Making

Actually, leadership is primarily a group activity. No leader in an organization, not even the accepted leader of the company, is in a position to formulate his decisions without consulting others. But the central thought of this method of winning leadership is that by making his decisions in conjunction with his group, a man can solidify his leadership.

Such a procedure tends to give the men confidence in the leader's proposals. By eliciting a free flow of premises at meetings, he can frequently uncover several he had overlooked. In the hunt for premises relevant to his proposals, the men think together and push their thinking farther down into details. They ask pertinent questions, bring out specific pieces of information; and, if the leader encourages them to do so, they will analyze and test and assign weights to each premise. The original proposal may have to be revised when new premises come to light; but, in the end, most of the men will back the final decision wholeheartedly. This is the type of leadership known as "democratic" leadership, one of the three widely discussed types alluded to earlier in this chapter. At the pricing conference, in the chapter on premises, we observed a group that was following this procedure; though nothing was said there about a leader, we can be sure that there was one (see pp. 63–64).

Thinking the decision out together tends to produce an objective consideration of the leader's proposal. If, in stating his proposal, he gives the impression that this is his final decision instead of a tentative one, and that the receivers will have no opportunity to think it through before saying, "Yes," the men's first reaction will be to oppose it. This will be specially true if, at first sight, they think that the proposal might endanger some of their personal goals. As we saw in the discussion of *hard proof* in the preceding chapter, they will try to think up unwanted consequences (objections) designed to dissuade the leader from carrying out the decision immediately. Postponement will give them time to think—to test out the decision in their own minds. The leader who senses that this is happening can sometimes save the proposal by requesting, "For the next fifteen minutes or half hour, let's make no reference to the unwanted consequences of adopting the plan; after the wanted consequences are sorted out, we can explore the unwanted ones."

Group decision making has a further advantage: When the program is finally accepted, each of these individuals is likely to feel that the plan itself is his own, for each has helped to create it. Seeing his own contributions fitted into the over-all plan is of great importance to a man because this constitutes proof to himself and others that he is contributing to the group's welfare; he is needed; and this, in turn, enhances his own stature. Furthermore, his loyalty to his leader is strengthened, for his leader has obviously demonstrated very good judgment in seeking his advice.

One variant of this procedure for achieving leadership of a group or committee was mentioned near the end of the chapter on authority —namely, gaining the acceptance of each member on a one-man-at-a-time basis. Another is to keep our subordinates, associates, and superiors informed about what we are thinking and what we hope to accomplish. This approach is time-consuming, but it offers others an insight into our thinking processes and a chance slowly to digest the premises we have in mind. It has the advantage of giving each receiver an opportunity to see plans as they unfold and to suggest changes before the plans have crystallized. The receivers can also feel confident that we have no nefarious schemes up our sleeve which might harm them; thus, they are more ready to lend their support whenever we propose some new plan to the group.

What the leader should be striving for is a decision that represents what the Quakers call "the sense of the meeting"—the crystallization of the proposed idea to a point where it meets the full approval of the group. To get his idea fully accepted, it must become the sense of the meeting that the proposal should be adopted. A formal vote should be unnecessary. After gaining the sense of the meeting, it is usually possible to frame a statement that reflects what the group wants to do, one that will elicit virtually unanimous agreement, a decision based on the leader's original premises as well as the new ones brought to light at the meeting. A showdown vote indicates that the proposal probably needs revision—that several members believe the unwanted consequences will preponderate. As a matter of fact, it often turns out that a vote on a formal motion gives a distorted idea of what the men *really* think is wise. A motion provides them with only two alternatives, a "Yes" or a "No," neither of which may be the most satisfactory solution.

Anticipating Dangers and Timing Proposals

In addition to using the methods already suggested, a man can win leadership by anticipating dangers to the organization and laying plans to meet them. He foresees these by visualizing in detail what his group's outside environment will be during the period ahead.[5] One of his jobs is to foresee dangers while they are still remote and lay plans to avoid these hazards or cope with them before they become present dangers. In this way, he gains a reputation for meeting problems the moment they come up, for "coming through" whenever a crisis arises.

But not all of the foreseeable problems are of equal importance. It is his responsibility to work on those that will have the greatest

---

[5] This task will be explored in Chaps. 11 and 12.

impact on the future of his group—the ones with the greatest "amount" of both wanted and unwanted consequences. The lesser problems can be passed on to his subordinates for solution, and the trivial ones can be shelved.

To achieve leadership, a man must also know when it is time to make a decision and put it into effect. If he waits too long to make an important decision, the company may be seriously injured. A delay in revamping one of the company's major products until after the competitors have changed theirs would be an example. On the other hand, it may be advisable to "hold things up" even though he may have promised to make the decision three weeks ago and his associates are now pressing him for directions. Quite often, a decision can be postponed without greatly upsetting the company's operation though, before he defers a decision, the leader should check the unwanted consequences of a delay. A man who wants to be a leader should not permit himself to be hurried into making an important decision. Obviously, he will never be able to gather all the information he would like; he is always having to make decisions on the basis of inadequate facts. But postponement enables him to gather more information, allows more time for the incubation process to take place, and permits him to recheck his newly created alternative to see if it is really as wonderful as it seemed at the time it was first conceived. Whenever he tries to hurry the creative process, his decisions are likely to prove unwise.

A man need not blurt out his new ideas the moment he conceives them. A proposal made when few in the organization can see its necessity will nearly always be rejected. A man cannot gain acceptance by crying, "Fire, fire!" when no fire is apparent to his associates. Frequently, however, this same proposal, if made at the time when the crisis is not only imminent but a source of great anxiety, will be swiftly adopted; under these circumstances, the men have wide zones of acceptance. We see quick action in Congress when a war or a depression threatens. On occasions of crises the members of an organization can themselves visualize with breath-taking clarity the somber picture of the future in case nothing is done. Consequently, they are often willing to accept a new alternative, which would be cast aside under more normal conditions.

Winning Leadership by Developing Responsibility and Integrity

The last of these suggestions, developing a reputation as a responsible person and one who can be fully trusted, is an elusive yet very telling and fundamental method of gaining a following, especially in a close-knit group where the men know one another well.

Basically, responsibility turns out to be *doing what others expect.* Each man in a group or an organization is entrusted with certain duties, some assigned formally, but most handed to the man informally by common consent. His task may be a small one—merely running an errand, for example. But whatever it is, others expect him to do it; and they insist that he bear the consequences if he does not, for the job is important to the welfare of the group. They also expect him to carry out his assignment in spite of unforeseen difficulties. A man gradually gains leadership when he proves that he is responsible. Once he has demonstrated his willingness and ability to carry out the first duties he is assigned, he is, by common consent, given more important tasks and thereafter tested on those.

There are two types of integrity which will aid in winning leadership—intellectual integrity and moral integrity. Let us look at intellectual integrity first. A leader must be completely honest with himself. Men quickly see through anyone who makes a practice of deceiving himself in reaching decisions about what he or his company should do; his decisions do not flow logically from the statements of cause-result relationships he implies or says he used, but instead from premises (motives) they suspect he used unconsciously or is ashamed to disclose. Nor can a leader allow himself to fall into the habit of deliberately trying to deceive his associates by misrepresenting to them the premises (especially those premises based on personal motives) he used in reaching a decision. Both kinds of intellectual dishonesty, subconsciously fooling himself, or deliberately trying to fool others, lead to loss of confidence. The recollection of lapses of this kind lies buried in the minds of his colleagues, so that each time he makes a new proposal they carefully probe for his hidden motives—his *real* premises—to make sure that they are not being misled.

No one is entirely free from intellectual dishonesty; but if we sometimes admit to this shortcoming, much of the stigma is removed. It breeds confidence if we point out the possibility that personal, perhaps even unethical, motives may be mixed up somewhere in a decision we are proposing. Poking fun at our own foibles once in a while, and enjoying with others a good chuckle over them, frequently restores lost confidence. Also, when we encounter an idea that we do not understand, we can often clear the air and raise ourselves in the estimation of our colleagues by freely admitting our confusion. Another evidence of intellectual integrity noted and filed away by associates for later use as a premise is a readiness to accept and act on a decision that will obviously injure us, or a group or an organization (the company excepted) to which we are extremely loyal. Likewise, a willingness to discard our own conclusion and accept another man's when the proof points that way is a mark of intellectual integrity.

Moral integrity is more difficult to frame in sharp terms. It partakes of honesty—of telling the exact truth—but, more than that, it consists in making good on promises, even when it "hurts." It is also broader than that. It has to do with acting in conformity with the moral codes which society has set up as proper behavior—with the group's ideas of right and wrong. In most groups, this proper behavior is measured in terms of whether the man's actions advance the welfare of other people, of society. Some features of these codes may now seem outmoded or unrealistic, inherited as they are from earlier centuries; but this does not mean that men will permit them to be flouted. In any case, even though the followers may not lay claim to any great moral integrity themselves, they demand it of their leader. Earlier generations used the word *character* in talking about moral and intellectual integrity.

Confidence in both the intellectual and the moral integrity of the leader is obviously essential. His followers must feel certain that he will act as they expect. A web of promises (*promises*, not premises—stated and implied agreements) is gradually built up over the years between a leader and his followers—expectations of behavior which are seldom mentioned but nevertheless are considered binding by the followers. Men want to be sure that their leader will fulfill his part of these agreements in accordance with moral laws as well as the letter and spirit of the agreements. If they lose this confidence, they gradually reject the leader, for they can no longer be certain that he will further their goals. When people find a man who consistently acts in accordance with their ideas of intellectual and moral integrity, they frame this series of actions into a premise: "Since he has always lived up to his promises and our codes, we know that he will behave 'properly' in the future, even though no verbal or written agreement exists." Here is suspension of disbelief. This, in turn, leads to habitual acceptance.

Most men never pass the initial tests of integrity and responsibility which their new associates give them when they first join the group, let alone the succeeding ones. In fact, it is in these fields of integrity and responsibility that people most often fail; they agree, inferentially at least, to act "properly" but then renege on their promises. Inasmuch as these basic tests are given each new employee by the members of an organization (informally, of course), and since few people possess the self-discipline necessary to pass more than the most elementary ones, the number of men who progress very far on the road to leadership is extremely limited.

It is evident from what has been said that few men are granted the privilege of attempting to employ *any* of the five other suggested methods of winning leadership. So those who pass these initial tests of responsibility and integrity must be regarded as valuable assets. These men must be nurtured if the company is to flourish. In the next chapter, we shall devote some attention to the ticklish job of teaching these selected individuals to become executive leaders—teaching them how to make decisions and gain acceptance—and creating an atmosphere that will encourage them to take the initiative in developing their leadership talents. Unfortunately, in many companies, such attempts are discouraged; and, as a consequence, those who have some sparks of leadership soon learn that it is prudent to stamp them out.

SOME REASONS WHY MEN FAIL AS LEADERS

Some men who seem to possess the necessary talents never succeed in winning even a small amount of leadership. All of us have seen men fail in their pursuit of leadership in spite of the fact that they possess integrity, brilliant minds, and an ability to think logically.

I should say that one of the chief reasons why such men fail is that they have never learned to live inside the skins of their fellow workers. A man cannot pursue leadership by thinking and acting egocentrically. It is essential that a leader take periodic imaginary trips with his followers. Such excursions provide a set of value premises without which no man can expect to achieve leadership. If a man makes no attempt to perceive these, his associates logically conclude that he has no understanding of their needs, no interest in furthering their goals.

Closely associated with this is a man's failure to listen. Some men become too imbued with the brilliance of their own proposals and so self-centered about their own goals and means that they talk about them continuously and brush aside, or scarcely hear, what others say. The hearer frames these incidents into premises for deciding to reject the man as a leader, for he is aware that the egocentric has failed to employ all the premises *he* considers important and thus concludes that the decisions the man conceives will not suit him. Indeed, he predicts that his own and his group's welfare would frequently be injured if he were to make a practice of accepting and following such a man's decisions.

A man sometimes expects to achieve leadership by assembling more facts than others. He has his head full of facts and an extra supply in the bulging briefcase he carries to all meetings. He presumes that because he can answer questions and supply accurate facts at the drop of a hat, others will look upon him as a leader. When they do not, he is perplexed; he *knows* he is an "authority," but no one pays much attention to him. What he fails to understand is that although people want facts, they need much more from a leader. A leader must start with facts, or the nearest available thing; but he must also employ value elements, then frame both types of elements into premises, conceive new alternatives based on these, choose the best one, and finally proceed to gain acceptance of his proposal.

We also frequently observe men trying to achieve leadership (or perhaps only popularity) by agreeing with what others say. Clearly, a man who does this lacks intellectual integrity; and men soon become aware of such a deficiency. Either he is misrepresenting what he himself thinks, or he has not thought through the problems far enough to have gathered premises and reached his own decision. In that case, he is certainly not a leader; to him, each new proposal he hears sounds better than the last. Some men may like him, others may merely tolerate him, but few will seriously consider him as a possible leader.

These reasons for failure appear to be negative statements of one or another phase of winning leadership. In view of this, there is probably little to be gained by pursuing this line of thinking further.

By now, it has doubtless become quite evident that this entire book deals with various ways of achieving leadership, for an executive must be a leader if he is to perform his tasks. His job is to set goals; to create ideas for achieving these goals; to learn how to make telling decisions; how to gain acceptance of decisions; and how to put them into effect.

More specifically, we have found that leadership is very closely associated with the authority concept we developed—namely, the prediction of the width of the receiver's zone of acceptance for a particular proposal and the use of simple authority, proof, and, if need be, sanctions. But in the conceptual subsystem explored in this chapter, we were dealing with the task of guiding the behavior of several people simultaneously, doing this repeatedly and consistently, and using proof and simple authority in almost all instances. We described the ideal leader as a man who had an aptitude for creating ideas for goals and means, who believed his group could flourish, and who made things happen.

There were indications that a man who is given the mantle of authority as a concomitant of his appointment to a position, or is looked upon as an authority because of his age, length of service, or financial position, enjoys an initial advantage in attempting to win leadership. However, it became clear that this is not enough. If a man is to win real leadership, he should endeavor to keep attuned to what is going on; attempt to build a long series of "good" decisions; use practical rationality in making decisions (consider more goals, alternatives and premises than others); employ group decision making at times; anticipate dangers and time his proposals; and most important, make a special effort to gain and hold a reputation for responsibility and integrity.

Intellectual and moral integrity appeared to be essential characteristics of a leader, together with a willingness to accept responsibility. This is because a large proportion of the relationships between the leader and the follower are what might be termed "unspoken contracts." If these fragile agreements are frequently broken by the leader, whether unconsciously or consciously, the follower loses confidence in the leader's willingness and ability to fulfill such contracts in the future. When we probed some of the reasons why men fail to achieve leadership, we discovered that we were repeating ourselves; we were simply saying that the men were failing to do certain things a leader must do.

I think that a man who is ranked high by his associates in the three aptitudes and the six practices that we have discussed would be considered an outstanding leader. But a man may be a good leader even though he falls short in several respects. And recall that almost every man enjoys some degree of leadership in the groups he joins. Men choose the best leader available, knowing he is not perfect; and they expect any leader to make some mistakes. Many businessmen have gained a deserved reputation as highly successful leaders, even though they have serious shortcomings when measured by our lofty standards; by comparison, they are much better leaders than their confreres.

Most of us have also known of inadequate leaders. And on occasion, we may have lived through the traumatic experience of working under a man to whom we would give failing grades in these several facets of leadership and/or who followed some of the practices that cause a man to fail as a leader. Such a man is soon supplanted by an informal leader, as we saw earlier, even though his superiors maintain the fiction that he is the actual leader.

In this chapter, we have been exhorting ourselves to improve certain patterns of behavior—no small task when our shortcomings have become ingrained. Evidently, constant vigilance will be needed if we are to make progress.

Success in exercising authority and winning leadership, however, is heavily dependent on a man's ability to communicate. We shall investigate that problem in the next chapter.

PROBLEM
ACHIEVING LEADERSHIP

In the Gould Metal Company, we became acquainted with three men: Mr. Gould, Mr. Hemple, and Mr. Willard. In answering items No. 1 and 2 below, use as a check list the aptitudes and the methods of winning leadership discussed in the chapter.

1. Choose either Mr. Gould or the two sales managers (do not try to distinguish between the two sales managers), and describe and analyze what he has (they have) been doing to win leadership in the company.
2. Discuss the shortcomings of your man—explain why you think he has not yet won the leadership he seeks, using specific examples from the case.
3. Sit down with your man, and show him how he *could* have handled *one* of the situations you used as an example in item No. 2 above.

Chapter **8**   COMMUNICATION
AND TRAINING

THE PURPOSE of *communication,* as we
shall use the term here, is to transfer from the mind of one person
to the mind of another the mental images needed for making decisions. Perfect communication is achieved when the receiver sees exactly the same image as the giver. When we communicate, we transmit pictures of separate elements (odd bits of information) and
premises whose causes or results must be inferred by the receiver;
also, we transmit complete three-part premises, and goals and means
(decisions) which the receiver can recast into his own premises
when making his own decisions. Most people use the more general
word *information* for these three types of ideas. For the sake of brev-
ity, we shall at times also use this catchall word.[1]

Out of the information that is communicated to us through our
eyes and ears we build those mental images which serve as our
miniature models of the real world and how it operates. And what
we say helps others fill in details of their own models of the real
world. To those of us who aspire to practical rationality in decision
making this incoming information about the real world is essential.
We and our associates conceive and try out our alternatives here.
And whenever we conceive an idea for a possible improvement in
the operation of our segment of this real world, we communicate
to others the new picture we have seen, trying to gain acceptance by

[1] A realistic brief description of communication problems and some useful generalizations about such problems, based upon a wide range of empirical data (most of it developed at the University of Michigan), will be found in Jay M. Jackson, "The Organization and Its Communication Problems," *Advanced Management,* Vol. 24, No. 2 (February 1959). Reprinted in Austen Grimshaw and J. W. Hennessey, Jr. (eds.), *Organization
Behavior* (New York: McGraw-Hill Book Co., Inc., 1960). In addition, Albert H. Rubenstein and Chadwick J. Haberstroh, *Some Theories of Organization* (Homewood, Ill.: The
Dorsey Press, Inc., and Richard D. Irwin, Inc., 1960), and Robert Dahl, Mason Haire
and Paul F. Lazarsfeld, *Social Science Research on Business* (New York: Columbia
University Press, 1959), contain references to several illuminating studies of communica-
tion. Also see Rensis Likert, *New Patterns of Management* (New York, McGraw-Hill
Book Co., Inc., 1961), chap. 4.

exercising authority and leadership. Our receivers then test out our proposal and decide whether they should help us change this aspect of the real world.

In this chapter, we shall make no attempt to deal with the art of communication, even though it is a significant aspect of our subject. We have already touched upon this in two earlier chapters. In our examination of the sixth stage of the creative process, the communication stage (pp. 54–55), we saw that the speaker should first picture in his own mind precise images of all the separate details which make up the idea he wants to communicate; all he then has to do is to describe these details in words, so that they will be fully understood by receivers. Again, in the chapter on authority, where we explored "easy" proof and "hard" proof (pp. 174–180), we were dealing with the art of communication—the communication of goals, alternatives, and premises.

Our definition of communication is somewhat broader than the one commonly used. In fact, it encompasses two types of communication. One is the transmittal of *temporarily* useful pieces of information; these are supposed to flow through the organization in a steady but ever-changing stream, to be cast aside once they have served their purpose in making the decision immediately at hand. Examples would be: orders received from customers; the amount of an item to be produced each day; figures on current shipments and sales, operating statements, cost data, inventories on hand, prices of raw materials, and specific proposals or directions for handling a particular problem. The other type of communication is what we usually call training. Here we are transmitting *permanently* useful pieces of information which are to be employed by workers or executives in making a large number of decisions over a rather long period in the future. Directions for the easiest way to assemble a standard product, rules and regulations, instructions as to methods of making decisions, and visual images of the company's long-term goals would be examples of permanently useful communications. The first type of communication is intended for immediate use; the second, for use at some later date.

The chief value of this chapter lies in its attempt to provide an orderly and useful conceptual framework into which the reader can fit the many things he already knows about communication, and to integrate these ideas with the concepts he has picked up in earlier chapters. Looking from a new vantage point at what the reader already knows may offer him fresh insights into some of the problems of communication and perhaps enable him to improve the communication in his own organization.

Incidentally, we are now well into our second group of subsystems —those dealing with gaining acceptance. Authority, the first subsystem, and communication, the third of the five subsystems in Part II, go hand in hand: To exercise authority, communication is essential. The same is true of leadership, the second subsystem. But whereas failures in authority and leadership result in rebellion, failures in communication result in overly high expenses and bad decisions. In view of what we have found to be true for authority, there is little need to add that information may flow downward, upward, sidewise, and diagonally in an organization.

Although the ideas about communication are straightforward enough (in fact, this chapter is a fairly elementary one), the problems of maintaining effective communication are knotty ones. In recent years, there has been a spectacular increase in the amount of information available to the members of most organizations—numerical data and verbalized information about the company and the political, economic, and competitive environment in which it must live. Yet, in many cases, only a small proportion of this information is fully utilized; much of it is being wasted. Frequently, the information does not reach the decider in time. Ordinarily, however, the difficulty lies deeper than that. Many of the people have not been taught how to employ the information fully in reaching decisions once they receive it. Communication is an essential first step in decision making.

It behooves a firm to devote a great deal of attention to communication. Most companies probably spend more money and more man-hours on communication—and get less from it per dollar spent—than on any other single activity. In many companies the aggregate spent on the various communication activities exceeds that spent on direct labor or the use (depletion) of equipment, for example, or on decision making. The salesman's sole task is to communicate premises to others—that is, to his customers and to his company. All advertising is communication. Communication includes the work and the records of the accounting department, all other record keeping, blueprints, and specifications prepared by engineers. Secretaries work at the task of communicating; and, of course, when two or more people in the company talk about a problem, they are communicating. Obviously, all writing and reading (of memorandums, letters, magazine articles, books, and so on) constitute communication. Most executives spend more of their time receiving and communicating elements of premises, the premises themselves, decisions, and goals than in the actual *making* of decisions. Gathering, transmitting, and filing these is particularly time-consuming and costly in large organizations because many people must be kept informed about what goes on, and most of these mental images must be communicated in written or oral form. In a small company the costs are less because much of the information is communicated to the decision makers by direct observation, and most of this is simply filed away under the men's hats.

These *visible* expenditures tell only a part of the story, however. Despite the large sums spent on communication, there are many failures in communication in every company. These failures result in bad decisions which may turn out to be more costly than the tangible communication expenses that appear on the profit and loss statement. Occasionally, the available information never reaches the decision makers or else reaches them too late, as already indicated. Moreover, men are frequently given erroneous facts, the result of mental lapses on the part of the givers, or misunderstandings about what information was needed, or deliberate misrepresentations. The costs of these wrong decisions are very real ones. A company plagued by stupid decisions will almost inevitably lose sales volume and operate under the handicap of abnormally high expenses; it also encounters trouble in competing against other companies for a position in its industry.

THE COMMUNICATION SYSTEM FOR TEMPORARILY USEFUL INFORMATION

In setting up a formal communication system, we are attempting to make sure that all the temporarily useful premises needed by the decider actually reach him, that they reach him in time, and that they are accurate. The task is greatly simplified by examining the destination of the communication first and working back from that. It resolves itself into six tasks: (1) deciding what premises the man at the "destination" needs in order to make the decisions he is responsible for, (2) determining the "best" sources or origins for these premises, (3) determining the "best" vehicles for carrying them accurately and rapidly from the source to the destination, (4) setting up a pathway over which they will freely and quickly move, (5) setting up information "feedback" systems, and (6) initiating the flow to make certain that the premises are actually transmitted.

Visualizing the Premises Each Decider Will Need— the Destination

By visualizing each decider in the process of making his decisions, it is relatively easy to form a clear picture of the premises he must receive regularly. For instance, before a lathe operator can decide what to do, he needs to know the type of bar stock to use, the dimensions, the tolerances, the number of units to make, the necessary machine settings, and the time when the job should be completed. An examination of the information that a man requires also provides an opportunity to eliminate incoming information that he never uses, so that communication can be cut to a minimum. Men are frequently overwhelmed by a snowstorm of unnecessary reports, directives, and memorandums.

Among the more important decisions a sales manager must make, for instance, are those connected with the supervision of his salesmen. He will need regular reports of each salesman's sales in both dollars and units, and similar reports for the accounts in each man's territory. He would probably find that he can use information about the customers called on, the number of calls made per day by the salesman, and the average size of sale. By comparing these data and framing premises from them, then adding other premises he has already accumulated, he can decide what each salesman should do about calling on his various customers. Note that he can, in turn, communicate these premises to his salesmen to prove that he has made a good decision—that the means he proposes will produce more sales.

The chief executive will probably require a somewhat different type of information. For example, he may need cumulative and comparative data on the company's total sales volume, in dollars and units; on total inventories; and on the current prices and price trends of the more important raw materials used by the company, especially if raw material costs constitute a large percentage of the company's expenses. Information on the company's current financial position will aid in deciding what expenditures can be made without injuring the company's credit. A constant flow of information about what is going on in the outside world will help him frame premises he requires for predicting the company's environment (to be discussed in Chapters 11 and 12). This picture of the future, in turn, will help him to create and test out in his mind possible company plans and to decide on means. He, too, can pass his information on to his subordinates, so that they can use it for their own decisions in their specialized fields.

As a final example of a destination, let us look at a potential customer—observe the premises he must receive if he is to make a decision to join our company as a member. (Recall that we include the customers in our definition of members of an organization.) The objective here is to provide him with pieces of information he can form into factual and value premises which, in turn, will lead him to conclude that the wanted consequences of buying our product will greatly outweigh the unwanted consequences, and that the spread between the two will exceed the spread he would enjoy if he were to join some competitor's organization. The cause element in the premises that he forms reads, "If I buy this product . . ." Our advertising department and salesmen supply him with result elements which he can incorporate in his premises. He is, of course, aware that most of these will point only to wanted consequences; and he may recognize that some are unreliable and therefore cast them aside; he will furnish his unwanted consequences. These results must be very real, very vivid to him. It is a waste of time to tell him, "If you buy our product, you will enjoy its high quality," or ". . . you'll like our service."[2]

Finding the Best Sources of Information

Once we have determined what information the decider will need, the problem of finding the best sources is half solved. Sources for the regular *standardized* information which must flow to a given decision maker every day can be readily determined. Information needed by the women in the billing department—here we are using commonplace examples—will most readily and accurately come from the shipping orders or directly from the customers' orders received by the sales department. These original orders also serve as the source of certain information required by the schedulers, and the scheduling department is the best source of certain information needed by the men in the plant. Obviously, these sources can supply such information most quickly and accurately.

For nonstandardized pieces of information needed in making his

---

[2] At the beginning of the customer's association with the company, the task of the sales department is to communicate proof, either through words or by demonstrations; but eventually, the company may be able to employ simple authority. Once the customer's zone of acceptance has become very wide (strong brand preferences or strong company loyalty), the cost of communicating premises to him is greatly reduced.

current decisions, a man will ordinarily have to ferret out his own sources—certain records, or certain *individuals* in the company who can supply it quickly and accurately. Nevertheless, he need not go about this blindly. A salesman, for example, is obviously a ready source of information about the needs of the accounts he calls on. The purchasing agent will know about the suppliers of raw materials and prices. Carl McGee in the scheduling department will have information about delivery dates. Certain cost-estimating men, product development engineers, and marketing research men in the company are likewise useful sources of information, as are executives. The workmen in the plant, union stewards, and union officials are sources often overlooked by executives; frequently, these men have accumulated a vast amount of valuable information.[3]

It is also necessary to look for the best sources for the *decisions* that must be transmitted to the destination. The role of executives and specialists as sources of decisions designed to guide the actions of others has been examined in earlier chapters, especially in the one on authority, so that this need not be amplified here. Sometimes, these decisions will be standing rules or orders; but the ones we are particularly concerned with at the moment are those that have to be supplied in a steady flow. Most of these come from employees of the organization; but many are available from such sources as business consultants, officials of the labor union, the company's attorneys, and the officers of its bank.

Choosing the Vehicles

A third facet of the problem of setting up a realistic communication system is the choice of the appropriate vehicle for communicating the premises from the sources to the users. All of us are aware that a person, or a telephone wire, or a piece of paper covered with black marks may serve as a vehicle; the problem is to determine which of the three will get the job done well enough and with the least expense.

---

[3] People's recollections can often supply approximations of facts, or even opinions, which are accurate enough to be formed into premises for the decision at hand. These and old records can be of great help as timesavers. Sometimes, old records—originally prepared for a quite different purpose—provide pertinent information; after mental allowance for their inadequacies have been made, they may be accurate enough to permit fairly valid decisions. The chief problem is to locate these records. Few people in an organization have enough imagination to realize that certain data gathered for an earlier study may provide some of the facts needed for the problem at hand. These old records frequently lie buried in the bottom drawer of a desk or at the back of an old filing cabinet. Government agencies, trade associations, business and professional magazines, and books are examples of some of the more obvious *outside* sources of information.

Information that is predominantly measured with value standards is, as we have seen, very difficult to communicate. For this, the human being is by all odds the best vehicle. The words a man speaks can be given shades of meaning impossible to convey in writing. Pauses, emphasis on certain words, tone of voice, pronunciation, and inflections can be used to transmit subtle nuances. The simple word, *yes*, for example, can be spoken in many different ways, each with a different meaning—to convey a question, uncertainty, surprise, agreement, anger, disbelief, for instance. Gestures with the hands or shoulders communicate shades of meaning. The face is a particularly telling communication medium—a frown, a smile, a grin, a raised eyebrow, tight lips, a quick look, a grimace, raised or lowered eyes, for example. Face-to-face communication has a further advantage. It provides for a two-way flow; this is especially useful in trying to transmit these difficult-to-express value premises. The receiver of the communication can indicate his perplexity and can ask questions. The source (giver) can then restate or amplify what he has said and thus make sure that his communication is understood. Face-to-face communication of value premises takes time, but this seems to be the only way complex ones can be accurately communicated.

Face-to-face communication is particularly necessary in communicating proof—especially when we expect the receiver's zone of acceptance to be relatively narrow and hard proof must be used. When we know that our intended receiver has all but made up his mind to reject a proposal, but is nevertheless willing to listen, we go and talk with him ("talk it over"), so that we can watch his responses as we unfold our proof. We realize that a telephone call or a letter would result in failure.

Sound waves, whether sent by wire or by air, are suitable for passing premises that are less subtle and less complex than those just described. The telephone possesses many of the advantages of the face-to-face method. Its chief limitation is that gestures and facial expressions cannot be conveyed. On the other hand, it is much faster and cheaper than carrying these premises on foot. Television as a means of communicating premises to potential customers is almost as effective as face-to-face communication; its chief limitation is the absence of a two-way flow. The same is true of radio. In neither case can the giver watch the receivers' facial expressions for evidences of perplexity, disbelief, boredom, or understanding; nor can he hear the receivers' questions.

The third major vehicle, the printed or written word, is particularly telling where the information to be transmitted is factual or where it is of a value nature but rather easily grasped.[4] Paper also buttresses our faulty memories. Detailed facts—those used in accounting or production records or by engineers, for instance—or the spelling of names, especially if more than two or three such pieces of information are to be communicated, almost have to be transmitted in writing to avoid error. The printed word is an adequate and also a very inexpensive vehicle in those cases where a proposal's premises, though not entirely factual, are few in number and demand no great mental effort on the part of the receiver. Advertisements and notices or announcements sent to employees or customers can be used to transmit these rather simple premises. But only in those cases where the receivers' zones of acceptance are already wide will they employ premises sent this way as their sole basis for taking action.

Pathways, or Channels of Communication

The fourth task in laying out a communication system for temporarily useful premises is to set up formal paths or channels of communication throughout the organization.

The layman ordinarily presumes that all messages start at the top and move down through the hierarchy step by step, or start at the bottom and move up; and that messages to be sent from a low level in one department to a low level in another department are channeled through successively higher executives until they reach a common executive and then are sent downward again. Such vertical up-and-down paths are commonly found, and they have their uses; they acquaint each person in the pathway with the information his subordinates and his superiors have available for premises. The trouble is that some of this information is almost valueless to most of the men in the channel. Each executive's desk becomes cluttered with a stream of memorandums, notices, and reports to the point where he almost completely ignores them, using instead the premises he already has, or ones he can readily gather by asking questions. Also, communications sent through these regular channels are often delayed; and if the communication is a verbal one, the persons in the hierarchy through whom it passes will at times "doctor it up" to make it more palatable to the person receiving it, or to avoid criti-

---

[4] The author of a book, however, can communicate quite complex value premises with the written word if he is skilled; but he is forced to employ a great many words in order to move his invisible images into the minds of others.

cism. (In a moment, we shall investigate more carefully some of these barriers to communication.)

To cope with such problems, it is often necessary, despite certain disadvantages, to use the most direct pathway. The main drawback is that some executives are fearful that direct communication will leave them uninformed or will undermine their "authority"—their prestige. In most organizations, however, where the men have worked together for many years and the idiosyncrasies of each are well known, compromises can usually be worked out that permit both speed and accuracy in transmission and at the same time assure an uneasy superior that he knows what is going on in his department. Frequently, the executives can agree on which information is to flow through them and which can go directly to their subordinates. Or copies of communications can be provided for those bosses who would otherwise feel that they had been bypassed.

A leader must rely heavily on direct channels (and on his men as vehicles) if he is to know what is really going on in his department. Were he to instruct the men to send him, via a subordinate, their ideas of what is happening, he would inevitably get a distorted picture. Direct communication is necessary where suggestions, arguments, questions, and an interchange of opinion will be needed before a decision can be made and put into effect. It is also essential for transmitting any touchy information that requires sensitivity and perception— requires an understanding of subtle or nonverbalized messages— whether they are to be sent upward, downward, or horizontally. The men use the most convenient channel (which is usually "direct") even though they may have been instructed to use some other formal channel. Top executives will normally frown upon these unofficial, informal channels, especially if the channel bypasses some of the executives, but they will eventually either pretend that these channels are not used or will give them a nod of approval.

At times, it is essential to set assembly centers astride some of the pathways, assembly centers responsible for gathering a mass of otherwise confusing facts and summarizing these into an orderly pattern (a report) for those who need them for decisions. Computers are playing more and more of a role here. And we have already delved into operations research enough to recognize that by feeding selected figures on costs, sales, and any other pertinent numerical information into a computer programmed with an appropriate formula, we can find out which alternative will be cheapest—within certain quite circumscribed limits, of course. Accounting departments, statistical divisions, and scheduling departments also secure and tabulate data from the original sources—from the salesmen (customers' orders), the purchasing department (receiving slips), the suppliers (invoices), or the workers (records of their production). Though assembly centers usually perform these essential tasks with the greatest dispatch possible, they are frequently subjected to a barrage of criticism because of delay in the transmission of badly needed information. "The accounting department never sends its reports to me until two weeks after the end of the month—long after I have to make my decisions."

Executives can go a long way toward improving communication by formally approving the use of direct pathways (where quicker) instead of the cumbersome formal up-and-down and roundabout pathways shown on the organization chart. Such approval also lends authenticity to the messages; nothing moves through these "legal" channels (or is *supposed* to move through them) except communications designed to advance the goals of the organization. In the next chapter, the chapter on informal groups, we shall come across this problem of channels of communication once again; such groups provide additional pathways which are essential to the life of the company.

Establishing a Feedback

When an executive sends a decision of his through a communication channel, he needs some way of learning whether it is being accepted and carried out—a "feedback" channel. He will have used one of the three types of authority to insure its acceptance, but this is no guarantee that the receiver will carry it out wholeheartedly. His feedback channels should tell him what changes, if any, he should make in his decision or in the type of authority he has been employing.

We have already observed that direct channels using face-to-face conversations provide a very effective pathway for information about what is going on and how the men are reacting to proposals. This feedback provides a quite natural method of establishing direction and control of his subordinates, one of the chief tasks of an executive, as we shall see in the concluding chapter of this book. When a department or company grows so large that direct observation or face-to-face reporting is impractical, we need a flow of written reports in words or in numerical form which will tell what is happening. Our task in either case is threefold: set up, with the subordinate's knowledge, a standard or goal we expect him to achieve when carrying out our proposal, periodically lay along side it the subordinate's actual performance—a feedback of what is happening—and then decide what remedial action, if any, is needed. This is one way of circumventing a pocket veto.

Initiating the Flow of Communication

Only a word need be said about the concluding facet of this problem of moving elements of premises, complete premises, and decisions from their origins to their destination, namely, the task of setting up the flow. The executive's basic task here is to establish an authority relationship with the men responsible for initiating the flow. It may consist of simple authority—of explaining, "I want you to prepare the information this way and send it through these channels to that destination before noon each day"—though he may at times need to employ proof or even sanctions.

This completes our examination of the task of setting up (or revising) a *formal* communication system for transmitting temporarily useful information. But be aware that these formal systems and channels carry only a part of the messages. In these pages we have tried, not always successfully, to confine ourselves to formal communication—executive-sponsored communication. However, much of the information about actual occurrences is carried through the informal "grape-vine" channels; for those, we shall wait until we know something about the company's informal groups, for they operate those channels.

Moreover, despite all our efforts to set up a fool-proof system for the formal transmittal of temporarily useful information, the flow is sometimes impeded. Let us examine some of the barriers that we shall doubtless encounter in any organizations we may work for.

AVOIDING SOME OF THE COMMON BARRIERS
TO COMMUNICATION

Unfortunately, no system for the communication of temporarily useful information, not even an ideal one such as that just described, will ever work perfectly. Most of the breakdowns in communication have their origin in human frailty, so that we have to learn to live with the failures. Certain barriers to communication are common in all organizations. Once these are recognized, however, it is possible to alleviate some of their ill effects by anticipating human weaknesses and allowing for and guarding against them, thus minimizing the damage. Most of the failures in the use of communication as a means of gaining acceptance can be summarized under five headings, under five types of barriers. Visualizing what should be done to correct these anticipated and commonly encountered problems, however, does not ensure that they will be corrected, for the task is no easy one.

Failure to Gain or Hold the Decider's Attention

Failure to gain the receiver's attention at the very outset raises one of the most obvious of these barriers. One way of gaining attention is to name a goal he is interested in or to promise to supply information or premises that will be useful to him. Unless the receiver is by habit willing to suspend disbelief temporarily, he will listen only if he can foresee the possibility that his own or his company's goals will be furthered. The moment he discovers that the message is of little value to him, he smiles and nods politely as the speaker progresses, but actually turns his mind to other problems. If the message is an advertisement, he tosses it into the wastebasket, or turns the page, or turns off the television set. Once this attention is lost, once the receiver turns a deaf ear, attempts to communicate further information are fruitless.

A subordinate frequently encounters this barrier in attempting to talk with his superior. To gain attention, he must displace the premises already in the man's mind—premises having to do with other problems—and substitute his own. The boss is ordinarily troubled with so many problems that, despite a resolve to listen carefully, his mind slides off to more urgent matters. If he becomes bored or is pressed for time, he plays with the papers on his desk as a signal for the man to leave. Though a superior has less trouble in gaining his subordinate's attention—he can use sanctions when necessary— he faces the same barrier to some degree; his subordinate begins to think about his own problems. A man giving a speech or a lecture often encounters this barrier.

Actually, a receiver automatically selects and remembers only the information he expects he will need; he hears whatever he thinks will further his goals and ignores or forgets the rest. This explains why marketing research men, when trying to determine the effectiveness of an advertisement, often count the number (percentage) of people who say they recall the message. But nose counting does not necessarily tell the whole story about an advertisement's effectiveness; the ultimate question is whether the hearer believes that the consequences he remembers will affect his goals enough to warrant taking the proposed action. Thus, an understanding of the receiver's background and goals is basic in gaining and holding attention.

To hold the receiver's attention, it is probably best, as we saw in discussing proof, to frame the premises into a pattern with some logical thread running through them—a thread that can be mentioned at the outset. Once the hearer becomes confused, he has great difficulty in picking up the pattern again and marching up the means-end staircase with the giver of premises. These threads can be simple enumerations—"I'm going to talk about three things"—or a series of means and ends leading to a goal that the receiver wishes to achieve.

Failure to State the Premises Clearly

Earlier in this chapter, it was pointed out that communication is not successful unless the hearer sees virtually the same mental image as the speaker. Most of us jump to the conclusion that the words we use to describe our mental images will call up the same ones in the mind of the man to whom we are communicating. This may be true when we are talking with members of our family or with our close associates at work, for we have learned their definitions. However, in the majority of other cases, this is fallacious. Except in the fields of science, there are few words which everyone defines alike. As we saw in discussing factual and value elements, there are scarcely any that are *completely* factual. Practically every element we use is measured in part (almost entirely, in many cases) with our personal measuring rods. Since these value standards differ for each man, the image that is called up in the hearer's mind when the element is mentioned will, of necessity, be somewhat different from what the hearer intended. And the farther to the right the element falls on the continuum shown in Diagram 5 (see p. 73), the greater the chance that it will be distorted in the hearer's mind and therefore misunderstood.

Unless the hearer is perceptive enough to make a reasonably accurate guess as to what the speaker has in mind when a value element is mentioned, he is likely to make an unwise decision, provided, of course, that he gives the element considerable weight. Ordinarily, if the speaker fails to state one of the elements in his premise clearly, the hearer receives a distorted image or a vague impression. Under such circumstances, some of the consequences the hearer envisaged when he made his choice will differ from those he expected, even though the premise the speaker *tried* to communicate was a very reliable one.

Few people stop to realize that the words and phrases a man uses and hears have, *to him, only* the meanings *he* attaches to them. The meanings with which he grew up, the meanings used by the social group in which he spent his formative years, are the ones that automatically come to his mind when he hears the words. When the speaker and the hearer each assume that the other man is using his personal definition—when they use terms that mean one thing to the speaker and a quite different thing to the hearer—misunderstandings are inevitable. In many cases, these are never discovered; neither the speaker nor the hearer is aware of what has happened. Of the five barriers to communication, this one, the failure to state things clearly, is undoubtedly encountered most often.[5]

One common source of misunderstanding is the use by a speaker of special definitions for everyday words. For instance, if we were to use indiscriminately the words *authority* or *premise* in the sense employed in this book, our hearers would get an entirely erroneous impression of what we have in mind. The use of a professional vocabulary or jargon such as that of accountants, lawyers, engineers, and scientists, likewise causes misunderstanding and confusion. Some of these difficulties can be avoided by thinking before speaking and then choosing words which, while perhaps not so precise, will paint in the receiver's mind a fairly accurate image of the idea we wish to convey.

The use of hollow words ("gobbledygook") which leave only a vague picture in the mind of the receiver is equally confusing. Words of a value nature or words with many definitions such as *poor, bad, proper, efficient,* and *best,* when used without stating the standards the speaker has in mind, and the use of general statements either provide the receiver with no information he can utilize in making his decisions or leave him with an erroneous impression. When these vague words and phrases have to be employed, examples will help the receiver to visualize the giver's idea. Some people also habitually use pronouns without sharply defining the references; the use of *nouns* instead of *it, those, he, them,* clears up such vagueness.

---

[5] Readers familiar with C. K. Ogden and I. A. Richards, *The Meaning of Meaning* (New York: Harcourt, Brace & Co., 1927), or with Stuart Chase, *The Tyranny of Words* (New York: Harcourt, Brace & Co., 1938), will recognize that in these paragraphs we are talking about the field known as "general semantics."

Serious misunderstandings frequently arise when two men start off a discussion in the belief that they are both talking about the same subject, whereas they are actually talking about two quite different subjects. Each has a different situation in mind, a different frame of reference. When a man discovers that he and his receiver seem to be talking at cross purposes, a quick description of what the subject is and the more obvious features of it, together with some examples, will ordinarily clear up the misconception. If a man makes a practice of prefacing each discussion with such a description, most of the arguments that arise from such misunderstandings can be avoided.

The above suggestions for reducing this barrier to communication can be summarized as follows: In using a value term or phrase, one that is likely to be misconstrued, first try to live inside the receiver's mind for a moment before writing or speaking and then choose words that will convey an accurate picture of our idea; the key task is to recast the statement into a more factual one, one that calls up in the hearer's mind explicit, relatively tangible images which are familiar to him.

Mental Lapses: Failure of the Decider to Acquire All the Necessary Premises

Even though the information a decider needs may be available in the organization, he frequently fails to secure it, as a result of mental lapses. Sometimes, the men who know of information or decisions that others could use in framing their premises either do not realize that need or else forget to forward the information. And the decider himself may overlook information he has already accumulated, or forget to ask for what he knows he should consider. Occasional mental lapses are almost inevitable. In the press of work a man's mind is not capable of bringing to bear on each project every piece of information and every idea he has encountered. Establishing a pattern of making written or mental notes as reminders seems to be the only way of surmounting this barrier.

A decision maker himself frequently forgets to explain exactly what he needs and why, when asking someone else to gather information for him. If a subordinate is forced to imagine what his boss wants, he will probably bring back information that is not quite right, even though he is both intelligent and conscientious. A clear idea of how the requested figures on sales volume, for instance, or expenses, or production are to be used provides the subordinate with a guide in gathering the information. Almost all the series of figures compiled by a company—all its old records—include in their totals certain data which are abnormal—nonhomogeneous or nonrecurring items such as a special order sold at a low price and pushed through the plant by using short cuts. When raw data are to be used for a special purpose, unusual circumstances such as these should be brought to the decision maker's attention, so that he can make necessary allowances. For instance, the data to be employed in operations research formulas will have to be "adjusted," or else the answers will be quite wrong.

Some bosses also occasionally forget to "button things up." When they make a change in procedures, they go over the new program with the men most obviously affected, but overlook the fact that the change will also alter certain small details of the work of other people.

Deliberate or Unconscious Distortion

People frequently distort the information they communicate to others. This is a device a man uses to protect himself against adverse criticism and to raise his prestige. He may also distort information for the purpose of furthering his goals or those of his group, his boss, his subordinates, or his company when his or their future welfare would be endangered if he were to tell the exact and whole truth. Probably no one is absolutely free from this type of dishonesty. Salesmen and advertising men often feel obligated to distort the truth; and employees, in dealing with their superiors, distort (and sometimes withhold) information that would reflect adversely on them and their groups.

In some instances the distortion may have been planned quite deliberately, but more often the response is instinctive and unconscious. In deciding which information to withhold from his superior, which to twist slightly, and which to pass to his superior in accurate form, a man frequently uses premises he is not consciously aware of and ones he would certainly not care to disclose to others. Both the deliberate and the unconscious distortions arise in part from the codes of behavior a man picks up during his formative years. For example, the boys' code, "Never tattle on another guy," is found workable in adult life. He knows that if he turns informer, he will be ostracized; so he will distort or misstate facts, when necessary, to protect members of his group. Incidentally, this gives him status; he is not a liar in their eyes, he is a hero.

In addition to protecting himself and his fellow workers, a man may try to "cover up" for his *boss*, or his department, or his company by turning in reports that look better than the facts warrant. And an executive may try to mislead *his* superiors in order to make his subordinates look better than they really are. We can expect to encounter distortions whenever outsiders are trying to encroach on a group in which there are strong loyalties—whether the encroacher be a person, or the company, or another department, or some informal group.

A man may also distort or hold back information to punish a superior or a staff man who has been jeopardizing one of his goals. This type of sanction—rewarding a superior by supplying accurate "inside" information (thus enabling him to make wise decisions) or punishing him by hiding information or supplying wrong information (thus making him look like a stupid decision maker) are very potent if the executive must depend on this one source of information.

Distortions are more readily discovered than might appear at first sight. We make due allowance for the fact that any man, despite his intention to be completely honest, will filter his information through the ideas he has stored in the three main reservoirs that we encountered in Chapter 5. And we soon learn to detect a man who regularly twists his communications, for we notice that what he says usually conflicts with what we already know. Once we discover this, we thereafter simply discount what he tells us, or else always double-check before accepting. The use of direct communication channels as pathways instead of the up-and-down ones shown in the formal organization chart helps to reduce the chances of distortion.

Distance as a Barrier in Communication

Two distance barriers are characteristically found in organizations. One is what might be called a "geographical barrier." The newly invented vehicles of communication have lowered this barrier in recent years; if time is important, telegraph, telephone, or air mail can be used. However, geographical distance produces two unwanted results. Sometimes, the information needed is never forwarded. The "owner" of the information may not realize that it would be useful; and in any case, sending it to others is a bothersome task. Distance also makes it difficult to pass along all the subtleties connected with the value premises. Geographical distance is just as much of a barrier when the source and the destination are both located in adjacent buildings as when one of the men works in the central office and the other in a branch office a thousand miles away.

Factual premises are relatively easy to understand when they are committed to paper, so the distance they travel harms them not at all. But the decisions made from a distance are seldom exactly right when most of the required premises are primarily of a value nature. This is the main reason why the men in a branch office or plant often say, "Those guys at the central office are certainly stupid." Indeed, these decisions may *not* be the best ones for the welfare of the company as a whole because the central-office decision makers do not have all of the value premises and those they do receive by mail or phone lack the subtle nuances which can be transmitted only through the eye and the ear.

The second distance barrier is what could be called a "social barrier." A janitor or an office clerk does not drop into the president's office and offer information or premises or proposals; it is "just not done." The men low in the hierarchy are frequently "scared to talk to him." They might show how "dumb" they are and be fired as a consequence. They ordinarily believe that the high executive will consider their premises trivial, so why waste his time? In any case, their immediate superior and fellow workers may suspect them of "apple polishing." An executive who says, "My door is always open," is puzzled when no one calls. For an explanation of this, he has only to recall how far away and unapproachable the middle-level and top executives seemed to him when he first started to work. Yet, as we have seen, in order to make solid decisions, the men at the top need much of the information gathered by the men at the bottom of the hierarchy, especially their value premises, and in particular the ones that would probably be distorted if they were sent through the regular channels.

Visiting with subordinates periodically in their own offices or places of work is one way of breaking down this barrier. The men feel more at home there and are likely to feel more free about revealing what they actually think, provided that they have confidence in the executive and recognize that he is not snooping. He has an opportunity to pick up difficult-to-communicate value premises relating to company problems as well as those that neither he nor his subordinates want to commit to paper for all to see. This also gives him an opportunity to gain some insight into the man's semipermanent goals and premises. An executive need not work in his shirt sleeves and drive an old car to reduce this social barrier. His task is to establish confidence on the part of the men that he will listen and understand, and on the part of the men's associates and their immediate bosses that this is not a spy system but a means of uncovering difficult-to-come-by premises for making decisions that will advance the goals of the company and the men. Needless to say, this confidence is hard to win.

TRANSMITTAL OF PERMANENTLY USEFUL INFORMATION: TRAINING

In the first half of this chapter, our attention has been centered on the creation of a formal communication system designed to transmit *temporarily useful information* for making specific daily decisions, and on the *typical barriers* to communication. From here on, we shall be investigating the task of communicating *permanently* useful information. As indicated early in the chapter, these permanent communications differ in only two major respects from the temporary ones; the temporary ones are designed for *immediate* use and for only *one* or *two* decisions, then thrown away, whereas the permanent ones are given the men *now* for use at a *later* date and for use in making a *great many* decisions. The latter not only reduce communication costs but improve the company decisions.

As an aid in keeping track of where we are during our examination of this notion of transmitting permanently useful information, the following outline should prove useful.

I. Communicating information to be used for making many similar (repetitive, or standardized) decisions: training workers—
  A. Training workers in the "one best way" to handle a repetitive physical task.
  B. Communicating (issuing) rules and regulations to be used by subordinates in making routine decisions.
  C. Use of manuals to communicate methods of carrying out regular work.
II. Communication of a method of thinking to be used for making one-of-a-kind decisions: training executives—
  A. Hiring men who have already received much of this information.
  B. Executive training and delegation of formal authority.
    1. Communicating such a method of thinking in the class room—training young men to:
      a. Make decisions.
      b. Gain acceptance of their decisions.
      c. Plan and put plans into effect.
    2. On-the-job executive training. (The paragraphs on this topic will bear careful study.)

C. Executive orientation.

D. Inducing the experienced executives to help train the young men.

In very broad terms we are here communicating information designed to fill out the men's mental image of the company and the way it operates, or should operate—the miniature model they create in their minds.

TRANSMITTING INFORMATION USEFUL IN MAKING REPETITIVE DECISIONS: EMPLOYEE TRAINING

Men who handle routine work, which requires them to make essentially the same decisions each day, can frequently be supplied with premises they can use rather permanently. Teaching those men and women who perform repetitive manual work a "one best way" to do it, or furnishing men who make routine decisions with certain rules and regulations they are to follow, or giving them manuals as guides, may not always work out well as might be expected; but in many cases the advantages outweigh the disadvantages.

The cost of deciding on a "one best way," or preparing rules, or printing manuals would be absurdly high if the employees were to use only once or twice the decisions contained in these forms of communication. But when these decisions are put to work as premises by many workers in making hundreds of decisions each day, the cost per worker-decision approaches zero. Moreover, the decisions of the workmen, based on these permanent, carefully worked out, standardized instructions, should be of better quality. Equally important, fewer supervisors will be required; and the company can employ less highly educated plant and office workers for these jobs.

Training Plant and Office Employees to Handle Routine Physical Tasks

Where groups of men or women will be performing the same physical tasks repeatedly, deciding on the "one best way" for their physical movements and training those people to use them—to use the industrial engineers' decisions as premises for their decisions about how to do the job—provides most of the advantages just mentioned.[6]

To be more concrete, let us suppose that we are able to standardize certain jobs heretofore done by men and women who used premises they had themselves picked up—used their own to decide how to per-

---

[6] Note, in passing, that there are probably many "best ways," many alternatives for handling a specific task, and that the ones chosen will always be subject to improvement.

form their work. Were we to decide on a one best way and train several workers to follow it, whether it be to stamp out the same piece on the same type of punch press day after day, or to assemble the same unit or handle certain uniform paper work in the office, the following advantages accrue: The cost of guiding each of the decisions the operators make is negligible; they are able to make better decisions about how to move their hands; they can make more such hand movements in an hour; and since the hourly pay rates for these workers is lower than for skilled workers whom we would otherwise need, direct labor costs are reduced.

But standardization of manual tasks is not a panacea; it often produces unforeseen, unwanted consequences. The proposed standardized body movements frequently prove awkward or fatiguing for the operator, so that he simply ignores the instructions. He will also rebel if he has conceived what he thinks is a better way (and his way *may* be better) or if his friends ridicule him for "letting those efficiency experts tell him what to do." And anyway, as the weeks pass he tends to slip back into old, established habits. Nor is the problem of determining a *proper* standard time easily solved. The conditions under which the men and women actually perform their jobs each day may differ considerably in many cases from those that existed at the time the original study was made. Frequently, the standards set are not completely accurate, even though scrupulous care was used in making what industrial engineers call "allowances." If the standards are too loose, the men cut their production to fit the standards. If the standards are too tight, the workers use sanctions—see that unexpected things go wrong. When the standards are not realistic, inequities show up in the men's pay rates based on these standards; predictions of production per man-hour are erroneous; consequently, the production schedules are not entirely accurate, and the cost estimates used for pricing may be misleading. Contrary to what many laymen suppose, in most medium-sized companies, there are relatively few standardized tasks really uniform enough and of long enough duration to warrant motion and time studies. In those companies where most of the men perform several types of jobs every day, the costs of setting standards for each, of formal training, and of record keeping mount up rapidly.

For jobs of such short duration that they do not warrant methods, motion, and time studies, this training can be done on an informal and simplified basis. It is not always necessary to make formal studies and set down written instructions for each job. A foreman can usually work out a practical procedure on the basis of past experience and train the men informally himself. Occasionally, fellow workers are also adept at this. Nor do records have to be maintained of standard versus actual time in order to gain benefits from training the people to follow the "one best way." Frequently, the men's contributions are higher under an informal system than under one where measured standards are set and actual production is compared with the standard.

Company Rules and Regulations as Permanent Communications

Company rules relieve executives of the task of making a great many of the recurrent daily decisions and also provide the subordinates with the "best" premises for reaching such decisions themselves. Rules and regulations are attempts on the part of executives to exercise authority—to induce the subordinate to follow certain courses of action under given circumstances. These are frequently called "company policies," but in this book we shall confine that term to statements of major long-range goals and means. In some companies, most of the rules consist of an accumulation of rather general decisions made over the years and handed down by word of mouth. In others, the rules are laboriously outlined in manuals, indexed, and called *Standard Practice Instructions* or *Standard Operating Procedures.* Supposedly, all the employee has to do is to go to this book and figure out which rule applies to the particular problem he faces, and then use the decision contained therein as the sole premise for his decision. The presumption is that if he always follows the rules, he will always make perfect decisions. Rules that two people who are relatives shall never be employed in the company, that each man shall retire at the age of 65, that prices of a certain product shall be quoted at 200 per cent of the out-of-pocket costs of raw materials and labor, that the books shall be closed on the last day of the month, or that employees shall be given a raise at the end of one year unless good cause is shown to the contrary, are illustrations of these rather permanent instructions designed to cover a large number of similar situations.

Some men consider rules a godsend. When they can look in "the book" and find out what to do, their lives are much simpler. Such a man feels confident that every decision he makes on the basis of the directives he finds there will advance the company's goals; even more pertinent to him is the fact that if he does as the book directs, he will never get into trouble. Rules enable those unfortunate men who lack self-confidence to make decisions of which they can be sure. Some bosses welcome these rules, too. The boss need not spend time and trouble examining each case himself; he can safely delegate these decisions to his subordinates. Also, supervisory costs are cut. In addition, the book contains rules about which everyone knows in advance, a body of "laws" which may be used in adjudicating disputes.

While the use of rules and regulations can help to smooth the operation of an organization, rigid adherence to them often leads to unforeseen and unwanted consequences. Where human beings are concerned, as we have had occasion to note, no two situations are precisely alike; however, the men who make a rule must, perforce, assume that all of the situations covered by that rule in the future will almost exactly duplicate the specific ones they had in mind when they framed the regulation. Hence, these rules often appear unrealistic to the men who are asked to follow them—"Made by some fellow who's never been away from his desk." Moreover, these regulations usually stipulate (or imply) that the applicable rule be the *only* premise used by the decider. But, as we have seen, in order to make good decisions in behalf of the company, several premises should ordinarily be employed. Thus, if the subordinate is required to follow the rule blindly, his decision frequently injures the company. In addition, insistence on blind or literal adherence to company rules may produce some of those undesirable consequences already noted in connection with the use of simple authority, such as doing only enough to "get by" the rule.

Rules appear to proliferate in organizations; this seems to be especially true in companies where the executives are unsure of their subordinates' decisions.[7] In such cases the rules are thought of as "red tape." Too many rules not only slow down decision making but often lead to a breakdown in men's respect for the regulations. When a man thinks that the use of a rule will injure him, he simply bends it or discards it and uses his own premises. However, to protect himself, he will usually try to make the records "look legal." If the man and his boss *both* realize that the strict application of the rule will harm the company's welfare as well as their own, the

---

[7] In one company where I have worked as a consultant, their "book" was almost a foot thick and contained rules governing every type of situation. It had not been thoroughly revised in twenty-five years. Moreover, in the earlier years, almost every infraction of the rules brought severe penalties. On the other hand, another very large corporation with which I have worked had no manuals except for an accounting manual and rules for standards of product quality.

chances are that they will look for a rule that permits them to do as they wish; or they will collaborate in breaking the rule and falsifying the record. Any reader who has been in the military services is familiar with these patterns of behavior. Such rule breaking and falsification frequently occur in business organizations run largely by rules and regulations—more often than management may realize.[8]

Manuals as Sources of Permanent Premises

Despite what has just been said, manuals *can* be of great assistance. If, instead of specific "how-to-do-it" rules, the statements are framed in terms of *goals* and simply outline the means and premises the men in the company should consider in making their decisions, many of the drawbacks enumerated above can be alleviated. In fact, there are three types of such manuals which can be used simultaneously. One is an orientation manual, the purpose of which is to provide the members with a statement of the long-term goals—for example, the exact niche the company hopes to fill and the major means the top executives have decided to employ during the next few years in attempting to fill that niche. It describes what the company thinks of as its permanent policies. In addition, this manual may include a brief history of the company's successes *and* failures, and thumbnail sketches of its past and present top executives. The company's past is a living thing, a source of premises for future decisions; and the executives should be described as real, knowable people. This orientation manual furnishes premises of use to old employees as well as new ones, and it may be of almost equal value when distributed to customers as a source of premises for their decisions about buying.

The second manual would contain what might be thought of as standard practice instructions—accounting procedures and quality specifications designed to ensure uniformity in handling a mass of detailed, standardizable work. In those cases where uniformity reduces the confusion and where, in other respects, the decision about how the job should be performed is a matter of indifference to employees, most of the men will follow the regulations without grumbling. The manual should give the chief reasons why these uniform procedures were adopted. But, equally important—and this feature is a departure from the orthodox manual—the men should be given

---

[8] In my work as a consultant, I have seen some instances where the emphasis on rigid rules has not only caused the men to be fearful of making their own decisions but has undermined their sense of honesty and personal integrity; telling lies—deliberate distortions—becomes an approved behavior pattern throughout the company.

explicit permission to *make exceptions* if it is entirely clear that the company would benefit, and if the work in other departments would not be upset.

The third manual is basically a job manual or, more exactly, a series of job manuals, each dealing with a major job classification— salesmen, design or production engineers, accountants, and so on. The chief purpose of this type of manual is to show how the "perfect" man would do the job. Each booklet would describe the crucial decisions the men in these jobs are called upon to make, indicate the types of premises they will probably find useful for each kind of decision, point out the best sources for these premises, and show some of the unwanted consequences to be borne in mind in making these decisions. The writer of the booklet must have lived with the men and their leaders for a time, for, to be really useful, such a manual must be framed in specific terms and must honestly attempt to help the men to make intelligent decisions. This sort of manual is of great help in training and retraining men. In addition, the men themselves can use it to appraise their own work; and their superiors and the personnel department can use it in evaluating the men before deciding on raises and promotions. It supplies all of them with a description of how the perfect man would do the job, and thus is a measuring stick for the quality of the men's decisions and the number of decisions they should be able to make each day.

Manuals of the three types mentioned can be used effectively only in conjunction with a staff of executives willing and able to think. Such manuals provide a tool for training a large segment of the company's employees—for teaching and encouraging them to make decisions of their own—but they are not a substitute for executive training.

DEVELOPING EXECUTIVES

This section deals further with the task of communicating permanently useful information to members of the organization. Here, however, instead of training workers to handle repetitive decisions, we turn our attention to the task of teaching lower-level and middle-level executives how to make decisions that are seldom exactly alike, the fairly complex ones which will affect the welfare of the company and its members in some major way. The objective is to reduce the burdensome but intangible costs arising from inferior decisions, the ones that never appear as expense items in the operating statement. The men will be making decisions like these: "What size raw material inventory shall we plan to have six weeks from now?" "Should we drop such and such a line?" "Should we set up a new branch?" "Should we develop this new product?" or "Should we reorganize our production planning department?"

In executive training, we are communicating a *method of thinking* which the men can use permanently. Ready-made decisions such as those taught employees who do repetitive manual work or those contained in rules and regulations are of very little practical use to them; they must build each decision anew, create solutions for difficult problems. What we really want are executive leaders.

Hiring Potential Executives

Fortunately, a company need not do all this executive training itself. Even a young, inexperienced college man will have gathered *some* ideas about how to think; presumably, a little of this has been communicated to him by his professors. Hiring inexperienced men who have already developed mental discipline and an ability to reason things out for themselves is undoubtedly less expensive than attempting to communicate this art to them after they join the company. Furthermore, as we discovered in our examination of the premise concept, in the search for executive timber, we are looking for men who have the ability to use both value and factual premises. Technically trained men who feel at home with both can sometimes be found, but as indicated before, many balk at value premises. The big problem is to secure men who can frame reliable value premises and use them with confidence. Liberal arts courses characteristically deal with this type of premise, so that most men with such training should have gathered a supply of these and should be able to use them with some assurance. Probably such men will never fully master all the technical premises used by the company's scientists and engineers, but they should be able to integrate the value premises they learn in college with the factual and value premises they will accumulate after they have been with the company for a while.[9]

A new, experienced executive hired from outside will presumably have accumulated an even larger array of facts, premises, and general conclusions. He can employ these in his work even though the

---

[9] Unfortunately, a company seldom finds it possible to put to use all the information that a new man in the organization has gathered from his previous training. And sometimes, a new recruit must *un*learn some of the premises he has been taught. Colleges, for instance, must teach a good many generalizations in order to give the student a usable, basic framework in his fields; but faculty members sometimes fail to tell their students that these generalizations are seldom precisely true in a specific application. The company has the job of teaching the man to uncover the specific pieces of information pertinent to the special problem at hand, frame these into premises, and then reason to a conclusion.

company's products and its customers and employees differ from those of his former company. In trying to select executive material from *within* the company, management is trying to do the same thing —select a man who already has many of the premises required on the new job.

Visualizing the job to be filled, and especially the kinds of decisions the man selected for the position will be making, then imagining the *perfect* man for the job, and thereafter imagining that each applicant is already working in that job, enables the executive to test out each man in his mind's eye. This is facilitated by trying to clarify the types of premises—factual and value premises—the man on that job is likely to use most. In hiring an engineer, for example, or an accountant, or a statistician, or a machinist, management is largely looking for men who can readily handle certain types of factual premises. In hiring a salesman, a personnel man, or an executive, management is endeavoring to find a man who feels at ease with value premises. A man with the potentials for handling *both* types of premises is the one to watch for; much of his basic training has already been communicated to him.

Training Executive Leaders and Delegation of Formal Authority

Probably the one most glaring weakness found in virtually all companies is a paucity of strong young executives who know how to lead. Yet they are essential if the company is to flourish in the years to come when the present top executives retire, leave, or die. Moreover, they can be used effectively during the interim to strengthen the company's ability to compete for a larger share of the business available. Characteristically, the older executives expect a young man to train himself by watching others and getting burned a few times. "He has to learn by his own mistakes," we are told; or, "Throw him in, and he will soon learn to swim." But the development of young executive leaders can be hastened and the quality of their decisions greatly improved by a training program. The task is to teach these men how to set goals, create ideas for achieving these goals, make decisions, gain acceptance of their decisions, and put their decisions into effect. Once this has been communicated, his superiors are more ready to delegate formal authority to him.

Class Room Training. Some insight can be gained by taking a formal course on the tasks of an executive. This book you are now reading has been written primarily for such a course offered at a college or university, or by a company. It is also hoped that men who have no opportunity to take such a course will read this book and find it fruitful. But, no matter how it is used, merely reading will not do much good. A man soon forgets what he reads unless he discusses the ideas with others and attempts to put them to work. Even in classroom teaching, it is almost essential to supplement any book on executive training with real problems drawn from business. Obviously, extra benefits can be gained by reading the assigned chapter and looking over the problem or case that goes with it, then discussing the applications with others. However, if a man is to enjoy *lasting* benefits, he must be willing to do a good deal of hard thinking before the class meets and reach a decision of his own based on the premises he finds in the chapter and the assigned problem.[10] Recall in this connection what was said earlier about thorough preparation before a meeting as a method of winning leadership in a group, and the task of a leader (here the instructor) in guiding and controlling the discussion.

A company that embarks on an executive development program will probably find that it must offer its own training course and lay plans for freeing certain of its middle-level and lower-echelon executives so that they, as well as the young recruits, can take the course. When the experienced men understand some of the concepts explored in a formal course such as the one described above, when they are in sympathy with the ideas and are willing to put them into practice, they create an atmosphere in which the promising younger men are encouraged to take the initiative. In addition, the caliber of their own work should improve.

On the Job Training.   But perhaps the main purpose of a formal training course is to prepare the seasoned executives to teach the younger men individually—teach them informally *on the job* by using everyday problems. Formal executive training programs frequently die an early death, primarily because medium-sized companies cannot always find enough promising men to justify holding formal classes after the course has been offered a few times; the men hired in the years that follow are left to fend for themselves.[11]

---

[10] Appendix A, "Check List for Writing Business Reports" (pp. 542–44), may prove helpful as a guide in preparing classroom assignments. See also Thomas C. Raymond, *Problems in Business Administration: Analysis by the Case Method* (New York: McGraw-Hill Book Co., 1955); and *The Case Method at the Harvard Business School*, edited by Malcolm P. McNair and Anita C. Hersum (New York: McGraw-Hill Book Co., 1954). These authors discuss the teaching of decision making solely by the use of cases.

[11] Another reason why training programs frequently prove disappointing is that the men forget to put the new concepts into practice. A carefully pursued on-the-job training program for subordinates provides bosses with an opportunity to use the ideas—and thus learn them more thoroughly themselves.

Fortunately, once the established executives have been trained, the company has at hand the machinery for training informally the new recruits who come in each year. Teaching subordinates is actually one of the most important jobs of an executive. But without some understanding of how decisions are made and how to gain acceptance of them, he has trouble in explaining these practices to a subordinate, even though he unconsciously uses the concepts himself. Without this understanding, executives tend to tell their subordinates, "Do it this way." As a consequence the young man never finds out what alternatives and premises his superior has taken into consideration. Hence, he is forced to return time after time for guidance; he never gains confidence in his own ability to make decisions.

An executive can do this on-the-job communicating very effectively by showing his subordinate how to solve some of the concrete departmental problems which arise. "In making this kind of decision, try to find premises of this type because of such and such. Probably you can get them from Fred. You are likely to find certain of Joe's premises rather shaky, but you can depend on Art for accuracy. You'll want to watch for such-and-such unwanted results in X and Y departments. You should give great weight to premises such as these because this and this is likely to happen," and so on, until the decision is reached. He also needs to teach the art of gaining acceptance and putting decisions into effect. He is attempting to make this young man the perfect man for the job.

More specifically, to teach a young man the decision-making process and the art of winning leadership, the best way is to begin by assigning him some simple departmental decisions, and when he has mastered these, turn to more and more complex ones. These small decisions contain exactly the same ingredients as the larger ones, as we have already seen. Initially, while the young man is new and fumbling around, his superior should help him to define his problem, and thus the goal, and proffer some likely alternative means for achieving the goal. His first assignment would be: "Gather pieces of information pertinent to these alternatives. Probably Mac can supply some; look in the file for others." After these are assembled, the superior can show how he frames the information into premises, weights them, and reaches his decision. Once these ideas are mastered, he can assign the man a relatively simple problem, tell him to define it clearly, think up some alternatives, gather his premises, reach a decision, and write a report, so that the two can sit down together and appraise the conclusion. At this stage the section head or department head is teaching his subordinate how to check his decisions. As soon as the subordinate gains the ability to cope with this particular type of small decision, the boss should instruct him to go ahead and make these hereafter but to come back for help whenever he feels unsure of himself. The executive now has a certain amount of confidence in the man.

Gradually, the young man can be given more difficult decisions, which require a broader and broader set of premises, and after a time, some that will affect other departments in the company. During each of these successively higher stages, the process described above of checking and guiding the young man will need to be repeated until eventually decisions of considerable complexity can be turned over to him. The goal is to teach him to make decisions that he had heretofore been afraid to make on his own—to teach him executive leadership.

The executive should *not* delegate this decision making, *should not delegate this authority formally,* until the young man has *won* from him the right to make each of these types of decisions. It is the subordinate's responsibility to win the confidence of his superior (and also of his associates)—confidence that his decisions will stand up when re-examined several months hence. However, before finally turning over this decision making, the seasoned executive should make sure that the subordinate knows three other significant things: (1) which decisions he is capable of making, (2) which decisions to take to his boss in tentative form for rechecking to see whether any important alternatives or premises have been overlooked, and (3) which problems he should hand over to the boss for decision after merely gathering as much pertinent information as he can find. Only then has the young man won the *full* confidence of his superior, won authority and leadership; only then is he ready for a formal appointment to a responsible job.

Executive Orientation

Executive orientation as a means of training has been indirectly touched upon in earlier chapters. In part this orientation consists of an attempt to teach practical rationality in decision making to the young executive—teach him to look for goals and premises beyond his own little cubicle in making his decisions. It is the executive's responsibility to give his men concrete pictures of the company's long-term goals, of the chief means the executives have chosen for achieving them, and the main problems "our" department as well as the other departments face in trying to achieve those goals.[12] He is teaching the man to look in four directions for sources of premises: to look upward in the hierarchy to the company's intermediate and ultimate goals, and the chief means the top executives have decided upon; to look to the "right" and to the "left" into the other departments whose work will be affected by his decisions; and to look down within his own department for local premises useful to him.

Orientation also includes keeping subordinates informed about current new developments both inside and outside the company, so that they can employ this information later whenever the occasion arises. Information such as the following often supplies men with useful premises: "The production section down on the first floor is overloaded with orders, but the one in the annex is working far below capacity." "The design department is working on an improvement in product No. 14." "The company is trying to decide whether to establish a new branch in the Southwest." "The company is planning to open up a new sales territory." "It's trying to solicit this type of customer." "The sales outlook is pretty gloomy, so all the other departments are going to have to cater to the needs of the sales department from now on." "Competitors have been raising their prices." "Freight rates may be increased soon." "Our inventories of products No. 3 and No. 7 are getting out of line." "The work of such and such a department will have to be changed in this way because of the new programs I told you about in the other department." With such information, subordinates should be able to make better company decisions.

Besides communicating to their own subordinates any developments that might affect their department, company executives on the same level of the hierarchy will often spontaneously set up horizontal channels to transmit a continuous flow among themselves of often quite subtle information which they can use to orient themselves— information they can use to fill in details of their mental images of the company and how it now operates. This orientation is essential in predicting the consequences of proposals they have in mind.

Information originating outside his own group provides a man with elements for premises which would never otherwise have occurred to him. With these additional premises which he secures from what we have called "orientation," he begins to think and act like a seasoned executive.

---

[12] The policy manual described a few pages back is a useful tool for orienting a new (or an experienced) executive.

Inducing Experienced Executives to Push the Decision Making Down in the Organization

Gaining the older executives' wholehearted support of a training program requires considerable forethought. Often, they will resent it. Teaching inexperienced subordinates calls for a great deal of patience; and, at the outset, it requires a great deal of time. Even more important, an executive who feels insecure about his job may fear that his subordinate will take over his job; and in many cases, he will wonder how he will keep busy after teaching this subordinate to make all his decisions.

In fact, their full approval is needed. The training program will be a failure unless the trainees are convinced that they will be rewarded by their immediate superiors or at least not punished, if they practice what they were taught. In many companies, creativity, self-reliance, and assumption of responsibility are covertly punished by some line executives. A young man dares not accept at face value the word of his superiors that the executives encourage initiative; the actions of management must bear out the words.

The training program will also be sabotaged unless the "old-timers" are reassured about their own welfare. Probably the chief executive will have to play a major role in convincing them that the program will produce valuable long-term results for everyone. He will have to prove to them that even though the task of teaching will be burdensome at first, their subordinates can be taught to handle intelligently many of those small decisions which keep piling up on their desks, the ones they have been taking home at night. He must also reassure them that their jobs will be safe. The task here is to show them that the ultimate objective of the executive training program is to raise the quality and increase the number of good decisions made by *all* executives, including those high up in the hierarchy. Their greater contributions should, in turn, lead to greater financial contributions from the customers; and this should lead to higher salaries as well as greater nonmonetary inducements for each of the executives.

Such a program has the effect of pushing the decision making down into the organization. The company and the men in the company gain several advantages from this, four of which stand out:

1. Each executive will have more time to think and plan. He is relieved of detail—of the task of gathering premises and of making those hundreds of small decisions which consume time. He can spend some of his hours with his

feet on the desk looking out of the window, trying out in his mind first one means-end staircase and then another, revising and revamping until he creates a plan that will come close to solving some of the problems he faces.

2. Certain decisions made down in the hierarchy will frequently be more realistic and telling than if they had been made by the executives higher up. The man on the spot has lived in the situation, so that he already has available most of the factual and value premises originating there. He already knows the value premises which are difficult to see and difficult to explain to others, and there is no distortion arising from passing these to others. Moreover, if the communication system and the training program are working properly, the man should have available most of the important premises which can be secured from sources outside his section or department. If a top executive were to make these decisions, only a few of these local premises would be likely ever to reach him; and several would probably be distorted.

3. A reservoir of executive talent is provided. Men low in the hierarchy get practice in handling the tasks of an executive. Consequently, when an executive is needed for a position, a competent one can be found within the organization. A company that promotes executives on the basis of seniority, or is frequently forced to go outside the organization for supervisors or executives, should regard these practices as danger signals; it is obviously failing to develop executives.

4. Pushing decision making down in the organization affords an outlet for men's creative drives. This practice uncovers talents and unleashes forces of great value to the company. Many young men of promise, as well as older men, feel frustrated in their jobs because they think that their capacities are not fully utilized; either they have not yet learned how to employ their executive talents fully, or their bosses will not permit them to do so. Opportunities to develop and use their creative ability supply satisfactions of great importance to men who aspire to high executive positions. These inducements, nonmonetary in nature, also increase his wholeheartedness and his contributions to the company.

SUMMARY

That communication plays a key role in gaining acceptance, that it is very costly, and that the costs of bad decisions can be reduced by improving communication has been the theme running through this chapter. In the sections dealing with the task of setting up a formal communication system and with the barriers to communication, the objective was to smooth the way for communications that would be used almost immediately as premises and then discarded. Later, the emphasis shifted to the communication of permanently useful premises. We discussed the reduction of communication costs by training men to use the "best" alternatives in their routine physical tasks and by providing rules and regulations and manuals that would guide them in making many of their small everyday decisions. We showed

how teaching men to become executive leaders could reduce the costs
of ill-advised decisions. No company can expect to solve its communication problems as well as it would like, but management can
greatly improve company communications by working presistently
on the weak spots. The informal groups in the company, which we
shall investigate next, supply additional pathways for communication; and they too serve as means of influencing the behavior of the
men in the company.

PROBLEM
COMMUNICATION AND TRAINING

Draw, from the Gould Metal Company case, examples of:
1. A system for communicating temporarily useful information.
2. The several barriers to communication.
3. The several types of permanently useful information that a company
   can profitably transmit to its members.

If you can find no suitable example, make up a plausible one for the Gould
Company or draw one from the Frisch Electronics Company case, the Midwest Feed Company case, or from your own experience.

Be prepared to describe how these examples tie back into the concepts
developed in Chapters 1 through 7.

Chapter **9** THE USE OF
INFORMAL GROUPS
IN GAINING
ACCEPTANCE

THE TASKS of overcoming resistance to change and deciding how to introduce changes center largely in the company's informal work groups. In this chapter, we shall be mentally testing out our new proposals on the members of these groups, seeking to uncover premises that will help us predict their responses. Workers frequently fight changes; the reason is that they and their jobs are peculiarly vulnerable; changes in the plant or office procedure often threaten their status in the company, and perhaps their very livelihood; yet they are virtually powerless to protect themselves. And such changes are frequent. A company is obliged to alter many jobs when it decides to drop an old product and produce a new one, when it decides to improve or lower its quality standards, introduce mass production or automation in the plant, or install electronic data processing equipment in the office to handle the statistical and accounting work. In view of the above, it is understandable that groups and their informal leaders frequently try to sabotage a new program. They use sanctions and the pocket veto to thwart changes.

Our objective in these pages will be to amplify our understanding of human beings, not to learn how to manipulate people. Nor are we interested in "life adjustment," though we shall certainly use our ingenuity to conceive and introduce changes that the men and women will welcome. Our problem is to induce these people to adopt changes that will further the company's welfare.

As a foundation, we shall begin the chapter with an examination of the nature of these informal groups. Then we shall explore five methods of employing informal groups to gain acceptance of our proposed program. First we shall examine the task of uncovering the goals of a group that will be affected by a proposed change and the means that are used by its members to achieve those goals; this will help us revise our proposal; if revision is not possible we shall at least know wherein the proposal jeopardizes their goals and the extent of the group's opposition. Next, we try to uncover those groups affected by the change whose members are very *loyal to the group* and thereafter frame proposals that will further the goals of these groups as well as the goals of the company; we hope that the men will carry out the proposal wholeheartedly when they see that the group will benefit. Third, we shall work with a quite elusive idea, the problem of devising standards that measure an individual's status in his group and at the same time measure his contributions to the company.

These are three of the chief uses of informal groups. Near the end of the chapter, we shall look briefly into two other uses—briefly, because we have already been introduced to these: the use of the informal groups' communication system and the use of its leaders.

These five dominate this, our fourth subsystem of Part II. The concluding pages will deal with morale and bring together most of the concepts thus far developed in Part II.

THE NATURE OF INFORMAL GROUPS

In this chapter, we view the company's employees in a new light. Instead of examining the goals and premises of *individuals* in the organization as we did in the first half of Chapter 5 (there we were examining their biological, psychological, and social needs, the goals of their outside organizations, and the reservoirs from which they draw their basic goals and premises), and instead of examining the goals and premises of *formal groups* (the salesmen, the customers, the research men, the plant workers, and so on) as we did in the second half of that chapter, where we were using the inducement-contribution concept, we here think of employees as members of *social groups*.

Executives coalesce into informal groups, just as do plant workers and office workers. And salesmen, research workers, and staff men frequently become members of such groups. We shall center our attention here on plant workers, primarily because these are usually the most intransigent.

Informal groups are regularly found in every business concern, except possibly those employing only two or three people. Their existence is essential to the well-being of a company.[1] They are not necessarily crosses to bear or something management must fight, as some people would have us believe. However, informal groups can harm the company when they act solely for the purpose of furthering the personal goals of their members.

The term *informal group* will be used here to designate a group of people who have been drawn together spontaneously—that is, without apparent direction—for the purpose of achieving certain goals they have in mind. Upon discovering their common goals, they unconsciously or consciously conclude that they can attain them better by working together than by working alone. Usually, the groups formed by employees coalesce because some of their needs are not otherwise fulfilled by the company. At times, men form groups to further certain company goals which they think are being slighted. The purpose may be entirely personal, however; the men may consciously or unconsciously feel that they are being "pushed around," so they band together for mutual self-protection. People in a community also coalesce into informal groups, just as do the employees; and employees are members of the community groups. We usually call these groups "cliques" or "factions" if we are not members of them.

The needs of the individual members of such groups are constantly changing; hence, informal groups are characteristically fluid. Each group lives only as long as its members feel that it serves their needs. Sometimes, a group lasts only a few minutes; or the need may be semipermanent, in which case the group will tend to approach what we call a "formal organization." Parenthetically, formal organizations usually start out as informal groups; the members discover that they have common long-term goals, so they set up something more permanent, such as a labor union, a government, or a company. Generally speaking, an informal group in a company has no official standing; it is not usually recognized and dealt with officially by management. Even though such a group may have coalesced to advance a company goal, it is not shown on the company's formal organization chart. In contrast with informal groups, the company's

---

[1] Mary Parker Follett did some of the earliest work in this field of informal organizations; her writings were later edited by Henry C. Metcalf and L. Urwick in *Dynamic Administration: The Collected Papers of Mary Parker Follett* (New York: Harper & Bros., 1940). More recently, Chester I. Barnard, T. North Whitehead, Elton Mayo, Fritz J. Roethlisberger, William Lloyd Warner, Carl R. Rogers, William F. Whyte, George C. Homans, Keith Davis, Chris Argyris, and A. Zaleznik have made notable contributions to an understanding of informal groups.

formal organization is made up of groups fashioned at the direction of management. The executives bring the members of the formal groups together to perform certain specific tasks which they anticipate will have to be carried on every day over a long period. The informal groups administer the company's needs which are infrequent or unanticipated, as well as to the men's personal needs which are not taken care of by these formally designated groups.

Two or three men who meet for lunch to talk over a company problem, or men or women who go out for coffee together, would constitute informal groups, according to this definition. So would a group of employees who meet once a week for bowling or poker. Men who eat lunch together on the loading platform and spend most of the hour damning certain company rules and regulations, or certain decisions, or their bosses, have formed an informal group. This also occurs when several men talk over the latest rumors, or their pay rates, or how to outsmart the company. Sometimes, the members of an entire department in a company are drawn together spontaneously, without company direction, to achieve some common goal; in this instance the men in the informal group would be identical with the men in the formally constituted group. Whether a committee appointed by the president to report back on a problem would be an informal or a formal group need not be resolved; certainly, such a committee would partake of both types.

Our definition does not attempt a sharp distinction between the nonofficial groups and these official groups. Here, as elsewhere, we are dealing with a subject that is essentially a matter of degree; the central purpose of the definition is not to supply rigid classifications but to provide insights that will enable management to reach intelligent decisions.

From the foregoing, it becomes clear that informal groups carry on many of the activities of the company. Indeed, they are the flesh and blood of the organization. They transform the company into a living, smoothly functioning organism; they contribute the vital activities not provided for by the skeletonlike formal organization. An understanding of the informal groups reveals how the formal organization *actually* operates; and the way it actually works ordinarily differs in certain respects from the way it is supposed to operate, as shown by the organization chart or as described by an officer of the company.

Much of this vital work is done automatically by the informal groups. However, once the executives become aware of the presence

of informal groups in their company, they can employ them deliberately in several ways to gain acceptance of proposed decisions.
Five of these ways will be discussed in this chapter.

EMPLOYING GROUP GOALS TO FRAME ACCEPTABLE COMPANY PLANS

An awareness of the presence of these informal groups enables an
executive to revise his plans to a point where they are more acceptable to employees than they might otherwise be. Inasmuch as these
groups are formed because the members have common goals, means,
and value premises, observation of them helps an executive to uncover premises these men use—the hopes and fears they think of—in
deciding how wholeheartedly they will carry out a proposal. He can
foresee which groups will welcome his plan and which will oppose it.

Once an executive realizes that informal groups exist in his company and habitually watches for their presence, the task of discovering them is a relatively simple one. Occasionally, they make themselves known to management through a spokesman or by a petition,
though more often management learns of such groups through rumor.
The majority of those executives who live close to their subordinates
can see and sense the groups that have been formed. Sometimes, however, there is little outward manifestation of their presence. In some
cases, to protect one another, the members try to conceal the existence
of their group; in other cases the individuals are but dimly aware
of the reasons for their feelings of oneness with each other.

To get a concrete picture of why particular groups have been
formed, it is necessary to look at the specific members of each group.

Groups Formed because of Similarity in the Men's Backgrounds

People with the same backgrounds frequently combine into informal groups chiefly because they think somewhat alike. They enjoy
one another's company. They feel comfortable when they are talking
together; no "foreign" ideas are interjected into the conversation.
They know what to expect from their fellow members.

An executive cannot do much about changing the goals of informal
groups formed for such purposes, but he can use them as guides in
revising his company proposals. After watching this type of informal
group for a time, he can gain considerable insight into their ultimate
and intermediate goals, and the means and premises the members
have tested and found workable. It may become evident that many

of the members are (or were) members of the same outside organizations. Or perhaps they have a common national heritage, or their religious or political or social philosophies are derived from similar
reservoirs.

Determining the prevailing economic occupational social strata of
the group's members may also provide clues; because of social conditioning, people of the same strata of a community usually adopt
similar goals and premises—social strata such as those named by
Warner: the lowest in the hierarchy, which he describes as the shift-
less unskilled people; the next lowest, the poor but honest wage
earners; the middle class made up of small businessmen and minor
executives; the recently prosperous and members of professions; and
at the top, the local aristocracy.[2]

Once an executive uncovers a common source, he can make an informed guess about the goals and premises that the group cherishes.
When, in Chapter 5, we embarked on the task of uncovering the
reservoirs of all the *individual* employees' deep-lying goals and value
premises, so that we could anticipate their decisions, we found that
the task would be an enormous one. As was pointed out there (p. 127),
the concept of informal groups enables the executive to reduce this
to manageable size.

Groups formed because the members have a common background,
a common cultural pattern, are likely to exist over a relatively long
period. But an executive can expect that the goals of each group will
gradually change and that the membership of these groups will
change. So he must periodically reappraise his ideas of each group's
patterns of thinking to make sure that the premises he forms from
his observations are still reasonably reliable.

Groups Serve Psychological and Social Needs

Joining an informal group gives a man psychological and social
shelter, a sense of belonging. When he identifies himself with, and
gives his loyalty to, an informal group, he is predicting that any
aid he gives that group will help to advance his own goals. Furthermore, no matter how much the members may quarrel among themselves, he can be fairly sure that when his welfare is threatened the
group will stand behind him. Membership also offers him considerable assurance that the company itself will be forced to provide for
his real needs. Indeed, this loyalty to an informal group frequently

---

[2] See W. Lloyd Warner and Associates, *Democracy in Jonesville* (New York:
Harper & Bros., 1949).

has the unexpected effect of strengthening a member's loyalty to company goals; for when he feels secure about his position in the company, he usually concludes that it is a pretty good company—it is helping him to achieve his own goals.

Belonging to a group may increase a man's sense of personal worth —his ego-satisfaction. If he works for a time in a group, he establishes friendships with other members, their cooperation becomes almost automatic, and they handle their work easily and pleasantly; thus he begins to feel that his group is best. He can hold up his head for another reason: He feels more like an independent, free human being, for instead of always acting like a subordinate, he can speak up and disagree with his boss upon occasion because of the backing he knows he will get.

These psychological and social satisfactions are of great moment to most people; thus, if our plan jeopardizes these, we can expect countermoves.

Groups Formed to Solve Troublesome Problems

The goal of informal groups formed because the members feel impelled to solve a company problem—because the men wish to change certain company practices, for instance—likewise serves as a guide in laying company plans. The men in these groups have picked up facts or near-facts about company problems from observation or hearsay, formed them into premises, and reached a conclusion that such and such should be done or should not be done. A group that discusses the way the boss treats them, or the company's practice of allowing "those young punks with stop watches to snoop around," or how to unsnarl the production schedules, would be an example of this kind of group. The goals of groups formed to cope with company-induced problems are usually just as fruitful as sources of premises for the executive's decisions as the goals of groups formed because of cultural heritages or psychological and social needs. They point to weaknesses in the present company program and provide the executive with premises for conceiving new alternatives to take care of smoldering grievances.

If an informal group has been formed to achieve goals that are of only passing interest to its members, management can largely ignore it. But if the goals are badly wanted by the group, are considered very significant as a means of furthering certain more ultimate goals, it behooves an executive to take one of two steps. He can make new plans which will help the members to resolve the troublesome problems, or else he can try to employ hard proof to convince the men that the means currently employed by the company will do a better job of furthering their goals than they at first realized.

When a group concludes that a change that is being introduced will interfere with the members' goals—when their zones of acceptance are very narrow or negative in width—the members will almost certainly band together more tightly than ever before and oppose the change, even though they are quite aware that the newly proposed means will forward company goals. Consciously or unconsciously, they will fight the company with all the many subtle sanctions they have available. Informal groups are masters of the art of reducing the members' contributions to the company to keep these in balance with the lower inducements which they believe they are receiving. When the group's goals are jeopardized, the members nearly always put loyalty to their group above loyalty to the company in the belief that group loyalty is a better way of assuring their future welfare.

When we stand back and look at the informal groups, we discover that they go quite far in furthering the hierarchy of basic goals suggested by Maslow (see p. 115). Certainly the group helps fill the first and most elementary need in that hierarchy—the biological or physiological needs. Moving up the hierarchy, the group helps fill a man's needs for safety and security—protection against the threat of arbitrary deprivation of what he already has won. The group also manages to contribute to the member's social needs, in addition to those lower in the hierarchy. And we have also seen that it helps a man satisfy his egoistic needs, his need to be a person whom he and other people can respect. Whether a group can contribute much to the topmost, and last-achieved need in the hierarchy, namely, a man's self-fulfillment needs, will depend largely on how high he manages to lift himself in the group—how close he gets to the position of group leader.[3]

EMPLOYING MEN'S LOYALTY TO THEIR GROUP TO FURTHER THE COMPANY'S GOALS

We have just noted that perception of the goals of the members of an informal group will help an executive revise his original idea and foresee the width of his subordinates' zones of acceptance. But when

---

[3] A. H. Maslow, *Motivation and Personality* (New York: Harper & Bros., 1954).

framing and revising our proposals, we dare not assume that these goals are of equal importance. The members may *all* give great weight to certain of the goals and little to others; and in any case they will each give somewhat different weights to the several goals.

The foregoing points to another phenomena of informal groups: The members of one group may be very cohesive, very loyal to the group, whereas another group may feel little loyalty because the goals they have in common are of little worth to them. In this chapter we are interested only in strongly loyal groups; the members of such groups frequently have worked in concert over a long period, have quite similar backgrounds, social needs, and problems, and believe strongly that the group's goals are important to their own welfare.

Though a strong group may give the executive more trouble than an amorphous group, it can be of more use to him. For instance, he can predict their responses more accurately. However, we are presently interested in the possibility that he *may* be able to employ the men's loyalty to the group's goals to further the company's goals. To accomplish this, the executive leader must conceive a proposal that will solve the company's problem and do a good deal to further the goals that the group talks about and thinks about most often. This is not easy, although we have already seen that, with a little forethought, most proposals can be revised so that they will serve several goals. We also realize that a man can seldom conceive a near-perfect solution, but that he can frequently create an idea for a partially successful means—a means that will forward to some extent some of the goals of the group and the company. To the extent that he succeeds, the members are usually willing to carry out the proposal. They willingly work for the good of their group, for, as we saw in the chapter on leadership, a man wins his group's approval and perhaps improves his chances of winning leadership by advancing his group's goals. Thus, a very good solution from their point of view would fall into the men's "trigger" zone of acceptance (they would immediately see a preponderance of wanted consequences) and a fairly good solution might perhaps fall in the 50–75 zone where the executive could use easy proof.

To utilize the men's loyalties fully, the executive may be able to incorporate other wanted consequences—for example, the furtherance of the goals of other groups that the men are loyal to. Recall that each member of an informal company group is also loyal to the goals of many other groups and that some of these are outside the company—his family, for example, or his union, or his fraternal and professional organizations. A man's acceptance will be whole-hearted when he is asked to undertake a task that will further the goals of several of his groups; for, under the circumstances, he knows that the members of each group will approve of what he does. Consequently, his contributions to the company will be large.

Sometimes, however, a man's loyalties are in conflict. An executive faces an almost insoluble dilemma when he finds that the best means of achieving the goals of one of his groups will cause injury to an-other group to which he is loyal. No matter what he does, he will be criticized by some of his friends in one of the groups for doing the wrong things; and if he tries to compromise, he may be virtually ostracized by both factions. Foremen who have risen from the ranks and are expected by their former "buddies" to advance their goals, but are also expected by management to further the company's goals, often face this dilemma. And a department head is sometimes asked to take actions that will help the company but will harm his depart-ment. If this man in the "middle" (or his superiors) cannot create an idea for a common means of advancing the goals of both groups to which a man is loyal, life can be miserable for him; he may eventually retire into his shell or resign to get relief from the pressure.

Very strong *departmental* loyalties sometimes produce conflicts of a somewhat different nature; yet these, too, can sometimes be turned to the company's advantage. Interdepartmental conflicts exist in nearly all companies. In some companies the sales and production departments are constantly at loggerheads; in others the clash is be-tween the accounting control and production departments; and so on. Where the membership in the informal groups and the formal groups is identical, the warfare may occasionally become so bitter that the members of the two departments spend most of their time bickering with each other; as a result the company's work slows down, and near-chaos ensues. It is likely that the internecine conflict originated because the individuals involved felt that only by strong depart-mental loyalty, instead of company loyalty, could they be assured of a satisfying future. To resolve problems of this nature, the chief executive will probably have to step in. Someone outside the fray will need to prove to the members of each department that actions in behalf of the company goals will, in the long run, ensure their welfare, even though these actions may temporarily injure the de-partments.

Department loyalties can be fastened to—and can exist side by side with—company loyalties, to the company's great benefit, just as in the case of other informal group loyalties. In fact, a man's pride in his own department and in its ability to meet difficult company problems successfully constitutes one of the most interesting phenomena found in organizations. Here, we can observe the marriage of two supposedly incompatible ideas—competition and cooperation. The departments are working together to make a larger pie for the company as a whole. Indeed, they are vying with one another to see which one can make the greatest contribution and, at the same time, working with the other departments to help them increase their contributions, too. The men can foresee that in this way they will each have a bigger and more satisfying piece of the pie than if they channeled their effort toward enlarging their own group's inducements at the expense of other departments. A company that consciously sets out to induce such cooperative competition cannot afford to be niggardly about sharing this larger pie with those who have created it; salaries must reflect this increased productivity.[4]

Men's desires for status largely explain why management can frequently employ loyalty to the groups' goals to further the company's goals. So this second use to which the executive can put informal groups is closely tied in with the one we turn to next. Ideally, the proposed task will raise the man's status in his informal groups, both inside and outside the company.

DEVISING STANDARDS THAT WILL MEASURE AN INDIVIDUAL'S STATUS IN HIS GROUP AS WELL AS HIS CONTRIBUTIONS TO THE COMPANY

The members of an informal group measure the status level of their own group as compared with other groups; and, in addition, they set up measures of status levels within the group and assign to each member a certain status level. This dual practice offers a third method of employing informal groups in gaining acceptance of proposed changes.

A man needs to feel proud of himself and what he can do. Everything seems right with the world when his friends tell him that he is steadily improving himself. This indicates to him that he is gaining in status in their eyes and that the future holds great promise. When he begins losing their respect, he recognizes this as a danger signal.

---

[4] In the next chapter, we shall investigate another approach to the solution of this problem—namely, changing the company's formal organization structure.

It signifies that he will go downhill in the future; and, as a consequence, he becomes apprehensive.

A man's interest in security—his family's and his own—is entirely understandable. In this uncertain world, it is quite natural to feel uneasy about the future. Losing a job, for instance, and having to accept a lower level job or a less steady job is a frightening experience for a man—or at least for most men. The drive to maintain or improve his status is frequently powerful, for the respect that other men accord him indicates their appraisal of his job security. As an extra fillip, high status helps a man exercise authority over his fellows, for they frequently look upon him as an expert.

The status of his group versus other groups in the community or in the company furnishes him with a broad-gauge first approximation of how well he will flourish. The group he belongs to provides him with more refined measures of how good he is and thus with a more exact projection of his future.

This is a somewhat complex idea, so we shall first examine these measures of status in some detail, then look briefly at the symbols that men use in measuring their own status and the status of others. With this as a background, we shall be able to get at the central point of this section—namely, how the group's status measures can be used in gaining acceptance of new proposals.

How a Group Measures Its Status versus That of Other Groups

Actually, each informal group in a community or a company ranks itself fairly high as compared with other groups. This is understandable. Prior to joining his group, each man had already decided which were the best means and goals for him. He joined the group in the first place because the other men were employing the same goals and means as he. Since all the members agree that their common means and goals are best, it is logical for the group as a whole to feel that their future is assured and that other groups will not fare so well. According to the measures used by each group, the members are quite certain that they will get along well—better than most other people.

This general statement calls for some illustrations. Some Negro groups look down on whites. "Whites are foolish—rush around tryin' to make money, fightin' each other to get ahead, doin' this and that, bustin' themselves. *We* know how to *live*. We know how to laugh and have a good time." Confirmed hobos probably look down on staid, settled folk in much the same way; they feel that hobos have the best goals and means. Groups from the working class sometimes talk about how much better off they are than the wealthy, just as certain groups among the wealthy frequently consider themselves above the working class. Some Swedish groups look down on Norwegians; and when Norwegians get together, they sometimes mention examples which "prove" that they are better than Swedes. College men occasionally feel rather smug when they compare themselves with non-college men, and noncollege men occasionally cite examples to "prove" that they are smarter than college men. Plant workers frequently rank themselves above white-collar workers, and white-collar workers usually think they are superior to plant workers.

This does not mean that a group is completely oblivious of how high the other groups rank them. The *total* community does rank each group, and it manifests its opinion in a variety of ways. This community ranking, however, is based largely on the predominant group's ideas of how successfully the several minority groups will achieve the goals adopted by the *dominant* group. If a colony of artists were to move to a farming area, it would probably be accorded a low status in the community, even though the artists really felt quite superior to the farmers. The farmers have seen with their own eyes—they *know*—that in order to flourish, a man must produce *food*. The artists produce paintings rather than food; therefore, their future is not assured—"Nobody can eat pictures." In some communities the men with the greatest amount of education and intelligence are rated highest, for the members predict that education and intelligence will produce a well-rounded, rich life; but according to the experience of the dominant group in other communities, men with school learning make impractical decisions.

That all groups could be best—that every group could enjoy the highest status—would seem absurd; yet, in a very real sense, this is possible. The reason for the anomaly is that there are no universal measures of status. Each group uses its own goals and its own set of value premises as standards. This is indeed fortunate; under these circumstances, almost every man can hold his head high. The members of each group can prove that they are as good as or better than most, and that their future is therefore assured. A minority group, for instance, seldom accepts wholeheartedly the standards used by the dominant group in the community or company. When other groups assert that their group is no good, they get angry or else shrug it off, saying, "They are just jealous of us."

The point of what we have been probing is that the status of their own group or groups is of great importance to people; when they see that their group's status is being reduced, they become panicky, for this means that their future is in jeopardy.[5] The old groups in a community or an organization often feel this way when a new group begins to grow in status. For example, the established groups sometimes feel that their welfare is endangered when Negroes first enter their company or community. The same thing occurs when a new nationality group first enters or when a low-income group begins to increase its income, or when college men are hired by a company that formerly hired only noncollege men. An insecure group closes ranks and prepares to fight if someone—company management or some other group—attempts to deprive it of either the means of achieving its goals *or* eliminates the measures the group has been using to prove that it is best. Similarly, when an executive makes a decision that deprives an informal employee group of its means of maintaining status, he can expect the members to rebel; for they foresee that if they do nothing to combat the change, they will sink to the level of a group they had heretofore scorned. On the other hand, if his decision enables the group to prove to itself and others that its status will be improved, he can anticipate wholehearted acceptance.

How Status Is Measured within the Group

Informal groups carry this ranking process a step further. The men accord each member within the group a rank that ranges all the way from the leader at the top down to the worst bungler. A man's status *within* his group is just as important to him as the status of his group; how he ranks provides him with an even more precise indication of what his future holds.

The members can easily rank one another because they live together day after day. They *experience* the value premises they need for deciding who are the most effective members and who are the least effective in achieving their common goals.[6] Moreover, inasmuch

---

[5] Schools and community leaders have made considerable progress in combating group or race prejudice; nevertheless, we see many manifestations of it. The reason for the outcroppings of fear and hate is that it is virtually impossible to prove to an established "in-group" that a rising group will not injure its welfare, for the value premises which the members use all point to an opposite conclusion.

[6] For an explicit description of the behavior of informal groups, including how the people rank their fellow members, see A. Zaleznik, C. R. Christensen, and F. J. Roethlisberger, *The Motivation, Productivity, and Satisfaction of Workers* (Boston: Harvard University Division of Research, Graduate School of Business Administration, 1958). To determine the rank accorded each person, these authors and other observers of informal groups have counted the number of "interactions" each individual has with other people who are inside and outside the group.

as the members have adopted common goals and means (often referred to as group norms), the men are usually in rather full agreement about the measurements they will use. Despite our earlier conclusion that each individual uses his own subjective measuring rods for his goals and the value elements in his premises, it now becomes evident that, within each informal group, these are really fairly uniform.

The members let one another know how each man stands, and each man uses this to gauge what he can expect of the future. The men defer to those who have furthered the group (the ones who have won leadership) and brush aside the proposals and premises of those who have usually been wrong. To gain status, each man tries to employ what the group believes to be the most effective means of attaining its goals; he tries to prove that he employs these means very tellingly. Each one savors any compliments about his effectiveness and repeats these to his family and friends as proof that his future is rosy. Conversely, he is forever on the lookout for, and seeking to counteract, any whisper that may lead people to conclude that his status or his reputation in the group is on the wane. A man's greatest fear is ridicule; this indicates to him that he is not needed—that his colleagues consider him inept in achieving the goals they regard as important and that he is on the verge of being expelled. The prospect of living alone in the world is a grim one. His security is no longer assured.

A goodly number of the status measures used by informal groups of *employees* represent what to them is clear proof of the man's present and future value to his *company*. His pay, length of service, and job rank are basic indicators. Other measures are the amount of responsibility he is given, the responsibility for handling an important task—for example, the keeping of certain records which a man and his group believe to be of great importance to management in making decisions. We see group status measures nearly everywhere we look; the gradations in skill, the gradations in title, the gradations in one type of job as compared with another, white collars versus work clothes, nearness of one's work place to the boss's desk—are all examples of such measures. Machinists rate one another on the basis of how accurately and easily each can turn out a machined part. Bookkeepers may rate one another on the basis of accuracy and neatness, salesmen on who gets the most sales. How effective each man is in forcing the company to make concessions, whether he owns a house, whether he has money in the bank or has a good education, are other illustrations of measuring sticks. Executives rate one another on how well they can make complex decisions which will stand up in retrospect and how rapidly they make them. "Fuddy-duddies" who cannot make up their minds, or who usually make impractical decisions, whether they be accountants, or executives, or shipping clerks, are ordinarily rated lowest among their associates.

Status Symbols, and Obsolete Measures of Status

Usually, a group that has existed for some time as a social unit begins to evolve symbols that are generally accepted by the group as measures of status levels. Several have already been mentioned: a telephone on the desk, a rug on the floor, the clothes a man wears, his title, the location of his desk with respect to the "top" man, his length of service. Such symbols are useful short cuts a man can use to prove that his status is high. The visible symbols are particularly convenient because a man and his family need say nothing to prove his status to others; their friends can *see* his status. Brief statements which help others to visualize his status ("Jim has forty men under him," or "Joe's the oldest machinist in the company," or "Our dad is the manager") are almost as handy as visible symbols. A man and his family need not boast; all they need to do is to mention the symbol.

Most men will strive mightily to secure these status symbols because, in their eyes, actual status and status symbols are synonymous. At the time the symbols were first adopted, they probably *did* reflect men's status. A man may eventually discover, however, and perhaps too late, that the symbols he has been striving for have lost their value as predictors of how he will fare. Unless these symbols are reappraised and revised periodically, they may prove to be entirely misleading. For instance, many people in the past have insisted on white-collar work in the belief that this would lead almost inevitably to a job as an executive, only to find later that it led neither to an executive job nor to a high income. When conditions change, a man must employ new means of ensuring his welfare; and he must therefore change the measures he uses. Inasmuch as conditions usually change slowly, men seldom fully recognize what has been taking place. They cling to their old symbols and strive for them, even though these have become archaic.

Ordinarily, status symbols are established early in the life of the informal group and are handed down without critical re-examination. Some of the status measures of a group in a plant, for instance, may have been established at a time when the industry was new and the technologies were in their infancy. In those early days the employees and the community could predict that the men who showed the greatest skill in making a high-quality unit would not only receive more pay and faster promotion but would keep their jobs when others were laid off; hence, they set up their status measures on the basis of skill in craftsmanship. As a company steadily improves its equipment and manufacturing processes, however—improves these to a point where almost any semiskilled man can produce a high-quality product—the individual skill once so badly needed is no longer essential to the company's welfare; and the old measure loses its predictive value. Yet the men are likely to assume that, because the measures worked once, they will always work; the status measure becomes "frozen."[7]

These obsolete measures of status frequently injure the company because the men who use them spend their energies in activities that are no longer of great worth to the company. For example, a group of lithographers using skilled craftsmanship as a status symbol may insist that every piece they turn out be perfect, even though the customers are entirely satisfied with what the lithographers would consider mediocre work. Employees often cling to the old measures because they can then boast about their status as skilled workmen and thus prove that they are needed. This largely accounts for the trouble management sometimes encounters in attempting to lower the quality of the company's products.

Employing Status Measures to Gain Wholehearted Acceptance of Proposed Changes

As already intimated, the decisions made by the company executives often have a strong impact on the status of an employee's informal group, on his status within his group, and on the status measures he has adopted. Few executives stop to think about this; nor are they always fully aware of the far-reaching effects of a decision that harms a man's status, though some make a practice of asking themselves, "What will his wife say?" in contemplating a change in a man's job. Changes in company status not only affect the position of respect a man holds within the company but also the position that he and his family hold in the community. A man is actually many

---

[7] Seniority is an example of a status symbol which has lately lost some of its value as a measure of how high a man really stands in his group or how much he contributes to the company. However, this "frozen" status measure still has predictive value in those companies where the unions have insisted on including it in the collective bargaining contract.

people—a member of the company, of his family, of his church, of his clubs, and of his group of friends. His status in the company, as represented by his title, the number of men who report to him, and his income, often helps to determine his status in those organizations. Hence, it is little wonder that a man is sensitive about his status in the company.[8]

Devising standards that measure an individual's status and at the same time measure his contributions to the company offers executives a very effective method of gaining wholehearted acceptance of a proposed change. An executive has available two general approaches. The first can be employed where the men already use group status measures which also measure the worth of their contributions; to the company; here the executive's task is to preserve these measures and to make sure that the changes in duties he proposes for the men will enable them to raise their status or, at worst, not lower it.

But, as we have seen, the men in certain groups adopt either inverted status measures or obsolete measures: They sometimes measure their status by how much they can harm the company, or by how well they perform tasks that now contribute but little to the company's welfare (obsolete measures). Here, the executive's task is to change the men's status measures—induce the men to substitute new status measures for the old, new ones which at the same time measure how much they contribute to the company. Manifestly, this second approach, conceiving and gaining acceptance of new status measures, is an arduous task. Let us probe further into these two approaches.

Where the men in the group already measure status largely by how much they contribute to the company, the executive's task of devising proposals that will be wholeheartedly adopted becomes a relatively straightforward one, provided that he is aware of their status measures. He can readily check in his mind's eye to make sure that no feature of the proposed task lowers the men's status as the group measures it, and then go ahead. One way to preserve a man's status when his job is changed is to issue a formal memorandum— for example, "Hereafter the following types of decisions are to be checked with Thomas McCue before they are carried out." In many cases, it is possible for the executive to revise his original idea of the job slightly, so that the men can continue to use their old group status measures.

---

[8] A man who is unsuccessful in securing what he thinks is adequate status in his work group or the company will frequently look for it elsewhere. He may seek high positions in his lodge or in civic organizations, or perhaps he will brag about how he gave his boss "a piece of his mind" the other day.

The objective is to remove all fear in the men's minds that the change may bode ill for them, and then go a step farther and make it clear that if they do an effective job, their status in the company will rise. Under these circumstances, their zones of acceptance will be wide; they already have many premises, most of which point to doing the job well, no matter what the obstacles. It may be necessary to introduce some proof; but, for the most part, the executive's proposal serves merely as a trigger. The men need no prodding thereafter. Actually, if the proposal is a means of achieving personal or group goals badly wanted by the men, it is not even necessary for them to grasp the importance of the new task as a means of achieving the company's goals.

For many men, the desire to raise their status in the community provides a strong incentive for accepting and carrying out proposed changes wholeheartedly. Indeed, the existence of community status measures probably accounts for a part of the drive of some men to make large contributions to the company; ascending the executive ladder raises a man's status in the community. Here, as with status levels within the groups, is a ready-made measure which the executive can employ; he can usually set up jobs in such a way that doing them well in behalf of the company helps the men to rise in the community.

On the other hand, if the men have adopted status measures which do *not* reflect their contributions to the company—where the ones they employ are oriented toward goals that will *injure* the company —or where they are using obsolete measures, the executive faces the unenviable task of substituting new measures for the old ones. Substituting low standards of workmanship for outmoded high standards, or high standards for low ones, would be examples. In these cases, and also in those instances where status in the group is measured regularly by how much the men can injure the company because of their feeling of resentment—where they use inverted measures— the objective is to replace these old status measures with new ones based on the effectiveness of their contributions to the company. And where members of entire departments have coalesced into informal groups which are loyal only to their respective departments, and the warring departments measure their status by how much they can harm other departments and help their own, the problem is to gain acceptance of new, company-wide status measures.

In circumstances like this, as by now we well know, the crucial and most difficult task is to conceive a new alternative that will further both the company and the men in the group. And we know that the task of gaining a hearing for the proposed change will be difficult, especially if hostility toward the company and some of its executives is the prevailing mood.

However, we are not here concerned with conceiving a new proposal; instead we wish to create ideas for new *measures* of the *status* of the individual *members* of the group. Clearly, these measures must grow out of the group's current work environment and the way the job is actually performed. In addition, it must be consonant with the group's standards of behavior and its habitual patterns of behavior. Furthermore, these will need to be reliable predictions of the members' welfare: The men must be able to see that the "cause"—doing the job better, as measured by these standards—will almost certainly produce the promised result, a rise in their status. Equally significant, we are interested only in measuring how well the men achieve goals that are *important* to the company.

Were we trying to induce the machine tool operators to increase their hourly production and lower their standards of workmanship, we might set looser tolerances and train the men in a new "one best way." But we can be sure that they will covertly go their old way unless they find that this change will further goals that the group deems important. Perhaps we can show that if the group can accomplish this, they and the rest of the men in the plant will be assured of jobs, whereas the company could not compete and would have to drop that product line and lay the men off were the old standards maintained. However, examples such as these are not very helpful as guides. The status measures that a group employs must grow out of the peculiar circumstances surrounding the particular job.

But conceiving the new measures is only a part of our task. After this has been done, the executive must also prove to the men (as well as to their associates, both inside and outside the company), that their status, as measured by this new yardstick, does in fact foreshadow a good future for them. This will probably require hard proof, and it may require sanctions.

The attitudes of the men's supervisor will probably play a large role in gaining acceptance of the proposed status measures. His perception of the width of the men's zone of acceptance, his ability to choose and exercise the appropriate type of authority, and the amount of his informal leadership will determine whether the men will give the proposed measures a fair trial. Ideally, he would use "laissez faire leadership" for men with wide zones, "democratic leadership" for men with medium sized zones, men who will ask questions and will want to know why, and "authoritarian leadership" for men with very narrow zones of acceptance. But whichever type he uses, he must, in the end, see that the men do, in fact, get the rewards they expected. And if he senses that the men are making contributions that are considerably below their capacity—that they have set quotas for themselves, for instance, and are chastising the "rate busters"—perhaps he can again try to ferret out goals that this group deems extremely important to the welfare of the members and revise the proposal once more, making sure this time that the men *are* rewarded according to the volume of production. The nonmonetary rewards are important to most men, but their efficacy is limited; the company's pay rates must play a substantial role.

If the proposed change is going to affect the status measures of a *large* proportion of the employees—when, for instance, one of the company's long-term goals or niches is to be altered—the executives should lay plans to acquaint both the community and the company employees with the purpose of the change. A public announcement of the new company goals provides the man's friends outside the company with a new measuring rod for evaluating his activities in the company and thus his probable status. "I see your company is doing big things. What will your job be like under the new setup?" When a man is asked such a question, he is given an opportunity to explain how important and essential he will be to the success of the company's program. A company-wide meeting prior to the public announcement furnishes a good chance to communicate to the employees the new company status measures which the executives will hereafter use in evaluating the men and their departments. Here is an example: "Under this new program the company will have to improve these products substantially. The salesmen will be responsible for lining up about 50 new accounts of such and such a type; the manufacturing department will be responsible for reducing its costs per unit by 10 per cent." Another purpose of this company-wide meeting is to invite suggestions for improving the plan before it is finally crystallized. A third purpose is to enable the men to think of the plan as theirs; and a fourth is to enable them to be "in the know," so that they can act as experts when their friends begin asking them about the new program. These goals can be partially achieved with printed material to be used for later reference—an abbreviated company orientation manual outlining the new company goals, why these goals were chosen, and what new means the company now proposes to employ.

In trying to change the status measures of only *one* of the company's informal groups, probably the best way is to set up a special meeting of the unit and invite the men to participate in devising new standards. The chairman of such a small meeting should be able to describe the set of conditions the group will be facing in the future, the crucial problems it will have to solve in the period ahead, and the tasks the men will have to perform extremely well if the company is to flourish. He must also be adept at eliciting a free flow of suggestions from the men as to new status measures which might be useful in evaluating each man's work. Without this free interchange, he may find the men sitting before him like bumps on a log. As a consequence, he may fall into the trap of trying to gain acceptance through the use of simple authority, or perhaps sanctions, instead of proof. Under these circumstances, he can expect only half-hearted acceptance of his proposal. What management is trying to do here is to encourage the group to set up its *own* standards and measures of two things: (1) measures for appraising the effectiveness of the decisions made by each man (how well their decisions on the job stand up when viewed as a means of achieving the goals agreed upon), and (2) of how *many* of these good decisions each man should make in a day or week. These standards and measures can usually be determined rather readily after examining the crucial tasks the men will have to perform. The third of the three types of manuals mentioned in the chapter on communication, the one describing how the "perfect" man would do the job, can be written up afterward to summarize the conclusions reached at those meetings.

Management has a tendency to think up and suggest status measures which appear unrealistic to the men. In fact, the executives' usual practice is to propose that sanctions be introduced, especially rewards that they believe will add to the men's status. When companies try to foist "phony" status measures upon employees, rewards that are of no value in the men's eyes or that make them look ridiculous—lapel buttons reading, "I'm a winner," for instance— the employees make fun of the measures. The status measures must be real and valuable to the men—either a recognition of their actual accomplishments in outdistancing rivals or valid symbols of those accomplishments. The men discard the measures if they cannot use them to prove to themselves—and to their associates, bosses, families, and friends—that their future looks promising.

Men's need for ego-satisfaction furnishes a touchstone for executives who are trying to create ideas for status measures *without* the

advice of the employees—that need, together with the basic require-
ment that the measures should reflect the men's success in making
their respective contributions to the company. Public recognition of
an individual's or a group's success in interdepartmental or inter-
branch competition furnishes some of these ego-satisfactions. Bonuses
will also serve as status measures, *provided* that they are based on
real contributions. And a system of cash or merchandise prizes, if
so based, can be used for short periods; sales managers frequently
use this approach with salesmen, though it can gradually lose its
effectiveness from overuse. Meetings called for the purpose of making
company awards heighten the ego-satisfactions. It is there that the
men enjoy the fruits of the status they have won, and it is by telling
their families and friends of such meetings that the fruits are sa-
vored. The practice of praising men for work well done, either privately or in a group, is one of the simplest and most effective means
of satisfying men's ego-needs, though a majority of executives completely overlook this.

Approbation not only makes a man more confident that he can
survive, more confident of his future but, in many cases, unleashes
energy not otherwise brought into play; it leads the man to increase
his efforts in behalf of the organization in the belief that this will
provide him still greater ego-satisfaction in the future. Praise, or its
equivalent, a feeling of being needed in an organization, is an inducement that costs nothing except a little trouble and thoughtfulness—a
thoughtfulness that can only grow out of sensitivity on the part of
the executive to the needs peculiar to each of the men whom he supervises. Incidentally, a boss also welcomes a sincere compliment from
his subordinates once in a while. Praise produces much of the "extra"
that seems to make a company forge ahead of its competitors; it
seems to produce that intangible we often call "morale"; and morale
largely determines the effectiveness of the company's sales department, office workers, and the product development and manufacturing divisions. When a man receives these additional inducements,
his contributions to the company usually rise sharply.

The status measures finally adopted must look logical to most of
the men after they have considered the effect of these on the status of
their informal groups, on their status within those groups, and on
their old status symbols. If the measures seem illogical after testing
them out in their minds—if they deem them valueless as predictors of
their welfare—they use the pocket veto. Executives who have revised
their plans to conform to the measures used by the groups can

usually point up the logic of the plans by using easy proof. Where the executives are trying to re-educate the men—trying to substitute new measures for undesirable ones, either by eliciting suggestions from the men or by conceiving the measures without their help—the executives must be prepared to use hard proof. However, it would be unrealistic to expect *all* the men to accept the new measures wholeheartedly. They are being asked to discard measures they have long accepted as reliable. The hope is that, as the time passes, all the men will find that the new measures are really reliable as predictors. Gaining the initial acceptance is only the beginning; the executives must follow through. It the men begin to suspect that company is not making good on its promises of a better future, even though they have adopted the proposed status measures, they will turn back to their old ones.

EMPLOYING THE INFORMAL ORGANIZATION'S CHANNELS OF COMMUNICATION TO GAIN ACCEPTANCE

The informal groups' communication system offers a fourth opportunity to utilize informal groups. That the informal communication system is a swift one, and that nearly all employees are regularly reached by this system, is evident to anyone who has ever worked in an organization. Many (not all) messages move up, down, and sidewise with incredible swiftness. The chief difficulty is the inaccuracy of many of the messages.

It is readily seen that the informal channels of communication are extremely valuable as a vehicle for acquainting the executive with some of the premises he requires. This is his most fruitful source of the personal value premises men are using. Equally important, it is his only source of those company premises which people fear to commit to the formal communication channels. An executive who is cut off from either of these types of premises will frequently make unrealistic decisions. Yet he needs to be ever watchful that the messages he receives are accurate; his job is to check these against what he already knows to be true and to ask questions until all his pieces of information fall into a logical, consistent pattern.

That executives can also employ the organization's informal channels of communication to transmit *their* messages to people in the organization, and to gain acceptance of the truth of these, is not so widely recognized. When the executives anticipate trouble in gaining acceptance because subordinates may be suspicious of their motives, they can employ these informal channels of communication for passing down through the organization the decisions they have made, and the goals and premises they used. Messages that reach employees *in*directly and *in*formally from headquarters (in confidence and "off the cuff," as it were) have the ring of truth about them; formal, written announcements are suspect—they can be skillfully, even craftily, worded so that they *look* palatable to those lower down in the organization. Executives can also use these channels to send those ticklish messages which would make them or their subordinates look bad if they were committed to paper or sent through the formal channels: "Pass the word along that the boys are staying out too long for their coffee breaks," for instance.

But sometimes the messages sent out by executives never reach their intended destinations. Members do not bother to pass along information which they believe will be of no use to others. Moreover, even valuable information may never get through. Information is transmitted from one group to another by people who are members of two or more groups, or who have friends in other groups. In the absence of these liaison people, the informal network fails to function.

If executives send messages through the informal communication system with a knowledge of its shortcomings and are vigilant about correcting garbled messages, it can serve them well. Employees tend to rely heavily on the grapevine because through it come pieces of information they badly need in making their personal decisions. Information that may affect people's welfare moves swiftly because each man knows that the next man can use it; and, in addition, he knows that he will be considered an expert, an "authority," when he passes the information on. The receivers form many of their premises from the information they receive in this way.

The chief problem is to prevent unfounded rumors. These usually start because the receivers have been furnished with only one element of a premise, or with only the decision. People need an explanation, need a picture of causes and results; if they do not get an explanation, they will often supply the best one they can think of and pass it along as true. A message may originally have read, "Art Lipinski was fired yesterday." The real reason may have been that he was caught stealing; but if this premise is not simultaneously sent with the decision through the organization, the message will soon read, "Art was fired because he's been arguing with the boss too much," or ". . . because he's been too active in the union." To a message that originally reads, "Orders for the new product have slowed down badly," someone along the line adds the words "so the men in

that department are going to be laid off." On the basis of this premise the men may decide to slow down production or begin thinking
about looking for other jobs. The men accept the statements they
hear through the grapevine as the "really true" premises and therefore use them for their own decisions, despite almost anything to
the contrary sent through official channels.

Sending along complete information helps to prevent unfounded
rumors; but correcting these inaccurate, though believable, cause-
result statements which are supplied by the grapevine is one of the
most knotty problems faced by management. Even the original fact
may become garbled along the way; and, in any case, management
seldom realizes that certain facts are known outside the inner circle
and that these have been embroidered. Virtually the only way executives can discover these is to keep the incoming channels of informal
communication open. Once the inaccurate pieces of information and
premises are known, corrections can be sent out, either informally or
formally. These may not be as fully believed as the original rumors,
but that is the fate of all attempts to set the record straight.

EMPLOYING THE LEADERS OF INFORMAL GROUPS

The use of the *leaders* of the informal groups constitutes the last
of our five ways of employing informal groups. Leaders can serve
the company at two points: as key men to talk with in attempting to
gain a group's acceptance of a proposed change, and as a source of
potential company executives.

Who the informal leaders are, and how to identify them so that
management can engage their assistance when it is needed in communicating premises to the group, sometimes proves a stumbling
block. If the grapevine has not already disclosed the leaders, they
may be guessed at by learning which man the men in the groups most
often mention. Actually, until a recognized crisis arises, the men may
not quite realize that they *are* members of a group, or who their
leader is. Under these circumstances, management may have to
suggest that they select a representative or a committee. Any man
chosen by management would inevitably be branded as a "company
man."

Why an informal group leader is able to play a key role in inducing his group to accept a new proposal becomes apparent by recalling that he has risen, and has been accepted, with the full consent
of the group because his followers can trust him to look after their
interests. A plan that the leader thinks is satisfactory will probably

be accepted, at least tentatively, even though several of his followers have reservations about it.[9] On the other hand, hard proof will have to be employed in those cases where the informal leader as well as his followers distrust management's motives, or where it appears to them that the plan will jeopardize their goals or status measures. The burden of proof rests upon management. Occasionally, the leader thinks the proposal will jeopardize his own *personal* status or goals, so he opposes the plan despite what seems to be incontrovertible proof that it will forward the group's goals as well as the company's. In those cases where the leader cannot be convinced, the only alternative is to communicate the proof directly to the men themselves, a procedure that is both time-consuming and frustrating.

Meetings with informal leaders must be carefully planned. Bringing an informal leader into the confidence of top management— asking him, for example, to attend the executive meetings at which the new decisions are actually being threshed out—is by no means a utopian solution. The informal group, as a consequence of such a step, may get an exaggerated idea of its own importance, which, when the crisis is over, will probably have to be deflated. What is more, an informal leader attending such meetings may easily go away with rather serious misconceptions, the result of barriers to communication. The informal leader is interjected into a group whose thinking patterns and vocabulary are unfamiliar to him. The executives will frequently make statements that are correctly interpreted and fully understood by their long-time colleagues, yet leave an erroneous impression on the visitor.

That the informal groups serve as a training place for leaders, and that these leaders may provide a source of potential company executives, needs little elaboration. Promoting informal leaders to the job of boss will usually work as long as the men understand that the company is not trying to proselyte their leaders, and as long as the executives realize that not all informal leaders will necessarily become effective executives. Men who possess only limited mental abilities frequently develop leadership traits, but they can seldom make discerning company decisions.

When the executives find a man who is intelligent and who has already won the leadership of an informal group, they can be reason-

---

[9] A union leader frequently faces the problem of gaining the union members' acceptance of a labor contract which is less attractive than the members had hoped for, yet is the best that conditions would permit. Notice, in passing, that a labor leader must be an informal as well as a formal leader. A union officer who loses his informal leadership is ordinarily voted out at the next election.

ably sure that he will be able to win the leadership of a formal section or department. He already knows how to gather value premises, and he understands men's goals; he can perceive what his associates believe they should do to achieve these goals, and he knows how to work out plans that will meet the needs of the group. If he is put through an executive training program such as that described in the preceding chapter, he should develop rapidly. Incidentally, many companies encourage their potential executives to join voluntary organizations in the community for the purpose of gaining experience in leadership and as a method of building self-confidence.

We have seen that informal groups can be very useful to executives in uncovering the goals, means, and premises that the members consider important; in harnessing to the company a man's loyalty to his informal group's goals; and in devising standards that measure a man's individual status as well as his contributions to the company. These groups can also be used as communication channels, and their leaders can be used as carriers of premises and as a source of potential executives. If the company executives are not sensitive to the needs of these informal groups, the members will frequently strengthen their loyalty to their groups in an effort to realize their personal goals. Characteristically, the result is lowered company efficiency and a decline in employee morale.

EMPLOYEE MORALE: EFFICIENCY VERSUS ADEQUACY

This is a convenient place to probe that vague, intangible thing called "employee morale." It ties in with several of the concepts we have been exploring in recent chapters, and thus it affords an opportunity to begin weaving some of our subsystems into an integrated whole.

High morale among the men in an organization appears to be an essential ingredient in its success. A change for the worse can seriously jeopardize the company, and a change for the better can call forth undreamed-of contributions. Indeed, a company whose members have only average ability but whose morale is high can frequently outdistance a firm with brilliant executives and low morale. Success in competition depends only partially upon men's ability. What really counts is the amount of that ability they channel into furthering the company's goals.

We shall not be able here to find answers to the riddle of morale, but the idea of *efficiency* versus *adequacy*, coupled with some of the insights we have been gathering, throws some light on why morale declines and what steps management may take to improve it. The objective of gaining acceptance—whether by employing authority, or leadership, or communication, or the informal groups—is to secure what we shall call *efficiency* in achieving company goals and, conversely, to avoid what we shall call mere *adequacy*. In these pages, we are equating *efficiency* with *high* morale and *adequacy* with *low* morale.

Morale is one of those amorphous words with vague definitions that we encountered when we examined the barrier named "Failure to State Premises Clearly." To avoid misunderstandings, we shall use the following definition from Webster: "When qualified by the adjective *high*, a confident, aggressive, resolute, often buoyant, spirit of wholehearted cooperation in a common effort." Clearly there are degrees of morale. Low morale would be evidenced by a minimal amount of these behaviors, including a minimum of zeal. Be aware that high morale is distinctly different from happiness or satisfaction, however; though high morale is usually accompanied by these two pleasurable feelings, neither of them will, of itself, bring about high contributions to a group or a company.

A quick, preliminary definition of efficiency might read like this: "The wholehearted employment of those means that will most certainly and most fully achieve a goal." The term *efficiency* is meaningful *only* when the actions taken are evaluated in terms of a specific goal. (We encountered this same thought in exploring rational behavior.) No action is efficient in and of itself. Loafing on the job is an efficient way of giving a man a sense of personal pleasure, but it is an inefficient means of achieving the company's goals. A given activity may be an efficient means of achieving one man's goals and an inefficient means of attaining another's. When we use the term *efficiency* in these pages, we shall usually be thinking of achieving company goals, though we cannot afford to neglect employees' personal and group goals.

Instead of defining *adequacy* as the dictionary defines it, we shall define it as "going through the motions," or more specifically, employing means that *appear* to be efficient means of achieving a goal but that in fact advance the goal much less than a superficial look at the records would indicate. The man who does a job at an adequacy level is doing only enough to get by. Notice that adequacy is *not* the antithesis of efficiency but instead a low level of efficiency.

As we shall use the terms *efficiency* and *adequacy*, they merge into one another. In fact, taken together, they are identical with the central idea lying behind the *bottom* graph of Diagram 7—the diagram on authority (see p. 159). There, we represented the highest level of contributions and wholeheartedness as 100 per cent on the scale; working at the highest level of ability is synonymous with what we are calling "highest efficiency." Adequacy begins to show up when efficiency drops approximately to the 40 per cent mark on the vertical scale. A level of 1 per cent would represent virtually no efficiency and very little adequacy.[10]

Some Reasons Why Morale Declines

There are at least three kinds of situations in which we can expect morale to decline—in which we can anticipate adequacy in achieving company goals instead of efficiency.

One is where a man foresees that his inducements are going to be lower than he had hoped. When, for instance, a man realizes that his status in the company or in his group is on the downgrade, he gradually loses his self-confidence and incentive to work at full capacity in behalf of the company. If he can see no hope of reversing the downhill trend—becomes confused because he cannot conceive a way of coping with the problem—he goes about his job with a heavy feeling in the pit of his stomach, the result of his anxiety over his future. Eventually, he begins to hate the company, his associates, and his job because they are not giving him the inducements he expected. The loyalty he once felt begins to wither away. His morale steadily sinks; he has trouble forcing himself to get on with his work; he eventually works only at an adequacy level. He reduces his contributions to the level of what he considers his very meager inducements, and his zones of acceptance for most of his superior's proposals are relatively narrow. If his old status measures are destroyed, we can expect a similar response, for without these, he can no longer tell what his status is and thus cannot prove that he is a valuable man.

A second situation in which we can expect that a man will work at an adequacy level is where his zones of acceptance are characteristically *very* wide—when they customarily fall in the *habitual ac-*

---

[10] Whether a man customarily works at an efficiency level or an adequacy level—where we should rate him on our scale—is based on value premises. A man's associates can evaluate his efficiency in achieving company goals, just as they can measure his status level within the informal group. The efficiency of a personnel man, for instance, or of an advertising man or a sales manager, cannot of course be measured *accurately* because we have no agreed-upon standards, though the man's associates can gain a fairly good idea of whether he is working at the top of his ability or merely doing enough to get by.

ceptance zone or the *indifference* zone—and his boss seldom uses proof. To his mind, there are few inducements for performing his job to the best of his ability. He believes that doing it superficially is a better method of achieving his personal goals than doing it thoroughly. The inducements he has for working in behalf of the company are scanty, so he automatically reduces his contributions.

In view of what has just been said about zones of acceptance, it will come as no surprise to hear that a third situation where we can expect morale to be low is one in which the men's zones of acceptance are typically narrow and/or sanctions are continuously employed. Sanctions will often induce men to work in behalf of the company, but their contributions will be meager—at the bare adequacy level, just high enough to avoid penalties or to win rewards.[11] That persistent threats of punishments will have an adverse effect on employee morale is fairly obvious. But that *rewards* used as sanctions can (and often do) have a similar effect is not so readily seen. Indeed, the constant use of ill-chosen rewards may prove more pernicious than the use of penalties.

This assertion about the sometimes pernicious effect of rewards rests on rather elusive premises; hence, it calls for some elaboration. Where the chief rewards a man receives are extra things bestowed by the boss in accordance with some rule or formula that measures only *one or two* of the many contributions a man should make to the company, he will usually do only the minimum amount necessary to win the reward. He tries to make his record *look* as though he had been performing that particular part of his job very well, even though he knows that his performance was slipshod. Moreover, he does not even pretend to perform the other parts of his job at anything above an adequacy level; "I'm not paid to do that," he retorts when he is criticized for his lack of efficiency. It is immaterial to him whether his actions, taken as a whole, actually help the company; in fact, to obtain the promised rewards, he may knowingly harm the company. A straight commission salesman will characteristically tend to confine himself only to the task of finding customers and closing sales, even though there are a great many other things an efficient salesman must do, as anyone who has worked in a sales department will testify.[12] Indeed, many such salesmen will make ex-

---

[11] The need to employ sanctions constantly, whether they be in the form of punishments or rewards, indicates the presence of low morale; the men's inducements and contributions are so low that the bosses are obliged to use sanctions to get the work done.

[12] This is one reason why companies frequently pay their salesmen a base salary and only a small commission on sales—only enough to keep the men constantly aware of the need for closing sales.

travagant promises to obtain an order, regardless of possible injury to the customer and the company.

Incentive pay systems for production workers occasionally result in adequacy, too. If the rewards are based on the number of units produced, and nothing else, the man's primary goal is to prove that he has done what the formula requires of him—and he does that part of the job with little regard for the actual consequences to the company. The troubles we have been discussing arise because management, through its system of rewards, has emphasized the wrong goals; or, at best, it has set up goals for the men which measure only *one* of the several tasks the men should perform well if the company is to flourish.

The injury to employee morale of such rewards may turn out to be much deeper—and more subtle—than just indicated. "Beating the system" occasionally becomes a normal, accepted practice. Few are the systems that cannot be twisted to the employee's advantage, even in those cases where the evaluations are based solely on factual premises. For example, a salesman can wait to mail customers' orders until the beginning of the following month for the purpose of increasing his commission or winning a prize. Or a subordinate and his boss will sometimes arrange the records of what the man has done so that he will receive the greatest possible rewards, even though he has not actually won them. If men are regularly given extra rewards in spite of the fact that everyone knows that they have consistently injured the company, or that their rewards are based upon twisted records, morale showly erodes away.[13] It becomes increasingly evident to them that trying to win the personal rewards afforded by the system is a much better way to get ahead than working conscientiously on behalf of the company. If the rewards are to be effective, they have to be won—and won fairly.

Perhaps the underlying reason why men respond as they do to the rewards type of sanctions is that they unconsciously think of them as somewhat akin to bribes. In accepting them, they lose some of their self-respect and their respect for the company.

The Task of Rebuilding Morale

The task of rebuilding employee morale, once it has sunk to a low level, is manifestly a challenging one for the executive. Conceiving

---

[13] Their *morals*—moral standards—are also lowered, as we saw when we were discussing the effect of the breakdown in the "authority" of rules and regulations; misrepresentation becomes proper behavior.

and carrying out a program designed to raise morale is no easy task; but, if it is successful, the results are often spectacular.

To raise employee morale in a section, or a department, or a company, it is evident, from what we have discovered, that an executive must do his best to make sure that his proposals will serve as means of furthering the goals of his men and their informal groups as well as of the company. Under these circumstances, each man sees considerable hope of raising his status by making the proposed contributions. He finds that he wants to do his job fast and well, and that doing it well calls for very little effort; indeed, it now requires much less effort than when he was working at a mere adequacy level. His heart sings as he works. The man's contributions almost unconsciously rise to match the new level of inducements. Not only does he require less time for each decision and thus make many more decisions than before, but he finds that he can readily handle more complicated decisions and that more of them are solid ones. In addition, he derives the added satisfaction that comes with creating.

When men's hopes rise, their morale goes up. Initially, the men may take a skeptical view of the new program; but as soon as they discover that the superior's promises of improved personal status have come true, they can see some purpose in contributing their best to the company. This now seems rational to them. In fact, they can now predict that if they do more and more in behalf of the company, their status will rise still further. They get pleasure from their work. They are going uphill rather than downhill. Instead of constantly complaining about the company's shortcomings, the premises they communicate to one another emphasize the wanted consequences of working efficiently. Gradually, they become more loyal to the company. Once this trend sets in, the executive sees more and more evidence of that remarkable phenomenon, a growth of pride in the ability of each group and of the company to do certain jobs well, and the conviction that by working together, they can cope successfully with almost any big job.

PROBLEM
THE ROLE OF INFORMAL GROUPS

The Wayne Hardware Supply Company, located southwest of Chicago's Loop area,* had been a highly respected organization since its founding in 1903. Under the guidance of Samuel Wayne, and later of his son Robert, the

---

* All names and the location of the company are disguised.

company had steadily grown. It was widely known among midwestern retailers as a well-run, medium-sized hardware wholesaler.

The company had long been handicapped by crowded quarters. From time
to time, the Waynes had purchased adjacent buildings and built new office
and warehouse space to take care of their expanding business. Eventually,
however, the cramped warehouse conditions, the awkward arrangement of
the warehouse buildings, the shortage of truck docks, the lack of parking
space, and the growing traffic congestion in the area, led the officers to erect a
large one-story office and warehouse building on a plot south of Chicago
adjacent to an expressway which circled the city. This, they believed, would
enable them to reduce their stockroom labor costs, costs which had been rising rapidly.

To the dismay of Mr. Robert Wayne, the move to the new warehouse had
proved disappointing. He knew his foremen were doing everything possible
to right the situation, but he thought that the prospects for improvement were
not good. The story of the changes in the warehousemen's work practices and
in their patterns of behavior—especially those of the order pickers—is as
follows.

The work in the warehouses consisted of bringing new stock in, storing it,
and assembling and packing the items that hardware stores ordered.

In the old buildings, warehousemen separated merchandise into two
classes: units that were prepackaged by manufacturers for ready shipment to
retailers, and loose or unpackaged items. Prepackaged items—bridge tables
and chairs, home appliances, and hand power tools, for example—were
brought in from the manufacturer on pallets and stored, as far as space would
permit, in two buildings. If an incoming shipment were too large for the
allotted space, the surplus stock would be taken to one of the out-of-the-way
lofts and brought down later when needed. Regular stock handlers normally
unloaded and "put away" the incoming merchandise, although the prepackaged order pickers helped with this work whenever necessary. To handle
outgoing orders for these items, the foreman would give each order picker
enough shipping orders to fill a hand truck, together with shipping labels or
tags for each item. The order pickers would push their carts through the
proper aisles, collect the items, affix the labels, mark the method of shipment
on the package, and push their truck loads to the shipping room where the
shipping clerks, who were located on the loading platform, would take over.

Handling the open-bin items was somewhat more complicated, primarily
because of the large number of such items and the many tiers of bins in
which they were stored. Wayne normally carried between 14,000 and 15,000
such items and each required a bin. As was the case with prepackaged units,
when a new shipment arrived, the stockmen, aided at times by the open-bin
pickers, filled the bin and stored the surplus stock in nearby but less convenient buildings. The order dispatchers of this department—these men
worked directly under the warehouse manager—would hand out shipping
orders to the department's order pickers. To assemble their orders, the men
would push their trucks through the various buildings and aisles and, when
finished, they would unload their assembled orders on wrapping benches
manned by packers.

Over the decades, the stockroom organization had varied widely in efficiency. After World War I, for example, when sales had grown steadily, the
backlog of unfilled orders increased sharply and delays and mistakes in
shipments became prevalent. Finally, Mr. Samuel Wayne replaced the rather
easygoing manager of the stock rooms with a man named George Deal. He
was autocratic and brusk, worked the men hard, closely supervised their
work, and, as the men resentfully expressed it, "was always yelling at us."
Contrary to what the Waynes had expected, the average number of items
assembled per man-hour began to decline rather steadily and the backlog of
unshipped orders continued to increase. To cope with this, Mr. Deal recommended that the company install an incentive pay system. With the help of
what the men sneeringly called "efficiency experts" he devised and installed
a bonus plan based on a rather complicated system of "earned points." The
men had strongly resisted the new foreman and his point system. It turned
out that the bonus incentives made little difference in the men's work rate.

By the late 1920's, the delays and high costs had became so serious that
Robert Wayne, now the president, discharged Mr. Deal and appointed in his
place the steadiest of the order pickers, Joe Ansolino, a man of about 30 who
was becoming a leader in the nearby Italian community. Mr. Wayne told Joe,
"Work out a plan that will straighten out the department, bring it to me for a
final check, and then put it to work. Clean house if you have to. I won't be
satisfied till we always ship every order before 11:00 A.M. of the day after
it's received."

Within a few weeks, most of the stock men and order pickers, and several
of the packers were replaced. For the stock and picker jobs, Joe selected men
in their late 20's or early 30's whose families he knew. The majority were
Italian, but upon the recommendation of the parish priest and one of the
Irish pickers whom he had retained, he tried out and finally hired six young
Irishmen. Neighborhoods of both nationalities had recently grown up within
a mile or so of the company. The bonus system was retained in a simplified
form. Gradually, the crew settled down.

Until the mid-1930's, Joe supervised all the men himself. He tried to give
each order picker a batch of shipping orders calling for items located in only
two or three warehouses; in this way, a picker could earn bonus points "without breaking his back on those ramps." As time passed, some of the order
pickers began helping one another to earn bonus points. A man who had orders calling for items that were concentrated in one or two stock rooms would
normally also need a few items which were stored in some distant building;
when this occurred, he would ask whoever was going that way to pick these
up for him. The group seemed to enjoy this departure and most of the men
eventually became participants. Several also took pride in their ability to
remember, without notes, exactly what extra items the others had asked them
to bring. Each man's reputation for helpfulness and good memory was frequently discussed.

In addition, the men appraised one another's skill in handling the trucks.
The order pickers had been obliged to push their trucks through connecting
passageways and steeply inclined ramps. Ascending a ramp called for powerful legs, and descending a ramp with a heavily laden truck required skill in

controlling the speed and a knowledge of the rough spots in the flooring. A side swipe or a collision in the narrow passages would scatter hundreds of items over the floor, effectively closing the ramp. While the pickers were reloading, the other pickers who were forced to wait would try to decide who was at fault; they also offered a variety of free advice.

By the time Joe Ansolino took over, the families of the Italian workers had become quite friendly with one another. And gradually, some of the Irish families began to visit back and forth, too. Good-natured rivalry eventually developed between the Irish and Italian communities. But regardless of their nationality, the men working in Wayne's warehouse were highly regarded by both groups, for they were assured of a steady job, the pay was all right, the men had a good boss, and everybody in the stockrooms was friendly.

The order pickers always watched their earned points quite carefully. When a man's pay per hour, including bonus, exceeded what the pickers considered was the then going rate in the area, one of the men who was thought of as a leader—perhaps Andrea Dondero or Tom O'Brien—would quietly speak to him. They would explain that "those guys upstairs are all right, but we don't want to give them any ideas." Whenever two or three pickers piled up too many points, they would take time off for conversation, a cigarette, and a rest. Their free time was gained by working steadily and fast and by the practice, mentioned earlier, of having others pick up the odd out-of-the-way items. They considered they had earned the rest periods.

Joe usually put the younger more agile men on the open-bin crew, for this required climbing ladders or crawling up the face of the bins (forbidden because of the chance of accident). Whenever a job as *packer* opened up, or a job as order picker for the prepackaged merchandise, the older and more responsible of the open-bin pickers were given first chance. These men were banteringly called the "rheumatiz squad," but even the oldest were tough muscled and active. The packers worked under the bonus point system along with the other men, but the time standards for this work had somehow been set very tight. To help the packers earn their bonuses and get a little free time for conversation and a smoke, most open-bin pickers, when unloading their accumulated items on the packing benches, would arrange these to facilitate quick packing in shipping cartons.

Pilfering of small items that could be used at home—electric fuses and sockets, small hand tools, screws and nails, paint brushes, and other items that would be unobtrusive in a man's pocket—was considered quite proper. Joe knew the men did this and he was quite sure the divisional merchandising managers and inventory clerks in the main office also suspected. However, neither he nor anyone else made any attempt to police the men. The men themselves policed the larger items: Items that were too large—that would be noticed if carried out at quitting time—were taboo.

During the depression of the early 1930's, Wayne Hardware Supply Company almost failed. Orders from retailers dropped to less than half of the 1929 sales. Consequently, cutbacks in expenses and manpower were necessary. Joe, who was assigned the responsibility for layoffs of the warehouse personnel, tried to keep men with young families and men who had the best work records. Hourly wages, bonuses, and work hours per week were reduced. In those years, the men abandoned their practice of setting their low work quotas, but they continued their cooperative work practices.

To cope with the low family incomes during the depression, the members of each nationality worked together more closely than before. Most of the families managed to keep a roof over their heads and secure enough food. These bonds were relaxed in the late 1930's, when jobs became more plentiful.

However, in the early 1940's, the members of each nationality united once more, this time to cope with new threats to their welfare. First, they began to notice that their respective communities were dying out. Their boys were going into the armed services and the children who stayed were taking jobs in other parts of Chicago. As the war drew to a close, these young people were also starting their own families, often with spouses whose backgrounds were quite different from their own. Many were moving to the new ranch-type houses in housing developments springing up on the outskirts of the city. In those areas, the neighbors of their sons and daughters were likely to be young people whose forebears had come from any one of several middle European countries. Equally disturbing, the fathers and mothers also noticed that the appearance of their own neighborhoods was rapidly changing. The houses that had once been kept neat, brightly painted, and spotlessly clean by their old neighbors were now being bought by landlords and indiscriminately rented to outsiders who had no interest in the property. Both groups had regularly consulted Joe Angelino about their neighborhood troubles with these newcomers, and he, Tom O'Brien, and Andy Dondero (now looked upon as leaders in their respective communities) would try to find solutions. On one occasion they even went to Mr. Robert Wayne about their dilemma, but even he could suggest no realistic permanent solution.

They had called upon Mr. Wayne, in part, because he had recently expressed to Joe his concern about the steady increase during recent months in the costs of order picking and the mounting backlog of unfinished orders. Instead of an average of 40 or 45 items per man hour, the average had slowly declined to around 35. And except for orders marked RUSH, RUSH, RUSH, two to four days were required to get an order shipped. In their conference with Mr. Wayne, Joe, and Tom and Andy (the latter were now foremen in the warehouse), attributed this to the low type of men they were having to hire. "These new guys don't give a hoot about the company and they wouldn't do an honest day's work for a thousand dollars." Joe had begun to bear down on the new men—acting, he admitted, almost as mean as George Deal, the old boss whom everyone had disliked. This, they agreed, had brought no improvement. When Mr. Wayne asked whether they thought stockroom labor costs could be reduced and shipments speeded up, Joe said he honestly believed that costs per item would probably go up instead of down, and that even though he might improve deliveries by hiring more men, he thought the men would try to maintain the backlog just to be sure they would never run out of work and be laid off.

Shortly after this conference Mr. Wayne had asked Joe, Tom, and Andy to come to his office again. After the usual preliminaries, he explained that he and the other front office executives had for several months been seriously studying the possibility of moving the offices and warehouse to a south Chicago suburb. The question was, how many of the good stockroom men would be willing to stay with the company. All three estimated that more than half would stay and that most of these would move to some suburb near the plant. Mr. Wayne spoke of the growing congestion inside and outside the present warehouse; he also indicated that if the company was to survive in the years ahead, it would have to make much faster deliveries in order to keep its customers and it would have to cut the merchandise handling costs. Failing this, the company would be forced to sell out or close its doors.

As stated earlier, the executives decided to build in the new location. A consulting firm designed the warehouse layout and labor-saving equipment with the advice of Joe and his two foremen. The three latter men relayed to the warehousemen descriptions of the many labor-saving features.

As the new building began to rise, the older men had become impatient to get into the new quarters. By the time the merchandise and the offices had been moved, a number of families had managed to sell their homes and find modern houses within driving distance of the warehouse. In most cases each family's new neighbors were young working class people who were newcomers to the area, "just starting out." Their social life consisted mostly of coffee klatches and backyard conversations; the talk usually turned to new household equipment, cars, the doings of the children, and the problems of getting the house "fixed up." The Wayne families now saw very little of one another.

The new warehouse was a model of efficiency. Its one floor was divided into two main sections. The active prepackaged stock was all stored in one section with an adjacent area for the surplus packaged stock. Storage for the open-bin items was similarly arranged. Because of the direct flow now possible, the work of handling the incoming and outgoing stock was substantially reduced. Also, the main aisles, which circled each storage section, were equipped with constantly moving drag lines recessed into the floor. Hand trucks with incoming merchandise could be attached to this chain and could be readily uncoupled and pulled aside while being unloaded by the stock men.

The trucks and drag lines were also used by the pickers for accumulating the items for the shipping orders. Both the packaged goods storage space and bin storage space were divided into several areas, each denoted by colors; order pickers were assigned to each area. Shipping orders usually required items from several areas and the trucks carried metal disks bearing the appropriate colors. As a truck with a green ticket approached the green area, for example, a "green" picker would pull it aside, get the items called for, and attach the truck again to the drag line. When the round was completed, the trucks were pulled off at the packing benches where the packers took over.

The old pickers formed the nucleus of the new crew. At first the men had been most enthusiastic about the new warehouse and its conveniences. They made several suggestions for the removal of the "bugs" that showed up during the initial weeks. Joe and his two foremen selected for each color area an experienced and reliable picker. They also hired several new open-bin pickers because some of the older men who moved with the company were now promoted to the packaged stock section or to the packing crew. Most of the new pickers were young family men living in nearby suburbs.

From the beginning, Joe and his foremen had been furnished with weekly reports of the average number of items per hour assembled by each picker, the total number of items assembled by each picker and by all pickers each week, and the number of unshipped orders which were 12 working-hours old, 20 to 28 hours old, and over 28 hours old. After the initial shakedown period, all the reports showed a steady improvement. For instance, the average number of items which the bin pickers assembled per man hour rose first to 50, then to 54, 57, and 59.

Thereafter, however, the trends were reversed. The average number of items per man-hour steadily declined to figures below 50. The men—especially the older men—began blaming this decline on the slowness of the stock men and the shortcomings of the layout and equipment. Nor were they willing to help the stock men move the new merchandise in; hence the stock men got behind. But most disturbing of all, they became touchy and morose and began criticizing and avoiding Joe and his foremen. This attitude gradually spread to the new men. The company had never had a union, but of late, organizers for a local warehousemen's union had been talking with the men. Upon the recommendation of the three leaders, Mr. Wayne gave the men a 5 per cent raise, bringing the warehousemen's pay rate well above the local scale; but the low assembly rate continued. In the meantime the consulting firm's time study men had been working out time standards for a new bonus point system similar to the old one. When this first went into effect, the men showed improvement, but this, too, was temporary. Joe and his two foremen now seldom went out on the floor; they spent most of their time going over their records trying to find out what had happened and attempting to decide how they could solve the problems they faced. They knew that Mr. Wayne would soon be pressing for a solution.

1. Group-versus-Group Status Measures
  a) In the 1930's, what status measures were used by the Italian and Irish communities?
  b) In the period immediately following World War II:
    1) What standards or measures were probably used by the old Italian and Irish neighborhood groups to measure their group status as compared with other groups which were invading their neighborhoods; how would the members try to demonstrate that their group's future was assured? Include those status measures that you discover in the case as well as any others you think they might have used.
    2) What would you suppose was their opinion of the reliability of these status measures as predictors of how the groups would fare in the future?
  c) After the Wayne families moved to the suburbs:
    1) What happened to their group status measures? How did each family measure its status as compared with other families?
    2) What do you think was their opinion of the reliability of these new community measures as predictors of their future security?

2. Status Measures within the Work Group

   a) What measures did the order pickers adopt to determine their individual status within their work group during the 1930's—what did they try to do best in order to make sure that they would be respected by their fellow pickers and their superiors and that their future welfare would be assured.

   b) How strong was their loyalty to their group? Why do you say so?

   c) Why did the number of items picked per man-hour go up shortly after the move?

   d) Why did it go down thereafter?

3. What does this case tell us about—

   a) The relationship between an individual's, a group's, and a company's goals and means, and the connections between these and status measures? (The concept of practical rationality may prove useful when you work out your answer to this question.)

   b) What does it tell us about monetary inducements offered employees?

4. What connections do you see between the ideas you developed in 3 a and b above and the idea of morale which is examined in the concluding pages of the chapter?

5. What steps might have been taken ahead of time to avoid, at least in part, the disappointing results noted at the new warehouse? (This question calls for hard thinking. Be specific.)

Chapter *10* THE
SEMIPERMANENT
FORMAL
ORGANIZATION
STRUCTURE

IN THIS chapter, we shall learn to gather premises which we can use in deciding what changes to make in the company's formal organizational structure. The structure serves as a fifth means of inducing people to adopt and carry out the improved programs that management has envisioned. The subsystem of concepts related to structure and the four related to authority, leadership, communication, and informal groups actually form an integrated body of thinking designed to coordinate and direct the activities the executives have decided to carry out.

Executives frequently change the company's organization structure to implement a new program. They also alter it to improve the employees' effectiveness in carrying out the current program. Typically, an executive never feels entirely satisfied with his company's formal organization structure. He frequently senses that something is wrong with the way some of the groups in certain departments are arranged and worries spasmodically about this, but he has trouble locating the precise nature of the problem. He may be aware, for instance, that one section of a department seems to be constantly falling down on its assigned job. Once in a while, the complaints about the section's inefficiency reach such a crescendo that he is obliged to take action. Seldom is a suitable alternative immediately apparent, however, because he cannot readily determine what the problem is. So, more often than not, he changes the structure on a "cut-and-try" basis— transfers the section to another department, for example—hoping that he will eventually hit upon a workable arrangement.

That experts believe organization structure to be one of management's most baffling problems is evidenced by the fact that probably more has been written on this subject than on any other phase of management.[1] The approach developed in this chapter grows out of that literature; but it differs in several respects from that of some of the more orthodox writers in the field, especially those who wrote in the 1920's and 1930's. We shall put to work the concepts we have already explored in an effort to uncover some of the elemental ideas underlying the concept of an organization structure—employ these as aids in deciding where in the company the problem lies and what changes to make in the structure.

Reshaping the formal organization structure into a more telling instrument for achieving the company's goals is, in practice, a complicated task—and a never-ending one—but once the fundamentals are understood, an executive is in a position to determine how to go about it in a realistic way. Our basic approach will be the now-familiar one of finding the alternatives (here, the possible combinations of the separate but intimately related parts of the organization) that will yield the greatest amount of wanted consequences and the least amount of unwanted. Each structure is actually a *set* of decisions—decisions about which people and how many should report to a particular executive and which groups of people should be included in a department or division. In every organization there are hundreds of possible alternatives—hundreds of combinations—each of which will produce somewhat different consequences. Clearly, the changes we introduce must be compromises; every combination will produce unwanted consequences.

CHARACTERISTICS OF THE FORMAL ORGANIZATION STRUCTURE AND PITFALLS TO WATCH FOR IN THINKING ABOUT THE STRUCTURE

The term *semipermanent formal organization structure*, as used in this book, means the long-term relationship of the parts of the organi-

---

[1] Many of the leading modern writers on management devote several chapters to the problems of formal structure. See, for example, Ralph C. Davis, *The Fundamentals of Management* (New York: Harper & Bros., 1951), chaps. 10–14; William H. Newman, *Administrative Action* (New York: Prentice-Hall, Inc., 1951), chaps. 8–17; Elmore Petersen and E. G. Plowman, *Business Organization and Management* (Homewood, Ill.: Richard D. Irwin, Inc., 1958), chaps. iv–x, xii; Harold Koontz and Cyril O'Donnell, *Principles of Management* (New York: McGraw-Hill Book Co., Inc., 1959), chaps. 6–14; William H. Newman and Charles E. Summer, Jr., *The Management Process* (Englewood Cliffs, N.J.: Prentice-Hall, Inc., 1961), chaps. 2–6; and Henry M. Albers, *Organized Executive Action* (New York: John Wiley & Sons, Inc., 1961), chaps. 4–9.

zation to the whole of the organization. The word *semipermanent* has been introduced to emphasize that the structure actually changes constantly. The term is a rather cumbersome one, so we shall ordinarily shorten it to *formal organization structure* or simply *formal organization*.

A formal organization structure is closely analogous to the structure of the human body. Each of its members (or organs) performs certain specialized tasks, each has its place, and each one is necessary to the well-being of all the others. As with the body, the tasks performed by the members of the organization must be coordinated if the organization is to flourish. An organization and a body are both organisms.

A company's formal organization structure is only a mental image. Nonetheless, it sets out which tasks each part (each individual, each section, and each department) should perform; the relative importance of each part of the organization; which of the individuals, sections, and departments are closely tied together and which are not closely related; and where in the organization each type of decision is lodged. The lines of the chart show who is to report to whom, show the *lines of formally bestowed authority*. It is almost always pictured as pyramidal in form. At the base rest a large number of specialists who work on the firing line, men who perform a rather wide range of relatively routine, though often highly specialized, activities. Above in the pyramid, directing their work, are layers of other specialists, managerial specialists. Indeed, we find specialization of tasks all through the pyramid. Each man does a distinguishably different job.

Because every man's task impinges on and also depends upon the work of other men in the company, the activities of these specialists must be coordinated. Management places most of the lower men in formally constituted groups to facilitate the passage of the premises they need. As already indicated, management also appoints middle-level executives whose responsibility is to aid in the coordination of their subordinates, men who are expected to exercise authority over these men and eventually become their leaders. In addition, still higher men are appointed to aid in coordinating the activities of this middle-management group. Commonly, an organization chart is drawn up in an effort to picture all these men and their relationships; it is a blueprint such as that used to depict the parts of a machine and their relationships.

The formal organization structure of a company is dynamic rather than fixed or permanent. That changes take place in the structure becomes apparent to anyone who compares a company's year-old organization chart with its current structure. In fact, a chart frequently becomes obsolete almost as soon as it is put on paper. Most of these changes in structure result from deliberate alterations in the departments, made with a view to improving the company's ability to flourish in its changing ideological and economic environment—changes that will be discussed in Chapters 11 and 12. Some changes are made because the organization expands in size; the activities of each person within the organization are likely to become more specialized as the company grows larger, and this calls for modifications in the structure. However, needed changes are sometimes made without the explicit direction or knowledge of the top executives. This frequently occurs when a department fails to perform its assigned duties. Informal groups in other departments, finding themselves hamstrung by the failure, begin to take over and discharge those tasks.

Changes in personnel also produce alterations in the structure. An organization is not a machine made of metal—not like a printing press, for instance, where each part is assigned a predetermined task and each replacement must be identical with the old one. The abilities of a new man on a job will ordinarily differ from those of his predecessor, so that it is necessary to fit the formal organization to the men and not the men to the formal organization. Also, many employees grow in stature while handling their assigned jobs—they are able to take on additional responsibilities—and this, too, calls for changes in structure.

Frequently, some of the features of a chart drawn up to represent an organization's formal structure seem illogical to the outsider—unless some man adept with a ruler has made it *look* logical by placing the activities in neatly balanced boxes on a piece of paper. Seldom does any organization conform to the pattern so often found in books (those in Diagrams 8A (p. 294) and B (p. 306) and 9 (p. 311) are no exception), not only because each company's structure is a unique instrument designed as a means of furthering its own chosen goals and is adapted to fit the employees, but because the structure reflects the history of the organization. Starting over with a clean slate is virtually impossible. The executives retain those features of the structure which have proved workable and try to revamp the others to make them more effective. Textbook discussions of organization charts and of organization structure sometimes leave the reader with a sense of unreality because these dynamic aspects are not fully explained.

As already indicated, one of the specific purposes of the formal organization structure is to set out the concrete duties which the employees are to perform rather permanently and to describe how they shall be integrated. However, by indicating the responsibilities of each individual, section, and department, the executives at the same time, by inference, make clear what each is *not* supposed to do; the structure provides a method of keeping people "out of one another's hair." In addition, the structure helps the formally appointed section heads and department heads to establish authority relationships because it shows who is to supervise whom, who is to be responsible for what duties, indicates where certain decisions are to be made and by whom, and supplies a flow-pattern for the formal communication of premises and decisions.

A second specific purpose is to make men feel that performing their proposed tasks is the normal, the accepted, thing to do; these may be new duties or modifications of their old ones or, perhaps, their present ones. The formal structure is itself a form of simple authority; though it is an intangible thing, its existence leads people to take for granted that the tasks they are asked to perform will further the company's goals: "Those executives upstairs ought to know—they're the experts in the field." Fortunately, as the men gradually become accustomed to performing their appointed tasks, they discover ways of using them to further their personal welfare as well as the company's, so many people eventually find that the change in the structure meets their personal needs reasonably well.

Executives should be aware of several pitfalls in thinking about formal organization structure and organization charts. Contrary to what is ordinarily assumed, an organization chart attempts to show only an *approximation* of the realities; it is not an accurate representation of the actual structure. We have already seen that charts quickly go out of date. But the misrepresentation is more pervasive than that. Because a company's structure is a very complicated thing, a chart that purports to describe it can really depict only the bare skeleton. Not all tasks can be fully shown on a chart; there are too many. Nor can the flow of information and the many subtleties in the authority relationships between people be represented by lines and boxes. Moreover, the *in*formal groups and the formal organization structure of the company are so closely entwined that they are virtually one in actual practice.[2]

The relative levels of the men in the hierarchy, as shown in the organization chart, are also likely to be misleading. A man or a department located high in the chart is not necessarily high in the actual organization hierarchy. The box may have been placed near the top merely to make the chart fit the sheet of paper. Nor does it mean that two men or two departments placed at the same level on the chart are actually equal; as we have seen, authority has to be won.

Executives sometimes erroneously believe that they can superimpose upon their organization a chart lifted from a book or a chart used successfully by some other company, or that they can devise a suitable formal organization structure from an armchair and hand the chart to the men in the company with instructions to adopt it. Charts taken from books or from other companies seldom prove practical because each company fills a different niche and each one's structure must be built especially to fill it. And people who devise an organization chart in an armchair tend to set up nicely symmetrical boxes which neatly balance one another, showing that each group of men is supervised by one man and that these several supervisors, in turn, are supervised by still another, and so on up to the top—just as we picture the organization of an army. Unfortunately, the men in an organization do not behave that way.

Nor is the company's formal organization structure and its chart always successful in constraining its members to play the clearly depicted roles which the chart has assigned to them. If the goals of a certain group are hampered by the structure, the members ignore it in their everyday activities, using instead their informal group's system of communication, its hierarchy of informal authority, and its leader.

Another pitfall is the assumption that a section, a department, or a division that has repeatedly failed to perform its duties can be brought up to par merely by changing the formal organization structure.[3] Appointing more supervisors for a section or a department, or removing some of the present echelons of supervision, does not neces-

---

[2] Mason Haire (ed.), *Modern Organization Theory* (New York: John Wiley and Sons, Inc., 1959), contains several stimulating, forward-looking, relatively abstract papers on human behavior in organizations, written by leading thinkers in the field.

[3] The use of the terms *section*, *department*, and *division* varies among companies. In these pages, we shall think of a section as a group of individuals brought together to do similar work, of a department as a group of sections, and of a division as a group of departments.

sarily solve the problem. Transferring a section from the jurisdiction of one department to another may prove equally disappointing. Moving the price-estimating section from the sales department to the accounting department or to the treasurer's department, or the methods section from the production department to the production planning department does not automatically produce fundamental changes in the effectiveness of that section. Improvements come only when the men in the group are furnished with the premises they need in making their decisions, and when they are mature enough to reach decisions that are equal to the needs of the company. Much of this effectiveness depends on the group's leader.

But the foregoing does not mean that a chart is of no use. It can be very helpful as a reflection of executives' ideas of what the organization structure is like. What we are saying is that a chart cannot be taken too literally, and that changing the structure does not automatically increase an organization's effectiveness.

WORKING OUT A SIMPLE ORGANIZATIONAL STRUCTURE

We shall begin our task of determining how to go about making changes in a company's formal structure—changes designed to improve it effectiveness—by exploring what we shall call a *simple organization structure*. In the second part of the chapter we shall introduce complexities into the structure; and eventually, in the third part we shall try to determine where in the structure the decisions should be made. Briefly, our task in this first part is to collect certain of the specialists into homogeneous groups and place supervisors over them, then tie these groups together in "bunches" and appoint superiors for those supervisors. Diagrams 8A and 8B (p. 306) exemplify the simple type of structure.

Starting to Build the Structure from the Bottom Up

The idea of building the structure up from the bottom of the hierarchy instead of down from the top provides one fertile source of insights useful in reshaping the company's organization structure. In trying to conceive a suitable organization structure, many people make the mistake of starting out at the top of the pyramid and working down. They begin with a preconceived idea that every company should have certain departments; that all the men who fabricate or assemble the product, for example, should automatically be placed together; that the record-keeping groups should always be brought together in another department; and so on. They jump to the conclusion

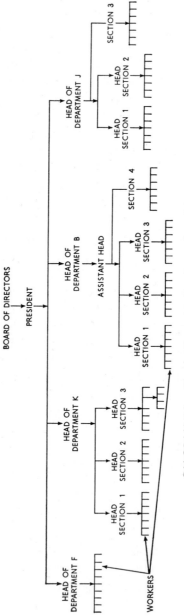

DIAGRAM 8A. Simple Organization Structure of Departments

that groups performing similar activities should always go together. It is possible that this arrangement will work out best for the company, but there is no way of telling until the company's needs have been analyzed. The chief purpose of a company's organization structure is to make sure that the work performed by the individuals on the firing line is well done, and the best way to do this is to begin with an examination of the tasks these people must do very well. *The superstructure—the hierarchy above these men—is erected to help them to do their jobs effectively.*

To make sure that these tasks are performed well, it is almost imperative, first, to learn the needs of the specific customer group the company intends to solicit. This provides premises for building a realistic organization capable of supplying those needs—for one of the main goals of a company is to enlarge the membership of the customer group. It is helpful to picture these customers as lying *beneath* a company's formal organization structure—*beneath* the pyramid. A study of their buying motives (goals) and buying habits (means) helps to reveal the premises they typically use in deciding which of the competing products to buy. Once these premises are clearly understood, management can determine which specific activities the men on the firing line (the salesmen, plant workers, engineers, and so on) must perform well—what types of decisions they will be called on to make, and what they must do if they are to induce these customers to join the organization and stay with it. The executives can then also decide the exact tasks which each of these groups must do *particularly well* if the company is to meet the needs of its prospective customer members better than its competitors.[4] This, in turn, helps them to determine which sections and departments will have to be large and manned by strong executives and personnel, and which can be left relatively small and weak.

Specialization

The idea of specialization furnishes another source of insights into the task of creating an effective "simple" organization structure. We

---

[4] Incidentally, the visual images of any necessary changes in the duties of the employees at the bottom of the pyramid also enable the executives to test in their minds ideas for changes in the structure. Will the new plan provide a better way of achieving the company's goals? How will the employees like the changes in the structure; will the changes lead to adequacy or efficiency?

The problem of determining the tasks the men in *our* company should perform extremely well will be taken up in Chapter 13 after we have decided on the company's niche in the economy. From a chronological point of view, this present chapter actually should follow Chapter 13, for the formal organization structure is really devised to make sure that those specific tasks will be carried out.

noted at the beginning that an organization is made up of various kinds of specialists and that one of the purposes of the structure is to help them to act in a coordinated way.

We can define a specialist as a person who is an expert in making the decisions called for in his particular field of activity; he is able to make a great many decisions in a day—many more than a non-expert—and most of these decisions will turn out to be more feasible than the decisions made by others. By concentrating his physical or mental efforts on one small segment of a larger problem or of a larger task, a man can usually become a specialist. Specialization contains the notion of thinking about, and doing, approximately the same thing repeatedly over a long period of time, thereby gathering the premises to reach more sophisticated decisions than a nonexpert in the field.

During the last several decades the tendency to specialize has become a dominant characteristic of our industrial civilization. There are probably two chief reasons why businessmen have eagerly adopted this approach, and these account for two of the three types of specialists we shall discuss here. One is that out-of-pocket labor costs can be sharply reduced by breaking a routine job into minute steps and employing division of labor.[5] Here, we are talking about a specialist in performing routine and predominantly manual activities, such as grinding burrs from a steel bar, or operating a calculating machine, or handling routine inquiries from customers. The man who operates a certain machine or assembles certain parts of a uniform product time after time not only uses specialized equipment, but he has the premises derived from learning the one best way and from going through the same operation so many times that he eventually accumulates a vast array of factual and value premises which enable him to do the work accurately and quickly. The same is true where the product of a department or a section is a stream of standardized facts—for instance, accounting data or statistical information, or a stream of rather routine, standardized decisions such as those produced by men in the customer complaint section or men who operate the company's data processing equipment. Procedures can be set up for making these routine decisions.

---

[5] Recall our conclusion (p. 137) that specialization and mass production largely account for the anomaly that the company's inducements and its members' inducements can both be increased. These savings in out-of-pocket costs are possible, however, *only* if there is a *mass market* for the product—*only* if customers are willing to buy it in large volume. In the absence of this, specialization of routine tasks is of relatively little value to a company as a cost-saving device.

A second reason for businessmen's interest in specialization is that, during the past century or more, the boundaries of our knowledge have greatly expanded. More precisely, we have been able to penetrate further and further down into specific areas of knowledge; we know more about the details in certain fields and how those details are interrelated. This has brought to the fore a second type of specialist, the professionally trained man who is an expert or an "authority" in a particular field of knowledge, the man whom we shall call the *mental* specialist. Such a man—whether he be a salesman, an advertising man, a design engineer, an organic chemist in the field of fats and oils, an expert on strength of materials, a production scheduler, a time and motion study man, a personnel man, an operations research man, an accountant, or a finance man—has developed a broad base of solid, detailed premises for reaching his decisions. He has penetrated down into his field, has at hand more factual and value premises than others, and is more aware of the interrelationship of these premises.[6] We shall think of these mental specialists *and* the routine specialists as the men on the firing line—the ones who are assigned places in groups or sections. The mental specialists include staff people; the routine specialists are roughly equivalent to plant and office workers.

Executives are also specialists (a third type of specialist) in *coordinating the decisions of others* and in conceiving and gaining

[6] Executives sometimes jump to the conclusion that the mental specialist should be assigned an assistant, a lower paid routine specialist whose job is simply to gather information for premises—do the "leg work"—so that the mental expert can devote all of his time solely to making decisions in his specialized field. This may prove a timesaver in those cases where most of the premises he requires are factual; but if his premises are of a predominantly value nature, he *has* to seek these himself in order to perceive the subtleties. In any case, as we have seen, a man's creative processes are frequently stimulated by a certain amount of routine work; this gives him time to think. Even top executives sometimes find it fruitful to "waste their time" going through the experience of compiling at least some of the figures they are going to use, for only in this way can they get the "feel" of what the figures actually mean.

Breaking up a section's work into several specialized jobs, another commonly adopted technique, may also prove inefficient. For example, specializing the work of the men in the home office sales department by assigning one man to check blueprints, another to follow up the orders as they move through the plant, and a third to handle customer complaints (specialization of duties) may lead to mistakes and waste motion in instances where the salient and difficult-to-come-by premises must be drawn from the customers. Here, specializing by customers instead of by duties will usually solve the problem. An inside office salesman who handles all the orders from certain specified accounts, and who follows each order from the moment the inquiry comes in until the product is delivered and installed in the customer's plant, accumulates a large body of premises relevant to each account and each order. He need not spend hours gathering data from others (his information is already in his head); the information is as accurate as he can make it; and he has all of the facts that are available, so that he can make his decisions more quickly and accurately.

acceptance of new alternatives. The majority of their decisions are based on a relatively complex set of premises. This is also true of mental specialists; but, unlike the latter, executives must be able to gather a very wide variety of premises from diverse sources instead of from only one field of knowledge. In addition, as we saw when investigating executive training, the executive's chief task is the making of complex decisions, the majority of which are unique; in this respect, he differs markedly from the routine specialist.

We can decide whether a group of manual or mental specialists should specialize still more than at present by paying particular attention to the effect of this on our company's sales volume and on its expenses. Upon examining the work done by our salesmen, for instance (these are mental specialists), we may realize that they could notably increase the company's sales—could compete for customer orders much more effectively—if, instead of selling all our products to each customer, our sales force were divided up and one group specialized in one of our product lines and a second and a third group specialized in our two other lines. Or if all our salesmen now serve four types of customer, we may find that by dividing the men up and developing four specialized sales forces, one for each market, the increase in their combined sales will more than pay for the added cost of duplicated travel expense.

On the other hand, cost reduction (not increased sales) may be the chief purpose in dividing into two or more groups the manual specialists who do a certain type of work. This is commonly practiced. Instead of having each man in the shipping department take a customer's order, go through the warehouse and accumulate all the items called for, pack the order, label it, make the shipping instructions, and arrange for shipment, it is less costly to divide up the men in the shipping department, instructing each group to specialize in one part of the task. These decisions are made in the same way as other decisions.

Forming Routine or Mental Specialists into Homogeneous Groups Headed by Executive Specialists

A distinguishing characteristic of what we are calling a *simple* formal organization structure is that the so-called "lines of authority" are rather clearly designated; each man is supposed to receive his directions from one giver, his superior. We have what is called "unity of command." In the second part of the chapter when we examine more complex problems of structure, we shall explore those enigmatic problems which arise when the company encourages its men to employ the premises supplied them by two or more specialists simultaneously in deciding how to get a particular job done.

Forming Sections.   We have already seen that, within limits, specialization enables men to handle the company's work more effectively. The work of the routine specialists who perform similar specialized tasks is also greatly facilitated by placing them in groups or sections where they can readily exchange premises and check one another's decisions. The men in such groups are working together for a common goal, they are employing similar means, they are likely to use many of the same premises, and the decisions they make will ordinarily have to dovetail. The men can share their experiences— teach one another the one best way. The same is true when mental specialists are formed into homogeneous groups. In some cases the specialists may be assembled into a group to take advantage of certain laborsaving equipment—machines and material-handling devices. But probably the larger and more universal problem which is solved by forming specialists into groups is that of communication.[7]

Management appoints a head for each group to help these routine specialists and mental specialists with premise passing and decision making. One of the responsibilities of the supervisor is to aid his men in transmitting to one another the premises that originate within the section, thus coordinating their work. Another is to coordinate the work of his section with that of other sections and departments in the company by looking upward in the hierarchy to the company's goals, and looking to the sections and departments to his right and his left for premises. He also makes certain that his men promptly receive the temporarily useful premises they require; and he keeps them informed about current new developments in other departments, so that they can make realistic decisions. This brings the section's work into line with the rest of the company's activities.

To win the authority that management has bestowed, the appointed head must not only be familiar with the specific premises which his specialists regularly employ, but he must feel at home with the particular *type* of premises they use. He must be able to think the way they think. In other words, a group of men who employ factual premises most of the time requires a superior who is adept in using

---

[7] Notice, in passing, that management almost automatically places men with similar educational and cultural backgrounds in the same groups because they are equipped to do similar work. This circumstance produces a valuable (though at times harmful) by-product—namely, a tendency for the men in each formal group to coalesce into an informal group.

factual premises; if most of the premises the men use are of a value nature their superior must feel comfortable with value premises. If the section head is less of an expert than they in gathering and handling their type of premises, the men will reject him as their leader; and he will fail in most of his efforts to direct and coordinate their activities. Few section heads are equally at home with both factual and value premises. This probably explains why an engineer is seldom put in charge of advertising men. Nor are salesmen commonly appointed as heads of production scheduling, accounting, or product design, for they are not at ease with the factual premises used there.

Span of Control. But a section head must have more than leadership if he is to achieve coordination. He must have time to give his specialists the help they need. The amount of time he has available for them *in part* determines how many men should be included in a single group. Contrary to what some of the early writers in the field of administration have suggested, there is no nice general answer to the question of how many subordinates a man should supervise—of what the optimum span of control should be. In the 1920's, authors sometimes mentioned seven as the right number. Actually, the average *is* around seven in many companies but under certain circumstances, 50 might be too few in one section, whereas, in another section three might be too many. In billing sections, where the girls gather most of their premises from the customer orders lying beside their billing machines, the supervisor will be called upon to help the girls only when some unusual problem turns up; in such a section, one man might be able to supervise 30 or possible 100 girls without trouble. On the other hand, three or four subordinates may be too many if the subordinates need close supervision or must secure most of their pieces of information from their superior, and if this information is complex and chiefly value in character.[8] And a supervisor who wastes his time or has trouble making decisions and gaining acceptance or who has failed to win informal leadership may have difficulty supervising even a small group, whereas a more capable leader of that same section could readily handle twice as many.

Appointing an Assistant. As indicated a moment ago, however, the number of subordinates a man can supervise personally is not the sole determinant of the optimum size of a section. If the group's

---

[8] Notice, in this connection, that a supervisor can be "cut in two." When only a few men are required in a section and they need little supervision, the company can use a working boss, a man who spends part of his time as a boss and the rest of his time as a worker. Supervisory costs are thus kept in line.

supervisor becomes too busy, an unofficial, informal assistant leader, to whom the men can turn for advice, will ordinarily be chosen by the group. When management finds that this has occurred, it is time to think about training and formally appointing an assistant. Ideally, this man has already received the on-the-job training described in Chapter 8 (pp. 240–242). He can handle the less complex decisions; he knows (1) which decisions he can safely make alone, (2) which he can make tentatively (he checks these with his superior before putting them into effect), and (3) which problems he should hand over to his superior (together with whatever data he has accumulated) because he lacks the necessary premises. If the group becomes so large that this no longer works, the head of the group may find it advisable to divide his routine or mental specialists into two sections and appoint section heads to help each group. In such a case the section takes on some of the characteristics of what we are calling a department.

Putting Sections Together into Departments and Appointing Departmental Heads

In this simple type of structure which we are now examining, everyone reports to only one superior. He serves as a communication medium in addition to his other tasks. But the formal structure itself also plays a major role in communication.

Using the Structure to Aid Free Communication. The chief purpose in tying together two, three, four, or more groups or sections of routine specialists or mental specialists, each with a supervisor, and placing these supervisors under a single head is to facilitate quick and accurate communication between the groups. (We are now beginning to move up in the structure depicted in Diagram 8A, p. 294.)

To make wise decisions about which *groups* of manual or mental specialists to include in a department, it is useful at the outset to visualize how the work is done by each section; while we watch, we note the key decisions the men must make, the temporarily useful information they will need in order to make their decisions, the sections which serve as sources of this information, and the most appropriate vehicle of communication. Ideally, we would always put these paired sources and destinations in the same department to ease the task of communication. However, there are obviously limits to this. It usually turns out that each section periodically needs information from almost every other section in the company; hence, when we place a section in one department, we automatically separate it from other sections that sometimes furnish it with needed information. Each alternative we try out—each combination—will inevitably produce unwanted as well as wanted consequences in the area of communication. Our task is to find the best combination.

Generally speaking, those sections which must promptly transmit to one another a large volume of varied and intricate factual premises, or which depend upon one another for many complex value premises, should be put together to form a department. The need to place together those sections made up of routine specialists or mental specialists which must communicate many *factual* premises rapidly and accurately can be illustrated by looking into a manufacturing department which is using mass production techniques. Each step in the fabrication and assembly process is closely dependent on the preceding steps and greatly affects the succeeding steps. In order to maintain a near-capacity production level in each of the several sections, a mass of factual information must flow back and forth between them. Also, each must be promptly informed about breakdowns in the flow and about revisions in plans. When these sections are tied together, the men can, for example, more readily go to other sections and explain why a certain part does not quite work when it gets to theirs; and they can conveniently send informally those premises that no one wants to inject into the formal communication channels.

The need for very close bonds between certain of the manufacturing sections is even greater in a company that produces in small lots to fill special orders for individual customers. Because of the varied nature of the work, unforeseen problems often arise; and the task of integrating each of the manufacturing steps required for each order is greatly multiplied. To meet this situation, the communications between the sections working on those orders must be particularly easy and free.[9]

We have seen that those sections which must communicate intricate sets of factual premises to each other can do a better job if they are joined into departments. *There is an even greater need to link together in one department those sections in the company which must depend on one another for the complex value premises they each require.* Tying them together facilitates the face-to-face communication

---

[9] Putting certain manufacturing sections together because this may reduce the job of moving heavy products from one section to the next (materials handling) is one premise, but not the sole premise, to consider in determining what manufacturing sections shall go together. It obviously has no bearing in deciding which of the company's *non*-manufacturing sections should be brought together in a given department.

so essential in conveying all the nuances of value premises. In laying sales plans, for example, the sales manager can profit from the many value premises accumulated by advertising men, salesmen, and market research men. Consequently, these three sections are typically included in one department. In a company making style goods—producing women's dresses, yard goods, books, or furniture, for instance —the sales executives must decide what particular products to include in the line each season, how much to charge, and how many units to manufacture initially. Then, after watching the weekly sales trends and gathering value premises from the men on the firing line, they must decide when and how much they will remanufacture when stocks get low. To gather these data, they must live close to the conditions—close to the sections that accumulate these value premises— so that they may see and sense those premises which are hard to put into words or into columns of figures; they must read between the lines and bring whatever they "see" into the picture.

Physical Location as an Aid to Communication. The foregoing points up a second method of assuring easy communication between sections (also between departments)—namely, contiguous physical locations. By locating sections (or departments) close together physically, it is possible to set up a pathway for the informal flow of value premises. Incidentally, in those cases where a section seems to fit equally well in either of two departments, the section can be located between them; and the decision as to which department head the section head is to report to can be made by flipping a coin.

Deciding Which Sections May Be Separated. What we have just been exploring also provides insight for decisions about those sections which need not be put together. Every section in the company will, as we saw, periodically require some premises from almost all the other sections; but in those cases where virtually all the information is of a factual nature (readily understandable figures or blueprints, for instance) or where the sections are called on to transmit only a few simple pieces of information each day or week, they need not be closely tied together. They can be placed in separate departments without jeopardizing communication because standardized factual information can be easily transmitted. Cost accounting, or the payroll section, for example, can be included in the treasurer's department, even though these sections secure practically all of their premises from production people. Or they can as readily be incorporated in the manufacturing department. The purchasing section can be placed under any one of several department heads, depending on convenience only, *in those cases* where the premises the buyers require are standardized and can be accurately described.

Uniting Groups Which Can Help One Another Solve Difficult Problems. The inexperienced layman is likely to suppose that groups which perform similar work should be formed into a department. After a casual inspection, he decides that the company's employees do four or five kinds of work—selling, production, accounting, and financial work, for instance—and accordingly puts together in one department the sections which perform the same kind of work.

Such generalizations often lead to ill-advised decisions. Merely because certain sections all deal with figures bearing a dollar sign does not mean that they should be formed into a department under the treasurer, nor does the fact that certain other sections handle the fabrication and assembly of the company's products necessarily mean that they should be incorporated in a manufacturing department. Actually, it may be advisable to assemble some of the products at the company's warehouse branches which are under the jurisdiction of the sales department. A section composed of mechanics whose job is to produce test models based on new designs created by the engineering department can often work more effectively under the engineering design department, even though they are really producing physical products—really manufacturing. Or it may be advisable to attach a group of engineers to the sales department if the product is a complex one and each unit is specially designed for a customer. In one company the product planning section will prove most effective if it is placed in the product development department; whereas in another company it must get most of its premises from men in the sales department and accordingly should be located there. The objective is to tie together those sections which will encounter the most difficulty in securing or transmitting the required premises, regardless of what kind of work they do.

Appointing the Department Heads. So far, we have noted two methods of assuring a free flow of premises between sections: linking together those sections which must transmit to each other the most premises and will most probably encounter problems in conveying these, and locating the sections together physically. A third is the formal appointment of department managers—executives whose assignment is to help the section heads to make their decisions, to coordinate the work of the sections with one another, and to integrate their work with the activities of sister departments. Theirs is the task of holding the organization together and moving it up the means-end staircases they have adopted. As was the case in selecting section heads, each department manager should not only be familiar with the specific premises used by the various sections whose bosses he supervises, but he should be able to think as they think. To win leadership, a sales manager must feel at home with value premises (though he must be able to use factual premises, too); and the heads of the manufacturing and the engineering departments must be particularly adept in the use of factual premises, though they must also know how to employ relatively simple value premises.

We have now examined certain steps we may use to create a picture of a more suitable structure for our company; we have achieved the stage of illumination in the creative process. The task now is to try out once more the various combinations of sections to make sure that the particular combination we have conceived does actually bring together the groups which will benefit most from propinquity. We are testing an interrelated set of decisions about the details of the formal structure. Note that when making these decisions, we must consider the strengths and shortcomings of the particular employees in each section and their supervisors. Recall that a simple *departmental* structure is depicted in Diagram 8A (p. 294). Next, we examine the other main type of simple organizational structure, the divisional structure.

Specializing by Product, Market, or Area: Divisional Structure

Before finally deciding on the company's organizational structure, we may want to consider the possibility of further specialization; a divisional type of structure may be preferable to a departmental type. Thus far we visualized only a departmental type, though we have vaguely referred to divisions. Actually, the divisions of a company (if any) are made up of departments, usually a set of parallel departments. As will be seen, divisions may be established for separate product lines, for different markets, or for geographical areas. A company frequently changes from the departmental to the divisional type of structure when it becomes overlarge and unwieldy. Diagrams 8A (p. 294) and 8B show the distinguishing characteristics of the departmental and the divisional types of structure. Both of these are "simple" organization structures; each man has only one boss.

In the departmental type of structure, the only type we have so far considered, the employees are in general (but by no means always)

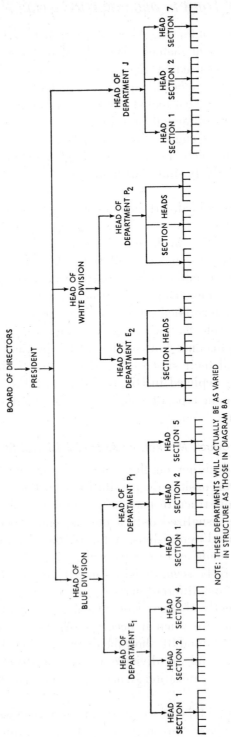

BOARD OF DIRECTORS

PRESIDENT

HEAD OF BLUE DIVISION

HEAD OF WHITE DIVISION

HEAD OF DEPARTMENT E_1

HEAD OF DEPARTMENT P_1

HEAD OF DEPARTMENT E_2

HEAD OF DEPARTMENT P_2

HEAD OF DEPARTMENT J

HEAD SECTION 1

HEAD SECTION 2

HEAD SECTION 4

HEAD SECTION 1

HEAD SECTION 2

HEAD SECTION 5

SECTION HEADS

SECTION HEADS

HEAD SECTION 1

HEAD SECTION 2

HEAD SECTION 7

NOTE: THESE DEPARTMENTS WILL ACTUALLY BE AS VARIED IN STRUCTURE AS THOSE IN DIAGRAM 8A

DIAGRAM 8B. Simple Organization Structure Made Up of Divisions arranged according to the kind of work they do. We form into separate departments the people (and sections) who do selling, manufacturing, product development, personnel work, and so on—though we have deliberately included in a department a section which did somewhat different work wherever this seemed best. The divisional type of structure is merely an elaborate departmental structure; it permits greater specialization of the employees.

The advantages for our company of a divisional type of organizational structure may become evident when we carefully examine the tasks that the men on the several firing lines must handle. Perhaps we discover that the men are overburdened with too much to learn or are forced to neglect some of their essential tasks; as a consequence, they are not able to perform their work as effectively as we should like. On the basis of this, we may conclude that employee proficiency would be increased if the sections in some of the departments were broken in two and the men in each half section were to specialize still more. Then they would be required to know only one field instead of two or three and would need to handle a narrower range of problems. We want to make sure that we can successfully compete for the available business. To achieve this, the men in each department must be as effective as their counterparts in competing companies.

In some cases, divisional specialization by *product lines* may yield a preponderance of wanted consequences. We organize two or more divisions, one for each of our product lines. Each will probably contain its own specialized sales, manufacturing, and product development departments.

For another company, we may decide to set up divisions for each of the principal types of *customers* (*markets*) we serve. For instance, one division might be made up of departments whose members intimately know the needs of the industrial market for their product and the other would contain departments which understand the needs of the consumer market.

Finally, for a company which serves a large area, we may decide to establish a division—an all-but-separate company—in each of three or four *geographical areas* in the United States or in other parts of the world.

In addition to the three variants just noted, many other combinations of these two fundamental organization structures, the departmental and the divisional structure, are possible. The divisionalization may be only partial. For instance, a company may set up two or three specialized manufacturing departments, one for each product line, but use only one sales force. Or it may use two or three separate sales departments each serving a different set of customers but have only one manufacturing department and one product development department.

The basic problem is to make sure that the additional income from the specialization will more than offset the additional costs.

Building the Top of the Hierarchy

When we approach the top management levels in the structure, where certain departments are to be brought together to form divisions, each with its own division head who is responsible to the chief executive, it will be observed that all of these men must be able to utilize both factual and value premises intelligently; they must feel at home in both. Generally speaking, as we have already seen, the higher the executive's position in the hierarchy, the fewer the factual premises available, and the more he must rely on value premises.

Unless the top executives—the division heads—are willing to accept the conclusions of their subordinates without reservations, willing to allow their subordinates to exercise simple authority over them a good deal of the time, these executives must be able to think and reason at practically any level of the organization's activities. We often read that all a top executive needs to do is to "hire a good man and give him the sole responsibility for running his department." However, unless the division head is familiar with the premises his department heads use and knows how to make well-considered decisions based on these premises, the departmental heads will be making the *real* decisions. Unless these top executives assume leadership of their divisions, the company tends to drift or else to go off in several directions simultaneously.

The president or chief executive is placed at the pinnacle of the structure to help the division heads (or in case there are no divisions, the department heads) decide what crucial tasks they and their departments must carry out. Provided that he has won his leadership, he takes the initiative in planning the company goals and in planning what each department must do to achieve those goals. He passes this mental image of goals and means to his subordinates, aids them in determining what specific tasks their several departments should do unusually well, and checks up periodically to see that each one does as planned, so that all the separate company activities fit together into an organic, interrelated whole. Much of Part III will be devoted to his tasks.

The role played by the board of directors, the group usually pictured at the very top of the organization chart, varies widely from company to company. More often than might be supposed, the directors are selected by the president, meet only as required by law, and perfunctorily approve what has already been decided by management. Ideally, these men help their subordinates (the president and other top executives) to solve their knotty problems. In addition to electing the officers, they can, if carefully selected, bring to the company a perspective and a wide range of value premises useful in making long-term decisions—pertinent ones which the top executives may have overlooked because they have been too close to their problems.[10]

COMPLICATING THE STRUCTURE OF THE ORGANIZATION AND RESOLVING THE CONFLICTS THAT RESULT

In a simple structure such as the one just investigated, emphasis is placed on formal authority and on unity of command—a single officially designated superior for each man. This makes for ease in determining which routine specialists and mental specialists should report to a certain superior, who the superiors are, and who is responsible for what, thus minimizing the conflicts within the organization. However, most medium-sized companies and virtually all large companies soon find that an organization with a simple structure cannot adequately handle the problems the company faces. It usually turns out that in order to maintain its position in the industry against the onslaught of competition, the company must gain the full benefit of the wealth of decisional premises available from mental experts; and this means that the top executives have to introduce a more complicated web of authority and communication than the one set out in a simple structure.

Executives frequently feel uneasy about approving the crossflow, for it violates one of the often-repeated organizational principles, unity of command; but the premises they gather from the realities they face every day *force* them, in practice, to assent—unofficially, if not officially. We have already seen that authority and communication have to flow in all directions in order to assure good decision making, and that in these days of specialization, no man is capable of

---

[10] For an incisive discussion of the role a board of directors *can* play, see Melvin T. Copeland and Andrew R. Towl, *The Board of Directors and Business Management* (Boston: Division of Research, Graduate School of Business Administration, Harvard University, 1947).

mastering and transmitting all the many specialized premises now available.

Although departures from the simple structure are nowadays vital to most companies, such departures do cause conflicts. These can be resolved, though the solutions are not easy; many companies manage to enjoy the benefits of cross-fertilization of ideas and at the same time the benefits of a smooth-running organization. Yet we cannot wish away these conflicts by simply saying that a man needs the very best premises and decisions he can get, and that these should come from the best sources; realistic plans have to be laid to make this happen.

Our objective here is to complicate the organization structure to the end that all employees will have available the best possible premises and, at the same time make sure that the receivers of the premises do not become confused by conflicting instructions. We are introducing duality of command—deliberately appointing two or even more men to guide the behavior of a given man. The majority of the problems arising from this procedure turn upon the question of which appointed expert is to make what decisions. The general solution suggested in these pages is to make certain that the various decisions made by the experts all dovetail. Essentially, these are jurisdictional problems. If left unresolved, they occasionally produce open and continuous warfare which shakes the morale of the entire organization. More often, however, these problems create an underlying atmosphere of conflict which periodically diverts men's efforts away from their task of achieving the company's goals.

Throughout this second part of the chapter, our underlying problem, though seldom stated, will be that of creating structures which will comfortably accommodate the mental experts who are to work closely with the men on the line. Such complications of the structure are commonly called line and staff arrangements. The basic difficulty here is that a man has two superiors, and this frequently causes dissention. We shall explore four rather typical staff arrangements and some ways of coping with the conflicts that normally exist. We shall begin our examination at the bottom of the structure again, but in this instance the only purpose is to provide a simple thread for our examination. Diagram 9 shows these four staff arrangements in an organizational chart.

The conflicts are deep seated; therefore, after noting some examples of the first (and simplest) of the four line and staff arrangements, we shall use this as a point of departure for probing into some of the

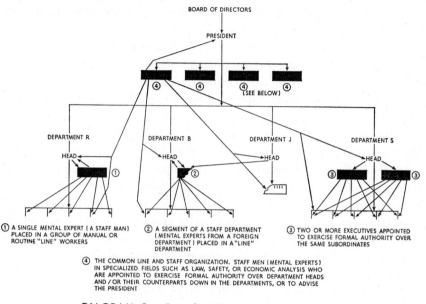

DIAGRAM 9.   Complex Organization Structure

origins of these conflicts. Actually, of course, when conceiving a complicated structure for our own company, we would not confine ourselves to these four types, but would conceive several promising combinations of the men and sections (just as for a simple structure), and choose the one whose details, we think, would yield the greatest amount of wanted consequences—always taking into consideration capacities and temperaments of the men who would be occupying all those little boxes.[11]

Introducing a Mental Specialist into a Group of Routine Specialists

Our first type of departure from a simple organization structure consists of interjecting into a homogeneous group of routine specialists a mental specialist whose goals and premises are quite different from those of the group, and having him thereafter report to a supervisor of the routine men—to a "line" man. (See Diagram 9, Example 1.)

[11] The subject of line and staff has engaged the attention of many students. Among these are the authors named in footnote 1 of this chapter, and Douglas McGregor, *The Human Side of Enterprise* (New York: McGraw-Hill Book Co., Inc., 1960), Louis A. Allen, *Improving Staff and Line Relationships* (New York: National Industrial Conference Board, 1956), and Robert C. Sampson, *The Staff Role in Management* (New York: Harper & Brothers, 1955). For an observer's realistic account of the relationships of line and staff men, see Melvill Dalton, *Men Who Manage* (New York: John Wiley & Sons, Inc., 1959), chap. 4.

Here are some examples: placing a personnel man permanently or temporarily under the foreman of the manufacturing department's assembly section, or under the sales manager; placing a metallurgist or a safety man in the production department; hiring a chemist to work in the plant on quality control; or interjecting a methods and time study man or a scheduler into the fabricating section of the production department.

With these examples in mind, let us now turn aside momentarily for our examination of the conflicts arising between line and staff. As already indicated, in many cases, this departure creates aggravating, chronic conflicts between the men in the "line" (the routine specialists and their appointed leaders) and the man on the "staff"—the mental specialist. The line men usually resent the staff men, and the staff men feel frustrated in trying to work with men in the line. Management's task is to establish a smooth working relationship between the two.

Inducing the supervisors in the "line departments" to accept the point of view expressed below will rest largely on the chief executive. His first task is to teach the idea that *all* sections and departments of the company, regardless of whether they are supposed to be line *or* staff, are *co-means* of achieving the company goals, and that the practice of emphasizing and drawing distinctions based on the line *versus* the staff is not an effective means of utilizing the company's man power. The objective here is to minimize these distinctions. Next, he has to prove to the heads of sections and departments that the mental experts can make decisions that will help them and their subordinates to do a better job. Third, he has to select the mental specialists with care, train them to make solid decisions in behalf of the line executives and their manual or routine specialists, and teach them how to gain acceptance and win leadership. The mental specialist must recognize that he has to win his authority—win it from the boss as well as from the men; it cannot be bestowed upon him. Finally, under the guidance of the executive, the mental specialist and the middle-management executive will have to learn how to sit down together and work out the specific problems the section or department faces. If this four-step program produces rebellion, it may be necessary to replace the executive, or the expert, or both.

In some companies the distinction (and conflicts) between staff men and line men have been drawn so sharply and have become so deeply embedded that re-educating the men poses a major challenge. An understanding of the origins of the antagonisms that commonly prevail aids in the re-education process. Such an understanding also sheds light on another problem—the roles of the "line" and "staff" men in the formal organization structure. As will become evident in the next few paragraphs, *I think the terms "line" and "staff" introduce distinctions that have not only outlived their usefulness but tend to confuse the problem of setting up a suitable organization structure.*

The line boss and the mental expert often find it difficult to think and work together. Because each frequently uses quite different premises, which lie outside the experience of the other, and because they seldom assign the same weights to those they both consider, they almost never reach identical conclusions. Moreover, each man, because of his intensive training, is sure that he is the expert; since neither is willing to concede that he is the novice, neither is able successfully to exercise authority over the other. Notice, too, that every time the supervisor allows the mental expert to guide his behavior, he loses status in the eyes of his men. Clearing up such deep-seated conflicts requires time and patience.

The antipathy is entirely understandable when it is seen also in the light of the historical development of American business. In the early 1800's the routine experts and their superiors were all-important; the only big job was the manufacture of the product. As a competitor against the family units which then produced their own clothing, household equipment, and food, the early manufacturer encountered little difficulty in selling his products, which were superior to the homemade products, and cheaper. However, as time passed and each manufacturer was forced to compete *entirely* against fellow manufacturers instead of against inefficient householders, the businessman found that his company must carry on several theretofore-unheard-of activities if it was to survive. Each of these started out as a staff activity—in the eyes of the owner a rather unnecessary undertaking, though of some slight help in solving temporary problems. Only when, and to the extent that, the premises and the decisions of these new men gradually grew in worth as a means of ensuring the company's welfare did they win for themselves a position of respect in the organization.[12]

---

[12] In *What's Ahead for American Business* (Boston: Atlantic Monthly Press and Little, Brown & Co., 1951), Sumner H. Slichter points out that the growth in importance of the so-called "staff" constitutes one of the major changes in American business practices. He emphasizes that staff men were introduced to help the line organization to make more effective decisions about "current operations, developing new policies, and making plans for the future."

In many companies, traces of these earlier patterns of thinking are evident today. The terms sales staff, advertising staff, legal staff, and engineering staff, for example, are still widely used. And plant foremen and superintendents still feel antagonistic toward the mental experts in their organizations. For one thing, the old guard loses status when the outsiders begin making some of the departmental decisions; and, understandably, they try to maintain their old positions. For another, in their eyes, these mental specialists have nothing to show for their work. The intangibles produced by them cannot be sold. According to the line men, the only thing that brings in money is the manufactured product which they make. More than that, since the mental experts do not handle the physical product, they do not really work; all they do is to sit around in offices and talk; they are *non*productive. But the most unfair thing of all, as they see it, is that "We have to *carry* these men; the profit and loss statement proves it. The only things they create are expenses; where do you see any record of the *income* they produce?" The men doing the *real* work have to bear the expense burden of such unnecessary, unproductive activities as advertising, personnel work, accounting, cost accounting, product development (or engineering) ; and motion and time studies, scheduling, production control, and quality control.

The patterns of thinking just described have led many people to accept uncritically two points of view—two "principles." One is that decision making should be the sole prerogative of the bosses in the line departments. On the basis of what we have so far seen in this book, this is not a solid conclusion; the fact that the work of a so-called "staff" man was not considered essential in earlier decades and the fact that he deals with ideas rather than physical products do not constitute adequate premises. The second "principle" is that the boss in the line should be granted the *sole* right to exercise authority; the mental specialist could advise but should not attempt to direct the behavior of, and communicate with, the subordinates in the line. The mental specialist could suggest new proposals to the supervisor, of course; but the supervisor had the privilege of brushing these aside. The application of these principles undoubtedly reduces the conflicts in the organization; but if the mental experts are *not* permitted to make decisions and exercise authority, *the money spent on them is largely wasted.*

Few companies today are in a strong enough competitive position to afford the luxury of permitting the men in the "line" to make *all* the decisions. At least *some* of the forward-looking competitors will employ mental experts to ensure more effective decisions, and they will see that these men go directly to the routine specialists in order to gain wholehearted acceptance of their proposals. Indeed, most companies have been obliged to give the mental experts increased responsibilities in order to meet the competition. This, together with the growing necessity of using proof instead of sanctions as a method of influencing the behavior of working men (mental experts are usually more adept at this than foremen), has gone a long way toward equalizing the effectiveness and authority of "line" and "staff" men, and breaking down the invidious distinctions between them.[13]

Transferring a Small Unit of Mental Experts from Its Home Department to Another

Breaking off a *segment* from one department and placing it in another department, a second type of departure from the simple organization structure, also falls within the framework of the "line and staff" idea we have been examining. These decentralized units, consisting of perhaps three or four mental specialists, carry out their regular duties even though they reside in another department. Here, we are primarily concerned with the relationships between the two department heads and their subordinates. (See Diagram 9, Example 2.)

Spreading some of these small groups of experts through the company in separate departments may cost us more than performing this work in a single unified department (though this is not necessarily so, as will be seen in a moment) because the men cannot take full advantage of mass-handling equipment and methods. Probably *centralized* accounting would cost less in a company using electronic data processing equipment. Nevertheless, when the structure is made more complex by transferring a segment of one department to another department, the decisions of the men from both departments are frequently improved to a point where the benefits greatly outweigh these higher costs.

The layman is likely to assume that all accounting activities, for

---

[13] What has been said should not be read to mean that the mental experts should take over the decision making. The ideal is to obtain *group* decision making. (The group in this first type of departure from the simple structure consists only of the boss and the mental expert.) In *The Practice of Management* (New York: Harper & Bros., 1954), p. 242, Peter F. Drucker points out that in several of the large corporations with which he has worked as a consultant, the mental specialists have taken over most of the decisions formerly made by the appointed bosses; they have become masters of the companies but do not know all the answers; as a result, those companies have lost some of their old effectiveness.

example, should be concentrated in one department to prevent duplication and to gain efficiency. But performing some of the accounting
work in a section attached to the sales department may require no
additional man power; the operators of billing and posting machines, supervised by a working boss, can frequently do their work
there as fast as in the home department. Equally important, their
working boss can quickly secure accurate premises for untangling
any snags that arise by going directly to someone in the sales department who knows the answers.

Sometimes, a sales manager insists that a unit of the credits and
collection section be placed in his department, knowing that credit
decisions have a marked effect on sales and that if credit men possess some of the value premises about an account in addition to the
factual premises found in the ledgers, they will make better company decisions. The credit men *may* be justified in extending credit
to a customer on the basis of the *value* premises the salesman brings
in, even though the account is past due; thus the company secures
sales that it would otherwise miss. On the other hand, on the basis of
the accumulated value premises, they may find it wise to cut off
credit, even though the customer's account shows no unpaid balance.
Moreover, when a sales manager always has at hand in convenient
form current figures on inventories, unshipped orders, and daily,
weekly, or monthly sales in units, he is in a better position to make
informed decisions about handling the orders that come in.

Occasionally, when a segment of a statistical or accounting department is transferred to a "foreign" department, the number of people
doing this kind of work can actually be reduced. In companies that
do not use this system, the department heads frequently compile their
own private records on the side—informal records of cumulative
expenses, production, stocks on hand, and so on—because they find
them useful in making their current decisions. They realize that this
duplicates some of the work done elsewhere in the company, but they
dare not wait until next week or the fifteenth of the next month for
these reports because by then it would be too late to take remedial
action. Usually, if two or three of the mental experts are transferred
to the department and given the responsibility for handling these records in the department, they can tie them into those of their home
department and communicate the totals to their central office, thus
eliminating the duplication.

The ability of data processing equipment to provide data promptly
to executives may reduce the need to place segments of the accounting

and statistical departments in foreign departments. But such equipment will not eliminate the need of moving small parts of other departments into foreign departments. For instance, to communicate effectively with our potential customer members, we may find it advisable to move a group from our engineering department into our sales department; or, to make sure the customers get what they ordered, we may decide to move a few men from the engineering department into the production department; and the personnel department, shipping, or credits and collections may be so segmented.

Conflicts often arise when a small unit is transferred to a foreign department, because there is no easy way of deciding which department head has jurisdiction—who has the last word—about the work of these small units. These conflicts are particularly acute in those cases where top management has insisted that a department admit into its inner sanctum a group from another department for the purpose of improving the department's decisions. Resentment usually runs high when a unit from the cost accounting department, for instance, or a group of quality control men, or a group from the personnel department is placed in the manufacturing department against the department's will. Which department has the final word over the men in this small section is a question that constantly bedevils the executives. The men in the group are responsible to the boss in the factory *as well as* to the head of their own department, but who has the final say? Or in a company that operates branches, who tells an accountant what to do when he is working permanently in a branch office under the local manager?

There are no easy answers to such questions. One approach is to ask the two department heads to formulate reasonable goals which will serve as means of furthering both departments and agree on broad rules which can be used in making on-the-spot decisions. For the accountants, these might include rules about what expense items to charge to certain accounts; for the credit men, what (broadly) should be the credit practices of the branches, and which decisions on credit should be made at the branch level and which at the central office. In the personnel field, these rules might set out agreed-upon methods of handling grievances, or a company-wide wage structure and current practices in granting raises based on the job classifications.

Once this is completed, the mental experts and the section or department head should be instructed to make their decisions in conference with one another, at least during the initial stages, using premises derived from the goals and rules that have been agreed upon. Such conferences provide for a merging of the premises that the staff men and the line supervisor have accumulated from their past experience; they each teach the others the premises they have garnered. Eventually, fewer and fewer daily conferences should be required; each man knows that the others, in making their decisions and putting them into effect, will give due weight to most of the premises they now have in common, that each will act within the framework of accepted goals and rules, and that each will make the decisions he can make best. When (or if) this mutual confidence and respect has been established, the executive can anticipate that the conflicts will abate between the department heads as well as between the experts and the section supervisors, and that the company will enjoy the fruits of this cross-fertilization program.

Introducing Duality (Not Unity) of Command

In the two line and staff arrangements already examined, the mental experts were working largely with routine or manual experts and were given the "right" to exercise authority over those men and their bosses, though in a very narrow specialized field. In the third and fourth types of structure, we are attempting to use highly placed executives to aid the free flow of available premises to mental experts and executives high in the hierarchy.

In the third type, we shall be deliberately vesting two departmental executives with formal authority to guide the behavior of a group of mental experts. The objective, once more, is to provide the subordinates with more alternatives and premises than they would otherwise have, and teach them how to use these in decision making. For instance, if ours is a company whose sales force sells all of the company's product lines or which sells to two distinctly different types of customers (industrial buyers, for example, and householders), we may decide, in the first case, to appoint a separate product sales manager for each line, and, in the second, to appoint a separate "market" sales manager for each market. These executives would work directly under the company's general sales manager, would become experts in their own fields, and would each be "given" formal authority over the salesmen; each man's responsibility would be to employ the appropriate types of informal authority over the salesmen and thus induce them to sell his own product line or to work effectively with his particular type of customer. (See Diagram 9, Example 3.)

We have already seen that duality of command often produces conflicts but that it offers some distinct advantages over so-called "unity of command." Writers in the field of organization have often said that a man should have only one superior. According to this "principle," if he has more than one boss, the orders given the subordinate frequently conflict. As a result, the subordinate chooses the one he will carry out; or else he is caught in a dilemma and does nothing.[14] Yet we do want unity of command in one sense; we want to make sure that we provide each subordinate with a unified, integrated picture of what he should do.

Salesmen who sell two or more quite diverse product lines are especially subject to conflicting instructions from product sales managers, so we shall use them as an example. To secure the maximum sales volume for each line, the salesmen need to be given information about the most likely buyers and furnished with a stream of premises which they can use in talking with customers. It is the product sales manager's responsibility to exercise authority over the salesmen with respect to his own line—to be loyal to his own line. However, the salesmen will find themselves in the middle unless plans are made to keep this authority and loyalty within bounds. For each product executive, wishing to increase his own volume and knowing that the business is there if he can only induce the salesmen to go after it, presses the men to give almost all their time and attention to his line.

Under these circumstances, the salesmen also need guidance from a man who will view each of the lines as a part of the whole—guidance on how to divide their time and efforts among the product lines and the customers for the best over-all interests of the company. Otherwise, each salesman will concentrate on his favorite products and customers. In addition, the men need training in the art of communicating proof to customers—training in salesmanship—and help in planning their sales routes each week. The executive who provides these premises—the man who manages the sales force's over-all activities—cannot show partiality for any one line; he must be loyal to the whole department and to the company as a whole rather than to just one product. Perhaps this is the chief reason why the man who

---

[14] In passing, it might be added that a *single* boss's orders can, and often do, produce these unwanted results. A boss occasionally gives a man conflicting orders or assigns him too much work. As a consequence, the subordinate has to make his own decisions about which jobs he will do; or else he becomes so frustrated that he accomplishes but little. Frederick W. Taylor, the father of scientific management, was an advocate of two or more bosses for a single man.

supervises the salesmen's activities is ordinarily appointed general sales manager.[15]

Unity of command does not happen automatically in a situation where there are several bosses; definite plans must be made to attain this goal. Conflicting instructions can be avoided if the several executives work out beforehand an integrated pattern for the premises and decisions they plan to transmit. They can determine which instructions or premises the men will need, which executive is best qualified to supply each of the premises; they can revise the premises until they harmonize, and then agree on how and when these premises will be forwarded to the men. This group decision making can be fostered by the formation of an executive committee made up of the executives. But in the absence of a formal committee, the conflicts arising from the antithetical premises are eventually resolved through the informal give-and-take which the executives learn after they have worked together; they learn from experience that they have to check with one another before taking action.

The Common Line-and-Staff Organization

Our fourth type of structure calls for a group of executives, specialists in their respective fields, who are located near the top of the hierarchy at a level directly below the president. This type may be useful if ours is a divisional type of organization with, for instance, several regional branches or two or more product departments whose executives, we believe, are deficient in certain fields and will need guidance in making decisions in those areas. A second objective may be to establish uniform policies throughout the organization. We would probably headquarter these staff men in the central office. (See Diagram 9, Example 4.)

Examples of men performing these duties would be a lawyer, a central office purchasing man who is an expert in buying and operating certain types of equipment (trucks or production machinery), and men who specialize in safety, plant protection, public relations, and so on. They often report directly to the president. Their responsibility would be to help the department heads of the various divisions or their own counterparts (if any) in the departments or the branches lay suitable plans and carry them out. It will be seen that

---

[15] Sometimes, a general sales manager loses his perspective, however, and temporarily backs one of his product-line sales managers, telling the salesmen to put all their efforts on that line during the coming month. As a consequence, the other lines have to be neglected.

the head of each department is responsible to the several central office staff men as well as to his division head. Or if the central office experts work largely with their counterpart subordinates in the branch, the subordinate branch men are obliged to try and satisfy both the expert and the branch manager.

This particular line-staff type of organization seems to engender considerable conflict—more perhaps than other types. In many companies these specialists are not very closely supervised by the president and they thus make many decisions alone. And while each man's proposals may be well chosen to further the particular activity for which he is responsible, his program may harm other company goals and means. Consequently, the zones of acceptance of the "line" men are often narrow and the experts tend to use sanctions and rules and regulations to induce their "subordinates" to carry out their respective programs. Moreover they frequently fail to talk over their proposed plan first with the men's superiors; nor do they always appraise the superiors' zone of acceptance, seek out his premises, and alter the master plan to suit the local needs. Sometimes they entirely bypass those managers who seem unwilling to cooperate.

Sometimes, instead of appointing staff men to help his subordinates, a company's president may appoint specialists who are to help *him* make *his* decisions. Examples would be an operations research man, a man responsible for long-term planning, an economist responsible for estimating sales, a tax specialist, or a man who is to spend his time looking for ideas for new products. In these instances the staff men only advise; and since we do not here have the problem of two or more bosses, there are no conflicts in formal authority.

There is little agreement among students of management as to what the line-staff relationship should be. Clearly, however, the actual role played by a staff man depends on his ability to win authority—to use concepts such as those we have been working with in this book. The location of his box on the organization chart does not determine his authority, any more than does a line executive's position on the chart.

Of course, when he is head of a section and has his own subordinates, he is vested with formal authority to direct their activities; in this case he must behave toward these men as would a line executive. And when a staff man learns to think in a company-wide perspective, he will probably be appointed as an executive in the line.

CENTRALIZED VERSUS DECENTRALIZED DECISION MAKING

We have investigated the task of building a simple organization structure and of complicating the structure by introducing duality of command—introducing staff men into the company's organization. Thus far, however, we have only partially explored the problem of deciding an equally important feature of the structure—namely, the level or point in the organization where certain decisions are to be made. Two facets of this have been left unnecessarily vague; one is the problem of determining *which of the company's decisions should be made* by line executives located *near or at the top of the hierarchy* (centralized) and which should be pushed down to a low point in the hierarchy (decentralized). The other is the closely related question of whether a *department* should be *supervised centrally*—whether a department should be located near the top of the organization structure (report to the chief executive, for instance) or be placed low in the organization structure under the supervision of a middle-level executive.

Recall that we have already encountered one facet of this problem of determining where in the hierarchy a certain type of decision should be made: which decisions shall be made by the company's staff men and which by its line executives. Our examination seemed to indicate that the men should use group decision making. This solution is of only limited value, however, in resolving the particular facet of the question which we face here.

Deciding Where in the Organization Structure Certain Decisions Shall Be Made

In these paragraphs, we shall sometimes visualize centralization as decision making at the top of the hierarchy, either by the chief executive or by an executive committee, and decentralization as decision making lodged lower down in the hierarchy. At other times, we shall think in geographical terms—of centralization as decision making by a department located in the central office of the company (geographically centralized decisions in accounting, credits, personnel, or purchasing, for instance), and decentralization as decision making at the branch. In both, however, we may use the same basic concepts in deciding whether we should try to centralize or decentralize certain of the company's decisions.

This is not an either-or question. In a particular company, it will probably become clear after an analysis that certain types of decisions can best be made centrally, while other decisions should be made down in the organization or out in the field; or that decisions once made centrally should, in view of changing conditions, now be decentralized, or the converse. Ideally, the decisions should be made at those points in the organization where the fullest set of premises is available, and where men capable of making these decisions are located. Generally speaking, I am personally inclined to urge executives, as far as possible, to push decision making down in the organization structure and outward geographically—to decentralize.

In endeavoring to decide where certain decisions should be made, the top executives will first want to ask themselves which decisions will make or break the company. By listing these in the order of their relative impact on the company's welfare and then conjuring up a picture of which "point" in the structure will likely have available the most complete set of premises for each of the various types of decisions, they can take a long step in improving the company's decisions. For example, the final decision as to the niche the company should fill would normally be placed in the president's hands, for he presumably has the most premises and the necessary perspective to weight them realistically. In this present chapter, we are inferentially placing decisions as to changes in the organization structure in his hands, too. Decisions about altering the task of a department, and altering its size and the character of its personnel with a view to making it over into a more effective instrument for achieving the company's goals, the subject of Chapter 14, are also in this book placed in the chief executive's hands. These are examples of crucial decisions affecting the long-run welfare of the company. The chief executive has (or should have) the most premises for making these.

But simply because a certain type of decision heads the list of critical decisions does *not* necessarily mean that the top executives are in the best position to make these. In certain companies, these decisions may actually turn out to be a mass of small everyday decisions, each one of which is based on a group of hard-to-come-by premises. In a bakery chain the make-or-break decisions are likely to be what kinds of bakery goods should be produced by a branch in order to increase sales volume in the local area—which ones will fit the local tastes—and what amount of each should be baked each day to keep "stales," a large expense item, at a minimum. These decisions cannot be made centrally; they must rest with the plant manager, for he has the necessary premises. In a metal-fabricating company producing specialized products to order, the decisions about what price to bid on each prospective order and how much engineering time to devote to each are likely to be the important ones; men who live with the premises pertinent to these decisions are the only ones in a position to make them. In a textile firm making yard goods, or any other firm making goods in which styles change rapidly, the salient problems are what styles to offer retail store buyers, how many units to produce initially, and the size of reruns, as well as the prices to charge; these decisions, to be solid, must be made down in the organization by the people who are closest to the value premises used by customers. If, in the foregoing instances, these decisions were made centrally—that is, by the topmost executives in the company— they probably would not stand up when examined in retrospect.[16]

On the other hand, where a company's products are uniform in character throughout the year and each product is bought by a large number of customers—toothpaste, for example, or fountain pens, or automobiles, or standard nuts and bolts—decisions about what products to offer, how many to make, when to restock, and what prices to charge, can often best be made centrally. Usually, these decisions can be based on statistical data such as the trends in the sales of the company's several products, information about what people like and do not like about each, data on which competitor's products are showing the greatest increases in sales, estimates of the industry's sales, and figures on the trend in the company's position in the industry.

The foregoing will suffice to point up the need to determine which of the company's decisions are crucial and how to decide where in the hierarchy that decision making should be lodged. There is no formula; each of these decisions on the location of decision making must be made on the basis of the premises inherent in the particular situation. To insist that all decisions in a company should be made centrally, or that all should be decentralized, would almost certainly lead to many bad decisions. Nevertheless, as I indicated earlier, wherever possible, I should advocate placing each type of decision in the hands of the *lowest* man in the hierarchy who is *capable of handling it*. Near the close of the chapter on communication and

---

[16] The above are examples of important selling decisions. In the meat packing industry, the *buying* decisions instead of the selling decisions are the most crucial to the success of the company; and these, too, have to be located far down in the organization, for the raw materials are not standardized; each animal is different. What proportions of salable meat and by-products a live steer will produce, and the quality of that meat, can only be predicted by a buyer who can inspect the animals; he is the only one in a position to decide what the company can afford to pay for a particular animal, though he must be guided by the current sale price of the meat he expects it to produce.

training, we noted that pushing decision making down in the organization structure—delegating formal authority (1) places decision making in the hands of those most likely to have available the needed factual and value premises; (2) gives young executives experience, and thus trains them for bigger tasks and strengthens their confidence in themselves; (3) provides a channel and an outlet for the men's creative drives; and (4) makes more time available to top executives for thinking and planning, once the men down in the organization are trained.

Raising and Lowering a Department's Level in the Hierarchy

Deciding how high, vertically speaking, a particular *department* or *section* should be placed in the organization, was the second of the two problems left unnecessarily vague in our study of structure. The question here is whether a department should be placed directly beneath (report directly to) the president—centralized in the sense that decisions can be greatly influenced by him—or whether it should be decentralized in the sense that the men are influenced largely by an executive lower down in the hierarchy. This idea can be illustrated by using two examples—one where the executive raises or lowers a department's status to adjust the company to changing business conditions, and the other where an entirely new department is being organized. Our task here is to decide on alterations in the major contours of those charts in Diagrams 8A and B (p. 294 and 306) and 9 (p. 311).

In general, the department or division whose tasks are currently of greatest importance to the welfare of the company should be most closely associated with the chief executive. Visualizing the tasks that the company must perform very well if it is to compete successfully for customers helps in deciding how high in the organization hierarchy a department should be placed. In one company the development of new products which will sell in large volume is most vital to its survival; and the chief executive will want to place the product development department nearest to him, so that he can give it all the help it needs. In another firm the selling and advertising activities must be given heavy emphasis. In still another company the manufacturing problems are the difficult ones; this may entail meeting customer specifications and rigid delivery dates to secure sales volume, or keeping manufacturing costs down to the bare minimum, so that the company can compete cost-wise and thus ensure sales volume. In a company selling perishables such as meats or other products with widely fluctuating prices (used cars would be another example), the central problem may be to learn what the competitors' prices are and to set its own selling prices at a level (in comparison with going market prices) that will keep its inventories under control—neither too high nor too low in view of anticipated price trends and sales volume.

A department's position in the hierarchy should not be regarded as a permanent one, however. Everyone in the company should understand that the level of each department may, at times, be lowered or raised to meet changing business conditions. During a period of depression (or even in so-called "normal" times) the problems of the sales department are paramount, and it should be raised to a position close to the chief executive. During such a period the tasks of the production department and the purchasing department will be comparatively easy; hence the men there can make their decisions with relatively little assistance, and these departments can be lowered in the organization hierarchy. On the other hand, during a war period or when sales volume is outrunning capacity, the positions of these departments in the hierarchy will have to be reversed. The chief executive may even be obliged to assume some of the duties of the purchasing department when materials are very short. Likewise, when the labor situation is tight, the industrial relations and personnel departments may have to be raised in status.

These same basic concepts are helpful in determining where to place a department newly organized to manufacture and market a new product. If it is decided that the new product should be pushed, and pushed hard, an effective way is to locate the department directly beneath the president so that he can help the newly appointed executives to make their decisions, assist the department in fending for itself, and give it status in the eyes of the other departments. Were the department placed under the jurisdiction of an executive located farther down in the organization, it might be handicapped by jealousy or lack of interest on the part of that executive, or by lack of mastery of its problems or lack of time on his part. If the chief executive wishes the department to flourish, he must see that it has full access to all the company's facilities—that it receives all the help it needs from engineering, production, sales, and advertising, for example.

What has just been said does not mean that *every* new department should be placed just beneath the chief executive. If a new department's future contributions are expected to be relatively small, it can often be placed under the aegis of a lower-level executive, albeit one who has the premises, motives, and time necessary to help it get started. Moreover, just because a new department is sometimes initially placed under the chief executive to hurry its development is no reason why it must remain there. It is the executive's responsibility to wean the department at an early date, so that he can turn to other problems.

POSTLUDE FOR PART II: A SUMMARY

Undoubtedly, every reader has by now discovered that he was already familiar with many features of the five conceptual subsystems explored in Part II. In these pages, we have simply tried to exhume these from the unconscious levels of our minds, break them apart, give them names, describe them, and arrange them in an orderly pattern. Our objective has been to understand the details of each subsystem more fully, so that we may employ them more tellingly in gaining acceptance. Condensing the subsystems covered in Part II and seeing how they fit together may add to the insights we have gained. Also, take note that the insights gained in Part II enable us to be much more rational than was possible at the end of Part I where we first grappled with the idea of practical rationality.

Before attempting to guide the behavior of another man, we found it helpful to predict the probable size of his zone of acceptance for our proposal. On that basis, we would then choose among simple authority, easy proof, hard proof, or sanctions as a means of guiding his behavior in the direction we wished. (In case it appeared that his zone would be negative in size, a revision of the proposal would be indicated.) By imagining that he had now heard what we planned to say to him, we were also able to make some predictions as to the amount of the receiver's contributions—whether at an efficiency level or at an adequacy level—in the event that we decided to make the proposal we had in mind and that we used the most appropriate type of authority.

It became evident that leadership was closely related to authority. The followers of a leader characteristically have wide zones of acceptance for many of his proposals; in fact, if he so desired, an established leader could use simple authority almost exclusively. We noted that a man who had developed certain aptitudes—a gift for creating ideas for goals, for believing his group could flourish, and for making things happen—possessed some substantial advantages. We also concluded that to gain leadership, a man should try to keep attuned to what is going on, to build a long series of decisions that seem farsighted in the eyes of his associates, propose goals that will stir their blood, use more premises and weight them more realistically than they, employ group decision making, anticipate dangers, and time his proposals. But, above all, he must demonstrate both intellectual and moral integrity.

Without effective communication—communication of the information the receivers will require in making their decisions—there is little chance of gaining acceptance of company programs. In working out a formal system for transmitting temporarily useful information and premises—those that would be used once and then discarded —we first investigated the premises needed at the destinations by the deciders; next, we determined which sources could furnish these promptly and accurately, chose the best pathway—noting that assembly centers astride the pathway may be helpful—then selected the best vehicles (the written word; or the telephone, radio, or television; or the person) and established paths for a feedback of information. Five commonly encountered barriers were examined—failure to gain the receiver's attention, problems of failure to understand what was said, mental lapses as to what premises the receiver would require in making his decisions, deliberate or unconscious distortion, and geographical and social distance. It became evident that training —the communication of permanently useful premises—was a method of reducing communication costs. For repetitive decisions, we explored two approaches: determining the one best way of doing a job and teaching the manual specialists to use this; and designing permanently useful, though flexible, rules and regulations, and setting these down in three types of manuals as guides to men's behavior. For decisions that are seldom alike (executive decisions), emphasis was placed on a way of thinking—training men to make complex decisions and to gain acceptance of them.

The company's informal groups serve as another effective means of gaining acceptance of proposals. These are the groups formed spontaneously to achieve goals the members hold dear; they are the flesh and blood of the formal organization. We discovered that they could be used to uncover the deep-seated goals and value premises the men in the groups use in deciding whether to accept a proposal wholeheartedly, and that men's loyalties to the goals of their group could be employed to further the company goals. Most important, they can be used in devising standards that will measure an individual's status as well as his contributions to the company. In addition, the informal group's quite remarkable communication system and the leaders who arise in those groups can be employed in gaining acceptance of proposals. Finally, we probed a short distance into the problem of improving the morale of the organization, concluding that high inducements, high efficiency, and high morale went together, and that low inducements, adequacy, and low morale were closely associated.

In the present chapter, our objective has been to improve the organization's semipermanent structure so that it will serve as a better means of communication, of gaining acceptance of plans for changes in their activities, of ensuring good decisions throughout the organization, and of coordinating the men's behavior. We erected a simple structure by starting at the bottom and forming the routine specialists and the mental specialists into homogeneous groups which could serve the customer's needs. Then we appointed supervisors (specialists in guiding the behavior of others) who could help them to make good decisions; tied together in a department those groups (or sections) which would encounter the most difficulty in transmitting their premises to one another (but asked ourselves if we could easily find a capable department head for this combination of sections, and if he would be too busy); appointed department heads who were to help the supervisors of these groups; and, finally, appointed a president and a board of directors. The executives at each level were vested with formal authority and were to help their subordinates. Before leaving the simple structure, however, we specialized the departments, specialized (and divided) them either on the basis of product or market, or geographically. Then we formed these bisected departments into divisions.

Next, to take full advantage of the premises developed by the company's mental specialists, we deliberately complicated the structure, at the same time trying to mitigate various types of conflicts which commonly accompany such departures from the simple structure. I urged that all sections and departments be thought of as co-means of achieving goals, and that attempts to draw distinctions between line and staff be discouraged. The first of the problems with which we dealt was that arising when a single mental specialist was placed in a group of routine specialists headed by a boss who did not fully understand the mental expert's premises. Next, we injected into a department a segment or a small unit which had originally been a part of a "foreign" department, and endeavored to work out some flexible rules which these men and the departmental executive could use as guides in making their on-the-spot decisions. Third, we appointed two or more executives over a group of subordinates and attempted to convert this duality of command into unity of command by preplanning the pattern of premises to be transmitted. Fourth, we looked into the common line-and-staff organization that is frequently used by very large organizations.

In the concluding section we turned to the question of whether a particular type of decision should be made low in the hierarchy (decentralized) or high in the hierarchy—centralized in the sense that these are made at the apex of the organization structure, either by the top executives or by the central office; and we also determined whether a given department should be located near the president or placed under the jurisdiction of an executive lower in the hierarchy.

Thus far in the book, we have been engaged in creating a complex, highly effective organization composed of human beings who are capable of utilizing all the ten conceptual subsystems developed in Parts I and II—an organization capable of ensuring the company's welfare. Our attention has been centered on developing executives who could make wise decisions and gain acceptance of their proposals, and on shaping the individuals into a highly integrated team, one that will be strong enough to cope with the problems the company will face in the period ahead. This is not to say that a forward-looking chief executive ever feels that he has created what he considers a perfect organization; manifestly, he cannot afford to be entirely satisfied with the caliber of his men. The job of teaching is a never-ending one. Nevertheless, we have now laid the foundation for the third major task of the executive—making company plans and putting them into effect—the one toward which Parts I and II have been pointing.

PROBLEM
CREATING A SUITABLE FORMAL ORGANIZATION STRUCTURE

The Chandler Book Publishing Company, located in an eastern seaboard city, was known as one of the larger and older book publishers in the country. Through the years the firm had grown to a point where the functions once performed by a mere handful of men were now carried on by about 1,000 men and women highly specialized in their fields.

Each year, this company published between 175 and 200 new titles; the sales of these, together with the sales of some 800 educational titles and 3,000 "trade" titles published in previous years, had lately totaled about 5,500,000 copies annually. A number of different types of books were published: "trade" books such as children's books, adult fiction, biography, travel books, and books on current social and political problems which were designed for sale to the general public; and educational books—grade school, high school, and college textbooks. Retail prices usually ranged from $3.00 to $10.00 per copy.

Briefly, the procedure was to secure manuscripts from authors, print them, and distribute them. To secure suitable manuscripts, the men and women performing the editorial work would try to find likely authors and urge them to prepare manuscripts, sometimes on particular subjects. They read, evaluated, and often suggested revisions in the manuscripts that were received, whether solicited or unsolicited by the publisher. Finally, in conference with top executives in the fields of sales, advertising, and production, they decided whether to accept and publish those manuscripts they deemed most promising. The selection of manuscripts that would precisely fit the requirements of the two broad groups of book buyers had become, through the years, one of the pressing problems the company faced. Gradually the company found that to compete it must specialize its editors. About 50 people were kept busy in this work.

In those cases where attractive design and type face were considered particularly important, the newly selected manuscripts were first channeled to men who read them to get a "feel of their personalities" and who then evolved title page arrangements, selected type faces and decorations, and chose cloth for binding; with certain types of books, they arranged with artists to make jacket drawings. The specifications thus developed accompanied the order to print. Where no special designing was called for, specifications were drawn up on a routine basis. This work required four or five people's time.

To print the books, it was first necessary to set type from the manuscripts and then cast plates (similar to those used on a newpaper press, except that they were flat intead of cylindrical). Thereafter, the books were printed, bound, and encased in a paper "jacket"; then the books were ready for warehousing and shipment. Securing the proper type of paper, scheduling of the work of typesetting, plating, printing, and binding entailed careful planning. Estimates were made of costs of manufacture for each printing order for a book before an order was finally confirmed. About 600 men and women were engaged in this work.

Selling trade books to the bookstores, department stores, and wholesalers, and textbooks to elementary schools, high schools, and colleges often began before the new books were actually printed. The characteristics of these books were explained by the trade salesmen to the buyers in the stores and wholesale houses, who in turn placed advance orders for delivery on the publication date, a date which was uniform throughout the country. Stores at that time also placed reorders for active titles already published. Bookstores and wholesalers in the largest cities were called upon every few days, those in medium-sized cities every two to three weeks, and stores in small cities perhaps two or three times a year. There are about 500 active retail store and wholesale accounts in the country.

In the grade schools and high schools the salesmen visited the teachers, principals, and superintendents; and in colleges the salesmen visited the professors. In order to talk intelligently about their own books, they had to know the competitors' books. Their objective was to interest the teachers in adopting one or more of Chandler's titles for use by the students. More emphasis here was placed on books already published—ones that had already met the critical standards of the profession. In all, the company made it a point to call upon the teachers in most of the several thousand educational institutions about twice a year. Somewhat over 100 men devoted their efforts to sales work of various kinds.

Advertising and promotion helped to pave the way for the salesmen. Material mailed to buyers in bookstores and to teachers flowed out continually. In addition, space advertising in book sections of newspapers and periodicals was run to influence the book-buying public. This work required the time of five or six people.

As orders arrived, continuing records were kept of the number of copies sold, of stocks on hand, of printing orders placed and where stocks appeared to be low, of promised delivery dates for reprintings. Orders for reprinting were placed on the basis of these data and any other information about the future sale of the books which the executives could gather. Four or five people were sufficient to prepare these data for the use of executives in making these decisions.

When orders came in, the credit of each purchaser was checked; after shipment, the invoices were mailed and the charges posted to the ledgers. Throughout the company, there was enough of this work to keep about 30 people busy. There was enough work in storing, wrapping, and shipping the books to occupy about 30 people in the organization. Twice a year, sales of each title were determined, the royalties due the authors computed, and checks mailed to the authors. About six people usually did this work.

Monthly financial reports of operating expenses and of income were built from the appropriate records originated by or passed along by members of the various sections and departments in the organization. Copies of these monthly reports were placed in the hands of men who held executive positions and who were in a position to take any corrective steps which might appear necessary. No formal budget was used; instead, decisions for changes in policy were made by the executives on the basis of trends in past expenses and sales records. The reports required the time of about 10 or 12 people.

PROBLEM A:

In the above case, you are given a list of the activities that various groups of people in the Chandler Book Publishing Company perform. These are rather permanent means which the executives have chosen for advancing the company's welfare.

Suggestions: First, visualize the customers we wish to serve, and look at their goals. Next, determine how we at Chandler can further those goals and how they decide which books to buy.

Then visualize in detail specific tasks performed by the men and women in each group mentioned in the case, particularly those tasks designed to induce authors and bookbuyers to join Chandler's organization; picture their training, the reservoirs from which they draw many of their goals and premises, and observe their informal groups. In other words, live down in the company.

Be sure to build your organization structure from the bottom up, instead of from the top down.

Problem: Your task in Problem A is to arrange the various groups into departments, and if you see fit, the various departments into divisions. You are to create a structure made up of many parts. There are hundreds of possible combinations, and for each detail you incorporate, you will foresee unwanted as well as wanted consequences.

1. Review the concepts developed in the three parts of the chapter, observe the several small groups of employees mentioned in the case, and begin trying out various combinations of these groups. You may wish to divide and specialize some of the groups. Eventually choose what you find is the best combination. Then set down the wanted and unwanted consequences that you can expect were Chandler to adopt your proposed structure.
2. Show, in an organization chart, how you decided to put these various groups of people together—which of these small groups (sections) you would put together under one boss to form departments for the purpose of ensuring coordinated activity between the groups in the departments and between the departments, and, if it seems appropriate, which of the departments should be formed into divisions.

PROBLEM B:

Problem B is intended to give you a chance to review Parts I and II of this book, an opportunity to see them as an interrelated whole, and some experience in putting to work all that you have learned.

The president of the Chandler Book Publishing Company had for some time been watching the growing demand for business books among businessmen and eventually became convinced that the company should enter this field. He was also convinced that in order to enter this specialized field successfully, the company should plan to set the program up on a rather large scale. (This company has adequate funds to finance a program of any reasonable size.) Keeping in mind the character of the company as described in the case, and using the concepts we have so far studied in this book as a framework for your answers, discuss the following:

1. Make a chronological list of the problems the president is likely to encounter in attempting to get this new business-book program started. How would you suggest that he go about avoiding them and/or resolving them ahead of time? Draw generously on Chapters 1 through 10.
2. Name the specific tasks that will have to be performed by the men who will handle the business books and about how many men, at the outset, will be needed to perform each.
3. Decide how these people should be fitted into the Chandler Book Publishing Company's present formal organization structure, give your main premises for this decision, and draw an organization chart showing this.

PLANNING AND PUTTING PLANS INTO EFFECT

WE NOW turn to a third area of decision making. In Part II, we were deciding how to go about gaining acceptance of our proposals. In Part III, we shall be deciding on a plan of action. A plan is merely a set of interrelated decisions woven into an embracing pattern. It is made up of a group of complementary means selected with a view to achieving one or more goals. Diagram 1 (see p. 19), with its several staircases, represents a plan.

Plans can range all the way from simple ones evolved in a few moments almost without thinking to plans of extreme complexity. The greater the difficulties lying in the path of achieving the goal, the more complex the plan must be. For example, each morning we set up an easily achieved goal—namely, a smooth face. Before shaving, we unconsciously go through a series of planning steps, in the course of which we decide on the goal and on the means—the actions—we shall employ to achieve this goal. Planning can range in intricacy, in time required, and in thinking effort, all the way from simple everyday plans to ones involving decisions as to a goal that will affect the happiness of millions of people and the means they are each to contribute in order to achieve the goal. Complex plans may require months or years of work and an extraordinary amount of thinking. The plan for the invasion of Europe on D-Day provides an illustration of what is doubtless one of the most complicated plans ever evolved.

In Part III, we analyze the task of conceiving and launching long-range company plans, which, in complexity, lie about halfway between the two extremes just mentioned. Our purpose here will *not* be to work out a plan; the company's top executives must find their own answers, for they are the only ones in a position to gather the pertinent premises. Instead, we shall confine ourselves to an investigation of the types of information they will find valuable and a frame of thinking composed of conceptual subsystems that they can use in laying out long-range plans and putting them into effect. We shall center our attention on major company plans; but the approach we shall examine, scaled down to appropriate size, is equally suited to smaller plans—ones that rest on lower steps of the staircase, such as those a section head or a department head must make if he is to handle his job effectively.

We are by this time aware that in order to take action, two decisions are necessary—*what* to do and *when* to do it—and that the ensuing action is not the same thing as these two decisions. Nevertheless, in everyday practice, planning (deciding what to do, and when), and putting plans into effect are not easily separated. In fact, drawing a line and saying, "Up to this point, we have been figuring out what to do; now we will begin taking action," is not only virtually impossible, but it misrepresents what actually goes on.

In observing an executive at work, we see only the overt action which takes place. To all appearances, he makes his decisions on the spot and acts on them immediately—even when the project under consideration is a major one. However, what one sees is deceiving. During the past weeks or months, he has undoubtedly spent considerable time planning; he probably reached his tentative decisions about what to do and when to act some time ago; and in the meantime, he has probably been mentally testing out and revising his plan and has unconsciously been taking active steps to implement it. For example, he has simultaneously been rechecking with his associates the various decisions he incorporated in the plan and has already made considerable progress toward gaining acceptance of the plan.

Whether checking the details and gaining acceptance should be called "planning" or "putting plans into effect" is immaterial. In any case a plan usually goes into effect piecemeal—one part of the plan is started today, and another tomorrow—so planning goes on while parts of the plan are being implemented. And the original plans often have to be changed after the plan is tried out, because some of the minor decisions included in it turn out to be impractical. Thus, it is evident that planning and action cannot be readily disentangled.

But all the foregoing should not lull us into the unrealistic belief that plans go into effect automatically. Executives frequently have trouble making the transition from planning to execution, even though here we have encountered difficulty in separating the two. A man finds himself in this predicament when he has not been able to conceive a plan that entirely satisfies him; he hesitates to take action; he is fearful that it will not work. Yet if the plan (or a revision of it) is not translated into deeds—if the newly created idea simply remains a dream—the executive eventually begins to lose confidence in himself. What is more, if as sometimes happens, he announces in an unguarded moment that the plan *has* been adopted, expecting it to go into effect of its own accord, the results are even worse. He has then publicly committed himself; but inasmuch as nothing happens thereafter, those who have looked to him as their leader lose faith.

It is essential that the executive *make* things happen. This calls for both fortitude and drive. And genuine self-confidence (not the pseudo self-confidence evidenced by bluster, desk pounding, and anger) comes only through careful study and planning. The executive gains *fortitude* because he *knows* his premises; he has "seen" the plan at work in his own mind and is confident that it will be successful. He acquires *drive* from his impatience to get the plan into operation, so that the company can enjoy its fruits. He must be both a creator and a doer, as noted in the chapter on the creative process.

Chapter 11

ANTICIPATING THE
COMPANY'S FUTURE
SOCIAL
ENVIRONMENT

WE ARE now embarking on our third and
final set of conceptual subsystems. Gradually we are building an
over-all framework for executive action.

Chapters 11 and 12 provide our first subsystem of concepts in Part
III, a subsystem designed to uncover information from which the top
executives can form premises when they are making the most important decisions of all—the company's long-range policy decisions.
These premises help in determining which long-term goals the company should adopt and which relatively permanent means the company should employ in reaching those goals. We shall use these later,
in Chapter 13, when we choose the company's intermediate goals,
particularly the market niche the company should fill; and again in
Chapter 14, when we set about fashioning the company's departments
into effective means of filling that niche.

The premises for these decisions are largely derived from predictions of the set of social and economic conditions in which the company will be living during the next few years. These environmental
conditions, in the main, will be determined by the goals, means, and
premises of certain groups of people *outside* the company—by what
they will be thinking and doing. The thoughts and actions of men
and women who are beyond the company's sphere of influence actually create the company's environment.

Our specific objective in this chapter is to learn to anticipate these
groups' responses to the long-term company goals and means which
we are considering—learn to imagine the effects our program will
have on those groups in the years ahead. Unless the company executives predict these consequences with a fair degree of accuracy, their

decisions will seem unrealistic when reappraised three or four years hence. In the preceding chapter, we saw that a company is an organism. But it is also a part of the fabric of living, changing things; and like any other organism, it must act within the changing pattern of that environment—adjust to it—if it is to flourish. Company executives cannot do much about altering the environment; so the next best procedure is to predict what it will be and adapt the company to it, thus enabling the organism to live within the forthcoming environment as comfortably as possible.

From now on we shall look at the company through the eyes of its president and its division heads. To do this well, we shall have to expand the boundaries of our concept of rationality; we must add to the goals, means, and premises we were taking into consideration in Part I when we were studying decision making and in Part II when deciding what to do in order to gain acceptance of our decisions. To win the leadership that was formally conferred upon the president by the board of directors, he (and we) and the other members of top management must now take into consideration the goals, means, and premises of groups entirely outside the company.

The big problem here is to conceive a *reliable* detailed picture of the company's forthcoming environment; we have to fling the mind forward into the years ahead to see what these groups will be thinking and doing. The only thing the top executives can be *entirely* sure of is that changes will occur. Nothing is known; all the features of the future environment are uncertain. The executives have to be content with informed guesses, which they hope will be reasonably accurate; moreover, the further ahead they predict, the greater the chance of error. They have to expect that the unexpected will happen. They are trying to answer questions that are commonly thought of as unanswerable—anticipate the behavior of large groups or categories of people. Theirs is the unenviable task of conceiving a *realistic, detailed,* mental picture of what the world will be like a few years hence when their current decisions about long-term goals and means have actually been put into effect. Ideally, it should be as replete with details as their image of the company's present world. Diagram 10 shows this idea pictorially.

More specifically, on the basis of past experience, executives can be reasonably sure that the social and political ideas held by men will shift and that, as a result, new legislation will be enacted. They can be equally certain that economic conditions in the nation and in the company's industry will change, that competitors will alter

ENVIRONMENT THREE TO FIVE YEARS HENCE

GENERAL
BUSINESS
CONDITIONS

ECONOMIC
CONDITIONS
OF THE COMPANY'S
INDUSTRY

ECONOMIC

CONDITIONS WITHIN
THAT INDUSTRY:
CUSTOMER NEEDS
COMPETITORS' BEHAVIOR
TECHNOLOGICAL IMPROVEMENTS

SOCIAL

IDEOLOGICAL

COMPANY'S
FUTURE
NICHES

POLITICAL

LEGISLATIVE

TODAY'S ENVIRONMENT

GENERAL
BUSINESS
CONDITIONS

ECONOMIC

ECONOMIC
CONDITIONS
OF THE COMPANY'S
INDUSTRY

SOCIAL

CONDITIONS WITHIN
THAT INDUSTRY:
CUSTOMER NEEDS
COMPETITORS' BEHAVIOR
TECHNOLOGICAL IMPROVEMENTS

IDEOLOGICAL

COMPANY'S
PRESENT
NICHES

POLITICAL

LEGISLATIVE

DIAGRAM 10.   Conceiving the Details of the Company's Future Environment their policies, that customers' needs and wants will change, and that technological improvements will continue. The question is, in what direction will they shift? These changes are evidences of modifications in the needs and goals of people and in the means they have decided to adopt. The top executives must mentally test out the many parts of their tentative plans to make sure that their company's proposed activities will be consonant with those goals.

Our main objective in Chapters 11 and 12 is to devise frameworks of thinking which will aid us in visualizing and anticipating the details of the two major facets of a company's environment—its social and its economic environment.

We shall begin this chapter with an examination of the general task of anticipating shifts in the company's environment, regardless of whether these be social or economic. But our main concern in this chapter will be to devise a framework for visualizing the details of the company's forthcoming social environment. The concluding pages of Chapter 11 will consist of examples of social trends.

THE TASK OF ANTICIPATING THE ENVIRONMENT

The executives of every company must, perforce, do some speculating about the company's future social and economic environment.[1] Otherwise, they would not stay in business. If pressed for an explanation of the success they have had in making policy decisions, a majority of the men would say, "I base mine on hunches." Commonly, their picture of the future covers only the next few months or so and includes only a few vague details. Yet men use this relatively scanty foresight as a source of premises for making decisions that will permanently affect the company's welfare—in deciding whether to train more workmen, expand the plant capacity, accede to union demands, buy new equipment, develop and market a new product, hire more salesmen, and soon. But short-run plans based on hunch are seldom as successful as they might be; and when an abortive plan has to be discarded, the company obviously loses much of the time and money it has spent in building a suitable organization and buying and installing the needed equipment.

---

[1] In this connection, readers may find interesting the chapter entitled "Foresight," in Alfred North Whitehead, *Adventures in Ideas* (New York: Macmillan Co., 1933), originally a lecture delivered at the Harvard Business School.

The literature on the businessman's task of visualizing the future is fragmentary, but many executives have alluded to this task and its importance. Stanley Stark's paper, "Executive Foresight," *Journal of Business of the University of Chicago* (January, 1961), pp. 31–44, weaves many of those references into an integrated pattern.

By anticipating the environment in detail for a relatively long period in the future, executives can usually choose investments that will serve as means of carrying out the company's immediate, short-run program and will be almost equally useful in furthering its long-range plan. Thus, their decisions will look much better when examined in retrospect.

The value of a description of the future environment as an aid in mapping out a course of action becomes evident from a re-examination of two examples introduced in Chapter 1. Although those were decisions resting rather low on their means-end staircases instead of near the top, they illustrate the point.

First, let us investigate the fisherman who is (or was) trying to decide which fishing gear to choose from among those displayed at the sporting goods store. (See p. 9.) If our sportsman should fail to visualize accurately the set of conditions which will actually exist while he is fishing, some of his decisions about lures and lines will probably look unrealistic when he views them in retrospect; when he actually goes on his vacation and starts to fish, he will find himself saying, "I wish I'd bought those other lures." Predictions of whether he will be fishing from a pier, a boat, or a bank, what weeds and other snags lie beneath the waters, the kind and size of the fish in the water, and the type of bait they will be striking, enable him to make more telling decisions about the gear he should buy. With these facets of the environment in mind, he can test the alternatives more accurately—he can anticipate the results of using each of the lures. He has no control over that environment, so he has to do the next best thing—predict what it will be and adjust his own decisions to fit it. Predictions of the physical environment, of which this is an example, are not overly difficult; this type of environment will change very little in the months and years ahead.

In contrast, when an executive is predicting his company's environment, he must visualize what *people* will be doing at the time his decision is finally translated into action, rather than the nature of the physical environment. The executive conference we attended, the one called because sales volume was lower than expected (see pp. 23–24), affords an illuminating example of this. The disappointing sales were occasioned, in part, by the *failure* of the executives to anticipate one important facet of the company's environment— namely, what their competitors would be doing about improving their products. In working out their plans a year or so earlier, our executives had evidently predicted in a vague way that their competitors would make no significant changes. From this picture, they drew premises that led them to decide to do nothing about redesigning their own products. Yet they knew from experience that this aspect of their competitor's behavior would be a salient feature of their own company's environment. While they could not be expected to predict these actions with accuracy, they could have secured some fairly useful ideas about them and could have gathered their information much earlier than they did. Had they done so, they would doubtless have made a different decision in the first place, one that would now seem more realistic. In fact, the problem of low sales, which prompted the conference, might not have arisen.

Uses of Predictions of the Company's Forthcoming Environment

In developing a long-term program involving major changes in the company's activities, which may require three, five, or perhaps ten years for completion, predictions of environmental conditions are even more essential than in the example just cited. When introducing a new over-all plan, the executives are committing the company to costly projects intended for use over a long period, so they cannot afford to make mistakes in these decisions. For these, they would welcome a vast array of factual premises; but the only ones they have available are of a virtually 100 per cent value nature. The causal connections and the result elements in those premises must be based largely upon the executives' mental images of what a wide variety of outsiders will do.

A realistic and detailed picture of the company's environment yields several wanted consequences. First it nurtures the six stages of the creative processes. Clearly, the creation of imaginative and farsighted ideas for the company's high goals and the intricate sets of stairsteps needed to implement those goals can play a major role in assuring the company's future welfare. The more detailed the picture, the more fruitful it will be as a source of ideas for promising alternatives. The details will also serve as a source of reliable premises when we try to foresee the consequences of adopting each alternative and as a basis for assigning weights to the consequences. These decisions will be more rational than they otherwise would be.

The executives cannot expect to be clairvoyant, of course; in fact, their portrait of the nature of the company's future environment must always be thought of as a tentative and progressively changing one. Yet, as we shall see later, it is usually possible to foresee the *direction* of many of the detailed changes; and this is much better than no information at all.

Second, this forecasting of men's actions enables the executives to set forth company goals which can be described in detail and used as clearly defined targets. For example, it helps them to discern and to describe promising market niches which will need to be filled in the years ahead and thereafter to decide in which of these the company can compete most effectively; they are looking for a growing market, in which they can secure a large share of the available business. As will become evident later, the executives, in choosing the most promising niche, require a wide range of premises, drawn from the anticipated actions of several groups or categories of outsiders. Among the more important are those brought to light by predicting which of the company's various types or classes of customers will increase their purchases in the future and which will be buying less of the kinds of products the company manufactures. When a company has set its sights clearly—when, for example, management knows exactly which classes of customers to court in the years ahead —the problems of deciding what means to adopt to fill the chosen niche are half solved. Chapter 13 will be devoted to choosing and describing the company's long-term goals.

Third, a long-term prediction of the environment helps the executive to decide what changes must be made in the company's organization and when these must be completed. Once they foresee the company's future niche, they can go about revamping the firm's assets —its physical means (plant and equipment) and its human means (labor force, office and sales forces, and executives)—into telling instruments for filling that niche. For example, once the executives know exactly the types of customers the company is going to serve, they can decide what changes must be made in the products, the kind of sales organization which will be required, and the modifications that will have to be made in the manufacturing department. But all these changes take time. And this largely explains why emphasis is placed here on rather long-term predictions of environment. The objective is to determine the niche and set the goals far enough ahead to allow time for making these changes in the company's activities —perhaps three or five years ahead. If the company is to prosper in that niche, it must be ready to fill it when the time comes.[2]

Reshaping the organization often seems to take an inordinate amount of time, frequently years. Employees are reluctant to change their ways; breaking comfortable habit patterns usually meets with

[2] For example, when a period of economic prosperity seems imminent, the executives should begin laying plans to reshape the company to fill an expanding niche in the prosperous environment—a niche in which it can flourish.

resistance, as we saw when examining informal groups. And even after men have wholeheartedly accepted the proposed changes in their duties, they have yet to learn to handle their new jobs. Moreover, new personnel with the ability to perform certain new tasks may have to be found and trained. This third purpose—the use of the picture of the company's environment as a basis for reshaping the company's departments—will be explored in Chapter 14.

Coping with the Apparently Unmanageable Task of Anticipating the Company's Environment

The concepts discussed in these next few pages are designed to supply a framework and a set of tools for thinking about, and coping with, what at first sight may seem to be an overwhelming task, trying to forecast the behavior of *very* large groups of people. For the most part, these are revisions or new applications of ideas encountered earlier in the book, now cast into a larger new mold. After exploring these concepts, we shall get on with the job of predicting the social environment.

The first is the concept of a perfect world. We have already seen that although each person has his own ideas of what would be perfect for him and the groups to which he is loyal, nevertheless there is reasonable agreement among men as to several of the desirable features. To this, we shall add the idea that men compare their present environment with their vision of the perfect environment, and then strive to get from where they now are to where they want to go, namely, achieve this perfect environment. Fortunately, the executive will need to watch for changes in behavior of only certain outside groups, only those whose behavior will have a marked effect on his company. Among the more obvious of these groups would be the company's future customers and its competitors. Once an executive glimpses the dominant goals of such a group and sees these in specific terms, he is in a position to anticipate some of the actions its members will take.

A second concept is a classification system which will comfortably contain (and not distort) the detailed predictions the executive must make. The one that we shall use is the idea of concentric rings; we shall begin with the predictions of changes in the ideas and actions of the largest groups which will affect the company's welfare and then, with this as a setting, turn to successively smaller segments within that environment. (Refer again to Diagram 10 p. 341.) For instance, in the main part of this chapter on the social environment, we shall examine trends in the ideology of the American public (the most inclusive group); and then within this, anticipate what the political parties will do; and, finally, what the Congress and the courts will do—successively smaller groups, each of which is strongly influenced by the actions of the larger, more encompassing groups. When we consider the second main feature of the company's environment—try to foresee economic conditions, we shall again begin with the largest classification—namely, general business conditions in the country as a whole. Then we shall turn to the next largest segment whose economic behavior will affect the company—expected economic conditions in the industry of which the company is a part. Finally, we shall explore details *within* our industry—try to predict the behavior of the competitors and customers in our industry. The future decisions of these successively smaller groups are the features of the company's environment which interest an executive most.

This second concept offers two advantages. First, by starting with the large setting and examining successively smaller rings within it, the executive is provided with a perspective that he would not otherwise enjoy. Second, this classification (or, for that matter, any other classification system) helps to reduce chaos to order. Unless a man's separate predictions are organized into a systematic framework, he gets lost in details. As we saw in the second and third stages of the creative process, we collect most of our detailed pictures of cause and effect in odd places and in no particular order. As isolated pieces of information, these are meaningless. By classifying them into homogeneous groups, an executive not only can remember them more easily, but he observes cause and result relationships between them which might otherwise be overlooked.

The third concept is that of ranking the detailed features according to the probable amount of their impact on the company's welfare. Fortunately, there is no need to project every aspect of the company's environment, because only a few will seriously affect us. For example, the coming of a war would have a marked effect on a company. However, changes that will occur in international trade balances and in tariff laws—even the notable changes induced by the European common market—probably will have relatively little effect on most medium-sized firms, those who sell and buy almost exclusively in the United States. The same is true of the majority of the forthcoming technological improvements; the only significant ones for our company are those that might be adopted by the company's suppliers, by the companies in its own industry, and the industry's customers. Ranking the features of the company's environment according to the amount of effect they may have on the company is of assistance in pointing up those the executive should watch most carefully. But executives will want to re-examine their lists periodically, because the relative importance of these factors keeps shifting as new conditions arise. No two companies' lists will be alike, of course; nor will the items in the lists be given the same weight.

A fourth concept, one that enables an executive to foresee more accurately the future goals (the perfect world) of the people in each of the groups and how they will behave in trying to attain their goals

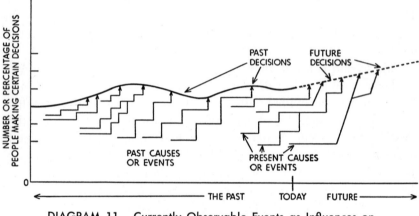

DIAGRAM 11.   Currently Observable Events as Influences on
People's Future Decisions

is the idea of projecting the details of the men's past actions into the future. Here, we are trying to determine what each brush stroke will look like. More specifically, we shall be endeavoring to predict whether more men in each classification, or fewer, will be deciding to take certain actions which will help or harm the company's welfare. The primary task is to uncover the recent events which the men in each category will use as sources of premises for deciding on their future actions, and especially their probable responses to our new plans. For instance, the recent trend in business conditions helps potential customers to predict whether they will have steady work and overtime pay or whether they will be laid off in the period ahead. This, in turn, furnishes them with premises in deciding whether to spend or save their money. These thoughts are pictured in Diagram 11.

As a minimum, the group's recent responses furnish a jumping-off place for predicting its members' future actions. But frequently, the trends in the group's behavior are reversed. Nevertheless, we are on reasonably safe ground in projecting the past trends into the future if we keep the caveats in mind. We do know that men gradually adopt new ideas or modes of behavior and slowly (and often reluctantly) abandon their old ones. For instance, 10 per cent of a group may adopt a new idea in the first year, a total of 15 per cent in the second, 25 per cent by the end of the third, and so on. It takes a long time for a majority of the members to conclude that the adoption of a new idea will advance their individual welfare. Recall that the rate of change in the ideas that men store in the reservoirs of their cultural heritage is almost imperceptible; men consider such ideas permanently true and seldom bother to reappraise them.

A number of the brush strokes can be described statistically. Here are some examples: the probable increase or decrease in the nation's population or in the population of a given region over the next few years; the expected changes in the amount of people's savings, or in the amount of money they will spend, or the number of new homes they will build. Published price series are statements in summary form of what people decided they would pay in *past* months or years. In *predicting future price* levels, one of the main facets of any company's future environment, we are anticipating whether people will pay more or less than in the past for given items.

But some of the most significant details of the group's probable future behavior can be described only with value measurements. For convenience, our examples of these environmental changes will be framed here as questions the executive needs to ask himself: Will more or fewer people be feeling uneasy about their jobs? Will more or fewer people feel resentful toward their bosses—be anxious about their personal liberties on the job, for instance? Will more people approve the actions of businessmen in general, and of our company in particular? The executive can make some reasonably solid predictions if he is perceptive, if he listens for indications of current causes which will lead people to change their minds. He can even draw a line on a graph such as that in Diagram 11, representing his ideas of the changing number (or percentage) of people who have held such ideas in the past and how many will hold such ideas in the future.[3]

---

[3] In the foregoing paragraphs, dealing with the idea of projecting men's past actions into the future, I have not touched upon some of the commonly used methods of predicting certain features of the company's environment. One is the use of surveys or polls, such as those conducted by marketing research organizations. By interviewing a representative sample of a group or category of outsiders, it is possible to obtain a reasonably accurate

Gathering, appraising, and using the predictions made by others, a fifth technique for coping with the problem of anticipating outsiders' behavior, can be described very quickly. In every company, there are men who live close to certain features of the environment and can make reasonably accurate predictions. Sales managers, for instance, and marketing research men, purchasing agents, and personnel men can often make shrewd guesses, based upon value premises, about the probable behavior of the environmental groups with which they frequently associate. In addition, newspapers, trade publications, business periodicals, and professional magazines carry articles written by specialists—articles on such subjects as expected business conditions, legislation, the outlook for a given industry, or forthcoming technological improvements. Here, the main problems confronting the executive are to choose which of the many articles to read and which to skim; to evaluate the predictions made by others; and to weave them into the integrated, detailed picture of the company's future environment which he is trying to paint.

The sixth and concluding idea, the idea of laying *flexible* long-term plans, is a tool designed to grapple with the problem of uncertainty—the likelihood that the completed visual image of the company's future environment may prove inaccurate. Obviously, since many of the details are conjectures, some are destined to be wrong. However, there is only a remote chance that *all* the details of the picture will turn out to be the exact *opposite* of those anticipated, unless the executives are framing a picture of what they *want* to see happen rather than what their observations have told them will occur. If some of the details prove faulty, not much is lost, for the success of the major long-term policies does not depend exclusively on the accuracy of each one of the brush strokes.

Yet it is entirely possible to misjudge one of the major components

statement of what those people *say* that they will do in the future. But the findings must be used with caution because the now existing causes which led these people to say that they would do such and such in the future—buy a certain product or vote for a certain candidate, for example—may change; consequently, the decisions they actually make and carry out later may differ from those they mentioned to the interviewer. Another method is the use of the idea of "leads" and "lags" in predicting certain features of the environment: "Gasoline sales are increasing (cause), so we can expect the sales of tires to increase shortly (result)." A third method is the use of computations based on formulas that have proved rather reliable in the past. The Dow-Jones theory for predicting turning points in security prices is an example of this. I have reservations about the use of formulas; my uneasiness stems from the fact that many of the premises that people consider in making their decisions cannot be expressed numerically. Inasmuch as these premises must be omitted from the formula, the predictions based on the formula often turn out to be erroneous. Incidentally, the adage that history repeats itself has been rather thoroughly discredited.

of the future environment—the coming of a war, for example, or the onset of a depression; such a misconception could almost wreck a company that has embarked on a long-term program resting on the belief that peace and prosperity will exist. To cope with this, executives generally try to lay plans that are flexible; they work out a program that will fit two or three types of environment. Their task is to visualize two or three most likely sets of future conditions, determine the company's best niche in each, and then begin building an organization that will be capable of filling *any one of the three.* Though ideally, the kind of company they envisage would serve as an equally effective means of filling any one of the three niches, in practice it is almost impossible to conceive such a program; so the next best thing is to design a company that will flourish best in the *most likely* of the three environments. For example, the executives may expect a marked improvement in general business conditions and accordingly set goals and start making changes in the company to take full advantage of that environment—perhaps expanding its plant or its executive group. But it would be suicidal to commit the company irrevocably to such a program. The changes made should be so designed that they will serve as reasonably useful means of prospering in the less likely environments—in the event that business activity levels out or a depression occurs. An ideal plan would be one that will make the company flourish, but at the same time can be terminated without significant loss, could be postponed even though the plan had been set in motion, and could be revised with some ease.[4]

Of these six, the first four make up the conceptual subsystem we shall be using to anticipate the company's environment: the concept of a perfect world, together with a comparison of the present world and the perfect world, and a prediction of what people will do to achieve that world; the idea of a classification system for the groups whose behavior we wish to predict, here the idea of the largest group and successively smaller groups within the larger; the third is the idea of ranking the features of the future environment to keep in mind the significant ones; the fourth is the idea of projecting the details of men's past actions into the future, predicting whether more people or fewer will be adopting a course of action. The fifth and sixth, finding out what other people think will occur and laying flexible plans, are intended to help us avoid costly mistakes.

[4] See Preston P. Le Breton and Dale A. Henning, *Planning Theory* (Englewood Cliffs, N.J.: Prentice Hall, Inc., 1961), p. 110.

In the pages that follow, where we embark on the top executives' task of creating a detailed picture of their own company's expected environment, we shall use the four interrelated concepts constantly.

FORESEEING THE COMPANY'S SOCIAL ENVIRONMENT

Our investigation of the executive's task of anticipating the company's social environment—more specifically, its ideological, political, and legislative environment—will intentionally be sketchy. Our purpose will be merely to nourish the creative process—to suggest some of the broad segments of these three features which executives can profitably examine and project. In the concluding pages of this chapter the reader will find a series of examples of specific trends in ideology and legislation, arranged in outline form, which should lend concreteness to the rather general discussion.

Though at first sight the ideology of a people—the largest and most elusive of the three concentric rings discussed in this chapter —may appear too remote to warrant consideration by company executives, further examination discloses that changes in ideology bear heavily upon the company's operations. We have already seen that men unconsciously pursue their ideals and that they frequently take these into consideration when they make decisions that affect the company. First, then, since most members of the organization (we are here using our special definition of members) will be somewhat influenced by the ideals expressed by people outside the company, an awareness of the national trends in ideology helps the executives to bring to light the goals and value premises these members will take into consideration—those we were attempting to uncover in the chapters titled "Anticipating the Decisions of Others," and "Informal Groups." Second, a recognition of trends in the public's goals gives the executives some insight into the public's probable reaction to certain company policies they are considering and thus furnishes some guidance in the area of public relations. Businessmen have become painfully aware that they must keep their company practices in tune with what the employees and the public think is "proper" behavior.

Third, an awareness of national trends can provide the executives with some fairly solid postulates about what the government's policies will be during the next few years; in the past half century the actions and attitudes of the federal, state, and local governments have become an increasingly important feature of the business firm's environment. Predictions as to the role the country will play in foreign affairs, what it will do to further the welfare of the nations in Africa, South America, and Asia, whether annual appropriations and tax rates will be increased or decreased, whether the government will continue to play an active part in combating booms and depressions, and whether there will be more government control of business, furnish company executives with foundational premises for laying long-term plans.

To foresee how the various groups who make such decisions will behave in the future, it is manifestly necessary to seek out the aspirations of these people—the ideals that have become their goals. "Since the course of history is largely guided by ideas, part of our analysis will be an exploration of the ideas likely to mold history in the near future."[5]

Among these aspirations are the people's ideas of what would constitute a perfect world. Many people in the United States would picture an ideal world as one in which some of the following conditions exist: where a man has freedom to think and act as he wishes, unhampered by arbitrary dictums; where there is orderliness and peace, made possible by laws that deal with everyone justly and alike; where no one goes hungry and all have access to medical care; where a man can feel a sense of dignity, can hold his head up and say, "I'm just as good as he is," and where he isn't being "pushed around";[6] or where there is prosperity ahead for him, his family, and his friends; where Christ's idea of peace and love of one's fellow men is all-pervasive, or the idea of a world that accords with those utopias conceived by Plato, St. Augustine, or Sir Thomas More. Although these ideals vary among individuals—there are no universals —and although they do change, most of them seem to be considered very desirable by the majority of people in the United States. No man expects to live long enough to see his idea of a perfect world come true; in fact, each person realizes that probably none of these images he carries around in his mind will ever become a reality. So he sets a more realistic goal—namely, to make the world a better place to live in, a world that is closer to the ideal than it is now. In the re-

---

[5] Quoted from Sumner H. Slichter, *What's Ahead for American Business* (Boston: Atlantic Monthly Press and Little, Brown & Co., 1951), p. 5.

[6] The Declaration of Independence pictures several rather permanent components of an ideal world. The Constitution, on the other hand, is predominantly concerned with some permanently useful, and quite specific, means of achieving that world—for example, that a man's fellow citizens and the people who run the government will not jeopardize that perfect world. Congress, the Supreme Court, and the administrative departments are constantly at work trying to inaugurate supplementary ways of achieving it.

maining pages of this book the term *perfect* will appear quite often, but it should always be interpreted in the light of what has just been said.

In addition to these aspirations, this anticipated environment we are discussing here also includes people's ideas about the most appropriate means of making these aspirations a reality—their ideas of the best patterns of behavior. These patterns of behavior, and the direction of the changes in them, provide an executive with an approximation of how people have gone about achieving their goals in the past and how they will proceed in the future.

We shall call these aspirations and patterns of behavior a people's *ideology*. They are based on the emotional conditioning of the individuals. They are the political and social philosophies, and the religious and moral precepts which tenant our cultural reservoirs. In these pages the word *ideology* will be used for a set of ideas which concern people's values. The anthropologist's way of thinking is helpful in this connection. He speaks of a man's universe or environment as a *culture;* and he defines this picture of a *culture* as the way a specific group or country thinks and feels; it is a society's picture of the goals it should try to achieve, and its ideas of the best way of attaining them. It is the group's knowledge stored up for future use in the memories of men and in books. An understanding of this *culture* goes beyond looking at the physical things (the subject of Chapter 12)—beyond the things people use—and beyond the paper records and statistics of what the people have done, though these are useful evidence. The ideological legacy with which we are concerned is what these people have inherited and retained in their minds as ideals worth striving for and workable ways of solving certain kinds of problems often faced by the people in the group. Many decisional habits developed by society to meet a specific problem are to be found in this ideological legacy and are handed down from one generation to the next.[7]

In these next few pages, we shall note some possible cause-effect relationships that may help us foresee some of these changes. But we

---

[7] For an able presentation of the approach used by an anthropologist in analyzing what a group's beliefs are and in predicting how these people will act in the future, see Clyde Kluckhohn, *Mirror for Man* (New York: McGraw-Hill Book Co., Inc., 1949). His book deals largely with the ideas contained in this paragraph. The passages quoted from Kluckhohn earlier (see p. 120–21) also bear on this topic. (Be aware that a culture includes *both* ideological and material things.) To get an idea of the complexity of the task of predicting change in a society, see Raymond Firth, *Social Change in Tikopea* (New York: The Macmillan Co., 1960).

must not allow ourselves to be lulled into supposing that reliable predictions are easy to make. In no society do behavioral habits form a tidy consistent pattern; moreover, the causes which bring about changes in men's ideas are many and complex. Because of this, we must here be even more chary of models than we were when we examined operations research as a tool for testing out possible alternatives for some of those low steps on a company's staircases. Yet we do know that some men alter their long-established goals and means when they are exposed to new alternatives which they think are better.

Foreseeing Changes in the Public's Ideology*

One way of gaining insight into the changing character of people's ideas of the perfect ideological world, and the means they plan to use in achieving it, is to turn to the sources from which they secure their ideas. Once an executive adopts the habit of watching for these, he finds them almost everywhere he looks. We shall examine three sources, two of them written; but remember that much of our cultural heritage is handed down by word of mouth by the family and other closely knit groups.

One source is the minds of the thinkers—that is, the religious, philosophical, and social literature we have inherited. Our aspirations and ideals are also embodied in the poetry, fiction, and plays that have endured. The world's writers reflect, as well as create, the ideas of a period. Most of us have neither the ability nor the interest needed to conceive new ideas or to reshape old ones. And most people only dimly realize what their own aspirations are, though they will recognize them once someone states them. Creative men who reshape old ideas and frame new ones which people recognize as useful often become leaders of thought. Their visions become a part of our cultural heritage. Sometimes, they are considered idealists or dreamers, mostly because practical men realize that the perfect world they are describing will never be entirely achieved. Yet they often conceive a new world which is so wonderful that people never forget the picture once they have caught a glimpse.

Very few read the writings of these men; but in spite of this, their ideas, at least those that make sense to people, eventually seep down. Those who read the originals often discuss these ideas, incorporate them in sermons and speeches, write about them in popular magazines, and include them in books that are more easily read than the originals. Most people who use these ideas in their daily lives are entirely unaware of the men who originated them; they often believe that the ideas are their own—ones they themselves created. The ideas of Adam Smith, Karl Marx, Darwin, Freud, John Dewey, and John Maynard Keynes, for example, have been adopted by millions of people who have never read the original works in which these ideas first appeared. Usually, a decade or more passes before a new idea is adopted by a large percentage of the people.

At least some of the company executives need to be aware of what the men at the frontiers have written; they must listen and read to see whether the ideas are being accepted by more and more people or are being discarded. The old and new literature which is now being read contains statements of society's current ideals—its current ideology;[8] the writings and ideas of authors which do not make sense to the people are quickly rejected. Those dynamic philosophic concepts which are in the ascendant and those on the wane are the ones that chiefly concern the executives. For example, whether Karl Marx's philosophy is gaining or losing adherents in Asia, Africa, South America, and Europe gives the executives some inkling of what our federal government's foreign policy will be in the future. Perceiving whether the proponents of Adam Smith's laissez faire philosophy are winning more followers or losing ground aids in predicting our government's domestic policies with respect to business. Ideas such as these serve as dominant threads in the fabric of public opinion.

Our written history provides a second source of premises for anticipating what the public's attitudes will be. The chronological approach used by most historians provides a sense of the main stream of past trends in ideologies and thus gives some additional insight as to where we may be going. For the most part, each new generation (or century) has revised the earlier ideologies, added newly discovered ones, and put these to work.[9] The history of ideas gives the executive some insight into the gradual rise and decline of certain pat-

---

[8] Marquis W. Childs and Douglas Cater have brought together a good deal of this thinking in their *Ethics in a Business Society* (New York: Harper & Brothers, 1954). This illuminating book also traces the changing pattern of people's attitudes toward businessmen. Incidentally, it is an admirable example of the way the ideas of the great thinkers are handed on to men who have never read the originals.

[9] Stringfellow Barr, *The Pilgrimage of Western Man* (New York: Harcourt, Brace & Co., 1949), Herbert J. Muller, *The Uses of the Past* (New York: Oxford University Press, 1952), and J. Bronowski and Bruce Mazlish, *The Western Intellectual Tradition* (New York: Harper & Brothers, 1960), are examples of books that illuminate the changing patterns of ideologies from early times to the present. Frederick Lewis Allen, *The Big Change* (New York: Harper & Brothers, 1952), is an example of social history dealing with the recent past in America.

terns of behavior which men have been employing to attain their ideal world. Although these generally change slowly and change direction only infrequently, the recent growth and effectiveness of the means of communicating ideas—books, periodicals, radio, and television—has greatly accelerated the rate of change as compared with earlier centuries.

Throughout history, men have created instruments for fulfilling their aspirations. Principal among these are their institutions. The changes in the character of these organizations grant us a third source of information for picturing the future environment. People shape and reshape institutions—municipal, state, federal, and world governments; church organizations; schools and colleges; libraries; charitable and health organizations; and business organizations—to improve their effectiveness in creating the perfect world. What these institutions are now asked to do for the public, as compared with what they were originally asked to do, offers clues to what people want, and thus insights into the company's environment. For example, as we shall see shortly, the American people have been modifying the character of the federal government over the decades—fashioning it into what they believe will be a more telling instrument for realizing their gradually evolving goals.

The public also notably modified the behavior of business institutions. The trends here are particularly pertinent to the chief executive. In these days a good product and conformance to the letter of the laws appearing on the statute books is not enough to assure the success of a company. The company's attitude and behavior toward the general public, its city, and its employees must conform to what the people think its behavior *should* be. To ignore the ideals and goals of these groups is to impose on the company an unnecessarily heavy burden. If these people believe that the company is injuring them, they will be against it and try to "cut it down to size" at every opportunity—place hurdles in its pathway. On the other hand, if they believe that the company is furthering their goals, they will rally to its support when critical voices are raised.[10]

Achieving and maintaining this harmony with the ideology of the public is by no means a one-man job. While the responsibility for ascertaining trends should be assigned to one or two men in the company who have a philosophical bent, all the company executives are responsible for the company's public relations and, by extension, its

---

[10] Here, the emphasis is on the *social* role of the business firm. Its *economic* role will be discussed in the next chapter.

employee relations. They can contribute by observing clues that indicate changes in ideologies and bringing these to the attention of
the other executives; they can help to reshape the company's program
to conform to those trends. Even more important, they must strive to
see that the actions and words of the various company executives are
in accord with the ideology; and they can make certain that the employees, the community, and—in the case of a large corporation—
the people of the nation are aware of the in-tuneness of the company's
program.

The other alternative is to change the public's ideas to conform to
the ideas of management; but, as stated early in the chapter, this is
usually much more difficult than modifying the company's program
to fit the public's ideology. Though some companies and some trade
associations have periodically attempted this through mass meetings,
study groups, sponsored publications, and advertisements, their efforts appear to have been relatively unsuccessful. Perhaps the primary reason is that, in the past, many people have distrusted the
motives of businessmen—suspected them of trying to "sell a bill of
goods" while working unremittingly for their own self-interest without regard to the public's welfare. (See pages 367–68 for a brief discussion of this trend.) When (or if) the business community rewins
the public's confidence—when its members demonstrate that, in making company decisions, they give due weight to the interests of the
public, the community, and the employees—executives can expect to
make more progress in changing people's minds.[11]

Foreseeing Changes in the Policies of Political Parties and the Government

An awareness of trends in ideology provides a basis for adjusting
the company's attitudes and practices to the public needs, as we have
seen. In addition, these ideological trends foreshadow changes in the
company's political and legislative environment. The latter actually
grow out of the ideologies; the ideology influences the programs of
the political parties, and many of the programs advocated by political parties are eventually incorporated into the governmental

---

[11] Some business leaders have lately become concerned about the tendency of their fel-
low executives to think in narrow terms and have taken the initiative in re-educating them.
Over the past few years, several conferences have been held at the Harvard Business
School to grapple with this problem. Most of the addresses have been published. See
Dan H. Fenn, Jr. (ed.), *Management's Mission in a New Society* (New York: McGraw-
Hill Book Co., Inc., 1959). Turn to Benjamin M. Selekman, *A Moral Philosophy for Man-
agement* (New York: McGraw-Hill Book Co., Inc., 1959), for a wise exploration of mor-
als in business.

policies and statutes. In a democracy the political parties—and through them, the government—serve as means of converting the national environment into what people think will be a better one. The features of this environment are constantly being remolded. Fortunately, however, there is an interval between the time when an idea is endorsed by a reasonable number of public leaders, its appearance in a party platform, and its final adoption (if adopted) as a government policy. This gives the executive an opportunity to foresee changes in legislation and governmental attitudes ahead of time and thus prepare for them.

By comparing the world that people are presently living in with the ideal world they would like to live in—or more exactly, by comparing the present world with the kind of world more and more people are striving for—it is often possible to anticipate what the political parties in a democracy will advocate. Every political party, if its members aspire to office, must be sensitive to the goals and means that the majority of the people have in mind—the kind of country the voting public would like to have. Changes in the ideas adopted by political parties are reflections of ideological trends. But more than that, these parties must themselves conceive and propose realistic and effective means of attaining these goals; they must become leaders of thought. To make sure of its future welfare—in a word, to gain enough members (voters) to win control of the government—a party must serve as an instrument for getting from where the country is now to where it wants to go, for achieving at least some of the features of the ideal world which the majority has envisaged.

A comparison of the platforms adopted by the Republican and Democratic parties each presidential year since 1930 reveals that both have been responsive to changes in people's ideas of the role the government should play. Both have gradually introduced new planks in their successive platforms which described new programs the government should undertake, ones they felt sure would lead to a better world. The rate at which the two parties have embraced these ideas has differed, and the emphasis they have each placed on certain specific means of achieving the goals has often been at variance. But both parties have shifted their central philosophies, and the trends in the philosophies of both have been moving in the same general direction. There seems little doubt that these changes were strongly influenced by the great driving power of the ideologies lying in people's minds.

The trends in the political philosophy of the parties, as expressed in the platforms and in political speeches, provide a preview of legislation. When a fairly large proportion of the men in both parties recognize that a specific governmental program will further the country's welfare, legislation follows.[12] As long as we have a democratic form of government, the programs of the parties will continue to foreshadow the legislation to come. And there is continuity in the legislative and administrative policies. President Kennedy made only minor changes in the Republican program of the 1950's. President Eisenhower and the Republican Party, despite the opposition of one wing of the party, embraced most of the program the Democrats had found they must follow in the preceding twenty years. Even though the Democratic Party in the mid-1930's introduced a large body of new legislation which differed in philosophy from what the Republican Party had theretofore advocated, it, too, carried over many of the ideas advocated by Republicans in earlier administrations. The Republicans under Harding, Coolidge, and Hoover found that they had to retain many of the policies advocated and put into practice by Wilson's administration.[13]

A sense of the trends in political philosophy and in past legislation is useful in predicting the statutes to come and in anticipating interpretations of the old and new statutes by the Supreme Court and the administrative departments. This part of the company's future environment and a prophecy of trends in the ideology help the executives to frame some quite specific long-term plans. That these furnish some salient premises for anticipating some of the environmental details mentioned earlier—such as increases in governmental expenditures for military needs, foreign aid, public welfare programs, and federal income tax rates—is fairly obvious. Following the trends in ideology, and anticipating laws and the interpretation of laws designed to regulate business firms' activities can also help the executives and the company attorneys to determine specific company policies—for instance, what the policies of the company should be with respect to unions; whether the company should set up an exclusive distributorship program and, if so, what kind; what its policies with respect to price leadership should be; whether it should use some

---

[12] See Chester A. Bowles, *American Political Parties in a Revolutionary World* (Cambridge, Mass.: Harvard University Press, 1956), for a discussion of this statement.

[13] This pattern is not confined to the United States. The Conservative government under Macmillan, Churchill, and Eden, for example, retained and continued to forward many of the programs introduced by the Labor government; and the Labor government carried over most of the policies of its predecessors.

variant of a basing point system of pricing; what its discount schedules for different types of buyers should be; or what its practices
should be with respect to labeling and advertising claims.[14]

In the future we can expect the federal, state, and local governments to play a large role in determining the activities of business
enterprises. For instance, there will probably be new laws and new
interpretations of old laws which will close off socially undesirable
avenues of action used by some companies, especially laws regulating marketing activities. (This does not portend the death of free enterprise, however; there are thousands of alternative courses of action which are not prohibited.) And as we shall see shortly, the government will probably take a more active part in maintaining a
stable rate of economic growth, in promoting high employment levels, and in damping the swings in business cycles. But the point here
is that when we have a picture of the probable laws and the legal
climate, we can be fairly realistic about the wanted and unwanted
consequences of adopting certain of the steps in our plan. Equally
important we can revise some of its features beforehand, to reduce
the number of unwanted consequences, especially the unwanted consequences of running afoul of the law.

The conceptual subsystem we have been using to foresee the company's social environment is relatively simple, even though the task
of actually foreseeing the ideas people will be living by and what
the government will do is itself complex. It can be summarized by
employing the means-end staircase concept. In Diagram 12 the ultimate goal, the picture of the ideal future world as seen by a majority of the public, is shown as resting at the top of the staircase.
But since this visual image exists in people's minds today, and since
it serves as a driving force for their action, the perfect world is also
shown at the left side of the diagram alongside the details of the
present world. People are constantly (though probably unconsciously) comparing their current environment with their evolving

---

[14] Executives are in a better position to modify legislation than to alter the trends in
ideologies. And when laws need to be changed, corrected, or adjusted so as to permit business to meet the people's changing needs, remedial action is manifestly in the public interest. Laws occasionally have to be amended because of ambiguity, or because Congress
failed to foresee the impact of certain sections or paragraphs of the statute, or because
conditions have gradually changed during the interim. A *particular* piece of legislation is
only *relatively* outside the company's control. Company executives, perhaps in concert with
men in other companies, can marshal evidence supporting their point of view, and then appear at hearings before congressional committees. It is their responsibility to see that the
bills affecting their welfare not only meet the needs of the public but are ones they themselves can "live" with.

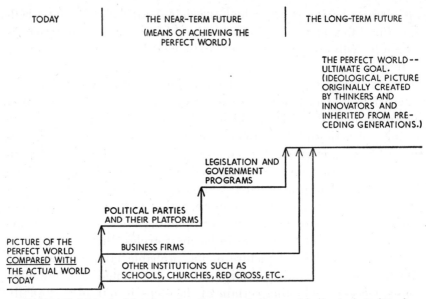

DIAGRAM 12.   Anticipating the Company's Future Ideological, Political,
and Legislative Environment

picture of the perfect world. Whenever shortcomings become clearly
apparent, they employ institutions such as business firms and political parties to modify the environment. They use moral suasion, laws,
and economic sanctions to recast the practices of business firms into
more telling means of creating their ideal world, and ballots and
political parties to change the activities of the government. In a
word, several of the important facets of the environment in which
the company must live during the years ahead are determined by the
decisions that people will make in an effort to further their ideologies; we have emphasized the roles that business and government will
play in achieving these ends. The task of the executive is to keep
the practices of his company in tune with the ideological, political,
and legislative features of the environment and to take advantage of
new opportunities brought about by the social changes.

SOME EXAMPLES OF IDEOLOGICAL, POLITICAL, AND LEGISLATIVE TRENDS THE EXECUTIVE MAY WATCH WITH PROFIT

This task of predicting the ideological, political, and governmental climate is, at best, an elusive one. To make the preceding discussion more explicit, I give below examples of some of the past and
current trends in ideology and legislation which I believe I see—

ones that, it seems to me, will delineate some significant facets of a company's future environment. Those listed seem reasonable to me now, and they may well come true; but five years from now, many of them will be outdated.

No two paintings will look alike because each man's experiences differ and because each man's projection, despite his best intentions, will reflect his own philosophy. Nor will an executive who is objective in painting his brush strokes approve of all the projected trends he observes, especially if they portend injury to some of his cherished goals. But he cannot afford to disregard the objectionable trends in laying out a long-term plan.

Our examination will commence with the details in the broadest area, that is, with people's thinking on world problems (Part I, below); and then we shall take up in succession a brief examination of trends in the American people's use of the federal government in domestic affairs (Part II), in people's attitudes toward business in general (Part III), and finally their attitudes toward their employees and bosses (Part IV)—successively smaller and smaller segments of the ideological and legislative areas. Ideological trends will be listed first, then the legislative trends which seem to have followed in their wake. Recall the conceptual framework depicted in Diagram 10 (p. 341).

Not all of these trends will have an equal effect on a company. The executive will need to rank these according to their probable impact, else he will become lost in a sea of information.

I. World Affairs

A. *Trends in Men's Thinking about the Role of the United States in World Affairs.* People's changing attitudes about the kind of world they would like to live in and the appropriate means of achieving it exert a profound effect upon our foreign policy. The instruments employed by nations throughout history to implement their foreign policy have been chiefly economic, political, commercial, military, and more recently ideological; their dominant goals have probably been peace and prosperity for the nation. The consequences of using these instruments are varying degrees of war or peace, and of prosperity or depression, for the country. Hence, men's ideas about how to ensure the country's national welfare have a strong influence on a company's future welfare.

1. In the years since World War II, people have gradually accepted the idea of giving economic and military assistance to coun-

tries who might be our allies in case of war as a means of securing the twin goals of world peace and prosperity.

2. Many people adopted the idea of assisting backward countries with educational, technical, and financial help, so that they could raise their standards of living and maintain stable, forward-looking governments. The goal was still a peaceful world without want.

3. Since 1925, there has been a growing distrust of the goals of the Soviet Union and of her means of achieving them, a trend temporarily reversed during World War II but quickly re-established after the war. Her behavior has been creating a mounting sense of frustration in America.

4. There is probably a growing concern about the possibility of a nuclear war. Men have been urging the government to devote more time, thought, and money to promoting peace and building up armaments—measures designed to preserve our not-quite-perfect world.

5. The idea of some sort of world government and a system of subsidiary regional organizations with the power to enforce decisions is gradually being accepted by greater numbers of people as one means (but not the sole means) of ensuring future welfare.

From the foregoing, we can conclude that in the next few years companies will be living in an environment of armed peace—of high taxes and fairly high employment because of armament spending.

B. *Legislation Dealing with Our Relationship with Other Countries.* The trends in these statutes have been quite consistent.

1. The laws adopted by Congress in the recent past indicate considerable willingness to further the prosperity of other nations, particularly for the purpose of maintaining world peace. The continued support of the Point Four Program (technical assistance program) and of the reciprocal trade treaties indicates that the United States has gradually abandoned isolationism and that it will continue to support attempts to maintain peace and prosperity in the world, perhaps for idealistic as well as practical reasons. These laws seem to grow directly out of the trends in ideologies discussed above.

2. The legislative trend has been unmistakable. Legislation intended to assist in maintaining world peace as well as world prosperity began with our membership in the United Nations and was carried further by the agreements with Greece, Turkey, and other countries to help those nations to maintain their independence. These were supplemented by the Marshall Plan and membership in the

North Atlantic Treaty Organization, the Organization for Economic Cooperation and Development, and in the Alliance for Progress designed to help Latin American Nations. These programs were implemented by congressional appropriations of staggering size, roughly equal to the government's total annual expenditures in the 1920's and 1930's, and were designed not only to secure peace and prosperity but to contain the Soviet Union. Although by the mid-1950's the number of congressmen who advocated more of this type of legislation temporarily declined, there was little evidence in the early 1960's that these laws would be repealed or that the appropriations would be substantially reduced.

3. During this period, Congress approved laws and increasingly large appropriations for research on, and the manufacture of, atomic and hydrogen bombs, guided missiles, space vehicles, and planes, to assure peace and protect against surprise attacks. This pattern of legislation seems destined to continue.

II. Domestic Affairs

A. *Trends in People's Ideas about Domestic Affairs and the Role of the Federal Government*

1. People seem to be taking the promises of the Declaration of Independence more literally than in the past. Lincoln's description of our government as a "government of the people, by the people, and for the people" is being adopted by more people as their guide in determining what they shall vote for.

2. With the passing of the frontier and the opportunity to "go West, young man," together with a rather steady increase in the average size of business concerns, progressively more people have concluded that they cannot establish a business of their own and that, as individuals, they have relatively little control over the means of improving their economic welfare. Consequently, over the decades, larger numbers of people have charged the government with responsibility for this, predicting that they will achieve their goals more fully by such action. The result has been the development of what many have called the "welfare state."

3. More and more people, including businessmen, think that the government should take steps to promote economic growth, maintain employment, mitigate the swings in business cycles, and regulate out-of-line prices; and that it should aid business firms, labor unions, individual workers, and farmers who run into trouble as a result of conditions over which they have little or no control.

4. For some years, there has been a growth in the idea that government should provide certain of the services the public wanted, especially the ones that business could not readily provide.

5. Although the ideas have not been entirely crystallized, there is some indication that more people now think that, in some cases, big organizations actually enhance the welfare of the public. The idea of world government has gradually been accepted as a possibility. Many church denominations have merged, as have labor unions; and their central offices have been given a larger role to play. And even though the general public is still suspicious of big business, many people are beginning to think that large corporations can also, if regulated, play a useful role in advancing the public welfare.

All these ideological trends furnish premises of value in laying out long-term company programs.

B. *Legislation Dealing with the Domestic Economic and Social Problems*[15]

1. Since the early 1900's, there has been a persistent effort through legislation to equalize the incomes of people by means of graduated income taxes and inheritance taxes, by supplying services free of charge to the public through governmental agencies, and by governmental assistance to the unemployed and the incapacitated. This upward trend leveled off during the Eisenhower administration but was resumed in the Kennedy administration.

2. Legislation has gradually crystallized the role of the labor unions. The Clayton Act was the first major piece of federal legislation; the role of unions was set out more fully in the short-lived N.R.A. legislation, and in the Wagner Act, later reshaped by the Taft-Hartley Act and the Landrum-Griffin Act. The protection of workers' interests has been a dominant note; but when labor grew rapidly in power, laws were passed to keep that power within bounds. Labor legislation of this nature will evidently continue as a feature of the environment of business firms.

3. The legislation of the past several decades designed to avoid booms, panics, and depressions has also been consistent. The control of money, credit, and interest rates through the Federal Reserve banks and the U.S. Treasury financing policies was made possible by legislation. And following the depression of the 1930's, legislation was enacted that attempted to restore economic prosperity—

---

[15] Donald S. Watson's, *Economic Policy: Business and Government* (Boston: Houghton Mifflin Co., 1960), is a book on this subject which I can highly recommend.

so-called "pump priming." We can expect similar legislation at the first indication of an out-of-hand boom or depression; the consequences of failing to take governmental action would be too grim, not only for the public and the political parties, but for business. This pattern of legislation also provides evidence that the proponents of Adam Smith's laissez faire philosophy are losing ground.

4. There has been a consistent pattern of legislation designed to maintain employment, not only by maintaining prosperity but by providing government employment or financial help during periods of excessive unemployment.

5. Since the 1890's, there has been more and more price regulation. In peacetime the government regulates (or supports) the prices of a growing number of commodities, especially agricultural products and the services provided by utilities; sets minimum wages for labor; insists that discounts offered by manufacturers be nondiscriminatory; and permits manufacturers to regulate the prices retailers should charge for their products.[16] In wartime, almost all commodities are price-controlled. During the depression the N.R.A. attempted to hold prices up. In spite of the widespread grumbling about wartime price controls and rationing, we can expect them again whenever foods or materials are in short supply.

It would appear from the foregoing that until business can demonstrate its ability to achieve the goal of general economic prosperity— achieve that goal as effectively as the government can—the American people will continue to charge the government with the responsibility of mitigating fluctuations in business activity, encouraging economic growth, and reducing unemployment.

III. Relationships between Government and Business

A. *Changing Attitudes of the Public toward Business as an Aid in Predicting What the Company's Environment Will Be*

1. It is apparent that, over the decades, people have gradually discarded the idea that business should be permitted complete freedom in choosing its own course of action; fewer persons believe that the public welfare would be furthered automatically if the government, through the courts, confined itself solely to the role of an umpire in settling disputes between companies. Confidence that the actions of businessmen would almost inevitably advance the public

---

[16] There are now indications that supporters of fair-trade and agricultural price legislation may be losing their influence.

interest began to wane during the period when Vanderbilt, Gould, Rockefeller, and others were practicing what the people considered unethical means of achieving their own goals. It was further weakened in the early 1900's, when people found that businessmen could not stop panics; and it was almost entirely shattered during the 1930 depression. This trend seems to have leveled off, but it is not yet on the decline.

2. During the first half of the twentieth century people were forsaking the idea that in a laissez faire economy the share of the national income received by each individual would necessarily be in direct proportion to the value of his contribution to society.

3. Through those decades, many people were of the opinion that conservative businessmen opposed virtually every proposal designed to improve the public welfare and that business would accept such changes only when forced to do so. Between the mid-1950's and the early 1960's, more businessmen began to recognize their responsibilities to their community and the nation.

B. *Governmental Regulation of, and Governmental Assistance to, Business Firms*

1. To make certain that an individual company does not harm the public, there has been a whole series of laws. Among these, the following are notable: the Sherman Act; the Federal Food, Drug, and Cosmetics Act; and the acts that set up the Interstate Commerce Commission, the Federal Trade Commission, the Federal Communications Commission, and the Securities and Exchange Commission. Their purpose has been to regulate the behavior of irresponsible executives. We can expect that these regulatory statutes will remain on the books and that others will be added whenever the public's welfare is jeopardized.

2. The regulation of the behavior of competing companies—rules of the game with respect to their behavior toward one another—for the purpose of protecting small companies was one of the objectives of the Sherman Act, and later of the Clayton and Robinson-Patman Acts. Legislation to help small business will probably be continued in the belief that such statutes will strengthen the economy.

3. Since about 1929 the government has steadily expanded the amount of data and has greatly improved the caliber of the information it makes available to businessmen. A vast array of economic data is compiled and published for the primary purpose of helping businessmen to predict the economic environment and thus to lay

realistic plans for the future.[17] These business indicators enable executives to foresee trouble spots in the economy before they become critical and to change their plans in time to avoid serious financial reversals. As more executives learn to use these, we can expect mixed business conditions more often—some industries periodically operating at full capacity and others at below capacity—and less chance of a general depression.

IV. Relationship between a Company and Its Employees

A. *Examples of Trends in the Thinking of Employees about the Companies They Work for and Their Bosses*

1. There has been a growing independence of employees in their attitudes toward management. It seems likely that this trend will continue and that executives will have to give this environmental feature heavy weight in laying their plans during the next few years. Workmen now feel more secure as a result of the growth in the power of the unions; the growing conviction that all men really do have equal rights also probably bolsters this pattern of thinking.

2. Fewer men are willing to accept the orders of the boss without question. More and more hold the opinion that the orders they are asked to carry out must be reasonable, must leave them with a sense of personal dignity, and must serve as a means of advancing their own goals as well as the company's.

3. More workers are convinced that they will have to rely more on unions and less on management for help in advancing their personal welfare.

4. Laboring men are more and more confident that they can take over large segments of the political power once held by the employers, in part because the number of wage earners has gradually outstripped the number of business owners and other voters whose future welfare was closely tied up with that of management, and in part because they are now learning how to use political techniques.

B. *Trends in Legislation Respecting the Relationship of Management and Labor*

1. The Clayton Act, the Wagner Act, and the Taft-Hartley Act were attempts to give workers greater freedom from arbitrary acts of management, as were the acts regulating hours of work, overtime, working conditions, minimum wages, and so on. There seems little

---

[17] For a partial list of publications, see Chap. 12, footnote 2, pp. 382–83.

evidence that this pattern of legislation will be altered in the fore-seeable future.

2. Legislation designed to regulate the relationship between management and employees has become more precise. The same is true of the rules for collective bargaining and rules designed to eliminate coercive actions by either party.

3. The fair employment practices acts adopted by the states rest on the belief that the equal rights granted under the Constitution must be protected; hence, these will undoubtedly remain on the statute books, though they may not be so easy to administer as their proponents had hoped.

Some broad conclusions about the future environment can be drawn from the detailed brush strokes described above.[18] There are unmistakable signs of a shift in people's goals and their means of achieving them. Interest in maintaining world peace has been rising steadily, whereas anxiety about the problem of attaining the perfect *domestic* ideological and social world which men sought during the first half of the twentieth century has remained approximately constant, perhaps because conditions have greatly improved since the early 1930's. The so-called "liberal" social and political philosophy which was widely espoused during the 1930's and 1940's probably waned in the 1950's and in the 1960's is apparently being superseded by a middle course philosophy in the role of government in domestic affairs. Nevertheless, there seems to be little disposition to strike much of the New Deal legislation from the books. The predominant goal now is the achievement of permanent world peace and prosperity. Consequently, the public, the political parties, and the government are concerning themselves with the search for means of securing those features of a perfect world. Foreign aid (primarily long-term loans and technical assistance) and heavy armaments have been temporarily chosen as means of attaining the new objectives.

With details in mind like those listed in the outline, the company's top executives can more readily test in their minds the alternative courses of action that they are considering as part of their long-range

---

[18] Bear in mind that other men's observations of trends will differ from mine in certain details and that their conclusions will therefore not coincide with mine. This paragraph is intended to illustrate the value to the executive of standing aside periodically—of playing the role of spectator instead of participant in the ideological-political controversies.

plans; they are in a position to anticipate the responses of the majority of the general public and of the government (including the community and employees), and thus they can revise their plans well ahead of time to meet the changing needs of these groups. A classification system such as the one used here helps to reduce to manageable size their task of gathering and extrapolating their own details of the ideological, political, and legislative world the company will face. And when seen as a part of the over-all pattern, any changes in the direction of the trends can more readily be detected, because reversals in trends commonly begin to show up in related aspects of the environment. These brush strokes aid the executives who must cope with the complicated task of developing and launching plans that will not only assure the company's welfare but serve the goals of outsiders who will be affected by the company's activities. But these details supply only one part of the picture. Executives also have to appraise the second main feature of the environment—the forthcoming economic-competitive conditions—if they are to lay realistic plans.

PROBLEM
ANTICIPATING THE COMPANY'S IDEOLOGICAL AND LEGISLATIVE ENVIRONMENT

To gain experience in putting to work the concepts unfolded in this chapter as well as those in the four later chapters of Part III, I highly recommend the "Superb Biscuits, Inc." case. This is a Harvard Business School case, published in George Albert Smith, Jr., and C. Roland Christensen, *Policy Formulation and Administration: A Casebook of Top-Management Problems in Business* (3rd ed.; Homewood, Ill.: Richard D. Irwin, Inc., 1959). Separate reprints of this case may be purchased at approximately 40¢ per copy, plus postage. When ordering, designate the case thus: (3G12) Superb Biscuits, Inc. Order from:

> Intercollegiate Clearing House,
> Soldiers Field Post Office,
> Boston 63, Mass.

The Superb Biscuit case takes us into a medium-sized baking company which is competing with the three large producers of packaged crackers and cookies. The young president and the other executives apparently have done some thinking about the company's changing ideological, political and legislative environment and are considering whether to adjust to the trends they foresee.

The questions listed below are intended to give the reader some practice in anticipating the ideological, political, and legislative environment in which a company will be living in the period ahead. More specifically, we are here searching for premises that may be useful later in the book when we shall be appraising the company's present policies and possibly working out a long-term plan for it. The case ends early in 1957; so, for our purposes, it will be necessary to transport ourselves back to that date (in other words, we have to imagine that we know nothing about what has occurred since 1957) and, on the basis of our knowledge then, foresee what this company's ideological, political, and legislative environment will be like in the period from 1957 to about 1962. Readers who are hazy about the trends in ideology and legislation during the preceding years (from about 1950 to 1956) and the impact it had on the American people should turn to a United States history which devotes a chapter or so to that period.

1. *a*) In recent years (that is, between 1950 and 1956), what have been the more significant trends in the American public's ideology:
   1) What are the dominant characteristics of the environment in which the American people have been living during the period 1950–56?
   2) In view of what people have been through, what would be their idea of an almost perfect world? To make this picture of a more perfect world as specific as possible, describe some of the salient details of a way of life which you think people in 1957 would very much like to enjoy.
   3) What ideas have been gaining adherents?
   4) Which of the ideas used by Americans as guide lines in preceding decades have been losing adherents?
   b) In the light of the premises you now (in 1957) have available, including those derived from answering 1*a* above, which of the ideological trends you enumerated in 1*a* 3) and 1*a* 4) will, in your opinion, continue for the next five years or so—until approximately 1962? (Here, you are endeavoring to describe in some detail the ideological environment in which Superb will be living. Try your best to exclude from your mind what *actually* occurred between 1957 and 1962 in answering this question, and also in answering Questions 2*b* and 3*b*, below.

(Begin thinking about the company's problem of adjusting its policies to conform to the changes you expect in people's ideologies.)

2. *a*) What have been the trends in the political philosophies (or programs) of the two major political parties prior to 1957:
   1) In the programs advocated by the Democratic Party?
   2) In the programs advocated by the Republican Party?
   3) Which features of these programs have been gaining adherents?
   4) Which features of these programs have been losing adherents?
   b) On the basis of the premises you gathered in answering Questions 1*a*, 1*b*, and 2*a*, describe the programs you believe the two parties will probably follow between 1957 and 1962.

(Also begin thinking about the impact of these on Superb Biscuits, Inc.)

3. *a*) Between 1950 and 1956 what new legislation has been passed and what old legislation has been implemented by larger appropriations:
   1) To benefit the consumer?
   2) To help and to control business?
   3) To help and to control labor?
   4) To advance the welfare of farmers?

(If some of the statutes you list were designed to forward the goals of more than one of these groups, so indicate.)

    b) On the basis of the premises you have gathered in answering all the foregoing questions:

        1) Will any of the legislation now on the statute books (January 1957) be repealed, be given much smaller appropriations, or be judged unconstitutional? If so, which laws?

        2) What will be the general nature of the new federal statutes which Congress will approve and which old laws will be implemented by large appropriations in the period from 1957 to 1962; what will be the objectives of this legislation?

(Begin thinking about the effects of recent and future legislation on Superb Biscuits, Inc. and its policies.)

Chapter *12*   FORESEEING THE
COMPANY'S FUTURE
ECONOMIC
ENVIRONMENT

IN THIS chapter, the objective will be to decide on the economic details of our imaginary picture of the company's forthcoming environment. In the preceding chapter, we filled in many of the ideological, political, and legislative brush strokes; that visual image, we said, helps us adjust the company's behavior to society's patterns of thinking and furnish premises for selecting social roles or niches consonant with the pattern, roles which would give the company (and society?) the greatest amount of wanted consequences and the smallest amount of unwanted.

We shall here attempt to frame premises useful in predicting the economic conditions in which our company will be living. This picture, in turn, will supply information for premises we can use in determining what role our company should play in the nation's economy. These will later help us decide on two long-term intermediate company goals which are of major concern to the company— (1) whether to expand or contract the size of the company in the period ahead, and (2) the kind of market niche the company should attempt to compete in. The decisions on the company's social and economic goals will be made in Chapter 13.

As before, we shall first try to see the details of the largest of the concentric circles—here, general business conditions. Next, we shall attempt to anticipate the economic health of our company's industry. Finally, we shall look *within* our industry—attempt to envisage the activities of our competitors, see the customers who buy our type of product, and forecast the forthcoming technological improvements.

We shall here, for the first time, deliberately include in our conceptual framework the *economic* goals, means, and premises that induce men to act. Heretofore, we have concerned ourselves chiefly with people's noneconomic motives and the personal problems which human beings encounter when they work together. Our practice will be to look at economic behavior as many businessmen do; their approach is much less formalized than that of a professional economist. For instance, instead of talking about the unchanging economic motives of people in general (maximization of profit, for instance) as would a professional economist, we shall be trying to foresee the economic goals and means that *particular* groups of outsiders will adopt in the period ahead—those of our competitors and the buying groups whose economic decisions will affect our company. As in Chapter 11, we shall try to paint in the details of their probable *future* goals, means, and premises so that we can later (in Chapter 13) test out our alternative long-term plans on these groups and forsee some of their economic responses. Readers familiar with economic theory should note that we shall use some of the less sophisticated concepts from macroeconomics; but in the microeconomic area, we shall employ a businessman's economic thinking pattern instead of the economic model known as the theory of the firm—instead of the familiar static equilibrium price theory.

Recall that as an aid in picturing the details of the company's forthcoming social and economic environment, we are employing a subsystem composed of four main concepts, concepts grounded on the subsystem developed in the five chapters of Part I. This new subsystem, as we have seen, is composed of:

1. The concept of the perfect world that people are currently seeking; this perfect world corrects the deficiencies that people see in their present environment. (Depicted partially in Diagram 12, p. 362.)
2. A classification system that will comfortably contain our detailed predictions of what the world will actually be like and what men will do to secure their future welfare. In Chapters 11 and 12, we happen to be using a system of successively smaller groups. (Facets of this concept are depicted in Diagrams 10, p. 341, 12, 13 p. 380 and 14, p. 397.)
3. Determining which changes in the future behavior of each group will probably affect our company most (ranking both the desirable and the undesirable changes to keep the task of predicting within bounds).
4. Anticipating the changes in each group's behavior by:
   a) Observing trends—whether more people or fewer have been adopting certain ideas of what the world should be like and of what courses of action they should adopt to further their future welfare.
   b) Probing for information about observable current changes in other people's actions which the people in each group will probably use in framing their premises when deciding on what action they should take

in the months or years ahead. (Facets of the ideas in 4a and b are depicted in Diagrams 11 p. 348, 12, 13, and 14.)

We shall continue to use these four ideas here, but as a further aid in foreseeing the behavior of the economic groups we shall introduce a new concept, the concept of the expected size of the annual gross margin which will be available to cover annual overhead and profits. This would be numbered 4c. (Facets of this concept are shown in the table on page 378 and in Diagrams 13 and 14.)

This new concept will first aid us in anticipating the behavior of all business firms in the aggregate and then of all firms in our industry; we shall also use it as a framework for deciding what market niche our company should attempt to fill. It combines into a single framework the effects of change in the four prime economic features of the company's environment—the available plant and man power capacity, the actual level of production and sales, the average selling prices per unit, and the average out-of-pocket costs per unit of all the nation's companies and of the companies in our industry.

THE CONCEPT OF ANNUAL GROSS MARGINS AS A TOOL

The idea of annual gross margin provides the executives with a central thread in trying to anticipate the nature of the first two of the three successively smaller segments of the economic environment which we shall explore. It offers a rather simple framework common to both which can be employed to organize the vast amount of information the executives gather, so that they can put this to work in visualizing the future.

A preliminary and quite general description of the notion of total margin would read as follows: It is the year's sales volume in units multiplied by the spread (or the margin, or the difference) between the average selling price per unit and the average out-of-pocket (or variable) cost per unit; it is the amount of money available to cover the annual overhead expenses and profits. In this book the money thus made available will often be called "the contribution to overhead."

We shall use this idea first to anticipate general business conditions in the United States—to predict whether, for *all* the nation's companies, the total productive capacity, the total volume of sales in units, the average selling prices, and the out-of-pocket costs per unit will be higher or lower than at present, and thus whether the annual gross margins for this particular group, American business *as a whole,* will be larger, smaller, or about the same—whether to expect prosperity or a depression. Second, we shall use this concept to predict these changes for all the companies in our company's industry as a whole, a segment within the national economy.

This idea is not of worth in foreseeing the behavior of two other groups—our competitors and our potential customers (these make up the smallest segment)—but later we shall employ this concept to prophesy those changes for our own company. It is the expected size of our company's annual gross margin which determines whether we should begin building for the future—spending money for plant, equipment, product development, advertising, and trained personnel, for example. Such expenditures (typically classified as "overhead") may not pay off immediately, but they will strengthen the company's ability to compete in the future. But the point here is that the size of the gross margins of all companies in the nation and the size of those enjoyed by the companies in our own industry will strongly influence the size of our own company's annual gross margin.

In order to keep our bearings in exploring this concept of annual gross margin, let us first agree on some definitions of terms we shall use and work out a simplified example of what we mean by *total* or *annual gross margin.* To make these ideas concrete, we shall picture them in their application to a single company.

Incidentally, the period under scrutiny could be weekly or monthly; but annual periods covering the past and the future will usually serve the purpose adequately in making predictions.

The first two terms are *out-of-pocket expenses* and *overhead expenses.* The determination of which are out-of-pocket expenses and which are overhead expenses constitutes one of the knotty problems of accounting. We shall think of *overhead* (or fixed expenses, or "burden") as the expenses the company has committed itself to meet almost regardless of the sales volume—for example, expenses for the year in salaries, rent, interest on bonds, local taxes, and possibly advertising and depreciation. (The depreciation expense item will not, of course, take money out of the till as do other expenses; it remains in the bank until it is spent for replacement of plant and equipment or for other purposes.)

We shall think of *out-of-pocket expenses* (sometimes called direct, or variable, or prime costs) as the ones that have to be paid out of our pocket each time an item is manufactured or sold. The most obvious are costs of raw materials, parts, packaging materials, inbound and outbound freight, pay for labor piecework, and commissions on sales.

Incidentally, variable labor costs will probably become less significant in the future. With the spread of automation, the proportion of
permanent workers on regular salary will probably increase, and
with growth of a guaranteed annual wage, piecework labor costs
and workers' daily wages, usually considered variable costs, will
also tend to become overhead or fixed costs.

Some expenses fall between these fixed and out-of-pocket expenses;
they are *semivariable,* a mixture of both. They vary somewhat in
proportion to sales or production volume, but not in a one-to-one
ratio—for instance, items like interest on short-term loans; cost of
power and light; salary expenses of employees who are kept on until
business becomes very bad, then laid off and rehired when business
improves; and wages of people who are hired temporarily when business is unusually good. Every one who has worked with break-even
charts encounters the problem of how to handle these semivariable
expenses; there is no easy solution. In our thinking here, we shall
cut the Gordian knot by lumping them in with the fixed or overhead
expenses.

Once the question of out-of-pocket and overhead expenses is settled, the fundamentals of this idea of annual gross margin can be
stated in a simplified example:

Sale price per unit...	$1.00
Less: Out-of-pocket costs per unit............................	0.25
Gross spread (or margin) per unit.............................	$0.75
Total annual (or monthly, or weekly) contribution to overhead— the total gross margin available to cover the period's overhead expenses and profits (assume 100,000 units produced and sold during the period); 100,000 × $0.75, the spread per unit, equals..	$75,000
If we wish to go a step further, we can subtract the total annual overhead (fixed and semivariable) expenses for the period; this, we shall say, amounts to....................................	60,000
Leaving the net operating profit before income taxes...........	$15,000

One of the chief objectives of the company—a dominant intermediate goal—is to make sure that the annual contributions to overhead will exceed the company's annual overhead or fixed expenses,
in other words, to make a profit—at least in the long run.

Our term *total gross margin* (or annual or monthly gross margin)
should *not* be confused with the item called "gross margin" which
appears in the company's profit and loss statement; that item is
customarily computed by subtracting the company's manufacturing
expenses for the period from the net sales; in accounting parlance,

it is the difference between net sales and costs of manufacturing, *including manufacturing overhead,* after adjustments for changes in the beginning and ending inventories.

To these terms, we shall add the term *capacity*—the amount of *units* that *could* be produced with the buildings, equipment, and man power that are (or will be) available. As stated earlier, the four chief elements we are trying to predict are these: the productive capacity available (how many units *could* be produced), the number of units that will *actually* be produced, the average sale price per unit, and the average out-of-pocket costs per unit. These are the elements that determine the annual gross margin. The changes from year to year in the levels of these four elements for all the nation's companies and for the companies in the industry cannot, of course, be set down in precise numerical terms, for there are no clear-cut figures published for these. The executive can make an estimate, however, of the *direction of the trends* in each of the four elements over the past months and years; and he can make some informed guesses about the levels for the months and years ahead. He can also set down his ideas as lines in graphs, even though he has no numbers available—graphs sketched out on the back of an envelope, as it were; at best, these will be only rough approximations of past and future levels. His task here is to determine whether each line will rise quite steeply in the future, rise somewhat, remain about level, decline somewhat, or decline rather sharply.

The set of diagrams marked 13A, 13B, and 13C illustrates the approach just mentioned. One such *set* of these three diagrams will be used to represent the economy as a whole, another set for the industry, and a third for the company. The topmost graph, Diagram 13A, shows two things: the executive's best estimate of the plant capacity of the nation (or of his industry or his company) and the level of *actual* production or sales in units. The dotted lines extending to the right represent his ideas of *expected* plant capacity and expected sales (or production) levels in the years ahead. The space between these lines represents unused capacity.

Diagram 13B represents his conception of the changing levels of average selling prices and out-of-pocket expenses per unit over past years, and an extension of these into the future. He will probably find that, in general, selling prices have risen when sales volume approached capacity and have softened when there was excess capacity; thus the expected size of the gap between the dotted lines in Diagram 13A—expected capacity versus production—provides some

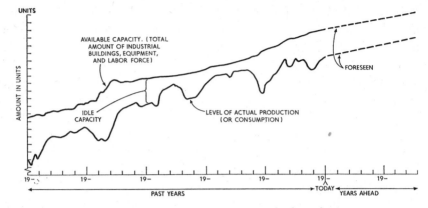

DIAGRAM 13A.   Capacity versus Level of Production

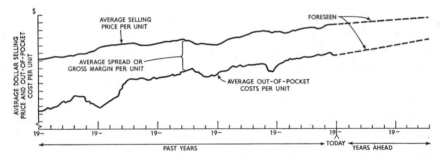

DIAGRAM 13B.   Average Gross Margin per Unit

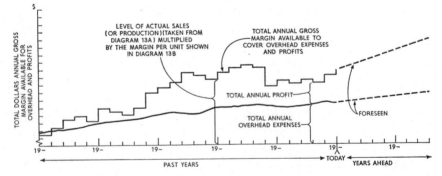

DIAGRAM 13C.   Total Annual Gross Margin

help in predicting the level of selling prices in Diagram 13B for the period ahead. From his experience and his picture of the nation's and the industry's future capacity and sales volume, he should also be able to foretell whether out-of-pocket costs for such items as raw materials, direct labor, packaging, and freight costs per unit will rise or fall in the period ahead, and by how much. The difference between these two represents the spread or gross margin per *unit* in the past and in the future.[1]

In Diagram 13C, the upper line represents the total annual (or monthly) gross margin available to cover the fixed expenses and profits. It is simply the number of units produced or sold (the lower of the two lines in Diagram 13A) multiplied by the gross margin per unit—the spread shown in Diagram 13B. The executive must concern himself with the size of the expected *total* annual gross margin for all the nation's companies and for the companies in his industry. Such predictions help him to make one of his major decisions—whether he should plan to expand or contract his organization. The lower line of Diagram 13C represents the total annual overhead expenses, past and projected. The space between those two lines represents profits.

Executives have available many sources of information useful in visualizing the past trends in the lines on these diagrams and for extrapolating them into the future. For example, for the economy as a whole and for many industries, there are figures indicating how many items people have decided to produce or to buy in the past, and index figures (using some earlier years as 100 per cent) which show whether people have decided to buy more or fewer than before. Similar data are available on selling prices of representative products and on the costs of raw material and direct labor. These past trends and other currently observable causes help the executives to predict what people will decide in the future. Newspapers and magazines are filled with these data; and the federal government, private organizations, and various trade associations also publish vast amounts of such information.

A man can get much more insight from published figures and from his own graphs if, instead of thinking of them as lines and numbers, he thinks of them as records of decisions already made and forecasts of decisions that will be made in the future by very specific groups of people facing very real situations. He needs to live inside the skins of these people in order to predict what they will do. And

---

[1] Contrary to what most laymen suppose, the gross margin per unit is practically never the same from one period to the next. Selling prices do not necessarily rise or fall parallel to out-of-pocket expenses. There is often a *general* relationship between the two, but changes in the price levels of each are also subject to quite separate and rather independent influences.

the figures and lines representing the past become much more meaningful if they are seen as a part of a rather long time series—viewed
as descriptions of changes in certain decisions made by certain specific groups of people over a rather long period of years. Separate
isolated figures showing only men's current decisions are virtually
meaningless unless they are related to the past.[2]

_____

[2] The following publications provide a wide range of such information. The list was
originally taken from "Talk about Reading," by Charles E. Bliss, in the *Harvard Business
School Bulletin* (Summer, 1952), p. 99. Professor Bliss did not mention the annual or bi-
annual publications, or the books listed.

GOVERNMENT PUBLICATIONS

Economic Indicators (monthly). Council of Economic Advisors. A succinct government
report, issued promptly, of the basic figures on national income and spending, prices,
employment, and so on, with charts.

Survey of Current Business (monthly) and its supplement, *Business Statistics Supplement*, which is issued biennially. The *Survey* prints current figures of the past twelve
months (only) for about 2,600 business indicators, as well as articles on special aspects
of business conditions. The *Supplement* brings together monthly and annual figures, and
covers several years.

The Federal Reserve Charts on Bank Credit, Money Rates, and Business (monthly) and
Historical Supplement with records going back to 1919. Largely designed for the bank-
ing profession, but many charts are included showing the changes in general business.

Economic Report of the President (usually semiannual) and its supplement, *Economic
Review of the Council of Economic Advisors*, brings together a large array of economic
statistics; and the text presents the conclusions about future conditions drawn from
these data by the Council.

The Bureau of the Census publishes an extraordinary quantity of data on specific industries, and on capacity, production, and distribution. These and the *Statistical Abstract*
and *Agricultural Statistics* are particularly useful in attempts to pinpoint the company's
"position" in its industry and its position in given geographical areas. Its *Industrial Statistics: Guide, and Finder Catalogue*, issued occasionally, shows examples of the many
types of data made available by the Bureau.

(All of the above may be obtained from the Superintendent of Documents, U.S. Government Printing Office, Washington, D.C.)

Monthly Letter of the First National City Bank of New York. Sent free on request. Presents orderly, intelligent, and often provocative analyses of current economic conditions.

The London Economist (weekly). Incisive articles, seldom dull; and because they are
written by foreign observers, these articles often prove unusually illuminating. *The London Economist* contains an "American Survey" section.

Fortune, Harvard Business Review, The Wall Street Journal, and *Business Week*, familiar
to all executives, often include articles dealing with general business conditions, as well
as special aspects of certain industries and companies.

TRADE PUBLICATIONS

Almost every industry issues trade publications which provide statistics and articles pertinent to the company executive's task of forecasting economic environment.

BOOKS

America's Needs and Resources, by J. Frederic Dewhurst, Thomas C. Fichandler, and Associates (New York: Twentieth Century Fund, 1955), presents an exhaustive picture
of the probable economic environment of the next several years.

(Continued on p. 383)

With this concept of annual (or total) gross margin as a background, the task of predicting the company's economic environment is greatly simplified. However, this does not mean that the painting-in of the details is a simple task.

GENERAL BUSINESS CONDITIONS

As already indicated, thus far in the book we have almost completely disregarded the likelihood that creature comforts and luxuries abound in the near-perfect world sought by most people—that man has economic needs. Men do not, of course, live solely for the aspirations and ideals we discussed in Chapter 11. The majority of our personal decisions and company decisions are concerned with means of achieving the material things which we visualize when we picture our perfect world. Securing these, we believe, will help to assure our welfare. We compare the physical details of this perfect (or better) world with our present physical environment, just as we compare our ideal or perfect social world with our present one, and then decide to take certain steps which will help us come closer to that perfect world. Most people in the United States glean thoughts about these material details from visiting the homes of their friends; from their observations of how wealthy people live; and from magazine articles, advertisements, and movies. Although we sometimes become confused and think of that material world as an end in itself, for the most part we look upon it as an intermediate goal—that is, as a means of gaining other goals that are somewhat more "ultimate" in nature, such as leisure; the pleasure of relaxing, loafing, and having fun; avoidance of unpleasant tasks; intellectual satisfactions; prestige among our fellow men; human dignity; self-fulfillment; the good life; and so on.

The sum of all people's decisions as to how they and their families and their companies will go about achieving that more attractive material world largely determines the over-all economic environment in which our company will be living. Men's past success in acquiring the perquisites of the wonderful material environment they want so badly can be measured by the long-term (upward) trend in the volume of goods manufactured and sold (gross national product), and the periodic deviations from this long run trend which are referred to as periods of prosperity and depression. Although some

---

Government Statistics for Business Use, edited by P. M. Hauser and W. R. Leonard (New York: John Wiley & Sons, 1956), describes the many series of data issued, where they may be found, and how they can be used.

economists believe the long-run upward trend will eventually level off, a majority hold the view that the upward trend will continue. In the years ahead, we can expect the United States to produce increasing amounts of material goods and services for the simple reason that people are determined to attain goals such as those mentioned; they will apply all the ingenuity they have and expend a great deal of their time and effort to invent means of securing them. And as soon as they have achieved a certain standard of living, we can expect them to revise that intermediate goal and set a higher one.[3] It is probably no accident that there has been a steady increase in the total amount of goods produced in the United States. Not only do people individually want more and more; this increasing production is also closely connected with increases in population, improvements in education and training, and improvements in people's ability to conceive new means of achieving their goals.

The Nature of Booms and Recessions

Executives are chiefly concerned with the possibility of a depression. The ideal environment would be one in which the nation's sales and production would show a steady month-after-month increase over the next few decades; and its capacity—plant, equipment, and man power—would expand at about the same rate, with capacity always just a fraction *above* the level of production. But on the basis of past experience, they can be fairly sure that the amounts people will decide to buy and produce will periodically fall well below the nation's productive capacity and at other times exceed the capacity. The possibility of a severe decline in demand hangs over an executive's head as a constant threat to the well-being of his company. Men who helped to guide a company through a depression—that of the 1930's, for example—or who watched their superiors do so, will not soon forget the sense of helplessness they felt in trying to cope with the problems they faced. Nearly every plan they devised to increase sales volume and widen the spread between selling prices and out-of-pocket costs proved abortive. Hence, it is understandable that executives continually worry about a depression and usually read

---

[3] Virtually the only physical limitation on the "more and more" is the amount of raw materials available—foods, metals, oil, fuel, lumber, and fibers for textiles—and even these may prove to be no serious limitation if scientists can continue to develop substitutes drawn from the earth, the sea, and the air. Available man power may also eventually limit production somewhat though, so far, we appear merely to have tapped the possibility of replacing men with machines, power, automated equipment, electronic computers, and electronic control devices.

nearly everything they encounter on the subject. Nor can a family that has gone through a major depression ever forget the searing experience.

In these next few pages, we shall be exploring a rather simplified, common sense, "shirt sleeve" approach for deciding whether general business will be better or worse—for predicting what the preponderance of business executives and families will do—an approach that an executive can use in extending the lines on his three graphs of the nation's business conditions.[4] That a man's predictions will never be entirely accurate in all details goes without saying; for the causes, causal connections, and results he is forced to employ in his premises are extremely complex and his premises are never entirely reliable. Moreover, the unforeseen—a threat of war, for instance—can quickly change the picture. Consequently, he has to keep revising his picture as new information comes to light.

Peacetime booms and depressions[5] are probably in part the result of cumulative mistakes made by the nation's business executives and the nation's families in predicting their future economic environment, and in part the result of new decisions they make upon discovering their faulty predictions. When they change their minds about the economic outlook, they shift their plan of action—find a better means of ensuring their welfare, using premises derived from their revised picture of the future.[6]

---

[4] For a somewhat more inclusive discussion, which synthetizes some of the best thinking of the theoretical economists, see the chapter entitled "The Business Cycle," in Paul A. Samuelson, *Economics: An Introductory Analysis* (New York: McGraw-Hill Book Co., Inc., 1948, 1951, 1955, 1958, or 1961) ; or C. Lowell Harriss, *The American Economy: Principles, Practices, and Policies* (rev. ed.; Homewood, Ill.: Richard D. Irwin, Inc., 1956), chap. 14. Wesley C. Mitchell, *Business Cycles: The Problem and Its Setting* (New York: National Bureau of Economic Research, 1927), still stands as one of the best books in the field. Wilson Wright, *Forecasting for Profit* (New York: John Wiley & Sons, 1947), though old, is quite useful in forecasting some of the specific economic environmental conditions for a company. Because of space limitations, no attempt will be made here to explore world-wide business conditions; we shall presently touch obliquely on some of those.

[5] Executives encounter relatively little difficulty in predicting the onset of business booms induced by wars, and the depressions that commonly follow; hence, at this point in the chapter, our discussion of the dislocations due to wars will be confined to a footnote. The most violent of the business fluctuations of the past 150 years are traceable to the strain placed upon the nation's productive facilities when they were suddenly called upon to supply large amounts of war materials in addition to normal civilian needs, and to the sudden reduction in armament orders when the war was over. These and other economic effects of the federal government's actions will be taken up briefly at the end of this section on general business conditions.

[6] The executives who do the buying for retail stores and wholesaling companies, as well as mine executives and farmers, also have to make such predictions. And what they decide also has a marked influence on general business conditions. This should be borne

Beginning of an Upswing

Tracing an upswing and a downswing in business and observing what businessmen and families usually seem to watch for in trying to create their respective pictures of the future economic environment provide a *modus operandi* for investigating some of the signs an executive should watch for in predicting what the nation's executives and families will do. A depression can be described as a period following an interval during which many executives have held over-optimistic pictures of the future. During that earlier period, they built additions to their plant, purchased and installed more equipment, and hired extra men and women in the expectation that most of these could be used at somewhere near full capacity in the future—at least until they had earned back enough to pay for the investment. Now they find that they must cut production considerably below capacity to keep their inventories in line with their revised idea of expected sales. In fact, they must cut the rate of production *well below* the *current* rate of sales, for only by producing *less* than they are currently selling can they reduce their inventories. They also reduce their purchases of raw materials and lay off workers, which intensifies the recession.

However, the moment the manufacturers' inventories drop to a point where they are in line with the very low level of sales they now expect, these executives must *increase* production in order to keep up with their current sales. They now increase their purchases of supplies and rehire people, which starts an upswing. The men and women rehired begin to view their future more optimistically and begin buying. As more people start buying, executives again predict better business and commence to rebuild their inventories and hire more people in preparation for the better future. Since sales now more nearly match the country's capacity, they can expect less pressure on their selling prices; in fact, some companies may even discover that they can raise prices without seriously reducing their sales volume. Costs of raw materials, parts, and packaging materials may rise somewhat, too, and possibly wage rates, though perhaps less than selling prices. But as a result of the expected larger sales and possible wider spread per unit, they can foresee larger *annual* gross margins for their own companies. When an executive observes these he has no trouble in deciding what the future trends will be and ex-

---

in mind in reading the paragraphs to follow because, to keep the central thread as clear as possible, no further reference will be made to their actions.

tending into the future those dotted lines on his three graphs of general business.[7]

Beginnings of Prosperity

If production and sales levels begin to approach the capacity to produce and eventually exceed capacity, an executive can expect a period of notable prosperity, and perhaps some price inflation. He knows this is coming when he sees building construction for industrial purposes beginning to expand, and the sales of industrial goods such as machine tools, electrical equipment, packaging equipment, materials-handling and processing equipment beginning to increase.[8] For one thing, he can now be sure that more and more producers of *consumers'* goods expect their sales volume to outrun their plant capacity and he can expect some of these executives to expand their plants. But he can *also* anticipate that the above-mentioned manufacturers of *producers'* goods, now expecting larger sales, will start hiring, and that when they near their productive capacity, they too will begin expanding their plants and buying equipment, thus adding to the country's sales volume (and to the number of persons employed) and to the annual gross margins which the nation's manufacturers are enjoying. Incidentally, the introduction of a popular new consumers' product may initiate or accelerate an upswing (or mitigate a downswing) because these manufacturers and their satellite

---

[7] Some idea of the percentage of the nation's plant capacity currently being utilized can be gleaned by comparing the present levels of Gross National Product and of the Federal Reserve Board's Index of Industrial Production with the highest previous level of each. The percentage of the capacity now in use (that is, the relationship between the nation's capacity and its actual production as shown by these figures), when supplemented by trends in the published figures on businessmen's *intentions to invest* in plant and equipment, provides a basis for predicting whether the nation's plant capacity will be increased. Unemployment figures and hours worked per week in manufacturing industries indicate the percentage of the nation's man power being utilized. The probable level of *production* in the future is foreshadowed by changes in the ratios of manufacturers' and retailers' inventories to sales volume, and by trends in the levels of consumer buying. Figures on both types of inventories are published. Indexes of department store sales are useful measures of trends in consumers' willingness to buy. Trends in the level of average *selling prices* are fairly well represented by the Department of Labor's Index of Wholesale Prices for Industrial Goods and its Index of Consumer Prices; their future levels can be estimated by noting the expected relationship between future capacity and future production levels. Changes in *levels of out-of-pocket costs* are reasonably well represented by the figures on Average Hourly Earnings of Employees in Manufacturing Industries and data on raw material prices. Current information for all the foregoing can be obtained most readily from the *Survey of Current Business* and the information on long-term trends from the *Supplements* and the Federal Reserve Board's *Chart Books*.

[8] Data relating to sales volume, unfilled orders on hand, production, inventories, prices, and so on, in the industries manufacturing producers' goods—that is, manufacturers' equipment and building supplies—can also be found in the *Survey of Current Business* and the *Supplement*.

service industries must enter the industrial market—all need to buy equipment, build raw material inventories, and hire men.

Responses of Consumers and Working Men When Business Is Improving

The consumers' decisions of the recent past to enlarge their purchasing have obviously been a key factor in the businessmen's decisions to expand—the decisions we have just watched them make. But at the same time the causes that led those families to change their view of the future from a pessimistic to an optimistic one are the actions we have just seen the country's executives taking. As executives begin rehiring, the new job holders begin to buy; and more of the men and women with jobs start spending a larger percentage of their income. Some families, foreseeing a more assured (and perhaps a larger) income, may buy household equipment or cars on the installment plan, or buy homes financed by mortgages.

The word about better times gets around very quickly, and the improved picture the consumers see is a very real one. Comments such as the following make a tremendous impression when people have lived through a recent lean period. "Joe's cousin got a job last week." "Mamie says four men over in her neighborhood will start work next Monday." "I hear that the plant on South Avenue is hiring." "Martha got a new living-room rug." "The Jensens are thinking of buying a new car." As the evidence of better times mounts, more families revise their pictures of the future. Their predictions of an improved environment, and their forthcoming decisions to buy more in the light of this, provide the executives in the consumer goods industries with premises for predicting larger sales.

The Turning Point and the Downswing

There is no way of foreseeing the turning point and a downswing with certainty. Even during an upswing the picture is always mixed; not all industries or all companies are expanding at the same rate; in fact, some may be cutting back, while others are expanding.[9] Moreover, the upswings and downswings are never smooth curves;

---

[9] Executives often become panicky when the sales of the companies in their *own* industry begin to sag. To them, it seems reasonable to expect, in view of what they are seeing every day in their own industry, that a country-wide recession or even a depression is in the making. Nor are the business conditions in a given region of the country necessarily representative of those in the nation as a whole. To keep his perspective about general business conditions, an executive needs to watch *total* business and visualize what *all* families are thinking and doing.

brief setbacks and short upward spurts are normal—and also misleading for the forecasters.

But when more and more of the producers of *industrial* goods begin to catch up on their unfilled orders for new equipment and building supplies and, as a consequence, lay off men, the executive can
be fairly sure that the crest of the business cycle has been reached; a
downturn is in the offing. At any rate, this is the time to be particularly watchful.[10]

A downswing begins in earnest when an increasing number of executives in the *consumer* goods industries realize either that they
have expanded their plant, equipment, and personnel far enough to
take care of their future orders, or that they may have overexpanded.
When this occurs, the sales of the construction and equipment industries are reduced very quickly and sharply and these *industrial*
producers must promptly and drastically reduce their payrolls and
inventories. In addition, some of the companies in the new industries which helped to accelerate the upswing eventually find that they
have virtually saturated their markets—almost everybody has one
of their products, and they now have only a replacement market—
so they, too, stop buying plants and equipment. The manufacturers
of consumer goods who find that they have overexpanded *also* start
laying off men so that they can bring their inventories into line with
expected sales.

Unless some of the nation's industries begin to expand their capacity at about the same time that others are contracting, the effect
on the economy can be cataclysmic. Greater numbers of consumers
now conclude that cutting down on buying, instead of buying more
as they had once planned, is a better way of ensuring their welfare.
In fact, many are forced to reduce their buying because fewer members of the family are working, the work week is shortened, pay rates
are in some cases reduced, and the amount of credit they can get is
limited. The word gets around that "Joe is laid off indefinitely," that
"Nobody is hiring," that "Such and such a company is going to shut
down for four weeks." As the word spreads and the evidence piles up,

---

[10] Although in our discussion of prosperity and depression the emphasis has been
placed on statistics, remember that all the details of the executive's picture of the *future*
must be built on value premises. His conceptions of expected levels in the four key elements he must watch—capacity, sales volume, selling prices, and out-of-pocket expenses
per unit—as well as his ideas of how families will view the future, are conclusions based
largely on value premises which he gathers from trying to live inside the skins of these
outside groups and from what he hears and reads. The economy is not a mechanical system, the behavior of which can be prophesied merely by extrapolating trends, computing
ratios, and watching for signs of reversals in these.

more and more families change their view of the future. Production and consumption eventually drop far below the nation's capacity to produce.

So much for the framework the executive can use in predicting what the rest of the nation's executives in the consumer goods and producers' goods industries will do about their plant, equipment, and labor force, their levels of production (Diagram 13A p. 380) and their prices (Diagram 13B p. 380). This simultaneously helps him to visualize the economic environment of households and business firms, and thus their buying decisions. These are understandable cause-result relationships—currently observable causes and their expected results—means-end staircases and premises used by other executives and by families and extrapolated by the executive into the future (see Diagram 11, p. 348).

The Role of the Federal Government in the Economic Environment

As already noted, the anticipated actions of government must also be brought into the picture. For the government can increase or decrease its purchases of goods; it has power, through taxation, to take purchasing power away from consumers and businessmen; and it can take many other actions which will have a marked bearing on people's view of the future. An executive's idea of what the government will do about economic conditions must be largely based on his view of future ideological and political trends and the resulting shifts in governmental policies, concepts that we have already explored.

The federal government, of course, is the largest single purchaser of goods and man power. An executive can expect it to increase its purchases when war threatens or the country's prosperity is endangered. A sudden increase in the amount of war goods purchased— or of roads, for example, or harbor improvements, public buildings, dams, and power projects—tells executives and workers that the level of business activity will soon rise, and that the percentage of the nation's plant and man power capacity in use will be enlarged. This, in turn, produces the other results—rehiring, for example— that we have already explored in connection with an upswing in business. A reduction in interest rates, a loosening of credit restrictions by changes in Federal Reserve bank policies and Treasury financing policies, and a reduction of tax rates, can also be anticipated if a recession appears on the horizon. Conversely, the executive can expect the government to reverse these practices (Congress willing) and reduce its buying if inflation impends—if demand seems destined to outrun plant and man power capacity—unless a war is imminent, in which case he can foresee a war boom, price controls, and restrictions on the use of raw materials and man power. All the governmental actions form a part of the web of general business conditions and contribute to (and often mitigate) the periodic deviations from the long-term upward trend in the economic environment of the company.

If we are to make realistic forecasts of the effects of our government's actions on the nation's level of prosperity, we shall also have to include the growing impact of our foreign policies. Increasing amounts will probably be spent on foreign aid. The chief reason is that the low-income people in the underdeveloped nations of Africa, Latin America, and southern Asia have lately glimpsed, and evidently intend to secure by some means—frequently by demonstrations and strikes against their own governments—a few of the material goods that we in America include in our idea of a perfect world. One way to reduce the chances of peoples' uprisings against a government that fails to offer the hope of a better life, and one way to prevent communist party domination in these countries, is to help them industrialize. Because only a portion of this money will be spent for American goods, this program will tend to be deflationary. But this deflationary pressure will doubtless be more than offset by the inflationary effect of our growing expenditures for nuclear weapons, missiles, and space vehicles.[11]

PREDICTING THE ECONOMIC CONDITIONS OF THE COMPANY'S INDUSTRY

By anticipating the economic conditions of his company's *industry* and seeing how these fit within the larger picture of general business conditions, an executive can make his visual image of the company's future environment even more concrete. The more detailed brush strokes which make up this second feature of the economic environment carry him a step further in his quest for information useful in conceiving and mentally testing possible long-term plans.

An understanding of the industry's history provides a background

---

[11] For a lucid and well-balanced account of the government's role in our *economy*, refer to Donald S. Watson, *Economic Policy*, (Boston: Houghton Mifflin Co., 1960). Readers interested in keeping abreast of the government's economic policies should consult the pamphlets published by the Committee for Economic Development, 711 Fifth Ave., New York 22, N.Y., which conducts continuing studies in this field.

that deepens the executive's understanding of the economic data. Knowledge of the practices that the companies in the industry have tried in the past, where they succeeded and failed, and why, affords perspective and adds flesh to the bare statistics which describe the economic changes that have taken place in our industry. It is helpful to read what has been written though the complete story is seldom recorded in books and magazine articles; the painful mistakes of the past are usually glossed over. About the only way to gain real insight is to listen to the tales of perspicacious elders in the industry; they will frequently disclose unpublished and unseen cause-result relationships useful in discerning what the future holds.

This history and the executive's conception of future business conditions is useful in drawing *preliminary* dotted lines on his set of three graphs (Diagrams 13A, B, and C, p. 380) representing his industry's future economic conditions. The industry's lines will rise and fall to some extent in concert with those representing the nation's economy. Its sales volume will be somewhat influenced, and the same will be true of its selling prices and out-of-pocket costs per unit; for the industry's selling prices will have to be kept in line with general price levels, and it must pay approximately the same as others for raw materials, purchased parts, labor, and transportation. However, not all industries reach their cyclical high points and low points simultaneously; graphs of *general* business conditions are simply averages or summaries of the level of business in *all* the nation's industries. As we saw earlier, sales in the industrial goods industries fluctuate much more widely than those of most consumer goods industries; and their curves are likely to flatten out and turn down earlier than those of industries supplying consumer goods. Moreover, the amplitude of the fluctuations in sales volume in each consumer goods industry differs; sales of home appliances are subject to much more volatile fluctuations than sales of food. By comparing the timing and the amplitude of the fluctuation of his industry with those of general business over the past few years, an executive is in a position to make a realistic modification of the probable levels of those preliminary dotted lines for his own industry which were drawn solely on the basis of expected business conditions.

In extrapolating his industry's volume, an executive can also profit from a study of the long-term trends in the proportion of the nation's total business secured by his industry. (See Diagram 14A p. 397.) For instance, he can expect the upward slope in the sales volume trend for his industry to be less steep in the future than that for the national economy if his industry has been losing position—if the needs of the householders and business firms served by his industry are now being supplied more satisfactorily by competing industries. In the home-heating field, for example, the coal industry has been losing position through the years to the oil and gas industries. It is frequently difficult to uncover these trends in the proportion of the nation's business secured by an industry; but once the executive has adduced the facts about the past, he can use these with considerable confidence to modify further his preliminary estimate of the industry's future sales volume because such a trend, once established, is likely to continue for several years.[12]

The line on the graph representing his industry's capacity in the past (the upper line in Diagram 13A) can be readily drawn by an executive who has lived with the industry for several years because he knows when it was operating at full capacity and the approximate volume then produced, and whether (and about how much) capacity has been added since. As a guide for extending the "capacity" line into the future, he has his estimate of expected industry sales volume and his knowledge accumulated from his experience and the rumors in the trade about the plans of certain competing companies to expand. When he compares his two dotted lines, he has an idea of how close to capacity the industry will be operating in the future.

The executive can make some useful predictions once he has formed a mental picture of the percentage of the industry's plant capacity likely to be in use. An industry in which the percentage of its capacity *in use* will probably be declining will be examined here because it offers some added insights.[13]

---

[12] The Federal Reserve Board's index of Industrial Production is broken down into durable and nondurable production; and those, in turn, are broken down by industries; but even these relatively detailed classifications include a wide range of products, the majority of which are not manufactured by firms in the company's *specific* niche. The previously mentioned *Industrial Statistics: Guide and Finder Catalogue*, issued occasionally by the U.S. Department of Commerce, Bureau of the Census, provides information about statistics compiled for a wide variety of products. For an extensive study of long-term trends and business fluctuations in several of the larger industries, see A. F. Burns and Wesley C. Mitchell, *Measuring Business Cycles* (New York: National Bureau of Economic Research, 1946). Incidentally, much less work has been done on an economic theory of the industry than on the theory of business cycles or on the economic theory of the individual firm. The approach used here incorporates a good deal of the thinking developed at the Harvard Business School.

[13] Usually, the capacity in a declining industry decreases very slowly. The equipment does wear out somewhat; thus, in this respect, its capacity declines; but most of the companies usually manage to stay in business despite operating losses, so the total capacity contracts less rapidly than might be expected. Typically, these companies first use up their liquid assets; thereafter, they finance their losses by spending very little of their depreciation money to replace outworn equipment. As a matter of fact, a declining industry's

An executive whose company is a member of a contracting industry can expect the annual gross margins of most of the companies, his among them, to shrink. Gradually, as each company finds that it is operating further and further below capacity, it lowers its selling price for the dual purpose of regaining some of the business lost to other industries and securing a larger share of the industry's dwindling business by taking it away from competitors.[14] To maintain sales, they will quote low prices even though the order may contribute only a small amount toward annual overhead expenses. Concurrently, the companies' out-of-pocket costs will probably increase because the companies' volume of *purchases* is lower. Thus the executive can expect the industry's gross margin *per unit* to narrow steadily. The industry's *annual* gross margin will contract even more rapidly, because its sales volume is also declining. Some companies succeed in staying the oncoming financial crisis by introducing lower-cost raw materials and laborsaving equipment; others may gain some respite by improving the decision making of the company executives, and some may *appear* to recover—though only temporarily—during a period of prosperity. When an industry is losing position in a nation's economy because of a change in consumers' tastes, these remedial steps halt only briefly the adverse long-term trends in the volume sold and the margin per unit and thus in the gross margin available to cover overhead and profits.

PREDICTING CONDITIONS *WITHIN* THE COMPANY'S INDUSTRY

A mental picture of the third and smallest facet of the company's economic environment—namely, what the groups *within* the company's industry will do—affords the most concrete premises of all for deciding which niche in the economy the company should essay to fill. By the time the executives have determined, (1) whether their

---

capacity *may* increase; some companies may introduce expense-saving devices which actually result in greater capacity in the industry. For example, even though cotton production in the United States has been declining, new mills for processing cotton *seed* have recently been built, using the new, more efficient solvent extraction process; but the old expeller-type plants are still in operation. And in spite of the reduced demand for cotton textiles, many cotton *textile* firms built plants in the South during the 1920's and 1930's to save freight and to secure low-cost labor; yet few of the old New England mills were dismantled; they somehow managed to keep open, even though they operated at far below their capacity and lost money year after year.

[14] But selling prices may decline in a rapidly *expanding* industry, too—even one that is operating at or near capacity—because it ordinarily can introduce mass production and mass distribution techniques as a result of its increased sales volume.

company has been gaining or losing position within its industry, (2) which groups of customers served by the industry will expand their purchases and which will contract, (3) what the individual competitors will be doing, and (4) the character of technological improvements which will be adopted by the industry, a majority of the premises will be available for deciding on its market niches. The future behavior of the groups we shall now examine will have a very direct bearing on the company's welfare.

Trends in the Company's Percentage of the Industry's Sales Volume

Whether the company has been gaining or losing position within its industry tells a president how strong all the competitors' organizations have been, as compared with his own. (See Diagram 14B p. 397.) If the company has gradually risen from fifteenth to seventh place, for instance, or if its volume has increased from 3 per cent to 8 per cent of the industry's volume, he knows that in certain specific respects his company has been serving the industry's customers better than most of its competitors, for a company's position is a result of the sum of the company's past activities with respect to customers.

Our fishermen (see p. 9), if he is still at the sporting goods store, is now making decisions that have been largely influenced by what the several departments of each manufacturer of fishing gear have been doing in the recent past to serve the needs of fishermen. And his decision is now helping to determine what the various companies' respective current positions in the fishing tackle industry will be. The decisions of our retail customers—the fishing tackle stores which our lie-abed salesman was planning to call on today (see p. 9; we have now given that salesman a product to sell)—likewise are influenced by what the various departments of each manufacturer have been doing. And their decisions will also help to determine the tackle manufacturers' respective positions. And the decision made by the competitor some months ago to improve his product—the product the executives decided was causing the company to lose sales (see p. 23)—is also now producing changes in our company's percentage of the industry's sales. Their decisions will continue to affect the company's position in the future.

Information on trends in the company's share of the market also provides some basis for estimating the company's future sales volume. If the executives have followed our advice, they have already predicted whether their own *industry's* unit sales and margins per unit will improve or decline in the period ahead, and by how much. The company's sales and margins will be strongly influenced by the level of the industry's sales volume and margins, which in turn, will be influenced by general business conditions. But this preliminary estimate of the company's annual gross margin will need to be modified in the light of the trend in the company's share of the industry's volume, by the new departures they expect their competitors to introduce, and by the changes in program they themselves plan to introduce in their own company. And the final estimate will need to be based also on value premises adduced by the sales organization and the top executives. If the picture of the company's annual gross margin which they draw from the foregoing looks *un*promising—if it will not cover their expected overhead—now is the time to start revising their ideas of the company's niche and developing a plan for revamping the company.

Visualizing What Specific Groups of Customers Will Do

The customers served by an industry are actually quite diverse;[15] in fact, they can ordinarily be segregated into distinct groups. They buy the industry's products for distinguishably different purposes, and the past trends in the volume purchased by each are dissimilar. (See Diagram 14B.) An examination of the past behavior of each group of customers in the industry and a prediction of what each will do about buying in the future provides the company's executives with details about a second feature of the expected environment *within* the company's industy. The executives can frequently determine which groups have been buying the industry's products in greater volume and which have been drying up. The premises derived from this information, together with the factual and value premises gathered elsewhere, provide a foundation for anticipating which groups' purchases will expand most in the future. It is also usually possible to learn whether the company has been getting its share of the business from each of the expanding groups. Finally, the executives can fill in other significant details of customers' expected behavior by gaining some idea of *why* each group buys the industry's product—what specific goals the product serves (buying motives)—

---

[15] In this book the word *customer* will usually be confined to ultimate consumer—the individual, or family, or company that actually uses up the company's product. Middlemen like wholesalers, jobbers, and retailers, though commonly called "customers" (or "accounts"), are not included in this definition. They will be called members of the *channels of distribution*. Recall that our *own* customers and middlemen were included in our broad definition of members of the organization.

and where and how they like to buy it (buying habits). (See Diagram 14B.)

Some examples of the different types of customers served by certain industries will make the foregoing more real. The flour industry serves bakeries, restaurants, institutions, and housewives.

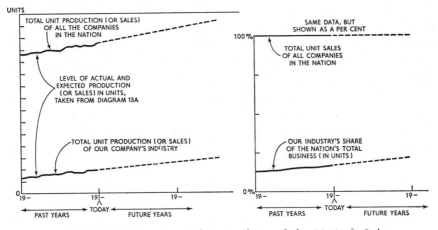

DIAGRAM 14A. Our Industry's Share of the Nation's Sales

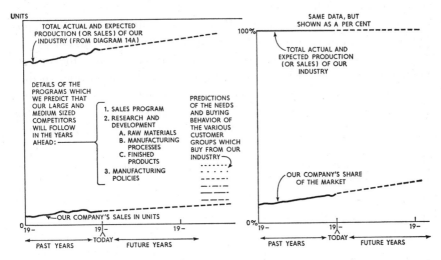

DIAGRAM 14B. Conditions within the Company's Industry

These groups can be broken down further; some housewives, for example (a decreasing number), bake bread, some bake only pastry; whereas some women would like to bake but hate the bother, and are therefore interested in short cuts such as "mixes." Most of these same distinguishable groups are served by the meat packing and the fruit and vegetable packing industries. The machine screw industry and the producers of materials-handling equipment serve practically all the metal-fabricating industries; but among these, some will expand and others contract. Manufacturers of electrical switches and controls may serve the machine tools industries as well as processing industries such as oil refining, sugar refining, and the chemical industries. A manufacturer of enamelware vessels or stainless steel containers may serve the housewife and the hospital and medical trade. The paint industry may serve householders—paint for either exteriors or interiors—as well as various commercial and industrial companies—paint for their buildings and their manufactured products. A classification of the industry's industrial buyers according to whether they are buying the industry's product as parts for the equipment they manufacture (original equipment manufacturers—OEM's) or for installation and use in their own plants, or only as replacement parts, also often uncovers useful details about the industry's customers and each specific group's future behavior.

The objective is to find customer groups whose purchases will expand *and* ones whose peculiar needs our company can fill better than the competitors. With such a niche, the executives can be fairly sure that the company's sales will increase. Furthermore, these potential customers are ordinarily willing and able to pay higher prices then those in groups whose volume is contracting; and the out-of-pocket costs of the units sold to each will be about the same, so that the spread per unit should be greater. On the basis of this the executives can count on larger annual gross margins—*if* they can get this business. As we shall see in Chapters 13 and 14, by anticipating the needs of these specific and quite diverse customer groups, the executives can also do a better job of developing products that will solve the particular problems of each group, and they should be able to revamp the channels of distribution and the manufacturing, inspection, and shipping departments in such a way that these customers get exactly what they want when they want it. As a result the company should be able to induce a larger and larger percentage of the industry's potential customers to become permanent members of its organization.

What Individual Competitors Will Be Doing

Predicting what the company's competitors within the industry will be doing—a third feature of the environment inside the industry

—is not so difficult as a layman might expect. Over the years, executives accumulate a great mass of information about the behavior patterns of their competitors; and they also frame pictures of the strengths and weaknesses of each. Normally, the work patterns of the people in the competitors' manufacturing, sales, and product research departments do not change radically from year to year; routines, once established, are seldom completely discarded. Furthermore, an executive can expect that a competitor will continue to outshine other companies in those activities for which it has already won a reputation—in product development, for instance, or in advertising—because this leadership is the result of decision-making skills which, once acquired, are not easily lost. Many of the weaknesses of each competitor will also probably persist, either because the executives are not yet aware of them or because they do not know how to correct them. Incidentally, an executive often fails to realize that competitors can find out as much about his company as he can about theirs, and that they are just as interested in gathering such information as he. See Diagram 14B.

This information reaches the executives through several communication channels. The company's salesmen tend to report the competitor's strong points; they explain, "If we could only do such and such as well as the Carson Company, I'd have booked that order." The buyers for the channels of distribution are also likely to slant their reports in the same direction because they want to keep their suppliers on the defensive. Executives can usually discover where their own company excels by ferreting out how they secured certain orders and why the competitors failed. Suppliers' salesmen sometimes reveal the strength and weakness of competitors, indicate how they are solving certain problems, and disclose which of their problems are not yet solved. By listening to the gossip at trade association meetings and reading between the lines of press releases and news stories, the executives can also gain insights into the problems competitors are facing and what they are doing to resolve them. Competitors' financial figures can often be secured from company reports to stockholders, reports from credit agencies such as Dun & Bradstreet, Inc., and (if the competitor is a large one) from studies published by Standard and Poor's Corporation and by the Securities and Exchange Commission. The information from the several sources just mentioned may be fragmentary; but because of their experiences in their own company, the executives are already familiar with most of the problems they hear about, so that they can usually fill in the interstices and thus paint a fairly complete and realistic picture.

The separation of these competitors into groups according to their size serves as a further tool in predicting what they will do. In most industries, there are usually three or four large companies. Characteristically, they handle the industry's standardized products, ones with very large potential sales volume selling at relatively low prices. They have evolved a system for mass distribution to those types of consumers whose needs are best served by the standard units, and they have set up production lines and specialized processing equipment geared to manufacture these the year round in large volume at very low cost. Most of them will have strong design and development departments, for improved products enable them to maintain their position in the industry; and they must constantly improve their manufacturing processes, perhaps by introducing more automation, if they are to keep their costs low. Moreover, the executives in those organizations have been selected and trained to make intelligent decisions about the problems of large-scale manufacturing and distribution. Since therein lies their advantage, we can expect them to continue with the same program in the future. Incidentally, large firms in *other* industries which at first thought would *not* seem to be competitors also bear watching. Interindustry competition can have a profound effect upon a company's future. Large companies in all industries are usually attempting to diversify their products and markets.

Consonant with the foregoing, our executive can also predict that these large companies will probably not try to secure orders for small-volume, specially designed, or custom-made products— women's style shoes, or a specially designed electric motor, for example. Their sales organizations, engineering men, and manufacturing departments are seldom capable of handling small, fussy orders. Even if a large company were to set up a special division to take care of such orders it would probably have trouble competing. Its selling and manufacturing costs would be approximately the same as those of smaller companies. But the new division would in all probability have to be governed by many of the company-wide rules and regulations, and would be plagued by failures in communication, both of which cause difficulty and errors in supplying exactly what a special customer wants when he wants it.

The medium-sized competitors, those against whom his own medium-sized company is competing most directly, are of dominant interest to the executive. Their actions in the future will probably affect the company very directly because they usually sell to virtually the same customer groups. Probably the simplest way of surmising their future behavior is to examine their past practices and extrapolate these into the next few years. More specifically, an executive can examine the *key* tasks which companies in the industry must perform to secure the types of customers they all serve, and determine which of the competitors have been performing those activities better or worse than his company. By using his own company as the standard, he can gradually build a quite specific mental image of their past behavior and, in particular, their respective weaknesses and strengths.[16] As indicated earlier, an executive can expect the majority of these competitors to continue with approximately the same programs in the future as in the past.

What companies that are smaller than our company will be doing also bears watching. The executives of a majority of smaller companies seem content to jog along in a routine way; their actions are consequently easy to predict. But a small company which has been taken over by an imaginative and dynamic executive can make rapid inroads because it is able quickly to adjust its organization to serve the needs of new customer groups and it can supply these needs very exactly. Probably no useful general statements can be made about such companies. An executive of a medium-sized company usually hears of them after they have taken over some of his customers. When this occurs, he must include them among the competitors he watches.

Making Mental Pictures of Forthcoming Technological Developments

A visual image of the forthcoming technological innovations in raw materials, in manufacturing, and in product design which will be adopted by companies in the industry fills in details of a fourth feature of the environment within the industry. The ones that will be put to use by the competitors will obviously have a marked impact on a company's welfare.[17] In a few industries, technological improvements in all three fields have come to a virtual standstill; in

---

[16] The pertinent questions to be asked here are almost identical with those the executive will need to ask himself in choosing the niches in which the company will be able to compete most effectively. See pages 418–23 for such a list. The idea is to select a niche in which the company can perform the key tasks better than its competitors.

[17] The adoption of technological improvements is but one way of competing. Parts I and II of the book are devoted to another—namely, building an effective organization by teaching men how to make decisions and how to gain acceptance of their decisions.

those businesses the problem of predicting is a fairly simple one. But in many industries the changes are very rapid indeed, and the task of anticipating the details of the company's technological environment requires insight.

One way to avoid glittering generalities about these expected alterations in the environment is to anticipate what *particular* competitors will do about adopting technological improvements in each of the three fields. By learning about the strong points of a competitor's research and development staff—where the abilities of the men in that department lie—and then looking back over the types of improvements that company has adopted in the past, an executive can make some reasonably solid conjectures about which type of technological improvements the competitor is likely to concentrate on. The established pattern of a research department's work can, of course, be changed by hiring new men; but this takes time.

The greatest uncertainty lies in the possibility of the discovery of newly created ideas; it is impossible to foresee *exactly* where the lightning will strike.[18] Yet, even here, there are some guide lines. The executives know that the industry is confronted with certain problems, they know which ones are growing almost intolerable, and they can expect solutions eventually because some extraordinary minds are probably already at work on these problems. But they cannot foresee *when* the solution will be found nor exactly what it will be.

Of the three types of technological improvements, those in the industry's raw materials are the easiest to foresee. Most of the new improvements are developed by the regular suppliers of the industry's raw materials, though products designed for use in some other industry can frequently be adapted.[19] Unless a new raw material is developed by one of the large competitors and kept secret for its own exclusive use, an executive usually learns of it from news reports in trade magazines or from suppliers' salesmen well before it is ready for market. He can attempt to guess which of his competitors will most likely adopt a given new product. He knows

----

[18] These men are working at the frontiers and employing at a high level the creative process explored in Chapter 2. We shall approach this problem from another point of view in Chapter 14, where the executive's task of building up his own product development department is investigated.

[19] In this paragraph, we shall think of raw materials as the materials a company buys either for further fabrication or for assembly: the products of the mines, forests, and farms; processed raw materials such as steel, textiles, insulation, or lard; and manufactured parts like screws, electric motors, or dress buttons used in the finished product. Of course, the finished product of one industry may serve as the raw material for another.

which companies have a tendency to adopt changes early, whether the product will help a certain competitor to correct some of the weaknesses in its end product, and what problems the competitor will face in converting its equipment to handle the raw material. This, and his knowledge of the abilities of the competitor's research men should enable him to make some shrewd, though tentative, guesses about a competitor's decision.

Technological improvements in the industry's manufacturing processes can also be foreseen to some extent. Among the current causes an executive can see about him, ones that will probably lead to the adoption of new processing methods, are the following: a new raw material that requires new equipment; development by the industry of new kinds of products; a steady increase in the labor rates paid by an industry whose labor costs loom large—the coal industry and the early bottle-blowing industry are examples. In a rapidly expanding industry, probably more and more specialized mass production equipment and more automation will be introduced. Generally speaking, a new processing method will be adopted rather widely if it solves some knotty problems or pays for itself in lower out-of-pocket costs within a few years. In addition, a specific competitor's decisions will be influenced by its ability to finance the new equipment and by the productive efficiency of its present equipment. The executive's pipelines for this information are similar to those mentioned for raw materials.

What the industry will be doing about adopting improved raw materials and processing equipment will primarily affect the industry's out-of-pocket costs—its raw materials and labor expenses. Improvements in the design of the industry's end products, a third type of technological innovation, will affect its sales volume and selling prices most.

Predicting what our leading competitors will do about improving their end products calls for considerable ingenuity, primarily because these are usually carefully guarded secrets. In Chapter 11 when we looked back on the conference held by the executives of the company whose sales were declining (p. 343), we chided those men for their failure to foresee a competitor's decision to improve its product. Obviously, there are no infallible methods of predicting these decisions; yet it is possible to make some tolerable guesses. The several sources of information already mentioned in connection with improved raw materials and manufacturing equipment will supply useful premises.

Another way is to watch for trends in the characteristics of the industry's products and project these into the future. For example, in many industries, there has been a tendency toward more specialization of end products. Once upon a time, we had two or three types of general-purpose soaps; now we have scores of special-purpose soaps. There has also been a tendency to design products to fit the person, rather than to design the products and then force the user to fit himself to them. The tendency to alter the exterior appearance with a view to heightening the products' aesthetic appeal has also been marked. Trends such as these move slowly; once they are detected, the task of predicting future alterations in product design is relatively easy.[20]

Predicting changes in what might be termed the *fundamentals* in the design of the industry's products is more difficult. (We touched on these briefly on page 402.) One approach is to search for the chief disadvantages the consumers encounter when they use the industry's product. For example, the product may need frequent repair or replacement (ideally, all parts should wear out simultaneously, like Holmes's "one-hoss shay"); or one of its basic parts may not perform smoothly. Another approach is to become acquainted with the basic research already done by people inside and outside the industry. And frequently, an executive hears of attempts to put to use old and all-but-forgotten scientific discoveries. Fortunately, fundamental research is usually evolutionary in nature. For instance, after the basic concept of television was discovered, several years elapsed before a practical product was perfected. The same thing has been true of atomic fission. Such slow development enables the executive to appraise well ahead of time the product's probable impact on his industry and on his company.

SUMMARY

So we come to the end of the executives' task of anticipating the company's environment. A synthesized visual image of the details of the two overriding features of the near-perfect world men aspire to— the social and the economic features—furnishes the executives with a picture of men's dominant goals and a view of the general nature of their future decisions. Predictions of the procedures the various

---

[20] This discussion is centered around physical end products, but remember that many industries produce ideas instead of material goods or services. For example, the movie industry, television, radio, and the theater produce ideas; and the newspaper, magazine, and book publishing industries are solely dependent for sales on the ideas they can communicate to their consumers.

groups of people will follow in an effort to attain that perfect world —the decisions of the several categories of men whose actions will affect the company—furnish the specifics.

Now that we have seen examples of many of the facets of the task of creating a detailed (though not necessarily accurate) picture of a company's forthcoming environment, it may be worthwhile to restate the four (five) interrelated concepts we have been using. Our subsystem for Chapters 11 and 12 contains: the concept of a detailed picture of men's current ideas of a perfect world; the idea of a comfortable classification system for the details of that future world and the details of how men intend to achieve it; a system of ranking the specific expected actions of these men according to their probable impact on the company; making detailed predictions by observing trends in the nature of the goals and means adopted by each group and by noting recent occurrences which the people of each group will probably use in deciding what course of action will further their future welfare; and by visualizing the expected annual gross margin of companies.

Some parts of the picture are supplied by anticipating the steps the general public will take in the fields of politics and legislation to further its well-being. Trends in men's ideas about the federal government's role in foreign affairs and about the use they will make of their government to improve domestic conditions, and trends in their attitudes toward the business community and their own employees and bosses, provide progressively more explicit details of this realm of the company's environment. These supply ideas for causes and results that will be useful in framing premises for determining the character of the niche the company should attempt to fill in *society*— its behavior as a social unit.

The economic decisions of these same people (classified, however, into quite different groups) will likewise shape the environment in which the company will have to live. In anticipating general business conditions, an executive is obliged to foresee whether the nation's productive capacity will be increased, how close to capacity the plants will be operated, and the trends in the spread between the selling price and out-of-pocket costs. These trends are helpful in determining whether the nation's businessmen as a whole expect an increase or decrease in their annual gross margin and thus whether they will expand or contract their purchases of equipment, labor, and raw materials. These actions simultaneously determine the number of jobs and the take-home pay which will be available, and this will influence the general public's decisions about buying. The size of the company's annual gross margin will be influenced by the decisions of both businessmen and consumers.

The economic conditions of the company's *industry* provides even more explicit brush strokes. Whether its industry's annual gross margin will increase or decrease, and whether it will be gaining or losing position in the national economy, will have a more direct effect on the company's annual gross margin than general business conditions. These trends and the expected changes *within* the company's industry —whether the company's competitors will be able to secure a larger or smaller share of the industry's market, what each group of customers served by the industry will do about buying the industry's products, what the company's large and medium-sized competitors will be doing, and the expected technological improvements—provide information out of which an executive can frame realistic premises for predicting the size of the company's annual gross margins in case it makes no changes in its long-term policies. Equally important, these economic conditions supply elements for premises which can be used in choosing two other types of long-term goals—whether to expand or contract the company, and what niches in the market it should try to fill in the years ahead.

PROBLEM

ANTICIPATING THE COMPANY'S ECONOMIC-COMPETITIVE ENVIRONMENT

As already indicated in the discussion that preceded the questions at the end of Chapter 11, the Superb Biscuits, Inc. case will be used throughout Part III. Here, we are employing it to gain practice in anticipating general business conditions, the economic conditions of the company's industry, and the conditions within the industry. As before, we shall imagine that we know nothing about what happened after January, 1957.

1. Anticipating general business conditions in the United States:
    a) Using the ideas lying behind Diagrams 13A, B, and C, p. 380 as a basis, prepare a set of three charts showing general business conditions in the recent past (1945 to 1956); extend the lines into the future— that is, to 1962. Though you may, if you wish, look up the data about the past, this will not be necessary; you may draw upon your general knowledge of changes through those years in the levels of the six lines you include in your charts.
    b) Explain briefly why you drew each of the six lines as you did for the years 1957 through 1962.
    (While working on Question 1, be thinking about the significance of your findings—the use to which they can be put by you and Mr. Kingsbury in laying plans for Superb.)
2. Anticipating the economic conditions of the packaged crackers and cookie industry:

a) Prepare a set of charts for the cracker-cookie industry, using Diagram 13A, B, and C, p. 380 as your guides. If you wish, look up data on this industry for the years prior to 1957. However, for our purposes the information in the case will be sufficient. Where no data is furnished, use your imagination in drawing the lines. You may find it advisable to go back to the year 1945. Extend these lines to 1962.

b) Explain briefly why you drew the lines as you did for the years 1957 through 1962. In preparing these charts, be aware that some of the past and future trends in the biscuit industry *may* differ substantially from those in the national economy.

(In answering Question 2, be particularly observant of the impact your answers will have on the plans you are to prepare later for Superb.)

3. Anticipating the actions of the customers and competitors *within* the cracker-cookie industry:

a) Past tendencies:

1) What have been the trends in Superb's percentage of the total United States sales of packaged biscuits and cookies? (Here we are looking at the effectiveness of *all* our competitors.)

2) Which types of crackers and cookies have been losing patrons; which do you imagine have been selling better? Have there been any trends in the volume of crackers and cookies purchased by the two main types of customers, housewives, and institutions? (Here we are examining the past behavior of the biscuit industry's customer groups.)

3) What have the large and the medium-sized competitors of the company, especially the large ones, been doing about setting up their systems for the distribution of biscuits? (For what types of products have their sales organizations been designed—standardized products or specially designed products?)

4) What have these competitors been doing about their methods of manufacture? Have they been turning toward, or away from mass production? (In Questions 3, 4, 5, and 6 we are trying to describe the past actions of competitors.)

5) What have these competitors been doing about: (a) product improvement and new products? (b) raw materials used in crackers and cookies? (c) manufacturing processes?

b) The period ahead—1957–62:

1) Which types of crackers and cookies are likely to gain in popularity and which customers using crackers and cookies will probably increase their purchases most in the future?

2) What changes, if any, do you anticipate in the present selling, manufacturing, and research programs of the company's largest competitors?

3) What improvements in cracker and cookie design, in cookie cartons and in the recipes (and thus in the taste) do you anticipate?

(Be thinking about the significance for Superb Biscuits, Inc. of your answers to these questions about expected conditions within the industry.)

Chapter *13*   DECIDING ON THE
COMPANY'S
LONG-TERM
POLICIES

WE ARE now well along in the most demanding of top management's tasks. What we are doing—visualizing in detail the future behavior of groups, employing these detailed images as a source of premises for conceiving long-term plans, then implementing these plans—calls for wisdom of the highest order. Such predictions and planning enable the skilled company president to map out courses of action which have a high probability of success.

Deciding on the company's long-term relatively permanent policies, the subject of the present chapter, is the first of the three remaining major tasks which we shall examine. A chapter will be devoted to each. The particular subsystems of concepts used in all three are recombinations of concepts which we have already mastered. We are merely employing them at the high levels in the staircases instead of lower down, and at the high levels in the executive echelons.[1] The details of the subsystem that we shall use are set out in the next four paragraphs.

Characteristically, a company's long-term plans have their genesis in a problem. The executives may have concluded, for instance, that unless something is done, the company will not prosper as they had once hoped, or that it will not live the long and prestigeous life they originally envisaged; in these cases their problem is that they are only partially successful in achieving the goals they had set some years earlier. On the other hand, they may have caught a glimpse of

---

[1] For other examinations of the task of planning see, David W. Ewing (ed.), *Long-Range Planning for Management* (New York: Harper & Brothers, 1958), Preston Le Breton and Dale A. Henning, *Planning Theory* (Englewood Cliffs, N.J.: Prentice-Hall, Inc., 1961), and Edwin C. Bursk and D. H. Fenn, Jr. (eds.), *Planning the Future Strategy of Your Business* (New York: McGraw-Hill Book Co., Inc., 1956).

a possible new major goal—a new situation they might advanta-
geously exploit, a new market niche, for example; here their problem
is to achieve a new goal.

The problems at the top of the staircases differ only in magnitude
from those which arise farther down on the staircases. And the new
means we adopt to solve the problem differ only in their complexity.
In these concluding chapters, we shall be conceiving plans comprising
several staircases, each with many steps, instead of simple plans consisting of improvements in, perhaps, only two or three of the steps far
down on the staircases. In other words, *planning is done by everyone
in the organization* and is necessary for every step in the company's
staircases; in Part III, we are dealing with a large and more complex
version of what the young executive or young staff man must begin
doing as soon as he starts on his first job.

To repeat, then: A plan originates from a problem that needs
solving. The executives in most companies are usually well aware
of these major problems. But in some instances the company's underlying problem is not clearly seen, even though the men see the sales
and profits dwindling. One way to sharpen the company's problem is
to crystallize the hopes that the executives once had for the company,
express these as intermediate goals, and try to find what companies
in our industry must do very well in order to be successful—find out
what they must do to achieve goals such as these. It may turn out
that we are much less skillful than competitors in performing the
salient activities. Or the investigation may disclose that we should
change some of our intermediate goals; gradual, almost imperceptible trends in environmental conditions may have rendered some of
them obsolete. For instance, had we been an executive of a railroad
during the late 1930's, we should probably have concluded that we
should subordinate one of our earlier goals of offering frequent, fast,
low-cost passenger service as a means of ensuring the company's welfare because of the growing competition of automobiles and air
travel.

Once we crystallize the problem we can leave the stage of confusion and proceed through the remaining five stages of the creative
process. We are here trying to conceive promising new alternatives
for many steps on several staircases; we may even have to visualize
some entirely new staircases. And in testing out these alternatives,
we are obliged to employ a much greater amount of practical rationality (per our definition on page 142) than before. We now need
many premises from groups we had heretofore ignored; in order to

secure a full complement of fairly reliable premises, we must foresee peoples' future social and economic environments and their goals, then imagine what effects or consequences our proposed plan will have on the outside groups. Moreover, we shall probably have to appraise the width of the zones of acceptance of virtually all the members of our organization instead of only a few, for nearly all will be affected by a major new plan. We want to make sure that the member groups will feel that their inducements will be enhanced or at least not be reduced and/or that the contributions they are asked to make will be the same or less. So much for our conceptual framework.

When we use the term *company policies* in the concluding chapters, we shall have in mind the long-term, high-level goals that the organization is pursuing and the major means it has adopted, including the relatively permanent guide lines for action that the executives have gradually evolved out of their accumulated experience.

Though there are many types of relatively permanent policies or goals that we could consider, we shall concentrate on three: First, we shall look into the task of determining our company's rather permanent role in society—in its community, its employee group, and in the nation. Most of our attention will be centered on the task of choosing a second type of semipermanent policy—selecting and filling a specific economic niche (or niches) during the next several years; though there are many economic niches, we shall concentrate on the task of deciding what market niche to enter. Finally, we shall view a company's business philosophy as a policy, as a group of semipermanent means adopted by the company to further its welfare.

These three types would all be classified as intermediate goals.

Recall our statement in Chapter 1 that one or more of the following are frequently chosen as intermediate goals: to become a leader in the industry; to accumulate cash reserves for the purpose of carrying the company through a depression; to maximize profit; and so on. But in our examination of the company's social environment, we began to realize that playing a commendable role in society was also a desirable intermediate goal. We looked upon all these as intermediate goals that would automatically further the company's set of ultimate goals—help it to prosper, for example, to gain prestige, or to perpetuate itself. We also noted in Chapter 1 that the intermediate goal most commonly emphasized is that of filling a promising market niche more successfully than competitors. We concluded that if the company reaches this goal, most of its other intermediate objectives, such as making a good profit or improving its position in its industry, will be obtained at the same time. The company's plans are largely fashioned to implement this major goal, though the means chosen are also selected with a view to furthering the other high goals.

Several reasons for setting long-term policies well ahead of time and stating them clearly have already been discussed, so all we need to do here is bring together some of the more pertinent ones. Stating these big goals in concrete terms—as seeable instead of vague and general goals—and setting them well ahead of time, enables the chief executive and his associates to conceive an integrated, over-all plan, foresee in detail the changes that must be made in the organization, and complete the alteration before D Day arrives. With a detailed plan in mind, management can also test it mentally on the various groups who will be affected to see whether the members will approve or oppose it. If the executives foresee that as a result of the proposed changes, a considerable proportion of any of these groups will transfer their loyalties to some competitor because their inducements have been reduced, it behooves them to revise their plan; otherwise, the company obviously has little chance of realizing its permanent goals fully. A description of a company's niches encompasses statements about the role it will play in furthering the goals of all these groups—in serving their *future* needs, not those of yesterday or today.

Testing a long-range program and revising it also sharpens the executive's mental image of its details; and this, in turn, enables him to describe in clear language the many intangible goals contained in it. The objective here is to make these goals real to the middle-level and lower-level executives. The goals will not serve as a guide until the executives and the mental experts in the company can see them distinctly and use them as sources of premises in making their company decisions.

These concrete statements of long-term company goals also help the executives and mental experts to make wise day-to-day, short-term administrative decisions. Men commonly choose these courses of action largely on the basis of expediency—on the basis of a narrow and limited set of premises. But with the long-term goals fixed clearly in their minds, their tendency (we hope) will be to reappraise each short-term decision to see whether they can convert it into a telling means of achieving the company's long-term goals as well as the one immediately at hand—and thus into a more useful decision. Whether to hire a given man as assistant chief of the product development department, or whether to accede to a distributor's request for an exclusive territory, or whether to buy a certain lot of off-standard raw materials offered at an attractive price, are examples of some decisions which can profitably be rechecked in the light of long-term goals. Before making a short-term decision, the men should ask themselves, and one another, such questions as these: If we adopt the proposal, will the long-range goals be harmed? Will it commit us to a program that will be of little use as a means of achieving those goals? If the proposal is to change the character of the equipment or man power in a department, for example, or the character of our distributors, will we later regret the decision because these changes channel the company's activities into blind alleys? Can we revise our proposal so that it will not only solve the immediate problem and forward the long-term goal we now have uppermost in mind, but also provide some by-products of value in achieving other long-term goals?

But we should continually remind ourselves that a plan is only a tool. We should be chary of any plan in which all the details are precisely set out and neatly buttoned up. It presupposes that we have been all-knowing about the forthcoming environment and the member groups' reactions to our proposals; thus we tend to follow the blueprint blindly. Actually, many of the decisions as to the best means for the lower steps can better be made as we go along, for we shall then know what the real situation is.

In any case, setting company goals is a continuing task. We have already seen that since the environment is constantly changing, the goals must be evolutionary in nature. (I hope I have not left the impression that goals should be re-examined and reset only once in every three, five, or ten years.) Long-term company policies are *relatively* permanent, not fixed and unchanging. Moreover, even when the company pursues certain of its intermediate goals over a rather long period, these are not all equally effective in advancing the company's ultimate goals; and the relative weights the executives assign to each will shift as environmental conditions change.

CLARIFYING THE COMPANY'S ROLE IN SOCIETY

Inasmuch as the premises for determining the roles the company is to play in its social environment—the niches it should try to fill there—were explored quite thoroughly in Chapter 11, we can deal rather quickly with the task of setting these intermediate goals. Let us begin with community goals.

That a company and its executives can and should play a leading part in community affairs need not be labored. Characteristically, however, many executives are reluctant to shoulder civic responsibility—responsibility for anticipating the town's needs, setting goals that will further its welfare, and playing a role in achieving those goals. Civic jobs are often accepted only when they cannot be gracefully evaded. But improving the local environment will manifestly aid the company in achieving its permanent goals.

Pinpointing the community programs which the company plans to support, and inducing the employees to take into consideration the side effects on these projects when making their company decisions, helps to implement the town's goals. Here are some examples of specific objectives: improving the community's cleanliness, appearance, and health not only by abiding by the letter of the local ordinances on building codes, sanitation, and public nuisances, but by acting in the spirit of the objectives lying beneath such ordinances; insisting on honest public officials and courts and the impartial enforcement of laws; trying to take steps that will strengthen the community's business firms and bring new families to the community; encouraging and supporting improved education, recreational facilities, and cultural advantages. Everyone, of course, gives lip service to these objectives, and a company obviously prefers a community that is striving for such goals; but these serve only as empty platitudes unless someone takes action. The company's executives are ordinarily respected and capable members of the community; if they willingly lend their leadership and see that their subordinates think and act in terms of the community as well as the company, the chances are that improvements will follow. As a rule, the revisions they make in their company decisions as a result of this extra thinking will involve little or no extra expense.

The company's conduct toward its employees—a second social group—and the role it plays in satisfying the social needs of its employees have also been treated at some length in earlier chapters (see p. 137 in particular); we shall therefore mention here only the interconnection between employee relations and community relations. The company's reputation in the community is largely influenced by the attitude of middle and top management toward its plant and office workers. Inasmuch as one of the objectives is to secure the cream of the community's work force, it is evident that the company must become known as a good place to work. This does not mean that management should behave paternalistically or mollycoddle its men. Contrary to what some people would claim, many workers look down on a "do-gooder" company or one that gives ground every time an employee complains. They respect a company that expects its employees to contribute at near 100 per cent of their ability.

The role that can be played by a medium-sized company in furthering the *national* welfare in time of peace is likely to be unspectacular, consisting mostly of behaving in conformance with the spirit and letter of state and federal legislation (including the payment of taxes for the nation's welfare) and the slowly changing ideology and mores of the public. In contrast, during wartime the spotlight picks up and publicizes each company act which in any way imperils the public interests, and people also watch for (and sometimes applaud) programs that help to win the war.

A company has certain rights, privileges and obligations in its community, state, and country. These determine its role in society.[2]

SELECTING THE MARKET NICHE

Whereas in the nineteenth century the chief intermediate goal of most companies was to "get the products manufactured," in recent decades businessmen have been giving precedence to *customers* and their goals. Finding and filling a suitable market niche undoubtedly has more bearing on a company's future welfare than any of its other intermediate goals. The main reason is that serving a consumer niche well should result in additional permanent customers. These particular members of the organization are hard to find. Their contributions are very essential to the company. Few firms feel that they have enough good ones. The turnover among customers is much higher than the labor turnover, and the expense of securing and keeping them is very heavy.

In deciding on the market niche, management is choosing the particular segment of the industry's market it plans to serve. A description of such a niche includes (1) the specific group of customers it intends to solicit and (2) the products (or services)—the particular features of those products—it intends to offer the customers. For example, if a furniture manufacturer is to flourish, the company has to decide whether to serve householders or institutions; whether to cater to those with low, medium, or high incomes, to buyers with conservative tastes or people who want the newest thing; whether it will make bedroom, dining-room, and living-room furniture, or

---

[2] For a fuller examination of management's role, see Dan H. Fenn, Jr. (ed.), *Management's Mission in a New Society* (New York: McGraw-Hill Book Co., 1959).

kitchen or recreational furniture. (The company can, of course, serve more than one niche.) A company manufacturing pneumatic rock drills must likewise visualize specific groups of users—men in coal mines or quarries, or men working for road construction companies, for instance—and then adapt its product to each of these markets. A company in the aluminum industry has to decide whether it will confine itself to supplying other companies with ingots and strip aluminum, whether to supply metal foil to the packaging industries or cooking utensils to housewives and/or the restaurant trade. A company *has* to specialize; few companies are capable of doing *everything* well.

The executives are looking for a niche (or niches) with several of the following characteristics—ideally, all of them. As already indicated, they are pre-eminently trying to find groups of customers whose needs will be expanding, who will buy more than in the past. In addition, the executives would welcome a niche in which the company can anticipate a wide margin between the prices the potential customers will pay for the product and the out-of-pocket costs of producing it. In a niche of this kind the company will enjoy an increase in the annual gross margin it has available to cover its overhead and profits. And in such a niche the company will be better able to survive a depression, for, if necessary, it can reduce prices to secure volume.

The executives would like to find a niche that is unique. Their task is to discover wanted things that other companies *will not* be supplying, not to ape the success formulas already adopted by others. And if they can find an infant market with large growth potentials and can fill it earlier than the competitors, they will gain the advantages accruing to a pioneer in that market. An ideal niche would be one that competitors cannot readily enter or, stated in positive terms, one in which a company can do a better job than its competitors.[3] In such

---

[3] I have profound confidence in the ability of medium-sized and small companies to flourish in the years ahead, despite the anxiety of some people about the steady growth of large corporations. (This does not mean, however, that I believe that they will automatically prosper; success rests on the ability of management—the ability to choose realistic niches and lay and execute plans to fill those niches.) There are numerous niches they can serve far better than most large companies. For instance, we saw earlier that medium-sized companies frequently have the advantage over large corporations in handling non-standardized products designed to serve the needs of small groups. In fact, some large companies (at least those in the industries with which I have been most closely associated: book publishing, livestock feeds, soy-bean processing, and meat packing) are more concerned about the inroads made in their business by smaller competitors than the possible encroachments of the other large corporations. In these industries, many of

a market, it can supply the customers' needs without undue strain; in fact, because of its competitive advantages, it should gradually secure a larger share of the available business.

Sometimes, new market niches are chosen in a hit-or-miss fashion. The company may, for example, accidentally secure a stray order from a buyer in a "foreign" niche at a time when it needs the business, and be tempted to seek more such customers. Or the company may discover a new use (or a new type of user) for one of its products. The outlook is promising. But unless virtually all of its departments can compete on an even basis with the firms already serving the niche, the company will soon be forced to withdraw.

Appraising the Company's Strengths and Weaknesses

In order to make realistic decisions about the specific market niche(s) the company should select, we try to foresee the consequences of entering the ones that promise the largest annual gross margins in the years ahead. We uncovered these in Chapter 12 (pp. 396–97) when we were predicting conditions *within* our company's industry—when trying to foresee which specific groups of customers would be increasing their purchases and would provide the largest gross margin per unit.

But we know that many of our competitors will also be soliciting orders in these markets. In fact, we can predict which companies will be our strongest competitors in each of the niches. Our earlier studies (p. 398–401) of the large and medium-sized companies in the industry gave us inklings of the dominant characteristics of their sales programs, product development work, and manufacturing practices in the period ahead. They will doubtless enter those niches (or continue in niches) where these can readily be employed.

Similarly, we seek market niches in which our particular assets or resources (our strengths) can be used to advantage and our shortcomings will handicap us least. We shall certainly wish to avoid a niche in which the industry's large companies or several companies of our own size have the advantage even though it otherwise looks very promising. Likewise, the discovery that there is a substantial market for a product is of little interest unless our company can fulfill that need. The discovery that there is, for instance, a large

---

the smaller companies have shown greater imagination in foreseeing special customer needs, more skill in catering to those needs, and greater drive in gaining the acceptance of their products; as a consequence, these companies together have been able to take over sizable segments of the markets formerly served by larger firms.

market among public utility companies for a method of removing scale from steam boilers is of no interest to a company unless it is capable of supplying that need.

An appraisal of the strengths and weaknesses of the company and its competitors helps the top executives visualize several of the significant consequences of entering each of the promising niches. These are readily brought to light by making a two-way comparison of the company's financial position, its sales organization, its product development men, its manufacturing department, and its top executives. First, we want to compare ourselves with our competitors; we want to know what kinds of tasks the people (and equipment) in each of our departments can do very well, what they can do only passably, and what they normally do very badly, compared with their counterparts in the large and medium-sized companies in our industry. Second, we want to know whether our handling of each of these tasks has been improving over the past decade, compared with our competitors', whether we have been just holding our own, or have been losing ground. The trends brought to light in this second way of comparison points to the company's activities that are likely to continue strong and those where we are losing ground and are likely to lose still more ground unless we take remedial action; we may decide we are so far behind we can never catch up, except at great cost, or we may decide to rebuild the department's personnel, and, perhaps, its equipment.

The questions which follow are intended to help the president and his associates embark on a realistic appraisal of their company.[4] Incidentally, the information thus elicited can be used again later, when we decide what changes we should make in each department and when the chief executive and treasurer set out to raise money to finance the new plan; the prospective investor will want to know the answers to these questions.

We begin with questions about the meaning of the trends during the past decade in certain items reported in the annual financial statements. Many of the company successes and problems begin to emerge when we compare these. The reason is that the trends in such items as the company's total sales, its variable and overhead expenses, and

---

[4] These questions are typical of those posed in the Administrative Policy course at the Harvard Business School when the students are analyzing a business case and planning a course of action. The Introduction to George Albert Smith, Jr., and C. Roland Christensen, *Policy Formulation and Administration: A Casebook of Top-Management Problems in Business* (3rd. ed.; Homewood, Ill.: Richard D. Irwin, Inc., 1959), contains an illuminating discussion of the approach used there.

profits, and if available, the trends in the sales and expenses of the company's separate product lines, serve as observable surface indicators of what has actually been occurring down in the operating departments; adverse trends are merely symptoms of deeper problems and weaknesses. These long term comparisons also may reveal that the company's financial position may become precarious unless the trends are promptly reversed.

I. THE ANNUAL FINANCIAL STATEMENTS

A. Operating statements

 1. How do the trends and cyclical fluctuations in our sales over the past ten years or so compare with those of the large companies and medium-sized companies in our industry? That is, have our sales been better or worse than would be expected in view of general business and economic conditions in the industry?

 2. What do the trends in out-of-pocket manufacturing expenses reveal? For instance, have the total annual costs of raw materials and direct labor been increasing or declining as a percentage of net sales? How does the trend in this *spread* between our sales and our variable manufacturing expenses compare with that of our large and medium-sized competitors?

 3. Are the manufacturing *overhead* expenses increasing disproportionately? Was this increase the result of a deliberate move, or have these costs gotten out of hand?[5]

 4. Do the trends in the company's gross profit from manufacturing look gratifying?

 5. What about the trends in the dollar amount, and in the percentage of net sales spent on selling and advertising? How do our trends compare with those of competitors? Ditto for the general administration and office expense. Did we *plan* these changes?

 6. Are the trends in net operating profits (both in dollars and percentage of sales) in line with those of competitors?

B. The annual balance sheets

 1. Have our liquid assets been increasing? What are the trends in the current ratio? What are the trends in the "acid test" ratio?[6] Are there any significant trends in the accounts receivable and in the inventory as a percentage of total assets and of sales volume?

 2. Is the ratio of notes payable and accounts payable to inventory and sales volume gradually mounting—in other words, are our creditors financing us more than in the past?

----

 [5] These *details* of competitors' operating statements are seldom published—usually, they are consolidated into one large item—but an experienced executive can make some useful guesses about such trends.

 [6] There are many other revealing financial ratios. Readers will find additional ones listed in almost any book on corporation finance.

3. Do the trends in the plant and equipment accounts indicate that we have been keeping abreast of competitors' expenditures for improvements?

4. In what balance sheet items are we better off and worse off than our large and our medium-sized competitors?

II. PRODUCTS AND PRODUCT DEVELOPMENT

A. The product lines in general

1. Is ours a dynamic, changing industry or a "settled" one as far as new products are concerned? Has the pace accelerated or slowed down over the past ten years? In general, have we taken the lead; or have we lost ground to competitors?

2. Have new competitors been developing products and entering our niches, or are firms leaving? How many of these are large companies from other industries, bent on diversifying their product lines?

3. Does our ability to compete against the products of other companies now depend more on patent holdings or on product design or on skill of workers? Are we losing these advantages?

B. Individual products or product lines

1. For which of our product lines have the market potentials been decreasing? Which have the brightest future?

2. Are there signs that the supply of any of the raw materials used in our products will soon dry up, indicating that we shall have to drop some of our products or else find substitute materials?

3. In which lines have we been doing a better job of anticipating customer needs and thus improving our position in the niches we are presently filling? In which lines have we been losing position? Have we been doing as well as competitors in finding replacements for product lines which are on the wane?

4. What particular features make our successful products more desirable than competitors'? Are we maintaining our position of leadership in these features, or are competitors catching up with us and forging ahead?

5. What kind of developmental work can our men perform best—and better than competitors?

6. What have been the trends in the past ten years in our dollar sales of each product line and in the proportion that each contributes to our total sales? How do these trends compare with the industry as a whole and with those of particular competitors?

7. What are the trends in the profitability of each line, and how do they compare? For example, which ones have been contributing an increasing amount each year to overhead and profits? Which have contributed more net *profits* after the assigned overhead has been subtracted.[7]

---

[7] Recognize the inherent limitations of these profit figures; the profits shown for each line are greatly influenced by the methods of allocating central office and manufacturing overhead to each product.

C. The personnel of our product design department

1. Who in our company has been taking the initiative in product improvements? How does the ability of this leader and of the specialists in the department compare now with that of our competitors? How did the men compare ten years ago?

2. Do the final decisions on products rest in the hands of men close to the necessary value premises; and do the men weigh these value premises, as well as the pertinent factual premises, in making their decisions?

3. Have the product design men improved their ability to develop products that the company's present sales organization (including its channels of distribution) can readily handle? Do they take into consideration the limitations of the company's manufacturing department? Do they know what these two departments can and cannot do? How does their ability and imagination in tailoring products to fit the customers' needs compare with their ability in prior years? How do our product improvements compare with those of competitors?

III. SELLING

A. Activities of the salesmen

1. What trends are evident in the number of active accounts? Are there any trends in the turnover of accounts—are we losing more customers than in the past, and which competitors have made the most inroads? Is there any increase in the number of new accounts added each year?

2. Has there been a decrease or an increase in the percentage of our sales to our top 10 or 25 accounts, and is this a result of a consciously pursued policy?

3. What have been the trends in the percentages sold direct and through dealers?

4. Have we been expanding or contracting the geographical area we serve; and have we been covering our potential customers in each area more intensely, or less? How does this compare with our competitors?

5. Are our salesmen better trained than formerly? How do they compare with competitors' salesmen in their ability to understand and resolve customers' problems, and to answer the unasked questions in the customers' minds? Are we controlling and directing them too much, or not enough—giving them less discretion, or more? Is this justified?

6. How does their morale compare with the morale of ten years ago, and with that of competitors' salesmen? What about the integrity of our salesmen? In communicating with customers and people in the office, do they have a tendency to distort the facts more often than they once did—to misrepresent—or are their statements more dependable? Is there any evidence that we are gaining or losing customers as a result of this tendency?

7. Have the relations between the sales department and the plant been deteriorating or improving?

B. Channels of distribution

1. Are we using jobbers, retailers, and manufacturers' agents as effectively as we once did, and have we been using these middlemen's salesmen as

effectively as competitors? Are there any significant undesirable or desirable trends in the percentage sold through each of these types of outlets?

2. Has our sales department become more successful in lining up new jobbers, retailers, and/or agents, and in inducing them to sell new products?

3. Are the employees of the channels of distribution we are using capable of transmitting to the consumers the premises we emphasize? Are they *willing* to do so?

C. Advertising

1. Do our catalogues and our consumer and trade advertisements serve the needs of the customers in our niche as well as they once did, and as well as those prepared by our competitors?

2. What about brand loyalty? Do we enjoy a growing reputation among certain types of potential customers—do more people believe our products will always solve certain of their problems better than our competitors' products, or are we losing that reputation to competitors?

D. Prices, discounts, and adjustments

1. What have been the trends in the prices the consumers pay for our products as compared with our competitors' prices? Are our prices consistently lower, or are they higher than those common in the industry; and is our price policy serving to increase the annual gross margin contributed by each product? Have we been making more price concessions, or less, than in the past?

2. How do the discounts (or the markups) we allow the various channels of distribution compare with those of earlier days, and with those of competitors? Are there any significant trends?

3. Do we adjust customers' complaints as promptly and willingly as competitors, or are we considered hard to deal with?

IV. MANUFACTURING

A. Changes in the character of the orders the department has been handling

1. Have lot sizes or lengths of runs in the plant been increasing or decreasing over the years?

2. Are the orders that are now put through more varied than in the past?

B. The plant equipment

1. Are we trying to use ill-adapted equipment—equipment that was originally installed to take care of orders quite different from those orders we described in A above? Have there been marked improvements in the industry's processing methods, and are we replacing our equipment at as fast a rate as most of our competitors?

2. Have we been altering the layout of the equipment to handle the changing character of the orders with a minimum of confusion and waste motion?

3. Have we been balancing our capacity and our sales, or do we have too much equipment for products that are drying up and too little for those

whose sales are increasing? Do we now have more bottlenecks than in the old days?

C. The workmen in the factory

1. What about the trends in labor turnover, in the number and gravity of the workers' grievances, and in the duration of strikes? How does morale compare, and has the union gained or lost influence with the men?
2. Have the informal groups and their leaders been working for or against the company? Are their status measures consonant with the welfare of the company?
3. How have our wage scales and fringe benefits compared with those of other plants in the area?
4. Has the percentage of skilled workers, by chance, been increasing, even though more of the work has become semiskilled? Are there any undesirable trends in average age?

D. The supervisors

1. Do the bosses have more ability now to cope with the factory problems and more interest in solving them?
2. How do their relations with their subordinates compare? Is there an atmosphere of strain? Have they been using more sanctions? Have they won authority and leadership?
3. Are the formal and informal communications improving? Have we been doing a better job of pushing the decision making down into the lower echelons in the plant and training young executives? Are we keeping up with competitors here?

E. Our ability to turn out the products required by the sales department

1. Are we meeting delivery dates and customer specifications as fully and as easily as we once did? Can we handle rush orders as readily as in the past? Is there more, or less, confusion in the plant—are raw materials and parts available, and are the production planning and scheduling more smoothly handled?
2. Are our costs of manufacturing individual parts in line with those of other manufacturers? Have we found it more and more profitable to buy parts from outsiders? Are we able to use more standardized parts than in the past?
3. Wherein lies the plant's greatest reputation in the trade—what can our workmen do best?

V. MANAGEMENT

A. The executives—top level and middle management

1. When seen in perspective, has management tended to push decision making down in the organization; or has it been inclined to centralize the control?
2. Have the executives become more imaginative, and have they been giving the company more of a forward thrust, more intellectual ferment,

than in the past; or have they been jogging along in the old routine? Are they more willing than competitors to take calculated risks—to enter new markets, for instance, or to expand the capacity of the organization?

3. What kind of reputation in the trade do the executives have for making wise decisions and keeping their promises?

B. The board of directors

1. Are the board members becoming rubber stamps, or are they increasing their contributions to the company? Have they been willing to ask more searching questions about proposed long-term company programs, about the environmental conditions the company will face, and about the ability of each department to carry out its part of a proposed program?

2. Are the loyalties of board members more divided than in former years —as a whole, are they working more in the interests of the company; or are their decisions influenced by a wish to advance their own personal interests?

Because most executives are harassed each day with a host of pressing, immediate problems, they fail to notice the almost imperceptible changes in the firm's physical and intangible assets which are brought to light by such questions. The key to an appraisal of a company's ability to compete lies in knowing the significant questions to ask about these trends. Among the men who do make a practice of examining trends, there is a tendency to confine their examination to the assets that can be measured and described in numerical terms—the tangible physical and financial assets. In the above questions, the quality of the invisible assets has been stressed, not only because they are commonly overlooked but also because they are usually of greater worth than the tangibles to the company.[8]

Choosing the Possible Niches

By the time the executives have visualized the forthcoming social and economic environment and diagnosed the company's comparative strengths and weaknesses, they will have some concrete ideas about the wanted and unwanted consequences of continuing in the present niche(s). And they will undoubtedly have formed some tentative ideas for several other promising niches[9] and accumulated an im-

---

[8] It is said that Andrew Carnegie once claimed that even if he lost all his money, plants, and equipment, he would be able to re-enter the steel business in a very short time, provided that he could retain his organization.

[9] The four main types of shifts in niches which a company can undertake are described in the next section of this chapter.

posing array of information, most of which will be useful in framing premises pertinent to one or more of the new alternatives. They are finally in a position to appraise the niches the company now serves and, if they find an opportunity in a better niche, to revise the company's intermediate goals to include this.

Listing and ranking the possible new market niches is a first step. Included here are descriptions of all the industry's promising markets, regardless of how effectively the company can compete for the business. An attempt to rank these markets, using as a basis the executives' consensus of which ones show the greatest promise, forces the men to examine and compare more thoughtfully the potentials of each.

A second step is to narrow down the alternatives. Those at the foot of the list, the ones with minimal growth potentials, can be discarded at once. Then the ones that can obviously be served more effectively by the large competitors or by certain of our medium-sized competitors would be crossed off the list. It is to be hoped that among those remaining, two or three will be worthy of further serious consideration—in which case, all the executives' travail will be well repaid.

A third step consists of imagining that the forthcoming environment has now arrived (imagining that they are already living in the period ahead), lifting their company over into that environment, and trying it out in each of these most promising niches. With their mental picture of the effects of each proposal on environmental groups and on the inducements and contributions of the several *member groups* in the company, and their forecast of where the competitors will excel and the peculiar advantages their company will enjoy, the executives should be able to foresee with considerable accuracy the effect on the company of the wanted and unwanted consequences of adopting each of the alternatives. Equally important, the executives are now able to determine whether they can transform the company into an effective competitor in those niches; they can now see which of the company's present assets must be augmented and whether some of the competitive weaknesses in the various departments can be remedied. Before reaching a final decision, they must feel confident that they can change the organization into one capable of performing the key tasks.

The picture of the company's advantages and limitations, and the changes that will have to be made in the company's present departments, forces the executives to be realistic in setting these long-term goals. It is their responsibility to set the goals at a level that challenges the organization[10] but demands no more of the men than they can produce when they are working at an efficiency level. The frustration accompanying an attempt to achieve an impossible goal, and the sense of failure when the plan that at first seemed so promising must ultimately be discarded, frequently drain the vitality of the men to a point where they thereafter prefer to vegetate. On the other hand, if goals are set too low, most of the employees, including the top and middle executives, will work at an adequacy level; they form the habit of handling their work perfunctorily. In both cases the morale suffers.

The company's welfare depends heavily on the market niche(s) it tries to fill. Its own annual gross margins in the years ahead will be strongly influenced by the annual gross margins available to companies which serve that niche—the expected sales volume, selling prices, and out-of-pocket costs of its industry, pictured in Diagrams 13A, B, and C, p. 380. And the expected trend in the size of the company's annual gross margin tells the executives whether they must begin dismantling their company, or whether they can start building for the future—investing *now* for returns that will probably not show up until later. For example, it gives them an idea of the amount of money they can safely spend on salaries for additional executives, supervisors, mental specialists, and salesmen—men the company will want to keep permanently; on the training of these men and of plant and office employees; on advertising and product development; and on interest, rent, and other long-term contractual obligations, including the reduction of mortgages. These decisions determine whether the company will be stronger or weaker in the future. Note, in passing, that the executives are here controlling the so-called "uncontrollable" fixed or overhead expenses by deciding ahead of time what they shall be—by planning these expenditures.

These are key decisions, involving large expenditures in money and time. If the leaders blunder—commit the company to niches in which it cannot compete, or to niches that are contracting—the consequences can be grim. Yet seldom are these decisions as irrevocable as they would appear. Actually, no experienced executive would consider launching his company on a long-term program involving its welfare in a major way without first making sure that the revamped company will be able to exist in the event that his predictions of the

---

[10] We encountered this same idea in exploring personal goals (see p. 116).

environmental conditions should prove to be wrong. Usually, the changes in the company can be so planned that they will be useful in case other less likely environmental conditions should develop and the company's economic goals must be revised.[11] Nor will the expenditures all have to be written off as complete losses in the event that the project proves to be abortive; in a majority of cases, at least, some of the newly acquired tangible and intangible assets can be used later.

Perhaps these safety factors explain why a good chief executive seems to feel confident about the outcome of a plan he proposes and why he can commit his company to a long-term program of great magnitude without torturing himself beyond endurance while making the decision, and without worrying unduly while the changes are being introduced. He also knows—and is urged on by the fact—that sometimes these basic decisions prove to be better than expected, even though the environmental conditions may be quite different from those anticipated.

SHIFTS IN THE COMPANY'S GOALS

Clearly, the most perplexing problem confronting executives bent on revising the company's long-term goals is to conceive ideas for more desirable ones. If they can think of none, any dreams they may have had of a stouter company will come to nought. We have by now accumulated a vast amount of pertinent information. This, when combined with the examples below should generate some of the sparks necessary to set off the creative process. The following pages also provide an overview of the several directions in which the executives may shift their company's goals—and these, too, may channel the mind into fruitful paths. The shifts available may be classified under four headings: (1) shifting the relative emphasis now placed on the goals of the various groups whose cooperation will be needed by the company, (2) filling its present market niche better than before, (3) shifting to a new niche, and (4) adding to the market niches the company now serves.

Shifting the Relative Amount of Emphasis Given to the Goals of the Several Groups Whose Cooperation Is Needed

We have already encountered one illustration of this first type of goal change—of a shift in the relative stress placed on the goals of

---

[11] Recall our discussion of flexible plans on pp. 350–51.

the various member groups which the company depends upon. We saw in the concluding section of the chapter on formal organization structure (pp. 326–27) that when raw materials and labor become scarce, the company usually increases its emphasis on achieving the goals of its suppliers and of plant and clerical employees by raising these departments to a point just below the president, and it reduces its emphasis on sales and lowers the level of that department because, under such circumstances, customers are usually hunting for goods and the department requires little help from the president. For example, in wartime, there are plenty of customers for refrigerators; the problem is to secure metal, parts, and man power, so the company is obliged to concentrate on furthering the goals of suppliers and workers.

Or the executive may decide that for the long-run welfare of the company, the weight now placed on the goals of the stockholders should be reduced. Over the years, most executives have held that the sole objective of a company is to maximize the profit for the owners. This is obviously an important objective; though individual stockholders nowadays seldom exercise much influence on the conduct of their companies, investors are nevertheless a very necessary group of company members, and a company must make money to survive. But investors are not the only group whose contributions are required and who must therefore be rewarded with enough inducements to persuade them to make those contributions. Sometimes, it is advisable to reduce profits and dividends, instead of maximizing them—to distribute more of the company's revenues to employees, executives, and suppliers, and/or to customers through lower prices.[12]

Or possibly, in the past, there may have been too little thought given to the goals of the company's bank, its transportation companies, the public as represented by the government, or the community in which the company is located. As we have seen, if the company is to prosper, it must serve some of the needs of *all* the

---

[12] Some readers may find the statements in this paragraph somewhat unorthodox. Teachers of economics, accounting, and almost all other business subjects say that *the* goal of a company is to maximize profits. In these pages, I too have frequently talked about profits—about increasing the annual gross margins and the planning of overhead expenses to ensure a profit. My own view, however, is that pointing to profits as a company's *sole* goal is a misleading simplification. Of course, businessmen must take profits into consideration in making decisions—but as I look back over my own experiences as executive and consultant, I now realize that although we (my associates and I) always spoke of profits in choosing among alternatives, we nevertheless also took into consideration the goals of all the other groups who contributed to the company, even though we seldom voiced these thoughts. One reason for our emphasis on profits was that we knew our associates would approve; it was proper behavior.

groups whose cooperation is necessary for its welfare; if a group thinks its inducements are unjustifiably low, its contributions will drop to an adequacy level—far below our expectations.

Filling the Present Customer Niches Better than in the Past

An examination of the premises pertinent to the three or four most promising alternative niches may lead the executives to decide that the company will best flourish by staying in its *present* niche. In fact, filling the present customer niche better than in the past—getting a larger share of the business—is probably a more common type of goal-setting decision than the three other types of goal changes we are investigating.

In those cases where the company's industry is expected to gain position in the national economy and its present niche in the industry also look promising, and when general business also seems destined to improve, the executives' problems are relatively simple. They can anticipate somewhat larger annual gross margins; thus, it is logical to set as goals an expansion in the size of the company and an increase in the share of the industry's volume. To implement these goals, the executives must determine the concrete steps they will have to take in order to gain this larger share and make certain that the company secures the needed tangible and intangible assets. (We shall explore this task quite fully in the next chapter.) For instance, the executives of a company in a new and flourishing industry which has sprung up as a result of the discovery of a major technological breakthrough (plastics, hybrid corn, electronics, and atomic fission would be examples) can anticipate a stream of further rapid improvements. To flourish in such an industry, they will have to place great stress on product development and improved manufacturing processes as means of attaining their intermediate goals. But before embarking on a large expansion program, firms in flourishing industries will want to double check their predictions of the level of general business.

The executives of a firm in an industry that is evidently drying up face a much more arduous task. To begin with, the company is probably already in a weakened condition. Nine times out of ten, the executives have failed to perceive the adverse trends in the industry's annual gross margin which largely account for the financial problems they now face. Nevertheless, they have become acutely aware that the going has been harder each year and that they have been forced by financial necessity to reduce the size of their company's operations. To pay their bills, they have cut expenses, probably on a catch-as-catch-can, day-to-day basis, hoping that something will soon turn up to solve their dilemma. In addition to reducing the labor and office forces and operating with old machinery, they have had to let most of their mental specialists go; product engineers, salesmen, purchasing agents, marketing research men, time study men, cost specialists, and younger executives have been dismissed whenever an opportunity presented itself, thus further reducing the company's ability to survive in the future. The executives now either do these tasks themselves or delegate them to subordinates who lack the necessary premises and are already overworked. Contracting the size of the company is a long and painful process, as anyone who has tried will attest. Executives are also loath to admit that they must cut back, for this proves that their earlier long-term decisions were wrong; these decisions now look like blunders. So it is understandable that the decisions to reduce overhead expenses are often made in a hit-or-miss fashion, long after the need has become urgent.

Nevertheless, the executives of firms in a declining industry need not stand transfixed, watching the specter of bankruptcy draw nearer and nearer. Usually, if the adverse trends are seen early enough, there is a solution that an imaginative executive can develop, a concerted over-all plan which will go a long way toward ensuring such a company's welfare. But a company like this will have to set goals that are quite different from those in an expanding industry.

One alternative, which requires fortitude, is to remain in the niche; adopt as a goal the orderly reduction in the size of the firm according to a definite program; and, at the same time, lay plans to strengthen the company to a point where it is equal to, or stronger than, the best of the competing companies. To maintain its sales volume, the firm must secure an increasing proportion of the sales of an industry whose sales volume is declining—no small feat if, at the same time, the company is to maintain its present gross margin per unit; the reason is that the competitors are also undoubtedly attempting to do the same things. To achieve these objectives, the executives will have to reduce the personnel and revitalize most of the sections in each department, perhaps replacing with new blood any unimaginative foremen or middle management executives to bring the company back to par.

A second way to cope with the problems of a company that has decided to remain in a waning industry is to wait out the contraction and at the same time keep the organization virtually intact—but this alternative is feasible only for companies with large cash reserves. Here, the expectation is that there will always be some customers in the niche, that most of the competitors will eventually close their doors, and that the company will thereafter secure most of the industry's sales. This program calls for liquid assets to finance operating losses over a period of years, and possibly money to purchase laborsaving equipment, to finance a change in plant location as a method of saving freight and labor costs, or to buy out bankrupt competitors. Some companies in the snuff industry followed this procedure; those who survived are now flourishing. In the flour-milling industry after World War I (the industry's capacity had expanded very rapidly prior to the 1920's), several smaller mills were either closed and left standing by the owners or sold to companies with liquid assets. More lately, the beer brewing industry has gone through this readjustment. As soon as an industry's productive capacity is reduced to somewhere near the new low level of consumption (we noted earlier that this may take 10 or 20 years), the surviving companies can expect a reasonably satisfactory annual gross margin.

A company facing a serious financial crisis will usually find that it is best to remain in the present niche. For instance, an almost bankrupt manufacturer of men's dress shoes would do well to set as its goal the grim one of survival—eagerly accept any orders it can readily find which will contribute a few hundred dollars to overhead, and cut out-of-pocket and overhead expenses to the bone. Were the executives to spend their precious time and money on finding and filling a new niche—women's style shoes, for example—the chances are that the company's creditors would force bankruptcy before the new objective could be accomplished.[13]

---

[13] Two reasons why companies run into financial trouble have been mentioned: the failure of the executives to recognize and adjust to the long-term adverse trends in their industry (or their inability to do anything about it if they *do* see the trends), and their tendency to reduce the size of the company in a hit-or-miss fashion when the financial pinch is felt. These situations can be remedied if they are seen before the company's liquid assets are exhausted—and most such organizations are worth saving. But a company in a dying industry which is *also* trying to serve a contracting niche in that industry, and *in addition* is losing position in that niche, faces a hopeless future. Here is concrete evidence that the executives are completely incompetent; they have been oblivious not only to long-term economic trends but to trends in the proficiency of the company's departments as compared with those of competitors; and, as a consequence, the organization has deteriorated to the point where it is incapable of competing. Manifestly, the goal should be to liquidate, or sell the company, before more losses are incurred. In the meat packing industry, one in which the margins per unit have been contracting over the decades, virtually all those packers who steadily lost position in the industry eventually went bankrupt or were merged with more successful competitors.

The majority of companies operate in industries and niches in which neither expansion nor contraction is anticipated. In those cases where the executives feel at home in their work and find it challenging, there is probably little reason for changing the niche; here, too, the goal of filling that niche somewhat better than before may be appropriate. Take, for example, a company in the garment trade industry which has been doing an intelligent job of designing and manufacturing daytime dresses for street wear by middle-income, middle-aged, slightly buxom women. (Note how specific this market niche is.) Such a company can expect a good future as long as its executives have the perception required to design dresses that will give the friends of their women customers an impression that they are reasonably young and attractive, that their taste is impeccable, and that their economic status is high. If the company can continue to design dresses exactly suiting the changing taste of these customers and can design more of these each succeeding season than its competitors, its share of the market will increase. To attempt to shift its niche —to design evening dresses for wealthy young debutantes, for instance—would probably invite disaster, primarily because these executives lack the value premises required to anticipate the tastes of those women.

Shifting into a New Niche

Although it may be feasible, in many cases, for a company to remain in its present niche even though it is expected to produce smaller and smaller annual gross margins—to stay on despite the shoals ahead—before so deciding, the executives may find it advisable to consider shifting to a new niche.

Shifting from one niche to another *within* the industry is probably easiest. The executives will never find that ideal one described earlier, but they may discover a market in which several of the company's assets can be used—including its trade reputation and the experience of its executives in making the decisions crucial for existence in the niche. Here are some examples: shifting from livestock feed to dog food; from a line of high-priced, beautifully packaged candies to a line of low-priced, simply packaged candies; from the manufacture of electronic equipment with the United States Defense Department as the sole customer to the manufacture of electric-eye door openers for home garages; from the manufacture of brass bellows used in the automatic mechanism for lighting gas stoves to the manufacture of thermostats used to control water temperatures in automobile radiators; from emphasis on the manufacture of complete pieces of equipment to the manufacture of replacement parts for that equipment (Electro-Motive Division of General Motors, manufacturers of Diesel locomotives, made this kind of shift); and from customers who buy in very large quantities to ones buying in small lots.

Shifting to a niche in an entirely different industry is another solution, though this ordinarily requires more capital—money to cover temporary operating losses. If the executives can find a new niche in which the company can use most of its physical assets as well as its intangible assets such as trade names, channels of distribution, sales organization, and managerial skills, the chances of success are high. Nevertheless, such a move calls for a great deal of planning and drive. The entire organization must learn a new business and must quickly become as proficient in decision making as the companies already in the field. Several well-known firms have succeeded in remolding their departments and entering a new industry. During World War I, Bendix Air Brakes Corporation moved into the aircraft field and, after the war, into the automatic washing machine field. Somewhat before that, E. I. Dupont de Nemours and Company had begun changing from gun powder, the sales volume of which was heavily dependent on wars, to the production of a wide range of chemicals and synthetic raw materials for industrial and home use. Lately, Armour and Company has been trying to shift to soaps and pharmaceutical products to offset the narrowing margins in the meat packing industry. After World War II, General Mills, Inc., attempted to enter the home appliance field in an effort to compensate for the steadily narrowing margins in the flour-milling industry. Apparently, it failed; at least, this product line was eventually sold to another company.

But both these types of changes in niche—a new niche in the same industry or one in another industry—will call for alterations in the company's activities. The company's products will usually have to be redesigned and new ones added to the line; the manufacturing department may have to be modified to handle the new orders; and in order to reach the new customers, the company may have to introduce major changes in the duties of the salesmen and in the character of its channels of distribution.

Adding Niches to Those the Company Is Already in: Diversification

For most companies, diversification, the fourth type of change in goals, is a somewhat less complicated step than any of the others;

and in most cases the chances of success are greater. Marketing a product that can be moved through the company's *present* sales organization and distributors and on through to its *present* consumers —a product that fulfills a somewhat different kind of need for those consumers—is a relatively simple way of entering a new niche; a toothpaste manufacturer adding a line of men's toiletries would be an example. The company embarking on such a program is nonetheless faced with two difficult problems. One problem is to secure research men (or editors or designers) capable of designing improved products for these new markets, each with desirable features which competitors cannot easily copy, and testing them in advance to make sure that they will be more acceptable than those already on the market. Another problem is the task of working out the "bugs" in the manufacture of the new products.

But a company that intends to diversify its market by serving an *entirely new* set of consumers—for instance, an oil company which now only supplies gasoline to filling stations, but intends to furnish coolants for machine tools—encounters a much more frustrating problem. In addition to the foregoing, it must set up a new sales force and entirely new channels of distribution. To build these requires years of patient work.[14] The purchase of another company or a merger offers a short cut to diversification, but the melding of the companies into a single integrated organization is not always easy. We need not go further into diversification except to mention the problems of a company facing a wartime situation.

During a war period the federal legislation controlling scarce raw materials, equipment, and labor is usually so framed, and the moral obligations are so great, that most firms are obliged to add a new niche to their present ones—to produce goods essential to the country's welfare. In choosing this temporary niche, the executives will need to think and plan in terms of two goals—the immediate goal of producing war materials, and the long-term goal of filling a suitable civilian market niche in the postwar world. To secure the premises required for choosing the dual goals, it is necessary to anticipate the environmental conditions the company will face in the postwar period as well as those during the war. If they plan to convert to the production of war goods, their task is to choose a type of government contract from among the many types available (that is, choose a specific near-term market niche) which calls for a labor force, equip-

---

[14] Near the end of the chapter on formal organization structure (pp. 326–27), we touched on the task of determining where in the structure to place a newly organized department to manufacture and market a new product.

ment, and an executive organization which the company can also use
after the war as a means of filling its *postwar* niche. And if they feel
constrained to expand the company because of the large volume of
business now available for the asking, they must also make certain
that they can later easily reduce its size—shrink the plant, man
power, and equipment—to fit the sales volume expected from the
company's postwar niche. Otherwise, their decisions will look shortsighted in retrospect; their new assets are of little value to them.
Executives who enlarge their company rapidly with a view to serving
a temporary market are frequently faced with the ordeal of reducing
its size and at the same time paying off the large, long-term financial
obligations (bonded indebtedness, for example) incurred to finance
the expansion, in addition to meeting the interest charges.

The executives of virtually every company either consciously or
unconsciously revise the firm's market goals periodically. The
changes made from time to time in the activities of the various departments are "seeable" evidence of this. Yet a man in a job located
far down in the organization's hierarchy seldom realizes that these
long-term decisions have been made and that management is now
implementing them. All he sees are the changes introduced in his
department, most of which seem pointless. In fact, he is likely to
resent the innovations because many of his status measures are destroyed and these new programs force him to make unfamiliar decisions. Whenever management adopts new long-term goals, it must
also lay plans to retrain the men and gain acceptance of new procedures.[15]

POLICIES DETERMINED BY THE COMPANY'S BUSINESS PHILOSOPHY

Our third type of policy, the company's pattern of behavior or its
business philosophy, likewise serves as a relatively permanent means
of furthering the company's welfare.

Companies develop characters and philosophies, just as do individuals. These are forged out of the company's cumulated experience
and its social and economic environment. They are the stored-up

---

[15] By now, it is evident that, chronologically, executives first anticipate the environment and set the long-term goals; then, they decide on the plan of action (the subject of
the next chapter) ; and finally, they attempt to gain acceptance of the changes. In other
words, chronologically, they first do the things discussed in Part III, then those in Part II.
Most of the human problems encountered in an organization arise as a result of decisions to make alterations in the company's program.

wisdom of the organization, the company's established ways of thinking and of doing things, the relatively permanent guide lines to
which the executives often refer when making their decisions.[16]

These are virtually never written down. When they are, they are
likely to sound pompous, in part because the ones chosen are not the
real policies. The executives may never even mention these; in fact,
they are likely to be amorphous ideas that have been handed down
and unconsciously learned by watching their superiors in the company. They learn that when they follow one of these policies the
outcome is successful and when they depart from it, many unwanted
consequences follow.

Over the years, the executives may have consciously or unconsciously evolved, and gained their subordinates' acceptance of, one
or more policies such as the following:

> To be a sharp bargainer and always drive for the best possible deal for the
> company.
> To think and act always in terms of the needs of our customers.
> To work with (or against) the labor unions.
> To be at the forefront in the development and marketing of improved
> products (or always be a follower).
> To encourage drive, creativity, and venturesomeness in the organization by
> setting new, exciting goals (or discourage this).
> To produce goods that are of medium grade (or quite low grade), which,
> though passable, are kept low in cost by cutting corners.
> To be a leader in the industry—to act instead of react, take initiative in-
> stead of merely trying to catch up with competitors.
> To be scrupulously fair to all employees and customers—moral integrity.
> To run the company conservatively, taking no chances.
> To inculcate the philosophy of change, of making changes in the com-
> pany's means of furthering its welfare: changes in its products, for exam-
> ple, or in its advertising practices.[17]

To try to enter a niche which is out of tune with one of the company's deeply imbedded policies is to court failure. An electrical
supply manufacturing company which has followed a philosophy of
concervatism in adopting changes would almost certainly fail in an
attempt to produce electronic equipment where technological change
is rapid. A company which has established high moral standards in
its dealings with customers and employees would have great diffi-

---

[16] Note the close parallel of this idea and the anthropologist's approach—the concept
of a social group's ideology which we explored on pp. 354–55.

[17] For a somewhat different approach to these ideas, see Manley H. Jones, "Evolving a
Business Philosophy," *Journal of the Academy of Management* (August, 1960), pp. 93–
98.

culty in competing in a market niche where it would have to follow unethical practices—collusion with other suppliers, or bribery of some kind—in order to secure orders.

It is very difficult to alter the established character and policies of a company. The top executives are obliged first to change their own patterns of thinking. To discard a long-followed philosophy of management, adopt another wholeheartedly, and use it constantly as a guide is no easy task. Equally important, they must teach the new philosophy to their subordinates, and do it by precept; they cannot say one thing and do another; middle management's and lower management's zones of acceptance for the new policy are likely to be rather narrow; hence it may be necessary to use sanctions as well as hard proof to induce wholehearted acceptance. Executives cannot expect to alter the company's character and policies by inserting self-laudatory publicity stories in the press, making pious speeches about the company's lofty ideals, and distributing booklets to employees and shareholders which make unjustified claims about the company's virtuous behavior.

It is now apparent that top executives decide on the company's intermediate goals in the same way as they decide on goals resting on lower steps of the staircase; they try to bring to light the most promising alternatives and choose the one (or ones) that will yield the greatest amount of wanted consequences and the least unwanted consequences. While choosing intermediate goals such as the types we have discussed in this chapter, however, the president must also necessarily be working out a plan to gain acceptance of the new goals as well as a plan for implementing them. In the next chapter we shall devote all our attention to implementing the company's economic goals: reshaping the departments into more effective means of filling the proposed market niche. But we must bear in mind that the success of his plan will depend on whether he can gain the wholehearted support of his associates and subordinates.

PROBLEM

DECIDING ON THE COMPANY'S LONG-TERM GOALS

1. Describe the market niches which Superb Biscuits, Inc. has been attempting to fill—the types of customers it has been trying to serve and the particular features of the crackers and cookies they were offering those customers.
2. What tangible and intangible assets does Superb now have; and how do these compare with what the company possessed in the eight or ten years

prior to 1957 and with those possessed by the large competitors in the industry? (Make informed guesses where necessary.)

Compare:

a) Its financial situation.

b) Its sales department and methods of distribution.

c) Its product development department and product lines.

d) Its manufacturing department.

e) Its top executives.

3. How do the market niches in the cracker and cookie industry compare:

   a) Which types of biscuits will probably increase most in sales?

   b) Which types of biscuits will probably yield us the largest gross margin per unit? Which the smallest?

   c) Which types of customers will probably expand their purchases most?

   d) Which types of customers will probably yield us the largest gross margin per unit? Which the smallest?

   e) Think about which combination of product type and customer type would yield us the largest gross margin per unit, and *also* think about the relative costs of selling to the various types of customers.

4. Among these niches, which ones will Superb be able to serve better than the large competitors?

5. On the basis of the premises you have now gathered, including those brought to light in answering the questions at the end of Chapters 11 and 12, and those you have uncovered when answering the above questions, what market niche do *you* propose for Superb?

6. Which type of goal shift are you proposing?

Chapter *14* REBUILDING THE
DEPARTMENTS
TO ACHIEVE THE
COMPANY'S GOALS

IN CHAPTERS 11 and 12, we were concerned with the task of anticipating the social and economic goals and behavior of groups outside the company. There we were employing a condensation of the five conceptual subsystems of decision making which we developed in Part I; but we added to it a new conceptual dimension, a new, rather complicated subsystem, to aid us in predicting the company's environment. In Chapter 13, we again used a condensed version of the conceptual framework of Part I and employed the premises we derived in Chapters 11 and 12 to decide on three types of long-term company policies: the role it should try to play in society, the market niche it should try to compete in, and the business philosophy it should adopt.

THE CONCEPTUAL SUBSYSTEM

In the present chapter we go a step further: condense and employ the subsystems developed in both Part II and Part I. And we shall impose on that framework another conceptual subsystem, a subsystem to be used as a tool for determining what changes we should make in the personnel and equipment now employed by each department. The objective is to plan an organization capable of coping with tomorrow's problems—to transform each department into a capable means of competing effectively during the next few years for a goodly share of the sales in the market niches the company has chosen.

Our superimposed framework consists of the following procedure for each department: (1) visualize the specific tasks it will have to perform unusually well (the ones in which it must excel if the company is to flourish), (2) conceive a picture of the ideal men, super-

438

visors, and equipment for carrying out those tasks, (3) compare the men and equipment now in the department with these ideal ones, and (4) decide what changes, if any, should be made.

We are now inserting real people into our plan—workers, supervisors, and top executives with both strengths and shortcomings. Obviously, we cannot expect to build perfect departments; people are human and compromises will have to be made; we are trying to attain an approximation of the ideal. Briefly, we shall be attempting to make realistic decisions about which of the present sections and departments should be strengthened, which can be cut down or eliminated, what new ones should be added, and which should remain unchanged because they are capable of handling their forthcoming problems. Our discussion of the changes to be made in the *equipment* will be confined to the manufacturing department, even though the other departments also use some equipment.

In this chapter we merely devise a plan, however. The *final* decision about the changes in each department's personnel and equipment will rest largely on whether the additional annual gross margin produced by these alterations in the company's departments will, in the long run, be greater than the additional annual overhead expenses incurred. The final decisions will be made in the next, concluding chapter after we have investigated and employed this concept.

Characteristically, manufacturing companies in the United States carry on seven major activities: sales, product development, manufacturing, personnel work, purchasing, controls, and financing. The top executives are charged with the responsibility for creating a near-perfect company by building departments capable of carrying out those activities. In this chapter we shall deal with each of these in turn, except for the financial department.[1]

Whenever we look into a department and take steps (1), (2), and (3) of the above mentioned four-step procedure, we find we have uncovered a great many premises of use in creating ideas for improvements in that department and choosing the most promising ideas. In order to perform step (1), namely, visualize the specific tasks each department will have to perform unusually well, we are obliged to recall in detail the nature of the company's expected social and economic environment and the specific characteristics of the market niche the company intends to fill. Our picture of the buying motives of customers in our market niche and our forecasts of our competi-

---

[1] Discussion of the treasurer's department will be postponed until Chapter 15 when we get into the company's financial problems.

tors' future behavior in the niche should be particularly revealing. This examination will point to the critical tasks that all companies in our industry must be able to perform unusually well, else they lose position in the industry and eventually fail. If our company is to flourish, we must see that the men and equipment in the departments responsible for those tasks are as good as, or better than their counterparts in the competing companies.

Here are some examples. In the livestock feed industry, the development of feeding formulas which will produce more pounds of meat than the competitors' feeds is usually the critical task; the task of selling—of finding potential farmer customers and passing the premises to them—is sometimes almost as important; manufacturing is a routine problem. In the book publishing industry the main job is to secure manuscripts for books that will interest large numbers of people. Selling, advertising, publicity, and manufacturing, though essential, are less important as means of achieving the company's goals. A furniture manufacturer, or a shoe manufacturer, or a rug manufacturer intending to shift into a niche in the high-fashion segment of the industry will have to strengthen its designing department and re-plan its manufacturing department to handle a wide variety of short runs. On the other hand, a manufacturer who intends to go into the low-price, high-volume segment of those industries must revamp and strengthen its manufacturing and sales departments to handle a volume of fairly uniform products. It behooves an executive to keep his eye on the *particular* things his company must perform better than his competitors in the niche and see that the departments assigned that task are equal to it.

Step (2), conceiving a picture of the ideal men, supervisors, and equipment for carrying out those crucial tasks, rests heavily on the creative process. Our task here is to visualize the specific characteristics and abilities that the ideal men and machines should have. We are trying to picture a combination of means which will *surely* be potent enough to carry out the crucial tasks more effectively than our competitors. Ideas for these begin to flow when we recognize our problem, start hunting for pertinent information, and on the basis of these, try to create a solution, create a perfect means or department.

Once in a while, when attempting to conceive the ideal group of men and machines, we may suddenly realize that some outside organization could carry out some of the crucial activities better than we. A company need not necessarily create all the means it requires. "Make or buy" decisions can have a marked effect on the financial success of a firm. It is frequently possible to buy the services of specialists who can do a better job than the company—to buy the services of wholesalers or retailers or of a truck line, or to buy certain standardized parts—and get a better job done at a lower cost than if the company had done the work itself. A company can also buy, on a temporary or permanent basis, the services of an advertising agency, a research organization, a bank, or a business consultant.

Step (3) in this conceptual framework, namely, comparing the men, supervisors, and equipment now in the department with the ideal ones we envisaged in (2), is a relatively straightforward task. We may find that some of the men and equipment in a department are already close enough to the ideal. These "good" departments will probably turn out to be the ones which we thought compared favorably with our competitors' and with the personnel of our same departments ten years ago (pp. 418–23). Recall that we chose a market niche in which we could fully utilize many of the abilities in which our company excelled. Hence, we doubtless already possess some men, equipment, and products that are fairly near the ideal for the niche we have chosen.

That two-way comparison also points to the places where each department falls short of the ideal. Or more exactly, it tells us where we are less effective than competitors and must either bring these up to par or be content with a slowly dying company.

Step (4) consists of deciding which of the men, supervisors, and equipment in each department should be retained, which will no longer be needed, and which should be altered. We are deciding on the size as well as the character of the department. Bear in mind that we shall probably want something less than the ideal we have pictured; securing the ideal may produce too many unwanted consequences. For instance, a group of ideal men and machines which would be potent enough to get customers' orders without fail might cost us more than the contribution they would make to overhead; or buying them might seriously deplete our cash assets.

When conceiving the changes, it is important to try to construct detailed pictures of the several departments simultaneously. It is, of course, essential to concentrate on one department at a time to avoid becoming confused. However, changes made in one department will almost always affect the other departments and these consequences must be weighed when deciding.

Before leaving step (4) we would, of course, attempt to test the plan ahead of time by imagining that all the changes in each of our departments have already gone into effect. The purpose is to see whether the revamped department's men, supervisors, and machines will be equal to the critical tasks ahead, whether the men will accept our proposed changes, and what revisions in the plan could be made to ensure their wholehearted acceptance. This examination often discloses unexpected shortcomings of the plan which can be corrected ahead of time.

Executives who follow such a conceptual framework when laying plans should succeed in building a reputation for laying *feasible* plans. This, in turn, establishes confidence in their leadership. In a company where new projects are hastily introduced and then either immediately revised or abandoned, the employees predict that accepting and carrying out *any* new proposal will prove to be a waste of effort, so they only halfheartedly back each new program and thus virtually kill it before it is launched. Frequent changes in programs also breed lack of confidence in the minds of the customers, channels of distribution, and suppliers. On the other hand, if management's proposals usually work out satisfactorily, a simple authority relationship closely approximating leadership is gradually established.

In this chapter, we shall be thinking in terms of a major overhaul of each department, even though this is seldom necessary. As a rule, such a drastic shake-up is required only if, in the past, the top executives have failed to perform most of the tasks discussed so far in this book and, as a consequence, the company faces a financial crisis. In such cases, to save the company, it may be imperative to bring in new executives, weed out the deadwood, cut the work force, and reshape all the departments in a major way, so that expenses can be cut immediately. But typically, the revisions in the company's activities are evolutionary in nature. Cumulatively, there may be many changes; but they usually consist of doing a little more of certain things the departments are already doing, and perhaps a little less of other things.

Once management has decided on the characteristics and the number of men required in each of the sections and departments (the task we embark on here), and once they have completed the tasks of selecting, appointing, and training the supervisors and middle-level and top executives for these groups (tasks that will be examined in the concluding chapter), putting the plan into effect becomes, relatively speaking, a formality. By the time the plan has been formulated and completed, most of the decisions as to necessary changes in the departments will have been discussed and agreed upon by the executives who are to put the changes into effect; the only step then required is a pull of the trigger by the chief executive. By then, each department manager knows exactly what changes he must introduce in the various sections of his department, which of his men will have narrow zones and which will have wide zones of acceptance, what the responses of the informal groups will be, and what type of authority he must employ in each case to gain the wholehearted acceptance of his subordinates. To achieve all this obviously takes time, but it is all a part of planning and putting the plans into effect.

RESHAPING THE SALES DEPARTMENT

Regardless of whether the company intends to strengthen its ability to fill its present market niche, or to change its niche, or to diversify its market, the chief task of the sales department is to induce customers to join the organization. If it fails in this, the company languishes. The large amount of money spent on selling and distribution in the United States indicates that executives consider these to be key activities. Estimates vary somewhat, but one reliable research group has calculated that about 60 per cent of the retail price of all the goods consumed in the United States is spent on selling. This was for the year 1929 and was an average; it included wholesaling and retailing expenses as well as the manufacturers' selling and advertising expenses, but *not* freight.[2] The percentage may differ somewhat today, but the main point here is that, in many companies, selling is the most expensive of its activities.

The objective of the sales department is to induce a particular kind of customer to join the company's organization. As we saw earlier, the company is looking for those customers who anticipate that the value they will receive when they buy the product (the inducements) will considerably outweigh the contributions they are asked to make —the costs in money and the trouble they must undergo—in buying and later in using the product. Moreover, the company seeks customers who want products that the company can produce at a relatively small out-of-pocket expense—low, that is, compared with the selling price these customers are willing to pay.[3] Under such circum-

---

[2] *Does Distribution Cost Too Much?* (New York: Twentieth Century Fund, 1939), p. 334. I know of no later equally extensive study. However, P. D. Converse in the "Puzzle of Marketing Costs," *Journal of Marketing* (April, 1957), p. 441 confirms these high costs. These data buttress what was said earlier about the large proportion of money spent by companies on communication; selling is largely communication.

[3] Farsighted executives will, however, also seek out certain orders which may show a loss—even an out-of-pocket loss—if they expect the customer's later orders to contribute to overhead, or if the sale of this "loss" item helps to secure orders for other products

stances, each unit sold makes a sizable contribution to the fund needed to cover the company's total overhead expenses for the period, and its profits. The larger the number of these customers, the greater the profits, and the greater the chances of flourishing.

The sales department also has the task of saving itself time by knowing which customers *not* to approach—those people whose inducement-contribution balance will probably *not* be improved by purchasing the company's product. To sell a customer who feels a strong loyalty to a competitor's product or who has little use for the product requires a great deal of proof and, in some instances, price concessions. More often than not, in such cases the sales effort ends in failure; or if it is successful, the success is temporary; there are no repeat orders.[4]

A sales department attempts to further the company's goal by performing some or all of the following tasks: (1) finding customers —individuals or families or companies—whose inducement-contribution balance is likely to be improved if they buy the product; (2) locating the *particular individuals* in the potential customer's organization who actually participate in deciding whether to buy our kind of product—one or more of the following: the father, mother, and/or children in the family; or an engineer, one or two production men, a financial man, and/or the purchasing agent in a company; (3) supplying each of these decision makers with lucidly stated premises which will help them decide to buy one of the company's products; (4) sending to their own company information about the needs of these potential customers; (5) making it convenient for the customers to buy, install, and use the product; and (6) making certain that the customers, after buying the product, do in fact secure the inducements they were led to expect, so that instead of vowing never to buy again, they will reorder and recommend the product to friends.

---

which do contribute to overhead (selling safety razors at a loss to get the blade business, for instance), or if selling at a loss is a method of entering a new niche. Narrow-visioned accountants sometimes insist that no order should be accepted unless it carries its proportionate overhead. Almost any company which rigidly follows this practice will eventually run into financial trouble; many premises beside out-of-pocket expenses and allocated overhead must be considered in pricing and in choosing what to sell and to whom to sell.

[4] Sales managers frequently hear from their salesmen that the company's prices are too high—" 'way out of line." This may, of course, be true, though the basic trouble *may* be that the salesman is trying to sell a customer who is wedded to the competitor; he is asking his company to lower the price asked—the contributions that the customer must make—as an easy way of closing the sale.

A sales department normally employs one or more of the four following groups of specialists: salesmen, channels of distribution, advertising men, and marketing research men. In medium-sized and small companies, some of the men usually serve as specialists in more than one field; for instance, the salesmen and the sales manager may do all the marketing research.

In making over these four "sections" of the sales department into effective instruments, an essential first step is to *be* the customers. One purpose is to discover the goals they are seeking to further when they buy a product like ours—the specific *buying motives* of each type of potential consumer. This will aid in choosing the premises that we should communicate to them. Another objective is to determine the typical *buying habits* of each group—whether they commonly buy directly from the manufacturer, through a jobber, or from a retailer, and why each group chooses to buy this way. Once these are understood, the characteristics and abilities of competent men for each of these four sales sections, as well as the number of men required in each, can be visualized rather concretely.

Making over the Sales Force

In most companies the salesmen are called upon to perform in varying degree all six of the sales tasks mentioned above. But the perfect salesmen for one firm during the period ahead may be distinguishably different from those of the ideal men for another company, because the relative importance and difficulty of these tasks will vary from company to company.

In one company the most urgent task ahead may be to locate prospective customers, whereas another company may already know all the customer prospects as well as the names and behavior patterns of the men in the customers' organizations who make the buying decisions. The former will require men with initiative, men who enjoy unearthing an unknown prospect and proving to him that he should buy the product. The latter company will need men who feel more at ease calling on known friends of the company who have already decided to buy—salesmen who like to follow a routine. In another company the most difficult job may be to prove to a customer that he should buy the company's product instead of a competitor's—this calls for a man highly skilled in the communication of premises. In still another firm (where the company manufactures to the customer's specifications) the salesman's task is to send back to his company a complete set of premises about the customer's needs (blueprints and specifications, for instance); this requires, perhaps, a technically trained man. And so on. A company's salesmen must be selected and trained with a view to performing the firm's critical sales jobs very well.

A company intent on improving its position in its *present* niche may set as its goal the molding of its sales force into a more telling tool than at present. Upon examining the probable buying motives and buying habits of the potential customers, and the probable sales programs of competitors, it may become evident that many of the present salesmen will not be able, because of temperament, or lack of ability or training, to perform their critical tasks as effectively as the salesmen working for competitors. In such a case the men with the requisite potentials would be kept and retrained; and new men who show promise of becoming perfect salesmen, can be selected and trained. And a determination of whether, under the new program, the sales force will need to spend more time, or less, in *total*, calling on the customers whom the company plans to solicit, provides a basis for deciding whether more or fewer salesmen will be needed.

Whenever a company plans to *change* its niche, a reappraisal of the present sales staff is a virtual necessity. The buying motives and buying habits of these new customers will undoubtedly differ in certain key respects from those the salesmen have heretofore been calling on; thus, it is probable that both the characteristics and size of the sales group will have to be changed considerably. And as we saw (p. 433), in those cases where the company is attempting to diversify its market, it may be advisable, for example, to build an entirely new sales staff alongside the old one.

The task of deciding on changes in the sales staff when the company enters a *new* niche can be clarified if we turn to examples. A company that has been making rotary pumps for the sugar industry and is now hoping to fill a niche in the oil-refining industry, will doubtless need salesmen with greater technical training than before. The men must be able to cope with a wide variety of more complex engineering concepts, and they must be familiar with the characteristic problems encountered in processing petroleum products. A company selling a standardized industrial product needs a routine man who will call on customers regularly; if it shifts to products that must in each case be designed to fit the customer's needs, it will need men gifted in the use of intricate factual and value premises. A company that has developed a new portable electric drill with special features such as high speeds and long life, and has concluded that customers would be willing to pay relatively high prices because of these extra inducements, will need salesmen who are self-starters, men who can locate prospects (go directly to machine shops in this instance) and use proof.

The salesman should also be reappraised when the company shifts into a new channel of distribution. After the electric drill just mentioned has become widely known and the company can safely change from direct selling to distribution through jobbers, the firm will need salesmen who can line up jobbers, induce the jobbers' salesmen to sell the item, and train them to do so—a job quite different from going into a machine shop "cold" and trying to sell. A livestock feed company which has decided to shift from selling direct to farmers to the use of wholesalers and retailers requires salesmen who can teach these middlemen to sell the product to farmers, a distinctly different —and more demanding—task than that of selling the product direct to the farmers. A refrigerator manufacturer formerly selling only through wholesalers who decides to sell direct to retailers not only needs more men, but men of a different kind; he needs men with a great deal of drive, who can work with the retail buyers in planning and executing sales promotion campaigns. Again, this is a task much more demanding than that of making sure that the wholesalers have ample stock.

These examples have been chosen to highlight the necessity of visualizing the crucial tasks the company's salesmen must carry out in the period ahead—carry out better than their counterparts in competing firms. The picture of the salesman's crucial tasks, in turn, provides a source of premises for deciding what the *perfect* salesman should be able to do well; and with this picture of the perfect salesman as a guide, the task ahead of selecting and training the men for the job begins to take shape.

Revamping the Advertising Department

The advertising men also aid in several of the six sales tasks mentioned. They can help to locate customers, help to supply them with ideas of the wanted consequences of buying our product, and also do something about keeping the customers as permanent members of the organization. As a matter of fact, in some industries—the cigarette industry and the soap industry, for instance—the advertising department, with the aid of the channels of distribution, does almost the entire job of selling; the company's salesmen play a minor role. But in any case, since advertising men can use only two communication vehicles—printed words, and words spoken over the radio and television—they are forced to confine themselves to the transmission of relatively simple premises. Their communication media—direct-mail circulars, catalogues, space advertising in newspapers and periodicals, electronic devices (radio and television), store displays, packaging designs, samples distributed to prospective customers, contests, and publicity stories—can be used in guiding the behavior of two important groups: the potential ultimate consumers and the employees of the company's channels of distribution.[5]

One of their tasks is to bring in leads—to induce potential customers to make their wants known to the company or to its middlemen. In some industries, as we have seen, locating customers who could profitably use the company's product is a major task; a company that sells *direct* to industrial buyers or householders uses advertising, in part, to induce these potential consumers to disclose their identity to the company so that its salesmen can call on them; and a company that sells through jobbers or retailers wants these potential consumers to communicate with a nearby middleman.

A second task is to communicate the wanted consequences of buying. In the chapters on inducements and contributions and on communication, we concluded that one of the central tasks of advertising is to transmit premises to potential consumers. The task of communicating premises to the company's channels of distribution—premises leading them to stock the product and make an effort to sell it—may be equally important.

Contrary to what many laymen believe, advertising does not necessarily produce increased sales volume. It is by no means true that the more a company advertises, the more it sells. Taking the country as a whole, my guess is that probably only one out of ten of the advertising campaigns initiated by companies produce enough total gross margin to cover the cost. The majority are discontinued after a brief trial period.[6] If potential consumers conclude that a company's product is not a desirable means of achieving their goals or

---

[5] For insight into the tasks of an advertising department, see Neil H. Borden and Martin V. Marshall, *Advertising Management; Text and Cases* (rev. ed.; Homewood, Illinois: Richard D. Irwin, Inc., 1959).

[6] This should not be read to mean that nine out of ten dollars spent on advertising in the United States is wasted.

that it is less desirable than a competitor's product, a battery of full-page advertisements, each containing all the proof a company can muster, will not change their minds. They simply ignore the advertising. Almost every company has learned this the hard way—by spending advertising money fruitlessly.

On the other hand, if the sales executive of the company finds that gradually more and more people are buying one of its products without much prodding—perhaps as a result of word-of-mouth recommendations or counter displays—he can usually expect good results from additional advertising. He can work on the assumption that the product is serving people's needs and that if the company communicates its proof to people who have not heretofore seen it, many will decide to buy. Advertising can also be useful, once near-saturation of the market has been reached, as a means of holding the company's loyal customers against the expected onslaughts of competition—to make certain that its proof is not supplanted by premises offered by a competitor.

After determining whether the emphasis should be placed on bringing in leads or on proving to people that they should buy the company's product, the executive is in a position to decide which groups of people should be sent the advertising messages, what premises should be stressed, approximately what proportion of the premises the advertising can carry, and which ones can best be carried personally by the salesmen. This helps him to form a concrete picture of the goals of the company's advertising section and, in turn, to determine the men's specific tasks in the period ahead: what kinds of advertising copy the men will be called on to prepare; whether more direct mail, or less, must be sent to ultimate consumers and channels of distribution (compared with last year); how much catalogue material will be needed; how much space will be used in trade magazines to reach industrial buyers and middlemen; how much and what kind of consumer advertising in local and mass-circulation media, and radio, and television will be required; and how much time will have to be devoted to store displays, packaging, and publicity stories.

Once the key advertising tasks are determined, the executive can create a mental image of the perfect section; then he can set about finding capable men either inside or outside the present advertising section. It may turn out that under the proposed plan the quantity and the nature of the work to be done may actually require fewer men in the department, or it may seem advisable to bring in an advertising agency—"buy" some of the advertising work rather than "make" it.

Deciding on Channels of Distribution

The company's middlemen, salesmen, and advertising men provide complementary means of securing consumer members. We have already seen that the character and number of these middlemen will have to be altered whenever the company changes its niche (p. 432). We want to place our products in the outlets to which customers habitually go for a product such as ours. Bear in mind that a company may decide to set up its own channels of distribution—its own branch warehouses and/or retail stores—but here, we shall assume that the company is "buying" the services of this "section" of its sales department.

Textbooks often list the following as some of the tasks or "functions" performed by the wholesaler, the jobber, the mill supply house, or the retailer: carrying stock, filling small orders, making deliveries, and taking credit risks. But, in addition, the company may employ these channels as active selling agents—induce them to find customers and pass premises to those customer prospects.[7]

Where middlemen are employed, a major task of both the sales force and the advertising men is to induce more outlets to perform these selling tasks and perform them more tellingly than in the past. For a company that is changing its niche, the first task of the salesmen and advertising men is to locate suitable middlemen and sign them up by proving to them that if they join, their additional annual gross margin will eventually exceed the additional expenses and trouble they will incur. We seek outlets whose salesmen regularly call on the potential consumers in the niche the company has chosen (they sell complementary lines of merchandise; thus the middleman's additional selling expense is kept at a minimum), and one whose salesmen are willing and able to communicate to those customers the wanted (and unwanted?) consequences of buying the product, thus maximizing the outlets' (and the company's) sales volume in the area.[8] The objective here is to see that each new middle-

---

[7] The discount given middlemen is generally commensurate with the amount of selling they are asked to do. This discount is their "pay" and also an "expense" to the company.

[8] Retailers and mill supply houses who carry and display a product also provide the prospective consumer with *an opportunity to gather premises by examining the product*; they do this in addition to passing premises to him orally.

man becomes a loyal member permanently wedded to the company's organization.

Once a middleman has joined the company's organization, his salesmen must be shown which consumers to approach with the product and what premises to employ, so that they can spend their time effectively. In those cases where the tasks of selecting and signing up distributors and training their sales forces loom large, it may be best to employ field supervisors or missionary salesmen who are specialists in this work rather than leave it to the regular company salesmen. In any event, the changes cannot be expected to "just happen." They have to be planned for, and men capable of doing the job must be assigned to the task.

Marketing Research

The funds allocated to the entire sales department are customarily divided among salesmen, advertising, channels of distribution (in the form of discounts),[9] and marketing research. Marketing research ordinarily takes a fraction of one per cent of sales. An examination of the allocation of these funds may disclose that sales volume could be increased with no commensurate increase in total expenses if the marketing research men were assigned some of the dollars now being spent less productively on projects carried on by the other three sales sections. For example, some of the money spent on advertising in the least productive magazines might be used more effectively on marketing research. At the same time, the executives should be aware that marketing research men cannot furnish watertight answers. The data they gather is at best only an approximation of the real facts; and in any case, these data provide only a portion of the premises the executives must use.

The central task of marketing research men is to aid the company in expending its money and efforts wisely. They can help the sales executives to channel the efforts of the salesmen, the advertising men, and the middlemen with a view to getting greater sales volume per dollar spent. If the marketing research men also have solid, practical training as economists, they can gather information about economic-competitive trends which the top executives may use in deciding on changes in the company's niche. In addition, they can furnish useful premises to other departments, such as product development

---

[9] The amount of money spent by a company on discounts may be determined by computing the *retail* value of the goods the middlemen buy from the company and subtracting from that the company's net sales to those outlets.

and manufacturing, as we shall see later. Most medium-sized companies require no more than two or three men; but when this is the case, it can be seen that the personnel must be unusually versatile.

Marketing research men can assist the sales manager in gathering a great many data pertinent in making sales decisions. For instance, they can help determine the number of potential consumers in a niche, what their typical buying motives and buying habits are, how many are located in each sales district, and what their buying power is—and they can sometimes furnish estimates of the competitors' respective sales volumes. From company records, they may determine past trends in the company's sales of each product to each specific group of customers. Items of information like these provide either cause or result elements for some of the premises required for setting sales quotas, comparing salesmen's expenses (these will be discussed when we take up the topic of controls), directing the advertising dollars, re-deploying the sales force, and reshaping the channels of distribution.

It is sometimes possible to appraise the results of new sales and advertising programs which are being tried out. However, since a company's sales volume is produced by employing several means simultaneously—salesmen, advertising, channels of distribution, packaging, and pricing, for instance—the decision about whether to extend the new advertising program must be based largely on value premises. It is virtually impossible to measure the effect of any *single* one of these means with accuracy.[10]

In planning the tasks and personnel for marketing research, the executive needs to start by determining what additional market data would be of most value to the sales manager, the product development men, the manufacturing department, and the chief executive. After eliminating the studies for which data are not readily available and ranging the remainder according to the usefulness of the information and the magnitude of the task of gathering the facts, an executive can gain some idea of whether the section should be enlarged or reduced in size, and what kind of men will be required.

An ideal marketing research man would need some very special qualifications—and men with all these qualifications are hard to find.

---

[10] Lyndon O. Brown, *Marketing and Distribution Research* (rev. ed.; New York: Ronald Press Co., 1955), and Donald D. Crisp, *Marketing Research* (New York: McGraw-Hill Book Co., Inc., 1957), provide useful insights into the tasks that can be performed by marketing research men. Unfortunately, some companies use marketing research men almost solely to adduce proof for use in advertising that their product is preferred above all other competing brands.

First of all, he must be able to visualize the key decisions the executives are to make and what relevant information he can furnish them. A man who cannot do this is virtually useless to the company. He will also have to be imaginative about possible sources of information. Usually, he can secure basic data from published sources; and there is often a great deal of information lying buried in company records. At times, it may be necessary to conduct a market study by means of interviews. The man needs to have some sense of how much time he should spend gathering the information, too, and whether approximate figures which could be easily gathered will serve almost as well as accurate ones. But more than that, a perfect research man would make concrete proposals to the executives and be aware of the task of gaining acceptance of them. His central task is to help the executive to make decisions that will stand up when they are reappraised three or five years hence; to do this, he must be more than a mere tabulator of data. One of the chief weaknesses of marketing research men is that they tend to employ in their premises only the figures they gather; they eschew value premises. Consequently, when they recommend a course of action, their proposals sound impractical. But the majority do not even bother to propose courses of action; they simply hand the executive a set of figures and hope that he will have the time and the intelligence to dig out relevant premises from the data.

In our examination of these four sections of the sales department, we have devoted most of our attention to determining the critical tasks the men will have to perform and to visualizing the perfect men (or outside organizations) for the jobs. Once this has been accomplished, it is relatively easy to compare the company's present personnel with the ideal. At this stage the executive can pinpoint the men who measure up, reshuffle or eliminate the inadequate men, hire new ones, and train this near-perfect personnel.

And now while we have in mind all these changes in personnel, we should pause to estimate the cost of the extra annual sales department overhead, if any, under this plan. (Bear in mind that it is still subject to revision.) The expenses will consist of additional salary and advertising incurred by the sales department. We shall want these figures in Chapter 15 when we try to determine whether the plan will bring in more than it costs.

The work of the four sections of the sales department is closely related to the work in the product development department, to which we turn next. In fact, many of the ideas about customers' goals and premises that are employed by the product development department are gathered for it by the sales department. If the sales group does not pass these on, it is failing in one of its vital tasks.

BUILDING THE PRODUCT DEVELOPMENT DEPARTMENT

Every company has, or once had, a product development department—in fact, if not in name. It may not now be active; most of the work may have been done by the founder before the firm was actually established. In some companies, this work is done by two or three salesmen, the executives, and a few skilled craftsmen who are able to put together a working model of a newly conceived product. Or the department may be the one that writers in the field of marketing usually call the *merchandising department*—the group of men who decide what items to include in the fall line, how many to make, when to reorder, and when to drop an item. In other companies the group is labeled *product design,* or *engineering,* or *research,* or *the research and development department,* or *the designers,* or *the editorial department.*[11]

We are already aware that the primary task of a company's product development department is to conceive products that will meet the needs of the consumers in the company's future niches, and meet them better than its competitors. However, the nature of this department's tasks differs sharply from company to company. In some firms the department must turn out a great many new products each year—scores of new books or new styles of fabrics, or hundreds of specially designed pieces of equipment. In other companies the objective is to launch only two or three new products designed for a mass market.

All product development men must employ the creative process, but the amount of creative ability demanded of them varies widely. In some companies, their work in the period ahead will consist of creating ideas for small modifications in products that already closely fit the customers' needs; women's slips would be an example. Other companies may need men capable of highly creative work—capable

[11] In some companies the men are charged with all three of the tasks mentioned in our earlier discussion of the forthcoming technological improvements in the industry (pp. 402–4)—improving the raw materials, revamping the processing equipment, and designing new products. In these pages, attention will be centered on the third task. The premises that were gathered when trying to anticipate the company's forthcoming technological environment should prove useful in deciding on the character of its product development department.

of conceiving quite new solutions to the problems consumers face or of anticipating needs that the consumers in the niche have not yet thought of; these might be long-term projects requiring five or ten years of development work.

In these days the future welfare of *all* companies depends heavily on the development of new products. Money spent in this manner can often go a long way toward improving a company's position in its industry and its profitability. In many companies, a portion of the money now spent on relatively unremunerative activities carried on by other departments will, when transferred to product development, produce increased sales volume and lowered costs, just as was noted in our discussion of marketing research activities.

Many executives have difficulty in converting a product development department into a smooth-running, effective instrument for advancing the company's goals. Consequently, we shall here go into the problem rather fully and re-employ several of the concepts already developed.

Understanding the Goals of Men

To most executives the product development department is enigmatic and perplexing. The specialists in this field appear to be both temperamental and unpredictable, and they often seem confused about what they are supposed to do. They frequently go off on tangents, bent on pursuing projects that the top executives feel sure will never be of any worth to the company. What is more, the practical results of their work are often disappointing. However, in a majority of cases the trouble that management encounters with its product development department lies not with the design men but with the top executives; some executives who have come up through other departments in the company make little attempt to understand the research men.

Once the top executives perceive the goals and premises these men regularly employ, much of this perplexity disappears. The scientists, engineers, or artist designers who go into industry—including those who are highly creative and temperamental—are just like other men in that they have certain personal goals which are strongly influenced by their past and present environment. Here are some broad generalizations about such men—offered, however, with some misgivings, because obviously no two men are alike. Their professional training is typically the salient feature of their environment, and they draw many of their premises and goals from this. Consequently, their zone of acceptance for a project will usually be narrow if it lowers their professional status, even though it clearly advances the company's goals. If they are assigned only routine tasks, they feel that their status in the profession and the company is endangered. They also believe that practically all their premises should be drawn from their professional training. Indeed, they are not particularly interested in any others; hence, they often appear naive about the premises employed by the company executives, such as, "If we adopt this research man's proposal, the costs will be so high that we can't sell it."[12]

The most creative men are ordinarily dedicated to the task of creating novel ideas or products which may be of value to *mankind*. If this also helps the company, so much the better. Their status among their professional associates is measured by these contributions. Earning a very large income or rising to the presidency of a company, two among the many conventional methods of gaining status commonly employed by businessmen, is relatively unimportant to them. In view of all this, it is little wonder that executives have difficulty in understanding and directing their research men.

Building a Hierarchy of Formal Authority

Selecting a department head for these men calls for above-average perception. Their superiors must be adept in the use of proof; the men who have been trained as scientists or engineers are taught that proof is the only admissible type of authority. Typically, these specialists—including those who design products with a view to enhancing aesthetic appeal—will pay little attention to a supervisor who has not won his leadership from them. They seldom respond to attempts to use simple authority, and they will rebel at the first hint of sanctions.

Imposing upon them a department manager who is unfamiliar with their frame of thinking leads to frustration and rebellion. In their eyes, his decisions will almost always prove unwise because he fails to give due weight to the goals and premises they consider important. They also have difficulty in making themselves fully understood by such a superior. They customarily use a very precise professional vocabulary; hence, explaining their own premises to the uninitiated

---

[12] Louis B. Barnes, in *Organizational Systems and Engineering Groups* (Boston: Harvard University, Division of Research, Graduate School of Business Administration, 1960), brings to light many of these goals and conflicts. Similar conflicts are felt by marketing research men; see Leo Bogart, "The Researcher's Dilemma," *Journal of Marketing* (January, 1962), pp. 6–11.

is extremely difficult. Also, the premises they use are very complex; and few of these men have been trained to organize and express their premises lucidly in laymen's words. Moreover, some scientists and engineers are rather contemptuous of value premises, especially those having to do with human behavior; they feel that these are irrational or emotional and should be suppressed.

Yet they need guidance in their projects, and need it badly. In some cases this guidance may be provided by asking their department head and two or three of the research men to work directly with management in deciding what products to develop, what each product's characteristics should be, and how much research money to spend on each.

Finding a suitable head for such a department is a difficult task. Ideally, he should understand the men's personal goals and be able to assign projects to the men that will advance their goals as well as the company's goals. He should also be familiar with many of the reliable premises they each commonly use in their specialized fields; or, at least, he must be able to grasp them when they are explained, so that he can help the men to solve their problems. And he should know how to explain the company goals and the part each project is to play in the over-all company program. What is more, he should be adept at giving recognition and showing approval—two powerful sanctions. And he has to be willing to push much of the decision making down into the hands of the men. In view of the character of these specialists and the difficulty—and urgency—of finding the right superior for them, it is not surprising that the executive frequently becomes exasperated with the research and design men and disappointed with the work they do. Almost all of the difficult problems we were discussing in Parts I and II of this book are encountered here in acute form.

Deciding on the Crucial Tasks of the Department

As a result of those ten-year comparisons we made of our own and our competitors' products and product development men (pp. 419–20) we have probably already accumulated some concrete ideas about the crucial tasks ahead for our company's product department. In the following paragraphs, we shall look at a few characteristic tasks of an engineering research department. For convenience we shall set these down roughly in the sequence in which they would be performed. In practice, we would list (or rank) these on the basis of which will be the most essential product development tasks our company will have to perform in the years ahead; this will determine the kind of personnel we shall need.

Conceiving new ideas for wide-margined products which will be widely bought, and deciding which ideas are promising enough to warrant development, constitute a first step and usually a key task for every company. However, we shall not assign this task solely to the product development men; finding new products is so important to the welfare of the company that we shall encourage all members of our organization to think up ideas and shall ask the top executives or a new products committee to decide which ones to pursue further. We shall digress briefly to look into these product decisions.

The product ideas in their original form need not necessarily be practical, but they should at least serve as sparks in initiating the creative process. Sometimes, customers make concrete suggestions for improvements in the company's products. In the case of producers' goods, inventive-minded men down in the customer's plant frequently discover that a slight change in the product would improve its efficiency. In the case of consumer goods, retail salespeople and men working for jobbers often make penetrating suggestions as a result of watching a mass of merchandise flow through their departments and hearing the comments of customers. The company's salesmen will often possess the insight necessary to visualize a new and needed product or to see where improvements can be made in the present product. The executives, especially if their minds are directed into this path, frequently come up with usable proposals. Inventors sometimes bring in interesting ideas. The men in the product development department, as a result of living constantly with the products, are always getting ideas for more suitable products— and theirs is the job of turning the impractical ideas of others into practical ones. Trade shows, articles in trade magazines and professional journals, and observation of trends in the character of new products being marketed by competitors and analyses of those products will sometimes provide the spark needed. Once in a while, it is possible to buy (or merge with) a young company struggling unsuccessfully to market a promising product.

Although marketing research is still an imperfect tool for predicting what the customers will need and what they will do about buying certain new products, it can sometimes produce information of signal value in making product development decisions. It is not indispensable, of course; products were developed and marketed long before the 1920's, when marketing research first came into its own; and hundreds of products are still developed and introduced successfully without benefit of marketing research. But these men can gather some helpful near-facts about consumers' probable reactions where few or none existed before—for example, which among several proposed products certain types of customers would choose, which features they like best, and what price they would be willing to pay. Remember, though, that these are sampling estimates of people's wants *in the recent past or the present;* hence the executive must extrapolate them into a picture of future demand in deciding on products; a man or woman who tells a poll taker, "I would buy that," may decide differently when faced with the *actual* decision about buying.

This initial step in deciding on the crucial tasks of the company's product development department—namely, this step of gathering ideas for new or improved products—necessarily includes decisions as to which ideas (which alternatives) to select. Department heads can be very helpful; since every new product decision affects the activities of all the departments, they should be able to foresee most of the wanted and unwanted consequences of adopting each proposal. And they can also tell whether their own departments will be able to cope with the problems they would face if the new product were adopted. Recall that when we discussed the possibility of shifting into a new niche and of adding niches (product diversification, pp. 432–34), we saw that we would have to make several changes in our departments.

The chief executive will usually be the man qualified to make the final decisions about new products. He is (or he should be) the one with all the necessary premises, and he is in a position to weight the departmental premises objectively.[13] But the decision does not stop there. In those cases where the product requires months or years of research and experimentation, it is the chief executive's responsibility to check the progress periodically and, when necessary, either redirect the work or discontinue it. As time passes, it may become evident that the demand will be smaller than anticipated, or that competitors have already developed a product with attributes similar to the one envisaged, or that the men have encountered some unfore-

---

[13] Note, in passing, that neither the chief executive nor the subexecutives can ever be entirely certain; their premises are scanty, and most of them are of a value nature; hence, their decisions will frequently prove unwise.

seen problems of design or manufacture, problems they have little hope of solving. But these last-named decisions will come later; let us return to the present.

By the time the new product has been chosen, the executives should have accumulated enough premises to enable them to take a second step—namely, to build a reasonably clear mental image of the characteristics of the new product, so that the design men can picture a concrete goal. Objectives such as, "Design furniture that will sell," "Design a better engine," "Develop a more effective antibiotic," "Create a new dress design," "Formulate a better livestock feed," or "Create a more tasty sausage," are too vague to be useful. The executive must see that the men have such information as the following: where the product is to be used and who, specifically, will use it; the day-to-day conditions under which it will be used, including ways in which the owners and operators may misuse it, and information about the limitations imposed by those considerations; the difficulties the consumers have encountered in using the competing products; and what the product should be expected to deliver to the user, in numerical terms wherever these "deliveries" can be measured, or in descriptive terms where no measurements are available. At this stage the executive and his developmental men are attempting to visualize the product as though it were already manufactured, and are "watching" it perform for a customer who has bought it. Thus, picturing in the mind's eye the details of a product that does not yet exist becomes a crucial task of many product research departments.

Simultaneously, the executives and research men are imagining it being fabricated and assembled and are trying to estimate the probable out-of-pocket costs for its manufacture in small volume and in large volume, assuming that the company's present equipment were to be used. In addition, they are trying to visualize the selling price the company can charge and what the out-of-pocket costs *should* be if the company is to secure an adequate margin, so that they can get a rough idea of each unit's contribution to overhead.

A third step may be to isolate and describe, as far as possible, the really knotty problems the product development men will encounter when designing the exterior (aesthetic) features or the interior (mechanical or chemical) features—the ones for which few known solutions are yet available. In a company determined to achieve product leadership, solving such problems will likely be the critical task. Initially, the men can safely lay aside the problems of design which have already been solved by others. The details of these can be worked out later.

The top executives will have very few premises to offer here; but they should sit in on the discussion, so that they can gain insight into the magnitude of the unsolved problems and determine whether the expected developmental costs will be justified. Sometimes, the research men already know what *procedure* they will have to follow in solving these problems; in cases of this kind, they can make some fairly accurate estimates of the size and the character of the tasks ahead. But where the problems lie at the frontiers of knowledge— at the frontiers of science, for example—the magnitude of the job can seldom be foreseen. They may succeed in inventing the idea rather quickly; but, in any event, the creative act cannot be hurried. Indeed, the experts may never find a useful solution. It is almost impossible for them or for anyone else to foresee the character of all the problems they will encounter, much less foretell the results. However, once the men have isolated and described the most difficult unsolved problems, they can anticipate what they will have to do and can thus channel their mental resources.

The three above-mentioned steps (finding and selecting product ideas, conceiving a mental picture of the product, and solving the knotty design problems) must also be thought through by executives who intend to ask an *outside organization* to handle a design problem. Executives frequently decide to approach a public or private research organization with a request to develop a new product simply because they have read that "research is a good thing." If they have only a vague idea of what they want done, if their goal has not been formulated in detail, they will probably be disappointed in the results. The experienced research organization can usually form some tentative idea of the time required to carry through the research, make an estimate of costs, indicate the results that may be expected, and proceed with the work with a minimum of fumbling once the company executives have thought through these three steps.

By the time these three preliminary steps have been taken, the executives of a company should be able to foresee in a general way what the department's chief tasks will be. One company may decide that the men should concentrate on the development of distinctly new products. Another company may conclude that the men should concentrate on bringing their present product line up to date. This would be a perennial task of a company in an industry where technological changes are continuous. Recall our discussion of this

problem when we tried to foresee trends in our company's technological environment (pp. 401–4). The executives may suspect that
some of the new raw materials or new parts recently put on the market should be tested and incorporated. Or the crucial task may be to
improve the interior mechanisms by incorporating recently developed technological improvements.

The objective in the foregoing instances has been to increase sales
by designing products that will fit the needs of the customer better
than competitors' products. But in another company the product department's crucial task in the period ahead may be to reduce manufacturing costs. These are not either-or objectives, of course; good
designers will always work with one eye on the customers and the
other on the abilities and limitations of the manufacturing department. Where cost reduction is paramount, the men might redesign
the product with a view to using lower cost raw materials or standardized parts instead of parts that must be specially manufactured.
Or they may try to see that unnecessarily tight tolerances are eliminated; that drill holes are changed to fit the drill presses; that
stitching is changed to save the time of the seamstresses; and that
parts are altered to ease the assembly job. They can also usually
make small revisions in the design, so that it will not be necessary
to tear the product apart in order to make repairs.

Before the product is actually announced to the trade and put into
production, models need to be tested.[14] Frequently, when the solutions to the separate design problems are brought together into one
"package," some unexpected and undesirable effects of one upon
the other come to light. In a food the vitamins may be reduced or
the texture or color may be undesirable; in a chemical formula using organics, unpredicted new carbon or benzine compounds may result; in a machine the vibrations may become unexpectedly violent.
Most of these can be checked in the laboratory. A second type of test
—testing the model under actual *working* conditions—is all too
often overlooked, or else hurriedly performed, possibly because of
the pressure to launch the product immediately. Whether the men are
designing a hat or a steam turbine, a piece of furniture, rubber
footwear, a new medical product, or a new type of processed food,
field tests often bring to light unwanted consequences that were not

---

[14] During the developmental period the sales department will have been at work selecting a suitable brand name and package—suitable, that is, from the customers' point of
view—and laying plans to launch the product.

observable in the laboratory or shop. Many companies jeopardize the future of their new products by marketing them prematurely. If the "bugs" are not removed before the product is offered, the resulting bad reputation makes the selling job unnecessarily difficult, even though the weaknesses are rectified as soon as they are discovered. At the other extreme, the research men sometimes insist on perfection before releasing a new product, in this way jeopardizing its sale by permitting competitors to establish their own similar new product.

Finally, it may be necessary to organize a group capable of effecting a smooth transition from the research stage to the stage of regular production.

Deciding on the Personnel

The picture of the key tasks ahead in product development serves as a basis for building or rebuilding the department. However, the character of this department in a company that expects to launch only a few products—perhaps no more than two or three a year—will probably differ markedly from the product development department of a company that must depend on a continuous stream of varied products for its existence. Personnel for three types of departments will be discussed here.

The first is the personnel for what might be called a skeleton department. Sometimes, medium-sized companies which plan to develop three or four products a year find it advisable to hire only one or two permanent men and to engage outside organizations for the actual designing. In this way, some of the problems mentioned below can be minimized or avoided. The chief responsibilities of the company's product man (or men) under such a plan are to keep management informed about new developments in research which might prove useful or injurious to the company, to help in the planning of projects that should be undertaken, to place the developmental work with the outside organizations best qualified to handle each phase of the project, and to follow up and coordinate this research work. Armour Research Foundation in Chicago, Mellon Institute in Pittsburgh, and Batelle Memorial Institute, Columbus, Ohio, are among the independent, nonprofit organizations engaged in scientific and engineering research. Some trade associations have established viable research programs. Also, the science departments of some universities will accept research projects (projects that lie close to the frontiers of knowledge are especially welcome); and there are several commercial concerns which specialize in product research.

Not all companies can get along with a skeleton department, however. In those industries where technological improvements are rapid, most companies—even those that expect to launch only two or three basically new products a year—find that they must carry on their own development work to keep ahead of competition. In this second type of department the tasks ahead demand design men who can perform highly creative work. The main problem here is to secure the necessary wide variety of inventive talents. The company needs depth of knowledge as well as variety of knowledge—several specialists—and, frequently, a good deal of expensive laboratory equipment. Added to this problem is the tendency of research and design men to run out of ideas; sometimes, a man's ability to create seems to dry up for reasons no one can fathom. As a result, new blood must be brought in periodically and the unproductive men transferred to other departments or encouraged to seek jobs elsewhere. Although the problems of maintaining an even keel in an unstable department such as this sometimes seem almost overwhelming, it is possible, by constantly shifting the personnel, to create a department capable of solving the design problems lying ahead and at the same time to adjust the size of the staff in accordance with the size of the projects they will be handling.[15]

In these cases where the company's development department will be responsible for creating solutions to problems requiring highly creative thinking, the executive's task of visualizing the ideal men and then selecting them is obviously quite complex. The character of the knotty problems the men will be called upon to resolve in the months and years ahead is difficult to predict and define concretely; and even after the executive has conceived a picture of the perfect men for these jobs, the tasks of comparing the present personnel with those perfect men, and of training and selecting new men equal to the job ahead, present serious problems. In choosing new

---

[15] A large company with diversified manufacturing facilities and several sales organizations can more readily afford to employ a large, permanent product development group capable of handling all of its problems, for in many cases the unexpected discoveries the men turn up can be used some time, somewhere in the organization, or the invention can be leased to other companies. But those companies, too, have a constant problem in maintaining a high level of creative activity among their product development men.

personnel, the executives will usually have to rely heavily on the recommendations of outside experts in the field. And they, too, can make mistakes.

The character of the third type of developmental organization—a company-operated design department which is to be responsible for turning out a large number of new products during the year, most of which will be adaptations of the company's basic products to meet the varying needs or changing tastes of the customers—can be seen much more readily. For instance, in companies selling machinery or electrical goods specially adapted to the customers' needs, these product men would have to be able to interpret the specifications sent in by the salesmen, secure additional information from the customer when necessary, question information that seems illogical, search through the files for designs already created for other similar applications, conceive the changes required, prepare the drawings and specifications, set up a list of materials and parts, and submit this information to the price-estimating men and the sales department for further action. A determination of whether these tasks will be more complex in the future, or less, provides premises necessary for picturing the ideal men for this department and enables the executive to compare the present members of the staff with these ideals, decide what changes in personnel will be required to convert the department into a more perfect one, and estimate how many men will be needed.

Before deciding on changes in the character of the design men, we shall doubtless want to appraise the group's present leader. To do this, we would need to think through his crucial tasks, visualize a perfect leader, and compare him with our present head. Possibly we shall need a new man. (Recall that in Chapter 1, we observed a president who was trying to find a replacement for the head of his product research department [pp. 418–20].) Finally, we shall want to estimate the additional annual overhead costs, if any (mostly salaries here), and try to judge whether these changes will make an annual contribution to overhead in excess of those costs.

REBUILDING THE MANUFACTURING DEPARTMENT

Although executives have to deal with a large number of detailed problems in reshaping the manufacturing department into an instrument for serving the proposed company niche, these are probably reasonably familiar to most readers of this book. Consequently,

we shall here paint with broad brush strokes, confining our attention to the main, over-all problems.[16]

Picturing the Expected Orders and the Department's Goals

By first imagining that the sales department has already been rebuilt, that the product development department has been recast, and
that the new or improved products have already been redesigned,
and *then picturing the nature of the orders that will henceforth be
sent in from old and new customers by the salesmen each day*, the
executive can lay a realistic foundation for refashioning this department. These images of the orders provide premises for answers to
questions like the following; and these, in turn, help to determine the
goals and character of a near-perfect factory for the period ahead.
Will the orders that will have to be handled by the plant call for a
wider or a smaller assortment of processing and assembling activities? Will they require the manufacture of more small lots, or will
there be more long runs than before? About how many of each
variety of order will have to be run through the plant each day or
week? Will the orders necessitate greater manual skill and greater
precision in the equipment, or less? Inasmuch as the character of
only a portion of the orders will differ from those received in the
past—and even these may not differ radically from the old—the
task of imagining their nature may be less difficult than might at first
appear.

Picturing the expected daily orders as they will flow through the
plant and imagining when the orders for new products will begin
coming in provides a basis for deciding on an *immediate* goal for the
department—decisions as to what changes are to be made in personnel and equipment, and the date when these should be completed.
These changes, however, are actually a means of achieving the department's more *permanent* long-term twin goals: (1) to get into
the customer's hands the exact products they want when they want
them, and (2) to produce these products at costs comparable to those
of competitors—the costs here being the out-of-pocket expenses plus
departmental overhead such as supervisory and equipment expenses,
and the salaries, if any, of industrial relations men, industrial engineers, or cost accountants, attached permanently to that department.

Gaining the plant personnel's acceptance of the first-named of these

---

[16] See W. Warren Haynes and Joseph L. Massie, *Management: Analysis, Concepts and
Cases* (Englewood Cliffs, N.J.: Prentice-Hall, Inc., 1961), for an unusually illuminating
examination of the use of management concepts in the plant.

twin goals, serving the customer's needs, is frequently a troublesome problem. Usually, the foremen and superintendents think their sole goal should be to keep the costs of production down. This accounts for some of those divisive conflicts between the plant and sales department mentioned earlier. When the sales department says, "We must change this product," or "This order must meet these unusual requirements and be delivered by this date," the manufacturing department's expenses usually rise. In the eyes of the plant superintendent this is an unnecessary expense, which not only jeopardizes the company's welfare but his own; he is afraid that he will be criticized because of the excessive costs. Nevertheless, if the company is to flourish, the factory men must be taught to be sales minded; the goal of giving the customer what he needs is often more effective than expense saving as a means of furthering the company's goal. The responsibility for teaching this will probably rest with the chief executive.

The factory has three major means available for achieving these dual goals—its physical plant and equipment, its workers, and its plant supervisors. All must be reappraised and where necessary, reshaped into more telling means.

Reshaping the Plant and Equipment to Fit the Expected Orders

The purpose in these next few paragraphs will be to point to some sources for pertinent premises the top executives need in deciding on the nature of their company's future physical assets. An investigation of possible locations for the plant, the size of the plant required, the character of the equipment the company will need, and its layout, provides a body of premises which the executives can weave together in conceiving an image of the perfect plant and deciding what alterations should be made in the company's present factory in order to convert it into something approaching the ideal.

Plant Location. When the new program calls for rather extensive changes in the character of the equipment and buildings, the executives are presented with an exceptional opportunity to reappraise the location of the plant. Ordinarily, it is impractical to think seriously about moving because of the expense. In some industries the location of a plant, however, may have a marked effect upon the company's ability to compete. Studies of the industry's economic trends in each of the several *regions* of the United States will often uncover premises pertinent to decisions on plant location. These may disclose that, almost imperceptibly, the present local sources of the company's raw materials have been drying up. Or such studies may disclose that the industry's manufacturing capacity in the area in which the firm is located will soon greatly exceed the raw material supplies available locally, or exceed the total *local* demand for the industry's products. Or they may show that the bulk of the consumers who use the company's products have moved to more distant locations. If any of these trends have set in, the executives may expect rising freight costs for themselves and correspondingly lower freight costs for competitors more strategically located. Or it may become evident that the kind of labor the company will need in the years ahead can only be found in good supply at a new location. These slow-moving changes, over which the company has no control, can profoundly affect three of its major out-of-pocket costs—costs of raw materials, freight, and labor—and, therefore, its gross margin per unit. As we saw in Chapter 4, operations research models may provide insights for plant location decisions. The model, however, will need to allow for these trends.

These environmental changes, together with operations research studies to determine the least costly location for a company attempting to fill the niche the executives have chosen, provide premises for reappraising the location of the plant. Yet a decision to move must be based on more than whether the proposed site will offer the cheapest combination of inbound and outbound freight costs, and low labor costs. For example, quick deliveries may be of supreme importance. And it is necessary to gain the acceptance of the executives who will be uprooted. Those whose wives and children are reluctant to leave their friends and relatives may resign, and the contributions of some of the men who decided to move with the company may be unexpectedly low—unless (or until) the families find a satisfying niche for themselves in the new city.

Size of the Plant. The size of the building and the amount of the equipment needed can usually be planned with considerable exactitude for a short period ahead—a year or two, for example. This decision as to size rests on a prediction of the expected sales volume, in physical units, for each product.[17] The executives can usually project next year's sales volume of each item in the product line with fair accuracy—the approximate increase or decrease compared with the past year's sales—and they can ordinarily anticipate the

---

[17] This estimate of sales in units can be used a second time in setting up the company budget and the departmental budgets, as we shall see in the next chapter.

seasonal variation in these sales.[18] Premises are furnished by an examination of past trends in the company's sales of each product, the nation's expected business conditions, the expected economic situation of the households or the industries the company has in mind as consumers, the new plans the company's sales department has laid for increasing (or decreasing) the sales of each item, and a prediction of what competitors will probably be doing about each type of product.

Once this sales estimate has been made, the executives can determine approximately how many of each of the *parts* for each of the finished products will have to be produced during the year, and how many each week. This then provides premises for deciding on the amount of machine time required for each type of product and its several parts, and thus for deciding on the character and amount of each type of equipment needed during the next year or so. As we shall see later, it also enables the company to predict what changes must be made in the character of the labor force and its size, so that provision can be made for selecting and training the men ahead of time.

Planning the size of the plant and equipment over a long-term period is patently much more complicated than planning the size for the next year or two. It may be possible to foresee the long-term trends in the volume of the industry's product which the nation will consume, but it is very difficult to predict whether another industry will develop a new product which can be substituted for ours. And it is equally difficult to foretell what percentage of our niche's business we shall secure in the next several years. About the only thing an executive can do is to try continually to anticipate economic-competitive conditions, as we did in Chapter 12; to revise his ideas when new conditions emerge; and to keep his capacity in line with his expected sales, making allowances, however, for anticipated cyclical fluctuations in general business conditions and the seasonal fluctuations in his own sales.

The Character of the Equipment Required. Whatever the location decided upon—and the decision may either be to stay, to move the entire company, or simply to establish a new branch—and whatever size the company's plant is to be, when the company's niche is

---

[18] Some of these estimates will be too high, of course, and others too low; but these errors tend to cancel one another. Thus the sum of the estimates of all the units will be more accurate than the individual components.

changed or redefined, the character of the equipment will ordinarily have to be reshaped.[19] In deciding on the equipment changes, we are trying to form a mental picture of the orders as they will move through the plant in the future, and thus to determine what jobs the equipment will have to perform day after day if the department is to turn out those orders promptly and at the lowest cost.

As we have seen, typically, the *medium*-sized company's goal is to fill a quite specialized niche. The orders such a company secures will ordinarily call for short manufacturing runs of a variety of nonuniform products. Indeed, most medium-sized companies enter this particular type of niche because few of their large competitors can profitably handle this kind of business. True, a medium-sized firm may be able to produce some of its *standardized* parts continuously the year round; and the same would be true of any large-volume product in their line. For these, they can employ a few highly specialized, semiautomatic or fully automatic machines; often, these machines must be made to order.[20] But typically, in these companies the orders received will be so varied in character, and the size of the runs will differ so widely, that versatile, multipurpose equipment capable of handling short runs rapidly and requiring a minimum of setup time will be needed. Only in this way can the plant produce at competitive prices.

After observing the expected orders as they will move through the plant and "watching" the specific tasks the machines will be called

---

[19] In the ensuing paragraphs, we shall be using for illustrative purposes a metal-fabricating plant, so that the reader will have to adjust the terminology to that of his own industry. Nevertheless, I have tried to frame the statements in such a way that they will be applicable to all types of industries, regardless of whether they fabricate and/or assemble pieces or parts to secure a usable product (machinery, clothing, pharmaceutical, electrical, or furniture industries, for example), or take things apart (meat packing, oil refining, lumber, and mining industries, for instance).

[20] Automation—the use of mechanical, electronic, or other devices as a substitute for machine operators' muscles and machine operators' decision making in the factory—can be employed to advantage by plants that expect to produce a uniform product in very large volume over a period of years, by companies that can expect automatic control devices to pay for themselves and pay the salaries of the mental experts they require, through savings in out-of-pocket expenses as a result of lower labor costs and a reduction in defective parts. These devices are used in two ways: (1) to guide a single machine in performing a series of operations on a part—positioning, fabricating, and discharging the piece, for instance—or in assembling several parts and seeing that this work is performed according to predetermined standards (quality control); and (2) to tie together the several machines through which the part moves in such a way that it is conveyed from one machine to the next without human guidance. The ideal in (2) is to convert the plant into one huge automatic machine, made up of many integrated though separate machines —a plant that presumably could be operated from a single control panel. In the paragraph above, we are concerned only with the first of these two—automation of the tasks performed by the separate machines.

on to perform, the ideal set of processing and materials-handling equipment can be visualized; and this picture can be laid alongside the company's present equipment. Once this is done, it soon becomes evident whether more, or less, of each type of equipment will be necessary and what new equipment must be bought. In some cases, it may become clear at once that a certain machine will seldom be used, or that a new and somewhat different piece of equipment must be bought.

But the decisions about whether to buy new machines or use the old ones are not always obvious. These less-evident decisions on equipment purchases rest on several factors; usually, the considerations that must be given greatest weight have to be based largely on value premises. One of these is the decision as to which of two machines—the best new one, or the one now owned—will produce the more desirable product in the eyes of the customers we expect to serve. A second factor is a decision as to the probable obsolescence rate of the equipment—what its usable life will be.[21] Once the second factor is determined, we can use engineering economy studies to learn which would be least costly. (See pp. 100–101.)

Equipment Layout. The layout of the equipment also must be based on the size of the expected orders. Although a medium-sized company can sometimes economically employ a full-scale production and assembly line similar to those described in most textbooks —one that is set in motion on January 1 and runs continuously through December 31 and, possibly, one that is highly automatic— it is not necessarily true that these will cut production costs. Actually, a job-shop type of layout, where each kind of equipment— drill presses, shapers, grinders, punch presses, for example—is located in its own separate room, may turn out the company's orders more speedily and at the lowest cost. Or what is sometimes called a *modified* or *flexible* type of production and assembly line may be the answer, one that combines certain features of the two extremes just mentioned. A flexible line can usually be employed where each order differs in certain respects from every other order; yet each one also requires the same *types* of parts and also, perhaps, some standardized parts which can be purchased outside or can be produced on

---

[21] Many companies set up a rule that every new piece of equipment must pay for itself in savings within a given number of years (three years, or six, or ten, for example) to guard against possible heavy loss from obsolescence. That a uniform formula of five years or ten years cannot be rigorously applied to all investments in new equipment is, of course, apparent; some machines will serve the company for only a year or two, while others will apparently be useful for twenty-five years.

specialized automatic machines and stored. In this case, the fabrication of the nonstandard parts is performed as the orders move through the plant and the standard parts are then fed into the assembly line. The central idea in plant layout is to take as much advantage of specialization of equipment and division of labor as the orders will permit and, at the same time, keep setup time at a minimum. Also bear in mind the possibility of arranging the layout to encourage the formation of informal groups in the hope that the members may adopt status measures that are congruent with the manufacturing department's goals.

Generally speaking, a company planning to fill a market niche that will absorb a *larger* volume of standardized products than the company has heretofore produced can shift its layout more toward a full-scale assembly line and greater automation. Conversely, if a wider variety and shorter runs are expected, the plant will obviously need to be shifted more toward a job-shop operation. But the changes in the character of the forthcoming orders *may* call for shifts in both directions—one section of the plant may be laid out as a flexible line and another as a job shop, each designed to take care of a distinctly different type of order. In any event, the layout is by no means irrevocably fixed, because most machines can be moved. The layout can be altered whenever the predominant character of the orders changes.

In the foregoing paragraphs, we have briefly noted some of the premises for deciding on the physical plant—its location, size, equipment, and layout. The cost of the proposed changes can readily be estimated. And the resulting savings in the labor cost per unit can also be computed. Thus we can estimate whether the additional annual contribution to overhead resulting from the change will exceed the added overhead expense. But all too often, the company fails to gain the expected savings from these innovations, even though they have been planned with great skill, because the executives have neglected to plan with forethought the character of the men and supervisors needed to handle the new kind of work and have failed to gain the men's wholehearted acceptance of the changes.

Rebuilding the Personnel in the Manufacturing Department

In reshaping the labor force and supervisors, and in determining the number of each type of men who will be required in the plant, the executive's first task is to picture those manufacturing jobs which will have to be performed extremely well in order to secure and keep the customers the company intends to solicit. Once this is clear, the kinds of manual skills needed in the labor force and the amount of decision making required of the men doing each job can be determined in some detail ahead of time. This is based on the images of the specific tasks the individual workmen will have to perform. A company planning to shift to longer runs, for example, has the task of recruiting more semiskilled help—probably young men and women who can be quickly trained to perform repetitive jobs, and whose abilities and ambitions are rather limited. As a minimum, however, they must be able and willing to discharge tasks in accordance with the "best way" formulas worked out by the motion and time study men.[22]

When the images of the ideal men (or women) for each of these jobs are laid alongside the present employees and their skills, many premises come to light for deciding which "unusable" men should be transferred to other sections or departments; which ones, if any, should be asked to seek work elsewhere because they are incapable of filling any of the jobs; and what kinds of new men and women must be hired.

In changing the duties of workmen, an executive frequently overlooks the possibility that even though they may be able to handle the new work very well indeed, their zones of acceptance may be narrow because they foresee that their inducements will be reduced or that the contributions they will be asked to make will be greater than at present. They may rebel because they feel that their status is endangered. Trouble obviously lies ahead if some of the company's skilled craftsmen, who have been accustomed to a variety of work and have regularly made a majority of their own decisions, are asked to perform semiskilled work. Or placing skilled men next to the unskilled help, or next to women, may in their eyes forebode a downtrend in their future welfare. But giving a man a job that is too difficult can be equally disastrous, even though he and his friends may look upon it as a promotion. As he futilely attempts to master the job, the tension mounts.

The reactions of the plant foremen to changes in their responsibilities are probably more often overlooked by executives than the responses of the workmen. These men are not equally at home in every type of foreman's job. The foreman of a machine shop, for example,

---

[22] This work of determining the "one best way" to perform each job and the plans for new equipment and improved layout determines, in part, the tasks ahead for the industrial engineering men—provides premises for deciding on the character of these specialists and the number needed, a subject that we shall explore when we discuss controls.

is ordinarily accustomed to making his decisions with a rather free hand; his tasks are characteristically those of passing out the work, seeing that it is done on time and according to specifications, and helping the individual workmen to gather the premises and make decisions. His incoming paper records are fairly easy to understand because his department requires few premises from outsiders and most of these can be transmitted orally. Typically, the reports he prepares are also relatively simple. Asking such a foreman to supervise a production assembly line, or even a flexible line, frequently leads to trouble. In this kind of job, many of his decisions are made *for* him by the production scheduling men and by the motion and time study men, so that he feels less essential than before. His status is lowered, and his contributions drop. Moreover, he finds the work more frustrating than before. To him, the decisions of the mental specialists frequently seem ill-advised; he accepts them with misgivings. The task of supervising a line also calls for more care in coordinating the detailed work of the operators. And he finds the job harder because he now employs premises handed to him on pieces of paper rather than premises he picks up by talking or by observation. Furthermore, he must make more elaborate reports than before; and, for him, paper work is difficult.

In the preceding paragraphs on personnel changes, we have dealt with the task of changing the character of the work force and their foremen in a company that is shifting toward standardized products which can be sold in larger volume; but essentially the same problems, in reverse, exist when a company is planning to shift away from mass-produced products to more specialized ones calling for shorter runs. In the latter case the chief task is to train the workmen and supervisors to make more of their own decisions.

This concludes our rather sketchy examination of the problem of rebuilding the manufacturing department. By the time the executives have completed this thinking process, they are in a position to stand back and view all of its several features as parts of an integrated organism. They now know the location and size of the plant they want; they can see in place the equipment they have chosen; they can visualize well-trained workmen operating the equipment; and capable supervisors.

Plans for changes in the character of the other mental experts— the industrial engineers, quality control men, and accounting men, for instance—who are to be charged with helping the manufacturing department will be investigated in the concluding section of this chapter, the section on *controls*. But before going into that, we shall look briefly at the industrial relations department and the purchasing department.

REBUILDING THE INDUSTRIAL RELATIONS DEPARTMENT

Having seen the changes that are to be made in the manufacturing department, we now have at hand the premises for deciding what changes, if any, should be made in the personnel-industrial relations department. In our minds, we see the workers' and foremen's crucial tasks in the years ahead; the picture, based on this, of the ideal workers and supervisors; a comparison of the men in the plant with the ideal; and the decisions as to what changes in jobs and personnel would be desirable.

This begins to define the character of the key tasks ahead for the personnel or industrial relations department and thus the types of men which will be needed there, as well as the size of that department. A prediction of the magnitude of their tasks of hiring and training men, shifting men from one job to another, settling labor grievances, and negotiating labor contracts rests on the premises drawn from an understanding of the trends in workers' attitudes toward their employers, and the other ideological as well as legislative trends discussed in Chapter 11, in addition to those uncovered by living inside the workers' skins.

In a company with high employee morale, low turnover, and few changes in work assignments, we would probably want a very small department, manned by men who have worked in the plant and who have a penchant for settling quarrels between workers, an ability to deal with unions, and only a mild interest in initiating a major overhaul of the work group. On the other hand, if we expect many changes in factory personnel and work assignments, the personnel men's critical tasks will be decidedly different. Here we should want more highly trained men and more of them. For in this case the factory's informal groups will be in a turmoil and they will probably adopt inverted status measures based on the amount of harm each man can do to the company.

Changes in the operators' jobs are likely to cause dissatisfaction in spite of careful attempts to revise the plan to fit the workers; thus, during the transition period, management can expect shop stewards and union officials to take an active part in protecting the interests of union members. Trying to gain acceptance by using a combination of the five conceptual subsystems explored in Part II should help in winning the wholehearted support of most of the men. The executive's job of building a personnel or industrial relations department capable of keeping the labor force on an even keel will not be further amplified in these pages, but this does not mean that it can be overlooked.

REBUILDING THE PURCHASING DEPARTMENT

Nor need the revisions in the purchasing department detain us long, not because these men's tasks are unimportant, for in some companies this department must be among the strongest and largest, but because the approach to be used is much the same as in the four departments we have already examined.

The character and size of the critical tasks lying ahead of it, as in the previous cases, determines how the department shall be altered. Obviously, a shift to a product using raw materials unfamiliar to the company, or an increase in the variety of the raw materials needed, or a decision to buy parts that were heretofore produced in the plant, can markedly increase and complicate its tasks. The same is true if the company plans to use more raw materials which must be bought from many small producers, or more that fluctuate sharply in price. The group's work is especially crucial in times of shortages. The department is a key one in a company where the raw materials and purchased parts constitute a large percentage of the selling price of the product.

The vital job of controlling raw material inventories to see that supplies are always available when needed, and yet not so large as to jeopardize the company's liquidity or cause inventory losses in the event of falling prices or as a result of obsolescence, is frequently assigned to them. We shall explore that part of their task when we discuss controls (p. 485–86).

On occasions when the decisions to purchase equipment, raw materials, or parts will be of great importance to the welfare of *several* departments in the company, the task of the purchasing agent becomes quite simple. Here, he must learn to play the role of a mere order signer and feel no resentment about his subordination. When the company is buying an expensive or complicated machine or choosing a new type of raw material, we want the decision made by the men whose work and departmental goals will be affected; they possess the premises needed to reach a decision. These might include any or all of the following: men in engineering, product design, sales, production, equipment maintenance, motion and time study, quality control, and costing, and those responsible for the financial affairs of the company. Their premises must be brought together and weighted so that a *group* decision can be made to fit the needs of all the departments.

RESHAPING THE DEPARTMENTS THAT CONTROL PRODUCTION AND SALES

The purpose of controls is to see that the company's activities turn out as planned. In using the term here, we shall be talking about the control of those activities which can be measured numerically. This type of control is often carried out by industrial engineers and cost accountants, and by marketing research men. They help management to see that the men achieve goals set for *production* volume, production expenses, and quality of product, and for *sales* volume and sales expenses.

We have already discussed several other types of controls, though they were not then so labeled. Executives employ authority, leadership, and communication to see that plans turn out as expected. The informal and formal organization structures are also employed to control men's behavior. In using those, an executive is trying to control intangible activities which can be measured only by accumulating value premises. It can be argued that the control of the unmeasurables is more vital to the welfare of the company than the control of the tangibles now under consideration, but this does not mean that we should dispense with numerical controls.

After investigating the tasks of control departments and the weaknesses and limitations of controls, we shall set about the task of developing controls for the manufacturing and selling departments.[23] In general, our objective will be to keep the controls to a minimum and to make them as simple as possible.

The Tasks of the Control Men

Trimmed down to essentials, controls consist of four tasks:

1. Deciding which *crucial* tasks the men in the plant and the salesmen may *not* perform as well as their counterparts in competing companies.
2. Deciding what will be the goal or standard or the 100 per cent for those tasks.

---

[23] I do not feel qualified to speak about the control of the activities performed in the product development department. My own guess is that, except for budgetary controls, attempts to employ numerical controls here will do more harm than good. Their products are ideas, and these can neither be counted nor be assigned a dollar value.

3. Comparing the men's actual performance with the goal or standard.
4. Taking remedial action.

Without the fourth step, there is no control, though executives sometimes think that controls are made up of only 2 and 3. The remedial
action might be any of the following: gaining acceptance of the
goals that were set in task 2, suggesting more effective means, raising
the goal if it is too easily attained, or lowering it if it is unrealisti-
cally high.

The specialists handling *production* controls, such as scheduling,
routing, dispatching, and so on, mostly deal with plant *volume*.
Those who handle motion and time standards, and cost estimating
and cost accounting activities, are the ones primarily concerned with
the control of the *out-of-pocket expenses* of the plant. These and
quality control and inventory control are all closely intertwined.
The men handling *sales* control ordinarily help to estimate sales
and set salesmen's quotas, both tasks dealing with volume; and they
also work on the problems of controlling the sales expenses.

These men normally help set goals for two of the four key items
in the table on page 378; we were there examining the concept of
annual gross margins. The first item in the table, the average selling
price per unit, is normally controlled by the company's sales executives.[24] The control men work only with the next two: the out-of-
pocket cost per unit, and the number of units produced or sold; they
set goals or standards for these and check up to see that these goals
are achieved. Together, these first three items determine the sum the

---

[24] Certain features of the task of controlling the selling price per unit have been
touched upon at various points; but nowhere have they been brought together. Let us take
a moment to assemble some of them. Choosing the niche in which the company will
operate, especially the particular kind of customer it will serve, and designing products
that will fit that niche, provide a company with considerable control over its prices. These
determine whether its prices will be high, low, or just above average as compared with
those of the industry as a whole. The main objective is to set prices at a level that produces the greatest contribution to overhead—at such a point that the sales volume in units
during the period ahead, when multiplied by the expected dollar margin per unit, will be
greatest. Once the products and customers are chosen and the relative price level is set,
however, a company will ordinarily find it advisable to raise and lower its prices in concert with those of the industry. If it attempts to hold its prices up when its competitors
are reducing their prices, it will usually lose position; its volume will decline, inventories
will pile up, and its overhead will exceed its annual gross margin. On the other hand, if it
fails to raise prices when prices are strong, the contributions available to cover its overhead and profits will probably be smaller than those enjoyed by competitors, and its
comparative financial position will be impaired. See Harry L. Hansen, *Marketing:
Text, Cases, and Readings* (rev. ed.; Homewood, Ill.: Richard D. Irwin, Inc., 1961),
chap. 17, for a well grounded examination of pricing. Malcolm P. McNair and Harry L.
Hansen, *Readings in Marketing* (New York: McGraw-Hill Book Co., Inc., 1956), offers
still further insights. Recall, also, the premises brought to light at the price-setting
session we attended (pp. 63–64), where the executives met to decide whether to raise the
price of one of their products.

company will have available annually to cover its overhead expenses and profits. We shall examine the task of controlling the fourth item, annual overhead expenses in the next chapter; note, however, that in this chapter we are beginning to watch (and control) the amount that the company will spend on overhead—the annual salary total, for instance, that each department will have to pay in the event our plan is adopted.

It is easy enough to decide on the *goals* for volume and out-of-pocket expenses. The big problem is to control men's activities so that these two goals are achieved. We are now well aware of what this entails; the five chapters on gaining acceptance were entirely devoted to the task of inducing members of the organization to carry out what we propose that they do. But recall, in particular, the conflicts that arise when attempting to complicate the formal organization structure by introducing mental experts, staff men—when we directed two or more men to exercise authority over another man. Some of these staff men who develop and handle the controls may work as single individuals interjected in a routine group under the group's boss; others may work as members of a small unit which has been detached from its home department and is placed in a "foreign" department; and still others may be acting as executive mental specialists with headquarters in the home office (see Diagram 9, page 311).

Men in the field of production controls frequently have trouble gaining the workers' and foremen's acceptance of the goals they set. Much of the difficulty can usually be traced to their tendency to use only factual premises when trying to prove that the goals should be adopted. The plant employees normally give such premises little weight, especially since these frequently prove only that the company's goals would be furthered. They are told some variant of the following: "If we achieve this very reasonable standard, we'll save the company about —— per year." The men are more interested in their own goals. Marketing research men also tend to subordinate value premises; they prefer good, solid, numerical data when setting sales quotas, for instance, and many of them feel uneasy when management changes their quotas to take account of value premises. "It's not scientific."

Limitations of Controls

One trouble with controls is that they are sometimes imposed when there is actually little need of them. It is not necessary to control every activity; no controls will be required for those jobs the men will automatically perform well enough to serve the company's needs. The activities that will have to be checked are those the executive has picked out as the critical ones in each department which the men are likely *not* to perform as planned. For instance, he may have anticipated that the company's decision to secure a new type of customer or to move into a new sales territory would not be carried out; to cope with this, it may be advisable to set goals such as, "Call on at least five of these new potential customers each week" (task No. 2, p. 477), and then see that tasks No. 3 and No. 4 are also implemented.

Controls are frequently continued long after they are needed because few executives stop to re-evaluate those they have instituted. Frayed nerves and unnecessarily heavy expenses for "burden" are the unwanted consequences here. As soon as the men habitually achieve the standards set, the controls can usually be reduced or discontinued. Occasionally (and ideally) an informal group will adopt these company standards as their status measures. In such a case, we must make doubly sure that these status measures do, in fact, presage a man's future welfare. Later, if the men's performances begin to fall to an adequacy level, the formal controls can be reimposed. And recall the deleterious effect on morale we uncovered (pp. 277–78) when too much emphasis was placed on sanctions, especially monetary incentives, for making only one of the several contributions a man is supposed to make to the company—measuring only the number of units he makes or sells, for instance.

The controls the company sets up do not work automatically. If the men who are furnished with the figures fail to use them regularly for guiding the behavior of their subordinates, the time and money spent on them are wasted. As indicated earlier, the figures are *not* controls in themselves. They are merely tools for describing the standards that are set and measuring the performance.

The cost of setting up and operating the controls has long been a serious limitation; these were a part of the "burden" (overhead) that the manufacturing people complained about. With the advent of electronic data-processing equipment, it would appear that the cost of furnishing management with information about performance would be sharply reduced. But many companies have found that they actually save very little money; the expense, in fact, is frequently greater. The equipment supplies *much* more data for the money spent, however, and furnishes it more promptly. The additional information sometimes produces an unwanted consequence, however. Executives are often tempted to ignore data when it proliferates; they lack the time to sort out the significant numbers and frame factual premises from these. Instead, they tend to rely only on the value premises they already have available.

The key to controls is the everyday use of the figures to frame factual premises for making decisions and for directing and redirecting the men's activities. The supervisors must be taught to use these, along with value premises, in their decision making, and then given enough time to gain acceptance of their newly framed decisions. Numerical controls are much more effective when only a few controls are employed. If a company tries to control everything, it is likely to control nothing. And in some cases, as we saw in an earlier chapter, men "fix up" the records to make it appear that they have met the standards.

Reshaping the Controls in the Manufacturing Department

Mental images of the crucial tasks to be performed in the plant—and, in particular, those that the men may not carry out automatically—provide the executive with premises for deciding what activities the manufacturing control men will have to watch. This in turn, determines the character and magnitude of their work in the period ahead. Most companies use four types of mental specialists in the plant: industrial engineers, accountants, quality control men, and inventory control men.

Industrial Engineers. An initial task of the industrial engineers is to make methods, motion, and time studies which will provide premises for deciding on the production standards and the one best way to perform the repetitive jobs in the plant. The standards they set are examples of permanently useful pieces of information transmitted to workers and supervisors, the ones discussed in connection with the training of manual workers (see pp. 232–34). (These are also used to set the labor cost standards.) A part of their job is to gain the workers' acceptance of each newly proposed "one best way" and train the men to follow it. Then, and only then, are these experts in a position to make the definitive time studies (that is, to compute the average time which will *really* be required to fabricate or assemble each part), set these as standards, and thereafter compare the actual time with these standards. The premises they frame from this information provide a basis for controlling the activities of each *individual* workman. In addition, these premises are used in deciding which machines and men should be employed to fabricate a given part, and the best sequence for performing the operations on a machine.

A second typical task of the industrial engineers is planning the plant layout. A third is production planning—seeing that the work done by the individual workmen in each section is coordinated and then that the work of the various manufacturing sections is dovetailed.[25] Production planning is a device for resolving problems of coordination which the executive foresaw at the time he was working out the changes in the manufacturing department. With the facts adduced from the motion and time studies, including estimates of setup time, industrial engineers can calculate how much time will be required to fabricate and assemble each of the parts required for each order. This, in turn, provides premises for deciding the best machine sequences and thus the routing of parts from one machine to the next and from one production section to the next, and for deciding on the schedule—the time when each job lot should be started and completed.[26]

Executives sometimes become overenthusiastic about the controls the industrial engineers can set up. In those cases where the executive foresees that a given section will consistently run into trouble in attempting to attain the standards set, it may be necessary to make daily comparisons of the actual performance with the standard. It is the executive's responsibility, however, to see that these controls are pared down as soon as practicable. As a matter of fact, in many instances, very simple controls can be used from the beginning. For example, the production planning may consist merely of communicating the standards or goals to the foremen and the workmen. And where the morale is high, the men themselves will frequently set the goals—quite high ones—and see that these are achieved; they take pride in the ability of the group to get the jobs done well and quickly for this raises the entire group's status in the company.

Cost Men. The tasks that the cost men in the manufacturing department will have to handle during the period ahead will also have to be pictured by the executive. Ordinarily their key tasks are

---

[25] Many companies employ motion and time studies solely for setting piece rates and paying production bonuses; but, to my mind, these studies are of even greater worth in production planning and cost controls. In an earlier chapter (p. 278), I expressed some uneasiness about the use of piece rates as the sole basis of rewards for high contributions.

[26] Note, in passing, that setting schedules that are too tight—assigning the men and machines more work than they can handle (some companies do this regularly in the belief that this will increase production)—is often worse than having no centralized production planning. Chaos ensues when every department is off schedule.

these: to make realistic predictions of the out-of-pocket costs of manufacturing a product—the time required to perform each task (based on the standards set by the industrial engineers), multiplied by the rate per hour for labor, plus the amount of raw materials required, multiplied by their costs per unit (here, they are setting a cost goal or standard); to make comparisons of the actual costs with the estimated costs; and, where the actual costs are too high, to work with the industrial engineers and foremen to uncover and correct the discrepancies. Upon investigation, they may discover in some instances that the workmen were actually performing their jobs very well but that the standards were improperly set. Perhaps the estimates for direct labor costs were invalid because they were based on unrealistic motion and time study data. Or the setup time may have been miscalculated, or their estimates of raw material costs may be fallacious because of unexpected wastage in cutting or because the number of rejects is higher than anticipated. In any case, here, as elsewhere, the figures showing the standard and the actual performance are merely tools for control; and full-scale, formal cost controls will be necessary only for those activities whose costs are likely to be higher than the cost standard set. It may turn out that the actual costs are usually so close to the estimated costs that only periodic checkups will be needed.

Once the cost accountant's tasks are pictured in detail, the executives can determine whether the men will have to set up more cost goals, or fewer, in the period ahead, and whether more or fewer comparisons with the standard costs will be required. As a minimum, most medium-sized companies will want figures on the average out-of-pocket labor and materials costs of the repetitive jobs; and the executive will want to communicate these to the foremen as guides or standards. For the *critical* routine jobs which may cost more than anticipated, they will probably find it desirable to follow the procedures just described—to set up formal standards and to check performances each day.

Some companies go a step further and allocate *indirect* or *overhead* expenses to each order or to each production department section every day or each month; but, often this is a waste of time and money. The foremen in the plant are in no position to do much about controlling departmental overhead expenses *per unit* such as machine burden, supervisory and specialists' salaries, or the central office overhead which is allotted to them, such as top executive salaries and selling and advertising costs—except through high levels of production. And even production volume is largely out of their hands; this depends on the orders received. These overhead expenses can best be determined and controlled by the top executives—the men who decide what will be spent annually on these activities. Keep in mind that we, in this chapter, are helping to decide on overhead expenses.

Mental pictures of the expected changes in the character of the forthcoming orders furnish the executives with an idea of the size of another job usually performed in part by cost accountants—namely, the task of estimating the costs for pricing purposes. A company that expects to sell more and more standard items, for example, can plan to reduce the number of men in the price-estimating section; whereas if it anticipates more special orders, the work of estimating costs as a basis for quoting prices will become more complicated. Some companies go a step further and allow this section to make decisions on the prices to be quoted on special orders. In such cases the practice is to provide the cost accountants with a formula; the prices are determined by their estimates of the out-of-pocket costs of raw materials, direct labor, and packaging, plus a fixed percentage of these to cover overhead and profits. The trouble with this is that although these facts provide useful premises, many other facts need to be taken into consideration, several of which are predominantly of a value nature, in quoting prices. For instance, quite properly, in practice, these percentage markups are strongly influenced by the price normally charged by competitors.[27]

Quality Control Men. Quality control may also require some attention. The executives may foresee that under the new program the number of imperfect parts and below-standard finished products will rise rapidly. If this is not controlled, the production schedules will be thrown off; and costs of raw material and direct labor will be higher than expected. And if standard parts are to be produced in larger volume, it may pay to introduce electronic or mechanical quality control devices, thus reducing the personnel in the department. Possibly the customers in the new niche may not require as high quality standards as the old customers, in which case quality

---

[27] Only by chance does a formula of out-of-pocket costs plus a predetermined percentage of out-of-pocket costs—100 per cent, for example—for overhead and profits give the "right" price. The goal is to secure a price that is quite close to the highest price the customers in the niche are willing to pay, so that the orders will contribute the largest amount to overhead. The right price may be higher than the figure computed with the formula, or it may be less. See the footnote on page 478 for other premises to be taken into consideration.

must be "controlled downward." In an earlier chapter, we noted the reluctance of workmen to lower the quality of their work because of the effect of this on their status. On the other hand, raising the quality may be essential in order to get business. Tightening the standards of quality is often resented because the work is more troublesome than before. After an examination of the tasks ahead in the control of quality, the executive can visualize the type of men needed, and whether more or fewer men will be required for the job of setting realistic quality standards and comparing the actual with the standard.

Inventory Control Men. Inventory control must be closely tied in with the work of men in purchasing, production control, and manufacturing. The purpose of inventory control is to avoid having in stock a ten years' supply of some raw materials, parts, or finished goods, and only an hour's supply of others. In most companies the man in charge of inventory controls must be able to use a wide range of premises. Records of the amounts of each item used or sold in the past provide premises that are helpful; but in most cases, these can be given very little weight. To keep inventories in line, the inventory man should know what the sales trends of each item will probably be in the *future*, what the seasonal characteristics of the sales may be, what changes in the design of products and what new, substitutable products are under consideration, what the relative costs of running a large lot versus a small lot would be, how much storage space will be available and when idle machines and men will be available—when the various sections of the plant will be working at capacity to turn out current orders, and when their work loads will be slack—as well as what changes can be expected in the character and the prices of the raw materials required for each product. The inventory man also needs to know about the company's financial situation. The man handling inventory controls must be able to gather value premises as well as factual premises from many sources if he is to make intelligent decisions.

The foregoing helps us understand why we cannot depend solely on operations research formulas to determine the lot size we should produce or purchase. The lot-size formula we used in Chapter 4 as a simplified example would, of course, be expanded to contain other measurable independent variables. But notice that most of the variables will have to be estimated each time the man places a manufacturing or purchase order and for each order he will make a different set of estimates; conditions are constantly changing, hence the task of preparing the data for the computer looms large. And after the calculations are completed, the "answer" must be revised to give due weight to value premises: What are the chances that the product development men will redesign the part before we use up the supply? (This premise would read "If we produce N units probably n of these will become obsolete and have to be discarded.) How soon will idle men and machines be available and how soon thereafter will they again be available? What effect will the impending strike of supplier A have on us?

Reshaping the Controls in the Sales Department

The task of planning and controlling the work of the sales force by means of statistics and accounting figures is somewhat less familiar to most people than the foregoing. However, here, as with manufacturing controls, the main objective is to control the volume and the expenses—in *this* department, the sales volume in each territory and the cost of selling that volume. And the procedure here, as in the production department, is to set up goals or standards for the volume and expenses, compare these with the actual results, and take any necessary remedial steps before it is too late.

But in this department, it is not possible to set standards that are demonstrably valid—these must be based largely on value premises —nor can the comparisons of the actual results with the expected results be so rigorously applied as in the plant. In the first place, the volume goals are estimates of future sales; and these are very difficult to determine with accuracy—more difficult than in the plant —for we are here prophesying the actions of a large number of people, whereas in the plant the predictions of volume produced are based on how the machines and their operators will behave. Moreover, the extent to which goals in a sales territory are achieved is by no means solely within the control of the salesman. For example, his actual sales will depend on the decisions of customers whose actions are, relatively speaking, outside his control. And his ability to achieve the goal is also strongly influenced by business conditions and the actions of competitors. Additionally, his sales depend on the efforts, past and present, of the men in the factory, in the product development department, in the advertising department, and in the channels of distribution, as well as on the decisions of his sales manager. For these reasons, the standards—for example, the sales quota in dollars and in units for the territory—should be thought of as goals rather than as definitive measuring sticks; and the salesman's results must be appraised not only in terms of these goals but in terms of the actions of people whose behavior he cannot be expected to control.

Men trained in marketing research will ordinarily be best qualified to estimate the total sales potentials of the company's market niche—but the sales manager will probably be the only one with enough premises to determine the *share* of the potential which his company should try to secure, and in this way set the salesmen's quotas. For the nation as a whole, he may, for example, be aiming for 10 per cent of *the potential* business available; but because of local conditions, he may decide that the quota for one territory should be 13 per cent of the potential and for another territory, 6 per cent. It will also be the sales manager's task to gain the salesman's acceptance of these quotas and help the salesman achieve them.

When a company is attempting to enter a *new*, unfamiliar niche, probably the most critical task will be to make sure that the salesmen find new potential customers. Data on the potential sales for our type of product in each territory, and the number and the names of potential customers, provide management with a guide in setting territorial objectives. And the comparisons of the salesmen's actual results with their territorial goals—with, for example, their quotas for dollar sales and the number of new customers they should secure —provides a means of checking up and deciding exactly what actions the salesmen must take in the period ahead to increase the company's share of the business.

To secure *intensive* coverage of the company's present niche, rather elaborate salesmen controls may be useful at times. For example, it may be worthwhile to assign quotas for each of the salesmen's *accounts* and keep cumulative records of the sale of each *product* to each account, so that the sales manager (or district supervisor) and the salesmen can go over these together to determine what specific steps the salesmen should take in selling each of the various products to each customer. The objective is to see that the territorial sales goals are achieved by the end of the period.

The keys to effective sales control are (1) comparisons from time to time, *during the period,* of the actual results to date with the goals the company expects to attain by the end of the period—progress reports, and (2) regular meetings with the salesmen *during that period* to appraise their work thus far and help them to replan their work for the remainder of the period. The objective is to see that the desired results are actually achieved; if they wait to check up until after the period is closed, nothing can be done. These elaborate controls, designed to achieve intensive coverage, can be discarded as soon as the men habitually perform their newly assigned tasks. When a new salesman is employed, it may be advisable to use these controls solely for him, but only so long as the sales manager feels that the new man needs guidance in handling the crucial tasks.

So far, we have discussed methods of controlling the sales volume. Fewer useful tools are available for setting sales *expense* standards and for checking up to see that they are met. Selling expenses typically increase out of proportion to sales when the company is introducing a new product, or when it is introducing one of its redesigned products to a new group of customers, or when it is expanding into new geographical territories. Management frequently attempts to control these expenses by putting the men on straight commission; in this way the ratio of sales force expenses to sales can be predicted and controlled precisely. But straight commission brings with it unwanted consequences. In many cases, some of the men cannot earn enough to live on; whereas other men are overpaid. And, as we have already seen (p. 277), men paid in this way are likely to concentrate only on turning in signed orders. Probably the simplest and the most workable sales expense control is the use of a percentage figure as a goal or general guide line—for example, "Direct selling expenses in the company as a whole and in each territory should run approximately 10 per cent of sales." In one year, it may be profitable to spend more than the allotted percentage on salaries and traveling expenses; in another, less. Or in a given *territory*, it may pay to spend more than the average. This "percentage method" does not tell the sales manager whether a given territory is a profitable one, but it serves as a useful measuring stick in comparing the selling expenses in the several territories and taking corrective action.[28]

Actually, these volume and expense control figures for the sales department provide only a partial description of goals and standards for salesmen, and of their effectiveness in achieving these goals and standards. The real test of a salesman's effectiveness is what he says and does in front of the customers. This is not readily measured; and, in any event, the results may not show up in the form of sales until several months or years have passed. Face-to-face supervision is the

---

[28] James W. Culliton, *Management of Marketing Costs* (Boston: Division of Research, Graduate School of Business Administration, Harvard University, 1948), offers a short but illuminating examination of the problem of allocating sales overhead expenses. He concludes that there are no easy solutions.

most effective method of controlling these nonmeasurable activities. However, numerical controls provide sources of very useful factual premises which can profitably be considered, along with value prem- ises, in directing and controlling the salesmen's work.

The crucial tasks which will need to be carried out by the various control groups, will furnish the executives with premises for conceiv- ing a picture of the abilities the various control experts should pos- sess. When this picture is laid alongside the men now doing this work a decision emerges as to which of the experts should be kept, what types of men should be brought in, how many will be needed, what retraining will be necessary, and who should be transferred or dropped.

The foregoing has been the theme running through this entire chapter. Our objective in reshaping these departments has been to work out the detailed plans in each department for implementing the company's long-term policies or goals which have been chosen—to provide the necessary means of reaching those goals. Our task has been to build the sales department, the product development depart- ment, the manufacturing department, the personnel and purchasing departments, and the several control departments into more effective instruments than before. So far, however, most of our attention has been devoted to revamping the men in the lower echelons of these departments—and the departmental equipment. Selecting the depart- ment heads and financing the program, two of the major tasks of putting plans into effect, will be explored in the concluding chapter, the one to which we now turn.

PROBLEM

Rebuilding the Departments to Achieve the Company's Goals

Although, ideally, you should work out a plan for revamping all the departments in Superb Biscuits, Inc., you can gain considerable experience by concentrating on only one department. Select any of the following de- partments, take into consideration the changes that you think should be made in the *other* departments, and work out a realistic plan for "your" depart- ment: sales, product development, production, or controls. Use the questions listed below.

Let us suppose that we have decided to continue to serve housewives and institutions, but to place substantially more emphasis on specialty cookies and crackers.

Your task is to conceive a plan for making your department into an even more telling instrument than it is now. Before trying to create your plan, review the premises you gathered in answering the questions at the end of Chapters 11, 12, and 13, and the decisions you have already made. You will find that you have accumulated information for an extraordinary number of useful premises. Remember it is now early 1957.

1. What will be the three or four crucial tasks of your department in the period 1957–1962? In other words, if Superb is to compete successfully in the niche we have chosen for it, what specific tasks will the men in your department have to perform extremely well—as well as, or better than their counterparts in the large and medium-sized competing companies?

2. In view of your answer to Question 1 and the premises you used there in reaching your decisions, what would the "perfect" personnel (and equipment, if any) for each of the sections in your department look like? More specifically, what characteristics would you want these men and their supervisors (and machinery) to have; and how many more, or how many less of each would be needed by your department in order to perform the crucial tasks for which it will be responsible? Give your premises for your decisions.

3. Describe the workers and supervisors (and equipment) now in the various sections of your department and compare these with those in the near-perfect department you envisaged in Question 2, above: which ones now approximate the ideal, which are not good enough, and which are *too* good?

4. What changes would you make in the character and number of men (and equipment, if any) presently in your department? In laying your plans, take into consideration the shortcomings of the company and the assets (tangible and intangible) which Superb now has. Be realistic about the assets it might be able to secure. Before making your final decision, test the plan in your mind; and revise it to a point where you think you can gain acceptance from the men in your department. It is your responsibility to conceive in detail a realistic department, one that you feel the company could build and one that could cope with the crucial tasks you see ahead.

5. List and sum the extra salaries and any other additional annual overhead expenses required by your plan. Subtract any reductions in these expenses. Be thinking about whether your plan's annual contribution to overhead would exceed its additional overhead expense, in case your departmental plan were adopted.

6. Briefly, wherein does your departmental plan differ from the company's present program?

Chapter *15*   IMPLEMENTING THE PLANS

IN THIS final chapter, we explore the executive's task *of implementing* the plans he has been developing. Here, we see the culmination of all the thinking and work he has been doing; the objective toward which the preceding chapters have been pointing is all but achieved. However, the fact that he performs this task last does not mean that he ignored it during the planning stage. We noted earlier that planning and implementing plans cannot be neatly disentangled. Among other things, the executive has probably developed and revised his plans with an eye to minimizing the task of gaining wholehearted acceptance of them. If this has been done, the transition from the stage of planning to the stage of action —of getting the men to carry out their parts of the plan—is already half accomplished.

The emphasis in these pages will be placed on the problems the chief executive and his associates must cope with in putting into effect a complicated, over-all company plan. The approach is equally applicable, however, to the task of executing a smaller, relatively simple plan—a plan such as any man further down in the organizational hierarchy might be responsible for. As emphasized earlier, the main difference lies in the fact that the latter plans deal with steps lower on the means-end staircase and require a much less elaborate set of means.

In addition to observing the culmination of the executive's long-range planning, we shall here see in use in one chapter many of the concepts that make up the fourteen conceptual subsystems we have explored.[1]

Our subsystem in this chapter consists of five steps. The approxi-

---

[1] For short integrative statements about management in general, see Robert Tannenbaum, "The Manager Concept: A Rational Synthesis," *Journal of Business*, Vol. XXII (1949), pp. 225–28; 233–40; and, see Edward H. Litchfield, "Notes on a General Theory of Administration," *Administrative Science Quarterly*, Vol. 1, No. 1 (June 1956), pp. 1–29.

mate time sequence in which these would be carried out will serve as our central thread. The steps are these: (1) reappraising the plan and making the final decision, (2) planning to put the plan into effect, implementing the plan by (3) building the top echelons of the organization, and (4) by financing the plan, and finally, (5), seeing that the plan works. We should be aware, however, that, in practice, parts of these steps will be carried on simultaneously. The over-lapping is actually more pervasive than that; as we saw in the Introduction to Part III, the president doubtless began thinking about these steps while still evolving his plans.

REAPPRAISAL AND THE FINAL DECISION

With the completion of his tentative plans for each department, the chief executive is in a position to stand aside and visualize how his imaginary company works as a complete unit. And he can now run a mental test to observe how his newly created organism will flourish in the forthcoming social-economic environment which he envisages.

He has created an idea for a complicated and very expensive alternative. Consequently, before going ahead, he will want to make certain he has foreseen most of the wanted and unwanted consequences of adopting it. He is now at stage five of the creative process—the stage of reappraisal. Our concern in this reappraisal will be twofold: Will the company's member groups and will the groups of outsiders behave as we predicted, and will the plan more than pay for itself?

Reappraising Our Predictions of People's Behavior

We shall want to take a second look at our ideas of the behavior of outside groups which determine the company's forthcoming economic environment. Are we now fairly sure that businessmen as a whole and householders as a whole will behave as we expected—will they decide (if this was our prediction) to expand their activities or at worst not contract their purchases of our types of products? Will the annual gross margins enjoyed by companies in our industry increase or at worst remain about steady? Do we have any late information which would lead us to change our minds about the probable behavior of our large and medium-sized competitors and the several customer groups in our niches? Do we detect any departures from our earlier picture of people's ideologies, the behavior of political parties, and of the probable legislation and court rulings?

What are the chances of war? In sum, do the niches we chose now seem as promising as when we originally decided on them?

We shall also want to reappraise the competitors' behavior; can we compete as effectively as they for a share of the business in the niches we have chosen. We have altered our departments (in our mind's eye), in the belief that they would provide effective means of achieving the goal of increasing our share of the business available in our niches. Our questions are these: Will the several altered departments be potent enough, taken together, to achieve the goal resting on the step above in our staircase? Are these changed departments the best means available for increasing our share of the market, all things considered, or should we further revise certain parts of our plan? Do we have in mind a reasonable number of means and goals for the necessary lower steps on the company's staircases or are we wish-thinking—expecting that some of these higher goals will achieve themselves? Are there any vague or missing steps in the staircases which lead up to our goal of creating departments which will be capable of performing the crucial tasks?

Before going ahead with the plan, we shall certainly want to *appraise the reliability of the premises*, especially those to which we gave greatest weight. The question we here pose is this: Will those many results or consequences which we envisaged *actually* occur in the event that we adopt the plan; do the premises now seem as reliable as they once did?

The following are examples of important consequences or results which might profitably be rechecked. Will the sales force actually behave as we had predicted; will the men conscientiously call on the new group of customers and work at an efficiency level instead of an adequacy level? In the light of the several facets of the forthcoming economic environment, will our competitors' salesmen and pricing executives behave approximately as we expected? And in the light of all the foregoing, will the new group of customers buy as much as we expected; will they actually decide that their inducement-contribution balance would be improved if they joined our organization? Will the informal groups in the factory and in the office think that the proposed changes in their work will increase the spread between their inducements and contribution? When the changes are completed and the groups have settled down to work, will the members feel their status is higher, or at least no lower than before? Will our out-of-pocket costs, then, be higher than we planned? Will the morale in our revamped product development department be high enough to make the men *want* to create improved products?

The premises used to decide on the topmost steps of the company's staircases will need to be scrutinized with especial care because they are all predominantly value and the consequences named in those premises are of great moment to the company. The cause element in practically all the premises is mostly value. (In most of the premises the cause would read, "If we adopt the plan.") In such premises we are obliged to use our personal yardsticks to measure most of hundreds of means that make up our proposed plan—such facets as the nature of the men we select, how skilled they are, how willing they are to perform the crucial company's tasks, for example. The character of the machinery we are planning to use and the number of people in each department are among the few facets of the cause (that is, facets of the plan) which could be considered factual. Virtually all the results are also predominantly value, as a rereading of the results which we questioned in the above four paragraphs will testify. And the same is true of the causal connections. In each case, to determine and demonstrate how the results flow from the causes, the speaker and his hearers are obliged to fall back on their own yardsticks, their own experiences. Recall the assertion in Chapter 3 (pp. 79–80), that top executives must depend heavily on value premises when selecting the company's topmost goals.

Appraising the Profitability and Estimating the Additional Cash Requirements

Before implementing the plan, we shall also want to test our unstated assumption that the plan will prove profitable. Whether the results named above will *actually* occur, and whether the hundreds of other results we envisaged will also occur, largely determines whether our predictions of sales, expenses, and profits will come true. Also, before making the final decision we shall want to be sure that the new investments do not seriously deplete the company's cash reserves.

Profitability. In making the final decision we should certainly give great weight to the premise, "If we adopt our long-term plan, we should sell about ——— units per year, enjoy an average gross margin per unit of about $———, spend approximately $——— on additional overhead expenses, and show a profit (loss?) the first year of about $———." The objective at this point is to recheck our plan, and revise it, if necessary, to make as sure as possible that the

increase in the company's annual gross margin which is produced by
the changes we plan to make in the niches and in the departments *will
be greater than the added overhead cost per year of* salaries, equipment, and other overhead expenses.

The executive can estimate the additional overhead expenses per
year fairly accurately at this stage in the planning. In fact, we (and
the president) were making such estimates in the preceding chapter
as we finished revamping each department. On the basis of the contemplated changes in personnel, the president can set down the probable annual salaries of the heads of any *new* sections or departments,
and of any additional salesmen, advertising men, product design
men, permanent plant workers and supervisors, secretaries, clerks,
and new staff men and women in the field of controls, as well as any
salary increases for replacements or for present employees who will
be promoted. Similarly, the executive can make a fairly accurate
estimate of the additional advertising called for under his plan; the
additional rent, if any; the probable extra depreciation on new equipment; and, eventually, when calculations of the additional funds required are completed, the added interest. Bear in mind that *the plan
may call for a cut* in the size of some of the sections and departments.
Also note that a company which plans to contract will be attempting
to reduce most of its overhead items.

Estimating the amount of extra gross margin the plan would contribute toward overhead and profits each year is somewhat more
complicated, though the executive's mental image of the rebuilt company operating in the economic environment he sees ahead, supplies
a great many premises. On the basis of these, he should be able to
estimate the number of physical units the company should sell annually in case the contemplated changes in the company's goals and
the various departments were put into effect.[2] (Note that whereas in
the preceding paragraph we were dealing only with the expected *increases* in next year's figures over this year's, in this paragraph we
are dealing, for the moment, with the *totals* for next year.) On the
basis of the expected economic-competitive environment and the character of the niches the executive intends to compete in, he can now
also predict whether the company's average selling price per unit
will be higher or lower, and by about how much—$2.00 more, or 50
cents less. And on the basis of the planned-for changes in design

---

[2] We worked out a sales forecast in the preceding chapter when we were deciding the
size of the plant and the amount of equipment needed (see pp. 468–69), and we shall
touch on this again when we take up budgets.

and in the raw materials and manufacturing procedures under the new plan, he can estimate the approximate level of out-of-pocket costs per unit—whether they will be 75 cents higher, for example, or 15 cents lower than at present. The company's expected total annual gross margin computed from these figures, *minus* the company's *present* total annual gross margin, gives the executive a reasonably solid figure, in dollars, of the *extra* annual gross margin the plan will turn in to the company.

The concluding step, finding out whether the extra income will exceed the additional overhead expenses, is a straightforward one. It consists of subtracting the expected increase in the annual overhead expenses from the anticipated increase in the annual gross margin.

This estimate of the profitability of the program obviously provides a key premise, one that must be weighted heavily in deciding whether to adopt the plan in its present form, revise it, or discard it. Here, we are predicting the effect of these changes on the company's profits. Such an approach also forces the executive to reappraise the details of his plan in a realistic light—*to examine separately the several changes he is considering in the departments to see whether each change will pay for itself.* When the individual changes are viewed in this way, he may notice that he has become overenthusiastic in his ideas of the results he can expect from some features of his plan; he recognizes that they will never contribute enough to overhead to pay for their costs, that they are what his colleagues will call "frills." To ensure profitability, he may eliminate certain means which now seem to promise only a small contribution to overhead—eliminate the less productive advertising, for example. Incidentally, revising the plan by destroying a feature of the "baby" he has so lovingly created, or cutting his creature down to smaller size, is often very painful.

The foregoing paragraphs should not be read to mean that the projected changes must produce an increase in profits the first year. Some of the first year's additional overhead expenses may properly be thought of as investments for the future, even though they are charged off as expenses. The plan is a long-term one; it takes time to harvest the expected fruits. No matter how brilliant the plan, the additional sales volume and the increase in the spread per unit will come slowly. The question is, will the new program more than pay for itself in the long run—in the next three, five, or ten years? What will be the effect on the forthcoming operating statements?

Effects on the Company's Cash Position. As indicated earlier, an examination of the effects of the proposed plan on the company's balance sheet is also called for. The objective here is to foresee whether the drain on the company's liquid assets will jeopardize the company's viability and whether more money will need to be raised. The additional investment in new equipment, including costs of installation, and in new building space, can be estimated in round figures rather easily. To this the executive must add the money necessary to finance the increased inventories and accounts receivable, and the expected operating losses of the first year or so. In addition, he would like to have a cushion of cash to meet any unexpected losses resulting from a strike, for instance, or from a short depression, or from some unforeseen failure in the plans.

The Final Decision

The decision as to whether to press his board of directors and his top executives for the adoption of his plan is made by the president (1) after he has re-examined his predictions of the behavior of the environmental and the company groups to make sure he has not deluded himself, (2) after he has made an appraisal of the profitability of the plan and revised it where needed and, in addition, (3) after he has determined whether his company can raise the money it will need. We shall here touch only briefly on this third problem, postponing our more complete examination of financing until later in the chapter.

When the chief executive sums up his estimates of new capital requirements and lays this figure alongside the company's cash on hand, the amount of money he must secure, the risks he is taking, and the size of the task of raising additional capital stand out starkly. It is at this point that he mentally reappraises the whole project. "This could wreck the company; what if the plans don't materialize?" And he can hear his board members and department heads, including his treasurer, expressing their own uneasiness: "If we try to finance these changes ourselves, we may go broke before the profits begin to come in—if they ever do." "If we have a depression, where will we be?" "If we go to outsiders for the extra capital we'll need, the present executives and owners may lose control of the company."

How the executive faces up to these decisive questions constitutes, in my opinion, the supreme test of his courage. His decision here is largely, though by no means entirely, irrevocable. To go ahead, he must have tested and revised his plan to a point where he is confident that it will work—confident that he can make the plan "happen." Before recommending to his associates and his board of directors that the project be adopted, he may want to check over the proposed investments once more to see if any of its features can be trimmed, postponed, or eliminated with but little injury to the program. At this stage (we are still in the fifth, the appraisal stage of the creative process), he also has an opportunity to lessen the risks by revising the plan so that it will to some extent fit two or three possible sets of most likely future environments.

Even after these two revisions have been completed—the revisions in the light of costs versus results, and the revision to make the plan flexible enough to fit a second or third niche with some chance of success—the chief executive may conclude that the risks are too great. If so, he can still turn back, for he has not yet committed the company to any moves. But if the planning has been realistic, the chances are that the company can make the proposed investments and commit itself to paying the additional overhead expenses—the annual interest charges, in particular, for these constitute a long-term contractual obligation.

PLANNING TO PUT THE PLANS INTO EFFECT

Let us suppose that the president has decided to proceed with his plan and that he has already gained the acceptance of his board of directors and has partially or wholly convinced most of his top management men. His next step in implementing the plan is to determine where to begin on this job of putting his program into effect. Two questions help to resolve this: Which parts of the plan are of most importance to the company's welfare and in what sequence should each part of the plan be started and completed?

Deciding on the Relative Importance and Magnitude of the Tasks Ahead

During the period when the executive was devising the details of his plan, those details on which he was working at the moment probably seemed the most important. After the detailed planning of each of the departments has been completed, it is therefore advisable to gain perspective by standing back and looking at the whole.

When the various parts of the plan are seen together it is relatively easy to rank the tasks lying ahead of the organization according to their relative importance as means of filling the company's chosen niche. These are *the long-term means* which the departments must certainly provide. The chief executive will want to give high priority to the changes in each department which were designed to help it perform effectively the most crucial of its tasks. With such a list, he can *also* tell what aspects of the plan—which department or section's work, for example—will need relatively little emphasis, the tasks that can be performed as well as necessary in a comparatively routine fashion.

But in addition, he has the task of visualizing the relative *magnitude* of the immediate tasks of reshaping the departments. Creating a new, near-perfect sales force may require the greatest amount of skill and work, or selecting and laying out the equipment for the plant, or strengthening the cost controls. By making another list, this one showing the tasks (ranged according to their magnitude) of converting the sections and departments into "perfect" ones, he can gain some additional perspective about the tasks he has ahead of him.

These two lists provide premises for determining the tasks to which he must devote most of his time and attention. It is easy to lose perspective at this stage; executives frequently discover, when they look back, that they have devoted an inordinate amount of attention to relatively trivial features of their plan, to steps that lie far down on the company's staircases.

Timing the Introduction of the Changes

The executive also wants the alterations completed by specified dates. The reason is that we are creating a company designed to flourish in the future—in the environment that we expect three or five years hence. If the edifice is not ready by the time that environment "arrives," or if it is ready *too early*, the "perfect" company, even if it is achieved, will not fit the environment in which it then finds itself.[3]

To make sure that the plan will be completed on schedule, it is necessary to work back from the date set for its completion—work back from D Day, as it were. But upon examining the separate projects included in the plan, it becomes evident that some of the changes

---

[3] Two cautions here: Once a man foresees a change in a feature of the company's environment, his tendency is to expect it to be consummated very soon, only to find later that he has inadvertently telescoped the time period; most environmental changes take place quite slowly, as we have seen. Second, the company must be able to serve its customers effectively between now and the arrival of the new environment—the environment is evolutionary; thus the changes in the department and the time schedule for introducing them have to be planned with this in mind.

will require a week to finish, others a month; and a few may require a year or perhaps two years before the transformation can be completed and the workers have accepted the change. The time required for each gives the chief executive a preliminary idea of a time schedule for starting each project.

The problem of timing would be fairly simple if it were merely a matter of starting a project early enough to finish it before the arrival of the target date for the entire plan. But usually, certain jobs must be completed before others can be started. For example, the new time studies may require only a week or two of work; but before they can be inaugurated, it will be essential to work out the jigs and the fixtures, decide on the "best" methods, and train the men to follow these methods. These tasks may require several weeks of work antedating the time study, so they must be started early if the time study is to be completed when planned. But this is by no means all. It may become evident that some of the other parts of the new program—for instance, the determination of standard costs to be used in quoting prices—cannot be started until after the time studies are completed, which may in turn mean that the time study and its antecedent work must be started even earlier than would otherwise be necessary. If new machines must be purchased and installed or new employees hired, these tasks, of course, must be completed before embarking on the motion studies, the training, and the setting of standard times. We have used the company's plant as an example here, but this same type of scheduling is useful in planning the changes in the other departments.[4]

In addition, the time schedules for changes to be made in each of the several departments will need to be synchronized. When these separate schedules are viewed as a whole, it may become evident that some will have to be revised so that they will all mesh. For instance, if the plan calls for major changes in the kinds and numbers of employees in the plant, the task of rebuilding the company's personnel department will have to be started very early indeed. But most of the changes in the sales department can usually be carried on simultaneously with those in the plant because the orders the salesmen will secure from the new type of customers they are soliciting (or for the

---

[4] In practice, it may *not* always be necessary to finish *all* the work on each of these prior projects immediately; only those parts of a given project which provide a basis for the succeeding steps have to be entirely completed. And it is often possible to use rough or approximate data temporarily, instead of accurate, completed data and thus, for the time being to short-cut some of the steps. However, in any case, some definite amount of time will be required; so the problem of scheduling is still with us.

new product) will obviously not swamp the manufacturing department at first. The objective is to match the orders received with the
ability of the plant to produce. The progress of the product design
department will likewise need to be matched with that of the plant
and the sales department. The same is true in scheduling the changes
in the controls.

These separate projects we have been discussing in connection
with timing are actually steps in some of the means-end staircases the
company has chosen, the goal of which is to revamp the company's
departments by a certain date. But in addition to showing the steps

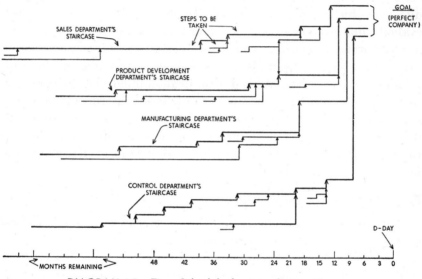

DIAGRAM 15. Time Schedule for Introducing Changes

and the sequence in which they are to be taken, this mental image
shows *when* each step in the staircases is to be started *and* completed,
it shows the deadlines. Diagram 15 will serve to summarize what
has been said about timing.

Once the chief executive has determined the relative magnitude
of the tasks ahead, and once he has worked out the problems of
timing, he is in a much better position to evaluate his department
managers to see which ones can handle the critical jobs and thus
tentatively decide on the men who will head the departments.

BUILDING THE TOP ECHELONS

Upon the completion of the first two steps for implementing the
plan—(1) reappraising and, if necessary, revising the plan, and (2)

setting up a plan to put the plan into effect—the chief executive should be ready to start acting.[5] His objective now is to bring the plan to the point where all he needs to do to start the action is employ simple authority; he needs only to pull the trigger. As indicated at the start of the chapter, two steps are still required to implement our plan—creating the top of the organization, and raising money. Here we shall work on the first of these.

Thus far in our plan, we (and the president) have conceived the perfect workers and the supervisors for the lower echelons of each department's management team. Our task here is to conceive and create a group of men to head these departments, and to head any divisions which we plan to establish. To implement this goal, we shall evaluate our present executives, find men for these top positions, bestow formal authority, change the formal structure where necessary, and show each man his duties, though encouraging his help in deciding how to carry out his duties. Bear in mind that the manager who would be ideal for one or more of these departments may *not* look anything like the perfect executive we have been picturing in this book; the perfect head for a department which is to handle routine work might be a conscientious, pedestrian sort of person who is meticulous about details.

Evaluating the Present Executives

Regardless of how remarkable a new plan may appear as a means of filling a new niche, or for filling the present niche better, it will fall short of expectations if any one of the department managers proves unequal to his assignment. So one of the main responsibilities of the chief executive is to secure or develop qualified men for those key posts—men he predicts will correspond closely with his idea of the perfect managers for the particular departments.

While working out the details of his plan, the chief executive was doubtless picturing the kind of manager that would be ideal for each department. And he was probably looking over his present executives, asking himself which of the revamped departments, if any, they would each be most capable of managing. He not only wants men who can create the kind of department needed, and who conform rather closely to his idea of a perfect manager for the department, but he wants managers who have the ability to win informal authority

[5] See Preston P. Le Breton and D. A. Henning, *Planning Theory* (Englewood Cliffs, N.J.: Prentice-Hall, Inc., 1961), chap. 7 and 8, for a discussion of the role of the Board of Directors and top management committees in implementing long-range plans.

from him and from their subordinates. Once he finds promising leaders, he can set up the top levels of the company's formal organization structure and appoint the executives by conferring *formal* authority on those men. We have already looked into these top management appointments twice, once in the chapter on formal organization structure when we erected the superstructure and again in our examination of the task of reshaping the product development department and choosing its leader.

The president is looking for certain broad-gauge qualities in his top executives as well as certain specific abilities. In the fourteen preceding chapters, we have dwelt at length on most of the fundamental abilities. But there are two or three other qualities which should be briefly mentioned. One has to do with the width of the men's zone of acceptance for the new program and the wholeheartedness with which the men will accept their new responsibilities. The chief executive would like to find men who can grasp the vision he has seen, and are eager to take on the duties he has in mind. At any rate, they must be able to see their own department's new goals clearly, agree that these goals are desirable as well as realistic, be able to understand thoroughly the picture of the new means to be employed (particularly the changes that are to be made in their respective departments), and must agree that these will be effective means of achieving the company's goals. If some of the men "drag their feet"—if they are not wholehearted in their support of the program—their departments will fall far short of the ideal he had visualized.

A second quality has to do with the flexibility of the men. The chief executive is looking for department managers willing to change their ways to meet new conditions, because most of the departments will have to be altered repeatedly in the years to come. For example, the chief executive will want a man who will sometimes be willing to accept, temporarily, what might seem like a reduction in his department's status if this seems essential to the company's welfare; he would like a sales manager, for instance, who agrees that his department should be reduced in importance during a wartime period when orders are plentiful. And he would like to have one who is constantly aware of changes in environmental conditions and selling techniques, and who is himself introducing changes in his sales organization to take advantage of them. An inflexible department head will eventually turn into a liability.

But the chief executive is also looking for certain specific abilities which have to do with running the departments after they have been revamped. By now, his ideas should be fairly concrete. He knows what new sections will have to be set up, which of the departments will have to be strengthened, in what respects they will have to be altered, and which ones must be reduced in importance. With these pictures of the characteristics of the departments as sources of premises, his task of visualizing the ideal top executive for each revamped department and determining whether the present heads measure up becomes relatively easy. He is seeking a man who can understand the premises that the men in the department will be using, who can help them to make intelligent decisions, and who can use the concepts in Part II of this book to gain their acceptance of the changes that are to be introduced. The new position should be a challenge to him, not a burden.

The chief executive's search for the ideal department head should, at the same time, be a search for a man who could be groomed into the "perfect" chief executive we have been envisaging in this book. This is a singularly important step for the long-term survival of the company, but it is frequently overlooked or postponed until an emergency—the sudden death or the retirement of the chief executive —forces immediate action.[6]

If the present manager of a department does not measure up to an approximation of the "perfect" department head, the chief executive first needs to ask himself whether the man has potential ability—that is, the ability to learn—and if, through guidance and executive training, the man can grow to a point where he can provide the particular kind of leadership required for the revamped department. He is asking himself where that man's principal weakness in handling the job will lie—in what specific activities he will most likely fail— then visualizing what training will be needed.

Most executives, no matter what their position in the hierarchy, are acutely aware of, and are constantly troubled by, the shortcomings of their subordinates. Yet the majority of their subordinates believe that they are very good executives or, at least, would be if they were

---

[6] See C. Roland Christensen, *Management Succession in a Small and Growing Enterprise* (Boston: Division of Research, Graduate School of Business Administration, Harvard University, 1953), for a discussion of this problem and the ways in which some small companies have (and have not) resolved it. Also see Melvin T. Copeland and A. R. Towl, *The Board of Directors and Business Management* (Boston: Division of Research, Graduate School of Business Administration, Harvard University, 1947), for suggestions about the role of the board of directors in evaluating and selecting the chief executive, and thereafter guiding him.

given a chance. In their eyes, their decisions have been excellent; in fact, they are usually wondering why they have not already been promoted. According to the premises these men are using, their conclusions about their own ability are quite obvious to them; and they are perplexed that their boss does not seem to agree.

The difference between the superior's and the subordinate's evaluation usually lies in the fact that even though the subordinate may be making decisions that take into consideration, and give due weight to, all the premises *he* has available, the man he reports to usually employs many more premises than he. To the man's boss, these additional premises are obvious, so he is irked when the subordinate fails to employ them; the man's decisions, when seen in the perspective of the company-wide picture the boss uses, frequently seem shortsighted and ill-advised. A chief executive is constantly, though often unconsciously, evaluating and comparing all his top executives on some such basis as this; hence, this evaluation we have been discussing is not an extra task.

No executive in any company is sacrosanct. What we have been saying about evaluating the ability of department heads to cope with the jobs ahead applies equally to the division heads and the chief executive. When it becomes apparent that the president of the company lacks the creative ability and leadership necessary to carry the company forward, it is the duty of those who are ultimately responsible for the welfare of the company to select a new man. In some companies, this group may be the board of directors, or more likely, certain members who have won for themselves a position of leadership on the board. In other companies the family that originally founded the company may be able to supply the guiding hand. In still others, it may be the officers of a bank that has become heavily involved financially, or a group of bondholders or stockholders.

Finding Men for Departmental Managers

The chief executive's most difficult task at this juncture is not to picture the ideal executive for the department, nor to evaluate his men, but to find executives who measure up. Clearly, the first place to look is within the company; these men have already accumulated a storehouse of useful premises derived from company sources.

It may turn out that the present department heads can be reshuffled so that the men's abilities will more nearly match the demands that will be made upon them. The principal problem here is to make sure that each of the transferred executives will feel at home with the types of premises, factual and value premises, predominantly used in his "new" department. A department head, however, normally accumulates many of the premises used regularly in the other departments. And a man with a perceptive mind can rather quickly pick up the endemic premises required in his new job once he has taken over the department. In fact, he frequently learns these *very* quickly because he is obliged to make telling decisions from the beginning. Furthermore, as an outsider, he can bring to the department a fresh perspective and a set of new premises. (If his predecessor has been on the job a long time, the chances are that the department has settled down to a routine.) A company-wide reassignment of these top jobs also helps each of the executives to gain a company-wide point of view; consequently, their decisions become more effective. Moreover, such rotations present new challenges to the executives, give them new interests, and help to prevent the formation of departmental cliques.

To fill the positions that are left unfilled after this appraisal of the present department managers, the chief executive will ordinarily look hopefully over the list of men further down in the organization who now hold less responsible jobs. If the company has conscientiously followed the practice of developing young executives, he will have several admirable prospects to choose from; but in most companies the list of potentials proves disappointing. It is surprising— and also disconcerting—to see how often companies are confronted with the embarrassing conclusion that they have no promising executive timber.

Going outside the organization in the hope of finding the ideal man is a hazardous business. No matter how thorough the interviews or how extensive the references, it is virtually impossible to uncover enough premises to be sure that the new man will be equal to the job. Ordinarily, these premises can be discovered only by working with the man for a period of time.[7]

---

[7] Psychological tests or placement tests can be of some help in identifying these executive candidates uncovered inside and outside the company, but even their strongest proponents carefully point out that such tests can be used only as aids. Because of the wide variety of tests available, and because I am an amateur in psychological testing, I hesitate to make generalizations about their merits; nevertheless, here are a few such generalizations, for what they are worth. Aptitude tests give clues to a man's ability to use factual premises in reasoning to a conclusion. It is difficult to build tests that will measure the man's ability to use value premises such as those an executive must employ. More than that, psychologists are not entirely sure about the aptitudes or characteristics a "good" executive should possess—what we should try to measure—or the relative weight to be assigned to each. But given such a list (the broad aptitudes I should consider most important are indicated by the chapter headings of this book), how does one construct a set

Appointing the Men: Bestowing Formal Authority

Seldom does a chief executive find a near-perfect department head. When he does, the appointment is, of course, a foregone conclusion; he feels a weight lifted from his shoulders. It is more usual to discover that in order to fill some of the vacancies, he must upgrade, albeit with misgivings, certain men he suspects are not fully qualified; he *hopes* that they may possess some highly desirable attributes which have not yet been detected and that, with experience and training they will overcome some of their weaknesses.

Sometimes, he is forced to make stopgap appointments in lieu of leaving the post vacant, because the several features of the plan need to be carried out according to time schedules. If he waits to find the perfect team of executives, certain parts of the plan will be seriously delayed. These makeshift arrangements give him time to look further for the ideal man, or perhaps to train one. But during this interval the chief executive will himself have to take over much of the actual direction of the department. This places an extra burden on him, and it usually produces uncertainty in the department; but the company can live with these unwanted consequences for a time if the chief executive has some plan for an eventual solution.

Probably the chief executive's most painful dilemma at this stage is the one of determining what to do with an executive who is no longer capable of leading his department. Often, the first thought is

---

of questions whose answers will measure these abilities—and also indicate the man's *potentials?* How does one measure the ability to lead, for instance, when there are no agreed-upon, objective, numerical measures for leadership? And above all, there seems to be no way of predicting the man's "drive" for doing the *particular* job to be assigned to him. He may have the necessary *ability*, but how can we predict whether he will work at the adequacy level or at an efficiency level? Tests of social aptitudes are subject to the same limitations. These tests, when used with a recognition of their limitations, do supply valuable information. Unfortunately, however, in hiring executive timber and promoting men, executives tend to assume that the test scores provide *all* the necessary premises; the results are displayed in numbers and bar graphs; thus, they are obviously scientific, and the answers they give *must* be right!

Several shortcomings of psychological tests in selecting executives are underlined by Mason Haire in R. A. Dahl, M. Haire, and P. F. Lazerfeld, *Social Science Research on Business* (New York: Columbia University Press, 1960), pp. 59–66.

Perhaps aptitude tests should be abandoned in favor of detailed appraisals of each man by his colleagues. See, for example, C. Wilson Randle, "How to Identify Promotable Executives," *Harvard Business Review*, Vol. XXXLV, No. 3 (May–June, 1956). This article based on rather extensive studies, lists some thirty attributes of a good executive which men generally agree upon, assigns them relative weights, then describes what appears to be a rather successful procedure for assessing a potential executive—a point-by-point rating by the men who know him best. The characteristics that are appraised can be measured only with value standards—"drive," for example—but these are defined quite precisely in this article, so that standards used by each appraiser are reasonably uniform.

to discharge him in the belief that he would be unhappy in a job carrying lower status. But it may turn out that he would be very well satisfied with a less demanding job, one he knows he can handle. In any case the company has a responsibility for the man's welfare. Perhaps he can be "saved" by transferring him to a department where routine decisions are sufficient for company survival. If the change in this man's job is a part of a major shift in department heads—a shift, so the announcement reads, "for the purpose of broadening every executive's experience"—the man can justify the change to his associates, family, and friends. If he seems incapable of heading any of the new departments and would be unhappy in other possible jobs, it may be necessary to help him to find a job elsewhere.

The tasks of selecting men for top management and middle management and taking care of the men displaced are so important to the company's welfare that the chief executive is obliged to work at them until they are resolved. The company can usually limp along if there are other weaknesses in the organization; but without skilled department managers who are able to cope with the departments' problems, or else a chief executive who has the time and energy to act in their stead, the company runs into real trouble in satisfying the needs of its several member groups.

We are now at the point where the chief executive is overtly implementing his plan. Once he is convinced he can find no better man to head a department or a division, he makes the appointment and gives the man a title. But even after the appointment, he, *in practice*, actually delegates a portion of the authority bestowed on him by the board of directors *only* when he is reasonably sure that the man knows which decisions he is to make himself and carry out, which he should make tentatively, but talk over with the president or others before carrying them out, and the ones he should immediately pass on to the president.

Establishing the Formal Organizational Structure

To help implement the plan, it may be advisable to change the company's formal organization structure. The capabilities, interests, and experience of each new department head will certainly differ from those of his predecessor. The foregoing, together with the probability that the new plan contemplates changes in the work done by some sections of each department and the likelihood that communications could therefore be improved between some sections by shifting them to other departments, may suggest that some revisions should be made in the structure. The picture of the improved structure evolves from the premises gathered during the planning stage and from the concepts we developed in Chapter 10, when we dealt with formal organization structure.

A public announcement of the formal appointment of the executives and of the structural changes, and an explanation of the reasons for these, serves the double purpose of giving these revisions the blessing of the company and implementing the plan. By this procedure, each man is made more aware of what decisions he, his superior, and his subordinates are supposed to make. He has a clearer idea of what the company expects him to do. Defining the executives' responsibilities and at the same time delimiting them not only helps to ensure that all the necessary decisions will be made, and that each shall be made by a designated individual, but it helps to avoid conflicts of a jurisdictional nature. The departures from what we called a simple structure—the places in the organization where the chief executive has complicated the structure by appointing two or more bosses for a single man—will obviously have to be discussed in detail directly with the managers if misunderstandings are to be avoided.

But as we now know, the formal appointment of the man—the bestowal of *formal* authority and the transfer to him of the responsibility for directing the work of a department—does not ensure that the appointee will succeed in exercising authority; if he cannot win his authority from his subordinates, the probabilities are that his department will never be converted into a near-perfect one.

Nevertheless, the chief executive has the responsibility for making sure that the lines of formal authority are actually functioning. Seeing that each executive in the hierarchy is backed up by his superiors serves as an effective adjunct (but only an adjunct) to the more fundamental resolution of this problem, namely executive training, which was discussed in the chapter on communication and training. The appointee will inevitably make some mistakes in dealing with his new subordinates. (Who does not?) But as long as he holds the job, his superior must, in public at least, defend and support his decisions, even though some injustices and other unwanted consequences may result. If that man's subordinates discover that they can get his decisions reversed by going over his head, he soon loses his worth as an executive. When he makes a mistake, however, it is the responsibility of his superior to sit down with him in private and show him the premises he either overlooked or failed to weight appropriately. With this additional training, he should be able eventually to improve his decision making, win his authority, and eventually win leadership. It may be necessary, in the end, to discharge a weak subexecutive; but until that time comes, his superior has little choice but to back him up.

These changes in organization structure and in authority do not take place overnight. An executive would be naïve to expect that. In fact, it is advisable to let the changes develop somewhat naturally. But this does not mean that the chief executive should not guide the changes, or that they are to be introduced at a rate chosen by the men. He must keep nudging the men into the organizational pattern he has in mind, using the spirit of the original plan, however, rather than the letter of the plan, as his guide. Recall that changes in the formal structure serve as a tool for gaining acceptance of proposed changes.

Directing the Department Heads

Our concern here will be to set goals for the department heads and use these to direct the efforts of those executives.

In the preceding chapter we were setting up formal systems to control the behavior of factory workers and salesmen. However, in devising those controls, we partially abandoned the traditional assumption that people hate to work and that accordingly every company should set up controls for almost every task; we decided that men would automatically perform some tasks because they *wanted* to; we would need to set goals and compare results only for those crucial tasks that they might *not* perform as well as necessary. In this chapter where we are dealing with high executives, we are going a step further and assuming that these men will readily see most of the company's goals and will want to work toward achieving all of them.[8] This prediction of their behavior seems reasonable in our case, for our executives were chosen, in part, because they had the capacity to see company goals and had a strong desire to achieve them.

The department heads and the division heads, if any, will probably know a few of the new goals and means contained in the new plan. But now that the chief executive has appointed them, he embarks more formally on the sixth stage of the creative process, the communication

---

[8] Douglas McGregor develops this idea of using goals to direct executives in *The Human Side of Enterprise* (New York: McGraw-Hill Book Co., Inc., 1960), chap. 5 and elsewhere. Also see Peter F. Drucker, *The Practice of Management* (New York: Harper & Brothers, 1954), pp. 119–36.

stage; he shows the men the whole picture of the new company he envisages, describes the new pattern of goals and means he has conceived, and indicates to each manager his ideas of what he thinks the department should look like. The second objective here is to induce the manager to accept the new departmental and company goals wholeheartedly through the use of what we called "easy" proof—by pointing out the company's new intermediate goals and showing him the pathways planned for achieving it. Here, among other things, the department head learns of the role each department in the company is to play in the program. Even more important, the chief executive is attempting to provide the man with a clear picture of exactly what changes are to be made in his department and what key tasks the department must be able to handle thereafter—and, at the same time, stimulate *him* to work out the details of the departmental plan. The man should leave these sessions with a feeling that the new program is very explicit as to what actions are to be taken and the time schedule for each, and with the feeling that it is his own plan as well as the boss's.

In explaining the manager's duties, it is helpful to separate them into the two groups: the changes that will have to be introduced and the crucial tasks the department must carry out day after day in the months ahead. Let us first sit in for a moment on their discussion of the initial task—achieving the immediate goal of a near-perfect department. And let us further suppose that the department head has caught the vision of the goal and is taking the initiative in conceiving the means of attaining it. "We will need ten men with such-and-such skills by this date and probably about five more within six months; I suggest this because . . ." "I'll ask George Reed to work with the personnel department in lining up these men and training them. George has his regular work to do, and this will be an extra load; but we can get John Zedlicka to help him if he gets bogged down." "We will need such-and-such equipment laid out in this way, and we must have it ready by mid-October." "We should be able to keep the costs of introducing this particular part of the change within such-and-such a figure." "I'll get Fred Metz to call these equipment manufacturers and ask them to send representatives before next Tuesday so we can get started on that job. I'll have men from cost accounting and the maintenance and engineering departments sit in on the sessions so they can help work out the details about the new type of equipment we will need."

Now, let us watch while they decide on the department's more permanent goals and means. The chief executive would hope that the department head would take the initiative here, too. "As I see it, our job in this department will be to make sure that these things (naming them) are done regularly and done extremely well. Evidently, these are critical in the success of the company's plan because of such and such." For example, at the session with the sales manager, the discussion of the department's permanent goals and means might run as follows: "The salesmen should hereafter concentrate on the customers in the —— industry; we will hope to get thirty new customers lined up before Christmas and about ten a month after that." "I'll transfer one of the salesmen into that new southern territory and ask him to sign up four new distributors within about three months; I think I can move Bill Yager over and get a new man for his territory." "The direct-mail campaign to these prospective distributors should get into full swing before the salesmen begin calling, and I'll start young Jordan on that." "Our sales volume from these accounts should run about $—— per month within a year, and we should sell about three hundred of J-42 and B-7." "We will, of course, continue calling on our regular customers and fighting for orders from them, but the big job we have to emphasize is getting these new customers." What the two executives are doing at these sessions is working their way by successive steps *down* the means-end staircase. Each lower step is more concrete than the one above it.

We have just been observing variants of the procedure which we labeled "group decision making" in the chapter on leadership. Although the president already has some clear ideas about appropriate decisions for many of the department's lower steps, the relationship which he is seeking to establish between himself and the department manager is that of two men working out the departmental plan together, though under the leadership of the chief executive. To maintain this relationship, the president will periodically have to suppress the temptation to "suggest" that certain of his pet ideas be included in the department head's plan. In the event the man proposes means that would jeopardize other parts of the over-all plan, the president will doubtless have to step in. But as long as the alternatives which the department head chooses for his stairsteps are strong enough to achieve the goals on the steps above them, and produce no serious harmful side effects, the president should adopt them wholeheartedly. He knows that under these circumstances only a simple pull of the trigger will be needed to implement the department's plan.

So much for the task of building the top echelons of our company. But this does not necessarily ensure that the plan will get under way. The subordinates in the department will have to do the work, so the departmental plan must include a procedure for seeing that the permanent crucial tasks are conscientiously performed. Otherwise, the men down in the department will tend to slip back into the old routines. In addition to appointing section heads and mental experts who will be responsible for supervising these jobs, it will probably be necessary to explain the reasons for the changes to the men at the bottom of the department's hierarchy, and work out a way of evaluating the performance of the new jobs in which the men may be derelict—set up some controls discussed in the preceding chapter and perhaps prepare a job manual.

SUPPLYING THE COMPANY AND THE DEPARTMENTS WITH FUNDS

Before actually launching the plan, we want to make sure we can get the necessary money. Recall that when we were reappraising the plan, we briefly considered, then laid aside, the task of fund raising (p. 497). The president and treasurer, we hope, began exploring the task of raising money well before the president took the step of forming his top management team and getting it ready to act.

Our second method of implementing the plan consists of two tasks: securing the funds that the company will need (raising additional capital), and providing each department with the money it will need (setting up budgets). Building the top echelons of the company was our first method.

Raising Capital to Finance the New Program

Although the executive will ordinarily have to go to outsiders for additional capital, some of the money—more than at first seemed possible—can frequently be raised within the company. For one thing, dividends can be reduced or halted so that the additional investments can, in part, be financed out of company earnings; this, incidentally, constitutes a type of forced investment on the part of the stockholders—their dividends are reinvested for them. Sometimes, money can be also raised by selling unneeded physical assets.

Temporary and Permanent Capital. Temporary capital can frequently be raised without recourse to borrowing. One way is to reduce repairs and replacements in plant and equipment to a minimum for a short time. Any depreciation charges that are not offset fully by expenses for repairs (or otherwise spent) show up in the balance sheet as cash; the effect of this practice is to use up, and in this way to "sell," some of the fixed assets by not replacing them. Reducing the inventories to a bare minimum, postponing the payment of bills, and tightening the collection of accounts receivable will also put cash in the bank. In an emergency, warehouse receipts on inventories and the hypothecation of accounts receivable will serve as sources of temporary capital. Once in a while, it is possible to lease equipment instead of buying it or to work out long-term financing arrangements with the equipment manufacturers.

But these stopgap measures are precarious—suitable *only* when the executives are quite certain that the earnings within the next two or three years will enable the company to repay these "borrowings" from itself and others. A company that plans to expand its sales volume rapidly is going to need *permanent* capital. In addition to financing larger inventories and accounts receivable and the new equipment, the firm is likely to need money to carry out product development work. Returns from the latter cannot be expected immediately; and, at best, they are uncertain. A young company in the throes of developing and perfecting its product and with little money available, will almost certainly need permanent capital. Trying to finance such a project out of profits entails some serious risks. The developmental work frequently takes more time and money than expected, and in its race against time the company is greatly tempted to market the product before it is perfected, in order to gain some income. We have already examined the consequences of such a move (see p. 463).

Sources of Capital.[9] The amount of permanent capital required largely determines where the chief executive should go for funds— to individuals or to an investment house. And in laying these plans, he must recognize that if the capital required is not large enough to warrant the issue of stock or long-term bonds which can be listed on a stock exchange, these new investors are probably committing themselves to rather long-term membership in the company. Financial men call this "partnership money," even though the company is a corporation. The investor in an unlisted security cannot withdraw at a moment's notice if the company's plans do not mature as expected;

---

[9] I am indebted to Mr. Harold F. Wood of A. G. Becker & Co., investment brokers, with main offices in Chicago, for much of the following material about raising capital. But I hasten to add that he would not fully agree with everything I have said, nor should he "be held responsible for the statements herein made."

in the event that he wishes to sell, he has to search out a buyer willing to take over his membership in the company.

Not many of the securities issued by medium-sized companies are listed on a stock exchange. One reason is size; to be eligible, a company must meet certain standards set by the exchange, minimum requirements such as the following: a certain net worth ($1,000,000 for example), certain average annual profits ($150,000, for example), public ownership of a certain percentage of the company's shares, and a minimum dollar market value of shares outstanding. In addition, the new stock and the company's financial reports will probably have to conform to the regulations of the Securities and Exchange Commission (a complicated and time-consuming task) because issues listed on exchanges will be sold interstate and thus fall under SEC regulations.

Although raising capital for medium-sized firms is difficult, the task is not insuperable. In the United States, there are several thousand brokers and dealers who sell securities in the over-the-counter market, and many of these participate in selling new securities. After the company's securities are sold to investors, they *may* be listed on one of the stock exchanges, but certainly this is not necessary. The volume of stocks and bonds (this includes government bonds) sold over the counter is greater than the sales on regular stock exchanges.[10]

We shall assume that our company is *not* one of those with a glamorous name or a type of product which seems to promise riches to naïve investors, and whose stock could therefore be sold without much effort. Our company probably has a reasonably promising product line, but no glamor. Hence, the men responsible for acquiring permanent capital—our president and treasurer, together with our attorney and firm of public accountants—can expect no quick and easy financial solution. To raise money, they must convince investors that our new plan is realistic and that it promises a reasonable profit. It is virtually impossible for a broker to sell the stock of a company which has neither a plan, nor a long record of good earnings. An executive with a new plan that requires outside financing must find investors who believe in him and believe he can actually carry out the plan.

The executive of a small company needing between $25,000 and $100,000 is in a relatively good position to raise funds. In normal

---

[10] See George L. Leffler, The Stock Market (2d ed.; New York: The Ronald Press Co., 1957), p. 4–5.

times, he can usually locate 5 to 20 men willing to invest $5,000 or so each. Frequently, the present stockholders will buy more stock. Sometimes, the company's banker or attorney will supply leads; and once in a while, a friendly broker is willing to suggest prospects. It is the company that requires between $100,000 and $300,000 or so which faces the hardest problem. Raising such a sum from individual investors would be an overwhelming task; yet it is impractical to float a stock or bond issue as small as this because, to prepare data, the company must pay legal and auditing fees which usually run between $20,000 and $50,000. Moreover, the underwriter's expenses of investigating and selling are so high, and his risk of carrying over unsold securities are so great, that relatively little is left over for the company. Brokers usually charge $7\frac{1}{2}$ to 8 per cent commission. One solution is a combination of bank loans, partnership money, and mortgage money—the latter borrowed, perhaps, from an insurance company under a contract that calls for repayment of the principal in equal monthly installments.

If the company needs a sum in excess of $300,000 or so, a small- or medium-sized investment broker which operates locally can be of considerable help. He and some of the other local investment houses may be able to sell the issue to their own local clients. With issues of this size, the practice is to sell shares only to investors residing in the state; when the shares are sold only intrastate, the approval of the Securities and Exchange Commission is not necessary. But instead of going to the trouble of issuing stock, the local broker may decide to act as a middleman in negotiating a combination of bank loans and insurance company loans. He has opportunity here to work out a variety of combination offers, including stock rights, options to purchase, and mortgages. Most insurance companies prefer self-liquidating loans of $1,000,000 and up.

Because of the flood of new issues in recent years and the readiness of the public to buy stock, brokers' investigations lately have become more cursory than in previous decades. Nevertheless, the reliable investment houses will want as much information as they can get before deciding whether to help a company raise new money.

Preparing Necessary Data. Regardless of the size of the sum required and the sources of the funds, the executive must be in a position to demonstrate just what makes his company "tick"—how and why it has been able to compete in the past and, even more important, how and why it will be able to compete in the future. The underwriter seeks detailed information which will provide him with the premises for deciding whether to float the issue, how much money should be (and can be) raised, and what kind of security would be most appropriate. His reputation among his clients and customers depends on how well his decisions stand up. This same kind of information, though perhaps less of it, will have to be prepared when the company intends to sell directly to individuals. A few of the more discriminating investors also may want rather complete data, so that they can make their own decisions—they may want proof rather than some expert's recommendations which they must take on faith—so that they themselves can determine whether the investment is the best alternative for their purposes. A company that has followed a planning procedure similar to the one we have been discussing in Part III will already have at hand practically all the information mentioned below.

The executives of the brokerage firm (and the individual investors?) first want a history of the company and copies of its operating statements, balance sheets, and the details of the surplus account for the past ten years or so, if possible. They will also ask about the background and the strong points and weaknesses of the company's executives, as well as the character and ability of the young management coming up. The young men are the ones on whom the investors will eventually have to depend for their returns.

But *most of all*, they will want a diagnosis of the company's departments, including its product lines—answers to most of those questions listed on pages 418–23 which the company executives pondered when they were appraising the company's strengths and shortcomings and comparing it with its competitors. The premises derived from these are the ones that will be given greatest weight. Incidentally, the tendency of investment houses is to stress information that can be cast in numerical form.

Having secured information on the company's history and its executives, and on trends in the financial statements and the competitive position of the company's product development, sales, and manufacturing departments, the broker (and the investor?) next wants to examine the purpose of the new financing. What is desired here is a description of the market niche the company is planning to fill, the premises underlying this choice, the executive's plan for improving the departments, and the expected costs of introducing the various changes versus the contributions these will make to overhead and profits.

Finally, it is necessary to show how the company expects to meet these obligations. A projection of earning power over the next few years provides the foundation for this—estimates of probable sales in units and dollars; the expected out-of-pocket costs of manufacturing as a percentage of selling price; the probable overhead in salaries and other fixed contractual obligations, including interest on the new loan, if any; and, out of this, an estimate of profits. They will also want to know what collateral the firm can offer as security if the loan is to be in the form of mortgage notes, and how the company plans to use the profits for paying off the loans. If stock is to be issued, estimates of the dollar earnings per share on the outstanding stock will be needed, even though the estimates of dividends must of necessity be conjectural; and they would hope for some inkling of when the dividends could be expected.

Not all the companies seeking investors will need to supply equally complete information on all the questions dealing with the company's competitive position which were listed on pages 418–23. Depending on the company, some of the topics can be covered in a sentence or two, while other facets will need to be discussed in considerable detail. The information described above would constitute the maximum demanded by a conscientious broker who is investigating a company with a view to issuing securities to the public. If the company is planning to raise the funds itself by offering securities directly to prospective investors, less elaborate information will ordinarily be required. But in such a case an attorney familiar with the issuance of securities should be consulted to ensure compliance with the rather complicated state and federal statutes and regulations relating to new security offerings.

Normally, a company will not require all the new money immediately, because the plan cannot be put into effect all at once. This is fortunate, for it takes time to sell securities such as these. If an underwriter is used, the executive's time schedule for introducing the changes in the departments provides a basis for scheduling the transfer of the new funds.

Selecting and Appointing a Treasurer. So much for the tasks of raising money to finance the new plan. But the task of preparing the financial reports for the new security issue and handling the details of issuing the securities in conformance with the legal requirements demands a great deal of care and planning, regardless of whether the funds are secured directly from investors or through a broker. If the chief executive concludes that his present treasurer and the treasurer's subordinates will be capable of carrying out the task, or that he and the treasurer will be able to do it together with the help of an attorney, all is well. He is now ready to assign that officer the responsibility for going ahead. But if he foresees that he and the treasurer will not measure up, he has the additional task of finding a man equal to the undertaking. One of the problems in selecting a treasurer is that fund raising is an intermittent assignment, so that the man chosen must be able to make major contributions in the interims. Preparing the company's regular financial reports is an obvious assignment; but, in addition, he can often be given the responsibility for the financial controls of the company—appointed controller. Budgeting, one important phase of that task, is the subject of the next section.

Supplying the Departments with Funds: Budgeting

Budgets are essentially financial tools for planning and implementing plans. Most companies employ several types of budgets; however, in these pages, we shall confine our attention to the most widely used type—the operating budget, which is made up of an estimate of the dollar sales, planned-for expenses, and expected profits.

It is helpful to look upon an operating budget as the counterpart of the company's operating statement. It is simply an estimated operating statement prepared at the *beginning* of the period, whereas the operating statement itself is prepared at the *end* of that period after the results are all known. The operating *budget* is a summary of the company's future plans, cast in terms of dollars. It provides a set of goals for the company—sales goals and expense goals. The operating *statement* provides a measure of how well these goals have been achieved—how well the actual performance compares with the standards that have been set in the budget. From the foregoing, it is evident that operating budgets are closely akin to the controls we were exploring in the preceding chapter. The major difference is that operating budgets are customarily designed to control the company's allover operation instead of only a small segment of its activities such as hand motions, for instance, or the sales in a given territory.

Preparing the Operating Budget. A company which has worked out a new plan using the pattern of concepts set out in Part III will have at hand all the data for its next year's budget. By now, the reader is aware that the initial step in preparing an operating budget is the forecast of sales for the period ahead—usually for the next six months or twelve months. Beneath this dollar sales estimate lies an estimate of the physical units of each product which the company expects to sell in the period—an estimate made by the top executives, with the help of mental specialists, of the increase or decrease in each product's sales as compared with last year. This is the estimate that was made at the time the executives were planning the size and character of the manufacturing department's equipment and man power (see p. 474). We have also already prophesied the average selling price per unit for next year—whether it would be $2.00 higher or 15 cents less than last year (see p. 495)—so we can now make a tentative dollar sales estimate.

The information for estimating the out-of-pocket and overhead expenses is likewise at hand. The number of physical units we shall manufacture, multiplied by the average cost per unit of raw materials, purchased parts, cartons, freight, and direct labor provides a basis for a tentative estimate of out-of-pocket manufacturing expenses. The department-by-department estimate of the additional annual overhead expenses which we made when trying to determine whether the new program would pay for itself supplies figures for estimating next year's overhead expenses (see pp. 495–96). We need no other data.

An executive cannot expect his next year's budget to be realistic if he simply doodles with the figures shown in the current year's operating statement or naively inserts in the budget some figures pulled out of thin air. As we saw earlier in the chapter when we began appraising the profitability of the new plan, the figures in the company's current-year operating statement are simply a summary of the dollar results of the behavior of the customers, the channels of distribution, and the various employee groups in the company. Thus the first task here is to review our predictions of people's behavior.[11]

Only if the next year's plans offer certain specific types of customers an increase in the spread between the monetary and nonmonetary inducements proffered them, on the one hand, and the contributions required of them, on the other, will the company's sales volume

---

[11] In this connection, it might be helpful to turn back to the illustration on pages 134–37 of the use of the inducement-contribution concept as a tool for predicting the actions of the member groups. There, we tested out a plan to improve one of the company's products—foresaw the reactions of potential customers, our salesmen, our product design men, and the men in the plant—and then predicted the effect on the *company's* inducement-contribution balance. In that example, it is evident that the company's sales and annual gross margin will increase considerably because the customers and salesmen will welcome the new product. But the annual gross margin will be smaller than *might be expected* because out-of-pocket manufacturing expenses will be higher than anticipated; the plant men, because of their resentment, will "accidentally" waste raw materials and make mistakes; they will reduce their contributions.

increase. If, in their eyes, the spread will be narrower, the executive can expect sales to decline; and he must revise his sales estimates accordingly. Similarly, to induce an employee group to make greater contributions, he must make sure that he offers them extra monetary and nonmonetary things so that they will automatically make the contributions the company will need. These employee contributions go beyond such obvious ones as time or effort; what the company wants from them is intelligent planning, sharp decision making, and an ability to put into effect plans that will help to achieve the company's goals. If the executive can induce the employees to make more of these contributions, he can be reasonably sure that the company's products and its sales program will meet the needs of the present and potential customer members, and that expenses will be kept down. If he concludes that he cannot expect each member group to take the hoped-for actions, he must either change his plans so that they will, or he must change his budget figures to correspond with the realities.

The Threefold Use of Budgets. As already intimated, operating budgets serve as instruments (1) for planning, (2) for implementing plans, and (3) for checking up to see that the plans are being followed.

Budgets help the executives to make concrete plans. Preparing a careful budget forces the executives to enumerate the specific means the company intends to employ in order to fill its chosen niche—the specific monetary and nonmonetary inducements which the company is obliged to offer, and the money costs of each. And when the department heads participate in making the over-all company budget, they also become more fully aware of the needs and the tasks of their sister departments.

Budgets are instruments for implementing plans in that they set concrete monetary goals for department's executives and places in their hands the funds that the departments will need. The sales estimate provides a concrete goal for the combined efforts of the sales department, and of the product development and manufacturing departments. The expense budgets prepared for the various departments set a goal as to the amounts they are to spend in achieving the sales volume. The actual transfer of this money to the department heads and division heads, if any, starts the wheels turning. As soon as the funds are made available for new equipment or for additional personnel, the department manager is in a position to put the new plans into effect. In fact, he not only has the "right" to act but the obligation to do so. If the plan calls for the expansion of a department, the budget forces the manager to spend *more* money than before—to spend it, however, only on those items which the company has decided it must have if it is to compete effectively. On the other hand, if a department's work is to be curtailed under the new plan, its reduced budget forces this contraction.

But most of all, budgets serve as instruments for checking up on the people in the departments to see that the plans are actually being carried out. Budgets are not in themselves controls, however, any more than were the controls discussed in Chapter 14. Only if the records of actual performance—the figures showing actual sales and expenses—are periodically compared with the expected performance (the budget) and appropriate action is taken before it is too late, do these serve as controls. This task of checking up after the new plan has been put into operation will be explored further in the final pages of this concluding chapter.

Limitations of Budgets.   As we have seen, executives can employ budgets to implement next year's plans. But as tools they have their shortcomings and limitations.

First, department managers and section heads tend to use their budgets as the sole basis for determining whether they are doing a good job, forgetting that there are other measures of achievement, some of which may be even more pertinent. They like to make a good record for themselves (in this respect, they are by no means unique); and many think they have proved their worth when they demonstrate that they have met the budget figures. Were this the sole test for deciding whether a department's efforts have been effective in achieving the company's goal, all would be well. But as we have seen, most departments must produce many intangibles which can never be measured in dollars; and failure to provide these to other members of the organization will jeopardize the company's welfare.

A second limitation is a supposition prevalent among many middle-level and lower-level executives that once the budget is adopted, it is sacrosanct, and that the company's main goal is to secure the profits set out in the budget. Conforming blindly to a budget will not necessarily further the company's well-being. It is essential to think of a budget as a flexible guide; the figures are based upon predictions. If these predictions prove untrue—for example, if sales begin to expand faster than expected—it would be absurd to hold rigorously to the budgeted expenses. Conversely, if it appears that sales will *not* reach the levels expected under the program planned for the year, it behooves management to reappraise the amounts of money originally allocated, distribute less than planned to many departments, and perhaps parcel out *more* than originally planned to other departments or activities. In budgeting, the objective is not to prove that the company can predict and control its financial results with exactitude, but to spend the money available from sales (and money secured from new investors) on those means which, in the light of unfolding events, will best further its permanent goals. Nor should a budget, even a revised one, necessarily be designed to provide the company with a profit. On occasion, a budget showing an operating deficit may serve the company's long-term interests best.

Third, an inflexible budget administered by an obdurate company official often serves as a strait jacket for the creative drives so vital to the welfare of an organization. This does not mean that management must give way to every whim of its mental experts and executives. But it is essential to give freedom and encouragement to imaginative and aggressive men, allowing them to strike while the enthusiasm is high and the opportunity is right instead of freezing the creative forces with the deadly response, "There's no provision for that in this year's budget; maybe we can include it next year." For a company to flourish in those industries where technological improvements are rapid, the budget must always be considered tentative.

Finally, executives rarely accept budgets wholeheartedly. Although almost everyone grants that budgets are a good thing—"All companies should operate on a budget"—my own guess is that comparatively few medium-sized companies consistently set up budgets, and still fewer actually pay close attention to them after they have been prepared.

One reason is that many executives believe budgets are intended as accurate forecasts of what will *actually* happen; and when they find that the actual results seldom resemble the budget, they conclude that budgeting and trying to follow the budget is a waste of time. They also feel ill at ease when they realize that the amount allowed their department for expenses does not serve as an unfailing guide to what they can spend. ("They told me I could spend $1,000 on this, but now they've changed their minds.") What is more, the amount that they must actually spend to get their projects completed is often quite different from what they were "supposed" to spend. After encountering a few such experiences, they conclude that they cannot guide their actions by the budget.

But a more fundamental objection—one that is very real, though seldom expressed by the executives themselves—is that the budget takes away a good deal of the department manager's freedom in making decisions. When budgeting is adopted, many of the decisions he had hitherto made by himself are now made by the group that prepares the budget. Even though he may play an important role in its preparation, the budget is usually a group decision. When he sees the budget as a whole, he may concur with the others that the budget is fair—though, more likely, he thinks it is fair to every department except his own—yet the fact that his actions are controlled by it lowers his status in his own eyes and possibly in the eyes of his subordinates. He is also fearful that an emergency may arise and that he will not have the money he will need to take care of it. Because of all this, it is usually difficult to elicit wholehearted acceptance of budgeting.

Despite these limitations, budgets have their uses—three of them, as we have seen. But the success of a budget depends heavily upon the interested support of the chief executive. His is the responsibility for gaining the men's acceptance of the idea of using a budget and making it work. Furthermore, unless he succeeds in getting his department heads and his accounting men to understand the fundamental purposes lying beneath the idea of a budget, the unwanted side effects frequently outweigh the wanted consequences of budgeting.

SEEING THAT THE PLAN ACTUALLY WORKS: THE FOLLOW-UP

Sufficient funds and a top management team such as we have envisaged, a team made up of men carefully tailored for the newly conceived organization, are powerful means of putting a long-term plan into effect. The men now know their assigned goals and means, and they know the time table. Hence they almost automatically initiate each part of the plan at the appropriate time. The plan is implemented without fanfare.

But launching the new program does not ensure that all its segments will thereafter be followed. To make certain that the plan works, it is necessary to do two things on a continuing basis. One is to see that the members of the organization are carrying out their respective assignments. The other is to make periodic revisions in the original plan so that it will fit the conditions that *actually* develop instead of those we predicted.

Checking Up

The purpose of the type of control discussed here is to see that the department heads and their subordinates do, in fact, carry out the planned-for changes and continuously work on the long-term goals and means. These are the changes and goals which the president and the department heads evolved for each department during the planning sessions that followed the formal appointments. In these pages, we shall again be using the idea of controls with its four facets—finding the crucial tasks that may not be carried out, setting a standard or a 100 per cent for this goal, comparing the actual performance with the goal or standard, and taking remedial action before it is too late. The chief difference is that we are now controlling top management instead of workers. And as was mentioned at the time the president was showing each executive what to do (p. 510), these men usually are more anxious than the workers to achieve the company's goals.

But these men do need guidance, for even though they *want* to achieve the standards or goals, they are not always as successful as they and their president would like. Their most obvious problem is to make certain that their subordinates perform as planned. They and their president have at hand the several methods of controlling and correcting subordinates' behavior which we studied in Part II, the most palpable of which is the use of the four types of informal authority; however, as we have seen, these are not always effective.

The Problem of Setting Standards. Beneath this task of guiding the executives' behavior lies the more subtle problem of measurement of the goals and performances of these men—the problem of discerning whether they are carrying out their most important duties. How, for example, does a top executive and his president determine whether he is training his subordinates to be better executives? How do the two of them measure his progress in raising the morale of his men? And how does he tell whether his subordinate is 100 per cent or 50 per cent successful in his attempts to win leadership?

Such activities are difficult to discern and easily overlooked, yet are obviously crucial to the success of the company; hence, the chief executive dares not *assume* that his men will automatically carry them out. His department heads have difficulty in appraising their progress in achieving intangible goals and correcting their own shortcomings. Moreover, without some direction and control, they are obliged to make their own decisions on the basis of the premises *they* can gather. And if they have no appraisal of their effectiveness in achieving their departments' goals, they have no reliable status measures for determining how valuable they are to the company. Clarence Randall points out that

"Every decent man wants to pull his own weight and he likes to be told he is doing his job well. . . . He can be deeply hurt if he believes he is being treated unfairly in the matter of compensation, but nothing moves him so profoundly as the inner satisfaction that comes to him when he can honestly say to himself, "That was a good job!"[12]

There is no easy way to set fair standards and measure the performance of these men. Consequently, the tendency is to check up on only those consequences of their activities that are predominantly factual—their sales, profits, or costs compared with the budgeted figures or last year's figures, for example—and reward (or punish) them on the basis of their achievements by these standards. Frequently these are unfair measurements of performance. One reason is that results of that kind are influenced strongly by decisions made elsewhere in the company or in the economy. The sales department's sales, for instance, are the result of the work of the product development department and production department as well as the sales department. Of even greater impact are the customers' buying decisions, the activities of competitors, and the fluctuations in business conditions. Similarly, the success of the manufacturing department, or of the product research, purchasing, and personnel departments, as measured by some factual standards, is strongly influenced by what others do. The levels of sales, expenses, and profits are clearly significant for the welfare of the company, but we can properly give these only a medium amount of weight in checking up on an individual executive.[13]

The chief difficulty in controlling top management's activities, then, is to find measurable or explicit standards which accurately reflect the more important goals of the organization. In their actual performance, the men will try to achieve whatever they think is being measured, regardless of whether it is significant, for they believe they are held accountable for those particular goals and no others.

Once the chief executive and his department heads learn to make allowances for the shortcomings of both factual and value standards, they can go a long way in setting reliable standards and measuring performance. They must, however, be willing to spend the time and thought necessary to describe the goals as concretely as possible. The goals and means that they chose for the department and the time schedule for starting and completing these projects, provide them

[12] Clarence Randall, *The Folklore of Management* (Boston: Little, Brown and Co., 1961), p. 62.

[13] See Rensis Likert, *New Patterns of Management* (New York: McGraw-Hill Book Co., Inc., 1961), pp. 75–76, for a somewhat different approach to this same problem.

with some standards against which they can each measure the department's actual progress. These standards can usually be framed concretely either with word descriptions or numbers (probably both); and as time passes, the men can compare what has really been accomplished with their picture of these goals, and then decide on the needed corrective action.

Setting Up Communication Systems. Once the standards or the methods of measurement for the crucial tasks are determined, it is fairly easy to choose a communication system capable of reporting actual performance and supplying an early warning of emerging problems. There are only two destinations for the messages—the president and his department head; but there will be many "origins," for the men will need a variety of pieces of information. Most of the information will be channeled from the several origins through assembly centers, but except for this, the paths would be direct. The appropriate vehicles would be tabular numerical reports, written reports, and oral reports.

Reports cast in numerical terms and issued at regular intervals serve as the mainstay of this system. Typical of these are comparisons of this year's figures to date with last year's, or comparisons of the actual figures to date with the budget, in physical units, dollars, and percentages—comparisons of the sales volume, production volume, and expenses, for instance. Among these are the numerical controls which the executive conceived for his workers at the time he was planning the changes in his departments. One trouble with many of the numerical reports submitted to executives by accountants and statisticians is that they often include details about trivial matters. The problem is to bring to the fore the significant figures—those that deal with the key activities most likely to get out of control—and to set them out separately and clearly, and in such form that the executive need not make his own calculations in the margin of the report. Moreover, numerical tabulations, as we have observed, never tell the full story where human beings are concerned.

Written progress reports prepared by the department heads—word descriptions of progress in achieving the goals—can be used to appraise many of the intangibles. They not only keep the president informed, but they force the subordinate to appraise his own progress—to gather pertinent information about what he has and has not accomplished—and to write this information down in an orderly form. At the outset the chief executive may have to show his subordinate how to write these progress reports—show him that what is wanted is a statement of the agreed-upon goals followed by the specific details about the progress the department has made in achieving them, together with indications of those places where the department may fall short of its goals, and suggestions for resolving those problems. One part of the report might deal with the advances made in implementing the changes that were planned, and another with the headway made in achieving the department's salient permanent goals.

In studying these reports, however, the executive needs to be aware that the man is being asked to evaluate himself, and that he is likely to report whatever will make him "look good" and pass over lightly, or entirely omit, the shortcomings—a case of conscious or unconscious distortion. This does not mean that the reports are of no value; actually, the chief executive, expecting this, simply supplements the reports himself, by asking questions and by direct observation.

Verbal reports—that is, conferences at which programs and progress are talked over—though time-consuming, are much more sensitive than numerical or written reports. An executive who knows what questions to ask can elicit value premises which are difficult to put on paper; thus, he obtains a truer appraisal of the current situation. A fourth type of report—direct observation—is much the most accurate and sensitive of all. One of the main advantages enjoyed by a small company over its larger competitors is that the chief executive need not rely on written or verbal reports; he sees and lives with the details of what goes on, and he can keep most of the facts in his head. In such a company the communication costs are reduced to a minimum.

Taking Remedial Action. The principal purposes in setting up a communication system are to make sure that red signals flash when things are not going according to plan and to take remedial action while the opportunity is still there. To take action, a session with the department head is essential. One objective is to trace back to their sources the causes of any symptoms of trouble which appear in the reports. These may be difficult to discover; but once they are pinpointed, the necessary corrective steps quickly become apparent. The difficulty can usually be traced back to inadequate means—subordinates who have failed in their duties, or else to one of the executives who has failed to assign someone to the tasks. But these sessions can be made even more fruitful. When the performance has been unusually good (and progress *is* sometimes better than expected), the two men may trace back to ascertain the causes, and having found them, do more of these things in the future.

Some executives use these sessions to badger their subordinates. This is common in companies which make a practice of preparing reports only at the end of a period already closed—only after the goal is supposed to have been achieved. Although these terminal reports can be used to help a subordinate to avoid certain glaring mistakes in the future, they all too often serve as a basis for a "why-in-hell-didn't-you" session. "Why didn't you sell your quota in that southwest territory?" "What are those salesmen doing? Living at the Ritz?" "Why didn't you keep the raw materials inventory in line?" "Look at all this down-time in the shop—weren't there enough orders in that big backlog to keep the men busy?" "If you can't do your job, I'll get somebody who can." Executives who employ this approach are usually men who have few premises for deciding *ahead of time* what should be done, or are either unwilling or unable to assist their subordinates in working out concrete plans for achieving the goals.

When taking remedial action, the president's purpose is not to second-guess the department head, but to help him find shortcomings in his department and take remedial action while there is yet time. Nor may he break that clause in the unwritten contract between him and his subordinate which, if written down, might read somewhat like this: "The president (or any superior) must give his subordinate at least one or two warnings before penalizing the man for failure to achieve agreed-upon goals. He must tell a man when his performance is below standard—tell him where he stands and why."

Most executives feel at home in checking up on departmental operations; but they are usually reluctant to check up on another important matter, a subordinate's idiosyncrasies and foibles, and help him to correct these. Almost every man unwittingly acquires a few habits which sometimes annoy others, ones that at times lead to friction. These habits reduce his effectiveness. For example, a man may habitually interrupt others, talk a great deal but say nothing (speak before he thinks things through), mispronounce certain words, use poor English, frequently arrive late for appointments, swear at inappropriate times, always glower, never say "please," habitually oppose new proposals (see only the unwanted consequences), or constantly criticize and never praise. Most men never notice their foibles until they are pointed out. More often than might be supposed, a man welcomes suggestions that will help him to correct these weaknesses. Talking them over frankly may prove embarrassing for both the man and his superior, but such a practice goes a long way toward converting a group into a smooth-running organization.

Checking up to see that the people are actually doing what they are supposed to do, and teaching them their jobs, are continuing tasks. However, once an executive habitually does those things he has been asked to do, and does them well, the need for checking up (except at relatively long intervals) is no longer an urgent one. He has won authority from his superior.

Making Periodic Revisions in the Plan

We end our book-long examination of executive decision making with an appraisal of the second of two tasks we have included in the follow-up, that of continually revising the plan after it has been put into operation. No plan ever operates as smoothly as anticipated; the unexpected can always be expected. *The failure of department heads (or lower executives) to achieve certain goals is only another way of saying that a problem exists;* some of the steps on the staircases we devised have not been powerful enough to achieve the goals on the steps above. These weak steps have to be replaced. It is here that new decisions—revisions in the plan—will be needed.

It is the president's responsibility to adjust the plan as he goes along, revising the steps whenever he finds a better way to advance the company's welfare. The idea is to think of the plan as a tool that the executives are to master and use; they must not let it master them.

The reasons for failure to achieve the goals set out in a plan can usually be traced to one or more of three causes.

One cause is that some aspects of the company's actual environment—some of the conditions outside its control—usually differ somewhat from those that were predicted. Under these circumstances, it is necessary to revise the original idea of the best niche and alter the planned-for changes in the company's departments in an effort to adjust to the set of conditions which are *now* seen ahead. As the company gradually aproaches D Day, the true character of the company's social and economic environment begins to unfold; and this new picture must supplant the earlier picture of the future. If the original plan was devised with a view to making it fit more than one set of conditions, however, the executives can expect (or at least hope) that the necessary alterations in the company's original plan will be minor.

A second reason is that even though the outside conditions may actually materialize as anticipated, certain features of the plan turn out to be unrealistic. As a result, when the plan is put into effect, "bugs" begin to show up. To foresee all the unwanted consequences at the outset is virtually impossible, even though several experienced men may have tested out the plan in their minds ahead of time. And in any case, once a man has conceived a plan, once he has gone through the stage in the creative process of "seeing all things in one" —the blinding flash—his tendency is to brush aside as of no importance some of the snags that may occur to him. "That won't happen; but if it does, we can take care of it when the time comes," he promises himself. In addition, it may become evident that some of the essential means—essential steps on the staircase—were either too vague or were completely overlooked, so that the plan has to be revised to include these. When the plan is put into operation, the executive is *forced* to deal with its shortcomings. He must alter his plan to meet the realities as they emerge.

A third source of difficulty arises from the failure of some of the individuals to carry out their parts of the plan. Here, the time schedules are chiefly affected. To unsnarl this problem, it may be necessary to shift personnel, or to hire temporary or new personnel, or to limp along with the task partially completed, though completed to a point where the company can "live with it" temporarily. The executive must expect such failures; in fact, he has provided a follow-up to bring them to light early. As soon as they appear, he goes about altering his original plans to meet the situation. The fact that the revised plan does not correspond exactly with the original one will injure the company very little, provided that the mistakes are caught promptly.

SUMMARY

In this chapter, we have been exploring the chief executive's climactic task. But let it be reiterated that the frame of thinking developed is just as applicable to the task of introducing small-scale plans as the large ones we have been discussing—the smaller-scale changes lying further down on the means-end staircases with which middle-level and top executives are constantly working.

We started out by reappraising the plan and making the final decision. One part of the reappraisal consisted of looking back to see if the groups outside and inside the company would really behave as we originally predicted. The other part consisted of determining whether the plan would bring in more money—more annual contributions to overhead—than the additional annual overhead expense. (Were we working on a small plan—on a plan to change the office procedure for preparing invoices, for instance—we should want to do this, too.)

Next, we spent a few minutes on planning to put plans into effect. There, we were trying to gain some perspective by ranging the several parts of the plan in the order of their importance and magnitude, in an effort to decide which should be given priority. And we were working out an integrated time schedule to determine when each change was to be completed and, in the light of this, when it must be started. (We would also do this [on a small scale] were we changing the office's invoicing procedure.)

Then we embarked on the task of actually setting the plan in motion. Our first project was to erect the top echelons of the organization. We began by evaluating the present top executives and comparing them with our ideas of near-perfect department heads, to decide who would be able to create and run the "perfect" departments we had visualized. At the same time, we looked inside and outside the company for executives to replace those found wanting. We bestowed formal authority on the men we chose, changed the structure of the formal organization to help the men carry out the changes, showed the executives what their duties and goals would be, and worked out with them a subordinate plan for implementing their goals. (A plan for a change in office procedure would call for some of these steps, too, though on a smaller scale; and we would, of course, be dealing with office workers and supervisors instead of with top executives.)

Our second project for implementing the plan was to provide the necessary money. Raising permanent capital for additional plant and equipment, for increases in accounts receivables and inventories, and for temporary operating losses turned out to be a major task. Nevertheless, we felt reasonably confident of success in view of our carefully selected market niche and our thoroughly thoughtout plans for revamping our departments so that we could compete effectively. We also provided the departments with the funds they would need to implement the program; we worked with budgets, specifically the operating budget, as a tool for planning, carrying out plans, and checking up after the plans were put into effect. (A plan for a change in office procedure would call for only a small change in the department's budget.)

By the time we reached the concluding section of the chapter, the chief executive had actually pulled the trigger; the plan was under way. The task there was to see that the plan was really working as anticipated. We had trouble in setting up reliable standards for these executives and measuring their performance. But we concluded that once we recognized the shortcomings of factual and value standards, we could appraise the men by watching how well they achieve their departmental goals. We were following up with tabulations of figures, written reports, conferences, and observation to see that the actual performances corresponded with the goals we had set. But we were also preparing to make changes in the plan. We saw that some changes in the niche, and thus in the departmental plans, would be necessary in the event that the environment had been predicted erroneously. Alterations in the original plan would also be called for if it became became evident that certain features of that plan were unrealistic or that some of the men had failed to carry out their assignments. (With a small plan, we would doubtless follow up in the same manner, though the procedures would be simpler.)

We should like to think that the executive's job is now completed, that he can now let the company run itself. But unfortunately, this is not the way things happen, as will be seen in the Postlude.

POSTLUDE

An executive's work is never done. When he has successfully finished a given project, he can rightfully take pride in his accomplishments and bask in the praise of men who realize what he has done— praise, by the way, that is seldom voiced; or if it is, it seems too fulsome. But he cannot sit back and relax. Long before he has put his plan into effect, he must begin the cycle anew. His job in the months and years ahead will be briefly described here, because this provides an opportunity to bring together in one place the concepts included in the several conceptual subsystems we have explored. We can here summarize the entire book in a few paragraphs and set out the executive's task in chronological order. (The actual chronology differs somewhat from the order of the chapters.)

Well before he has achieved his objective of creating a near-perfect company for the environment he saw ahead—an environment that has now virtually arrived—he must begin to reappraise the niche he has chosen. His task is to picture the company environment for the next few years and decide whether new opportunities have now arisen—decide whether he should propose a revision in the long-term goals he has been striving for. An examination of the trends (and the possible reversals of the trends) in ideologies, political philosophy, and governmental policies, supplies many value premises of moment to him in determining the company's future long-term policies. Even more important, he must constantly be observing the general economic trends of the nation and the economic trends of his industry—the expected sales volume versus capacity, and the spread between selling prices and out-of-pocket costs. Within his industry, he must also be watching for changes in the volume bought by the several classes of customers served by the industry, for changes in competitors' selling and manufacturing programs, and for technological developments.

On the basis of what he thinks will happen in the outside environment, he is in a position to revise the company's long-term goals or select better goals for the period still further ahead, set a new D Day and begin trying once more to reshape the men, equipment, and supervisors now in the various departments and sections into more telling instruments for filling the niches he now sees are most promising—the various sections of the sales, product development, and manufacturing departments, and the purchasing, personnel, and control departments.

During the coming period, he also has the continuing task of improving the effectiveness of the men in the organization. He wants to make sure that the executives at all levels of the company will be capable of making decisions that will stand up even better than before, and that they will gain wholehearted acceptance of their decisions. A company never has too many executives who are *too* good. The stronger the executive group, the better the company can compete, and the more it will flourish; when the executives improve, the company almost automatically expands—they *produce* the expansion.

As a foundation for improving the decision making of his men, the executive can show them how to crystallize concrete statements of the company's ultimate and intermediate goals, how to form means-end staircases for the lesser decisions that have already been made, and how to look for weak or missing steps of the staircases for the purpose of pinpointing the decisions which will now have to be made. Teaching them to create ideas for heretofore unthought-of alternatives consists of establishing the idea that the company welcomes creativity, then of showing the men how to recognize the stage of confusion and how to cut through this confusion by crystallizing the statement of the problem and the goals; how to hunt for information pertinent to the problem; how to go through the incubation stage by organizing this information into premises, weighting them, and arranging the premises into homogeneous groups; how to set the mind on the task of creating an idea for a new alternative that may solve the problem, hoping that a new idea will suddenly come to light; and finally, how to revise and communicate the idea.

The key task of deciding what means (or goal) should be placed on a step of a staircase can be clarified by explaining the idea of alternatives and showing the men how to go about choosing among the most promising alternatives, including any new ones they may have conceived. The first step here is to uncover the premises germane to each alternative by trying out each one in the mind and separating these premises into two lists, one containing premises pointing to wanted consequences, and the other to the unwanted consequences of adopting each of the alternatives. The second step is to explore the reliability of the premises—determine whether the result will actually occur—a procedure that is aided by analyzing the three elements of the premises (cause, causal connection, and result) to see whether the speaker and his hearers are measuring these with objective, factual standards or subjective value standards. The executive will want to teach his men that factual premises are often unreliable (the consequences named will not occur), and that many value premises are quite reliable (the consequences named will occur). The final step is to teach the men to weight the wanted and unwanted consequences which will flow from adopting a given alternative and to choose the alternative(s) which will provide the greatest amount of wanted consequences and the smallest amount of unwanted consequences.

To improve their decision making, he will also want the men to know where mathematical models—operations research formulas in particular—can be useful and how to avoid their pitfalls. They can be used to advantage when the effects of many causes must be taken into consideration simultaneously, when the many causes can be described numerically, where the causal connection, that is, the relationships between these causes and their effects are stable and unchanging, and where the result is readily quantifiable. The men need to understand that operations research does not render decisions; it shows the executive only one of the consequences of adopting an alternative—usually the cost or the profit—and shows which alternative will be best on that basis alone. The executives also need to understand and make allowances for the many assumptions that are imbedded in the formula, and when making their decisions, they must remember to consider and give appropriate weights to the other consequences of adopting the cheapest or most profitable alternative.

In operations research, the emphasis was on finding and using factual premises. But the executives will have much more occasion to uncover and take into consideration the intangible goals and the value premises that their colleagues and subordinates will use. The president will want to make sure his executives take into consideration the effects their proposals will have on their colleagues' and subordinates' individual biological, social, and psychological needs, the effects the proposals will have on the goals of the organizations to which those men are loyal, and the compatibility of their proposals with those men's cultural heritages—their ethnic or nationality heritage, their religious and moral heritage, and the political, social, and economic philosophies they have adopted. He will also want his men to sort out the several member groups which make up the organization, and take into consideration the probable effects of their proposals on the inducements and contributions of each of these groups as well as on the company, noting how well the proposal they make compares with the inducements offered and contributions demanded by competitors.

Eventually, the men should be capable of using all the foregoing conceptual subsystems, melding them into the concept of practical rationality.

His task of teaching the men how to gain acceptance of their decisions is particularly difficult. They must learn to foresee the width of their receivers' zones of acceptance, to recognize which decisions must be discarded before they are proposed; and once they find a proposal they believe will be accepted, they must learn to choose the appropriate type of authority—simple authority, "easy" or "hard" proof, or sanctions—and to foresee what level of wholeheartedness and contribution can be expected. He will want to develop leaders, men with aptitudes for creating ideas for goals, for believing their groups can flourish, and for making things happen. He wants men who can think through the alternatives and premises before speaking out, who gradually build a long series of good decisions, who anticipate dangers, who possess moral and intellectual integrity, and who are willing to accept responsibility. Leadership has to be won by the executives; it cannot be conferred.

To gain acceptance of company decisions, plans for a communication system and for training also have to be worked out. For the communication of information that will be of only temporary use to the decider, the appropriate sources, pathways, and vehicles have to be chosen; and provision must be made to reduce barriers to communication, barriers such as failure to gain attention, misunderstandings of what is meant, mental lapses, distortion, and distance. To provide the routine manual specialists with permanently useful premises, the executive can see that the workers are trained in the "one best way," and that company policy manuals, standard practice instructions, and job manuals are provided and followed. For executives who will be making one-of-a-kind decisions, the communication of a thinking method akin to that described in this book is almost essential.

Empathy with the informal groups in the company will also aid the executives in deciding how to proceed in gaining acceptance of their proposed changes in the factory and the offices. Once they uncover the goals of these groups, they should be able to revise their company proposals to make these more compatible with the group's goals. They may even be able to employ the members' loyalty to their groups' goals to implement the company's goals by devising a single means that will advance the goals of both. Or they may manage to set up status measures which will measure the height of the men's status in their group and also the amount they contribute to the company. The executives must also be taught to use the informal groups' communication channels and the informal leaders.

Making changes in the formal organization structure is a fifth method of gaining men's acceptance of proposed changes in the company's procedures. Beginning at the bottom of the pyramid, a first step is to form into groups (or sections) the manual and the mental specialists who, under the new plan, will be employing similar premises, and the selecting as a leader for the section a man capable of helping the group carry out its assignments at the level called for. A second step is to place together in departments the sections which, under the new plan, will have to transmit the largest volume of premises to one another and will have the most difficulty in communicating these, then finding and appointing a department head capable of leading and directing the department's section heads. If the executives believe the company could compete better were the men more specialized, they may decide to split up some of the departments, forming divisions which may be specialized by product line, type of customer, or geographical area. In addition, complicating the formal structure by introducing staff men may help in gaining acceptance of the proposed changes in the work of the sections and departments, and making sure the work is performed in accordance with the new plan. Here the top executives are formally bestowing on a staff man the authority to guide certain aspects of the behavior of men in the line, men who already have an appointed superior. This formal provision for the cross-flow of authority and communication from two or more superiors helps to ensure that the best available premises are supplied directly to each man and thus improves the decision making.

The executive's *new* long-term program for the *forthcoming* period —the changes he plans to introduce in the various departments—will actually go into effect piecemeal. But for this new program, just as with the one now completed, the chief executive has the task of re-appraising his plan to see whether the people affected will actually behave as expected and to see if the plan will pay its way; deciding which of the changes are most important; working out a time schedule; visualizing perfect department heads for the new program, measuring his present executives against the "perfect" ones, selecting and formally appointing the executives, and showing them what their jobs are to be; raising the new capital required for the new plan, providing the department heads with the money they each need to introduce changes and carry on their work; and finally pulling the trigger that launches the project. And once more, he ends the cycle by checking to see that the new plans are being carried out.

From what we have seen in the pages of this book, it is evident that a forward-looking executive lives in an exciting world. For one thing, his job is an ever-changing one. Because the company's environment, its proposed plans, and the problems of putting them into effect are in a state of constant flux, no two days, or weeks, or years are ever the same. What is more, instead of performing his activities in the neat, consecutive series described in the Postlude, he is usually performing most of these activities simultaneously. Not only does each new cycle overlap the cycle nearing completion, but he is usually working on several features of a plan at the same time, and these are in various stages of completion.

Furthermore, the executive's job continuously poses new challenges. There are always new goals to achieve; and in any case, he never quite achieves any of the goals he sets. Consequently, he is always tantalized by what can yet be done. Nor are there clear-cut answers to any of his problems; yet he is constantly trying to make decisions that will stand up in the years ahead. And he is never fully successful in gaining wholehearted acceptance; people being what they are, this task is never finished.

But most of all, this is an exhilarating profession. It provides a man with an outlet for his creative drives. Once he has experienced the excitement of creating the ideas for a new plan, of conceiving the means of carrying it out, and then of seeing the plan materialize, he never forgets the feeling of gratification. Once he gets a taste of the experience of creating results that he and his fellow men can enjoy, he is exactly like any other creator; he feels frustrated unless he can continue to conceive new ideas. It is easy to understand why many executives become so engrossed in their work that they sometimes neglect their families and friends, and overlook their civic and social responsibilities. Yet this need not occur, nor need the executive burn his life away with pressures and tensions. The solution is to develop younger executives who can gradually assume some of his responsibilities.

PROBLEM

Putting the Program into Effect

1. Should we recommend the adoption of the plan? (The reappraisal.)
   a) Will each of the outside groups which constitute Superb's social and economic environment really behave approximately as we originally predicted?
   b) Will each of the groups inside the company actually accept the changes we propose in their duties? Which groups will have the narrowest zones of acceptance and thus may reduce their contributions?
   c) Add up the increases we are proposing in Superb's overhead expenses per year, estimate our present average gross margin per unit and probable number of pounds we now sell annually to determine the annual contribution to overhead we have recently been receiving, make similar estimates for the period ahead under the new plan, and determine whether the proposed plan will more than pay for itself. (Restudy pp. 376–79 before trying to answer this question.)
   d) Should we go ahead? (For purposes of teaching, we shall suppose that our decision is to carry out the plan.)
2. Working out a plan for putting our plan into effect.
   a) List the chief changes we plan to introduce in the company and rank them according to the magnitude and difficulty of the task of carrying out those changes.
   b) To give yourself experience in timing, choose one department and work out a time schedule for starting and completing the changes proposed in that department, bearing in mind that your schedule will need to be synchronized with the time schedules of other departments.
3. Forming the top echelons of the organization as a means of implementing the plan.
   a) Describe the ideal manager for each department, bearing in mind that the ideal man may be one who is gifted in doing routine work, compare

the present manager with the ideal, and decide which men will be
reasonably capable of creating and leading their (or another) department, which can be retained, and which should be replaced.

b) Where do you think we should look for the new department head(s)?

c) We shall suppose that you and Mr. Kingsbury have now formally appointed the department heads that have been chosen. What changes, if
any, would you propose in the formal organization structure that is
depicted in Exhibit 5 of the case? Give two or three of your main
premises.

d) Choose one of the department heads. What specific goals would you
set for him, and what would be some of the means you think he should
place on the lower steps of his department's staircases? Here you are
directing these executives—showing them the plan, a plan which indicates what to do and when to do it.

4. Supplying funds as a means of implementing the plan.

   a) Funds for the company—permanent capital.

      (1) What capital investments are called for in the plan, including the
          funds for increases, if any, in accounts receivables and inventories?

      (2) What would be the effect on our balance sheet and our credit stand-
          ing if we were to finance these out of the cash we have (see Ex-
          hibit 2)?

      (3) Where should we go for help in raising additional capital? Do you
          think we can convince those investors to put money in Superb?

   b) Funds for the departments—operating budgets.

      (1) What would you tell Mr. Kingsbury that a budget would do for
          Superb?

      (2) What would probably be the width of each executive's zone of
          acceptance for a budget?

      (3) How would you propose going about gaining their acceptance of
          the idea of budgeting?

Let us now assume that the department heads have been implementing the
plan; they have for some time been working on the task of putting each part
of it into effect according to the agreed-upon schedule.

5. Seeing that the plan actually works.

   a) Checking up (supervision).

      (1) Examine one "new" department only. Which of its tasks are most
          crucial to the success of Superb *and* which will also be hardest to
          carry out?

      (2) How would you describe the standard (or the goal or the 100
          per cent) which you think the department head should attain
          in performing these difficult crucial tasks.

      (3) To keep Mr. Kingsbury and his department heads informed about
          your department's progress in achieving the foregoing standards
          or goals, what kinds of reports would you propose for each of the
          main goals?

   b) What features of our long-range plan for your department do you
      think we shall most likely have to revise because:

      (1) Unexpected changes have occurred in the economic environment.

    (2) It turned out to be unrealistic.

    (3) Some of the men in the department failed to carry out their part of the plan.

Explain why you think so.

6. If you were offered a suitable job in the company and you knew Mr. Kingsbury had adopted our plan, would you accept or reject the offer? Why?

Appendix 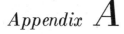 CHECK LIST FOR
WRITING BUSINESS
REPORTS

BELOW is a check list which I have gradu-
ally evolved over a period of years as an aid in writing reports when
one is asked to recommend a decision to his superiors. In most cases
a man writing such a report faces a more arduous task than is indicated by the check list, however. Before doing anything else, he must
crystallize the problem, gather the pertinent information about the
problem, and conceive some alternative solutions. In business cases
prepared for classroom use, cases such as those prepared by the
Harvard Business School, most of this preliminary work has already
been done.

1. Appraise your opening paragraph. Note, though, that the statements contained in it are framed *after* the decision-making process has been completed.
   a) Are your decision (or proposal), and your subconclusions (that is, the
   three or four chief "becauses" underlying your decision), briefly stated
   in the *first* paragraph of the report?
   b) Are your decision, and your subconclusions, clearly stated and concrete? Or are they indecisive, or unduly vague or qualified?
   c) Does your decision come to grips with the central problem you are trying to resolve—with the question, if any, with which you were asked to
   deal?
   d) Is your decision consistent with, and supported by, and does it grow out
   of, the premises embodied in the report? Or does it conflict with, or fail
   to grow out of, the premises?
2. How about the organization of your report?
   a) Is the organization clear and simple, so that the reader can easily grasp,
   and afterward remember, the three or four chief subconclusions you
   embodied in the report? That is, (1) do the subconclusions in the first
   paragraph correspond with the topic sentences of the paragraphs that
   follow; and (2) do the premises in each paragraph further reinforce
   the subconclusions?
   b) Is the topic sentence (the first sentence) of each paragraph framed as

542

a conclusion that grows out of, and is supported by, the premises contained in the paragraph?

c) Did you include in each paragraph *only* those premises which were pertinent to the conclusion contained in the topic sentence? Do those premises demonstrate why you think the consequence named in the paragraph's topic sentence will occur?

d) Are the topic sentences of each paragraph framed so that they, in turn, read as premises that support your major decision; do they (or a variant of them) also appear in your first paragraph as a subconclusion?

e) Is the report cohesive—is each paragraph related to what precedes and to what follows, and are the sentences in the paragraphs so related?

(Parts 3, 4, and 5, which follow, are intended to help you with your discovery and your analysis of three types of factual or near-factual material, and with the effectiveness with which you used this material in your report.)

3. How about your use of pertinent numerical data?

a) Were all the figures that are pertinent to the decision included in your report?

b) Were the figures accurately read; and were your calculations, if any, accurate?

c) In using sets of figures, were the cause-result relationships between them stated clearly in words and thus used constructively as premises in reaching subconclusions and showing why you reached them?

d) In predicting what the cause-result relationships of the sets of figures used would be, did you call to the reader's attention whatever assumptions or limitations there may be in your premises—in other words, did you indicate how reliable they are?

4. How about your use of nonfigure statements which are predominantly factual?

a) Did you gather nonfigure statements pertinent to a solid decision and frame them into premises?

b) Were the statements you gathered from the people in the company fully understood?

c) Were these statements interwoven with the figures from Part 3 above and framed as premises for the conclusion in your topic sentences? Or were they used merely as a rehash of those statements?

d) Did you think through, visualize concretely, and state clearly the cause-result relationships which you have framed?

5. How about your use of information that is predominantly of a value nature?

a) Were the effects of current and probable future business conditions faced by the company used as premises?

b) Were competitive conditions in the industry, as well as competitors' probable reactions to your proposal, considered?

c) Did you sort out and see clearly and in detail the goals of the people in each of the various groups (for example, the ultimate consumers, the channels of distribution, the salesmen, the men in product development, the men in the plant, and in the various control departments and the executives who are likely to be affected by your decision?

　　d) Did you put yourself in the shoes of the members of each of these groups and revise your decision to a point where you were sure that the people in the groups essential to the success of your plan will support it?

6. Appraise your report before writing the final draft.
　　a) Is the report objective?
　　　　(1) Or did you make up your mind too early—that is, before you had examined all the alternatives and their wanted and unwanted consequences?
　　　　(2) Is your conclusion one-sided because you have unconsciously excluded some of those premises which should have been brought to light in Parts 3, 4, and 5, or so weighted them as to bias your conclusion?
　　　　(3) Did you include premises which would weigh against your proposal?
　　　　(4) Did you mention reasonably possible alternatives and give your premises, briefly, for discarding them?
　　b) In the report, is there considerable evidence of thinking through and of seeing the impact of your proposal on the *whole* of the company's activity?
　　c) Did you avoid the use of broad general statements and principles as premises for any of your conclusions? (The answer here should be "No.")
　　d) Are there proposals or statements in your report which are not consistent with one another?

7. What about the writing?
　　a) Is the report concise, nonrepetitive, with each word contributing its part to the whole?
　　b) Is the report easy to read?
　　c) Is the idea in each sentence clearly expressed?
　　d) Are there awkward constructions?
　　e) What about sentence structures and grammar?
　　f) What about your choice of words?
　　g) Are the spelling, proof reading, and punctuation correct?
　　h) What about the neatness of your report?
　　i) Have you confined your report to 750–1,000 words?

Appendix *B* GLOSSARY

THE PURPOSE of this glossary is to provide a brief description of terms used in the book the meanings of which are not immediately apparent or to which I have attached special definitions. In many cases these are concepts that are difficult to summarize accurately in a short statement; hence, if the reader is encountering the term for the first time, he should turn to the pages in the book for a more precise description. In the book itself I use these terms only after they have been explained; hence the glossary will not be needed by those who read straight through.

Authority (pp. 162–63 and Diagram 7). A successful attempt by one person to guide the behavior of another person in a chosen direction. An authority relationship exists when (and only when) that other person so modifies or alters his behavior. Every person in an organization exercises authority from time to time. Authority, as the term is used here, means informal authority; it is not "given" by a superior and has nothing to do with formal appointments or titles. In an organization this authority is most often exercised "downward" in the hierarchy (that is, by the boss over his subordinates) but it is very frequently also exercised "upward" (men often manage to alter the behavior of their boss). In addition, men often exercise authority sideways and diagonally in the hierarchy. And Mr. A. may exercise authority over Miss B. on one occasion and on another Miss B. can (and often does) exercise authority over Mr. A. People utilize three types of authority (see Diagram 7) in an effort to guide the behavior of another person: simple authority (they merely request or suggest that the other person do a certain thing)—see pp. 165–66; "easy" or "hard" proof (they explain the reasons why the other person should behave as proposed)—see pp. 173–80; and sanctions (they either offer rewards to the person to induce him to carry out the proposal or make outright or implied threats of punishment)—see pp. 169–70.

Contributions to overhead and profit (pp. 376–78). This term refers to the gross margin (the dollar difference) between the selling price of the company's products and the *out-of-pocket* expenses (which see) of manufacturing and selling its products. The contribution *per unit* is the spread or gross margin contributed to the company's coffers each time a single unit is sold. The *annual* or *total* contribution to overhead and profits is the annual or total gross margin; it is determined by multiplying the number of units sold in the period by the average spread or gross margin per unit. This annual or total figure is the amount the company has available to cover all its overhead expenses and profits.

Communication (pp. 212–13). The transfer from the mind of one person to the mind of another of mental images of whatever information is required by that other person when he is making his decisions. Some of this information is sent through the organization in a steady stream; each piece of information is intended to be used in making only one or two decisions—used only once or twice and then discarded. Other images are transferred in the hope that they will be used many times in the future for making a large number of decisions—permanently useful information. Training is an example of the latter.

Efficiency versus adequacy (pp. 274–76). Efficiency, as used here, is defined as working at or near top capacity to achieve a specific goal—the whole-hearted employment of means that will most certainly and most fully achieve that goal. Efficiency can be appraised only in terms of a given goal. Adequacy is defined as going through the motions of trying to achieve a goal, doing only enough to "get by." Adequacy is not the antithesis of efficiency but instead a low level of efficiency; it is a half-hearted attempt to achieve a goal.

Factual premise (pp. 67–72 and Diagrams 4 and 5). Before examining this, the reader should study the description of the word "premise." The term *factual* refers *solely* to the question of *what types of standards or measurements* the speaker and his hearers employ when they visualize each of the three elements (the cause, the causal connection, and the result) in a premise they are considering. If, when the cause and result are mentioned, all of the people at the meeting see virtually the same image—if they are all using virtually the same "objective" description such as inches or dollars or objects to which they can point—the cause and result are factual by this definition; they are images that have been demonstrated; there is no ambiguity. Similarly, if the speaker and his hearers use objective measures to demonstrate or test whether or not there is a connection between the cause and result, this element, too, is factual. There are very few premises whose elements are all factual; at least *some* of the measures a man employs when he visualizes each of the three elements are *value* measures (which see). Nevertheless, if the *majority* of the measures used by the men are factual, we are for convenience, calling the premise a factual premise; it is predominantly factual.

Gross margin (pp. 376–79). See *Contributions to overhead and profits.* Do not confuse this with the term "gross margin" which often appears in companies' operating statements.

Inducement-contribution concept (pp. 130–34 and Diagrams 6A and 6B). A ledger-like arrangement of premises pertinent to a new proposal or program—premises as seen through the eyes of the various groups of people in the organization who will be affected (for example, customers, middlemen, employee groups, and stockholders), and as seen from the company's point of view. It is useful in testing out a proposal in the mind to foresee whether the various groups who will be affected will oppose or welcome it, and how their subsequent behavior will affect the company's welfare. Those groups in the company who foresee that the inducements they expect to receive as a result of the new program (the wanted consequences) will outweigh the contributions they will be asked to make to the company (in their eyes, the unwanted consequences) and who also foresee that the difference between their inducements and contributions under the new program will be greater than under the current program, will almost certainly make wholeheartedly the contributions that the executives had expected from them. Their contributions to the company will be greater than before. Any groups that foresee that the spread between their inducements and contributions will be reduced can be expected to make fewer contributions than at present; they will "drag their feet," make just enough contributions to "get by."

This reduction in their contributions will adversely affect the company, for the contributions made to the company by these groups are its inducements—the things it wishes to secure, its means of achieving its goals. The executives would like the groups to make their contributions wholeheartedly (at the top of their ability), for then the company will be better off; the inducements it receives will increase. This concept is an adaptation of the equilibrium concept that has been widely used by scholars.

Informal group (pp. 248–50). Two or more people who have been drawn together spontaneously—without apparent direction—for the purpose of achieving some goal(s) they consciously or unconsciously hold in common. These goals may be entirely personal, but in many instances the groups form for the purpose of advancing (or thwarting) a company goal. In virtually all cases such groups are nonofficial in the sense that management does not formally recognize their existence.

Intermediate goals (pp. 13–16). A group of goals chosen by individuals or organizations which, in their eyes, will almost automatically and inevitably further their ultimate goals. These are the relatively permanent means they have chosen to employ in their efforts to attain their ultimate goals.

Means-end staircase (pp. 16–20 and Diagrams 1 and 2). A connected series of progressively higher goals arranged in the form of stairsteps, the topmost of which serves as a means of achieving one or more of the intermediate goals of the individual or the organization. Actually, however, the goal that rests on *any* given step of the staircase serves as a *means* of attaining the goal resting on the step just above it. Hence, any given step serves as *both* a means and a goal; in a "good" staircase, each step is a decision as to the best means of achieving the goal on the step just above it, each is powerful enough to produce the step (goal) on the step above it, and each serves as a goal during the period when the person or organization is determining the means that is to rest on the step just *below* it. Note that each step on the staircase is a decision that has been made but has not yet been fully implemented.

Member groups of the organization (pp. 129–30). *All* the groups of people who make contributions to the welfare of the company. These include the company's customers (that is, the ultimate consumers of its products); its wholesalers (or jobbers) and its retailers, if any; its suppliers of raw materials, parts, and equipment; its transportation companies, banks, and so on, *as well as* employee groups such as salesmen, office workers, accountants, plant workers, engineers, shipping clerks, executives, etc., and the owners of the company—the partners or the holders of its stocks and bonds.

Niche of the company (pp. 412–16). The roles the company is attempting to play in its economic and social environment. A description of a company's market niche would consist of an enumeration of the particular *types of consumers* the company attempts to solicit and the products (or services) it is offering them, along with a description of the *particular features* of those products, features designed to fit certain of their specific needs. Its niche in the social environment is the role it attempts to play in satisfying the needs of its employees, its community, and its nation. Filling its chosen niches very well is usually the company's chief intermediate goal.

Out-of-pocket costs or expenses (pp. 377–78). Sometimes called direct expenses or variable expenses. These are the expenditures which the company must make *each* time it manufactures or sells a *single* item (or unit)— what it must spend for raw materials, purchased parts, direct labor, freight, and selling commissions. This definition, incidentally is similar to, but somewhat broader than, the commonly used definition; most writers confine the term to direct manufacturing costs only.

Overhead expenses (pp. 377–78). Money which the company has agreed to pay out regardless of the number of units it produces. In this book, they are always shown as *totals* for the period under consideration, *never* per unit. Nor is there any attempt to draw a distinction between the semivariable and the fixed expenses; they are all lumped together and called "overhead expenses."

Policies (pp. 234, 410, and 434). The company's intermediate goals and the relatively permanent means the company executives have adopted to implement those high goals.

Premises (pp. 60–63 and Diagram 3). Statements or assertions germane to an alternative, ones which a man takes into consideration when he tests out alternatives in his mind in an effort to reach a decision. They are his predictions of what he believes will happen in case the alternative is adopted. He says to himself "Were I to choose alternative A, these things will occur." "Were I to choose alternative D, these things will occur." In its most complete form, a premise is a sentence which contains three elements, a cause (for example, "If I adopt alternative A"), a result (for example, "the men in the shipping room will have to work harder"), and a causal connection which, according to the statement, is asserted to exist between the cause and the result (the last named—the causal connection—is seldom stated in actual words). Some of the premises a man thinks of when considering each alternative point to wanted consequences or results, and others to unwanted consequences. Moreover, there are two types of premises, those which are predominantly factual and those predominantly value. The terms *factual* and *value* refer *solely* to the question of how the speaker and his hearers measure the elements contained in the premise. (See references to these in the Glossary.)

Rationality (pp. 141–48). This concept serves as a summary of the decision-making process. It consists of taking into consideration the most desirable, long-term goals, setting up means-end staircases for achieving those goals, examining the steps on the staircase to discover missing or weak steps, creating ideas for new and better alternatives for those weak or missing steps, and choosing the best alternatives after uncovering most of the premises, both factual and value, germane to each, and testing these premises for reliability (validity), then weighting them. To be as rational as possible, a man would have to take into consideration all the goals, all the alternatives, and all the premises germane to those alternatives and goals— all, that is, that he could encompass *within the time he has available to make up his mind.*

Rebellion (p. 172 and Diagram 7). The opposite of a successful attempt to exercise authority. When an individual believes that his welfare will be seriously jeopardized if he behaves as proposed, he either refuses outright or conveniently forgets to do as bid; he rebels by managing to avoid doing as proposed.

Reliability of a premise (pp. 82–86). The determination of whether the result named in the premise will actually come true in the particular instance under consideration. Past experience is the only basis we have for appraising the reliability of a premise.

Sanctions (pp. 169–72 and Diagram 7). One type of authority (which see). These are either offers of rewards or threats of punishment.

Specialist (p. 296). A person who is an expert in making the decisions called for in his particular field of activity. *Manual or routine specialist:* a person whose primary task is to decide how to move his hands in order to get a certain job done, or whose task is to make repetitive, routine decisions. *Mental specialist:* a person, usually a staff man, who has penetrated deeply into a particular field of knowledge and as a consequence has accumulated a great wealth of alternatives and premises pertinent to that field and consequently can make excellent decisions within that field. *Executive specialist:* a "line" man, an expert in co-ordinating the decisions of other people and in directing their behavior; ordinarily these experts must rely heavily on value premises in making their decisions.

Status measures (pp. 257–62). The measures which an informal group devises to predict how the group will fare in the future, and how each member of the group will prosper. If, according to those standards, the group or a man in the group is losing position, it (or he) will unconsciously take steps designed to reverse the trend—often quite drastic steps. If they see that they are maintaining their position or rising on their scales of measurement, they feel safe about their future welfare; they can predict a rosy future.

Ultimate goals (pp. 11–13 and 115–17). Rather permanent objectives, usually rather distant ones that are somewhat intangible and quite big, which a man or an organization has consciously or unconsciously decided to pursue. These are their description of what they think of as an almost perfect set of conditions, ones they think would be wonderful. They believe that if these goals are achieved, their *future welfare* will be assured.

Value premise (pp. 74–78 and Diagram 7). As in the case of a *factual premise* (which see), the question to be answered here is how the speaker and his hearers measure the cause, the result, and causal connection that are mentioned in the premise they are considering. In a value premise they each measure these three elements with their own personal (or subjective) standards instead of with widely adopted "objective" yardsticks. For the most part these value standards are the man's private inventions, ones he has developed himself to measure intangibles and unseeable things such as prestige or freedom. These value measures are drawn from the personal experiences of the speaker and his hearers; the men carry these measuring rods around inside themselves; each man's yardstick differs from those used by the other men. There are very few premises whose three elements are all measured *exclusively* with value standards; usually the speaker and his hearers employ at least a *few* factual measures. But if the majority of measures used to describe each of the three elements are value, we nevertheless call it a value premise; it is predominantly value. A value premise can be just as reliable as a factual premise.

Zone of acceptance; the width of the zone of acceptance (pp. 157–60 and Diagram 7). A prediction, made prior to an attempt to exercise authority over another person, of his probable response to a specific proposal. The question at issue here is whether (1) he will be strongly averse to the proposal we want him to carry out, or (2) whether he would be reluctant but would probably accede under pressure, or (3) whether he would raise questions about it and would want these answered before accepting, or (4) would act on it without much if any hesitation. In the first-named instance we would say his zone of acceptance is negative in width—less than zero; in the last instance (4) we would say his zone is somewhere near 100 per cent in width; in number 2, the width would extend from 0 per cent to approximately 25 per cent in width; in number 3 from about 25 per cent to 75 per cent in width. This concept is used in determining which type of authority to use in gaining his acceptance of the proposal.

INDEX

*This book has been set on the Linotype in 12
and 10 point Bodoni Book, leaded 1 point.
Part and chapter numbers and titles are in 14
and 30 point Bodoni #175. The size of the
type page is 27 by 46½ picas.*